DANIEL A. WREN, Ph.D., University of Illinois, is Professor of Management at Florida State University. He previously taught at the University of Illinois and is the author, with Dan Voich, Jr., of *Principles of Management—Resources and Systems*, published by The Ronald Press Company.

THE EVOLUTION OF
MANAGEMENT THOUGHT

DANIEL A. WREN
FLORIDA STATE UNIVERSITY

THE RONALD PRESS COMPANY · NEW YORK

Library of Congress Catalog Card Number: 75–168592
PRINTED IN THE UNITED STATES OF AMERICA

To Leon, my link with the past;
to Karen, my link with the present;
and to Jonathan, my link with the future.

Preface

My purpose in this book is to bring together into one source the whats, whos, whys, and hows of the evolution of management thinking over a wide span of years in order to acquaint students studying in this area with our rich intellectual heritage.

I have tried to make the book an unfolding story about the lives and the times of those who are our intellectual forefathers. These individuals have left us a heritage which we often take for granted, frequently do not acknowledge, and sometimes reject because we do not think yesterday's solutions have any practical value for tomorrow's problems. But these men and women were pretty much as we are: they were attempting to cope with the manifold problems of administering mass assemblages of human and physical resources; they were trying to develop philosophies and theories about human behavior and motivation; they were agents for change; and they were struggling with man's age-old problem of allocating scarce resources to meet the goals and desires of organizations and men. Our problems today are basically the same, only the proposed solutions have changed as we have learned more, as we have sharpened our diagnostic tools, and as cultural values have changed.

This book traces the evolution of management thought from its earliest, informal days to the present by examining the backgrounds, ideas, and influence of the major contributors. In so doing, it outlines and depicts the significant eras in the development of management thought and analyzes the various trends and movements throughout this development. In addition, it illustrates the impact of environmental forces on the development of ideas. Management is an open-ended activity in that what is done and thought is affected by the prevailing economic, social, and political values and institutions. Moreover, those who are actually "doing" and "thinking" in turn affect the environment, and it is this dynamic interaction which is emphasized.

Throughout, the organization is chronological, in order to demonstrate the evolutionary nature of management theory and practice and to show how assumptions about men and organizations change with shifting economic, social, and political values and institutions. Finally—in keeping with the concept that management theory is a product of past historical forces—the concluding chapter summarizes the functions of the manager and discusses the history of management as a prologue to the future.

I would be remiss if I made no acknowledgment of my own indebtedness to those who have helped me in my own evolution of thinking. Professor Robert G. Cook of the University of Missouri gave me an excellent introduction to management history. At the University of Illinois, Professors Joseph Litterer, Dwight Flanders, Harvey Huegy, and M. J. Mandeville encouraged me to approach problems from an interdisciplinary and environmental point of view. Professor Mandeville, though retired, furnished excellent insights from his own broad acquaintance with the body of management knowledge. Professor Huegy provided guidelines against which to measure my own thinking. Professor Albert Wickesberg of the University of Minnesota gave comments and suggestions which were very helpful and sincerely appreciated. Professors John Mee and Richard Whiting willingly shared materials and ideas; Kenneth Trombley helped on some of the finer points of the life of Morris L. Cooke; Fritz Roethlisberger clarified some origins of Human Relations ideas; Ernestine Gilbreth Carey reviewed what I had written of the Gilbreths; Ralph C. Davis gave generously in writing of his own evolving ideas; and William B. Wolf was of invaluable assistance on the life and work of Chester Barnard.

Charles A. Rovetta, Dean of the School of Business, Florida State University, has been one of my most faithful supporters and has created a climate in which one can do creative scholarly work. Jack T. Dobson, Chairman of the Department of Management, has aided this climate and has been most considerate in work assignments. There have been others—almost too many others for full acknowledgment—who have played their roles: Susan Works, Linda Miller, and Vicki Vetter typed most of the manuscript; Ron Moitzfield, Roger Kerr, Clay Parham, Patsy Owens, Homer Ooten, and others have furnished insights and research assistance; and my graduate classes have served as guinea pigs and devils' advocates throughout the evolution of this book. Various publishers have been very generous in allowing me to quote or reproduce from their books; specific credit is given in the form of footnotes throughout the text. To all of those above, and to those whom I have omitted, I am deeply grateful.

DANIEL A. WREN

Tallahassee, Florida
January, 1972

Contents

agement Education: *Principles of Manufacturing.* Charles
Dupin: Industrial Education in France: *The Pioneers: A
Final Note.*

Part II: The Scientific Management Era

Part IV: The Modern Era

EARLY MANAGEMENT THOUGHT

Part I will cover a wide span of time and trace developments in management thought up to the scientific management era in America. After a brief introduction to the role of management in organizations, we will examine examples of very early management thought and then demonstrate how changes in the economic, social, and political environment were setting the stage for the Industrial Revolution. This revolution created certain management problems in the embryonic factory system and led to a need for the formal study of management. The genesis of modern management thought will be found in the work of early pioneers in management thought who sought to solve the problems created by the factory system. We will conclude Part I by tracing this genesis of management thought to America and examine our early experiences with the factory, some early management writers, and the cultural environment of America before the scientific management era.

1

A Prologue to the Past

Management is as old as man, but formal study of the discipline of management is relatively new. Management is essential to organized endeavors, and for a broad working definition let us view management as an activity which performs certain functions in order to obtain the effective acquisition, allocation, and utilization of human efforts and physical resources in order to accomplish some goal. Management "thought," then, is the existing body of knowledge about the activity of management, its functions, purpose, and scope. The purpose of this study is to trace the significant periods in the evolution of management thought from its earliest informal days to the present. The study of management, like the study of men and their cultures, is an unfolding story of changing ideas about the nature of work, the nature of man, and the functioning of organizations. The methodology of this study of management will be analytic, synthetic, and interdisciplinary. It will be analytic in examining men, their backgrounds, their ideas, and their influence. It will be synthetic in examining trends, movements, and environmental forces that furnish a conceptual framework for understanding men and their approaches to the solution of management problems. It will be interdisciplinary in the sense that it includes—but moves beyond—traditional management writings to draw upon economic history, sociology, psychology, social history, political science, and cultural anthropology in order to place management thought in a cultural historical perspective. The author's objective is to place management thought in the context of its cultural environment and thereby to understand not only *what* management thought was and is, but also to explain *why* it developed as it did.

Management history as a separate area of study is generally neglected in most schools of business administration. A smattering of history is taught at various levels but the area generally lacks depth, direction, and unity. Henry Wadsworth Longfellow said "let the dead past bury its dead," but there is much to be said for resurrection. We live and study in an age which is represented by a diversity of approaches to management. The student is presented with quantitative, behavioral, functional, and/or systems approaches in the various courses he takes. While such a variety of intellectual inputs may be stimulating, it typically leaves the student with a fragmented picture of management and assumes that he has the ability to integrate these various ideas for himself. In many cases, this burden is far too great. A study of evolving management thought can provide the origins of ideas and approaches, trace their development, provide some perspective in terms of the cultural environment, and thus provide a conceptual framework which will enhance the process of integration. A study of the past contributes to a more logical, coherent picture of the present. Without a knowledge of history, an individual has only his own limited experiences as a basis for thought and action. History should therefore equip the perceptive person with additional alternatives and answers to build into his decision-making model. Intellectual flexibility and a mental set for the inevitability of change can be facilitated through the study of the past. Present pedagogy can be improved, knowledge expanded, and insights gained by examining the lives and labors of management's intellectual forefathers. Theory, a legitimate goal in any discipline, is based upon the warp and woof of men's ideas in the fabric of management. By tracing the origin and development of modern management concepts, we can better understand the analytical and conceptual tools of our trade. In understanding the growth and development of large-scale enterprise, the dynamics of technology, the ebb and flow of cultural values, and the changing assumptions about the nature and nurture of man, we can better equip young men and women with the skills and attitudes they need to prepare themselves for future positions of responsibility. The study of management history not only furnishes insights into our own culture but also reveals notions of how management skills and knowledge might be applied to other organizations and to other cultures.

Today is not like yesterday, nor will tomorrow be like today; yet today is a synergism of all our yesterdays, and tomorrow will be the same. There are many lessons in history for management scholars; the important one is the study of the past as prologue.

A CULTURAL FRAMEWORK

How have our concepts of managing organizations evolved throughout history? To understand this evolution, this dynamic process of change and growth, we need to establish a cultural framework of analysis for the evolution of management thought. Management is not a closed-end activity since the manager operates his organization and makes decisions within a given set of cultural values and institutions. Thus management has "open-system" characteristics in that the manager affects his environment and in turn is affected by it.

Culture is our total community heritage of nonbiological, humanly transmitted traits and includes the economic, social, and political forms of behavior associated with man. Generally, we speak of a specific culture within geographic or physically contiguous boundaries, such as that of the United States, or Mexico, or that of Germany. However, there are "levels" of culture, such as the "Western" culture and "Eastern" cultures of the world. Or there may be subcultures within one culture, such as a "middle class" culture, that of the "hippies," or of other groups sharing a common set of cultural forms of behavior. Here the term "culture" will apply to a set of people having in common an economic, social, and political system. Culture is the broadest possible concept for study, and here the study of management will be confined to more specific economic, social, and political ideas which influence the job of managing an organization. Man's behavior is a product of past and present cultural forces and the discipline of management is also a product of the economic, social, and political forces of the past and present. Cultures are generally taken for granted, much like the goldfish who takes the water in his fishtank as a natural state of affairs. Modern individuals examine present organizations, read contemporary authors, and yet they have little appreciation of the background of our technology, political bodies, or arrangements for the allocation of resources. Management thought did not develop in a cultural vacuum; the manager has always found his job affected by the existing culture.

To study modern management, the past must be examined to see how our communal heritage was established. The elements of our culture were described above as economic, social, and political. In practice, these elements are closely interrelated and interact to form our total culture; they are separated here and throughout the following pages only for ease of presentation. Here our attention shall be confined to the portions of our culture which apply most directly to management and omit other cultural phenomena such as art forms, music, and so on.

The Economic Facet

The economic facet of culture is the relationship of man to resources. Resources may be man-made or natural; the term denotes as well both tangible objects and intangible efforts which have the capability of being utilized to achieve some stated end. Physical resources include land, buildings, raw materials, semi-finished products, tools, and equipment or other tangible objects used by man and organizations. Human thought and effort are also resources because they design, assemble, shape, and perform other activities which result in the production of some product or service.

Every society has the economic problem of a scarcity of resources and a multiplicity of economic ends. The mobilization of these scarce resources to produce and distribute products, services, and satisfactions has taken a variety of forms throughout history. Heilbroner has characterized these methods of allocating resources as by tradition, by command, and by the market.[1] The traditional method operates on past societal precepts; technology is essentially static, occupations are passed down from one generation to the next, agriculture predominates over industry, and the social and economic systems remain essentially closed to change. The command method is the imposition of the will of some central person or agency upon the rest of the economy about how resources will be allocated and utilized. The economic commander-in-chief

---

[1] Robert L. Heilbroner, *The Making of Economic Society*, Englewood Cliffs, N.J.: Prentice-Hall, 1962, pp. 10–16.

may be the monarch, the fascist dictator, or the collectivist central planning agency. What is to be produced, what prices and wages will be, and how economic goods and services are to be distributed are decisions to be made by some central source. The *market* method, which Heilbroner has noted as a relatively recent phenomenon, relies upon an impersonal network of forces and decisions to allocate resources. Prices, wages, and interest rates are set by a bargaining process between those who have the product or service and those who want it; all resources flow to their best reward and no central agency nor prior precepts need to intervene.

In actual practice, modern societies display a mixture of the elements of tradition, command, and the market. Much of our total cultural heritage has been influenced by tradition and command as the predominant economic philosophies. However, we will see later that the market philosophy created the need for the formal, systematic development of a body of management thought. In brief, the state of technology and the source of decisions about the societal allocation of resources have a large bearing upon how the manager goes about his job. A tradition-directed economy would circumscribe the role of the manager with prior precepts; the command orientation would make him an executor of central decisions; but the market system opens the way to the innovative utilization of resources to meet a multiplicity of ends.

The Social Facet

The social facet refers to the relationship of man to other men in a given culture. Man does not live alone but finds advantages in forming groups for mutual survival or for the furtherance of personal goals. In forming groups, the initial input is a variety of people of differing needs, abilities, and values. Out of this heterogeneity, some homogeneity must evolve or the group will not survive. Thus all participants form a "contract" which encompasses some common rules and agreements about how to behave to preserve the group.[2] The unwritten but nevertheless binding contract would define assumptions about the behavior of others and expectations about the return treatment of the individual. It would include some agreement about how best to combine and coordinate

[2] Pitirim A. Sorokin, *Society, Culture, and Personality,* New York: Cooper Square Publishers, 1962, pp. 371–373.

efforts to accomplish a given task, be it the making of an economic product or achieving the satisfactions of social fellowship.

Values, or cultural standards of conduct defining the propriety of a given type of behavior, are another part of social interactions. Thus ethics in interpersonal relations is an age-old problem. Economic transactions, deeply imbedded in man's social trust in man, are an integral part of a societal contract. Values shift from one time period to another and from one culture to another. Managerial efforts are affected by the relationships between man and the group, and by the social values prevailing in the culture.

The Political Facet

The *political* part of culture is the relation of man to state and includes the legal and political arrangements for the establishment of social order and for the protection of life and property. The absence of state and order is anarchy; unless there is some provision for protection of rational man from irrational man, the result is total economic, social, and political chaos. Where order begins, anarchy ends. Political institutions to bring order and stability take a variety of forms, ranging from representative government to a monarchy or dictatorship. Political assumptions about the nature of man change from one end of the continuum of self-governing man to the other extreme position of direction from one man or a ruling body at the top which imposes its will on others based on the assumption that man cannot, or will not, govern himself. Provisions for property, contracts, and justice are also key concepts in the political aspect of cultures. In a democracy, man typically has the right of private property, the freedom to enter or not to enter into contracts, and an appeal system for justice. Under a dictatorship or monarchy, the right to hold and use private property is severely restricted, the right to contract is limited, and the system of justice depends upon the whims of those in power. The cultural role of management is affected by the form of government, by the power to hold or not hold property, by the ability to engage in contracts for the production and distribution of goods, and by the appeal mechanism available to redress grievances.

Interacting to form any culture, the economic, social, and political facets are useful tools of analysis for examining the evolution of management thought. The manager is affected by his cultural environment, and the ways in which he allocates and utilizes resources have evolved within the changing views about economic, social, and political institutions and values.

MAN, MANAGEMENT, AND ORGANIZATIONS

From this introduction to the cultural environment of management, let us turn more specifically to the basic elements of our study. Even before man began to record his activities, he encountered the necessities of managing his efforts and the efforts of others in cooperative endeavors. As an overview, Figure 1-1 places man in a state of nature and traces his quest for need satisfaction through organizations. Management, an activity essential to organized endeavors, facilitates the operation of organizations in order to satisfy the needs of man.

Man

Man is the fundamental unit of analysis in the study of mankind, the study of organizations, and the study of management. Man has always faced a relatively hostile environment characterized by scarce food supplies, inadequate shelters, and in general a scarcity of other resources with which to satisfy his manifold needs. Man is not biologically stronger than many of the species which exist or existed on earth. To explain his survival one must look beyond his physical powers for other characteristics which can explain the proliferation of the human race to the point where man today can control and manipulate his environment, within certain natural physical boundaries which themselves are constantly being challenged as we seek outer space and expand our technology.

The solution to the question of why man, of all the creatures who ever existed, has survived is found in man's ability to reason, his ability to cope with the problems of reality. In the long evolutionary process, it was not always the most *physically* fit who survived, for they were still inferior to the behemoths and the carnivorous animals, but it was the most *mentally* fit who are our forefathers. Paleoanthropologists tell us that the first true man, *Homo erectus*, appeared some 500,000 years ago. Evidence uncovered at Olduvai Gorge by Dr. Louis Leakey and Mary Leakey suggests that *Homo erectus* became a capable tool and weapon maker, mastered the use

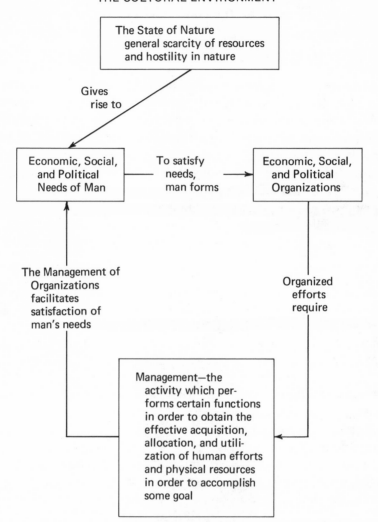

Fig. 1–1. Man, management, and organizations.

of fire, had a low level of conceptual thought, had powers of speech, and engaged in activities which required a marked degree of planning and cooperation. His brain was at the evolutionary mid-point in cranial capacity between the chimpanzee and modern man; other evidence shows a steady evolution in brain size toward the present and strongly suggests that man's mind has been his main means of survival. These were the men who fashioned equalizing clubs and spears for defense, who formed implements for tilling the soil, and who developed organizational means which gave man a differential advantage over his natural enemies.

Man is not only *Homo sapiens* but also *Homo faber*, man the maker, the doer. He is active, not passive, creative, not idle, and ever-changing in his quest to better himself and his species. Man's most basic needs are economic ones, those necessary to physical survival in a harsh world in which food, drink, shelter and other fundamental needs of life must be obtained. With cultural advancement, these economic needs become more complex but they still form a base of man's existence. Beyond these basic needs, which are essential to existence itself, he has social needs. These needs for affiliation most probably arose out of physiological drives in the sex act and the selection of a mate. The family became the most elementary unit of man's group relationships and he found satisfactions as well as new duties in this organization. Survival of the family became a goal and man found that he could better protect and enhance his welfare by forming groups or tribes for mutual advantage in food-gathering, defense, and family care activities.

Early man found that the knowledge and skills of one generation must be transmitted to the next if the species was to survive. Such were the elementary beginnings of education and the transmission of knowledge. In forming groups and living with his fellow man to minister to both economic and social needs, he found need of rules and means to insure the viability of the organization. He formed elementary political units which had agreed upon codes about economic, social, political, and often religious behavior. It was out of these economic, social, and political needs of man that organized activity began. Man found advantages in participating and cooperating with others to achieve his own goals.

Organizations and Management

As man has evolved, so have organizations. Man found that he could magnify his own abilities by working with others and thereby better satisfy his own needs. The inputs of various skills and abilities into the group led to the recognition that some were better at some tasks than others. Group tasks were *differentiated*, that is, there was a division of labor to take advantage of these varying skills.

Once labor was divided, some agreement had to be reached about how to structure and interrelate these various work assignments in order to accomplish group objectives. Quite logically, the group also *stratified* tasks and developed a hierarchy of authority or power. Perhaps the assignment of work to others was made by the strongest, the eldest, or the most articulate of the group who became the earliest leader. In any case, the group had to achieve some unity of agreement about what was to be done, how, and who would be responsible for accomplishment.

This most elementary appearance of the first organization reflected essentially the same common elements of organizations throughout history. First, there had to be a goal, a purpose, an objective, or something to be accomplished. Perhaps it was the annual berry-picking, the hunt, the sowing of a crop, or the defense of the group from marauding nomads. Second, people had to be attracted to the purpose or the common will in order to participate. They had to perceive that it was in their best interest to work toward the group goal. The first bonds of organization were in man's attraction to the group as a means of satisfying his own needs. Third, the organizational members needed something with which to work or fight. These were the resources or means to the end and comprised the people themselves, the weapons, the tilling implements, or whatever. Fourth, there was a need for a structuring of the various activities of the participants in order that their actions would interact and be interrelated in achieving the common goal. If each proceeded without timing and coordination of effort, the result would be chaos. Finally, the group discovered that results could be better achieved if someone had the assigned task of keeping the whole group on its course toward the goal. Someone had to resolve differences of opinion, decide on strategy and timing, and maintain the structure of activities and relationships toward the objective. This emergence of an activity of *managing* apart from the activities of *doing* was to become an essential aspect of all types of cooperative endeavors. Management as an activity has always existed in order to make man's desires manifest through organized effort. Management facilitates the efforts of man in organized groups and arises when men seek to cooperate to achieve goals.

Man has always participated in organizations and organizations have always existed to serve the ends of man. These ends are manifold and are reflected in organizational arrangements for the satisfaction of economic needs and wants, for the provision for individual and social desires, for the transmission of knowledge from one generation to the next, and for the protection of life and property from internal and external threats. As man's conceptual ability has been refined through evolution, he has also refined his understanding of the art of arranging physical and human resources for guidance toward purposeful ends. We call this art management, and its evolution is the focal point of our study.

SUMMARY

Our ideas about man, management, and organizations have evolved within the context of various cultural values and institutions throughout history. The development of a body of knowledge about how to manage has also evolved within a framework of the economic, social, and political facets of various cultures. Management thought is both a process in and a product of its cultural environment. Having these open-system characteristics, management thought must be examined within this cultural framework. In nature, man has economic, social, and political needs which he seeks to satisfy through organized efforts. Management is an essential activity which arises as individuals seek to satisfy their needs through group action, and it facilitates the accomplishment of goals for the individual and the group. Various organizations such as the family, the tribe, the state, and the church have appeared throughout history as means to man's ends. Man creates organizations to enlarge upon his own specialized talents, to protect himself, to enrich his life, and to satisfy a variety of other needs. To reach these ends, organizations are formed of people who have a common purpose and who are attracted to the group in order to satisfy their needs. These organizations must be managed and our study will focus upon how our ideas about management have evolved over time.

2

Management Before Industrialization

Historically, industrialization is a relatively recent phenomenon. Man existed for eons before he made the great advances in power, transportation, communications, and technology which came to be known as the Industrial Revolution. Before industrialization, man's organizations were primarily the household, the tribe, the church, the military, and the state. He did engage in small-scale economic undertakings but nothing on a scale to compare with what would emerge as a result of the Industrial Revolution. Nevertheless, man still found a need for management in the conduct of military campaigns, in household affairs, in the administration of government, and in the operation of the church. It is in these organizations that we see the earliest notions of the management of men in organizations. In examining pre-industrial management, two themes consistently appear: (1) the relatively parochial view of the management function; and (2) the low esteem of commerce held by the prevailing cultures. This chapter will examine these first attempts at management in early civilizations and will discuss the changing cultural values which would lead to the Industrial Revolution.

MANAGEMENT IN EARLY CIVILIZATIONS

Egypt

The Egyptians developed extensive irrigation projects as an adjunct to the annual inundation by the Nile, and their engineering feats of the pyramids and canals were marvels superior to anything the Greeks and Romans later developed. Mining and most engineering projects were state monopolies and required the development of an extensive bureaucracy to administer state affairs. The labor supply consisted in part of freemen and in part of slaves. Strong cultural traditions bound freemen to occupations, and chains took care of other labor problems. Under the state-controlled system, accounting for receipts and expenditures became quite a problem. A visitor to the Louvre will recall having seen the statue of the squatting, nearly nude Egyptian scribe, pen in hand and another behind his ear, recording an inventory, noting sales receipts, or perhaps preparing his master's income tax. Such were the humble beginnings of modern business functions. The pharaoh based his authority on divine right and delegated state administration to a vizier who acted as prime minister, chief justice, and head of the treasury. Beneath the vizier, an elaborate bureaucracy was developed to measure the rise of the river upon which every part of the economy depended, to forecast the grain crop and revenues, to allocate these revenues to the various governmental units, and to supervise all industry and trade. Here were some rather sophisticated (for the times) methods of managing through forecasting, planning work, dividing the work among the various people and departments, and establishing a "professional" full time administrator to coordinate and control the state enterprise.

The Hebrews

The Hebrews have recorded some early management practices in the Bible which may be studied by modern administrators. Moses, employing an exception principle, delegated the judging of misdemeanors to subordinate tribal leaders and acted himself only on major cases. The exodus from Egyptian bondage was quite a managerial task; although divine intervention at perilous points is rarely available to today's managers. The Ten Commandments were some rules for organizational conduct to preserve group solidarity. Joseph, again through recourse to a source not as readily available for modern management forecasting, was able to engage in long-range planning to store grain for the "seven lean years." These examples reflect intuitive management knowledge applied to meet the necessities of the moment but which were not generalized in managerial practices of the day.

Greece

Will Durant captured the essence of the rise and fall of many civilizations with his "a nation is born stoic, and dies epicurean."[1] In the stoic phase of the cycle, adversity breeds cohesion and deprivation fosters initiative. Self-control, thrift, hard work, and an orderly life bring prosperity. As affluence reigns, self-control becomes self-indulgence, thrift becomes a vice, industry and perseverance yield to opportunism, and social order breaks down. Epicureans take no thought for the morrow and decline begins; the fall comes not from without, but from internal decay. The cycle was true for Greece and for Rome. America was founded by stoics, the Puritans; does the past foretell the future?

The institutions, art, language, drama, and literature of Greece form a significant part of our own culture. However, Greek economic philosophy was anti-business and trade and commerce were considered beneath the dignity of the Grecian ideal man. Work, being ignoble to the aristocratic or philosophical Greek, was to be carried out by slaves and less than respectable citizens. Manual workers and merchants were excluded from citizenship in the Greek democracy because of the low esteem of manual and trade occupations. Government administration was based solely on the election and participation by all citizens and the prevailing philosophy discouraged "professional" experts as administrators.

Socrates observed that managerial skills were transferable between public and private affairs. In this early recognition of the universality of management, Socrates noted that "the conduct of private affairs differs from that of public concerns only in magnitude"; both involved the management of men and if one could not manage his private affairs he certainly could not manage the public business. However, the Greeks may have followed the Socratic notion of universality too far. Military and municipal leaders were regularly rotated, creating chaos in governmental affairs and becoming a terrible burden when threatened by the better organized, more professional armies of Philip of Macedonia and Alexander the Great and the government of Sparta.

In his *Politics*, Aristotle noted that "He who has never learned

<hr>

[1] Will Durant, *The Story of Civilization, Part I: Our Oriental Heritage,* New York: Simon and Schuster, 1935, p. 259.

to obey cannot be a good commander."[2]   In his discussion of household management (*oeconomia*) he, like Socrates, spoke of the similarity between the art of managing a state and managing a household. Both involved the management of property and of slaves and freemen with the only difference being the magnitude of the total operation. In his *Metaphysics*, Aristotle developed the thesis that reality is knowable through the senses and through reason. By rejecting mysticism, Aristotle became the father of the scientific method and established the intellectual foundation for the Renaissance and the age of reason. Eventually this spirit of scientific inquiry would form a basis for scientific management.

Greece fell before the Romans, a hardy stock of people from the banks of the Tiber. It destroyed itself first by depleting its forests and natural resources, by internal moral decay, by political disorder, and by decimating its leaders through revolts and counter-revolts. Stoicism, like its later Christian counterparts Calvinism and Puritanism, produced the strongest characters of that time. Despite the anti-trade philosophy, the age of Greece illustrates the first seeds of democracy, the advent of decentralized participatory government, the first attempts to establish individual liberty, the beginnings of the scientific method for problem solving, and an early, though sketchy, insight into the notion that managing different undertakings requires essentially the same managerial skills.

Rome

Rome was born stoic and conquered the decaying Hellenic civilization. The Romans developed a quasi-factory system to manufacture armaments for the legions, for the pottery makers who produced for a world market, and later for textiles which were sold for export. The famous Roman road system was built to speed the distribution of goods, as well as to speed the movement of troops to dissident colonies. The Romans inherited the Greek disdain for trade and left business activities in the hands of Greek and Oriental freedmen. A growing external trade required commercial standardization and the state developed a guaranteed system of measures, weights, and coins. The first resemblance of a corporate organization appeared in the form of joint-stock companies which

---

[2] Aristotle, *Politics* (translated by Benjamin Jowett), Chicago: Great Books of the Western World. Encyclopaedia Britannica, Inc., Vol. IX, p. 474.

sold stocks to the public in order to carry out government contracts to supply the war effort. There was a highly specialized labor force which, with few exceptions, worked in small shops as independent craftsmen selling for the market rather than for individual customers. Free workers formed guilds (*collegia*) but these were for social aims and mutual benefits, such as to defray the cost of funerals, rather than for establishing wages, hours, or conditions of employment. The state regulated all aspects of Roman economic life: it levied tariffs on trade, laid fines upon monopolists, regulated the guilds, and used its revenues to fight a multitude of wars. Large-scale organizations could not exist since the government prohibited joint stock companies for any purpose other than the execution of government contracts.

The Romans also had a genius for order, and the military autocracy ran the empire with an iron hand. Behind this authoritarian organizational structure lay two fundamental concepts—discipline and functionalism. The latter provided for a specific division of work among the various military and governmental agencies and the former provided a rigid framework and hierarchy of authority to insure that the functions were carried out. The contributions of Rome to our heritage lay chiefly in law and government which were manifestations of this concern for order. Roman law became a model for later civilizations and the Roman separation of legislative and executive powers provided a model system of checks and balances for later constitutional governments.

The Catholic Church

The Roman Catholic Church could be considered a legacy of Rome in an indirect manner. Gibbon held that Christianity was the chief cause of Rome's fall because it destroyed the old faiths of Rome which had given character to the Roman man and stability to the Roman state. Christianity was more probably the effect rather than the cause of Rome's downfall and it brought consolation to poverty, hope to slavery, and the promise of a better afterlife. Christianity became a legacy for mankind guiding the morality of Western culture to the present.

The Catholic Church itself posed some interesting organizational problems. As the faith spread, novel sects grew and the first blush of a youthful theology threatened to become an adolescence of diver-

sity.   In the second century A.D., leaders recognized the need to
define more rigorously the objectives, doctrine, conduct of Christian
activities, and the conditions for membership in the organization.
Leaders developed scriptural canons (i.e., what scriptures were
authentic and inspired), doctrine (i.e., catholic or "universal" orthodox belief), and sought to establish an organization and a central
source of Church authority.   Early congregations operated independently, each defining its own doctrine and conditions for membership.   However, the Church at Rome claimed final authority,
since it had been founded by Peter and Christ had said that upon
that rock (Greek, *petra*) he would found his church.   Little is
known of that period of struggle between decentralized and centralized authority in the church.   The outcome was centralized doctrine and authority in Rome and the Papacy.   However, the conflict
between centralized and decentralized authority has reappeared
throughout history not only in the Catholic Church but in other
organizations.   In modern organizational terms, the Catholic
Church leaders perceived a need to "institutionalize" the organization: that is, the need to specify policies, procedures, doctrine, and
authority.   The problem is a recurring one even today: the need
for unanimity of purpose, yet with discretion for local problems
and conditions.

Feudalism and the Middle Ages

Renaissance writers coined the phrase "Middle Ages" to refer
to what occurred from the decline of Rome to the Renaissance
period.   Slavery became uneconomical in the late Roman period:
the upkeep of slaves was costly and they showed no particular
enthusiasm for their work.   The abolition of slavery came not with
moral progress but with economic change.   Development of free
men as tenant farmers proved to be more economical for the landholder, for they were less expensive to keep and avoidance of starva-
tion yielded a crude but effective incentive system.   The growth of
large estates and the political disorder following the fall of Rome led
to an economic, social, and political chaos ripe for the emergence of
the feudal system.   Feudalism as a cultural system prevailed from
about A.D. 600 to about A.D. 1500.   At the base of the feudal system
was the serf who was free yet tied more than the slave before him
to his master.   The serf tilled a plot of land owned by the manorial

lord, much like modern share croppers, and was given military protection in exchange for a portion of the products of his labors.   The
feudal system tied man to the land, fixed rigid class distinctions,
established an age of landed aristocracy that was to endure to the
Industrial Revolution, forced education to a standstill, made poverty
and ignorance the hallmark of the masses, and completely stifled
human progress until the age of reformation.   It is no wonder that
some historians prefer to call this period the "Dark Ages."

The Catholic Church dominated medieval life and provided the
hope of an afterlife as the only consolation for this one.   The Church
also became the largest landholder in Europe and employed serfs;
as Durant said, "feudalism feudalized the Church."[3]   With the
Church as superstate, the admonitions of doctrine against lending
for interest, against desiring anything from this world other than
subsistence, and against materialistic trade and profits, continued the
opinion of business as an evil necessity.   The complete domination
of life by the Church led men to think not of this world, but of the
other; not of gain, but of salvation.   The self-interest of trade
diverted men's thoughts from God to gain, from obedience to
initiative, and from humility to activity.   The seeds of doubt and
despair were sown and only a great cultural revolution could pave
the way for an industrial society.

The Revival of Commerce

Feudalism gave birth to the Crusades and in turn, died as a
result of them.   Two centuries of religious fervor had left Jerusalem
in the hands of the Moslems and Europe was seething with the
potential for change.   The Crusades also stimulated commerce by
opening new trade routes and exposing parochial, feudal Europe
to the wealth of the East.   The Crusades weakened Christian belief.
Embarking on their journeys with invincible religious conviction,
the Crusaders returned with the realization that the Middle Eastern culture was superior in manners, morals, trade, industry, and
warfare.   The results of this cultural confrontation led to a more
secular life in Europe through weakening religious bonds.   Interest
arose in exploration and a new spirit of trade and commerce arose to
fill the land of feudalism.   New markets, new ideas, the rise of

---

[3] Will Durant, *The Story of Civilization, Part IV: The Age of Faith*, New York:
Simon and Schuster, 1950, p. 564.

towns, the first seeds of a new middle class, freer circulation of money and credit instruments, and the resurgence of political order created the soil for the Renaissance and the Reformation.

Old cities were revitalized by trade, and new cities arose as trade centers. Industrial growth followed the securing of trade routes and textiles became a leading facet of economic growth. The first method of industrial organization was the *domestic* system of production. Under the domestic or "putting out" system, a merchant procured the raw materials, farmed them out to individual workers or families who, using their own equipment, would complete the product in their home and then deliver it to the employer for a wage. Indeed, the domestic system of production lingers even today in the weaving of tweed cloth in Ireland and Scotland. The faults of the domestic system lay in the simple tools and technology, with little incentive to improve them, and in the inefficiencies of small-scale production with a limited division of labor. As the volume of trade grew, the domestic system proved inefficient and the need for more capital, the benefits to be gained from specializing labor, and the economies of scale of a centralized workplace would lead to the factory system.

Growing trade also required a rationalization of the methods of keeping accounts. Luca Pacioli (Venetian) in 1494 wrote *Summa de Arithmetica, geometrica, proportioni, et proportionalita*. This was the first system of double entry bookkeeping and arose out of the need for merchants to know their credit and debit positions in general and in relation to specific persons or accounts.[4] Pacioli's system was the first information system for management; it told the entrepreneur his cash and inventory position and enabled a check on his cash flow. It did not tell him his costs and it was not until the twentieth century that any advancements were made upon Pacioli's system. In Siena, Venice, Genoa, and Florence, bankers such as the Peruzzis and the Medicis loaned the funds and established the clearing houses for the bookkeeping transfer of accounts. The greatest obstacle for banking was the prevailing prohibition against interest but commerical necessity overcame religious sanctity and devious loopholes developed so funds could flow. By 1400, most states had repealed prohibitions against interest, and with respect to

---

[4] R. Emmett Taylor, "Luca Pacioli", in A. C. Littleton and B. S. Yamey (eds.), *Studies in the History of Accounting*, Homewood, Ill.: Richard D. Irwin, 1956, pp. 175–184.

the Church prohibition, it became something which remained in the canons but not enforced and hence ignored by all.

Feudalism was dead, interred by the expansion of trade, the growth of urbanization, the creation of a merchant class, and the development of strong central governments. But the age of industrialization had not yet arrived. New wine was fermenting, straining the old societal containers. What man needed now was a new spirit, a new sanction for his efforts.

THE CULTURAL REBIRTH

The new wine that was straining the cultural containers was a trinity of forces which would eventually lead to the Industrial Revolution and a new culture for mankind. These forces established the cultural foundations of a new industrial age which brought man from subservience to new-found freedoms in economic arrangements for the allocation of resources, in his social relations, and in political institutions. One facet of this cultural trinity, the market ethic, brought forth the notion of a market-directed economy. The rediscovery of the ancient classics and renewed interest in reason and science epitomized the Renaissance and broke the ancient hold of theology on man through the Protestant Reformation and the subsequent Protestant ethic. The liberty ethic established new concepts in relations between man and state through constitutional government. These three "ethics," or standards for cultural conduct, interacted in practice to change cultural values toward man, toward work, and toward profits. The outcome of this cultural rebirth was the creation of a new environment which would lead to the need for the formal study of management.

The Market Ethic

Economic thinking was basically sterile during the Middle Ages since localized, subsistence-level economies needed no economic theory to explain their workings. Early man perceived the main factors of production as land and labor, and even the latter did not pose much of a problem. Capital as an input factor was scorned and its return damned. Any idea that management was a resource input to the organization was completely lacking in early economic thought.

In the sixteenth and seventeenth centuries, the re-emergence of strong national entities began to reshape economic thought. As new lands were discovered through explorations, new trade routes and new products created an international market. This revolution in trade resulted in the economic philosophy of mercantilism and injected the government into a central role of financing and protecting trade in order to build strong national economies. This economic chauvinism meant that the state intervened in all economic affairs, engaged in state economic planning, and regulated private economic activity to a large degree.[5] Mercantilism eventually fell of its own weight. Much of its planning went awry because it tried to keep alive uneconomic enterprises, because it curbed private initiative, because it built elaborate bureaucratic, red-tape controls, and because it fostered wars and trade rivalries and destroyed the very markets it was trying to create.[6] The mercantilists were a philosophical contradiction to the emerging eighteenth century "Age of Enlightenment." The mercantilists thought only of the state while the philosophy of the enlightenment was a champion of individual rights and viewed all human institutions in terms of the contribution they could make to the happiness of each individual.[7]

In the eighteenth century, the Physiocratic school of economic thought emerged to challenge mercantilism. Francois Quesnay, its founder, maintained that wealth did not lie in gold and silver but sprang from agricultural production. He advocated *laissez-faire* capitalism, meaning that the government should "let alone" the mechanisms of the market; for him, economics had a natural order and harmony and government intervention interfered with the natural course of events. Adam Smith (1723–1790), a Scottish political economist, was not a Physiocrat *per se* but was influenced by their view of a natural harmony in economics. In his *Wealth of Nations*, Smith established the "classical" school and became the father of liberal economics.[8] Smith thought that the tariff policies of mercantilism were destructive and, rather than protecting industry, these policies penalized efficiency by a state fiat and conse-

5 John Fred Bell, *A History of Economic Thought*, 2d ed., New York: Ronald Press, 1967, p. 53.

6 Shepard B. Clough, *The Economic Development of Western Civilization*, New York: McGraw-Hill Book Co., 1959, Chapter 11.

7 John Bowditch and Clement Ramsland (ed.), *Voices of the Industrial Revolution*, Ann Arbor: University of Michigan Press, 1961, pp. iv–v.

8 Adam Smith, *An Inquiry Into the Nature and Causes of the Wealth of Nations*, Chicago: Great Books of the Western World, Vol. 39, Encyclopaedia Britannica, 1952. Originally published in 1776.

quently misallocated the nation's resources. Smith proposed that only the market and competition be the regulator of economic activity. The "invisible hand" of the market would insure that resources flowed to their best consumption and their most efficient reward and the economic self-interest of each person and nation, acting in a fully competitive market, would bring about the greatest prosperity to all.

For Adam Smith, the specialization-of-labor concept was a pillar of this market mechanism. He cited the example of the pin-makers who, when each performed a limited operation, could produce 48,000 pins a day, whereas one unspecialized worker could do no more than twenty pins per day. He admitted that this was a trifling example but he found the same principles of division of labor operating successfully in many industries:

> This great increase of the quantity of work which, in consequence of the division of labour, the same number of people are capable of performing, is owing to three different circumstances; first, to the increase of dexterity in every particular workman; secondly, to the saving of the time which is commonly lost in passing from one species of work to another; and lastly, to the invention of a great number of machines which facilitate and abridge labour, and enable one man to do the work of many.[9]

The division of labor concept benefitted all of society and provided an economic rationale for the factory system. When markets were limited, a household or domestic production arrangement could meet market needs. As the population grew and as new trade territories became feasible, a greater division of labor was possible and the factory system as a productive device began to gain momentum.

When his writing appeared in the early stages of the Industrial Revolution, Smith found a large number of vocal supporters and fertile soil for his liberal economics. He was in tune with the philosophy of the Enlightenment and the newly emerging group of entrepreneurs who wished to sweep away the restrictions of mercantilism and the controlling power of the landed aristocracy. England found in the market ethic an economic sanction for private initiative rather than mercantilism, competition rather than protection, innovation rather than economic stagnancy, and self-interest rather than state interest as the motivating force. The market ethic

---

[9] *Ibid.*, p. 4. Smith also enunciated the first marketing principle when he noted that the division of labor was limited by the extent of the market, *i.e.*, there would be no economic rationale in having 18 men producing 48,000 pins per day if the market could only absorb 20,000 per day. *Ibid.*, Chapter 3.

became one element in this trinity of forces which created the cultural environment for the flowering of the industrial system.

The Protestant Ethic

The loosening of religious bonds by the Crusades and the spread of general prosperity through the revival of commerce was bound sooner or later to lead to a revolt against the Church. It began in Germany with Martin Luther and shook the world. By no stretch of the imagination could Martin Luther be considered as pro-capitalism. He agreed with the church in condemning interest, considered commerce a "nasty business," and spoke out vehemently against the Fuggers, the leading industrial family in Germany. John Calvin was inspired by the reformation attempts of Luther and, like Luther, he followed the Augustinian creed of predestination and brought to the Reformation a somber view of the smallness and weakness of man. He viewed as ideal a combination of church and state which led to his theocracy of Geneva and clearly repudiated the philosophy of the Renaissance. His concept of the "elect," those predestined to be saved, gave a new spirit to his followers. Since all was predetermined, each should believe that he was of the elect and, based on this divine election, each would have the courage to face the tribulations of any harsh world. Did the stern Protestantism of Luther and Calvin provide the religious sanctions for capitalism? Certainly their ideas did not espouse the cause of capitalism, but, (as often happens when disciples are given free rein) did their ideas create a new man for a new age?

Max Weber would answer in the affirmative by stating the case for Protestantism creating the spirit of capitalism.[10] Weber began his search for an explanation of the capitalistic spirit by noting the overwhelming number of Protestants as business leaders and entrepreneurs, and as the more skilled laborers and the more highly technically and commercially trained personnel. In Weber's view, Luther developed the idea of a "calling" in the sense of a task set by God, a life task. This was a new idea brought about during the Reformation which became a central dogma of Protestant denominations. It discarded Catholic notions of subsistence living and

---

[10] Max Weber, *The Protestant Ethic and the Spirit of Capitalism* (trans. by Talcott Parsons), New York: Charles Scribner's Sons, 1958. Originally published in Germany (1905) and revised in 1920 to include answers to various critics.

monastic asceticism by urging the individual to fulfill the obligations imposed upon him in this world, i.e., in his "calling" (German, *Beruf*). It placed worldly affairs as the highest form of moral activity for the individual and gave the performance of earthly duties a religious significance and sanction. Every man's occupation was a calling and all were legitimate in the sight of God. Weber did not say that Luther intended capitalism to follow from his concept of the calling; on the contrary, it was later connotations which led to refinement of this idea into a success-oriented spirit of capitalism. The calling did place a new interpretation on the purpose of life for man; instead of waiting in his station for the Judgment Day, the worker should pursue whatever occupation he had chosen, not for the purpose of material gain beyond needs, but because it was divine will. The result of this Protestant dogma was a worldly asceticism which asked man to renounce earthly sensuality to labor in this world for the glorification of God. Each man must consider himself as one of the "elect" and if he did not his lack of confidence was interpreted as a lack of faith. To attain self-confidence, each individual must engage in intense worldly activity for it and it alone dispelled religious doubts and gave certainty of grace. In practice, this came to mean that God helps those who help themselves.

The Catholic layman, in contrast, fulfilled his required religious duties conscientiously. Beyond that minimum his good works need not form a rationalized system of life. He could use his good works to atone for particular sins, to better his chances for salvation, or as a sort of insurance premium for his later years. To make a sharper distinction, Weber described the demands of Calvinism:

> The God of Calvinism demanded of his believers not single good works, but a life of good works combined into a unified system. There was not place for the very human Catholic cycle of sin, repentance, atonement, release, followed by renewed sin. Nor was there any balance of merit for a life as a whole which could be adjusted by temporal punishments or the Churches' means of grace.[11]

The Calvinist was therefore required to live a *life* of good works, not an inconsistent series of wrongs balanced by repentant rights. Weber saw this as a keystone in developing a spirit of effort and gain; man was no longer able to give free rein to irrational impulses but was required by dogma to exercise self-control over his every

[11] *Ibid.*, p. 117.

action. One proved his faith in worldly activity and he did it with zeal and self-discipline.

This new Protestant asceticism, which Weber also characterized as Puritanism, did not condone the pursuit of wealth for its own sake for wealth would lead to pleasure and to all the temptations of the flesh. Instead activity became the goal of the good life. Numerous corollaries developed in practice: (1) that the waste of time was the deadliest of sins since every hour wasted was negating the opportunity to labor for the glory of God; (2) willingness to work: "he who will not work shall not eat"; (3) that the division and specialization of labor was a result of Divine Will since it led to the development of a higher degree of skill, to improvement in the quality and quantity of production, and hence served the good of all; and (4) that consumption beyond basic needs was wasteful and therefore sinful: "Waste not, want not."[12] According to Weber, each of these ideas had a significant impact on the motivations of men leading to a spirit of enterprise.

Intense activity moved men from a contemplative life to one of continuous physical and mental labor. Willingness to work placed the motivational burden on the individual and his self-directed, self-controlled life gave him an internal gyroscope.[13] The specialization of labor placed each man in his calling, required him to do his best, and the non-specialized worker demonstrated a lack of grace. The Protestant ethic postulated that God desired profitability, that this was a sign of grace, and to waste anything and reduce profits, or to forgo what might be a profitable venture, worked against God's will. By not seeking luxury, each man created a surplus or profit from his labors. The created wealth could not be consumed beyond a person's basic needs and thus the surplus was to be reinvested in other ventures or the improvement of present ones.

Protestantism resulted in specific guidelines for the creation of a capitalistic spirit.[14] According to Weber, man had a duty to work, a duty to use his wealth wisely, and a duty to live a self-denying

---

12 *Ibid.*, p. 157–173.

13 *Cf.*, David Riesman, Nathan Glazer, and Reuel Denney, *The Lonely Crowd*, Garden City, N. Y.: Doubleday and Co., 1950, pp. 29–32. Riesman and his associates characterized the product of the Protestant ethic as "inner-directed man."

14 Peters has classified Weber as an "apologist" in that he, along with Adam Smith, sought to justify the activities and the acquisitive motivation of individual businessmen. See Lynn H. Peters, *The Acquisitive Motivation of the Businessman: Classical Views—Apologetic and Critical*, Madison: Bureau of Business Research, University of Wisconsin, Vol. 3, No. 2, (March, 1966), pp. 6–12.

life. An unequal distribution of goods in the world was Divine Providence at work since each man had unequal talents and therefore reaped unequal rewards. Wealth was no assurance of heaven and the poor need not worry as long as they performed their calling properly. For Weber, the spirit of capitalism was created by the Protestant ethic which equated spiritual worth and temporal success. With no room for self-indulgence and with the tenets of self-control and self-direction, a new age of individualism had been born.

Critics of the Weberian Thesis

Every thesis generates its antithesis and Weber's Protestant ethic is no exception. R. H. Tawney reversed Weber's thesis and argued that capitalism was the cause and justification of Protestantism, not the effect.[15] Tawney noted that Catholic cities were chief commercial centers and Catholics were leading bankers and that the "capitalistic spirit" was present in many places far in advance of the sixteenth and seventeenth century influences that Weber discussed. According to Tawney:

Is it not a little artificial to suggest that capitalist enterprise had to wait, as Weber appears to imply, till religious changes had produced a capitalist spirit? Would it not be equally plausible, and equally one-sided, to argue that the religious changes were themselves merely the result of economic movements?[16]

In Tawney's view, the rise of capitalism was action and reaction, molding and in turn being molded by other significant cultural forces. The Renaissance brought a new focus on reason, on discovery, on exploration, and on science; all were challenges to the monolithic authority of the Church. The Renaissance contributed the humanist's views that made life on earth more important and brought the promise of a new social order in which there would be mobility for man; it signaled the mastery of man over his environment rather than the reverse case of the Middle Ages.[17] Growing economic life posed new problems for Church doctrine and merchants and tradesmen engaged in profit-making activities regardless of dogma. Perhaps, then, the Reformation was an attempt to create materialistic loopholes for the emerging merchant class.

[15] R. H. Tawney, *Religion and the Rise of Capitalism,* London: John Murray, 1926.
[16] R. H. Tawney, "Foreword" to Max Weber's *The Protestant Ethic,* p. 8.
[17] Tawney, *Religion and the Rise of Capitalism,* pp. 61–63.

With two sets of assumptions two different conclusions are reached: one, Weber's notion that the Church changed and then the spirit of capitalism abounded; or two, Tawney's view that economic motivation was steam pushing on the lid of church authority until the safety valve of a change in dogma (i.e., the Reformation and its later proliferation into various sects) could sanction economic efforts.   Tawney's criticism spawned other support for the anti-Weberian viewpoint.   Fanfani argued that the market system and capitalism had existed for over a hundred years before the first Protestant Church was formed.[18]   H. M. Robertson took the position that "Protestantism did not influence capitalism, but capitalism influenced the social ethics of Protestantism . . ."[19]   The Jewish case against Weber was presented by Werner Sombart, who suggested that everything Weber ascribed to Puritanism might be equally ascribed to Judaism, and probably to a greater degree.   Sombart suggested that Puritanism was essentially a modified form of Judaism and that the Jews were historically earlier and more significant to the spirit of capitalism than the Puritans.[20]   Weber of course rejected this by saying that Judaism led to "speculative pariah-capitalism" while Protestantism led to a more constructive form of capitalism.[21]

Modern Support for Weber

Despite the criticisms of Weber's thesis there is modern evidence that Protestants hold different values toward work.   In his *Achieving Society*, McClelland began a search for the psychological factors which were generally important for economic development.[22] The factor he isolated was the "need for achievement" or the short-hand version "*n* achievement."   McClelland's study was both historical and cross-cultural and his findings support Weber's thesis. First, McClelland found that high *n* achievement was essential to

---

[18] Amintore Fanfani, *Catholicism, Protestantism, and Capitalism*, New York: Sheed and Ward, 1955, p. 183.

[19] Hector M. Robertson, *Aspects of the Rise of Economic Individualism: A Criticism of Max Weber and his School*, New York: Kelley and Millman, 1959, p. 183 (first published in 1933).   Another who follows essentially the same thesis is Kurt Samuelson, *Religion and Economic Action* (trans. by Geoffrey French), New York: Basic Books, 1961.

[20] Werner Sombart, *The Jew and Modern Capitalism* (trans. by M. Epstein), London: T. Fisher Unwin, 1913.

[21] Max Weber, p. 271.

[22] David C. McClelland, *The Achieving Society*, New York: Van Nostrand Rinehold Co., 1961.

engaging in entrepreneurial activities; second, that high n achievement in a society was significantly correlated to rapid economic development; and third, that certain ethnic, religious, and minority groups showed marked differences in n achievement. He found that Protestants produced children with higher n achievement than Catholics, and Jews produced children with higher n achievement than either one. McClelland concluded that "individualistic" religions, for example the Protestant ones, tended to be associated with a high need for achievement, while "authoritarian" ones, such as traditional Catholicism, tended to have a lower need for achievement. He did concede, however, that at the present there are wide variations and subcultures among various modern Catholic communities.

What was involved in the need for achievement was not so much the need to reach certain goals, such as wealth, status, respect, etc., as to enjoy the satisfactions of success. Wealth was a way of keeping score, not the goal. The entrepreneurial personality was characterized by special attitudes toward risk-taking, willingness to expend energy, willingness to innovate, and a readiness to make decisions and accept responsibility. Historically the concern for achievement appeared in a culture some fifty or so years before a rapid rate of economic growth and prosperity. McClelland found this to be true in ancient Greece (before its golden age), in Spain in the Middle Ages (before the age of exploration), and in England during two different periods. The first period was from 1500–1625 when Protestantism and Puritanism were growing in strength in England and this was occurring concurrently with a rising need for achievement. The second period came in the eighteenth century just prior to the Industrial Revolution. The reasoning that McClelland used to support Weber was basically thus: (1) the Protestant Reformation emphasized self-reliance rather than reliance on others in all facets of life; (2) Protestant parents changed child-rearing practices to teach self-reliance and independence; (3) it has been empirically demonstrated by McClelland and his associates that these practices lead to a higher need for achievement in sons; and (4) a higher need for achievement leads to spurts of economic activity such as that which Weber characterized as the spirit of capitalism.[23] Therefore, McClelland was able to draw a relationship

[23] *Ibid.*, pp. 47–53.

empirically between the influence of Protestantism and Weber's "spirit of modern capitalism."

Lenski has summarized the criticisms of Weber, evaluated them, and presented the evidence both for and against Weber.[24] On balance, he found evidence more in favor of Weber than against him. Lenski examined vertical mobility and concomitant characteristics of aspirations, ambition, and attitudes toward work in an attempt to define the relationship between religious affiliation and the ability of people to move upward in the job world. The findings resulted in a ranking of: first (most mobile) Jews; second, Protestants; and third (least mobile), Catholics. Lenski's explanation resided in the differences among the above three groups with respect to "achievement" motivation and their attitudes toward work. Jews and Protestants showed a positive attitude toward work and derived satisfactions from work. Catholics held neutral attitudes toward work and indicated that it was done for some other purpose than the satisfaction that came from work itself. In Lenski's view:

Catholics continued to regard work primarily as a necessary evil; a consequence of Adam's fall and a penalty for sin. By contrast, Protestants come to view it as an opportunity for serving God, or, in the Deist version, for building character.[25]

The implications of McClelland's and Lenski's findings can be far-reaching for modern man. Not only did they find empirical support for Weber, but their work suggests that achievement values can be taught and instilled in various societies. In underdeveloped nations and in America's ghettos, inculcation of achievement values would provide means for self-help programs to speed the progress of or the adjustment to industrialization.[26]

The Liberty Ethic

Given the postulates of economic freedom and the sanctions of individual rewards for worldly efforts, the political system must be conducive to individual liberty. The divine right of kings, the aristocracy of the manor lord, the exercise of secular authority by the church, and serfdom as a birthright were not favorable conditions

---

[24] Gerhard Lenski, *The Religious Factor: A Sociological Study of Religious Impact on Politics, Economics, and Family Life*, Garden City, N. Y.: Doubleday and Co., 1961.

[25] *Ibid.*, p. 83.

[26] For examples of how this might be done, see David C. McClelland and David G. Winter, *Motivating Economic Achievement*, New York: Free Press, 1969.

for developing an industrialized society. In the Age of Enlightenment, new political philosophers began to stimulate the thoughts of men with such new ideas as equality, justice, the rights of man, a rule of reason, and notions of a republic governed by the consent of the governed. These were radical ideas in those times, ideas that threatened the existing order with a profound revolution in the views of the relationship between man and state.

Before this facet of the cultural rebirth, political theory called for the domination of the many by the few and found its best proponents in Machiavelli and Thomas Hobbes. Nicolo Machiavelli, an out-of-office administrator and diplomat in the city-state of Florence, wrote *The Prince* in 1513.[27] He was an experienced observer of the intrigues of state and papacy and set forth a "how to do it" book for a ruler or any aspiring ruler. *The Prince*, dedicated to Lorenzo di Piero de Medici, was an exposition on how to rule, not how to be good or wise, but how to rule men successfully. Machiavelli's basic assumption about the nature of man was indicative of his rationale for the type of leadership he advocated:

> Whoever desires to found a state and give it laws, must start with the assumption that all men are bad and ever ready to display their vicious nature, whenever they may find occasion for it.[28]

To cope with this brute man, the ruler was justified in pursuing any leadership style that suited his purpose. He should be concerned with having a good reputation, but not with being virtuous; should he have to choose between feared and loved, he would find it better to be feared; and above all, he must be like a lion and a fox, employing force and deceit. For Machiavelli, it was the end and not the means which was important; if the ruler succeeded, he would win approval and his villainies would be forgotten. "Machiavellian" has come to connote the unscrupulous, crafty, and cunning in policy. For that time, and perhaps for this one, Machiavelli has personified the command philosophy of governing men.[29]

Thomas Hobbes' *Leviathan* (1651) was a later argument for a

---

[27] Nicolo Machiavelli, *The Prince* (trans. by Luigi Ricci), New York: New American Library, 1952.

[28] Nicolo Machiavelli, *Discourses on Livy,* trans. by Alan H. Gilbert, reprinted in *Machiavelli: The Chief Works and Others,* Durham, N.C.: Duke University Press, Vol. 1, 1956, p. 203.

[29] An interesting analysis of Machiavellian practices in modern corporate life may be found in Antony Jay, *Management and Machiavelli,* New York: Holt, Rinehart, and Winston, 1967.

strong central leadership.[30] He began his analysis with man in a state of nature, without civil government, and proceeded to the conclusion that some greater power, the *Leviathan*, must exist to bring order from chaos. This man or body became sovereign; since it was given all rights by the governed, its powers could not be revoked, and it became an absolute sovereign. It made no difference to Hobbes whether the sovereign be civil or ecclesiastical, as long as the central power regulated all overt conduct and expression, both civil and religious. The sovereign ruled all, and the individual was subordinate to the system.

In the history of human liberty, John Locke's essay *Concerning Civil Government* (1690) must stand as a great contribution to political theory and as an effective instigator of political action. It served to state the principles of the English "bloodless revolution" of 1688 which brought about substantial fundamental changes in the British constitution. It also set the stage for the American Revolution of 1776 by inspiring the authors of the Declaration of Independence and furnished inspiration to Jean Jacques Rousseau's *Social Contract* and the ensuing French Revolution. Perhaps no other one man has had such a profound effect on political theory and action. Locke attacked the divine right of kings, whose proponents traced this right to Adam's God given right to rule his children, and set forth some new concepts of authority:

> . . . who shall be judge whether the prince or legislative body act contrary to their trust? . . . To this I reply, the people shall be judge . . .[31]

This notion found more explicit support in the Declaration of Independence:

> We hold these truths to be self-evident, that all men are created equal; that they are endowed by their creator with certain inalienable rights; that among these are life, liberty, and the pursuit of happiness. That to secure these rights, governments are instituted among men deriving their just powers from the consent of the governed.

Locke's work is so broad that it is possible only to sample his main contributions: first, that men were governed by a natural law of reason and not by the arbitrary rules of tradition or the whims

---

[30] Thomas Hobbes, *Leviathan, or Matter, Form, and Power of a Commonwealth Ecclesiastical and Civil*, Chicago: Great Books of the Western World, Vol. 23, Encyclopaedia Britannica, 1952.

[31] John Locke, *Second Essay Concerning Civil Government*, Chicago: Great Books of the Western World, Vol. 35, Encyclopaedia Britannica, 1952, p. 81.

of a central authoritarian figure. Second, that civil society was built upon private property. The law of nature and reason commanded one not to harm another's possessions and men entered into a civil society in order to preserve more perfectly their liberty and property and this was then protected by both natural law and civil law. Since man had a natural right to property, the state could not take it away from him, but must rather protect his right to it.

Locke was a Puritan in the England of Cromwell. His writing must have affected that of Adam Smith and most certainly established the basis for Rousseau's writings. In the emergence of the philosophical Age of Enlightenment, he put forth a new civil order for man: one, a law based on reason, not the arbitrary dictates of men; two, a government deriving its powers from the governed; three, liberty to pursue individual goals as a natural right; and four, private property and its use in the pursuit of happiness as a natural and legally protected right. These four ideas interwove in practice to form a solid political foundation for industrial growth. It provided a sanction for *laissez-faire* economics, it sanctioned the pursuit of individual rewards, guaranteed the rights of property, gave protection to contracts, and provided for a system of justice among men.

SUMMARY

Early management thought was dominated by cultural values which were anti-business, anti-achievement, and largely anti-man. Industrialization could not emerge when man was bound to his station in life, when monarchs ruled by central dictates, and when people were urged to take no thought of individual fulfillment in this world but to wait for a better one. Before the Industrial Revolution, economies and societies were essentially static and political values involved unilateral decision making by some central authority. While some early ideas of management appeared, they were largely localized. Organizations could be run on the divine right of the king, on the appeal of dogma to the faithful, and on the rigorous discipline of the military. There was little or no need to develop a formal body of management thought under these non-industrialized circumstances.

Three forces were interacting and combining to provide for a new age of industrialization. Characterized as "ethics," or standards governing the conduct of men, they illustrate how economic, social, and political attitudes were changing during the cultural rebirth. Economically, the market ethic discouraged state domination of trade, encouraged competition, fostered the ethic of individual initiative, and placed self-interest and exchange at the core of market activities. Socially, the Protestant ethic shifted the motivation of man from other world wishes to this world salvation through effort. Achievement in the "calling" was sanctioned as the duty of man. Politically, the liberty ethic placed man in a participatory role in government, encouraged private property, discouraged rule by dictatorial whims, and introduced more freedom and individualism in all spheres of human life. Together, these three ethics created an individualistic ethic which would form the core of management thought for many years.

This cultural rebirth would establish the preconditions for industrialization and subsequently the need for a rational, formalized, systematic body of knowledge about how to manage. The emergence and refinement of the market economy required managers to become more creative and to be better informed about how best to administer an organization. Faced with a competitive, changing environment, the manager had to develop a body of knowledge about how best to utilize resources. Men began thinking of individual gain and had to be accommodated in some rational administrative framework. The emergence of modern management had to be based on *rational* ways of making decisions; no longer could the organization be operated on the whims of a few. This change did not come suddenly but evolved over a long period of time as the culture changed. How these changes came about and how they affected the evolution of management thought is the subject of this book. It is an intriguing story.

3

The Industrial Revolution: Problems and Perspective

The Industrial Revolution heralded a new age for man and society. The cultural rebirth had created new social, economic, and political conditions which were ripe for advances in science and technology. Subsequent improvements in technology made possible large combinations of physical and human resources and ushered in the factory system to replace the domestic system of production. This chapter will examine the salient characteristics of the Industrial Revolution and the managerial problems it created, and attempt to achieve some perspective on the consequences of this cultural revolution.

THE INDUSTRIAL REVOLUTION IN ENGLAND

Industrial progress is always closely tied to advancements in science and technology. In the fifteenth century, Johann Gutenberg (1400–1468) developed the first metallic movable type for a printing press and opened the door to an information revolution which has yet to cease. While medieval scientists attempted to deduce physical laws from the writings of Plato, Aristotle, St. Augustine, and the Bible, a new age of scientific inquiry began in the sixteenth and seventeenth centuries as church bonds loosened.

Francis Bacon (1561–1626) made an appeal for direct observation and the use of inductive rather than deductive logic; Nicholas Copernicus (1473–1543) challenged the Church's geocentric explanation of the universe and substituted a heliocentric one; Galileo Galilei (1564–1603) experimented with pendulums and the speed of falling objects; William Gilbert (1540–1603) experimented with magnets and laid the basis for electrical theory; William Harvey (1578–1657) learned that the heart pumped the blood through the body; and Isaac Newton (1642–1727) developed calculus and stated laws of motion and gravitation. This scientific revolution emphasized the spirit of observation and inquiry and established the foundation for the technological revolution which was to follow.

Even since man began to improve his methods of tilling the soil, of making weapons, or of weaving cloth, there have been advancements in technology or the art of making and using tools and equipment. Technology has been evolving and advancing for thousands of years but a "revolution" came in late eighteenth-century England and marked the beginning of a more rapid advance in technology than ever before. The essence of this revolution was the substitution of machine power for man power and it brought about marked changes in everyday human life. Phyllis Deane, in pin-pointing the emergence of the Industrial Revolution, illustrated the difference between pre-industrialized societies and industrialized ones. Pre-industrial societies are characterized by low per capita income, economic stagnation, dependence on agriculture, a low degree of specialization of labor, and very little geographical integration of markets. Industrial societies are characterized by rising or high per capita income, economic growth, low dependence on agriculture, a high degree of specialization of labor, and a widespread geographical integration of markets.[1] Using these factors as indicators, Deane concluded that the shift in England from a pre-industrial to an industrial nation became most evident in 1750 and accelerated thereafter.

Why England?

What underlying conditions enabled England to be the great watershed dividing pre-industrialized and industrialized societies?

[1] Phyllis Deane, *The First Industrial Revolution,* London: Cambridge University Press, 1965, pp. 5–19.

England had a constitutional government which was sensitive to the *laissez-faire* desires of businessmen and devoted to protecting and expanding trade in the larger world markets. The agricultural policies of the government encouraged large-scale farming and as farm machinery improved, farmers were displaced from the land to become available for factory work. Internal tolls on the use of roads and canals were abolished and the government encouraged the abandonment of old guild restrictions on output which stifled innovation and competition. In contrast France continued to encourage the guilds and their practices. The advocates of free enterprise held power in Britain's Parliament and legal barriers to the spread of commerce were broken down. Science and free inquiry were encouraged and practical applications of research in physics and chemistry were being made. On the Continent, abstract research was the order of the day and this inhibited industrial development there. In England, banks, exchange facilities, and joint stock companies grew, the currency was stable, and the profits from the colonies, slave trading, and the mining of gold and silver were being reinvested at an ever increasing rate. Liberty in England had created a new religion and this growing spirit of self-reliance epitomized the Protestant ethic.[2] The ascetic life demanded of Protestants yielded a surplus of funds for reinvestment and furnished capital for the industrial age. England also derived much of its initial investment capital from Switzerland, a land of thrifty and hardworking Calvinists. For example, by 1790 inhabitants of the city of Berne alone had invested 440,000 pounds in London.[3]

Social values in England were shifting to sanction profit-seeking and achievement. Crouzet, comparing England and France, says that vertical mobility was higher in England as class barriers were being lowered while France kept its relatively closed society. In France, the nobles were forbidden to go into commerce, in England they were encouraged; the French continued to hold business in low esteem, while England became the "workshop of the world": and England was characterized by a spirit of acquisitiveness, while France was more easy-going.[4] Recalling McClelland, who

[2] Herbert W. Schneider, *The Puritan Mind*, New York: Holt, Rinehart and Winston, 1930.

[3] William O. Henderson, *J. C. Fisher and His Diary of Industrial England 1814–1851*, New York: Augustus M. Kelley, 1966, p. 18.

[4] F. Crouzet, "England and France in the 18th Century: A Comparative Analysis of Two Economic Growths," in R. M. Hartwell (ed.), *The Causes of the Industrial*

stated that "the shortest way to achieve economic objectives might turn out to be through changing people first,"[5] Hagen has suggested:

In my judgment, the Industrial Revolution occurred first in England and Wales not simply because the circumstances facing Britain were different from those facing Continental countries but because British people were *inwardly* different from those on the Continent.[6]

Hagen characterized this difference as being one of a willingness to innovate, to place trust in one's own capacity, and to perceive oneself as a thinking and emotion-feeling organism. These attitudes led to changes in the English political system, in the economic sphere of life, and in social institutions. This creative spirit inspired people to gain power and status through economic activity and moved them to reject authoritarian governments.[7] Applying Rostow's terminology, the "preconditions for take-off" had been met and England created an industrial society.[8]

The Age of Machines

The physical elements of the Industrial Revolution were coal, iron, transportation, machinery, power, and factories; the human elements were the entrepreneurs with a zeal for innovation and profits and a largely agrarian and handicraft labor force. Iron and coal are the sinews of industry and England had ample quantities of both. Early blast furnaces used water-driven power to fan the coke.

Revolution in England, London: Methuen and Co. Ltd., 1967, pp. 139–174. Crouzet's thesis is supported in C. Landes, "French Entrepreneurship and Industrial Growth in the 19th Century," *The Journal of Economic History,* IX, No. 1, (May 1949). He attributed the relative economic retardation of France in the nineteenth century to a lack of entrepreneurs.

[5] McClelland, *The Achieving Society,* p. 337.

[6] Everett E. Hagen, "British Personality and the Industrial Revolution: The Historical Evidence," in Tom Burns and S. B. Saul (eds.), *Social Theory and Economic Change,* London: Tavistock Publications, 1967, p. 37. Italics added.

[7] *Ibid.,* pp. 41–42. Hagen also presented an interesting hypothesis about the relationship between child-rearing and economic change. He equated traditional with authoritarian societies and invoked psychoanalytical theory to suggest that child-rearing practices in traditional societies tend to develop passive, dependent, non-innovative children. The cycle is renewed from generation to generation and perpetuates the traditional society (cited by Burns and Saul, pp. 2–3). This appears to be compatible with McClelland's idea that high achievers are the children of fathers with low dominance.

[8] W. W. Rostow, *The Stages of Economic Growth,* London: Cambridge University Press, 1960, pp. 4–12.

In 1760, an enterprising John Smeaton replaced the water-driven bellows in his furnaces with one partially driven by steam and increased his iron production from 12 to 40 tons per furnace per day. Iron declined in price with added productivity and new uses were found: in 1763, the first known railway, the first iron bridge in 1779, and the first iron ship in 1787.[9] Birmingham, close to large coal and iron deposits, became the leading city in the English iron industry. Transport was costly and difficult and the construction of canals greatly reduced the cost of commercial traffic in Britain so that cities sprang up along the waterways.

The growing market for textiles proved a boon to further innovations. Increasing imports of cotton and a larger world market made mechanical improvements imperative. John Kay began the mechanization of weaving by his "flying shuttle" in 1733; in 1765, James Hargreaves changed the position of the spinning wheel from vertical to horizontal, stacked the wheels on top of one another, and wove eight threads at once by turning them all with one pulley and belt. He called his gadget the "spinning jenny" (Jenny was Mrs. Hargreaves) and added more wheels and power until he was weaving 80 threads at once. Resistance to technological advancement by workers appeared early in industrial history in the "Luddites," followers of the mythical General Ludd. The Luddites sought to stay the advance of history by smashing the new-fangled machinery. For example, operators of the old hand spinners were convinced that the new "jenny" would put them out of work; they raided Hargreave's house, smashed his machines, and he fled to Nottingham where a shortage of labor allowed him to install his machines.[10] In 1769, Richard Arkwright developed a "water frame" that stretched the cotton fibers into a tighter, harder yarn. His factories grew with this innovation until by 1776 he employed 5,000 workers, including many children who could operate the very simple machinery. Unfortunately, Arkwright also had problems with the Luddites at his new steam-powered plant at Chorley; a mob of spinners burned it to the ground, but before the ashes were cold, he was rebuilding.

[9] A. P. Usher, *An Introduction to the Industrial History of England*, Boston: Houghton-Mifflin Co., 1920, p. 323. Another excellent history of technological advancement is R. Whatley Cooke Taylor, *Introduction to a History of the Factory System*, London: Richard Bentley & Sons, 1886.

[10] Leonard M. Fanning, *Fathers of Industry*, New York: MacFadden-Bartell Inc., 1964, pp. 21–22.

The revolution in textiles drew from advancements in iron and power; iron made sturdier frames and enabled the enlargement of capacity to go with the extra power from steam. The steam engine was not new; Hero of Alexandria (circa A.D. 200) developed one for the sake of amusement. Others had built models but had mechanical problems. James Watt developed the first workable steam engine in 1765 but finances and moving from the prototype to an industrial installation took 12 years. During this time he formed a partnership with Matthew Boulton, a leading English ironmaker, and they perfected steam power for Boulton's foundry. In 1788, Watt patented a "fly-ball governor" which adjusted the flow of steam to promote the uniform speed of the engine. This first cybernetic control device operated on a centrifugal principle; as the engine sped up, arms on a rotating shaft raised and the steam intake vents closed, reducing power intake; as the engine slowed, the arms dropped, allowing more power.[11]

The historian Arnold Toynbee has noted that two men, Adam Smith and James Watt, were the most responsible for destroying the old England, building a new one, and launching the World toward industrialization. Smith brought about the revolution in economic thought; Watt, the revolution in the use of steam power.[12] Harnessed to the wheels of a hundred industries, the steam engine provided more efficient and cheaper power; power for ships, trains and factories, revolutionizing English commerce and industry. Steam power lowered production costs, lowered prices, and expanded markets. A spirit of innovation led to inventions, inventions led to factories, and factories led to a need for direction and organization. The expanded market called for more workers, more machines, and a larger production scale on a regular basis. Capital was needed to finance these larger undertakings and the men who could command the capital began to bring together workers and machines under one common authority. Labor was divided, each man specializing in some task; parts of products had to become interchangeable such that the division of labor would lead to a common final result. Out of the division of labor would come the need for the direction and coordination of efforts. The "factory system" as a method of production was born, the age of

[11] Ibid., pp. 30–37.
[12] Arnold Toynbee, The Industrial Revolution, Boston: Beacon Press, 1956, p. 89; originally published in 1884.

machines began, and the infant capitalism toddled forth to create an abundance such as the world had never seen.

Management: The Fourth Factor of Production

Before the Industrial Revolution, economic theory focused on basically two factors of production, land and labor, and recognized capital as an input factor only as Church bonds loosened. The physiocrats recognized a "farmer-entrepreneur" but held that manufacturing and commerce were "sterile" and unable to produce a surplus. Adam Smith recognized the entrepreneur as a factor but treated his return or the surplus he created as a return to capital. Jean Baptiste Say (1767–1832), a French economist, was the first to explicitly recognize a fourth factor of production. Say noted that some "adventurers" (entrepreneurs) owned the undertaking but more frequently than not they owned only a share, having borrowed from others or having formed a partnership. The "adventurer" thus became a manager for others and assumed an additional risk in combining the factors of land, labor, and capital:

> . . . at one time he must employ a great number of hands; at another, buy or order the raw material, collect labourers, find consumers, and give at all times a rigid attention to order and economy; in a word, he must possess the art of superintendence and administration . . . There is always a degree of risk attending such undertakings . . . [and] the adventurer may . . . sink his fortune, and in some measure his character . . .[13]

For assuming the added risk in combining the traditional three factors of production, the "adventurer" received a separate reward for administration in addition to a return of his own invested capital.

Some authors make a further distinction between an entrepreneur and a manager; Fritz Redlich, for example, said the entrepreneur made "strategic" decisions, those pertaining to broader competitive policies of the total firm; while the manager made "tactical" decisions concerning the use of resources within the broad policy framework.[14] Jospeh Schumpeter saw the entrepreneur as an innovator-manager who was the prime mover in bringing about economic change by introducing new products,

---

[13] Jean Baptiste Say, *A Treatise on Political Economy*, New York: Augustus M. Kelley, 1964, pp. 330–331; originally published in 1803.

[14] Fritz Redlich, *The Entrepreneur*, Cambridge, Mass.: Harvard University Press, 1957, pp. 50–51.

new methods of production, new markets, new sources of raw material supplies, or a new organization of industry.[15] Professor Collins and his associates viewed the entrepreneur as an organization builder and innovator and distinguished between those who "build" (the innovating entrepreneur) and those who administer the organization after it has been built ("the bureaucratic entrepreneur").[16]

The early entrepreneur was the fourth factor of production in the sense that he was an "innovator" as well as a manager. As his organization grew, the entrepreneur found that he alone could not direct and control all activities and he began to delegate some of them to a level of submanagers. These submanagers were the first non-owning, salaried managers who had the responsibility of making decisions within a broader framework of policies established by the entrepreneur. It was in the process of delegation that many problems were to arise as the entrepreneur expanded his organization and took on an increasing number of lower level managers.

MANAGEMENT PROBLEMS IN THE EARLY FACTORY

The emerging factory system posed different management problems than ever encountered before. The Church could organize and manage its properties because of dogma and the devotion of the faithful; the military could control large numbers of men through a rigid hierarchy of discipline and authority; and governmental bureaucracies could operate without having to meet competition or show a profit. The managers in the new factory system could not resort to any of these devices to insure the proper utilization of resources.

The Industrial Revolution spawned a number of industries and the early 1800's were characterized by the growth of these firms in an ever increasing competitive environment. For the firm, the

---

[15] Joseph A. Schumpeter, *The Theory of Economic Development*, Cambridge, Mass.: Harvard University Press, 1936, p. 66 passim.

[16] Orvis F. Collins, David G. Moore, and Dareb B. Unwalla, *The Enterprising Man*, East Lansing, Mich.; Bureau of Business Economic Research, 1964, pp. 19–20. The whole subject of entrepreneurship has been dealt with at length under the sponsorship of the Harvard Center for Entrepreneurial Studies, in the journal *Explorations in Entrepreneurial History* (two series), and in a collection by Hugh G. J. Aitken (ed.), *Explorations in Enterprise*, Cambridge, Mass.: Harvard University Press, 1965.

pressure for size came from the need for economies of scale to compete more effectively. Some advocated resisting the pressures for size; for example, a report of the Committee on Woollen Manufacturers of 1806 stated that the development of large factories would not lead to many advantages for the entrepreneur. By continuing the domestic system, the entrepreneur could save much capital investment and would not need to "submit to the constant trouble and solicitude of watching over a numerous body of workmen."[17] Competition still demanded growth but the retarding factor was the lack of a pool of trained managers who could cope with large-scale factory problems. Hence the size of the early firm was often limited by the number of people the entrepreneur himself could effectively supervise. The result was a dual line of advance for the factory system: on the one hand, technology and capital made a larger scale of production possible and forces of competition made a larger size imperative; on the other hand, the enlargement of operations created a myriad of managerial problems.

The Search for Managerial Talent

The shortage of managerial talent posed all sorts of problems for the early entrepreneurs. Judging from early literature, the salaried manager, i.e., those in the layer of management below entrepreneur, were usually illiterate workmen promoted from the worker ranks because they evidenced a greater degree of technical skills or had the ability (often the physical strength) to keep discipline. Typically they were paid only a little more than the other workers and more often than not were attracted to the managerial position because it gave them the power to hire wives and children to work in the factory. Untrained in the intricacies of managing, the manager was left on his own to develop his own leadership style. Problems were met and solved on an *ad hoc* basis, and only a few managers could learn from the experiences of others in solving factory problems or handling people. The general view of leadership was that success or failure to produce results depended upon the "character" of the leader, upon his personal traits and idiosyncrasies, and not upon any generalized concepts of leadership.

[17] Sidney Pollard, *The Genesis of Modern Management: A Study of the Industrial Revolution in Great Britain,* Cambridge, Mass.: Harvard University Press, 1965, p. 11. Pollard's research into the early factory is quite extensive and is the most thorough of all works pertaining to early managerial problems created by the factory system.

Other sources of management talent provided little enlightenment. Entrepreneurs used relatives in managerial positions frequently, presumably based on the assumption that they were more trustworthy or would act to preserve their potential inheritance. This device also served as a training ground to secure ownership and control in the family for the next generation. Another source of talent was the "counting-house"; entrepreneurs recruited likely looking bank clerks and tellers thinking they probably had both business and financial acumen. For developing managers, the entrepreneurs relied on osmosis and experience on the job to furnish these recruits with the necessary knowledge.

The matriculation of England from an agrarian to an industrial society meant that there was no "managerial class" or in modern terms, no "professional" managers. First, there was no common body of knowledge about how to manage. The training of managers supplemented experience on the job with teaching the fledgling manager the techniques of production, the sources and characteristics of materials, the operations of machine processes, trade practices, and the legal obligations of the firm. This training was oriented toward a specific industry, cotton, woolen, mining, or whatever, and did not lend itself readily to generalization. The manager, trained in one industry, found himself bound to that industry since he would need to relearn his skills if he moved to another. Second, there was no common code of management behavior, no universal set of expectations about how a manager should act. Codes were developed for specific industries and gave advice about the manager's responsibility for safety, for the security of the plant and equipment, design standards for engineering, and for procedures to follow in safeguarding the owner's interests.

James Montgomery of Glasgow (Scotland) prepared what were most probably the first "management" texts.[18] Montgomery's managerial advice was largely technical in nature; he advised how to discern quality and quantity of work, how to adjust and repair machinery, how to keep costs down, and how to "avoid unnecessary severity" in disciplining subordinates. He noted that a manager must be "just and impartial—firm and decisive—always

---

[18] James Montgomery, *The Carding and Spinning Masters' Assistant; or the Theory and Practice of Cotton Spinning*, Glasgow: J. Niven, Jr., 1832; and James Montgomery, *The Cotton Spinner's Manual*, Glasgow: J. Niven, Jr., 1835. Montgomery's contributions are discussed and portions of the 1832 work are reproduced in James P. Baughman (ed.), "James Montgomery on Factory Management, 1832," *Business History Review*, Vol. 42, No. 2 (Summer, 1968), pp. 219–226.

on the alert to prevent rather than check faults after they have taken place . . ."[19] This latter comment on controlling was very perceptive and indicated an early understanding that the control function is essentially looking forward rather than backward. However, Montgomery's advice was for the cotton industry and, like most other early writers, he did not seek to develop any generalized principles of management.

Early managerial salaries also left much to be desired. The first-line supervisors, or "overlookers," were paid little more than the workers. Often the white collar salaried managers were paid on the basis of their social class rather than on the extent of their responsibility. By 1800, however, Pollard noted that the shortage of talent had forced payment based on the job and not the man.[20] By 1830, the salaries of non-owner managers had risen rapidly and compressed the differential between their pay and that of the owner managers. In England, but not in France or Italy, the status of the entrepreneur was rising, inducing many young men to seek their fortunes in commerce, or at least to become a junior partner in a large firm. The second- and third-generation offspring of the founder-entrepreneur changed their style to give more status to the salaried manager. They tended to delegate more and depended more upon the salaried manager. Perhaps their affluence, built by the success of their forefathers, made them less desirous of becoming personally involved in daily activities; or perhaps the firms had grown to such a size and the fund of managerial talent had reached a point where they could find more reliable subordinates than their predecessors. In the early factory, the problems of finding and developing managerial talent were acute. There were no business schools for recruiting, no systematic programs for developing people into managers, and managerial skill was judged a localized, idiosyncratic matter.

The Labor Problem

The managerial problem was acute but the problems with labor made even the strongest "bull-of-the-woods" supervisor blanch. The factory had to attract the laborer from rural to urban life; and the peasant, with his traditional family ties and heritage, his long

[19] Baughman, quoting Montgomery, p. 226.
[20] Pollard, p. 139.

links with the past and his community, had to absorb a whole new culture in his shift to the factory.

Broadly conceived, the labor problem had three aspects: recruitment, training, and discipline. In itself, the recruitment problem was multi-faceted. The existing labor force consisted of unskilled agrarian workers who had a definite aversion to factory life and work. This aversion was largely due to the necessity of abiding by the rules and rigorous discipline that factory work required; although certainly much of it also came from the distaste for the noise, dirt, and apparent squalor in many of the factories themselves. The shift from a small workshop, from the farm, or from a family-operated operation, was a drastic one for the worker. He had to pull up roots from a long-familiar milieu and go to the brawling, bustling city for employment. He was required to accept a new culture and not exactly an inviting one at that. As Sombart has noted, men who were non-accumulative, non-acquisitive, and accustomed to working for a subsistence income had to be made obedient to a cash stimulus for the prospect of maximization of income; further they had to be stimulated within the bounds of a predictable, controllable manner set by management.[21]

Andrew Ure and others complained that factory work was uncongenial to the typical worker who was accustomed to the domestic or agrarian life and did not look kindly upon the monotony of factory jobs, the year-round regularization of hours, and the constant demands of attention to his work. Workers tended to be restless, shiftless, and deviant. The firm of Roebuck and Garrett, for example, moved their factory from Birmingham (England) to Scotland because they found the Scots to be more reliable and obedient.[22] Further, personal inclinations and group mores of such long-established groups as the handloom weavers and the framework knitters were opposed to factory discipline. The factory broke their cohesiveness and exacted a different pace and quality of work.

The Shortage of Skilled Labor

The other facet of the recruitment problem resided in the extreme shortage of skilled labor. The paradox of early nineteenth

[21] Werner Sombart, *The Jew and Modern Capitalism* (trans. by M. Epstein), London: T. Fisher Unwin, 1913, pp. 809, 829–831.
[22] Pollard, p. 161.

century England was a large amount of unemployment existing simultaneously with employers begging for help. It was structural unemployment partially in that the former agrarian workers did not possess factory skills but largely it was due to the refusal of workers to accept factory life. Some skilled labor did exist in small, scattered guilds and workshops; however, these craftsmen preferred this arrangement to the routine of factory work. Employers had to offer all sorts of inducements to these men and had to make major concessions to keep them on the job. The loss of strategic or key craftsmen could shut down the whole factory. James Watt had pressing problems with finding men who could cut and fit the valves and cylinders to the proper tolerances; indeed, many of his early failures were of execution, not design. Arkwright kept his skilled people working extra hours because they were so scarce. Many iron mills kept their furnaces going even in slack times in order to keep from losing their labor force. These practices cast doubt on Marx's claim of the "reserve army of the unemployed"; the unemployment problem was a technological one and also one of personal inclination. If the worker had the skills, or if he were willing to work in the factory to learn these skills, he need not have been unemployed. It was necessity, not malice, that led early entrepreneurs to employ domestic servants, women, children, parish paupers, displaced farmers, and anyone else they could obtain. Employers used every possible medium to advertise for workers and one authority reported that children and paupers were employed only after other sources of labor were absorbed.[23] The employers were desperate and hired anyone who appeared to be breathing; Robert Owen, upon hearing of a shipwreck of 200 emigrés bound for America, sent a messenger with an offer of employment for the whole lot![24]

Training

The second major problem was that of training. Once the personnel was recruited, they had to be taught the new skills of an industrial life. Literacy was uncommon and basic educational skills were lacking; drawings, instruction sheets, and procedures for machine operation demanded some ability to read, figure, and

[23] Stanley D. Chapman, *The Early Factory Masters: The Transition to the Factory System in the Midlands Textile Industry,* New York: Augustus M. Kelley, 1967, p. 168.
[24] Pollard, p. 173.

to respond with predictable results. Training was conducted largely by oral instruction, demonstration, and trial and error. The new employee learned from someone else, usually a co-worker, how to operate a machine or process a piece of material. Standardized methods were unheard of and each worker blithely followed the precepts of someone else who knew little more than he. The shortage of skilled men, such as machinists, millwrights, and instrument makers, was of course a serious problem. Even more serious, however, were the *new* skills required by the factory since no previous jobs had exactly the same skills as the new ones. To transfer the worker's existing skills to new ones met both problems of learning as well as resistance to the new methods. The traditional prejudices against anything new added to management's discomfort. Finally, workers were not accustomed to abiding by the accuracy and tolerances demanded by the technique of interchangeable parts upon which many factories were based. Even the relatively crude measuring tools required instruction for use. The craftsman, accustomed to individualizing his work, resisted the standardization of parts, methods, and tools required by the interchangeable-parts method of production.

The haphazard acquisition of knowledge from co-workers or inept supervisors, the lack of standard methods of work, and worker resistance to new methods posed serious problems for efficient factory operation. Employers resorted to developing their own schools to teach elementary arithmetic and geometry and other skills needed in the factory and not available in the populace. With this knowledge of the early factory it is easier to explain a number of managerial practices which modern writers often use to criticize early factory pioneers. Jobs were de-skilled, *i.e.* specialized and divided into minute tasks, because of the ease of teaching them to the worker. The goal was not only efficiency but also to solve the practical problems of finding and training personnel. Job enlargement would have been totally impractical for the early factory worker. The establishment of centralized, even autocratic, leadership was in large part probably necessitated by the need to get predictable results from an unwilling work force. Participation by the worker in decision making would have been impractical; of course even benevolent autocracy, though practiced by some, would have been an improvement. Not fully accustomed to democracy in their daily life and with memories of the authority of the feudal lord, the workers probably saw little change in their relations with their new superiors. The workers, lacking skills and motivation, would have frustrated a twentieth century manager who espoused participative or democratic leadership. Viewed in its cultural perspective, the early factory probably demanded autocratic leadership to cope with the vagaries of the existing labor force.

Discipline

The third problem, and by no means the least one, was that of discipline. Accustomed to the craft traditions of independence and the agrarian mores of self sufficiency, workers had to develop "habits of industry" such as punctuality, regular attendance, the acceptance of a new regime of supervision, and the mechanical pacing of work effort. Instead of supervision by the traditional aspects of craftmanship and the hallowed master-servant relationship, the factory substituted a different discipline. It demanded intensity rather than spurts of work, accuracy and standardization rather than individuality in design and methods, and the use of equipment and material of others, not pride in one's own tools of production. Apparently the new habits did not come easily: worker attendance was irregular, "feast days" which were common traditions in the domestic system caused large-scale absenteeism for factory operators, and workers tended to work in spurts by laboring long hours, collecting their money, and then disappearing for countless days of dissipation. To combat the feast-days problem, some early employers resorted to using the traditional holidays for company-sponsored outings and feasts to build company loyalty, to break the monotony of the work year, and to cement personal relations. For example, Arkwright held a feast for 500 employees at his Cromford mill in 1776 and Matthew Boulton hosted 700 at his Soho plant. Punctuality, or "time-thrift" in the early employer's terms, posed all sorts of problems. Employers levied fines for tardiness and often resorted to locking the plant gates and workshop doors at starting time. The old liberty of hours under the domestic and agrarian systems was gone forever.

Methods of discipline were often quite rigorous by modern standards. Efforts to cope with disciplinary problems fell into three categories and, upon close inspection, appear to have changed only in application, not theory, up to the present day. The offering of positive inducements ("the carrot"), negative sanctions ("the stick"), and efforts to build a new "factory ethos" became the methods for bringing deviant workers into the fold. For the carrot, early employers developed two devices, subcontracting and payment by results. Subcontracting will be examined in greater depth later, but in essence it involved the employer contracting with an overseer for certain bits of work. This transferred responsibility for keeping the workers going to the overseer who had an incentive to accomplish a specified amount of output with the least possible costs. Individual piecework, or payment by results, appeared at an early point in the factory system. By 1833, 47.5 per cent of the cotton mill workers were on a piece-rate incentive.[25] Establishment of the concept of payment by results represented a major psychological break with tradition. The old attitude that the worker must be kept at the subsistence level and that the best worker was the hungriest one was replaced by an early concept of "economic man." This notion held that monetary incentives brought out the best in man and that he would work harder to get more. Economic man was born, to survive for many years. The piece-rate system engendered, even in these early years, the same animosities which are seen today. Employers resorted to the "speed-up," to rate-cutting, the quality of work often deteriorated, and employer-employee friction often arose over the standards and the computation of payment.

The "stick," negative sanctions, became a practice for which the early industrial system is frequently criticized. Corporal punishment, especially of children, was used, though authors disagree on its frequency and severity. The subcontracting system may have contributed to many of these abuses since the owner relinquished control and often left disciplinary policy in the hands of unlettered overseers who took their job of getting out production a little too seriously. Graduated fines were more common methods of discipline: one plant fined workers 30 cents for being absent Monday morning, and 70 cents for singing, swearing, or being drunk.[26] Since wages often amounted to two or three dollars a week, this was a fairly large portion of the worker's pay. Disciplinary policies probably varied widely between factories and

[25] Pollard, p. 190.
[26] *Ibid.*, p. 187.

fluctuated according to the relative scarcity or abundance of workers. Skilled workers, who were in short supply, were probably not dealt with too severely and labor shortages in general also must have diminished the employer's ability to be too harsh. It must be remembered that the prevailing attitude toward children, even in respectable homes, was that they should be seen and not heard, and that to "spare the rod" was to "spoil the child." In the context of the period, employers treated children as they were accustomed to being treated at home;[27] although that does not condone what did happen.

The third method of discipline was general in conception and oriented toward creating a new factory ethos. The goal was to use religious morals and values to create the proper attitudes toward work. The encouragement of moral education, even on company time and in early company towns, reading of the "good book," regular church attendance, and exhortations to avoid the deadly sins of laziness, sloth, and avarice were methods of inculcating in the working population the right habits of industry. A coalition of employers and ministers exhorted the populace to guard against the moral depravities which were not only sinful, but led to a lackadaisical, dissipated work force. The Quaker Lead Company, for example, punished workers for "tippling [drinking], fighting, and night rambling."[28] Doubtless this moral suasion emanated from more than a concern for the soul of the worker. Pollard presented a succinct statement of these attempts to create a new ethos:

The drive to raise the level of respectability and morality among the working classes was not undertaken for their own sake, but primarily . . . as an aspect of building up a new factory discipline.[29]

Management Functions in the Early Factory

In addition to the difficulties of staffing the factory with a reluctant labor force, the task of acquiring competent sub-managers, and the avoidance of the Luddites, early managers faced planning, organizing, and controlling problems similar to those of the modern manager. The Luddites became rather impotent after 1813 when a mass trial and a mass hanging ended that movement. Workmen's "combinations" were forbidden by law and early employers resorted

27 Chapman, p. 203.
28 Pollard, p. 193.
29 *Ibid.*, p. 197.

to a "black-list" and the firing of anyone who conspired to form a union. Although employers could agree on what to do with threats from labor, they did not attempt to share their knowledge about how to manage other aspects of their operations.

In planning operations, the early factory required more far-sightedness than the domestic system. As the factory system developed, the new industrialist became more rational, more pragmatically interested in laying a foundation for long-term growth rather than short-term speculative gains. Early mines required long-range planning to develop the veins and early factories required costly equipment. As capital was "sunk," the business-man had to be more rational and more aware of the long-term implications of his decision. Examples of planning in industry are few and those which do exist are largely technically oriented rather than comprehensive in company scope and application. Robert Owen and Richard Arkwright led the way in pre-planning factory layout. Their "requirements," or principles if you prefer, emphasized the orderliness of the work flow and factory cleanliness. Factory technology demanded the planning of power sources and connections, the arrangement of machinery and space for a smooth flow-through of work, and the reduction of confusion through bins and well-placed stores of materials.[30] The firm of Boulton and Watt also stressed factory layout and developed detailed systems for controlling stocks of materials and parts. They engaged in rudimentary work study for production planning, for work flow, and for assembly methods at their Soho factory (the engine works).[31] The use of standardized, interchangeable parts made planning necessary, both in design and execution of the assembly. James Watt, Jr., saw at an early stage that standard parts would lessen the tasks of controlling work and that detailed planning and proper initial execution would insure that the final product would meet specifications. Standard parts also eased repairs for the customer and reduced both the company's and customer's inventory of spare parts, thus simplifying the stock control system.

In organizing, managers were limited to a large extent by the

[30] Jennifer Tann, The Development of the Factory System, London: Cornmarket Press, 1970.

[31] Erich Roll, An Early Experiment in Industrial Organization: Being a History of the Firm of Boulton and Watt, 1775–1805, London: Longmans, Green and Co., 1930. The development of relatively advanced managerial techniques at Boulton and Watt is credited to the sons of the firm's famous founders, Matthew Robinson Boulton and James Watt, Jr. Ibid., p. xv.

caliber of the subordinate managers. Early departmentation, or the grouping of activities, was often based on the number of partners or relatives. With a gesture toward egalitarianism, each became a department head with one or two salaried managers below him supervising the workers. Some companies did develop what would be called a typical line structure with a single director and other managers below him in an orderly organizational box format. Robert Owen followed such a format by developing four "under managers" who supervised the workers at New Lanark when Owen was on one of his many visits to New Harmony in America. William Brown, manager of his own East Mill establishment at Dundee, Scotland, illustrated an early example of building an organization. Brown's success was attested by the fact that his mill became the center of management consulting for the woolen industry. Brown, like James Montgomery, went beyond the technical aspects of factory operations to discuss problems of supervision and organization. For his own mill, Brown stated:

The first and great object to be aimed at by the Manager of East Mill is PROFIT. The chief requisites to profit are—a good quality of yarn—large quantity—little waste—moderate expenses—and a good state of the machinery.[32]

To insure profitability, Brown formed eleven departments (such as flax preparing, tow spinning, warehouse, mechanic, etc.) and developed an eighteen page job description for his immediate subordinate manager describing precise details of daily routines and duties of all employees. These instructions included how to check on work performed, quantities of materials used, quality of work, and a variety of other supervisory responsibilities. Further, Brown's advice to his under-manager stressed technical as well as administrative knowledge, social skills, and how to keep discipline without severity. Unfortunately, his observations on management were not published at the time although many of his essays on the techniques of woolen production were. In early management writings, the stress was on techniques and advice concerning managerial skills was infrequent and parochial.

In controlling performance, entrepreneurs faced numerous problems. Needing to delegate authority to cope with larger-

[32] Dennis Chapman, "William Brown of Dundee, 1791–1864: Management in a Scottish Flax Mill," in *Explorations in Entrepreneurial History,* Volume 4 (1st series), 1952, p. 228.

sized enterprises since they could no longer personally oversee all operations, the shortage of trained and trusted submanagers posed problems of accountability. Adam Smith observed that it was a rare salaried manager who would exercise the same vigilance over other people's money as he would over his own. Accounting knowledge had not advanced since Pacioli and its use as an aid to the manager was an almost unheard of phenomenon. Books were kept to account for earnings, wages, material, and sales, but there is no evidence that the manager knew how to use the accounting function as an aid to decision making. The accounting information he had was in gross form, undigested and erratic. Charles Babbage did suggest a descriptive cost accounting system but it was not until the twentieth century that accounting and management thought developed to the point where costs and information became a focal point of study. This lag in knowledge is really not surprising since the prevailing view was that it was the personality of the manager that meant success or failure, not accounts nor procedures.

Pollard cited numerous examples of business failures occurring when the "principals," or owners, left the management of firms up to a salaried staff of managers. These managers were often dishonest, absconding, and alcoholic, and their mismanagement led many early entrepreneurs to establish a "contracting out" system in an effort to insure control. The entrepreneurs set a contract price for the finished work and let the contractor manager pay his own workers, procure his own materials, and assume all factory risk.[33] Working to keep costs down to insure a profit as the margin between his contract price and his costs, the subcontractor had an important incentive which was lacking under the direct factory work system. Contracting out provided control for the entrepreneur and motivation for the contractor without necessitating direct supervision by the principal. Of course there were disadvantages in practice; the contractor often stressed short-run return to the detriment of worker safety and this practice often led to a deterioration in the condition of mines or in the maintenance of equipment. The drive to produce more or speed up the worker gave rise to abuses and some very crude managerial techniques which often led to dissatisfaction and riots. Yet many early man-

[33] Pollard, pp. 19–23.

agers kept this system rather than try to supervise a large-scale operation directly.

Through trial-and-error experience, early entrepreneurs attempted to cope with the problems of managing a factory and a work force. The emphasis on technical rather than managerial problems was probably due to the crude state of the technological art and the pressure to keep abreast of competition and to make the new gadgets work. Management was deemed a localized matter, not subject to generalization, and success was thought to depend upon the personal qualities of the manager, not upon his grasp of broader principles of management. Management was a personal art, not a discipline; pragmatic, not theoretical; and parochial, not universal.

There were some individuals who were attempting to fill this void in management knowledge; their efforts will be the subject of Chapter 4. But first, let us try to gain some perspective on the cultural impact of the Industrial Revolution.

CULTURAL CONSEQUENCES OF THE INDUSTRIAL REVOLUTION

The revolution was not only technological but cultural. The new machines, the new factories, and the new cities shook man's tradition-based roots and demanded his participation in a new era. In the hearts of many there is an idealization of the agrarian life before industrialization. Critics have charged that capitalism, together with its offspring—the market and factory systems—has robbed man of a golden age of equality and freedom. More specifically, the criticisms have been that man was enslaved to the owners of capital, that man became little more than a commodity in the marketplace of life, that capitalists exploited child and female labor, and that industrialization created poverty, urbanization, pollution, and a host of other societal ills. Let us examine some of these criticisms and attempt to gain a perspective on the cultural consequences of this new age of industrialization and capitalism.

The Condition of the Worker

Economics earned its sobriquet, "the dismal science," during the early nineteenth century. Thomas Malthus set out to disprove the optimism of Adam Smith and liberal economics with his famous "population" argument. Malthus postulated that population increases in geometric proportion while the food supply at best increases only arithmetically. The population is limited by the means of subsistence and the masses tend to reproduce beyond these means, preventing any improvement in their condition. Government relief of the poor only encourages a population increase, food prices go up, and the poor are no better off. The only answer for Malthus (he was not very optimistic about the outcome) was to restrict the supply of labor and to encourage self-restraint in the reproduction of the masses.[34] His was a hopeless view of man as no more than a commodity in the market place of life who was basically powerless to overcome his disadvantage. David Ricardo did not appear much more optimistic; his "iron law of wages" said that in the long run real wages would always tend to stabilize at some minimum level which would provide the worker with just enough means to subsist.[35] The "Utopian socialists," such as Robert Owen, saw man as powerless in his environment and wanted to replace the individualism of the market with a communal life. The Utopians did not write of the necessity of revolt but felt they could achieve change through their writings and by example. An opposite view was developed by Karl Marx and Friedrich Engels, who advocated the need for force as the midwife of history. Because man was powerless, in their view, and because he was being kept at the subsistence level by the exploitation of the factory masters, workers must combine to break their chains. While the writings of Marx and Engels are more political essays than economic analyses, they did reflect the economist's dismal view of the world at that time.

Was man powerless and exploited to the poverty level by capitalism? The subsistence level for the masses was not new; they had spent the previous thousand or more years in essentially the same status but as agrarian peasants tied to a feudal landlord. The Industrial Revolution did not create poverty; it inherited it. The rise of capitalism was creating the means for releasing man from drudgery through labor-saving machines, making man more productive and better paid for less exertion of effort.[36] Further, it is

[34] John Fred Bell, A History of Economic Thought, 2d ed., New York: Ronald Press Co., 1968, pp. 180–186.

[35] Ibid., p. 221.

[36] Friedrich A. Hayek, "History and Politics," in F. A. Hayek (ed.), Capitalism and the Historians, Chicago: University of Chicago Press, 1954, pp. 15–16.

difficult to agree with Marx and Engels that the worker was exploited by the factory owner for basically two reasons: first, the severe shortage of labor which would have diminished the manager's power to do as he liked with his labor; and second, the fact that workers' real wages were steadily rising from 1790 to 1830 and the workers' lot was improving "well above the level of mere subsistence."[37] For those who were willing to enter the factory and learn its new skills, the new machines and methods made them more productive and raised wages; in turn, added industrial efficiency reduced the prices of goods and raised real wages. The increasing use of incentive payment plans held out a promise of economic betterment for man; no longer tied to remitting a tithe to the feudal lord, an individual could, through effort, enhance his own well-being. It is also likely that wages were rising to reduce the onus of factory work and to overcome the short supply of labor. Was man powerless? Was he a commodity exploited by the new entrepreneur? His lack of power appears to have been more of a reluctance to accept the new discipline of the factory; as for the commodity angle, no employer of the time would have agreed that he could buy and sell labor as he pleased.

Child and Female Labor

Child and female labor were not inventions of the Industrial Revolution. The domestic system required the participation of all and feudalism was built upon the family as the basic economic unit. One authority noted that child labor was at its worst in the domestic system long *before* the factory system.[38] Up to 75% of the labor force in many factories depended upon child and female labor. However, it is doubtful that employers made any profit on child labor whose upkeep usually cost more than they produced.[39] Employers would have preferred a mature, stable, adult work force but these individuals were scarce and hard to attract. Concern in Britain over child labor practices led to two famous Parliamentary investigations; the first in 1819 at the behest of Robert Owen, and chaired by Sir Robert Peel, himself an extensive employer of children in his factories; and that of the Sadler Committee of 1832.

---

[37] T. S. Ashton, "The Standard of Life of the Workers in England: 1790–1830," in Hayek, p. 158.

[38] R. Whatley Cooke Taylor, p. 402.

[39] Stanley D. Chapman, p. 171.

Extensive and detailed evidence was given before these committees.[40] Children often began work at age five and occasionally spent a fourteen-hour day at the factory. This practice was widespread, being found in the cotton, wool, flax, and silk mills, and existing legislation concerning child labor provided no enforcement mechanism. In their testimony, witnesses described the hours (long), wages (low), working conditions (often extremely poor), and the methods of discipline (often harsh). One witness testified that children often fell asleep at work and were kept awake by an overseer who grasped the child by his legs and dipped him head first in a barrel of water.

Female labor, attracted to the factory for the wages to build a dowry, for the opportunity of finding a husband, or driven to the factory to supplement the family income, fared little better in some cases. Mantoux depicted the early entrepreneur as

. . . tyrannical, hard, sometimes cruel, their passions and greeds were those of upstarts. They had the reputation of being heavy drinkers and of having little regard for the honour of their female employees. They were proud of their newly acquired wealth and lived in great style with footmen, carriages and gorgeous town and country houses.[41]

Mantoux is guilty of over-generalization; ample examples can be given, such as Josiah Wedgewood, Matthew Boulton, James Watt, John Wilkinson, Robert Owen, and a host of others for whom there is no evidence that they played loose and fancy free with their female employees.[42] Only one specific case was cited in Parliamentary testimony and the tenor of the critics' position was that of the "temptations and opportunities" presented by the presence of both male and female in the same workshop.[43] Evidently if the workers had been segregated by sex, no testimony would have appeared at all. There was great concern that unemployed girls would be forced by circumstances to prostitution; but a Doctor Hawkins presented evidence for Manchester that of the fifty prostitutes who had been apprehended in the past four years (1829–

[40] For some excerpts, see E. Royston Pike, 'Hard Times': Human Documents of the Industrial Revolution, New York: Praeger Publishers, 1966, especially pp. 100–218.
[41] Paul J. Mantoux, The Industrial Revolution in the Eighteenth Century, trans. by Marjorie Vernon, New York: MacMillan Co., 1928, p. 397.
[42] See W. O. Henderson's Diary of J. C. Fischer, p. 57. Undoubtedly some of these individuals existed, as they do in all ages, but Fischer maintained that they were not representative of the era.
[43] Pike, p. 285, with the lurid title of "Seduction in the Mill."

1833), only eight came from the factories, while twenty-nine came from the ranks of former household servants.[44]

Evidence concerning child and female labor is contradictory; most testimony hints of the moral degradation of factory life but the hard statistics are lacking. It appears that emotional and religious overtones were given more credence, isolated instances were ballooned, and no rigorous empirical investigation to compare the past with the prevailing state of affairs was undertaken. One cannot condone child labor whether it be of the domestic system or of the factory system. Employers of the times were driven to employment of children and females by the low level of technology, and the great demand for unskilled labor. What the critics overlooked was the fact that capitalism was slowly but surely allowing the release of children from the workforce. As better machines were developed to perform the simple jobs, it became uneconomical to employ children. It was an economic force—broadening capitalism, not legislative fiat nor a moral rebirth—that freed the child from the looms.[45] As for legislation and governmental bodies, it was the Poor Law Authorities, a government office, which sent the paupers into the factories! The paupers were poor or deserted children legally in the care of the state; to relieve the state of the burdens of maintenance, they were sent to whomever would accept their care and feeding.

There is evidence that the factory system led to a general rise in the standard of living, something lacking in the previous thousand years, to falling urban death rates and decreasing infant mortality. These factors led to a population explosion in England in that its inhabitants increased from six million in 1750 to nine million in 1800 and to twelve million in 1820. Further, infant mortality before the age of five had fallen from 74.5% in 1730–1749 to 31.8% in 1810–1829. Since there were no significant medical advances apparent during the period, one can only conclude that people were better able to feed, clothe, and care for themselves.[46] Heilbroner has pointed out that factory life, even with

[44] *Ibid.*, p. 297.

[45] W. H. Hutt, "The Factory System of the Early Nineteenth Century," in Hayek, p. 184.

[46] Margaret C. Buer, *Health, Wealth and Population in the Early Days of the Industrial Revolution, 1760–1815,* London: George Routledge & Sons, 1926, p. 30. Cited by Robert Hessen, "The Effects of the Industrial Revolution on Women and Children," in Ayn Rand, *Capitalism: The Unknown Ideal,* New York: American Library, 1966, p. 104.

urban poverty, represented an improvement over life in an agrarian and domestic system.[47]   Poverty was not new, it had just been collected in one place, the city, and made more easily visible to the legislators, intellectuals, and others.   Isolated and scattered, agrarian poverty did not shock the sensibilities, but next door and down the street, it became a problem.   Heilbroner further answered the critics of the Industrial Revolution in saying that the age of criticism was based on political and not economic unrest.   England of that period was characterized by a surging interest in rights and justice and in political reform; the populace had "a critical temper of mind before which *any* economic system would have suffered censure."[48]   This criticism was directed at the entrepreneur, not because he was to blame, but because he was a convenient symbol of change.

One cannot tax capitalism with the unsavory conditions and practices of the Industrial Revolution.   The factory system inherited child and female labor, poverty, and long working hours from the past, it did not create them; the new age of industrial capitalism was creating through the factory a method for man to gain leverage for a better life.

SUMMARY

The Industrial Revolution created a new cultural environment and a revised set of problems for management.   Man's needs were becoming more complex as he sought to adjust to life in the city and to the new rigor of the factory.   Organizations were being reshaped by the demands for heavy infusions of capital, by the division of labor, and by the need for economical, predictable performance.   Organizations needed to innovate and compete in a market economy and this created pressures for growth and the economies to be obtained from large scale production and distribution.   Economic theory recognized that the entrepreneur-manager performed a distinct role in combining the traditional three factors of production in the ever-growing factory system. With size came the need for managers, the need for a capable, disciplined, trained, motivated work force, and the need for

[47] Robert L. Heilbroner, *The Making of Economic Society*, Englewood Cliffs, N.J.: Prentice-Hall, 1962, p. 85.
[48] *Ibid.*, p. 86.

rationalizing the planning, organizing, and controlling of operations in the early enterprise. The problems were present and the next chapter will examine some early management pioneers who proposed solutions for coping with the growing factory system.

4

Management Pioneers
in the Factory System

A prevailing theme so far has been the relationship of management thought to its cultural environment. The factory system posed new problems for owners, managers, and for society at large. This chapter will focus on four individuals who pioneered in proposing solutions to the manifold pressures of coping with the earliest large scale industrial organizations. History leaves a notoriously scanty scent. Records and memorabilia are lost or destroyed, notable ideas may never be committed to writing, and judgments must be made on perhaps a small part of what actually occurred. Of the early management pioneers, history has provided us with the best records for four men, Robert Owen, Charles Babbage, Andrew Ure, and Charles Dupin.

ROBERT OWEN: THE SEARCH FOR A NEW HARMONY

Robert Owen (1771–1858) was a paradox in the turbulent era of the Industrial Revolution.[1] A successful entrepreneur himself, he attempted to halt the surge of industrialism and the evils he saw in it as he called for a new moral order based on a social reorganization. He had a vision of a new industrial society which was to be a

[1] This description of Owen's life and work is based on his autobiography: Robert Owen, *The Life of Robert Owen*, London: Effingham Wilson, 1857; reissued by Augustus M. Kelley, 1967 (Volumes I and IA).

combination of agricultural and industrial commune and harkened back to the lost days of a more primitive man. Philosophically, he viewed man as powerless, held in the grips of revolutionary forces of the new age of machinery which destroyed man's moral purpose and his social solidarity. His struggle was a long and frustrating one and he appears in history as a King Canute ordering the waves of progress to recede.

Early Managerial Experiences

A self-made man imbued with the self confidence which typified the early entrepreneurs, Owen, at the age of 18, founded his first factory in Manchester during an age of war prosperity when many were getting rich. There was a great impetus in cotton trade and the new water frame, the weaving machines of Arkwright and Crompton, and the power sources of Watt made large factories feasible. Owen teamed with a mechanic named Ernest Jones, Jones taking the technical responsibility and Owen the management; and Owen described his introduction to managing:

I looked very wisely at the men in their different departments, although I really knew nothing. But by intensely observing everything, I maintained order and regularity throughout the establishment, which proceeded under the circumstances far better than I had anticipated.[2]

Jones proved a burden to the firm, and Owen set out on his own after buying up Jones' share. His firm became profitable but he decided to become a salaried manager and sold his equipment to a Mr. Drinkwater and became employed by him. Still with a modicum of experience, he applied himself to the new position:

I looked grave, inspected everything very minutely . . . I was in with the first [workers] in the morning, and I locked up the premises at night. I continued this silent inspection and superintendence day by day for six weeks, saying merely yes or no to the questions . . . I did not give one direct order about anything. But at the end of that time I felt myself so much master of my position as to be ready to give directions in every department.[3]

Owen, left on his own by Mr. Drinkwater, made a success of the mill. He rearranged the equipment, bettered the conditions of the workers, and achieved a great deal of influence over his

[2] *Ibid.*, p. 31–32.
[3] *Ibid.*, p. 39.

subordinates. He later attributed his success with the workers to his "habits of exactness" and to his knowledge of human nature. He left Drinkwater in 1794 or 1795 to establish a new partnership, the New Lanark (Scotland) venture. At New Lanark, he encountered the ubiquitous problem of scarcity of labor and noted: "It was most difficult to induce any sober, well-doing family to leave their home to go into cotton mills as then conducted."[4] Perhaps this difficulty in attracting labor influenced his personnel policies; he began forming his visions of a new society. At New Lanark, he employed between four and five hundred parish apprentices, the pauper children furnished by the Poor Law authorities to whomever would take them. The children worked 13 hours per day including an hour and a quarter off for meals. Owen continued to employ children but tried to improve their living and working conditions even though he could not persuade his partners to accept all of his reforms. His reform efforts aimed to reshape the whole village of New Lanark, including the streets, houses, sanitation, and the educational system.

At New Lanark, Owen encountered the same disciplinary problems as other manufacturers. Similar to the attempts of others to create a new factory ethos, he tried to use moral suasion rather than corporal punishment. He developed one particularly unique device, the "silent monitor," to aid discipline. Under this system, Owen awarded four types of marks to each superintendent and each of them in turn rated his subordinates. These marks were translated into color codes of black, blue, yellow, and white in ascending order of merit. A block of wood was mounted on each machine and the four sides painted according to the code. At the end of each day, the marks were recorded, translated, and the appropriate color side of the block turned to face the aisle. Anyone passing, and knowing the code, could immediately assess the workers' last day's effort. This wooden albatross worked to motivate laggards to overcome their deficiency and supposedly to induce the white block "good guys" to maintain theirs. It was most certainly a precursor of modern management's public posting of sales and production data to instill departmental pride or to encourage competition.

[4] *Ibid.*, p. 79.

The Call for Reform

Pre-dating Mayo, Roethlisberger, Likert, and others who have urged concern for the human resource asset of the firm, Owen set forth his rationale for a new philosophy:

> . . . you will find that from the commencement of my management I viewed the population [the labor force] . . . as a system composed of many parts, and which it was my duty and interest so to combine, as that every hand, as well as every spring, lever, and wheel, should effectually cooperate to produce the greatest pecuniary gain to the proprietors . . . Experience has also shown you the difference of the results between a mechanism which is neat, clean, well-arranged, and always in a high state of repair; and that which is allowed to be dirty, in disorder, without the means of preventing unnecessary friction, and which therefore becomes, and works, much out of repair . . . If, then, due care as to the state of your inanimate machines can produce such beneficial results, what may not be expected if you devote equal attention to your vital machines [the human resource], which are far more wonderfully constructed?[5]

Owen chided his fellow manufacturers for not understanding the human element. He charged that they would spend thousands on the best machines, yet buy the cheapest labor. They would spend time improving machines, specializing labor, and cutting costs, yet make no investment in the human resource. He appealed to their pecuniary instincts, claiming that money spent on improving labor "would return you, not five, ten, or fifteen per cent for your capital so expended, but often fifty, and in many cases a hundred per cent."[6] He claimed a 50% return at New Lanark, and said it would shortly reach 100%. He claimed that it was more profitable to show such concern for people and that it also served to relieve the "accumulation of human misery." Owen's venture at New Lanark was profitable but there is at least one doubter about whether or not this was due to his personnel policies. One biographer noted that profits in the cotton spinning industry at that time were so large, averaging 20% or more on capital invested, that *any* personnel policy could have been profitable. "In fact the margin of profit was so wide that we need scarcely look for any other explanation of Owen's success as a manufacturer."[7] Whatever the reasons for his own success, Owen deplored the commercialism of life. He declared an intellectual

---

[5] *Ibid.*, Appendix B. p. 260.

[6] *Ibid.*, p. 261.

[7] Frank Podmore, *Robert Owen,* New York: Appleton-Century-Crofts, 1924, p. 642.

war on capitalism and also attacked the Church because it condoned the evils of the new industrial age. These views branded him as a radical and made it more difficult for him to persuade others of the need for reform. Owen felt that the crucial error of all established religions was the preaching of the doctrine of human responsibility. He held that man was the creature of his environment, relatively incapable of escaping it without a moral rearmament through education. Contrary to the church view that good character was promoted by the promise of rewards and punishment, especially in the hereafter, Owen felt that character developed solely if the material and moral environment of men was proper. To these ends, he became more active politically about 1813 and proposed a factory bill to prohibit all employment under age ten and to limit hours to 10½ per day with no night work for children. His proposal was too radical for other manufacturers and politicians of that time. After many political intrigues, the bill became law in 1819 but instead of applying to all factories, applied only to cotton mills and set the age limit at 9 and not 10. With no provision for inspection to insure compliance, the law was toothless.

A biographer suggests that, frustrated in his attempts to reform society, Owen became slightly "mad" in 1817.[8] Failing to change Britain, he sought the openness of America and established the first cooperative community based on his principles at New Harmony (Indiana) in 1824. That venture too was doomed to fail within three years and Owen found himself both financially and emotionally broken. Owen had thought that what he had learned and applied in his cotton mills could be applied to the whole society but he was unable to persuade others that his new moral order was realistic and not utopian. As a reformer, Owen devised laws for relief of the poor and proposed solutions to unemployment problems. He proposed "Villages of Cooperation" (like New Harmony) which would have a communal sharing of surplus and be based on agriculture. He fought against the Malthusian doctrine of overpopulation, saying that, if all shared, none would hunger. He deplored the evils of the division of labor; in his ideal system, each man would do a number of different jobs, switching easily from one to another. For him, it was the evils of the

[8] G.D.H. Cole, *The Life of Robert Owen,* third edition, Hamden, Conn.: Archon Books, 1966, p. 197.

wage system and capitalism that caused life at a subsistence level. In 1834, Owen led the British Trade Union movement which was a working class movement based on the idea of collective action to control the means of production. He failed. Nevertheless, Robert Owen, a Utopian Socialist, a King Canute ordering the waves of industrialization to recede, sowed the first seeds of concern for the human element in industry.

CHARLES BABBAGE: THE IRASCIBLE GENIUS

To call Charles Babbage (1792–1871) an irascible genius is to pay him the greatest compliment for he fitted both qualities and emerged as a significant figure in management thought long before Frederick W. Taylor. Largely technique oriented like his contemporaries, Babbage's application of technological aids to human effort has earned him a place in history as the patron saint of operations research and management science. He theorized and applied a scientific approach to management long before the scientific management era in America. Born in Devonshire as the son of a wealthy banker, he used his inheritance in a life-long quest "into the causes of all those little things and events which astonish the childish mind."[9] He remarked that his first question after receiving a new toy was invariably "Mamma, what is inside of it?" and he also invariably broke open the toy if the answer did not appear satisfactory. The value of his work was recognized by few of his contemporaries, and he was generally considered a crackpot by his neighbors. His personal traits were not endearing to those who disturbed his cogitations. In retaliation against the ubiquitous English street organ grinders, he blew bugles and created a commotion outside his house to scare them away. One contemporary, perhaps a neighbor, wrote: "He spoke as if he hated mankind in general, Englishmen in particular, and the English Government and organ grinders most of all."[10]

[9] Charles Babbage (autobiography), *Passages From the Life of a Philosopher,* London: Longman & Green, 1864, reprinted in Philip and Emily Morrison (eds.), *Charles Babbage and His Calculating Engines,* New York: Dover Publications, 1961, p. 9.

[10] No author, "The Cranky Grandfather of the Computer," *Fortune,* March, 1964, p. 112–113. The life and peccadillos of Babbage are pieced together from this source: from Morrison and Morrison, *op. cit.;* and from an excellent biography by Maboth Moseley, *Irascible Genius: A Life of Charles Babbage, Inventor,* London: Hutchinson & Co. Publishers, 1964.

The First Computer

Babbage's scientific output was phenomenal.[11]   He demonstrated the world's first practical mechanical calculator, his "difference engine," in 1822.   Ninety one years later its basic principles were being employed in Burroughs' accounting machines. Babbage had governmental support in his work on the difference engine but his irascibility cost him the support of government bureaucrats for his "analytical engine," a versatile computer that would follow instructions automatically.[12]   In concept, Babbage's computer had all the basic elements of a more modern version.   It had a store or memory device, a mill or arithmetic unit, a punch card input system, an external memory storage, and conditional transfer.[13]

Babbage's computer never became a commercial reality nor did he develop a punch-card machine.   However, Herman Hollerith, inventor of the earliest practical punched card tabulating machine, perhaps had read Babbage's work or even more certainly knew of the Jacquard loom which was developed in 1801 by Joseph-Marie Jacquard.   The Jacquard loom, still in use in the textile industry, used "pattern" or punch-cards in which a hole signaled the loom to lift a thread and a blank corresponded to a depressed thread, thus guiding the machine weave.   In short, the Jacquard loom anticipated by one hundred or so years the zero/one, on/off, yes/no, binary system of the modern digital computer.   Babbage probably borrowed the Jacquard concept but demonstrated foresight in his use of punch-cards for the storage of information as well as the guidance of machine operations.   For more than a century Babbage's computer concepts lay dormant, awaiting the development of electronic technology.   In 1939, Howard Aiken,

[11] Babbage was recognized as a genius by his contemporaries and the prevailing theory of the day was that there had to be physiological differences in the human brain which would explain variations in human intelligence.   Accordingly, Babbage willed his brain to the Royal College of Surgeons (England) who, after a post-mortem examination, found nothing extraordinary in Babbage's brain mass or structure.   Babbage's brain is still preserved by the Museum of the Royal College of Surgeons.   Maboth Moseley, p. 257.

[12] Babbage conceived the analytical engine in 1833 and worked on it intermittently throughout the remainder of his lifetime.   Jeremy Bernstein, *The Analytical Engine,* New York: Random House, 1963, p. 36.

[13] "Conditional transfer" in computer terminology is the "if" statement: *i.e.* instructions to the computer that "if such and such occurs, follow this path: if not, proceed in the normal sequence of control."

then a graduate student in physics and now professor emeritus at Harvard, began to work on a large-scale computer. With the help of International Business Machines, he completed it in 1944. He was well along in his work when he discovered the work of Babbage and found that the irascible genius had been there before him by more than a hundred years.

One of the few bright spots in Babbage's life was his friendship with Augusta Ada, Countess of Lovelace and daughter of the poet Lord Byron. The Countess was attractive, had a gift for mathematics and engineering, and was one of the few who really understood Babbage's work. She wrote treatises on his work, expressed his ideas better than he could, and actually wrote programs for the computer. Together with Babbage, she developed a sure-fire system for betting on the horses; unfortunately, the fillies did not fit the system and the Countess had to pawn her jewels. Undaunted by the Countess' loss of the family jewels, though the Count of Lovelace was upset, Babbage continued his work and developed gaming programs for his computer which were a forerunner of modern business gaming techniques. He limited his research to developing a computer program to play tick-tack-toe and chess but he saw that the machine (he called it an "automaton") could be programmed to make the best possible combinations of positions and moves, including anticipation as far as three moves in advance. Development of this automaton to play chess and tick-tack-toe certainly must have brought him to the fringe of probability theory in programming for player positions and decision alternatives.

Analyzing Industrial Operations

Inevitably, Babbage's inquisitive mind and wide interests led him to write of management. Babbage was more of a starter of projects than a finisher, as his computer work demonstrates. He frequently lost interest in his projects once his initial curiosity was satisfied, an unfortunate characteristic of many men of his genius. His most successful book was *On the Economy of Machinery and Manufactures* in 1832.[14] Babbage became interested in manufacturing and management as a result of his problems of supervising

---

[14] Charles Babbage, *On the Economy of Machinery and Manufactures,* London: Charles Knight, 1832; reprinted by Augustus M. Kelley (New York), 1963.

construction of his own "engine" and visited a wide variety of English factories. He described in great detail the tools and machines, discussed the "economical principles of manufacturing" and, in the true spirit of inquiry for an operations research man, analyzed operations, the kinds of skills involved, the expense of each process, and suggested directions for improving the then current practices.

Babbage, like Adam Smith, was fascinated by the principle of division of labor and felt that all advanced civilizations had achieved their positions through this process. For Babbage, the division of labor brought more efficiency because:

1. *Of the time required for learning* . . . the greater the number of distinct processes, the longer will be the time which the apprentice must employ in acquiring it . . . If, however, instead of learning all the different processes for making a needle, for instance, his attention be confined to one operation, the portion of time consumed unprofitably . . . will be small, and all the rest of it will be beneficial to his master . . .

2. *Of waste of materials in learning.* A certain quantity of material will . . . be consumed unprofitably, or spoiled by every person who learns an art . . . if each man commit this waste in acquiring successively every process, the quantity of waste will be much greater than if each person confine his attention to one process . . .

3. Another advantage resulting from the division of labor is, *the saving of that portion of time which is always lost in changing from one occupation to another.* . . . Long habit also produces in the muscles exercised a capacity for enduring fatigue to a much greater degree than they could support under other circumstances . . .

4. *Change of tools.* The employment of different tools in the successive processes is another cause of the loss of time in changing from one operation to another . . . in many processes of the arts the tools are of great delicacy, requiring accurate adjustment every time they are used; and in many cases the time employed in adjusting bears a large proportion to that employed in using the tool . . .

5. *Skill acquired by frequent repetition of the same processes.* The constant repetition of the same process necessarily produces in the workman a degree of excellence and rapidity in his particular department, which is never possessed by a person who is obliged to execute many different processes . . .

6. *The division of labor suggests the contrivance of tools and machinery to execute its processes.* When each process, by which any article is produced, is the sole occupation of one individual, his whole attention being devoted to a very limited and simple operation, improvements in the form of his tools, or in the mode of using them, are much more likely to occur to his mind, than if it were distracted by a greater variety of circumstances. Such an improvement in the tool is generally the first step towards a machine.[15]

[15] *Ibid.,* pp. 170–174.

Babbage also saw that the division of labor could be applied to mental as well as manual operations. He cited as an example G. F. Prony, Director of the École des Ponts et Chaussées (School of Bridges and Roads), who successfully divided his workers into skilled, semi-skilled, and unskilled categories for the purpose of preparing an elaborate set of mathematical tables. By this method, Prony could conserve his high-powered mathematicians by giving them the more complex tasks and shifting to those who could only add and subtract the more menial, but necessary, chores.

As a management scientist, Babbage was interested in machinery, tools, the efficient use of power, developing "counting machines" to check quantity of work, and economy in the use of raw materials; these he called the "mechanical principles" of manufacturing. He developed a "method of observing manufactories" which was closely akin to a scientific, systematic approach to the study of operations. The observer must prepare a list of questions about the materials used, normal waste, expenses, tools, prices, the final market, workers, their wages, skill required, length of work cycle, and so on.[16] In essence it was the same procedure as that an operations analyst or a consultant would use in his approach to an assignment. Babbage also discussed the advantage of large factories where capital investment made for more efficiency and the proper location of these factories with respect to sources of raw materials. On the human side, he recalled the Luddite movement and pleaded with the workers to recognize that the factory system worked to their betterment:

It is of great importance that the more intelligent amongst the class of workmen should examine the correctness of these views; because . . . the whole class may . . . be led by designing persons to pursue a course, which . . . is in reality at variance with their own best interests.[17]

He attempted to show the mutuality of interests between the worker and the factory owner somewhat similar to what Taylor was saying 75 years later:

. . . the prosperity and success of the master manufacturer is essential to the welfare of the workman . . . whilst it is perfectly true that workmen, as a class,

---

[16] Babbage's list begins on p. 115 and continues through p. 117. It should be noted that Babbage's discussion of "expenses" has the appearance of an early form of cost accounting. However, it differed from modern cost accounting in that it *described* costs rather than providing for an analysis of what costs *ought* to be as under a standard cost system.

[17] *Ibid.*, p. 230.

derive advantage from the prosperity of their employers, I do not think that each individual partakes of that advantage exactly in proportion to the extent to which he contributes to it . . . it would be of great importance, if . . . the mode of payment could be so arranged, that every person employed should derive advantage from the success of the whole; and that the profits of each individual should advance, as the factory itself produced profit, without the necessity of making any change in wages.[18]

Babbage's profit-sharing scheme had two facets: one, that a portion of wages would depend on factory profits; and two, that the worker "should derive more advantage from applying any improvement he might discover", i.e. a bonus for suggestions. The worker would receive a fixed salary based on the nature of his task plus a share in the profits, and the suggestion system would use a committee to determine the proper bonus for production savings. Babbage saw a number of advantages in his proposal: (1) that each worker would have a direct interest in the firm's prosperity; (2) that each would be stimulated to prevent waste and mismanagement; (3) that every department would be improved; and (4) that only workmen of high skill and character would be admitted since "it would be the common interest of all to admit only the most respectable and skillful." In effect, the work group, operating under a profit-sharing plan, would act to screen out undesirables who would reduce their share. Finally, Babbage saw his scheme as removing the necessity for "combinations" of workmen since their interests would be the same as the employers. With this mutuality of interests between worker and manager, neither would oppress the other and all would prosper.

Beyond his significant scientific contributions, Charles Babbage made significant advancements in understanding the problems of the emerging factory system. His analytic, scientific approach to the study of manufacturing, his recognition of the need for new incentives to enlist the cooperation of the worker, and his search for new harmonies between manager and worker place him as a man of vision in management.

ANDREW URE: PIONEERING IN MANAGEMENT EDUCATION

History has left us with relatively little knowledge of Andrew Ure the man, although it is known that he was an educator with a Ph.D. in the physical sciences. In Glasgow in the mid-eighteenth

---

[18] *Ibid.*, pp. 250–251.

century, a Dr. Anderson had lectured on science and through his will founded an institution to educate the working man on science. One of the lecturers at this new institution in Glasgow was Dr. Andrew Ure, considered to be one of the best teachers in England at that time. Educational pressures for technically trained white collar workers and managers soon shifted the composition of Dr. Ure's classes from the working man to clerks, warehousemen, small tradesmen, and shopkeepers; it was from these classes that managers for the ever growing factory system were to be recruited. Ure knew the French engineer and management writer Charles Dupin and when Dupin visited Great Britain in 1816–1818, Ure escorted him around the Glasgow factories. Dupin commented that many of the managers of these factories were Ure's own students. This fact was acknowledged by Ure who said that his students were "spread over the [United] Kingdom as proprietors and managers of factories."[19] Dupin's work was influenced by Ure and in turn, it will be suggested below that Dupin influenced Henri Fayol.

Principles of Manufacturing

Ure, deeply concerned with industrial education, set out to prepare for publication a systematic account of the principles and processes of manufacturing. The essential principle of the factory system was the substitution of "mechanical science for hand skill . . . [and to provide] for the graduation of labor among artisans."[20] Although Ure devoted a large portion of his book to the technical problems of manufacturing in the silk, cotton, woolen, and flax industries, he eventually dealt with the problems of managing. Obviously pro-management in his analysis, Ure sought an "automatic plan" to prevent individual intractable workers from stopping work as they pleased and thereby throwing the whole factory into disorder. According to Ure, workers must recognize the benefits of mechanization and not resist its introduction. To establish this automatic plan, management must "arrange and connect" manufactures to achieve a harmony of the whole. In every

---

[19] Andrew Ure, *The Philosophy of Manufactures: or an Exposition of the Scientific, Moral and Commercial Economy of the Factory System of Great Britain,* London: Charles Knight, 1835; reprinted as an Economic Classic by Augustus M. Kelley, (New York), 1967, p. viii.

[20] *Ibid.,* p. 20. *"Graduation of Labor"* referred to upgrading the skills of the worker in order to do more complex work.

establishment there were "three principles of action, or three organic systems; the mechanical, the moral and the commercial."[21] While these formed no clearcut notions of organizing work, Ure did seek to place them in the harmony of a "self-governing agency." "Mechanical" referred to the techniques and processes of production; "moral" to the condition of personnel; and "commercial" to sustaining the organization through selling and financing.

The mechanical part of manufactures was treated extensively by the scientist Ure; the moral aspect brought out the pro-management side of the educator. The factory system of Ure's day was under attack from a number of sources and Ure set out to defend industrial practices. He argued that factory operatives were better treated "as to personal comforts" than artisans or other workers in non-industrial establishments. They ate better, enjoyed more leisurely labor because of the machines provided by the factory owner, and were better paid. Instead of appreciating this largesse, they engaged in strikes, sabotaged equipment, and caused capital losses for their employers, thus working against their own continued employment. Rebutting the investigations into child labor, Ure noted that most of the witnesses had never visited the factories; he also engaged in some character assassination, charging that one witness was an atheist, one a tavern keeper, and one an assaulter of women. For positive evidence, Ure noted that children lived in well-kept cottages, received both practical and religious education, were better fed, and enjoyed better health than otherwise available in the general community. Children employed in agriculture were paid half the factory wages and kept in sloth and ignorance. Citing medical investigations sponsored by the Factory Commission, Ure concluded that the incidence of disease, the dietary habits, and the general state of health of all factory workers were better than in the general population.

To illustrate worker non-appreciation of employer's concern for their health, Ure cited an instance in which large ventilating fans had been installed in one factory to reduce the foulness of the air. Instead of thanking the employer, the workers complained that the fresh air had increased their appetites and therefore they were entitled to a corresponding wage increase! The factory owner reached a compromise with his workers by running the fan only

[21] *Ibid.*, p. 55.

half the day, thereafter hearing no more complaints about either the foul air or appetites. In terms of the evidence presented in Chapter 3, Ure was probably more right than wrong concerning the condition of labor. He was a defender of the factory system, seeing more benefits accruing to society than there were disadvantages. His instruction in management was largely technically oriented and he exhorted workers not to resist but to accept the advance of mechanization. In Ure's work, there are very few generalizations about management, and his concern for the management of certain industries, e.g. textiles, reflects the parochial views of other early writers such as Montgomery and Brown.

CHARLES DUPIN: INDUSTRIAL EDUCATION IN FRANCE

A second individual who pioneered in industrial education was the French engineer, Baron Charles Dupin (1784–1873). As noted above, Dupin had visited Great Britain (1816–1818) and observed the results Andrew Ure was obtaining in preparing individuals for factory management. In 1819, Dupin was named Professor of Mathematics and Economics at the Conservatory of Arts and Professions (Paris).[22] He must have immediately initiated his own curricula, for in 1831 he wrote: "For 12 years I have had the honor of teaching geometry and mechanics applied to the arts, in favor of the industrial class . . . on the most important questions to the well-being, education, and morality of the workers, to the progress of national industry, to the development of all means of prosperity that work can produce for the splendor and happiness of our country."[23] Dupin cannot be credited with much originality in developing management principles. His contribution occurs in the influence he had on the course of industrial education and, though there is no direct historical support, perhaps on the later work of Henri Fayol. Fayol is generally credited with being the first to distinguish between technical and administrative skills and the possibility and necessity of teaching administration. Yet examine this passage from Dupin, eight or so decades earlier:

It is to the director of workshops and factories that it is suitable to make, by means of geometry and applied mechanics, *a special study* of all the ways to

---

[22] *La Grande Encyclopédie,* Volume 15, p. 81.
[23] Charles Dupin, *Discours sur le Sort des Ouvriers,* Paris: Bachelier Librairie, 1831, p. 1. Translated, the title is *Discourse on the Condition of the Workers.*

economize the efforts of workers. . . . For a man to be a director of others, manual work has only a secondary importance; it is his intellectual ability (*force intellectuelle*) that must put him in the top position, and it is in instruction such as that of the Conservatory of the Arts and Professions, that he must develop it.[24]

The "special study" would be the classes Dupin and Ure were teaching and Dupin clearly distinguished this type of program from manual or technical instruction. Fayol, himself educated as an engineer in France, could possibly have read Dupin and gleaned his own notions of teaching administration.

John H. Hoaglund reported that by 1826 Dupin's materials on management had been presented in 98 French cities to 5,000 or more workers and supervisors.[25] Since his *Discours* was not published until 1831, the number of people he influenced must be greatly expanded. In his earlier publications, Dupin adopted the style of Babbage and Ure in emphasizing the advantages of specialization of labor:

It is a precious art in foremen and manufacturers to know how to break a job into its simplest elements, and nevertheless to keep them as small a number as possible, to assign each part to separate workers. This advantage may be pushed farther in large establishments than in small ones, because there are more workers to be separated into distinct working rooms. When such a division of work is put into operation the most scrupulous attention must be exercised to calculate the duration of each type of operation, in order to proportion the work to the particular number of workers that are assigned to it.[26]

He wrote of the need for clear, concise instructions to workers, of the need for producing the desired level of work with the least expenditure of worker energy, and of the necessity of studying each type of industry in order to find and publish the best results of industrial practice.

The *Discours* was not so much an examination of management as it was an exhortation to remove industrial strife. Dupin recognized worker "uneasiness" over the introduction of mechanization into French industry, discussed the work of James Watt, and encouraged workers and managers to recognize the benefits of

[24] *Ibid.*, pp. 12–13. Emphasis added.

[25] John H. Hoaglund, "Management Before Frederick Taylor," *Proceedings of the Academy of Management,* December, 1955, pp. 15–24; reprinted in Paul M. Dauten, Jr., (ed.) *Current Issues and Emerging Concepts in Management,* Boston: Houghton Mifflin Co., 1962, p. 28.

[26] Charles Dupin, *Géométrie et Mécanique des Arts et Métiers et des Beaux Arts,* Paris: Bachelier III, 1926. Cited and translated by John H. Hoaglund, *ibid.,* p. 30.

mechanization to themselves and to society. Regarding the dangers of technological displacement, he noted that before Watt's engine (1780), British industry employed fewer than one million men; by 1830, over three million were employed in industry and combined with machinery equivalent to the power of seven million men. For Dupin this was ample proof that mechanization created jobs rather than destroyed them. Evidently the French had their own Luddites and Dupin indicated that such resistance to mechanization was futile; the solution called for was widespread industrial training to permit the agrarian and unskilled worker to share in the prosperity of industrialization: "He who perfects the machines tends to give them the advantage over the worker; he who perfects the worker, gives him the same fighting chance, and makes the machine serve his well-being, instead of having to suffer from their competition. Let us concern ourselves with man involved with the difficulties of the work and of the industry."[27] These were insights not only applicable to early nineteenth century France but also to a world of the twentieth and the twenty-first centuries.

The Pioneers: A Final Note

The four pioneers discussed above were formulating the seeds of a management discipline. But, at their best, these were sparse and rudimentary. What were the reasons which prevented the formalization of a body of management thought during this early stage rather than some three-quarters of a century later? Why did Taylor get the credit for being the father of scientific management and not Charles Babbage? In perspective, the reasons are manifold: first, the stress of early writings was on the techniques and not managing *per se*. In an age of expanding technology, it was difficult for early writers to separate the managerial function from the technical and commercial aspects of running a firm. Management was more concerned with finance, production processes, selling, and acquiring labor, all of which were indeed critical at the time, rather than with developing principles or generalizations about management. An analogy might be that of a young child learning to walk: the motor urge is so great and consumes so much of his energy and attention that his development of speech is

[27] Dupin, *Discours*, p. 9.

retarded.   As the skill of walking is perfected, speech develops. The early entrepreneurs were just learning to walk in the new factory system; the technical and human problems consumed so much of their time that they had little left over for being articulate in stating generalizations about management.   Second, the period was dominated by the technical genius, the inventor-pioneer, and the owner-founder.   Success or failure was more likely to be attributed to his individual characteristics rather than to any generalized ideas about what skills a manager would need.   Each industry and its problems were considered unique and hence the principles derived by one entrepreneur were not considered applicable to different situations.   Finally, the state of the art of disseminating knowledge must be considered.   Few were literate, books were expensive, and schools were either classically oriented toward developing scholars or technique-oriented toward the artisan.   Scholars read the books of other scholars; it is not likely that Babbage, Dupin, and Ure were widely read by the practicing manager. The classes of Ure and Dupin undoubtedly reached into some factories but this was probably only a minor fraction of the total management market.

SUMMARY

In England, and France to a lesser extent, can be found the genesis of modern management thought.   Robert Owen appealed to the heart as well as to the pocketbook in his search for a New Harmony between the human factor and the age of machines. Charles Babbage appealed to the mind, became the Grandfather of Scientific Management, and applied a scientific approach to management before Taylor.   Andrew Ure taught his experiences and observations and developed managers for the new factories.   Dupin learned from Ure, started management classes in France, and perhaps influenced Henri Fayol.   With the genesis of management thought in England, the exodus of our story will be the study of management in America before Taylor.

5

Early American
Management

The nineteenth century in America was an age of dynamic growth and expansion of the factory system. A colony of mighty England twenty-four years before the beginning of this age and torn by half a decade of internecine strife in mid-century, America was to become the world's leading political and industrial force by the close of the century. Pre-Civil War America may be characterized as the emergence of the industrial system and post-Civil War America as an age of changing cultural values as industry grew toward maturity. This chapter will explore the emergence and growth of American industry, the work of some early management pioneers, and the changing cultural environment as a prelude to the emergence of the scientific management era.

ANTEBELLUM INDUSTRY AND MANAGEMENT

To the landless peasants and underpaid workmen of Europe, America loomed as a land of golden opportunity; thousands, then tens and hundreds of thousands tore their family roots from the soil of Europe to make America a cultural potpourri. Efforts to develop colonial manufactures was frowned upon by England for it posed the possibility of dangerous competition for England's early factories. After the Revolution, America sought independence both politically and economically. The War of 1812 severed America economically from England and spurred the growth of indigenous manufacturing operations.   Conditions for industry were ripe; America was a land rich in natural resources, a growing labor supply, and a political system which encouraged the creation of wealth as a way of life. Many merchant capitalists had made their fortunes in trade; and these funds, aided by the dictums of thrift of early Puritanism, made increasing amounts of capital available for manufacturing. Technological advancements were rapid and the Americans became known for their inventiveness as well as their Yankee ingenuity. Eli Whitney's cotton gin (1794), Paul Revere's method of producing cold rolled copper (1801), Robert Fulton's steamboat (1807), Jethro Wood's iron plow (1819), Cyrus McCormick's reaper (1831), Thomas Davenport's electric motor (1834), and Charles Goodyear's rubber vulcanizing process (1839) were examples of this inventiveness and the foundations of a subsequent dynamic economic system.[1]

The Industrial Revolution in America had three facets: power, transportation, and communication. The foundations of steam power had been built in England but soon took on a powerful upward surge in America. A craze of canal building in the 1820's and an ever expanding rail network opened new markets for producers. As the market expanded, mass production based on interchangeability of parts and division of labor became more feasible. The lowered costs of transportation and the new markets helped break down regional monopolies and barriers, stimulating entrepreneurs to explore and develop new production techniques. In communication, Samuel F. B. Morse' telegraph (1844) enabled the coordination of the many transactions of a growing economy.

Daniel Boorstin has characterized the early Americans as "transients." They were willing to "make anything, do anything, go anywhere."[2] Native resourcefulness was rampant and this restless and ingenious spirit drove the early American to explore and

---

[1] For early technological history, see: Roger Burlingame, *Machines That Made America*, New York: Harcourt, Brace, Jovanovich, 1953; John W. Oliver, *History of American Technology*, New York: Ronald Press Co., 1956: and Victor Clark, *History of Manufactures in the United States: 1607–1860*, New York: McGraw-Hill Book Co., 1916.

[2] Daniel Boorstin, *The Americans: The National Experience*, New York: Random House, 1965.   Another study of the American character is Alexis de Tocqueville, *Democracy in America*, New York: Alfred A. Knopf, 1945 (originally published in 1835).

open the West, to invent, and to adapt to the ever increasing flow of new nationalities. The social lid of tradition-bound Europe was loosened by American opportunity; progress, success, and "get up and go" became the watch-words of the new culture.

Early Industrial Development

England sought to prevent industrial development by prohibiting the sale of manufacturing equipment and the emigration of skilled labor to America. Samuel Slater, a textile engineer for Richard Arkwright, disguised himself as a "farmer" on his emigration papers, memorized detailed blueprints of the textile equipment, and reconstructed the necessary equipment upon his arrival in America. Together with Moses Brown, a Quaker merchant of means, he launched America's first textile factory in 1790 with a 72 spindle mill at Pawtucket, Rhode Island. On a visit to England, Francis Cabot Lowell had also observed textile manufacturing; he copied the designs of mechanical weaving equipment, brought them surreptitiously to America, and established the Boston Manufacturing Company at Waltham, Massachusetts. Other factories and other entrepreneurs followed until the New England textile industry grew to rival that of England.

In textiles and other industries, labor posed a problem as it had in England. The labor force was largely unskilled, since England attempted to prevent skilled workers from leaving the country.[3] To attract labor, early textile manufacturers developed two distinct labor relations policies: the "Rhode Island system," begun by Slater at Pawtucket and later at Fall River (Massachusetts); and the "Waltham system" of Lowell and his associates. The Rhode Island system was patterned after English practices of employing the whole family if possible and it therefore resulted in more child labor. In contrast, the Waltham system was designed to attract female labor to the factory by establishing company "boarding houses." Workers in the textile factories were mainly "Yankee" girls and they were brought to the factories from the neighboring farms by agents touring the countryside and emphasizing the moral and educational advantages of factory work.[4] The girls had to be

[3] Theodore Marburg, "Aspects of Labor Administration in the Early Nineteenth Century," *Business History Review* Vol. XV, No. 1, (February, 1941) pp. 1–10.

[4] Thomas C. Cochran and William Miller, *The Age of Enterprise*, New York: Harper and Row, 1961, p. 19.

in at 10:00 p.m. and their moral conduct was carefully watched by a housemother. Evidently, the Waltham plan was less successful in keeping a labor force since Ware estimated that the girls working in New England cotton mills stayed on the average one year.[5] Growing immigration, however, provided a steady source of replacements for the eastern factories. The Western frontier was a safety valve which presented opportunities for workers who found the wilderness more attractive than the factories. Consequently, the American factory did not demonstrate in the same depth the evils as did the English factory. Employers were paying high wages to attract and hold their labor, child labor was not as prevalent (perhaps since there were no "Poor Law Authorities" to encourage it), and abuses were less frequent and less severe.[6] The American worker was less resistant to the introduction of machinery and the Luddites found few followers, except in Pittsburgh, where some hand loom weavers rioted and destroyed their machines. Guilds were less entrenched and the American employer found innovation more acceptable to the worker.

Textiles represented America's entry into the industrial age but railroads and the steel industry were not far behind. The iron rail, flanged wheel, and the puffing locomotive began to develop around 1830. Opposed initially by the canal supporters who were fearful of its competition, the rail industry by 1850 had brought a new dimension to American life. It all started with Colonel John Stevens of Hoboken, New Jersey, who obtained from the New Jersey legislature America's first railroad charter in 1815.[7] Deemed "eccentric," he could not obtain financial backing until 1830 when he built the 23-mile-long Camden and Amboy Railroad. Stevens made numerous other technical contributions and earned the title "Father of American Engineering." He also endowed the Stevens' Institute of Technology (Hoboken, N.J.) which was to become the *alma mater* of Frederick W. Taylor and Henry L. Gantt, pioneers in scientific management. After the Camden and Amboy,

---

[5] Norman Ware, *The Industrial Worker: 1840–1860,* Glouchester, Mass.: Peter Smith Co., 1959, p. 149.

[6] Ross M. Robertson, *History of the American Economy,* New York: Harcourt, Brace, Jovanovich, 1955, p. 184. Based on his own research, Ware agreed with Robertson that there were fewer evils in the American factory system.

[7] An interesting account of John Stevens' various activities, including his anticipation by three years of Fulton's steamboat, may be found in Dorothy Gregg, "John Stevens: General Entrepreneur," in William Miller (ed.) *Men in Business,* New York: Harper and Row, 1957, pp. 120–152.

other lines such as the Chesapeake and Ohio and the Baltimore and Ohio were built and expanded until by 1850 there were 9,000 miles of track reaching all the way into Ohio.[8] The new age of rails was sweeping away local trade barriers, opening up new markets, and revolutionizing trade and communications.

Steel is the sinew of any industrial economy. Iron, because of its impurities, caused many problems for early machine designers and factory owners. The race to improve iron production proceeded, as is often the history of invention, on separate concurrent paths in England and America. William Kelly of Kentucky began his experiments in 1847 and perfected a system of refining iron by subjecting it to a blast of hot air in a specially built furnace. Unfortunately, Kelly did not apply for a patent until 1857, two years after Sir Henry Bessemer had obtained his patent in England. The Bessemer process, based on the same idea, was quite an improvement over the very slow process of "puddling" iron, or the removal of carbon and other impurities by passing heated gases over the molten iron. Until 1908 and the perfection of the "open hearth" method of making steel, the Bessemer process formed the basis for the world's steel industry. The Americans made the most of their ingenuity in production; in 1868 the United States produced 8,500 tons of steel, Britain 110,000; in 1879, the countries outputs were nearly equal; but by 1902, America produced 9,138,000 tons and England 1,826,000. American industry was showing its mettle.

THE RAILROADS: PIONEERING IN AMERICAN MANAGEMENT

The railroads were truly America's first "big business." The textile industry, though growing and dominating the Northeast, never developed into companies of the size and scope of the railroads. The management of textile firms was largely tied to England's early managerial methods, and perhaps the New England entrepreneurs read Montgomery, Brown, Ure, or Babbage for advice on managing cotton manufactures. The railroads, however, posed completely new problems; developing slowly in England concurrently with advances in America, there was no body of literature nor an extant fund of practical experience. The railroads

[8] John F. Stover, *American Railroads*, Chicago: University of Chicago Press, 1961, p. 29.

were the first American business which grew to such a size and complexity that means had to be developed of coping with massive financial requirements, of developing integrated systems of trackage and station agents, of spreading large fixed costs, and of handling a labor force dispersed over a wide geographical area.[9] These factors required managers to develop ways of managing America's first industry of larger than local scope. Railroad pioneers had to develop the first organizational structures of any size and substance and likewise developed the nation's earliest professional managers. Unlike textile and other plants, railroad operations were dispersed and could not be controlled by frequent personal inspection of the hundreds of stations and thousands of miles of track, thus making communications a significant problem. The investments in track and rolling stock were immense and required extensive long-range planning to prevent large fixed capital outlays from being placed in the wrong market area. Passenger safety and the prevention of damage or loss in transit of cargo were critical to successful operations. Scheduling of service required planning and coordination, and standing rules and policies had to be developed to guide the decisions of lower organizational elements.[10] With these immense problems of allocating and utilizing resources, it is no wonder that railroad managers were forced into developing a management system.

Daniel McCallum: System and Organization

Two individuals, Daniel C. McCallum and Henry Varnum Poor, emerge as the most significant figures in the systematization of early railroad management, although others such as Charles Perkins and Albert Fink also made some lasting contributions. Daniel Craig McCallum (1815–1878) was a misplaced poet; born in Scotland and essentially uneducated, he assumed responsibilities as General

[9] Evidence of the scope of railroad problems may be made by comparing America's largest industry of the 1850's, the Pepperell Manufacturing Company (textiles), with some of the rail companies. Pepperell had expenses in excess of $300,000 in only one year during the 1850's; the New York and Erie spent $2,861,875 and the Pennsylvania spent $2,149,918 in 1855. Pepperell employed an average of 800 workers, the Erie 4,000, and by the 1880's, the Pennsylvania employed close to 50,000. (Alfred D. Chandler, Jr. (ed.), *The Railroads: The Nation's First Big Business, Sources and Readings*, New York: Harcourt, Brace, Jovanovich, 1965, p. 97).

[10] *Ibid.*, pp. 9–10. Another excellent source on railroad history is Leland H. Jenks, "Early History of a Railway Organization," *Business History Review*, Vol. 35 (Summer, 1961), pp. 153–179.

Superintendent of the Erie line in 1854 and developed his management system. He resigned from the Erie in 1857 and in 1862 he was asked by Secretary of War Stanton to manage the nation's railways with the power to seize and operate any railroad necessary to the Union's war effort.[11] By the end of the war he was a Major General and his major feat was supplying Sherman's 200-day Atlanta campaign. During the Atlanta campaign he found time to write the poem "The Laying and Running of the Rail":

> The steam horse is a wonder—
> His voice as distant thunder,
> See him fly o'er hill and dale![12]

So much for the poet. What was this "system" that McCallum developed for the Erie? McCallum had gone to work for the Erie in the early 1850's as Superintendent of the Susquehanna Division and had developed an early set of procedures to govern that segment's operations. Faced with growing problems of rail integration and a high accident rate, the Erie management made McCallum General Superintendent of the Erie line in May 1854. In June of 1854, the workers struck for ten days; not for shorter hours nor more pay, but in defiance of McCallum's institution of his system. Evidently he wasted little time in putting his ideas into practice!

To McCallum, good management was based on good discipline, specific and detailed job descriptions, frequent and accurate reporting of performance, pay and promotion based on merit, a clearly defined hierarchy of authority of superiors over subordinates, and the enforcement of personal responsibility and accountability throughout the organization. He stated his principles of management as:

1. A proper division of responsibilities.
2. Sufficient power conferred to enable the same to be fully carried out, that such responsibilities may be real in their character.
3. The means of knowing whether such responsibilities are faithfully executed.
4. Great promptness in the report of all derelictions of duty, that evils may at once be corrected.
5. Such information, to be obtained through a system of daily reports and checks that will not embarrass principal officers, nor lessen their influence with their subordinates.

---

[11] Personal data on McCallum is based on "Big Business Takes the Management Track," *Business Week*, April 30, 1966, pp. 104–106.

[12] *Ibid.*, p. 104. McCallum had his poetry privately printed.

6. The adoption of a system, as a whole, which will not only enable the General Superintendent to detect errors immediately, but will also point out the delinquent.[13]

MaCallum developed a high degree of organizational specificity to carry out these principles. First, he separated and identified each grade of worker as to task and required each worker to wear a prescribed uniform with the insignia of his grade. Second, he developed comprehensive rules to limit the ability of individuals to do their tasks as they pleased. Rule No. 6, for example, required the engineers to stop their engines and personally see that the yard switches were properly set. The engineers saw this as an encroachment of their esteemed position; McCallum perceived it as a control device for safety.

Finally, McCallum developed a formal organizational chart (which he later put on sale to the general public for a price of $1.00). The chart took the form of a tree and depicted the lines of authority and responsibility, the division of labor among operating units, and the communication lines for reporting and control. The roots of the tree represented the Board of Directors and the President; the branches were the five operating divisions plus the staff service departments of engine repairs, car, bridge, telegraph, painting, treasurer's, and secretary's offices; the leaves were the various local freight and ticket forwarding offices, subordinate supervisors, crews, foremen, and so on to the lowest element. Adherence to the formal lines of authority was to be absolute:

The enforcement of a rigid system of discipline . . . is indispensable to success. All subordinates should be accountable to, and *be directed by their immediate superiors only*; as obedience cannot be enforced where the foreman in immediate charge is interfered with by a superior officer giving orders directly to his subordinates.[14]

McCallum saw no exceptions to this unity of command principle; to do otherwise would break down his control system, which was based on personal accountability.

McCallum also developed information management to probably the highest state of the art for the times. He used the telegraph to make operations safer as well as to facilitate administration by requiring hourly reports to show the position of every train

---

[13] Daniel C. McCallum, "Superintendents' Report," March 25, 1856, in *Annual Report of the New York and Erie Railroad Company for 1855*, Chandler, p. 102.
[14] McCallum, *Annual Report*, in Chandler, *The Railroads*, p. 104.

in the system, daily reports on passengers and cargo, and monthly reports to give management "statistical accounts" for planning, rate making, and control. He designed a clever cross-check control system by requiring both freight and passenger conductors to report on train movements, loadings, damaged freight, etc.; by comparing the reports, he could readily see discrepancies and any dishonesty.

McCallum's system was successful, from management's point of view, but it incurred the wrath of the operatives. A swelling chorus of dissension forced his resignation, with that of the President, in July, 1857. However, McCallum earned the highest praise of Henry Varnum Poor, the eminent editor of the *American Railroad Journal* and spokesman for the industry. Poor later had some doubts about the system but thought that it was a step in the right direction. Others followed McCallum's pioneering work: Albert Fink developed a cost accounting system which used information flows, classification of costs, and statistical control devices which became a model for modern corporate control.[15] Charles E. Perkins, President of the Chicago, Burlington, and Quincy Railroad, made refinements in McCallum's organization by pointing out the limits to how much work a manager could supervise and the necessity to push authority and responsibility downward in the organization, and proposed a means of resolving conflicts between lower elements by moving them to a higher common level of authority.[16] McCallum's work, despite his problems, is a striking example of early management efforts to cope with large corporate systems. Unfortunately, soon after McCallum left the Erie, it fell into the hands of the piratical *troika* of Daniel Drew, Jim Fisk, and Jay Gould. In later years the Erie became the byword for poor management.

Henry V. Poor: A Broader View of Management

Henry Varnum Poor (1812–1905), through his editor's position on the *American Railroad Journal*, essayed to become the conscience of America's first large business. Whereas McCallum spoke of internal operating problems, Poor looked for broader

[15] Albert Fink, "Classification of Operating Expenses," in *Annual Report of the Louisville and Nashville Railroad Company* (1874), *ibid.*, pp. 108–117.

[16] From the personal papers of Charles E. Perkins, written in 1855, *ibid.*, pp. 118–125.

principles of railroad operations including financing, regulation, and the role of the railroad in American life. Poor was well educated and came from a more select background than McCallum; his biographer tells us that Poor was thoroughly imbued with the romance and optimism of nineteenth century America.[17] As editor of the *Journal* in the pre-Civil War years, Poor made it the leading business periodical of the day and a reliable source of information for the railroad investor as well as the manager. His editorials discussed railroad developments, problems, needed reforms in operating practices, and presented detailed financial and operating data. After the war, his *Manual of Railroads in the United States* continued his efforts to further the dissemination of financial and operating information. His life was marked throughout by the critical age of railroads coming from infancy to maturity and by their amazing impact on opening the West and tying America together with a web of steel.

In its early years, the Erie was one of Poor's favorite targets, for it was poorly managed and financed. The advent of McCallum's reforms soon made Poor the biggest booster of the Erie as an example of proper management. Poor saw a need for managerial reform through development of a group of professional managers rather than speculators and promoters to build the nation's transportation system. Poor looked for a science or "system" of management and from McCallum's work Poor gleaned three fundamental principles: organization, communication, and information.[18] Organization was basic to all management; there must be a careful division of labor from the President down to the common laborer, each with specific duties and responsibilities. Every person would be directly accountable to his immediate superior; Poor repeatedly used the terms "responsibility" and "accountability" in his editorials. Second, communication was devising a method of reporting throughout the organization to give top management a continuous and accurate accounting on operations. Finally, information was "recorded communication"; Poor saw the need for a set of

---

[17] Alfred D. Chandler, Jr. *Henry Varnum Poor: Business Editor, Analyst, and Reformer,* Cambridge, Mass.: Harvard University Press, 1956. An interesting sidelight is that Professor Chandler is the great-grandson of Henry Varnum Poor.

[18] *Ibid.,* pp. 146–147. Chandler's work is based on Poor's editorials in the *Journal* and will be cited here without referring to specific dates and issues of that *Journal.* In the case of Poor's three principles, for example, Poor was influenced by McCallum and not vice versa. *Ibid.,* p. 147.

operating reports to be compiled for costs, revenues, and rate making. This third principle was an early appearance of a "data bank" concept in management literature in the sense that management would build up a fund of data on operations to analyze the present system and to provide a base for changes to improve service. One can readily see the influence of McCallum on Poor's writing and can trace the development of the third principle through Albert Fink's efforts to install statistical control systems in the corporate structure.

Just as McCallum's work was becoming widely known, in large part due to Poor's editorials, Poor began having his doubts about whether organization, communication, and information were adequate principles to encompass the task of management. Poor visited England in 1858 to view its railway system and upon his return he wrote concerning: "the grave difficulties of adapting human capabilities and current business practices and institutions to the severe requirements demanded by the efficient operation of such large administrative units."[19] Both in England and on the Erie Poor saw developing the worker resistance to the discipline required by systematic management. The tighter control required to bring order from chaos, the limiting of individual discretion in the performance of tasks, and the rigid hierarchical specifications of a formal organization, were all leading to worker protests against the tyranny of the system. This protest was not new in the annals of management history, nor has the issue ever been fully resolved to this day. Poor, however, thought these protests were too extreme and defended the need for systematization: "We can see no other way in which such a vast machine can be safely and successfully conducted,"[20] i.e. except through order, system, and discipline.

Accordingly, Poor began to look for some broader principles to overcome the dangers of "regarding man as a mere machine, out of which all the qualities necessary to be a good servant can be enforced by the mere payment of wages. But duties cannot always be prescribed and the most valuable are often voluntary ones."[21] Close prescription of duties and the bureaucratization of management reduced incentives and inevitably would lead the railroads, in

---

[19] *Ibid.*, p. 155.
[20] *Ibid.*, p. 155.
[21] *Loc. cit.*

Poor's view, to the problems inherent in the rigid managerial structures along the patterns of the military and the government. Poor's solution was a leadership which would overcome dullness and routine by infusing the organization with an *esprit de corps*. Top management should become "the soul of the enterprise, reaching and infusing life, intelligence and obedience into every portion of it. This soul must not be a fragmentary or disjointed one—giving one direction to the head, another to the hands, and another to the feet. Wherever there is lack of unity there will be a lack of energy—of intelligence—of life—of accountability and subordination."[22]

In anticipating Fayol's unity-of-direction principle by 60 years, he regarded the problems of top management as those of assuming and of getting subordinates to assume a total systems view of the organization. Leaders must not only know all aspects of railroad operation and administration but also needed to be able to handle men, to know the total system, and to prevent inter-departmental conflicts which destroyed unity of purpose. The breakdown in leadership came from two sources: one, selection on some basis other than ability or training and, two, the lack of an information system to pinpoint weak managers. Poor's pleas for professional managers to manage well the property of others were not too dissimilar to the problems Adam Smith had pointed out nearly a century before.

As spokesman for the industry, Poor lashed out against the promoters and speculators who manipulated and "watered" stock for short-run gains at the expense of the total industry. He reflected the *laissez-faire* spirit by calling for unrestricted competition. Rates should not be regulated by government and the only legislation necessary was that to protect "honest rational men" from the dishonest promoters. He insisted that the rapid development of the American railroad system was "proof that reliance on the self-interest of individuals operating under conditions of unrestricted competition resulted in the greatest good for the greatest number."[23] Through publicity to inform stockholders and the public, through professionalization of management, and through protection of the rational from the irrational, the railroads could achieve their proper role in the economy.

[22] *Ibid.*, p. 157.
[23] *Ibid.*, p. 260.

Henry Varnum Poor was truly a remarkable man who came to grips with the broader problems of management and its environment. He stated issues which face management today and will be there tomorrow. His position that the role of government was to protect, not to control, illustrates an ever recurring problem of management *vis-à-vis* government. His search for order out of chaos without destroying individual incentive and dignity is yet a current problem too. Long before Frederick Taylor he called for a system; long before Elton Mayo he called for a recognition of the human factor; and long before Chris Argyris he called for leadership to remove the rigidities of formal organization. He was one of our most outstanding early contributors to management thought.

Antebellum Management: A Final Note

Early American entrepreneurs faced in common the problems of financing expansion, of bringing a reluctant labor force into the new factory regimen, of finding capable salaried professional managers, of coping with a growing national market brought on by the transportation and communication revolutions, and of resolving the problems caused by the new machines and production processes. Appropriately enough, the first inklings of systematic management arose in the railroad industry where the first large accumulation of resources appeared and where a system had to be developed to allocate and utilize this mass of resources. The Industrial Revolution in America had established a number of industries which would form the basis of America's industrial might. Oliver Evans had developed an automated flour mill in 1787 and America soon became the breadbasket of the world.[24] Samuel Slater, Francis Cabot Lowell, and William Pepperell formed the early textile industry; railroads were expanding and steel technology advancing; Goodyear had vulcanized rubber, Elias Howe, Jr., had developed the sewing machine, Philip D. Armour was making Chicago into the meat-packing capital of the world, the Du Ponts were operating a powder mill at Brandywine, Morse was refining the telegraph, and Cyrus H. McCormick was perfecting the reaper.[25] It was a dynamic era for inventors and entrepreneurs.

[24] John Chamberlain, *The Enterprising Americans,* New York: Harper and Row, 1961, pp. 51–53.

[25] William T. Hutchinson, *Cyrus Hall McCormick,* New York: Appleton-Century-Crofts, Vol. I (1930) and Vol. II (1935).

THE POST-WAR ERA

The great scar that divided the United States from 1861 to 1865 is a convenient dividing point for the study of management in early America. The two periods form distinct eras and Maurer has suggested that the entrepreneurs of the first half of the nineteenth century were models of the *laissez-faire* doctrine of Adam Smith.[26] They did not pursue unrestricted self-interest and the maximization of short run profits but the last half of the century brought a new breed of businessmen who were not Adam Smith models. These "looters," as Maurer called them, formed pools and trusts to share or monopolize the market, corrupted legislators who were willing partakers of the largesse, and were more interested in manipulation than management.

The "Robber Barons"

Virtuous conduct seldom makes news. Historians and journalists are awed by the extraordinary and more frequently than not overstress it to the detriment of those quiet, sturdy, responsible people who, unheralded, are the true productive builders. Matthew Josephson, among others, developed the idea of "robber barons" to such a point that the public is quick to equate any capitalist with these tycoon-tyrants.[27] The robber barons are of interest for a number of reasons: first, they characterized a stage in the economic development of America; second, they reflected the "rags to riches" social aspirations of many Americans; and finally, their practices served to bring about changes in the relationship of business to government and of business to its total cultural environment.

It is not by coincidence that the most flagrant of the corrupt practices came in the railroad industry. Rail lines criss-crossed the nation and, with large fixed costs, it was inevitable that there would be price wars. Government land grants and subsidies had encouraged building in marginal return areas where greater economic pressures would be brought to bear. Duplicate lines

[26] Herrymon Maurer, *Great Enterprise: Growth and Behavior of the Big Corporation*, New York: The MacMillan Co., 1955, pp. 36–38.

[27] Matthew Josephson, *The Robber Barons*, New York: Harcourt, Brace, Jovanovich, 1934; Stewart H. Holbrook, *The Age of the Moguls*, Garden City, N.Y.: Doubleday and Co., 1953; and Gustavus Myers, *The Great American Fortunes*, New York: Julian Messner, 1939.

serving these areas and crossing at key terminals increased competition. Finally, the granting of operating franchises opened the
gate to collusion between the railroad promoter and the legislator.
Railroad expansion became more frequently a political decision
rather than an economic one. There were other "barons," of
course, but the railroads characterized an economic age in which
businessmen sought to evade the economics of Adam Smith and
turned to collusion instead of competition and to bribery in place
of service. Josephson noted that honesty toward customers,
respectability, and conservatism in business practices, all those
characteristics of the early American entrepreneur, were beginning to depart in the 1840's. The new breed of businessmen left
home early to seek their fortune; for the most part they came
from the aggressive Yankee race of New England, had grown up in
relative poverty, were immigrants or the sons of immigrants, were
acquisition motivated, and were puritanical and pious men who
took their Calvinistic origins seriously.[28] There were exceptions—
some were contradictions in character such as Daniel Drew who
spent his evenings, often drunk, in a cheap hotel room reading
the Bible and chewing tobacco. They all saw the potential of growth
in the burgeoning economy and vowed to take advantage of it. It
would be impossible to chronicle all of their activities but some
thumbnail sketches will reveal the nature of the manipulating and
looting entrepreneur.

Commodore Cornelius Vanderbilt gained control of the New
York and Harlem line by bribery of the New York State legislature
and by stock manipulation. He later built the New York Central
system, watered the stock, increased his fortune, and once
remarked: "What do I care about the law? Hain't I got the
power?"[29] Daniel Drew has the dubious honor of being the first to
engage in the practice which came to be called "watering stock."
He had purchased a herd of cattle with an enlistment bonus he
had received from his Civil War Army days. In transporting the
herd to market, he fed them salt to make them thirsty, then offered
them all the water they could drink and sold at a very large profit
some temporarily overweight cattle. Together with Jay Gould and
Jim Fisk, Drew turned to railroading and soon gave the Erie line its

---

[28] Josephson, pp. 30–32 and Holbrook, pp. viii–x.
[29] Josephson, p. 72. It was Cornelius Vanderbilt's son William who uttered the
infamous phrase "The public be damned." *Ibid.*, p. 187.

reputation for mismanagement in the days following Daniel Mc-
Callum. This deadly trio of Drew, Fisk and Gould cared nothing for
the operations of the railroad; they were simply after the money
they could make from their financial scheming. The Western rail-
roaders were especially malignant; led by Collis P. Huntington and
aided by Leland Stanford, Sr., they purchased the favors of legislators who could grant them free government land, give franchises,
and pass enabling legislation. One year Huntington paid $200,000
to get a bill through Congress; he later complained that Congress
was costing up to a half a million dollars a session and moaned, "I
am afraid this damnation Congress will kill us."[30]

Not all of the "barons" were railroad men. John D. Rockefeller
combined audacity and cunning in building his South Improvement Company and the Standard Oil colossus. By conspiring with
the railroads, he was able to extract rebates on his freight and to
receive rebates on the oil that his rivals shipped.[31] Andrew Carnegie was a steel baron who at one point owned or controlled two-
thirds of the nation's young steel industry. The Homestead strike
earned Carnegie a poor press when he met union efforts with a
force of Pinkerton detectives (hired to protect the plant) who were
brutally stoned and beaten by the striking workers; State troops
moved in and secured the plant for a wholly non-union crew. In
the process 14 had been killed and 163 wounded. Others, such as
Philip D. Armour in meat packing, Henry Clay Frick in coal and
coke, and J. P. Morgan, Sr. in finance, represented some questionable practices of entrepreneurship.

The robber barons were an enigma; what was their *raison
d'être*? They were religious men:

> It would be false to deny or overlook the strong religious impulse shared
> by most of the great possessors of money, who were nearly all apparently true
> believers, godly men and generous champions of the Church.[32]

They were generous men: Rockefeller was financing missionaries
to China at the same time his workers were being shot and burned
at the Colorado Fuel and Iron battle. They lived ostentatiously in
what Thorstein Veblen saw as "conspicuous consumption."

---

[30] Maurer, p. 44. They kept two sets of accounts, one for "legal" expenses, and
one for "extra legal" expenses, Josephson, p. 357.

[31] *Ibid.*, pp. 115–119. See also Ida Tarbell, *History of Standard Oil*, New York:
Harper and Row, 1905.

[32] Josephson, p. 317.

Ignorant of art, they bought it by the boat load. Philanthropic with everyone but their workers and their competitors, they blazed across the pages of entrepreneurial history marking a new era for America.

The abuses of these men unleashed a reform movement which changed the character of management's relation to its environment. The robber barons were playing a "game" of commerce, out to destroy others, at whatever price had to be paid, in a form of jungle warfare. The classical economics of Adam Smith envisioned a rational man who pursued his self-interest but not at the price of the loss of the self-interest and integrity of those with whom he was trading. The robber barons were not following the *laissez-faire* precepts of the classical school but colluded with government to gain monopolies and formed pools and arrangements to prevent, not further, competition.

The Creative Entrepreneurs

In rebuttal to the robbers and looters, there existed in the last half of the century quiet Americans who were revolutionizing the industrial structure. Some had their faults, but to a large degree their lives were marked by production, not destruction, and by the creation and management of wealth, not its manipulation. Again we can only sample from their lives to see a more refreshing view of American entrepreneurship. Thomas Edison immediately emerges as one of the most dynamic. His early work on automatic printing equipment to go with Samuel F. B. Morse's telegraph led to advances and the development of Western Union. Unfortunately, he was "conned" by Jay Gould, who had gained control of Western Union; Edison emerged after a court suit with $1 for his pains.[33] Edison made improvements on Alexander Graham Bell's telephone and was shortly engaged in a patent fight which eventually led to the sale of his ideas to the rapidly growing Bell system. He was more richly rewarded in this case, receiving $100,000 for American patent rights and $145,000 for his English rights. At Menlo Park, his stream of inventions was unparalleled; the phonograph, the dictaphone, the electric light (initially financed by J. P. Morgan), the motion picture camera, and a host

[33] Jonathan Hughes, *The Vital Few*, Boston: Houghton Mifflin Co., 1966, pp. 162–164.

of others. His work formed the basis for such modern giants as General Electric, Consolidated Edison, and all the other "Edisons."

Andrew Carnegie must be considered a creator and innovator despite his faults. He built a management accounting system to parallel his integrated steel works because he recognized at an early stage that, with the proper information about costs, management could gain a competitive advantage. He used this information to lower costs and prices in order to enlarge his market and outstrip his competitors. Carnegie plowed back his profits, refused to speculate in stocks, scorned financiers, and ran a tight ship. Carnegie believed in high wages for it was then that he found workers at their most productive level: "I can't afford to pay them [the workers] any other way [than high wages]."[34] He never understood the Homestead strike and blamed the trouble on Henry Clay Frick who was his partner and President of Carnegie Steel. Frick closed the plant (Carnegie was touring abroad when the dispute arose), hired the Pinkertons, built a fence around the property, and refused to budge. The bloody strike and its aftermath gave steel a bad name that endures even today. Carnegie had a knack for developing managers, however; Charles Schwab and W. E. Corey, both Carnegie protégés, were to become presidents of U. S. Steel. Carnegie eventually sold out to the Morgan interests, resulting in the formation of U. S. Steel in 1901. Carnegie's philanthropies are legendary but he was also a dominant figure who brought integrated management to the steel industry.

The latter part of the nineteenth century witnessed the beginnings of careers of other creative entrepreneurs, whose influences would spread into the twentieth century. The automobile, a late nineteenth-century phenomenon, was not the invention of Henry Ford; but innovations in auto production techniques were largely due to his efforts.[35] Ford took the concept of interchangeable parts, arranged the work space so that work flowed by the workers on a moving belt, each worker performing a highly specialized task, and brought the concept of mass production to large-scale American industry. Perhaps this moving assembly line concept was the introduction to a second Industrial Revolution.

[34] *Ibid.*, p. 241.
[35] Henry Ford is a favorite subject for historians. For example, Allan Nevins, *Ford: The Times, The Man and The Company*, New York: Charles Scribner's Sons, 1954. Nevins notes, however, that it was not Henry Ford alone, but a group of men and a series of experiments before the idea was perfected. *Ibid.*, pp. 469–476.

The story of these creative entrepreneurs is probably enough as a rebuttal to the robber barons, but there were others: Walter P. Chrysler in automobiles; in retailing, Wanamaker, the Filenes, Sears, Montgomery Ward, and J. C. Penney; the DuPonts, who expanded from gunpowder to other ventures, and a host of others.[36] These were the men, the productive men, who were building America. Relatively uninterested in speculative schemes to get rich quick, they operated in a long-run manner designed to create useful products at lower costs and prices to serve a growing America. The creative entrepreneurs are the true heroes of the American industrial story.

The Economic Environment

No nation can undergo a transformation of society as America did in the nineteenth century without substantial repercussions. An examination of America's response to industrialism is necessary in order to understand the forces that would shape the twentieth century. American economic conditions encouraged a rapid growth in corporate size, and mass markets and mass production had ushered in an era of intense competition. Aggressive entrepreneurs responded by overbuilding capacity which further intensified price competition. To protect themselves from this sharp competition, business sought to combine through pools, trusts, mergers, and holding companies to insulate themselves from the market. The doctrine of *laissez-faire* was a one-way street in practice; government should do nothing to regulate business but everything to aid it. There were large land grants to the railroads and legislation which supplied protection for industry against foreign competition, thus fostering domestic monopolies.

The farmers, like the businessmen, also undertook collective action to protect themselves from economic adversity. The Granger movement, in a large part, aimed at state supervision of railroad rates and was intended to give the farmer greater control over his environment. Farmer cooperative ventures also consti-

[36] The contributions of these men are chronicled in many places; for example: John Chamberlain, *The Enterprising Americans*, New York: Harper and Row, 1961; Hughes, *The Vital Few*; Boris Emmet and John Jeuck, *Catalogues and Counters*, Chicago: University of Chicago Press, 1950; and Tom Mahoney and Leonard Sloane, *The Great Merchants*, New York: Harper and Row, 1966.

tuted a persistent effort of the farm movement to protect itself. Joining the farmer and the businessman, labor also attempted to organize for concerted effort. The National Labor Union, headed by William H. Sylvis, sought to supplant the wage system with cooperative production in which the workers would pool their resources, supply their own labor, and manage the factories. The Noble Order of the Knights of Labor, organized in 1867, sought an eight-hour day, the establishment of a Bureau of Labor Statistics, protection of child labor, a graduated income tax, government ownership of railroads and telegraph lines, the abolition of national banks, and a system of cooperation to take the place of wages. The American Federation of Labor, organized in 1886, was a federation of craft unions which concentrated on the pursuit of immediate economic gains for the worker on the job rather than on distant political reforms. Under Samuel Gomper's leadership, the union membership increased from less than 200,000 in 1886 to over 2,865,000 by the time of Gomper's death in 1924.[37]

In essence, the new age threatened everyone with the unknowns of change. Worker, farmer, and businessman alike organized for collective action. Producers joined to control the conditions under which they sold their products; distributors combined to wield influence over marketing and transportation; and laborers formed trade unions to bargain with management. This organizational revolution revealed the degree to which industrialism had shifted the context of economic decisions from personal relationships among individuals to a struggle for power among well-organized groups.

Corporations possessed enormous potential for growth and, as industrialization proceeded, they grew in size, scope, resources, and power. Alfred Chandler has developed an interesting thesis about the historical growth of large corporations and their subsequent organizational forms. By tracing the history of various firms, he delineated four phases in the history of the large American enterprise: one, "the initial expansion and accumulation of resources"; two, "the rationalization of the use of resources"; three, "the expansion into new markets and lines to help assure the continuing full use of resources"; and finally "the development of a new structure to make possible continuing effective mobilization

[37] Philip A. Taft, *The A.F.L. in The Time of Gompers*, New York: Harper and Row, 1957, Chapter 3.

of resources to meet both changing short-term market demands and long-term market trends."[38] Hence the cycle runs to accumulate resources, rationalize resource utilization, expand resources, and re-rationalize resource utilization; presumably *ad infinitum.* For different companies, the cycle starts and ends at different times, depending upon the state of technology and the firm's ability to react to and capitalize on market opportunities. During the latter part of the nineteenth century, many major industries were forming and would fit into Chandler's phase I or "resource accumulation stage." Although Chandler did not make the analogy, the stage was set for phase two and scientific management, which will be the subject of part two.

The Social Environment

In the era under consideration, social Darwinism was deemed by some to be the prevailing social philosophy. In 1859, Charles Darwin published his great work, *On the Origin of Species by Means of Natural Selection, or the Preservation of Favored Races in the Struggle for Life.* This book set forth his theories concerning evolution and natural selection through the struggle for existence. Social scientists seized Darwin's theories in an attempt to apply them to human society and the result was "social Darwinism."[39] Two men were primarily instrumental in spreading the implications of Darwin's theories to fields other than biology. Herbert Spencer was an English philosopher who advocated the preeminence of the individual over society and of science over religion. The other was William Graham Sumner, a professor of political and social science at Yale, who became the most vigorous and influential social Darwinist in America. Since the most striking phrases of Darwinism were "struggle for existence" and "survival of the fittest," both Spencer and Sumner suggested that nature would provide that the "most fit" in a competitive situation would win. This process would lead to the continuing improvement of mankind since the progress of civilization depended upon natural selection and that in turn depended upon the work-

---

[38] Alfred D. Chandler, Jr., *Strategy and Structure: Chapters in the History of the Industrial Enterprise,* Cambridge, Mass.: MIT Press, 1962, p. 385. A similar thesis is put forth by Edith T. Penrose, *The Theory of the Growth of the Firm,* London: Oxford University Press, 1959, although her work is more on the economics of growth and not on corporate structural changes.

[39] Richard Hofstadter, *Social Darwinism in American Thought,* Boston: Beacon Press, 1945, p. 4.

ings of unrestricted competition. According to Sumner, competition was a law of nature which "can no more be done away with than gravitation."[40] In the struggle for existence in a competitive society, money was the measure of success; this explained the huge fortunes millionaires acquired in a competitive system. Being the most fit, their huge fortunes were the legitimate wages of efficiency. Thus, through unrestricted competition, the fittest would survive and move up the social ladder of success and the unfit would occupy the lower class structures and would eventually be eliminated through evolution. This process would be slow and gradual and society must not try to interfere with the process of nature.

To prove his case for linking social Darwinism to managerial philosophy, Hofstadter quoted some leading businessmen. To John D. Rockefeller he ascribed these sentiments:

The growth of a large business is merely a survival of the fittest. . . . The American Beauty rose can be produced in the splendor and fragrance which brings cheer to its beholder only by sacrificing the early buds which grow up around it. This is not an evil tendency in business. It is merely the working-out of a law of nature and law of God.[41]

James J. Hill implied that the absorption of smaller railroads by larger railroads represented the industrial analogy to the victory of the strong. He also stated that "the fortunes of railroad companies are determined by the law of the survival of the fittest."[42] Andrew Carnegie, one of Spencer's most prominent disciples, after reading Darwin and Spencer, stated:

I remember that light came as in a flood and all was clear. Not only had I got rid of theology and the supernatural, but I had found the truth of evolution. "All is well since all grows better" became my motto.[43]

Others have attributed the practices of American businessmen to the notion of social Darwinism. Witness, for example, the views of two renowned business historians:

This philosophy [Spencer's] had served American industrialists well in the late decades of the nineteenth century; so well indeed, that they had been able to learn no other despite changing conditions, so well that they were reluctant to surrender it even when its application to the life around them had become obscure.[44]

40 *Ibid.*, p. 57.
41 *Ibid.*, p. 45.
42 *Loc. cit.*
43 *Loc. cit.*
44 Thomas C. Cochran and William Miller, *The Age of Enterprise: A Social History of Industrial America*, New York: Harper and Row, Torchbook edition, 1961, p. 128.

These historians charged that American society saw its own image in that tooth-and-claw version of natural selection and that its dominant groups were therefore able to dramatize this vision of competition as a thing good in itself. Ruthless business rivalry and unprincipled politics were to be justified by the survival philosophy.

Are these allegations true? Another esteemed historian has suggested that "Darwinsim may have done no more for the business community than to furnish a new terminology for old ideas."[45] He claimed that businessmen were pragmatic doers who worked out the rules as they met them; they read or heard little of Spencer, Darwin, Sumner, or Adam Smith, and cared little for abstract social and economic theories. Raymond J. Wilson agrees with Kirkland; "It is not true that this commitment [to competition] was grounded on Darwinian premises."[46] Few knew enough of Spencer or Darwin "to turn biology to the uses of self-justification." Further, Wilson claimed that only Andrew Carnegie was a true social Darwinist business man. Even as a Darwinist, Carnegie put forth a gospel of wealth and stewardship which characterized many of the leaders of the day who accumulated fortunes and then endowed foundations, colleges, libraries, and other philanthropies. The "American Beauty rose" analogy attributed to John D. Rockefeller was made by his son in the early 1900's and not during the heyday of social Darwinism. James J. Hill did make his "survival of the fittest" statement but only during an interview in 1922 for his memoirs, not while he was actively in the railroad business.[47]

What can be concluded about the effect of social Darwinism on the thought and practices of the businessman? The peak of social Darwinism in America saw businessmen and others trying to avoid competition through cooperative efforts of pools, Granges, and unions instead of allowing the laws of nature to run their course. Businessmen, being of a practical bent, have never been noted for their interest in the social theories of the intellectuals;

[45] Edward C. Kirkland, *Dream and Thought in the Business Community, 1860–1900*, Ithaca, N.Y.: Cornell University Press, 1956, p. 14. Another who shares this pragmatic view is Peter d. A. Jones (ed.), *The Robber Barons Revisited*, Boston: D.C. Health and Company, 1968, pp. v–xi.

[46] Raymond J. Wilson (ed.), *Darwinism and the American Intellectual: A Book of Readings*, Homewood, Ill.: Dorsey Press, 1967, p. 93.

[47] *Ibid.*, pp. 94–99.

here again social Darwinism falls short.   Another strike against the proponents is the known pious nature of the entrepreneurs, at least on Sunday, and the thought of Darwinian concepts appealing to them is doubtful.   Social Darwinism may have provided a rationalization for some practices, but the conclusion that it was the dominant philosophy is tenuous.

The social value which was imbedded in the culture was a need for achievement.[48]   This value, aided by the economic sanction of *laissez-faire* competition and the pro-business political environment, did bring about some unsavory practices which fed the pens of the muckrakers.   However, beyond those who may have used social Darwinism as justification for their misdirected achievement drives, there were many, many more who were turning America into an industrial giant, building firms to serve the consumer, creating products and services, and creating organizations which would benefit man.

The Political Environment

Politically, America was undergoing a great transformation in the relationship between business and government.   Some historians have argued that the Populist-Progressive era of reform was an attack on corporate wealth to promote greater economic opportunity for all.[49]   Another has suggested that the reformers were attempting to cope with societal change and "they centered their fire on the business leader . . . [who] was a *symbol of change* which they could conveniently attack, rather than the essence of change itself."[50]   The businessman was a target in the age of reform. The first attempts to reform business practices came very logically with the railroads.   In 1869 Massachusetts passed the first statutes regulating railroads, the Granger laws of the seventies brought regulation to others, and the Interstate Commerce Act of 1887, which proved generally ineffective in practice, became the first national regulation.   Beyond the railroads, the Sherman Antitrust Act of 1890 sought to check corporate trusts and monopoly

[48] McClelland, *The Achieving Society,* pp. 150–151; McClelland and his associates found that *n* achievement in America rose quite rapidly between 1850 and 1890 but declined thereafter.

[49] For example: Charles Howard Hopkins, *The Rise of the Social Gospel in American Protestantism: 1865–1915,* New Haven, Conn.: Yale University Press, 1940.

[50] Samuel P. Hays, *The Response to Industrialism: 1885–1914,* Chicago: University of Chicago Press, 1957, p. 188.   Italics added.

practices "in restraint of trade." Poorly defined and narrowly construed, it was generally ineffectual.

The voices of reform earned their title of "muckrakers." Their protests were not only against business but also against the practices of corrupt governments and their failure to provide justice. Lincoln Steffens unfolded a trail of political corruption in his *The Shame of the Cities*; Ida Tarbell criticized the unethical practices of Standard Oil; Thomas Lawson exposed Wall Street in *Frenzied Finance*; Upton Sinclair aimed at the nation's heart and hit its stomach in *The Jungle* (resulting in the passage of the Pure Food and Drug Act); and David Phillips described the close connection between industrialists and lawmakers in the *Treason of the Senate*. In essence, the reform movement aimed at coping with the cultural upheaval caused by large scale enterprise, "spoils" government, and the abuse of the many by the powerful few, whether in business or in government. The result was a decline in *laissez-faire* and a growth in governmental regulation of life.

Historically, the struggle between unrestrained competition on the one hand and government regulation on the other poses some interesting questions. Henri Pirenne has suggested that there is a cyclical relationship throughout history between economic freedom and state control of economic activities. Basically he has said that each historical era develops a different class of entrepreneurs who, having risen from lower social classes, are prepared to undertake risk ventures in order to better themselves. These men are not the sons of previous capitalists but eager young men who sense unmet market needs. As their enterprises grow, they are aided by economic freedom. As they become successful and entrenched, two things happen: one, they abuse their freedoms and become more regulated by public authorities; and two, they become more status and security conscious as they gain more wealth. Becoming less daring and cornered at every turn by regulation, the entrepreneurs eventually wither away as they lose the innovative zeal and fail to react to changing economic conditions. They are replaced by other new young eager men who repeat the same cycle. As a corollary to this rise and fall of entrepreneurs, Pirenne characterized cycles of recurring economic freedom and control: relatively *laissez-faire* freedom appearing in the eleventh, twelfth, fifteenth, and nineteenth centuries; public

control and regulation being dominant in the thirteenth, four-
teenth, sixteenth, eighteenth (mercantilism), and the twentieth
centuries.[51]   In brief, Pirenne's thesis was that unrestrained competition in one century led to abuses and eventually to regulation
in the next century.   Pirenne did not analyze how regulation
withered away, allowing the cycle to repeat itself.   More precise
research should be attempted, but intuitively it would appear that
overregulation stifles innovation and to restore progress added
motives must be made available through a loosening of economic
restraints.   Libermanism in Russia, for example, could be a form
of this removal of restraints.   If Pirenne's cycle holds true, the
manager of the twenty-first century may operate under fewer
governmental restrictions.

SUMMARY OF PART I

Part I of this study has been an examination of management
thought prior to the scientific management era in America and
may be visually conceptualized as Figure 5-1.   Man, a fundamental
unit of our study, has manifold needs and wants which he seeks
to satisfy through organized endeavors.   In organizations, management is an activity which performs certain functions in order to
obtain the effective acquisition, allocation, and utilization of human
efforts and physical resources in order to meet the organization's
objectives and to yield positive benefits to organizational members.
The cultural environment, characterized as having economic, social,
and political facets, shapes values and forms institutional arrangements which have a large bearing upon man, upon organizations,
and upon management as an activity.

Early civilizations reflected some early attempts to relate man
to organizations but generally placed a low value on economic
activity and held a parochial view of the management function.
The cultural rebirth brought a new view of man, of economic
activity, of social values, of political arrangements, and established
the preconditions for the Industrial Revolution.   This technological and cultural revolution created the factory system to replace
the domestic system and posed managerial problems on a scale
never encountered before.   Broadly viewed, these problems may

[51] Henri Pirenne, "The Stages in the Social History of Capitalism," *American
Historical Review*, Vol. XIX, (April, 1914), pp. 494–515.

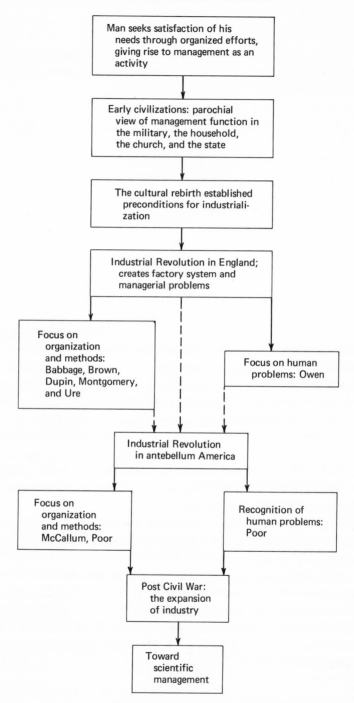

Fig. 5–1. Synopsis of early management thought

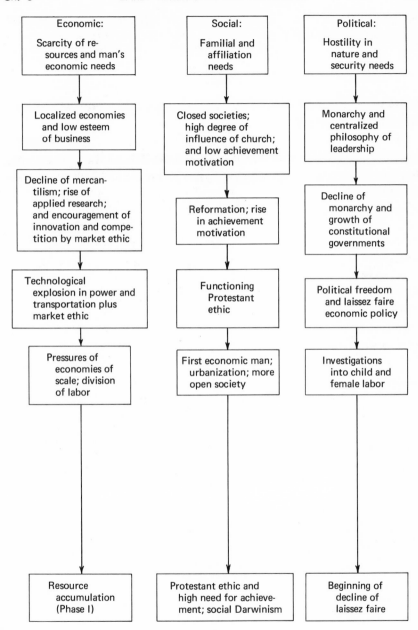

Economic:	Social:	Political:
Scarcity of resources and man's economic needs	Familial and affiliation needs	Hostility in nature and security needs
Localized economies and low esteem of business	Closed societies; high degree of influence of church; and low achievement motivation	Monarchy and centralized philosophy of leadership
Decline of mercantilism; rise of applied research; and encouragement of innovation and competition by market ethic	Reformation; rise in achievement motivation	Decline of monarchy and growth of constitutional governments
Technological explosion in power and transportation plus market ethic	Functioning Protestant ethic	Political freedom and laissez faire economic policy
Pressures of economies of scale; division of labor	First economic man; urbanization; more open society	Investigations into child and female labor
Resource accumulation (Phase I)	Protestant ethic and high need for achievement; social Darwinism	Beginning of decline of laissez faire

and the cultural environment.

be grouped in three categories: (1) the organizational and methods problems of melding technology, materials, organizational functions, and productive processes in an efficient manner; (2) the human problems of acquiring, developing, stimulating, and controlling human behavior toward preconceived ends; and (3) the managerial problem of fusing both of the above facets in order to accomplish objectives.

Throughout our study of management thought, we will see that various writers will shift their relative emphasis on the importance of the organization and methods facet *vis-à-vis* the human facet. This does not mean that these two facets are mutually exclusive but that it is a matter of relative focus and this to a large degree will be influenced by the cultural environment. For example, Charles Babbage was concerned with the human problems of the factory but his primary concern was with the analysis of production techniques. Robert Owen, on the other hand, was more concerned with the impact of industrialization on people. Likewise, Henry Varnum Poor was more concerned with the systematization of the railroads but recognized the interaction of the organization and methods facet with the human facet.

Figure 5-1 illustrates in summary form management thought before Scientific Management. It shows the interaction of the cultural environment with early ideas about the management activity, depicts the relative emphases of management pioneers, and provides the basis for the beginnings of the scientific management era in America.

II

THE SCIENTIFIC MANAGEMENT ERA

Part II will begin with the work of Frederick W. Taylor and will examine management thought in Europe and America up to the early 1930's. Taylor provided the major thrust for an era which will be characterized as a search for efficiency and systematization in management thought. Around Taylor there were others, such as Carl Barth, H. L. Gantt, Frank and Lillian Gilbreth, Morris Cooke, and Harrington Emerson, who were spreading the gospel of efficiency in America. Though the work of Taylor and his followers dominated this era, there were also some early behavioral contributions and these will be examined as a prelude to the emergence of human relations in industry. Next, we will examine the work of Henri Fayol and Max Weber who wrote during the scientific management era but whose discovery for the development of management thought came much later. We will conclude Part II by examining the critics of Taylorism and by presenting a conceptual viewpoint of the economic, social, and political conditions which comprised the cultural environment of scientific management.

6

The Advent of Scientific Management

The last decades of the nineteenth century resulted in unprecedented accumulations of resources in American industry. Electrical power for the factory came into vogue, heavy capital equipment became widespread, mechanization was being substituted for hand labor leading to higher potential productivity, and mass production techniques were emerging to reshape man's concept of technology and production. With resources accumulated and technology developed, the major impediment to added industrial productivity was in the crude forms of developing, organizing, controlling, and administering this mass of resource efforts. At no place in the firm was this more crucial than in the production shop itself. Labor was highly specialized, standardized methods and procedures were in short supply, and there was little emphasis on coordinating, integrating, and systematizing work.[1] It is no coincidence that engineers became the source of early efforts to systematize management. Engineers designed the equipment, supervised its installation, advised on its utilization, and provided

[1] Two excellent analyses of these industrial problems preceding Taylorism may be found in Joseph A. Litterer, "Systematic Management: The Search for Order and Integration," *Business History Review*, Vol. 35 (Winter, 1961), pp. 461–476; and Joseph A. Litterer, "Systematic Management: Design for Organizational Recoupling in American Manufacturing Firms," *Business History Review*, Vol. 37, (Winter, 1963), pp. 369–391.

111

the major source of assistance in solving management problems.[2] Accordingly, the first management writers emphasized techniques and methods of shop efficiency, for these appeared at the time to be the major industrial problems. One engineer stands out during this era of a need for systematic management and, although he had a strong supporting cast, he emerges as the "Father of Scientific Management."

FREDERICK WINSLOW TAYLOR: THE EARLY YEARS

Frederick Winslow Taylor (1856–1915) was born in Germantown, Pennsylvania as the son of a fairly prosperous lawyer who was of Quaker stock and a mother who traced her Puritan ancestry to a Plymouth, Massachusetts, ancestor who arrived in 1629.[3] This Quaker-Puritan stock and training gave Taylor an unusual preparation for his life's work: an intense spirit of inquiry for the truth, an urge to observe and verify facts, and a Puritan zeal to eradicate the evils of waste and slothfulness. Taylor's early education was liberally sprinkled with the classics, with the study of French and German, and with occasional trips to Europe. As a young man, he was "enamored of scientific investigation, research, and experiment . . . [with] a passion for improving and reforming things on the basis of fact, and early was filled with a divine discontent with anything short of the *one best way*."[4] He put to careful study and analysis the game of croquet, the best method with the least fatigue of taking a cross-country walk, and devised other ingenious devices which were early evidence of the intensely meticulous nature which became his hallmark in later work.

His parents intended that he follow his father's profession of law and duly enrolled him at Phillips Exeter to prepare for Harvard. The competition was stiff and Taylor's zeal and restless energy led to late nights and long hours, eventually impairing his eyesight.

---

[2] The role of industrial engineers and the early "works management" movement is very capably discussed in Leland H. Jenks, "Early Phases of the Management Movement," *Administrative Science Quarterly*, Vol. 5 (December, 1960) pp. 421–477.

[3] The life of Taylor is presented in complete detail in Frank Barkley Copley, *Frederick W. Taylor: Father of Scientific Management*, (2 Volumes) New York: Harper and Row, 1923. A more recent work on Taylor uses a "psycho-historical" approach to examine his life and conflicts: see Sudhir Kakar, *Frederick Taylor: A Study in Personality and Innovation*, Cambridge, Mass.: M.I.T. Press, 1970.

[4] Copley, Volume I, pp. 55–56.

Though he passed the Harvard exams with honors, his poor health and eyesight forced him to turn away from law school and into an apprenticeship as a pattern-maker and machinist with the Enterprise Hydraulic Works of Philadelphia.[5] He started his four year apprenticeship at no wage (since his father was a "man of means") and was making the grand sum of $3 a week when he finished his apparenticeship in 1878. Living an ascetic life which would have pleased Ben Franklin (for he neither smoked nor drank stimulants such as alcohol, coffee or tea), his apprentice years were grueling; he attributed his success to "character," which to Taylor was "the ability to control yourself, body and mind. . . . the ability above all to do things which are disagreeable."[6] His early concern with self-control, with character, and with doing even the tiresome and dull things because they developed a person, were manifestations of a later concern for discipline and adherence to the "one best way."

At Enterprise, Taylor developed an empathy for the worker's point of view; he could swear with the best of them and admired their sense of pride in workmanship.[7] However, he saw about him what he called the "bad industrial conditions," which consisted of worker soldiering on the job, the poor quality of management, and the lack of harmony between workers and managers.

Taylor at Midvale

Taylor moved to Midvale Steel (Philadelphia) in 1878 as common laborer. The economic consequence of the financial panic of 1873 still lingered and jobs were scarce. The steel industry had developed slowly and was reaching its apex in the 1880's with the introduction of better machine tools and power. Midvale, under the presidency of William Sellers, was one of the leading steel firms of the era. At Midvale, Taylor would rise from common laborer to clerk, to machinist, to gang boss of the machinists, to

[5] *Ibid.*, pp. 77–79. Professor Kakar suggests that Taylor's change of plans was not due to failing eyesight but due to his rejection of his father's choosing his profession for him. Thus Taylor was passing through an adolescent "identity crisis" and in this manner sought to establish his own independence and personality. Kakar, pp. 26–27.

[6] Copley, p. 84.

[7] Copley, pp. 88–93 and p. 4. Kakar's analysis holds that Taylor's swearing and identification with the workers served as an outlet for his "aggressive impulses" against his family whose life style he was repudiating. Kakar, pp. 36–37.

foreman of the machine shop, to master mechanic in charge of repairs and maintenance throughout the plant, and to chief engineer —all in six years; a meteoric rise for this intense young man. The twelve years at Midvale (1878–1890) were years of experimentation which provided the basis for his system of shop management and for his experiments with metals. Realizing his lack of scientific education, he enrolled in a home study course from Stevens Institute of Technology of Hoboken, New Jersey. He never attended classes except to take examinations and graduated with a degree in mechanical engineering in 1883. In total, it was two and a half years of study, all while pursuing his full-time duties at Midvale.

Taylor had no training in management and relied solely upon his own investigations as to what should be done. His frontal attack on shop problems led to an early confrontation with the workers. When Taylor became gang boss, the company had established a piecework incentive system which Taylor knew to be ineffective from his own working days. Midvale management felt that the workers would control their own behavior and would be properly motivated once given the piece-rate incentive. Taylor knew otherwise; he knew their output was only a third of what was possible and he set about to correct the situation as soon as he received the authority. To see a worker operating at less than what he could do was morally shocking to the Quaker-Puritan Taylor. To do less than your best was bad for the character and probably this was a greater sin to Taylor than any mere unused capacity of machines or men.

The restriction of output at Midvale was classified by Taylor in "natural soldiering" and "systematic soldiering." Natural soldiering proceeded from "the natural instinct and tendency of men to take it easy"; while the systematic form came from the worker's "more intricate second thought and reasoning caused by their relations with other men."[8] Natural soldiering could be overcome by a manager able to inspire or force men to come up to the mark. Systematic soldiering posed a different problem and managers for years had been attempting to cope with the tendency to conform to group output standards. Why do men soldier? Taylor answered as follows: first, they believed that to work faster would throw

---

[8] Frederick W. Taylor, *Shop Management,* New York: Harper and Row, 1903, p. 30. Reissued as part of Frederick Winslow Taylor, *Scientific Management,* New York: Harper and Row, 1947. Pagination is the same in both editions.

large numbers of men out of work; second, the defective management systems then in use forced the worker to work slowly to
protect his own interests; and third, because of the adherence to
rule-of-thumb work methods handed down from generation to
generation.[9] Taylor placed the blame on management, not on the
workers, for he thought that it was management's job to design
the jobs properly and to offer the proper incentives to overcome
their soldiering.

In no small part, systematic soldiering arose out of a "lump of
labor" theory that postulated a limited amount of work in the
world and that to do more today left less to be done tomorrow;
i.e., you could work yourself or your fellow man out of a job if
you worked too fast. A daily or hourly wage system encouraged
soldiering because pay was based on attendance and position, not
effort. To work harder brought no reward and actually encouraged
the lazy man. Piece-rate systems, old long before Taylor, sought to
encourage individual incentive and initiative by paying each on
the basis of his output. Such systems had been generally failures
before Taylor; standards were often poorly set, employers cut the
rates when workers earned too much, and workers hid their short-
cut methods and improvements from management to protect
themselves. With ample experience of cuts when they exceeded a
certain amount of income, workers developed a consensus about
how much each should produce and earn, not only to protect themselves but undoubtedly also to avoid the ridicule of the less capable.
The workers perceived that management envisioned some maximum sum of pay and any earnings beyond that would lead to rate
cuts. Taylor did not blame the men; in fact he sympathized with
them, because he felt that it was the wage *system*, not the men,
that was at fault.

Taylor's initial experiences as a machine shop foreman resulted
in a bitter encounter with the workers. He told the men that he
knew they could do more and that he was going to see that they
did. Taylor started by showing them how to use the lathes to get
more output with very little more effort by using his methods. He
failed in retraining those machinists because they refused to follow

[9] Frederick W. Taylor, *The Principles of Scientific Management*, New York:
Harper and Row, 1911, pp. 15–16. Reissued as part of Frederick Winslow Taylor,
Scientific Management, New York: Harper and Row, 1947. Pagination is the same in
both editions.

his instructions; he then turned to training common laborers who, after learning the method, joined the group and resisted increased production. Taylor admitted "I was up against a stone wall. I did not blame these laborers in my heart; my sympathy was with them all the time . . . ;"[10] but he had a job to do and the obstreperous workers only challenged the young Taylor. He turned to more drastic means by cutting the rate to make the men work harder to earn the same pay. The men retaliated by breaking and jamming the machines; Taylor countered by a system of fines (the proceeds going to a worker benefit fund) for equipment damage. Eventually Taylor not only won the battle with the machinists but learned a valuable lesson as well. Never again would he use the system of fines, and he later established strict rules against rate cutting. More importantly, the young Taylor realized that a new industrial scheme was essential to prevent such bitter labor-management encounters. It was at this time that Taylor began his search for a science of work.

The Search for Science in Management

Though sympathetic with efforts to soldier, Taylor thought that he could overcome it by a careful investigation of work which would then be used in setting rates. Once the workers saw that the rate was properly set, they would know that it was based on facts and not whims and that this would reduce their motivation to soldier. The problem was in defining a full and fair day's standard for each task. Taylor set out to determine scientifically what the men *ought* to be able to do with their equipment and materials, and this became the true beginning of scientific management, *i.e.*, the use of a scientific fact-finding method to determine empirically instead of traditionally the right ways to perform tasks. Initially, Taylor probably never envisioned that any theory would ensue nor that this step was the beginning of further applications to many jobs and industries. He did it because he felt that this would be a way to overcome the worker antagonism and resistance he encountered earlier. He had the worker's interests in mind when he thought that management should have the responsibility

[10] Copley (I), p. 162. Kakar notes that this battle with the machinists reflected his own internal conflicts and anxieties, that is, a struggle to control them while trying to control his own rebellious strivings. Kakar, pp. 61–62.

for determining standards, planning work, and devising incentive schemes; he abhorred the previous methods of setting a rate based on past performance, leaving it up to the worker to motivate himself to meet that rate, and cutting the rate if the worker earned too much.

Time study became the foundation of the Taylor system and some have questioned Taylor's claim to originality. Charles Babbage had demonstrated the use of a watch in recording the labor operations and times necessary in the manufacture of pins. Copley said that Taylor probably had never heard of Babbage when Taylor began his time studies in the early 1880's.[11] In 1912, a subcommittee of the American Society of Mechanical Engineers issued a report on time study which made no mention of Taylor's work but referenced Adam Smith and Charles Babbage. Taylor contributed to a discussion of this report in an effort to clarify his concept of time study and to answer the doubters of his originality.

Time study was begun in the machine shop of the Midvale Steel Company in 1881. . . . It is true that the form of Tables 1 and 2 [the Babbage contribution to the A.S.M.E. report] is similar to that of the blanks recording time study, but here the resemblance ceases. Each line in Table 2, for instance, gives statistics regarding the average of the entire work of an operative who works day in and day out, in running a machine engaged in the manufacture of pins. This table involves no study whatever of the movements of the man, nor of the time in which the movements *should* have been made. Mere Statistics as to the time which a man takes to do a given piece of work do not constitute "time study": "time study," as its name implies, involves a careful study of the time in which work *ought* to be done . . . [rather than] the time in which the work actually was done.[12]

Taylor's distinction supported his claim to originality since he was using time study for analytical rather than descriptive purposes; that is, future versus past uses of data. Taylor's time study formed the basis for his scientific approach to the job and had two phases: "analytical" and "constructive." In analysis, each job was broken into as many simple elementary movements as possible, useless movements were discarded, the quickest and best methods for each elementary movement was selected by observing the most skilled workman at each, and the movement was timed and recorded.

[11] Copley, p. 221. For support of Copley, see Lyndall Urwick and E.F.L. Brech, *The Making of Scientific Management*, Vol. I, London: Management Publications Trust, 1943, p. 37; for the opposite view, *i.e.*, that Taylor must have known of Babbage, see John Hoaglund, "Management Before Frederick Taylor," pp. 23–25.

[12] Copley, pp. 225–226.

To the recorded time, a percentage was added to cover unavoidable delays and interruptions, another percentage to cover "the newness" of workmen to a job, and yet another percentage for rest periods. It was in the determination and addition of these percentages that most critics said Taylor's method was not "scientific" since these were based on the experience and intuition of the time study observer. The constructive phase involved building a file of elementary movements and times to be used wherever possible on other jobs or classes of work; further, this phase led to consideration of improvements in tools, machines, materials, methods, and the ultimate standardization of all elements surrounding and accompanying the job.[13]

Whereas Babbage was content with gross times of actual performance, Taylor's method broke the job into component parts, tested them, and reconstructed the job as it *should* be done. Taylor thought that such scientific study of the job would form a "proof" to the worker to overcome resistance. In a later defense before his critics, Taylor denied that he sought exactness: "All we hope to do through time study is to get a vastly closer approximation as to time than we ever had before."[14]

The Quest for New Incentives

Since management relied heavily on engineers for advice in the factory, it is not coincidental that associations of engineers were the first to examine and write about managerial problems. The American Society of Mechanical Engineers was founded in 1880 and became the first proponents of the search for systematic, scientific management. An important point for the group came in 1886 with a paper by Henry R. Towne, President of the Yale and Towne Manufacturing Company, on "The Engineer as Economist."[15] Towne stressed that the engineer must look beyond the mere *mechanical* efficiency criteria of an economic (*i.e.*, costs and revenues) nature. Engineers employed by industry must broaden their intellectual interests to learn to think and act as economists who were concerned with broader questions of total resource utilization. Since there were no management schools nor management associations, Towne suggested that the A.S.M.E. become a clear-

---

[13] Taylor, *Shop Management*, pp. 149–176.
[14] Copley (I), pp. 234–235.
[15] *Transactions*, A.S.M.E., Vol. 7 (1886), pp. 428–432.

ing house for information on managerial practices. Towne's ideas affected the thinking and life of Taylor, who had joined the A.S.M.E. in 1886. It had less impact on future papers for the A.S.M.E. as only four other papers were presented on management up to 1895. One was another Towne paper on "gain sharing" in which he contended that profit sharing was not an appropriate solution to the problem of greater worker productivity. In profit sharing, savings from worker efforts in one department could be offset by a lack of diligence in others. Instead, Towne proposed to determine costs and productivity for each work unit or department and to return to them the "gains" according to their own performance. Towne's plan guaranteed a wage rate to each employee, plus a 50-50 split of the "gain" in the worker's department.[16] Another significant paper was Frederick A. Halsey's "The Premium Plan of Paying for Labor," in which he attacked the evils of both profitsharing and individual piece-work systems.[17] He saw a lack of motivation in profitsharing and abuses in the piece-rate system. Halsey proposed that incentives be based on past production records, plus a guaranteed minimum wage, plus a premium for doing more work. The premium would amount to about one-third more than the daily or hourly rate and leave two-thirds of the added value to accrue to the employer, who would be therefore less inclined to cut the rate.

Enter Frederick Taylor at this point. Taylor's first formal statement of his new system was "A Piece-Rate System" in which he attacked both the Towne and the Halsey plans.[18] The weakness in both, in Taylor's view, was that they sought to induce the worker to produce more by sharing the gain from their extra efforts with management. Taylor proposed a new system consisting of three parts: one, observation and analysis through time study to set the "rate" or standard; two, a "differential rate" system of piece-work; and three, "paying men and not positions." In Taylor's opinion, profit sharing failed because: (1) it discouraged personal ambition because all shared in profits regardless of their contribution; and (2) the "remoteness of the reward." Taylor's second criticism of profit sharing was an early insight into the psychological principle of temporal contiguity, i.e., the timing of the reinforcement with regard to the behavior, and reflected Taylor's view that a share

16 Henry R. Towne, "Gain Sharing," Transactions, A.S.M.E., Vol. 10, (1889).
17 Transactions, A.S.M.E., Vol. 12 (1891), pp. 755–764.
18 Transactions, A.S.M.E., Vol. 16 (1895), pp. 856–883.

of the profits at the end of the year gave no incentive for maximum daily performance.

In this paper, Taylor had clearly put the onus on management to take charge, to accept its responsibilities, and to move away from the old system of leaving the work up to the worker. A rate setting department planned the work and divided it into its various elements and set a rate or standard for each element. Based on thorough study, this rate moved job performance from guesswork and tradition to a more rational basis. The principle of the differential rate worked two ways: it forced those who did not meet the standard to receive a very low rate of pay, and greatly rewarded those who did attain the standard.[19] The incentive became that of following the proper methods and making the standard in order to be rewarded. The notion of paying men and not positions was designed partially to overcome soldiering but mainly to individualize the worker by paying for his efforts and not for his class of work. Taylor's paper of 1895 on the piece-rate system outlined his view on unions, an opinion he never changed, and one which would bring him a barrage of criticism:

> The writer is far from taking the view held by many manufacturers that labor unions are an almost unmitigated detriment to those who join them, as well as to employers and the general public. The labor unions . . . have rendered a great service not only to their members, but to the world, in shortening the hours of labor and in modifying the hardships and improving the conditions of wage workers. . . . When employers herd their men together in classes, pay all of each class the same wages . . . the only remedy for the men lies in combination; and frequently the only possible answer to encroachment on the part of their employers is a strike. . . .
>
> This state of affairs is far from satisfactory and the writer believes the system of regulating wages and conditions of employment of whole classes of men by conference and agreement between the leaders, unions and manufacturers to be vastly inferior . . . to the plan of stimulating each workman's ambition by paying him according to his individual worth, and without limiting him to the rate of work or pay of the average of his class.[20]

Taylor had no personal vendetta against unions *per se* (a view often misconstrued), but saw no necessity for them under his system of incentive management. Unions, to maintain their group soli-

[19] The "high" rate was set such that the average employee who met the standard earned 125 per cent of the base standard pay: the "low" rate, for those who failed to meet the standard, was set at 80 per cent. C. W. Lytle, *Wage Incentive Methods,* New York: Ronald Press Co., 1942, pp. 179–180.

[20] Taylor, "A Piece-Rate System," pp. 859–860; also in *Shop Management,* pp. 185–186.

darity, must insist on a "common rule" and a standardization of wages and conditions for all. Individualized treatment is a threat to the group. For Taylor, this view prevented each man from fulfilling his personal desires because he was to be treated as one of the masses. Men should be inspired to better themselves à la the Protestant ethic, not lumped into one class and treated like everyone else.

This early paper on incentives and the proper relation between worker and manager anticipated his philosophy of mutual interest between those parties. Countering a "more-less" assumption that if the workers got more, the employer naturally got less, Taylor saw a mutuality of interests rather than natural conflict between labor and management. This was his statement of the "paradox of high wages and low costs" which, on the surface, appear to be diametrically opposed concepts. Instead of the employers' practice of buying the cheapest labor and paying the lowest wages possible and the worker's desire to gain all he could get for the least he could give, Taylor advocated paying the first-class man a high wage, thereby inducing him to produce more under standard, efficient conditions with no greater expenditure of effort than formerly. The result was more productivity, hence lower per unit labor costs to the employer and higher wages to the worker, thus satisfying both parties to the transaction. To summarize his system of payments, Taylor said the aim of each establishment should be:

(a) That each workman should be given as far as possible the highest grade of work for which his ability and physique fit him.
(b) That each workman should be called upon to turn out the maximum amount of work which a first-rate man of his class can do and thrive.
(c) That each workman, when he works at the best pace of a first class man, should be paid from 30 per cent to 100 per cent according to the nature of the work which he does, beyond the average of his class.[21]

The First Class Man

This new notion of a "first class man" formed a basis for the scientific selection of workmen and caused Taylor much grief in trying to explain it to others. In testimony before a special Congressional committee, Taylor defined his first-class man:

I believe the only man who does not come under "first-class" as I have defined it, is the man who can work and will not work. I have tried to make it clear

21 *Shop Management*, pp. 28–29.

that for each type of workman some job can be found at which he is first class, with the exception of those men who are perfectly well able to do the job but won't do it.[22]

Under these terms, a "non-first class" worker would be either one who was physically and/or mentally unsuited for the work assigned, (in which case he should be retrained or transferred to another job for which he was suited), or any worker who was unwilling to give his best. In setting rates for each job, Taylor set the standard at the pace a first-class man "can keep up for a long term of years without injury to his health. It is a pace under which men become happier and thrive."[23] The first-class pace was not based on spurts of activity nor on strain but on the normal pace that a worker could sustain. Basically, Taylor was laying the foundations for sound personnel management, *i.e.*, the match of men's abilities to the job.

It was management's task to find the work for which the employee was best suited, to assist him in becoming a first-class worker, and to provide him with an incentive to give his best. Taylor's views on the first-class man were closely intertwined with his personal philosophy of "the will to get there" or that success drive which was the basis of his own life. It was his observation that the major difference between individuals was not in brains, but in *will*, the drive to achieve.[24] The first class man was a man with ambition who was suited to his work, not some "superhuman," as the term came to connote to many people.

The Task Management System

At Midvale Taylor was laying the foundations of what he preferred to call task management. An essential ingredient was time study and the development of a science of work; a second ingredient was the selection of men who could meet those standards when motivated by the differential piece rate. But the system was yet incomplete and Taylor began to build further. Taylor defined management as "knowing exactly what you want men to do, and

---

[22] *Hearings before Special Committee of the House of Representatives to Investigate The Taylor and other Systems of Shop Management under Authority of House Resolution 90,* Washington, D.C.: U.S. Government Printing Office, 1912, p. 1451.

[23] *Shop Management,* p. 25.

[24] Copley (I), p. 183.

then seeing that they do it in the best and cheapest way." Taylor added that no concise definition could fully describe the art of management but that "the relations between employers and men form without question the most important part of this art."[25] He saw unevenness in the quality of management in the shop and challenged the assumption that if you hired the right man the methods would take care of themselves. Management had the explicit responsibility to design the work system so that the greatest productivity was possible rather than relying upon the offering of incentives to induce people to produce more.

Recognizing that his work system depended upon careful advance planning, he developed the concept of "task management," a term he preferred over its later designation as "scientific management." Task management consisted of two parts: (1) each workman each day was given a definite task with detailed written instructions and an exact time allowance for each element of the work; and (2) the worker who performed the task in the time allotted would receive extraordinarily high wages while ordinary wages would go to those who took more time than allotted. The task was based upon detailed time study, and methods, tools, and materials were standardized. Once the tasks were defined and assigned to first-class individuals, the total work system had to be organized. An immediate problem of organization was the pressure that task management placed on the manager to minutely plan the work and guide it toward completion. To cope with this increasing complexity in managing, Taylor developed a unique form of supervision called "functional foremen." Taylor specified nine qualities that made up a "well-rounded" foreman:

> Brains;
> Education;
> Special or technical knowledge; manual dexterity or strength;
> Tact;
> Energy;
> Grit;
> Honesty;
> Judgment or common sense; and
> Good health.[26]

Taylor thought that to find a man with three of these traits was not too difficult; with five or six, more difficult, but with seven

[25] *Shop Management,* p. 21.
[26] *Ibid.,* p. 96.

or eight almost impossible. This led him to abandon the military type of line organization of a single boss and to develop his functional foreman concept, for he hypothesized that not all foremen's duties required all these traits.[27] By specializing the foreman's job, physical and mental demands on the incumbent would be accordingly reduced. Initially, Taylor employed assistants to prepare instruction cards and perform other detailed tasks for Taylor as foreman. As his system evolved, he gave more and more responsibility to these men by further segregating the functions and delegating them. The result was a new organizational technique of functionalism rather than the previously typical hierarchical "military" arrangement. The typical manager of that day was not much of a planner; layout largely dictated planning; no one had developed task planning to the degree that Taylor had. Taylor's new style began with a distinction between the planning of work and its performance, a notable advance for the times. The "foremen," a rather misleading term because each was little more than a specialized clerk, were given final responsibility over some aspect of the work, thus negating the military hierarchy of one boss for the workers.

Taylor divided the responsibility into two major areas, performance duties and planning duties. In the performance segment of supervisory responsibilities, the "gang boss" had charge of all work up to the time that the piece was placed in the machine; the "speed boss" began his work when the material was in the machine and he determined the tools, the cut, and machine speed; the "inspector" was responsible for quality of work; and the "repair boss" was in charge of care and maintenance of the machinery. In the planning department, the "order of work route clerk" determined the flow of the work and the exact order of work by each class of men and machines; the "instruction card clerk" furnished written information on tools, materials, the piece rate and premium, and other operating instructions; the "time and cost clerk" sent the time ticket for recording times taken and costs incurred and insured the return of this data; the "shop disciplinarian" kept a record of each man's "virtues and defects," served as a "peace-

[27] Whiting has found that Taylor's concept of the functional foremen was also used as early as 1884 by John Richards, owner and manager of the San Francisco Tool Company. Richards, apparently also having difficulty in finding well-rounded foremen, created five separate functional areas in the shop with one man in charge of each. Richard J. Whiting, "John Richards—California Pioneer of Management Thought," *California Management Review*, Vol. 6, No. 2 (Winter, 1963), p. 37.

maker," and performed the employment function of selecting and discharging employees.

The functional foreman concept (Figure 6-1) was an expediency; it provided a shop with supervision in a relatively short time versus the long-range search for and development of well-rounded

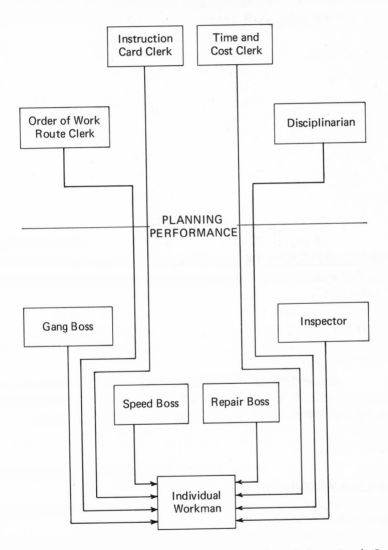

Fig. 6–1. Taylor's functional foremen. (Adapted from Frank B. and Lillian M. Gilbreth, *Applied Motion Study*, New York: Sturgis and Walton Co., 1917.)

managers. Taylor saw no conflict in his system with the unity-of-command idea of the military. To him, *knowledge* must prevail; orders were given to workers on the basis of the specialized knowledge of the clerk or boss and not on the basis of the authority inherent in the position. Hence there was no conflict since each man had only one boss on any one particular aspect of his job, such as speed of machine, repairs, etc. With his general objectives of harmony and mutuality of interests between workers and management, Taylor foresaw that the spirit of cooperation would obviate any inherent conflicts under the functional arrangement. Training of bosses would be easier since each had to learn only limited duties. Evidently Taylor was encountering a problem seen frequently in the earlier factories, the shortage of management talent.

Taylor had little difficulty in selling his functional principle to the workers; the bosses, however, resisted the system because it contracted their authority and range of activities.[28] Taylor did not specify that *one man* had to be in charge of each function; in smaller units, one man might perform all of the planning tasks or some other grouping of duties. Taylor's purpose was to focus specialized management knowledge on the work. As his concept has evolved to the present, this is now done by *functional authority* over a task, not over the man, and without circumventing the supervisor. Taylor's functional foreman concept never became widespread in practice and its failures did not arise from confusion of workers or a violation of unity of command but from the recognition that it failed to develop well-rounded managers who could cope with a variety of shop problems through the use of staff assistants. In essence, functionalization was an attempt at decentralization, intending to strip authority from the general manager to place it in the hands of specialized lower level managers.

This early attempt at decentralization of authority was designed to bring about a shift in the duties of the general manager. As a corollary to this re-definition, Taylor developed a special role for the general works manager. He was to avoid the minutiae of shop management, leaving that to his specialists, and concern himself only with "exceptions." The "exception principle" was one of Taylor's more important contributions:

Under it the manager should receive only condensed, summarized, and

[28] Copley (I), p. 292.

invariably comparative reports, covering . . . all of the exceptions to past averages or to the standards . . . both the especially good and especially bad exceptions . . . leaving him free to consider broader lines of policy and to study the character and fitness of the important men under him.[29]

For Taylor all authority was based on knowledge, not position, and the exception principle enabled a check on who was and who was not meeting his delegated responsibility.

Onward and Upward

The years at Midvale had been full ones; his fulltime duties and meteoric rise on his job, teaming up with Clark to win the U.S. Amateur doubles tennis championship in 1881, the M.E. degree from Stevens Institute in 1883, marriage in 1884, scientific studies of the art of cutting metals and machine belting, and the essentials of task management all yielded a busy twelve years for Taylor. In 1890 he left Midvale to become General Manager of the Manufacturing Investment Company, a converter of wood products into paper fiber. Perceiving a need for a new profession of a consulting engineer for management, he left his job at Manufacturing Investment Company and set up his own practice which lasted from 1893 to 1901. During his consulting period he built a wealth and variety of experience in various industries which facilitated the refinement of his emerging system and eventually his philosophy of management.

One of Taylor's clients was the Simond's Rolling Machine Company, where he conducted his experiments in the manufacture of bicycle ball bearings. In the finishing room, 120 girls inspected the final product for flaws; a most tedious job for 10½ hours per day. Over a period of time, Taylor began to improve the selection of the girls, shortened the work day gradually to 8½ hours, introduced morning and afternoon rest periods, and put them on piece work. The interaction of the variables in the situation were complex and it would be impossible to fix causes and results. However, the outcome was that thirty-five girls did the work of 120, accuracy improved by two-thirds, productivity increased from 5 million to 17 million bearings per month, wages were averaging 80 to 100 per cent more than formerly, and "each girl was made to feel that she was the object of especial care and interest on the part of man-

29 *Shop Management*, p. 126. Copyright 1947, Harper and Row; by permission.

agement."[30]   Taylor's efficiency methods were working.   They were working so well, in fact, that Taylor soon had to learn to cope with the problems of displaced labor which his methods were bringing about.

Taylor at Bethlehem

The Bethlehem Steel Company maintained its main plant in Lehigh, Pennsylvania, a community largely composed of Pennsylvania Dutch.   It was to this environment that Taylor as a consultant brought his methods in 1898, developed with Maunsel White a self-hardening steel for machine tools, and continued to build his philosophy of task management.   Taylor came to Bethlehem largely at the instigation of the entrepreneur Joseph Wharton, founder of the first school of business, who owned one quarter of Bethlehem's stock.   Bethlehem's management was in poor shape, since promotions were made and positions held because of influence rather than ability.   Taylor's early attempts to install his methods met immediate resistance from management, although he early earned the nickname of "Speedy" Taylor from the workers.   For assistance, Taylor called in loyal lieutenants such as Dwight V. Merrick, who became in later years a leading authority on time study, and Henry L. Gantt, who had worked with him at Midvale. Taylor never felt that Gantt fully grasped the underlying philosophy of his system; however, he respected Gantt's abilities and knew that he at least understood how to implement Taylor's methods.   Pursuing his metal cutting experiments jointly with installing his management system at Bethlehem, Taylor also called in Carl Barth, a mathematical genius, to help him with his research.   Taylor's relations with Barth, as with Gantt, were often less than genial.   Taylor hired Gantt and Barth not because of compatibility, but because they had the skills he needed.   The outcome was mutual respect but not always mutual agreement.   While Barth was developing a slide rule to solve the complex equations involved in handling the multitude of variables in cutting metals, Taylor was proceeding to systematize the utilization of yard labor at the mill.

[30] Taylor, *Principles*, pp. 95–96. This comment leads to the possible conclusion that Taylor, not Mayo, discovered what came to be known as the "Hawthorne effect," *i.e.*, that concern for and attention to the worker by the experimenter led to a substantial increase in productivity.

The yard gang, consisting of four to six hundred men, depending upon the season, was engaged in unloading raw materials of ore, limestone, sand, etc. from incoming rail cars as well as loading finished products on rail cars for shipment. The workers were all paid basically the same wage of $1.15 per day and the foremen were workers promoted from the ranks. Taylor was challenged when informed that these men were "slow and phlegmatic, and that nothing would induce them to work fast."[31] Taylor attacked the pig iron handling by a gang of 75 men first. It was a simple job in which the worker picked up a "pig" of iron weighing 92 pounds, walked up an inclined plank, and placed the pig in the car for shipment. Taylor felt that here was a good chance to show that his methods could be applied to even the simplest task. At Midvale, he had set out to discover some "law of fatigue" which would determine how much rest a worker needed when performing arduous manual tasks; he failed at Midvale, but tried with the help of Barth to find the law at Bethlehem. Barth was doubtful and amused at Taylor's ideas, but he went along, perhaps to escape the intense wrath of Taylor. Using his slide rule, Barth found that the pig iron handler could work under a heavy load only 42% of the day and that 58% of the day must be spent "free of load" or not actually toting pigs. Before Taylor undertook to apply his system, the handlers were loading on the cars an average of twelve and a half long tons of pig iron per man per day. After analyzing his data, Taylor concluded that a man *should* be able to load 47 to 48 long tons per day with no greater fatigue due to the rest pauses.[32] He contrived an incentive piece rate which would enable the worker to earn about 60 per cent more, or $1.85 per day, if he met the standard of 47½ tons per day.

To institute his new method, Taylor had to select his first class man. He chose a physically fit Dutchman who placed a high value on a dollar. "A penny looks about the size of a cart-wheel to him," was the comment of one worker. Taylor chose to call the man

[31] *Shop Management*, p. 47.

[32] *Principles*, pp. 60–61. Taylor furnished proof for the mathematically skeptical. Forty-seven and one half long tons (one long ton = 2,240 pounds) at 92 pounds per pig = 1156 pigs per day. Forty two per cent of the day "under load" = 252 working minutes ÷ 1156 pigs = 0.22 minutes per pig. The pigs were moved an average distance of 36 feet. Therefore, 36 feet in 0.22 minutes (13.2 seconds) means that while *under load* the worker was traveling at a rate of 1.84 m.p.h. (normal walking pace is about 4 m.p.h.).

"Schmidt" and the following passage depicts Taylor *vis-à-vis* the worker:

"Schmidt, are you a high-priced man?"

"Vell, I don't know vat you mean."

"Oh yes, you do. What I want to know is whether you are a high-priced man or not."

"Vell, I don't know vat you mean."

"Oh, come now, you answer my questions. What I want to find out is whether you are a high-priced man or one of these cheap fellows here. What I want to find out is whether you want to earn $1.85 a day or whether you are satisfied with $1.15, just the same as all those cheap fellows are getting."

"Did I vant $1.85 a day? Vas dot a high-priced man? Vel, yes, I vas a high-priced man."

"Oh, you're aggravating me. Of course you want $1.85 a day—every one wants it! You know perfectly well that that has very little to do with your being a high-priced man. For goodness sake answer my questions, and don't waste any more of my time. Now come over here. You see that pile of pig iron?"

"Yes."

"You see that car?"

"Yes."

"Well, if you are a high-priced man, you will load that pig iron on that car tomorrow for $1.85. Now do wake up and answer my question. Tell me whether you are a high-priced man or not."

"Vell—did I got $1.85 for loading dot pig iron on dot car tomorrow?"

"Yes, of course you do, and you get $1.85 for loading a pile like that every day right through the year. That is what a high-priced man does, and you know it just as well as I do."

"Vell, dot's all right. I could load dot pig iron on the car tomorrow for $1.85, and I get it every day, don't I?"

"Certainly you do—certainly you do."

"Vell, den, I vas a high-priced man."

"Now, hold on, hold on. You know just as well as I do that a high-priced man has to do exactly as he's told from morning till night. You have seen this man here before, haven't you?"

"No, I never saw him."

"Well, if you are a high-priced man, you will do exactly as this man tells you tomorrow, from morning till night. When he tells you to pick up a pig and walk, you pick it up and you walk, and when he tells you to sit down and rest, you sit down. You do that right straight through the day. And what's more, no back talk. Now a high-priced man does just what he's told to do, and no back talk. Do you understand that? When this man tells you to walk, you walk; when he tells you to sit down, you sit down, and you don't talk back at him. Now you come on to work here tomorrow morning and I'll know before night whether you are really a high-priced man or not."[33]

The other pig iron handlers were not quite as eager as Schmidt even though he succeeded at his task. Taylor's opposition came,

[33] *Ibid.*, pp. 44–47. Copyright 1947, Harper and Row; by permission.

strangely enough, not only from the workers but from management and from the citizens of the city of Bethlehem. The owners saw that the work force could be cut to about one fourth its previous level if Taylor had his way. As Taylor told it:

> "They [the owners] did not wish me, as they said, to depopulate South Bethlehem. They owned all the houses in South Bethlehem and the company stores, and when they saw we were cutting the labor force down to about one fourth, they did not want it . . . I said: You are going to have it . . . You employed me with the distinct understanding that is what I was going to do . . . [they responded] Well, we did not think you could do it."[34]

Taylor continued to clash with Bethlehem management and it was only the strong influence of Joseph Wharton that kept him in his position as long as he stayed. As Schmidt continued to earn his high pay, the resistance of the other workers began to fade like the tan from a winter vacation. They gradually came around to Taylor asking to be shown the new method to earn the $1.85 per day. Only about one man in four proved to be a first-class man and Taylor pruned the yard gang accordingly; to those who protested the displacement of the remainder, Taylor indicated they were shifted to other company jobs for which they were better suited and then went on to earn higher wages.

Taylor had his critics for his handling of Schmidt. A young Socialist named Upton Sinclair wrote the editor of *The American Magazine* to protest "that he [Taylor] gave about a 61% increase in wages, and got a 362% increase in work."[35] Sinclair protested that this was exploitation and that the solution was for the workers to "take possession of the instrument and means of production" in order to get full value for their effort. In his response to Sinclair, Taylor put forth his philosophy of scientific management, saying that Sinclair's sympathies were inappropriately focused and that he overlooked the larger benefits of the system. Schmidt earned more with no greater effort because he had been taught *how*. The *method* enabled greater productivity and it was not exploitation or speeding up the worker but improvement in the *method* which freed the worker from wasteful efforts. Hence Schmidt's added earnings were for working no harder. Taylor's defense was a larger societal view that *all* benefitted, the worker by receiving higher wages with no greater expenditure of effort, management by hav-

---

[34] Copley (II), p. 46.
[35] February 24, 1911, cited by Copley (II), pp. 50–51.

ing greater profits, and the consumer by paying lower prices for products. The worker earned more because someone else taught him how and established the proper procedures. The primary concern for Taylor was the total benefits derived for all people, worker, employer, and consumer.[36] Taylor did not feel that he had done Schmidt an injustice, and the eagerness of other workers to become "high priced men" seemed to bear this out.[37]

Another part of Taylor's work at Bethlehem earned him the further animosity of management. Taylor introduced a cost accounting system and referred to it as "in general the modern railroad system of accounting adapted and modified to suit the manufacturing business."[38] Taylor did not claim originality for his accounting system, borrowing from McCallum, Fink, and especially from Captain Henry Metcalf. At the Frankford Arsenal (near Philadelphia), Metcalf had developed an extensive control system in 1881. Metcalf's system consisted of a separate card for each expense, every order, every receipt, and for each transaction. The system focused responsibility and accountability by pinpointing the outflow of authority for work from the central headquarters, combined with a strict inflow of data on the work on that authority.[39] Similarly, Taylor's system called for a rigorous classification of costs and the reporting procedures clearly reflected his exception principle. His thinking had an impact on the accounting profession by stimulating their interest in costs. Taylor abhorred the futility of *post-mortem* accounting which gave the manager annual, semi-annual, or monthly reports, considering these as being too late for managerial action. He moved the cost accounting function to his planning department and thereby generated his cost reports coincident with daily operations reports. Costs then became an integral part of daily planning and control, not a subject for analysis after a long period of time had passed. The system was effective, in fact, so effective that management tried to throw the system out. Apparently Bethlehem management did not like such an accurate appraisal of their performance.

[36] The complete response is quite lengthy and may be found in Copley (II), pp. 51–55; and also in *Principles*, pp. 136–140.

[37] Rumors in 1911 that Schmidt died as a result of working for Taylor were completely refuted; a physician testified that, at age 44, Schmidt was still in good physical condition and working 10 to 12 hours per day. Copley (II), p. 55.

[38] *Ibid.*, p. 364.

[39] Henry Metcalf, *The Cost of Manufactures and the Administration of Workshops, Public and Private,* New York: John Wiley and Sons, 1885.

Taylor eventually lost the struggle with Bethlehem's management and left the company in 1901 despite entreaties from Wharton. In that same year, Bethlehem was sold to Charles M. Schwab, a Carnegie protégé, who ordered the Taylor system abandoned. As production fell afterward, some lower level supervisors returned to Taylor's ideas, deceived Schwab by saying their practices were not based on Taylorism, and succeeded in restoring productivity.[40]

TAYLOR: THE PERIPATETIC PHILOSOPHER

In 1901, Taylor moved his wife and three newly adopted children from Bethlehem to face a new world. Financially assured by his patents and his savings from past earnings, Taylor turned to the task of articulating his system in print and lectures.[41] A man of action and clearly uncomfortable at the demands of a desk and pen, he began the preparation of *Shop Management*, which appeared in 1903. About him Taylor witnessed various adoptions of his system; among the more notable was the work of James Mapes Dodge at the Link-Belt Company and that of Wilfred Lewis at the Tabor Company, a manufacturer of molding machines. Other conversions to the Taylor system were occurring steadily and must have brought some pride to the post-Bethlehem Taylor. During these years Taylor was not connected with any particular firm. In his spare time, he landscaped and renovated Boxly (near Philadelphia) as the new family home, developed new mixtures for soils for better golf greens, thoroughly investigated the best grasses for them, and set out to design some new concepts in golf clubs. He developed a putter with a "Y" shaft, experimented with lengths and thicknesses of shafts, and spent a great deal of time in practice on the links, or more euphemistically "experimentation."

In 1906, Taylor became president of the prestigious American Society of Mechanical Engineers. His fame was spreading and those who were to spread the Taylor gospel were gathering. Henri Le Chatelier, Horace K. Hathaway, Morris L. Cooke, Sanford E. Thompson, Frank Gilbreth, and others were joining the

---

[40] Copley (II), pp. 159–163. Based on a letter from Taylor to General William Crozier.

[41] Kakar concludes that this step in Taylor's life was a reaction to his perceived failure at Bethlehem Steel and was a typical reaction in terms of a person's life cycle. That is, a striving to overcome the depression of failure, a turning from "work to good works," and an attempt to prove his self-worth. Kakar, pp. 162–166.

earlier apostles, Gantt and Barth. Asked to teach a course at Harvard in the area which was to become the Graduate School of Business Administration (1908), Taylor refused, saying that his system could be learned only in the shop. Professor Edwin Gay, soon to be Dean of the school, told Taylor that the course on scientific management would be taught with or without him, period. Taylor succumbed, though he was never entirely happy about teaching his system in a classroom. Taylor was not anti-business education but felt that experience was the only way to learn his own particular system.

Although he detested travel, he began to travel widely and lectured to a variety of groups. His lectures on "Success" at the University of Illinois in 1909 capsulized his views on business education:

> I have selected some ten or fifteen instances . . . illustrating the all important fact that the ordinary qualities of common sense, character, grit, endurance, etc., count far more in attaining success than book learning or intellectual attainments.[42]

Taylor's Harvard lectures began in 1909 and were given each winter through 1914. An interesting, though not polished speaker nor writer, he illustrated his material with anecdotes, punctuated them with curse words from his early mill worker days, and must have appeared as quite dramatic within the staid ivy covered walls. For all his lectures, Taylor never accepted a penny of reimbursement, not even for traveling expenses. Likewise, he refused payment for the years of consulting he did in the Navy shipyards at Brooklyn and in the Army's Ordnance Department.

The Eastern Rate Case

Taylor also found his system getting some extraordinary free publicity. The Boston lawyer Louis D. Brandeis was becoming noted in the early twentieth century as "the people's lawyer." In 1910, when the Eastern railroads asked the Interstate Commerce Commission for an increase in freight rates, Brandeis took up the cause of the shippers and brought about an unusual series of hearings which thrust Taylor's task management into the public eye. At a loss for a name to apply to the Taylor system, Brandeis, Gil-

---

[42] Copley (II), p. 294.

breth, Gantt, and several other engineers met at Gantt's New York apartment to discuss the matter. Brandeis noted that Taylor frequently used the phrase "scientific" in his work: the others agreed with Brandeis and "scientific management" was the outcome. Brandeis' argument before the Interstate Commerce Commission was based on the inefficiency of railroad management and his proposition was that no rate increase would be necessary if the railroads applied scientific management. Proof of his case was a parade of witnesses who testified to the efficiencies to be gained; James M. Dodge, H. K. Hathaway, Henry R. Towne, and Harrington Emerson were some of the proponents of adopting more efficient management methods based on the Taylor principles. Taylor accepted the Brandeis-coined phrase "scientific management," but with reluctance, fearing that it sounded too "academic." The phrase caught on with the press, however, and Taylor gained a place in the public spotlight. The hearings, with the decision going against the railroads, concluded that it was too early to judge the merits of the new management system; nevertheless, the publicity furnished an impetus to Taylor's ideas that had both desirable and undesirable characteristics. Harrington Emerson's testimony that the railroads could save a million dollars a day by applying scientific management had great appeal to cost conscious manufacturers and to the public. On the other hand, organized labor, especially the entrenched railway brotherhoods, were rising up to protest the introduction of these methods. For management to admit to using scientific management was to invite labor trouble.

Watertown and the Congressional Investigation

The railroad hearings brought publicity but had some unusual repercussions. As noted above, Taylor was serving to bring his system to improve the efficiency of governmental units, especially the Brooklyn Navy Yards and the Army Ordnance Department. Taylor had failed in bringing more efficiency to the Navy Yards and received a few verbal bruises from the naval bureaucracy as his reward. At the head of the Army Ordnance Department was General William Crozier, who had read Taylor's work and saw its applicability to Army arsenals. Crozier chose as test plants the arsenals at Watertown, Massachusetts and Rock Island, Illinois. The time studies and other procedures were going smoothly at

Watertown but trouble was brewing elsewhere. At Rock Island, a representative of the International Association of Machinists appeared to agitate the workers against time studies. The national union offices took up the fight against Taylorism in all government offices and sought to resist its introduction in other enterprises. As early as 1911, organized labor began to wage an all-out war on Taylorism. At this time, the public interest in scientific management was at its height due to the hearings on railroad rates. Taylor wrote to Crozier to install the system at Watertown carefully, step by step, despite the resistance at Rock Island, including sounding out the sentiments of the workers in each department before beginning the time study. Dwight Merrick was doing the study and attempted to begin an analysis of the molders at Watertown. One of the molders refused, citing "the organization" (the union) as the reason for his refusal; he was fired, and in August of 1911 the first strike under Taylorism occurred at the Watertown Arsenal. Taylor attributed the whole problem to a mistake in tactics; the sentiments of the molders had not been examined nor had they been briefed on the purposes of the time study. Taylor did not blame the union but thought the cause was a premature attempt to make the study without following his recommended technique of consulting the workers first.[43] However, the agitation continued, and it was represented to Congress that the Watertown strike was due to unsatisfactory treatment of labor due to the introduction of the Taylor system. As a consequence, the House appointed a special committee to investigate. It consisted of three men, William B. Wilson, a former official of the United Mine Workers, then chairman of the House Labor Committee, and later Secretary of Labor under President Wilson; William C. Redfield, a manufacturer who later became Secretary of Commerce under Wilson; and John Q. Tilson, the only Republican member, as an umpire.

The hearings began in October, 1911, and ended in February, 1912. Taylor spent twelve hours scattered over four days in the witness chair. As Copley stated "terrorism was in the air" as the unions set out to harass Taylor. From the testimony one can see the hostility and sharpness in the questions and answers. For exam-

---

[43] Milton J. Nadworny, *Scientific Management and the Unions: 1900–1923,* Cambridge, Mass.: Harvard University Press, 1955, p. 80, agrees that the workers were not objecting to the time studies and the production bonus but to the *method* of introducing the system.

ple, this clash ensued over "the first-class man" with the Honorable Mr. Wilson, the labor man, presiding. (Previous to this testimony, there were some questions and discussion on the effect of scientific management on worker displacement.)

The Chairman.   Is it not true that a man who is not a good workman and who may not be responsible for the fact that he is not a good workman, has to live as well as the man who is a good workman?

Mr. Taylor.   Not as well as the other workman; otherwise, that would imply that all those in the world were entitled to live equally well whether they worked or whether they were idle, and that certainly is not the case. Not as well.

The Chairman.   Under scientific management, then, you propose that because a man is not in the first class as a workman that there is no place in the world for him—if he is not in the first class in some particular line that this must be destroyed and removed?

Mr. Taylor.   Mr. Chairman, would it not be well for me to describe what I mean by a "first-class" workman.   I have written a good deal about "first class" workmen in my books, and I find there is quite a general misapprehension as to the use of that term "first-class."

The Chairman.   Before you come to a definition of what you consider a first class workman I would like to have your concept of how you are going to take care, under your scientific management, of a man who is not a first-class workman in some particular line?

Mr. Taylor.   I cannot answer that question until I define what I mean by "first-class."   You and I may have a totally different idea as to the meaning of these words, and therefore I suggest that you allow me to state what I mean.

The Chairman.   The very fact that you specify "first-class" would indicate that in your mind you would have some other class than "first class."

Mr. Taylor.   If you will allow me to define it I think I can make it clear.

The Chairman.   You said a "first-class" workman can be taken care of under normal conditions.   That is what you have already said.   Now, the other class that is in your mind, other than "first-class," how does your system propose to take care of them?

Mr. Taylor.   Mr. Chairman, I cannot answer that question.   I cannot answer any question relating to "first-class" workmen until you know my definition of that term, because I have used these words technically throughout my paper, and I am not willing to answer a question you put about "first-class" workmen with the assumption that my answer applies to all I have said in my book.

The Chairman.   You yourself injected the term "first-class" by saying that you did not know of a condition in normal times when a "first-class" workman could not find employment.

Mr. Taylor.   I do not think I used that term "first-class."

Mr. Redfield.   Mr. Chairman, the witness has now four times, I think, said that until he is allowed to define what he means by "first-class" no answer can be given, because he means one thing by the words "first-class" and he thinks that you mean another thing.

The Chairman.   My question has nothing whatever to do with the definition of the words "first-class."   It has to do with the other class than "first-class" not with "first-class."   A definition of first-class will in no manner contribute to a proper reply to my question, because I am not asking about "first-class," but the other than "first-class" workmen.

Mr. Taylor.   I cannot describe the others until I have described what I mean by "first-class."

Mr. Redfield.   As I was saying when I was interrupted, the witness has stated that he cannot answer the question for the reason that the language that the chairman uses, namely, the words "first-class" do not mean the same thing in the Chairman's mind that they mean in the witness's mind, and he asks the privilege of defining what they do mean, so that the language shall be mutually intelligible.   Now, it seems to me, and I think it is good law and entirely proper, that the witness ought to be permitted to define his meaning and then if, after his definition is made, there is any misunderstanding, we can proceed.[44]

Then the Chairman, Mr. Redfield, and Mr. Tilson engaged in spirited discussion of whether or not Taylor should be allowed to define his terms; Redfield and Tilson prevailed and Taylor proceeded to his ideas of a first class man and concluded:

. . . among every class of workmen we have some balky workmen—I do not mean men who are unable to work, but men who, physically well able to work, are simply lazy, and who through no amount of teaching and instructing and through no amount of kindly treatment, can be brought into the "first-class."   That is the man whom I call "second-class."   They have the physical possibility of being "first-class", but they obstinately refuse to do so.

Now, Mr. Chairman, I am ready to answer your question, having clearly in mind that I have these two types of "second-class" men in view; the one which is physically able to do the work, but who refused to do it—and the other who is not physically or mentally fitted to do that particular job.   These are the two types of "second-class" men.

The Chairman.   Then, how does scientific management propose to take care of men who are not "first-class" men in any particular line of work?

Mr. Taylor.   I give it up.

The Chairman.   Scientific management has no place for such men?

Mr. Taylor.   Scientific management has no use for a bird that can sing and won't sing.

The Chairman.   I am not speaking about birds at all.

Mr. Taylor.   No man who can work and won't work has any place under scientific management.

The Chairman.   It is not a question of a man "who can work and won't work" it is a question of a man who is not a "first-class" man in any one particular line, according to your own definition.

Mr. Taylor.   I do not know of any such line of work.   For each man some line can be found in which he is first-class.[45]

In another instance, Taylor was being questioned by Mr. John R. O'Leary (third Vice President of the International Molder's Unions of North America) on the fines he had levied on workers at Midvale Steel:

[44] *Hearings*, pp. 1452–1453.
[45] *Ibid.*, pp. 1455–1456.

Mr. O'Leary.   Did I understand you to say that you had the permission and cooperation of the men in putting in that system?

Mr. Taylor.   Yes . . . they ran it, invested the funds, took care of the sick; they furnished the doctor and nurse . . .

Mr. O'Leary.   What did they charge the men who were injured, for the Doctor?

Mr. Taylor.   Not a cent.   The services were all free.

Mr. O'Leary.   Are you aware that there have been many suits instituted against the Midvale Steel Co. to recover those fines, and that they were recovered?

Mr. Taylor.   No; I am not aware of it.

Mr. O'Leary.   Are you aware that men are fined a dollar for going to the urinal?

Mr. Taylor.   I have not the slightest idea that is true.   Who ever said that told an untruth.   Nothing of that kind was done while I was there.[46]

No support for O'Leary's charges ever appeared in any other testimony.   Later, Mr. Redfield queried Taylor about his financial interest in the installation of the scientific method at the Tabor Company:

Mr. Redfield.   You have 120 shares out of a total number of how many shares issued by the company?

Mr. Taylor.   I really do not know what the capitalization is.   My friend Mr. Tabor here says there are about 1,500 shares in the company.

Mr. Redfield.   You have, then, about a one-fifth interest?

Mr. Taylor.   Oh, no.

Mr. Redfield.   Then it is not a majority interest?

Mr. Taylor.   No; and I never have received a cent from it.

Mr. Redfield.   Is it, or is it not, a fact that it is a part of the application of the Taylor System that it will be utilized indirectly for the sale of the products of any company in which you are interested?   If it is, we want to know it.

Mr. Taylor.   Why, no; what a ridiculous—why, no.

Mr. Redfield.   The charge was made in the testimony at Boston.

Mr. Taylor.   It is absolutely untrue.

Mr. Redfield.   That is what I want to know—if it is true or false.

Mr. Taylor.   Why, absolutely false.

Mr. Redfield.   We want to know if this thing is being worked to fill your pockets, directly or indirectly . . .

Mr. Taylor.   It is absolutely false.   I have never had a dollar of dividends from the Tabor Manufacturing Company . . .[47]

As Ida M. Tarbell, the muckraker of the Standard Oil days, declared:

One of the most sportsmanlike exhibits the country ever saw was Mr. Taylor's willingness to subject himself to the heckling and the badgering of labor leaders, congressmen, and investigators of all degrees of misunderstanding, suspicion and ill will.   To a man of his temperament and highly trained

[46] *Ibid.*, pp. 745–746.
[47] *Ibid.*, p. 1504.

intellect, who had given a quarter of a century of the hardest kind of toil to develop useful truths, the kind of questioning to which he was sometimes subjected must have been maddening.[48]

From Miss Tarbell, this was quite a compliment. Baited, insulted, and made to appear a beast, Taylor staggered from the stand at the close of his testimony. Taylor's pride was sorely wounded, his life work reviled before a congressional committee. There was no victory for anyone in the final report of the committee. Phrased in good political double talk, the report said that it was too early "to determine with accuracy their [Taylor's and other scientific management systems] effect on the health and pay of employees and their effect on wages and labor cost."[49] The committee found no evidence to support abuses of workers nor any need for remedial legislation. It did refer to possible abuses, perhaps as a bone for opponents, but presented no evidence that they had occurred.

Despite the recommendation that no legislation was needed, pro-labor forces began introducing riders to appropriation bills specifying that no part of the Taylor system could be used under operating funds granted by that bill. In considering appropriation bills for the Army and Navy in 1914-1915, a heated debate occurred in the Senate. Among the anti-Taylor, pro-rider advocates was Henry Cabot Lodge, descendant of the early Massachusetts textile tycoons, who spoke of ending "the days of slavery" brought about by men such as Taylor who thought it "profitable to work the slaves to the last possible point and let them die."[50] Such demagoguery clearly indicated his ignorance of what Taylor was attempting. The rider failed in the Senate, but was restored in conference between the two Houses. After that, Congress after Congress continued to attach such riders to Army, Navy, and Post Office appropriation bills.[51] Taylorism and the attempt to bring efficiency to government agencies was clearly crippled.

---

[48] New Ideals in Business, p. 315, cited by Copley (II), p. 347.

[49] Hearings, p. 1930.

[50] Copley (II), p. 351. Mary Barnett Gilson, an early employment counselor and later lecturer at the University of Chicago, called Senator Lodge an "exhibitionist" who tilted at windmills. M. B. Gilson, What's Past is Prologue, New York: Harper & Row, 1940, p. 55.

[51] Such anti-scientific management legislation persisted until 1949 when time study and incentive bonus restrictions were removed from the statutes through the efforts of Senator Taft (Ohio) and Senator Flanders (Vermont). Nadworny, p. 103.

The Mental Revolution

In the first decade of the twentieth century, great national concern was voiced by President Theodore Roosevelt and others over the depletion of America's resources. This national impetus exceeded a mere concern for natural resources to a much larger need for what the President called "national efficiency." Taylor, who had for almost three decades fought against the misuse of both physical and human resources, found himself as a result of the railroad hearings the man of the hour. Taylor wrote to meet that need for national efficiency in his *Principles of Scientific Management* where he stated his objectives as:

First. To point out, through a series of simple illustrations, the great loss which the whole country is suffering through inefficiency in almost all of our daily acts.
Second. To try to convince the reader that the remedy for this inefficiency lies in systematic management, rather than in searching for some unusual or extraordinary man.
Third. To prove that the best management is a true science, resting upon clearly defined laws, rules, and principles, as a foundation. And further to show that the fundamental principles of scientific management are applicable to all kinds of human activities, from our simplest individual acts to the work of our great corporations, which call for the most elaborate cooperation.[52]

"The principal object of management," said Taylor, "should be to secure the maximum prosperity for the employer, coupled with the maximum prosperity for each employee."[53] Taylor deplored short-run short-cuts which gave one side advantage over another; his mutuality of interests emphasized a long-term growth of both parties to insure prosperity for each. In *Principles*, Taylor was becoming a philosopher, looking beyond mere shop-level efficiency to show how scientific management, when applied to the lowest level, could then be generalized to bring about prosperity on the national or even international level. Taylor recognized that the "efficiency experts" were giving scientific management a black eye. He warned that "the mechanism of management must not be mistaken for its essence, or underlying philosophy."[54] This

---

[52] Taylor, *Principles*, p. 7. Copyright 1947, Harper and Row; by permission. This third point is a statement of the universality of scientific management but it does not necessarily hint at the same level of universality of management that will be seen later in the work of Henri Fayol.
[53] *Ibid.*, p. 9.
[54] *Ibid.*, p. 128.

philosophy was based on a mutuality of interests and had four basic principles:

First. The development of a true science.
Second. The scientific selection of the workman.
Third. His scientific education and development.
Fourth. Intimate friendly cooperation between the management and the men.[55]

But neither these principles, nor any single part of Taylor's system, could be isolated as a major factor:

It is no single element, but rather this whole combination, that constitutes scientific management, which may be summarized:
Science, not rule of thumb.
Harmony, not discord.
Cooperation, not individualism.
Maximum output, in place of restricted output.
The development of each man to his greatest efficiency and prosperity.[56]

A good many "efficiency experts" suddenly appeared in 1911 promising great cost reductions and improvements to those employers who would hire their services. Taylor deplored these experts, fearing, and properly so, that they promised quick panaceas without grasping the fundamental attitudes that had to be changed and the necessity of gaining acceptance and the step-by-step study, re-study, and installation of his methods. Taylor made a marked distinction between true scientific management and the efficiency craze; the difference was in a "mental revolution" on the part of the employer and the employee, something which came about from mutual respect over a period of time and not from the adoption of the mechanics of the system. At the hearings, Taylor tried to clarify first what scientific management was *not*, and then what it was:

Scientific management is not any efficiency device, not a device of any kind for securing efficiency; nor is it any bunch or group of efficiency devices. It is not a new system of figuring costs; it is not a new scheme of paying men; it is not a piecework system; it is not a bonus system; it is not a premium system; it is no scheme for paying men; it is not holding a stop watch on a man and writing things down about him; it is not time study; it is not motion study nor an analysis of the movements of men; it is not the printing and ruling and unloading of a ton or two of blanks on a set of men and saying, "Here's your system; go use it." It is not divided foremanship or functional foremanship; it is not any of the devices which the average man calls to mind

[55] *Ibid.*, p. 130. Copyright 1947, Harper and Row; by permission.
[56] *Ibid.*, p. 140. Copyright 1947, Harper and Row; by permission.

when scientific management is spoken of. The average man thinks of one or more of these things when he hears the words "scientific management" mentioned, but scientific management is not any of these devices. I am not sneering at cost-keeping systems, at time study, at functional foremanship, nor at any new and improved scheme of paying men, nor at any efficiency devices, if they are really devices that make for efficiency. I believe in them; but what I am emphasizing is that these devices in whole or in part are not scientific management, they are useful adjuncts to scientific management, so are they also useful adjuncts of other systems of management.

Now, in its essence, scientific management involves a complete mental revolution on the part of the workingman engaged in any particular establishment or industry—a complete mental revolution on the part of these men as to their duties toward their work, toward their fellow men, and toward their employers. And it involves the equally complete mental revolution on the part of those on the management's side—the foreman, the superintendent, the owner of the business, the board of directors—a complete mental revolution on their part as to their duties toward their fellow workers in the management, toward their workmen, and toward all of their daily problems. And without this complete mental revolution on both sides scientific management does not exist.

That is the essence of scientific management, this great mental revolution.[57]

What was the result of this mental revolution?

The great revolution that takes place in the mental attitude of the two parties under scientific management is that both sides take their eyes off of the division of the surplus as the all-important matter, and together turn their attention toward increasing the size of the surplus until this surplus becomes so large that it is unnecessary to quarrel over how it shall be divided. They come to see that when they stop pulling against one another, and instead both turn and push shoulder to shoulder in the same direction, the size of the surplus created by their joint efforts is truly astounding. They both realize that when they substitute friendly cooperation and mutual helpfulness for antagonism and strife they are together able to make this surplus so enormously greater than it was in the past that there is ample room for a large increase in wages for the workmen and an equally great increase in profits for the manufacturer. This, gentlemen, is the beginning of the great mental revolution which constitutes the first step toward scientific management.[58]

Taylor knew that his prime antagonists were the leaders of labor, not the laborers themselves, and was convinced of a conspiracy among union leaders to oppose his system. He made repeated offers to Samuel Gompers, President of the American Federation of Labor, to come and see plants using scientific management and to get the facts for himself; Mr. Gompers refused.[59] The same was

---

[57] *Hearings*, p. 1387.

[58] *Ibid.*, pp. 1388–1389.

[59] Copley (II), pp. 403–404. In his testimony before the committee, Gompers categorically denied the existence of soldiering and labor resistance. *Hearings*, p. 27. Gompers' biographer, Philip Taft, has suggested that Gompers *himself* was not

true of John Mitchell of the mine workers. Taylor stuck with his early ideas that unions were fine in theory but lacked in practice any semblance of openness to improve the economic system. In Taylor's view, union philosophy and that of scientific management were directly antagonistic in that unions built and encouraged antagonisms setting the worker apart from management, while scientific management encouraged a mutuality of interests. To Gompers, "more, more, more" meant labor's gains came from the employer's pocket; for Taylor "more" came to both through improved productivity.

Taylor and the Human Factor

In answer to charges of the coldness and impersonality of scientific management and in rebuttal to omission of the human factor from his management equation, Taylor spoke on systems and men:

No system can do away with the need of real men. Both system and good men are needed, and after introducing the best system, success will be in proportion to the ability, consistency, and respected authority of the management.[60]

On human relations:

No system of management, however good, should be applied in a wooden way. The proper personal relations should always be maintained between the employers and men; and even the prejudices of the workmen should be considered in dealing with them.

The employer who goes through his works with kid gloves on, and is never known to dirty his hands or clothes, and who either talks to his men in a condescending or patronizing way, or else not at all, has no chance whatever of ascertaining their real thoughts or feelings.

Above all is it desirable that men should be talked to on their own level by those who are over them. Each man should be encouraged to discuss any trouble which he may have, either in the works or outside, with those over him. Men would far rather even be blamed by their bosses, especially if the 'tearing out' has a touch of human nature and feeling in it, than to be passed by day after day without a word, and with no more notice than if they were part of the machinery.

The opportunity which each man should have of airing his mind freely, and

---

unalterably opposed to scientific management. According to Taft, Gompers yielded to the influence of the "socialist" President of the International Association of Machinists, William H. Johnston, because the Machinists were the largest and most powerful affiliate in the AFL. Philip Taft, *The A. F. of L. in the Time of Gompers,* New York: Harper and Row, 1957, pp. 299–300.

[60] *Shop Management,* p. 148.

having it out with his employers, is a safety-valve; and if the superintendents are reasonable men, and listen to and treat with respect what their men have to say, there is absolutely no reason for labor unions and strikes.

It is not the large charities (however generous they may be) that are needed or appreciated by workmen so much as small acts of personal kindness and sympathy, which establish a bond of friendly feeling between them and their employers.

The moral effect of this system on the men is marked. The feeling that substantial justice is being done them renders them on the whole much more manly, straightforward, and truthful. They work more cheerfully, and are more obliging to one another and their employers. They are not soured, as under the old system, by brooding over the injustice done them; and their spare minutes are not spent to the same extent in criticising their employers.[61]

On resistance to change:

Through generations of bitter experiences working men as a class have learned to look upon all change as antagonistic to their best interests. They do not ask the object of the change, but oppose it simply as *change*. The first changes, therefore, should be such as to allay the suspicions of the men and convince them by actual contact that the reforms are after all rather harmless and are only such as will ultimately be of benefit to all concerned. Such improvements then as directly affect the workmen least should be started first. At the same time it must be remembered that the whole operation is of necessity so slow that the new system should be started at as many points as possible and constantly pushed as hard as possible.[62]

Taylor stated that it took from two to five years to install his system fully. Scientific management was not an overnight panacea and required diligence and understanding when installations were attempted. Three weeks before his death, he spoke to the Cleveland Advertising Club:

Scientific management at every step has been an evolution, not a theory. In all cases the practice has preceded the theory . . . all the men that I know of who are connected with scientific management are ready to abandon any scheme, any theory, in favor of anything else that can be found which is better. There is nothing in scientific management that is fixed.[63]

If there was a "one best way," Taylor in the twilight years knew from experience that it came after much experimentation and perhaps even then was not rigid but subject to further examination.

Worried by the declining health of his wife, bedeviled by the antagonism of organized labor, and frustrated by the efficiency experts who borrowed the techniques and forgot the philosophy, Taylor's last days were nigh. In a drafty drawing room of a rail car

---

[61] *Ibid.*, pp. 184–185. Copyright 1947, Harper and Row; by permission.
[62] *Ibid.*, p. 137. Copyright 1947, Harper and Row; by permission.
[63] Copley (II), p. 348.

while returning from one of his speaking trips, he caught pneumonia. He died in the hospital one day after his fifty-ninth birthday. In a grave on a hill with a view of the steel smokestacks of Philadelphia, his epitaph reads "Frederick W. Taylor, Father of Scientific Management."

SUMMARY

Frederick W. Taylor, the father of scientific management, and his associates represent the first age of synthesis in management thought. Management has been characterized as a process of fusing the physical resource or the technical facet of organizations with the human resource facet in order to achieve organizational objectives. Prior to Taylor, no other person had developed to the same degree a systematic approach to management's problems and coupled it with a philosophical framework.

On the technique side, Taylor's scientific approach sought to analyze existing practices, study them for standardization and improvement, and rationalize resource utilization. On the human side, Taylor sought the highest degree of individual development and reward through fatigue reduction, scientific selection, matching men's abilities to jobs, and through incentive schemes. He did not neglect the human element, as is so often suggested, but stressed the individual and not the group side of man. Taylor's synthesis came through his call for a "mental revolution" which sought to fuse the interests of labor and management into a mutually rewarding whole.

7

Spreading the Gospel of Efficiency

Space and time rarely allow the full measure of a man and his work. This is true of Frederick W. Taylor and also applies to those who worked with and followed Taylor in propagating the scientific management movement. Taylor became the rallying point and this chapter will focus on six individuals who were prominent in the embryonic days of scientific management: Carl G. Barth, Henry L. Gantt, the dynamic duo of Frank and Lillian Gilbreth, Harrington Emerson, and Morris L. Cooke. These were the individuals who were in the vanguard in spreading the gospel of efficiency.

THE MOST ORTHODOX: CARL BARTH

Of all the disciples in the vanguard of the scientific management movement, Carl Georg Lange Barth (1860–1939) was the most orthodox. Barth was recruited from his position as a mathematics teacher by Taylor at the suggestion of Wilfred Lewis for purposes of handling the complex mathematical problems in Taylor's metal cutting experiments. Born in Norway, Barth was a stern man whose rimless glasses and close-cropped beard gave him a Teutonic professorial look. He was even more demanding than Taylor on standards and waste, to such an extent that Taylor pleaded with Barth to display more "tact." Barth joined Taylor at Bethlehem and his first assignment was to help Henry L. Gantt with the feed

147

and speed problems which had plagued Taylor since Midvale. Barth's solution was "a combination of a crude or embryonic log-arithmic slide rule and a set of tables" of formulae which allowed the instantaneous solution of any machine feed and speed problem. The operator, knowing the power of the machine and the cutting tool being used, could determine the proper rate at which the material to be processed could be fed into the machine and the proper speed of the lathe. Taylor credited Barth's "mathematical genius" for solving the variables and complexities of metal cutting.

When Taylor left Bethlehem at the urging of top management, Carl Barth went with him and assisted in the first installations of scientific management at the Tabor Manufacturing Company, the Link Belt Company, Fairbanks Scale, Yale and Towne, and later at the Watertown Arsenal. He also assisted George Babcock in installing scientific management in the Franklin Motor Car Com-pany (1908–1912) and thus was a pioneer in the rationalization of that infant industry. Barth lectured on scientific management at Harvard (1911–16 and 1919–22) and was "exceedingly proud of being accused of being Mr. Taylor's most orthodox disciple."[1] He resisted any tampering with Taylor's precepts and later maintained that only those who had worked directly with Taylor, such as him-self, were the "direct disciples" who fully understood the task management system.[2] Carl Barth's contribution to management thought was confined to his faithful execution of Taylor's precepts; his slide rule was unique and helpful but was confined to a narrow aspect of the whole philosophy of scientific management. It was the work of others that would lead to more unique derivations in the gospel of efficiency.

THE MOST UNORTHODOX: H. L. GANTT

Henry Laurence Gantt (1861–1919) was born into a prosperous Maryland farm family and, when the Civil War left the family desti-tute, Gantt learned at an early age the demands of hard work, frugal living, and the self-discipline required to make one's way in the

---

[1] Carl G. Barth, "Discussion," *Transactions of the A.S.M.E.*, Vol. XXXIV (1912), p. 1204.

[2] Carl G. Barth, "Discussion," *Bulletin of the Taylor Society*, (September, 1920), p. 149.

world.[3] Graduating with distinction from Johns Hopkins in 1880, he became a teacher of natural science and mechanics at his old prep school, McDonagh (1880–1883). He returned to college at the Stevens Institute of Technology, gained his degree as a mechanical engineer in 1884, became a draftsman for an engineering firm, returned to his teaching post at McDonagh during 1886–1887, and then joined the Midvale Steel Company in 1887 as an Assistant in the Engineering Department. It was here that the then twenty-six-year-old Gantt met and began to work with a man who would have a significant influence on his future career, F. W. Taylor. Taylor and Gantt were an unusual team; they had mutual interests in their quest for science in management and developed a deep mutual admiration for each other's work. Gantt, however, was more cautious than Taylor in approaching problems, a sign interpreted by Taylor as pussyfooting. Gantt was also prone to severe headaches and to outbursts of irritation throughout his entire life. However, he grasped the essence of Taylor's work and, though they clashed at times, became a prime disciple of Taylor. Working closely with Taylor at Midvale, following him to the Simond's Rolling Machine Company to become Superintendent, and joining him again at Bethlehem Steel, Gantt's early years and work were closely related to Taylor's. After 1901, however, he became a consulting industrial engineer on his own and, although he espoused the views of scientific management, his later years were bringing the development of a different Gantt. During his lifetime he published over 150 titles, including three major books, made numerous presentations before the 'A.S.M.E. (becoming vice-president of that group in 1914), patented more than a dozen inventions, lectured at Stevens, Columbia, Harvard, and Yale, and became one of the first successful management consultants.[4]

The Task and Bonus System

Gantt's ideas were largely influenced by Taylor, and the same elements appear in his early writings. The stress on the mutuality

[3] Biographical data on Gantt is from L. P. Alford, *Henry L. Gantt: Leader in Industry,* prepared originally as a memorial volume for the A.S.M.E. and later published by Harper and Row (New York), 1934.
[4] A complete bibliography of Gantt's work may be found in Alford. Much of Gantt's work is reprinted in a subject heading format by Alex W. Rathe, *Gantt on Management,* New York: American Management Association, 1961.

of interests between labor and management, the scientific selection of workmen, the incentive rate to stimulate performance, detailed instructions on work, and all of the other familiar concepts are reflected in Gantt's work. Gantt also sought the efficient utilization of labor through scientific investigation and "harmonious cooperation" between labor and management. In his words:

. . . the only healthy industrial condition is that in which the employer has the best men obtainable for his work, and the workman feels that his labor is being sold at the highest market price.[5]

On this road to high wages and low costs, Gantt saw some different possibilities for incentive systems. His view on unions paralleled that of Taylor but he was more persuasive and philosophical in stating the issue:

If the amount of wealth in the world were fixed, the struggle for the possession of that wealth would necessarily cause antagonism; but, inasmuch as the amount of wealth is not fixed, but constantly increasing, the fact that one man has become wealthy does not necessarily mean that someone else has become poorer, but may mean quit the reverse, especially if the first is a producer of wealth. . . . As long . . . as one party—no matter which—tries to get all it can of the new wealth, regardless of the rights of the other, conflicts will continue.[6]

The "more, more, more" of organized labor hence became an antagonistic force unless it cooperated in producing more for the benefit of the other party to the transaction, management, and vice versa. Gantt was not convinced that the differential piece rate of Taylor was adequate to the task of bringing this desired cooperation to the operative workers. Instead, Gantt devised his "task work with a bonus" system which paid the worker a bonus of 50 cents per day if he did all of his work assigned for any particular day.[7] Further, the foreman was to be given a bonus for each man who made the standard plus an extra bonus if *all* the men made it. Thus, if 9 of 10 workers made the standard, the foreman would

[5] H. L. Gantt, *Work, Wages, and Profits,* second edition, New York: Engineering Magazine Company, 1916, p. 33.

[6] *Ibid.,* p. 55.

[7] Gantt later discovered that this plan offered little incentive beyond meeting the standard. To overcome this defect, he modified the plan to pay the workman for the time allowed plus a percentage of that time if he completed the job in the allowed time or less. Hence, a workman could receive four hours pay for doing a three-hour job in three hours or less. *Ibid.,* p. 165. For a detailed explanation and the computations necessary to Gantt's task and bonus plan, see C. W. Lytle. *Wage Incentive Methods,* New York: Ronald Press Co., 1942, pp. 185–200.

receive 10 cents per man or $.90; if all ten made the standard, he received 15 cents per man or $1.50. To Gantt, this extra bonus for the foreman was for "bringing the inferior workmen up to the standard [and] made him devote his energies to those men who most needed them."[8] This is the first recorded attempt to make it in the financial interest of the *foreman* to teach the worker the right way. From his own schoolmaster experience, Gantt learned the importance of teaching and he felt that the bonus system would shift the foreman from a "driver" to a teacher and helper of his subordinates. In this shift from concern for production to concern for the worker through instruction and subsequently improved production, Gantt's work stands as an early landmark in early human behavioral thought. In Gantt's works: "Whatever we do must be in accord with human nature. We cannot drive people; we must direct their development."[9] Like Taylor, Gantt encountered more resistance from the foremen than from the workers. The main managerial obstacle was their reluctance to define and give tasks precisely and to exert the higher caliber of work which management must do to make the system succeed. As under the Taylor system, Gantt's plan called for the scientific investigation of the task, analysis and study of movements and times, standardization of conditions, and winning worker cooperation. Gantt's addition was the more direct involvement of management through a direct financial interest.

The "Habits of Industry"

In teaching the worker, Gantt felt the foreman should do more than increase the worker's skill and knowledge and added an ingredient to industrial education called the "habits of industry." These habits would be those of industriousness and cooperation which would facilitate the acquisition of all other knowledge. This too called for a break with the past and Taylor's influence is seen once more:

the general policy of the past has been to drive; but the era of force must give way to that of knowledge, and the policy of the future will be to teach and lead, to the advantage of all concerned.[10]

[8] *Work, Wages and Profits*, p. 115.
[9] *Ibid.*, p. 124.
[10] *Ibid.*, p. 148.

The habits that must be taught the worker were those of "doing promptly and to the best of his ability the work set before him."[11] Stress must be placed on the pride that comes from quality as well as quantity of work. Gantt cited an example of a group of girls who, working under the task and bonus system, formed a society of bonus producers with group admission available only to those who consistently earned the premium. To Gantt, this was the proper condition for all workers since he was also concerned with worker morale. However, this could come about only after management had created the proper atmosphere of cooperation and confidence with the employees. The results of his inculcation of "habits" were higher wages, increased skill, and greater pleasure and pride for the worker, coupled with lower costs and greater productivity for the employer. Beyond these tangible manifestations of efficiency, the harmonious cooperation between labor and management created that intangible élan or morale so vital to successful cooperative endeavors.

Graphic Aids to Management

As a former schoolmaster, Gantt was oriented toward the dramatization of data through graphic means. One of his early subjects for graphing was the "fixing of habits of industry" through horizontal bars illustrating the progress of workers toward meeting the task standard. For each worker, a daily record was kept of whether he made the standard and received a bonus, recorded in black, or did not, recorded in red. The graph served to aid both management and the worker since progress as well as reasons for not making the bonus were recorded, enabling management to pinpoint deficiencies and feeding back progress data to the worker. In converting shops or departments from day work to task work, the progress of the shop could be seen by everyone as the chart contained progressively more and more solid black lines. As this method of charting succeeded in getting better performance, Gantt expanded his visual aids to include a chart on the daily production balance, cost control, quantity of work per machine, quantity of work per man in comparison with the original estimates, the expense of idle machinery, and others. However, his major break-

[11] *Ibid.*, p. 154.

through in charting came when he was serving as a dollar-a-year consultant to the Department of the Army during World War I.

The conversion of American industry to wartime production did not come quickly and smoothly. America had the productive capacity, but the integration and coordination of private industrial efforts with the governmental agencies were haphazard. Plants were scattered all over the nation, shipments were late, warehouses crowded or disorganized, and the Ordnance Department and the Navy were utilizing their resources poorly. Gantt had had some contact with governmental work before the War. In 1911, with Charles Day and Harrington Emerson, he was commissioned to study the organization and management of Navy shipyards. Their efforts went for naught when the Secretary of the Navy announced that he would never allow scientific management in the shipyards. The reader will recall that this was the period of the Congressional hearings and the general ill-will against the efficiency movement. Gantt had also served as a consultant to General William Crozier at the Frankford Arsenal just prior to the War. Crozier, influenced by Gantt's graphic displays, developed a series of "progress and performance" charts to aid in managing the Ordnance Arsenals. However, Crozier was removed from his position in 1917 and his successors allowed the system to lapse. When Gantt gave up his lucrative consulting work to aid the war effort, he puzzled over the problem of keeping track of the vast work of the various departments. Scheduling was especially crucial and management lacked the necessary information to control and coordinate private contractor's efforts with those of the government agencies. Gantt spent three months trying to unravel the mess before the thought came to him that:

We have all been wrong in scheduling on a basis of *quantities*; the essential element in the situation is *time*, and this should be the basis in laying out any program.[12]

The first published Gantt chart depicted five items of war materials and the scheduling of orders placed, orders completed, and issuances from stores or inventory. A portion of this chart appears in Figure 7-1.

The heavy line for each item carried forward to October indi-

[12] L. P. Alford, p. 207.

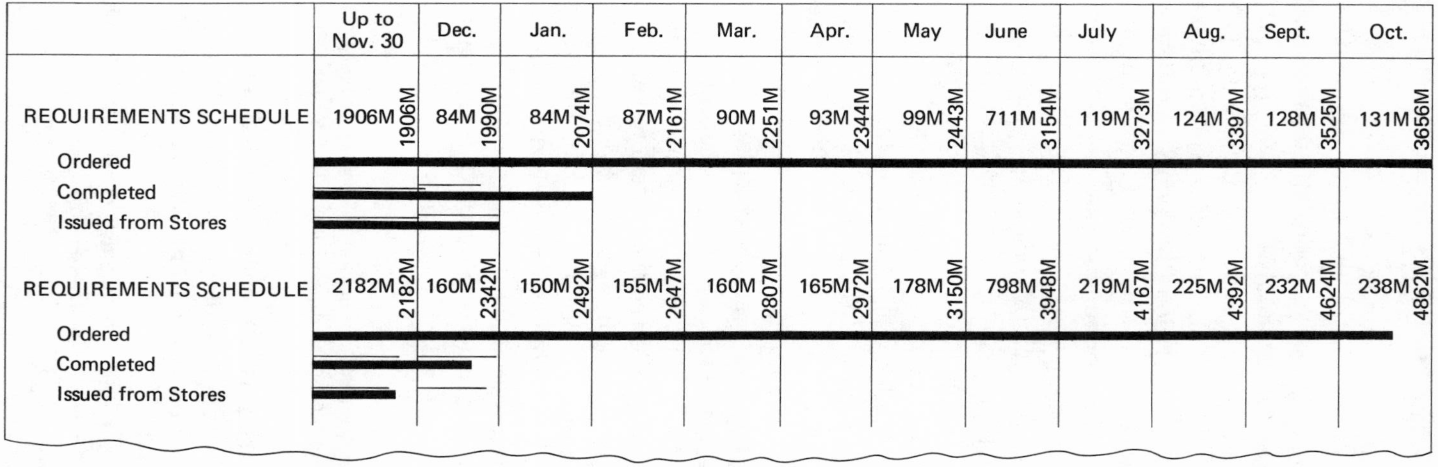

	Up to Nov. 30	Dec.	Jan.	Feb.	Mar.	Apr.	May	June	July	Aug.	Sept.	Oct.
REQUIREMENTS SCHEDULE	1906M	1990M / 84M	2074M / 84M	2161M / 87M	2251M / 90M	2344M / 93M	2443M / 99M	3154M / 711M	3273M / 119M	3397M / 124M	3525M / 128M	3656M / 131M
Ordered												
Completed												
Issued from Stores												
REQUIREMENTS SCHEDULE	2182M	2342M / 160M	2492M / 150M	2647M / 155M	2807M / 160M	2972M / 165M	3150M / 178M	3948M / 798M	4167M / 219M	4392M / 225M	4624M / 232M	4862M / 238M
Ordered												
Completed												
Issued from Stores												

Fig. 7–1. First published Gantt chart. (*Originally in Industrial Management*, February, 1918. Reproduced, and described in Alford, *op. cit.*, pp. 211–213.)

cated the accumulated needs as expressed in orders received. The vertical figure at the end of each month showed cumulative requirements up to that date and the horizontal figure for each month represented the amount to be supplied during that month. On the first item, total requirements to the end of October was 3,656,000 while the monthly requirements varied from 84,000 in December to 711,000 in June. For "completed" and "issued from stores," the heavy line represented *actual* progress while the light line indicated planned performance. Taking December 31 as a check point on the first item for example, *actual* performance is one month ahead of schedule, leaving a balance in stores; and it can be seen that the second item is behind schedule, thus indicating that corrective action is needed to get that item back on schedule.

Gantt's graphic aids to management planning and controlling were revolutionary for this period in management thought. In a ready graphic form, management could see how plans were progressing and take whatever action necessary to keep projects on time or within budget authorizations. Gantt never patented the concept, nor profited from it, but his achievement did earn him the Distinguished Service Medal from the government. A member of Gantt's consulting firm, Wallace Clark, popularized the idea of the Gantt Chart in a book that was translated into eight languages, formed the basis for the Russian central planners to control their "five-year plans," and provided the whole world with a graphic means of planning and controlling work.[13] All subsequent production control boards and charts drew their inspiration from Gantt's original work; the modern variation became Program Evaluation and Review Technique (PERT), which was a computerized, more intricate scheme but nevertheless founded upon the principles of planning and controlling times and costs. In Washington, the war effort took a measurable turn as the result of Gantt's contributions. Materials flowed more smoothly, boat-building blossomed, and America's productive might was brought to its greatest outpouring of goods. Surely these must have been some consolation here for the man whose efforts to systematize governmental operations had been spurned so few years before.

[13] Wallace Clark, *The Gantt Chart: A Working Tool of Management*, New York: Ronald Press Co., 1922. For further information on Wallace Clark, see Harold Smiddy, "Wallace Clark's Contribution to International Management," *Advanced Management*, Vol. 23 (March, 1958), pp. 17–26.

Gantt: The Later Years

After the death of Taylor, Gantt began developing some very different ideas regarding the role of the industrial engineer and the business firm as an institution. In 1916, he deplored the failure of American industrial leadership which, in his opinion, was caused by the rise of leaders to power based on their influence and not their merit. Gantt's new leadership would be based on fact, not opinion, and on ability, not favoritism. The industrial engineer would be the new leader, not the financier nor the labor leader, because only the engineer could cope with the American problem of production as the creation of wealth. The engineers would be an educated elite to lead America, not with a concern for profits, but by stressing productive efficiency. Gantt's own notions regarding these changes were partially due to his reading of Thorstein Veblen but mostly attributable to Charles Ferguson.[14] In 1916, Gantt formed an organization called the "New Machine" whose membership comprised engineers and other sympathetic reformers who sought to acquire political as well as economic power. Charles Ferguson, Gantt's inspiration, was a minister who had served as an idea man for Colonel Edward M. House, President Wilson's adviser. Ferguson was a "joyous mystic" who preached a "religion of democracy" which would summon forth "an aristocracy of the capable to put down the rule of the mob and destroy privilege."[15] Gantt's New Machine operated on the premise that the engineer would form this "aristocracy of the capable." In a letter to President Wilson, the leaders of the New Machine called on the President to transfer the "control of the huge and delicate apparatus [i.e., industry] into the hands of those who understand its operation," to set up employment bureaus for better placement of men, and for "public service banks" to extend credit on the basis of ability and personality rather than property.[16]

Once the New Machine was rolling, Gantt lost his concern for mere factory matters and sought broader areas for reform. He attacked the profit system itself and on this point he appears to be largely influenced by the swirl of world events. In 1917, the Czar was overthrown and collectivism came by violent bloodshed in

[14] Alford, p. 264.
[15] Samuel Haber, *Efficiency and Uplift*, Chicago: University of Chicago Press, 1964, p. 45.
[16] Alford, pp. 269–277.

Russia. America herself had a "great red scare" in 1919 and anarchists were seen lurking everywhere. The Socialist Eugene Debs was something of a folk hero, there had been Communist uprisings in Bavaria and Hungary, the "Wobblies" (the International Workers of the World) were provoking labor unrest, and most Americans were firmly convinced that the Bolsheviks were about to overturn society. In the preface to his last book, written in 1919, Gantt said:

The attempt which extreme radicals all over the world are making to get control of both the political and business systems on the theory that they would make the industrial and business system serve the community, is a real danger so long as our present system does not accomplish that end . . . in order to resume our advance toward the development of an unconquerable democratic civilization, we must purge our economic system of all autocratic practices of whatever kind, and return to the democratic principle of rendering service, which was the basis of its wonderful growth.[17]

Gantt said that businessmen had emphasized profits, sought monopolies, and had forgotten to give "service" to the community. He said the businessman "has forgotten that his business system had its foundation in service, and as far as the community is concerned has no reason for existence except the service it can render."[18] Gantt's answer was that America could be saved without revolution by forming "public service corporations." These corporations would be financed by public money and profits would be returned to the community. Gantt did not specify any industries, nor the extent of such a plan, but he felt that this plan would insure that both labor and management would get their deserved shares and the "push and pull" wastes of competition would be eliminated. As he saw the situation: " . . . *the business system must accept its social responsibility and devote itself primarily to service, or the community will ultimately make the attempt to take it over in order to operate it in its own interest.*"[19] This position posed a paradox, for in an interview shortly before his death, he said:

I am in favor of an organization similar to a cartel system. If in every industry we had a committee consisting of representatives of producers, distributors, and consumers, such a committee could fix prices with due regard to supply and demand . . .[20]

[17] H. L. Gantt, *Organizing for Work*, New York: Harcourt, Brace, Jovanovich, 1919, pp. iv–v.
[18] *Ibid.*, p. 5.
[19] *Ibid.*, p. 15.
[20] *New York Sunday World*, October 12, 1919, cited by L. P. Alford, p. 298.

And further:

> . . . the engineer, who is a man of few opinions and many facts and many deeds, should be accorded the economic leadership which is his proper place in our economic system.[21]

Unfortunately, Gantt's ideas in his later years are vague and contradictory. On the one hand he called for service and social responsibility; on the other, a socialistic device of public service corporations. He wanted labor and management to receive rewards according to "services rendered," yet he would want a committee to fix prices of products. He would replace autocracy with democracy yet felt that a managerial elite, composed primarily of engineers, would be the most capable in running the system. In November, 1919, Gantt was stricken with a "digestive disturbance" and died at the age of fifty-eight years. After Gantt's death, the New Machine dissolved. Henry Laurence Gantt, the most unorthodox of Taylor's followers, had come to the ultimate conclusion that the mental revolution must be in the hands of the engineer and that the mutuality of interests was to be found in cartels and public service corporations.

PARTNERS FOR LIFE: THE GILBRETHS

Frank Bunker (1868–1924) and Lillian Moller Gilbreth (1878–   ) formed a husband and wife team that brought not only color but significance to the early management movement. Frank was the son of a Maine hardware merchant and he learned early the virtues of frugality and thrift characteristic of New England puritanism.[22] When he was three, his father died and the family moved to Boston where he was educated at Andover and the Rice Grammar School. He prepped for the Massachusetts Institute of Technology, passed the qualifying exams, but decided instead to become an apprentice bricklayer at the tender age of 17. He rose to become chief superintendent of the Whidden Company and then launched his own career as an independent con-

---

[21] *Ibid.*, p. 296.

[22] Biographical information on the Gilbreths is from Edna Yost, *Frank and Lillian Gilbreth: Partners for Life,* New Brunswick, N.J.: Rutgers University Press, 1949. Popularized versions of their lives may be found in *Cheaper by the Dozen,* by Frank B. Gilbreth, Jr. and Ernestine Gilbreth Carey, New York: Thomas Y. Crowell Co., 1948; and (same authors) *Belles on Their Toes,* New York: Thomas Y. Crowell Co., 1950.

tractor in 1895 where his work formed the basis for his first investigations and publications. Though working independently of Taylor, Gilbreth's early work closely paralleled what Taylor was doing.
In his later years, he formed his own management consulting company and became closely associated with the scientific management
movement. It was to the good fortune of modern management
that Frank married Lillian Moller for they formed a complementary
team whose combined intellectual interests and assets brought a
new dimension to the inchoate field of management. Lillian was
the daughter of a German-born sugar refiner and spent her early
years in Oakland, California. Her family was relatively prosperous
and she was schooled early in the responsibilities of home and children. Lillian was an exceptionally bright student, receiving her
bachelor's and master's degrees in English from the University of
California. She interrupted her work on her doctors' degree for a
trip east; on that trip she met Frank, and their marriage in 1904
brought together two people who lived a most significant partnership, reminiscent of the Curies. After the marriage, Lillian decided
to change her academic interests to psychology, for she thought
that this field would best complement the work her husband was
doing. Combining marriage and the ever growing family (there
were eventually twelve children) with her assistance to Frank's
work, Lillian continued to do her research on her doctor's thesis and
finally submitted it in 1912. The greatest blow came when the
University of California informed her that the thesis was acceptable
but that she would have to return to campus for a year of residency
before the degree could be granted. Lillian had been led to believe
that this requirement would be waived in her case but the
university officials were steadfast. Frank was furious and began
shopping around for a publisher. The *Industrial Engineering Magazine* published it in serial form (May 1912–May 1913) and it was
eventually published in book form by the firm of Sturgis and Walton with the proviso that the author be listed as "L. M. Gilbreth"
with no mention that the author was a woman.[23] The thesis-turned-
book, *The Psychology of Management*, stands in the literature as
one of the earliest contributions to understanding the human factor

---

[23] Yost, p. 213. Lillian, like many women of that period, faced discrimination at
every turn. Though she had earned a Phi Beta Kappa key at California, her name
was omitted from the list of recipients. The "key" was later granted by the
university.

in industry. Eventually the California authorities agreed that she could spend her "residency" in any college which gave an advanced degree in industrial psychology or management. These were scarce at that time but Frank discovered that Brown University was planning to offer a Ph.D. degree in "Applied Management;" after the proper preparation and waiting Lillian received her Ph.D. in 1915. This was not the culmination but the beginning of many years of hard work. Frank's work became more famous and Lillian's work on fatigue and psychology was a valuable supplement. Even after Frank's death in 1924, Lillian has continued to this day to be the "First Lady of Management." In 1931 she was the first recipient of what became an established, much-sought-after award, The Gilbreth Medal, originally given by the Society of Industrial Engineers, and later an award of the Society for Advancement of Management. She was Professor of Management at Purdue University (1935–48) and her other contributions, honors, honorary degrees, and awards would fill many pages.[24] Here were two, and then one, of our most esteemed contributors to management thought.

Systematizing the Construction Industry

Though Frank Gilbreth was a contemporary of the founders of the scientific management movement, his own early work was done apart from any knowledge of what was happening at Midvale Steel. One of the first things he noted as a bricklayer's apprentice was the diversity in methods and speeds used by the workers. One set of motions was used for working fast, another for the slow pace, and yet another for teaching others how to lay bricks. Though bricklaying was one of man's oldest occupations, Gilbreth set out to develop in writing the best ways of laying bricks, handling materials, rigging scaffolding, training apprentices and in general improving methods while lowering costs and yet paying higher wages. The essence of the system of work he was developing as a superintendent, as a contractor, and later as a consultant was published as the *Field System*, the *Concrete System*, and the *Bricklaying System*.[25]

[24] Lillian Moller Gilbreth celebrated her ninety-third birthday May 24, 1971.

[25] Portions of these are reprinted in William R. Spriegel and Clark E. Meyers (eds.), *The Writing of the Gilbreths*, Homewood, Ill., Richard D. Irwin, 1953, pp. 3–65.

The *Field System* was an accounting system without a set of books. It was designed to aid the construction contractor by showing costs, costs related to estimates, and the total cost of the job each Saturday up to the previous Thursday. No bookkeepers were needed since the original memorandum or receipt was filed and there was no general ledger. Gilbreth developed other facets of the field system and included detailed instructions for its use, even including a rule about no smoking on the job and the admonition that whistle blasts at starting and quitting time should not be over 4 seconds long. He established a suggestion system including a $10 first prize each month for the best idea on how to improve work, give better service to customers, or secure additional construction jobs. Included in the field system were provisions for photographing working conditions at the time of any accident for use in lawsuits or other claims. Another part of the system was a "white list" card. This was an early appraisal form for workers which the foreman filled out on both desirables and undesirables. In an intermittent, transient trade such as construction, the Gilbreth "white list" became a valuable source of information for employers. Though his advice was quite detailed and applicable to construction, it was indicative of Gilbreth's desire to rationalize the workplace and is reminiscent of what the whole scientific management movement was attempting.

The *Concrete System* contained detailed advice to concrete contractors. Gilbreth wrote here too of directing the workers, including the necessity of "athletic contests" between work groups to give them a spirit of competition in completing the job. The total job was divided into equal groups of men who competed to finish a wall or build concrete pillars. The *Bricklaying System* was also technical but brought forth a new facet of study to the young Gilbreth. The original concern was with the training of young apprentices and Gilbreth saw the wastes of hand-me-down instruction from experienced workers. He proposed the remedial step of finding the best way of laying bricks through motion study, followed by instruction and insisting that the emphasis be placed on *learning* the right way before maximum output was expected of the young worker. This early work was but a prelude to his later in-depth analysis of motions and fatigue. One characteristic of Gilbreth's life-long quest was that he asked the workers to help improve methods and achieve motion economy for *their own sake* as well as for management's. He not only taught the workers how to handle bricks but *why* that way was best. He thought pride was an essential part of learning a trade and that this came only if you knew your trade well. He stressed economy of effort, not speed, and sought to show how to improve productivity with no greater physical exertion. The result of his extensive analysis of bricklaying showed that motions could be reduced from 18½ to 4 and that men could increase their output from 1,000 to 2,700 bricks laid per day with no greater effort. Like Taylor, Gilbreth found that the conditions of work greatly affected output; accordingly, he developed different types of scaffolding to suit the job, precise instructions on mortar consistency and trowel usage, and a "packet system" for proper conveyance and placement of bricks for the worker. Being a trained bricklayer himself undoubtedly helped Gilbreth win worker cooperation; however, he demonstrated early the need for worker involvement in making improvements, including incentives to do so, an emphasis on training, and finally the need to systematize without speeding up the worker.

Extending Motion and Fatigue Study

In 1907, after he had developed the rudiments of his construction systems, Gilbreth met Frederick Taylor. They had a great deal in common and Gilbreth soon developed into one of Taylor's most fervent advocates.[26] Their work interests were essentially parallel although they differed in terminology: Taylor called his work "time study" and Gilbreth called his "motion study." In practice they were measuring the same thing, with similar objectives of eliminating motions to reduce fatigue and improve productivity. Gilbreth maintained that the stop watch was not an essential ingredient to his system and his bricklaying studies were of motions only. After Gilbreth came into contact with Taylor and began to refine his own system, he developed more and more intricate uses of the time dimensions of work. In one of the many amusing anecdotes about the Gilbreths in *Cheaper by the Dozen*, the children wrote that Frank was always the "efficiency expert" at home

[26] Nadworny has presented evidence that Gilbreth admired Taylor but not vice versa. Taylor and his followers distrusted Gilbreth because his consulting and micromotion analysis conflicted with Taylor's time study. Only after Taylor's death was there a *rapprochement* between micromotion study and time study. See Milton J. Nadworny, "Frederick Taylor and Frank Gilbreth—Competition in Scientific Management," *Business History Review*, Vol. 31, No. 1 (Spring, 1957), pp. 23–34.

and on the job. He buttoned his vest from the bottom up, instead of top down, because the former took only three seconds and the latter took seven. He used two shaving brushes to lather his face and found that he could reduce shaving time by 17 seconds. He tried shaving with two razors, found that he could reduce the total shaving time by 44 seconds, but abandoned this scheme because it took two minutes per bandage applied to the cuts. His children suggest that it was the two lost minutes that bothered him and not the cuts.[27]

At Providence, Rhode Island, while Lillian was working on her doctorate, Gilbreth turned his attention away from construction and extended motion study to the general field of manufacturing. Fatigue became a major focus of attention and he received help from Mrs. Gilbreth in studying its causes and effects. The prevailing theory of the period was that fatigue was caused by a toxin generated by physical exertion and released in the blood. Every motion caused fatigue; hence any elimination of motions reduced fatigue. Gilbreth's analysis proceeded to isolating worker variables such as anatomy, habits, mode of living, etc., and variables in worker surroundings such as clothes, colors of walls, lighting, heating, tools, etc. He finally isolated 15 worker variables, 14 variables in the surroundings, and 13 "variables of motion" such as acceleration, length, path, etc. As he developed his study, he found it difficult for the human eye to follow motions and the study of gross movements was inadequate for the preciseness he needed.

He developed two techniques to overcome this deficiency: one, a list of micro-motions of the most elementary motions; and two, the use of motion picture cameras and lights. Gross analysis of movements, such as "reach for tool," told Gilbreth little about the elements of that move. Accordingly, he developed a list of 17 basic motions, each called a "therblig" (Gilbreth spelled backward with the "th" transposed) such as "search," "select," "transport loaded," "position," "hold," etc.[28] These fundamental motions could not be further subdivided and gave Gilbreth a

[27] Frank B. Gilbreth, Jr. and Ernestine G. Carey, *Cheaper By The Dozen*, p. 3.

[28] In 1851, Charles Babbage published his *Laws of Mechanical Notation* which contained methods for studying machine movements. According to Mrs. Gilbreth, Frank was an admirer of Babbage's work and Hoaglund suggests that Gilbreth applied to human movements the same ideas and symbols that Babbage used for machine movements. John H. Hoaglund, "Management Before Frederick Taylor," reprinted in Paul M. Dauten, Jr. (ed.), *Current Issues and Emerging Concepts in Management,* Boston: Houghton Mifflin Co. 1962, p. 27.

more precise way of analyzing the exact elements of any worker movement.

The second technique used the then infant technology of the motion picture camera. Gilbreth placed a large-faced clock, calibrated in fractions of minutes, in the camera's field of vision of the worker being studied. The pictures enabled Gilbreth to time the smallest motion of the worker. This was the beginning of what Gilbreth called "micro-motion" study.

He also developed the "cyclegraphic" technique of attaching a small electric light bulb to the hand, finger, or arm of the worker which allowed photographs to show a path of light through space as the worker moved. His "chronocyclegraph" used a flashing bulb which showed acceleration and deceleration of movements by appearing in the film as a series of pear shaped dots. Gilbreth found these laborious, meticulous methods necessary to improve methods, demonstrate correct motions, and to train new operators.[29]

One should not confuse the techniques with what the Gilbreths were trying to build. Their search for efficiency and economy included flow charts of both products and men's work, a three-position plan of promotion, and the impact of motion study on the worker. All of their techniques were focused on eliminating waste in industry. The promotion plan was designed to prepare men for advancement and as a morale and incentive booster. Each man was considered to hold three positions in the organization: first, the position he last occupied and in which he was now serving as a teacher to his successor; second, his present position; and third, as one preparing for the next highest position. The system required charting promotion paths and records for appraising performance, and kept the worker from getting lodged in blind alley jobs. The psychology of motion study was to impress upon the worker the benefits of reducing fatigue and improving pay through motion study. According to the Gilbreths, monotony came not from performing the job the same way each time, but from the "lack of interest" of management in the worker. Motion and

[29] The preceding material is a summary of more detailed descriptions found in F. B. Gilbreth, *Motion Study*, New York: Van Nostrand Reinhold Co., 1911; and F. B. and L. M. Gilbreth, *Fatigue Study*, New York: Sturgis and Walton Co., 1916; and F. B. and L. M. Gilbreth, *Applied Motion Study*, New York: Sturgis and Walton Co., 1917.

fatigue study displayed management's interest and facilitated the elimination of monotony.

Support for the Scientific Management Movement

During 1911, a number of A.S.M.E. members were finding it difficult to get papers on management recognized by that organization. A rump faction, led by Frank Gilbreth, formed a separate organization, first called the Society to Promote the Science of Management, then after Taylor's death, The Taylor Society.[30] Gilbreth was a vocal supporter of Taylor's in the Eastern rate hearings and participated in coining the term "scientific management." Like Taylor, he preferred the term "Taylor system" but his *Primer of Scientific Management* was designed to answer questions about this "new" phenomenon made famous by the rate hearings and the Congressional investigation. In the Foreword, Louis Brandeis said:

. . . the Primer will prove of greatest value in helping to remove from the minds of workingmen misapprehensions which have led some well-meaning labor leaders to oppose a movement from which labor has most to gain.[31]

Gilbreth proceeded in the *Primer* to pose common questions about scientific management and to provide answers in very basic terminology about the philosophy and practice of scientific management. No new information was provided but the expository device of questions and answers reflected an excellent approach to win over adherents to the cause. The following are merely examples:

Q. *Does it [scientific management] not make machines out of men?*
A. . . . Is a good boxer, or fencer, or golf player a machine? He certainly approaches closely the 100% mark of perfection from the standpoint of the experts in motion study. It is not nearly so important to decide whether or not he is a machine as to decide whether or not it is desirable to have a man trained as near perfection as possible . . .[32]
Q. *Does not the monotony of the highly specialized subdivision of work cause the men to become insane?*
A. . . . No, he will not become insane, for if his brain is of such an order that his work does not stimulate it to its highest degree, then he will be pro-

---

[30] In 1936, the Taylor Society and the Society of Industrial Engineers merged to form the Society for Advancement of Management.
[31] F. B. Gilbreth, *Primer of Scientific Management*, New York: Van Nostrand Reinhold Co., 1912, p. vii.
[32] *Ibid.*, pp. 49–50.

moted, for under Scientific Management each man is specially trained to occupy that place that is the highest that he is capable . . .[33]

Q. *Does not the "speed boss" speed up the men to a point that is injurious to their health?*

A. "Speed boss," like "task," is an unfortunate name . . . the speed boss does not tell the men how fast they shall make their motions . . . [but he does] tell the men at what speeds their machines shall run.[34]

Q. *If Scientific Management is a good thing for the workers, why do the labor leaders all oppose it?*

A. They do not all oppose it. Some oppose it for the simple reason that they do not understand it; the others have visions that Scientific Management is something that will reduce the value of their jobs,—and all are afraid, because of the bad treatment that workmen as a whole have had in the past, that Scientific Management is simply a new 'confidence game,' presented in a more attractive manner than ever before . . . they simply cannot imagine Dr. Taylor or any other practical man working for their interests unless there is a "comeback" somewhere . . .[35]

Like Taylor, Gilbreth reaped the wrath of labor as he became more closely aligned with the scientific management movement. He had never encountered any strikes under his methods until 1910. Unlike Taylor, who thought that standards were the sole prerogative of management, Gilbreth had enlisted the cooperation of organized labor on the jobs. The continued ill-will of labor and the necessity to get to a campus for Lillian's work resulted in his leaving the contracting business and becoming an efficiency engineer in his own consulting company in 1914.

The Psychology of Management

Dr. Lillian Moller Gilbreth played an important role in her husband's work and earned as well a substantial reputation on her own.[36] Her doctor's thesis, published in book form before she received her degree, applied the findings of psychology to the workplace. She was not the originator of industrial psychology,

[33] *Ibid.*, pp. 53–54.

[34] *Ibid.*, p. 65.

[35] *Ibid.*, pp. 87–88.

[36] For instance, Dr. Gilberth made significant contributions to the field of home economics by applying the principles and techniques of scientific management to the home. See Lillian M. Gilbreth, *The Home-Maker and Her Job*, New York: Appleton-Century-Crofts, 1927; and *Management in the Home: Happier Living Through Saving Time and Energy*, New York: Dodd, Mead and Co., 1955. The married reader might develop more empathy for the resistance F. W. Taylor encountered by reading these books and applying Dr. Gilbreth's advice to the work of his wife!

since Hugo Munsterberg had opened up that field earlier, but she brought a human element into scientific management through her training, insight, and understanding.

She began by defining the psychology of management as "the effect of the mind that is directing work upon that work which is directed, and the effect of this undirected and directed work upon the mind of the worker."[37] Heretofore, management had been considered an area in which no one could hope to succeed unless he had the inherited "knack"; with scientific management, it became possible to found management on laws and to study it in the classroom. Successful management "lies on the *man*, not on the work," and scientific management provided a means to make the most of man's efforts. Dr. Gilbreth characterized three historical styles of management: (1) traditional; (2) transitory; and (3) scientific. Traditional management was the "driver" or "Marquis of Queensbury" style that followed the unitary line of command and was typified by centralized authority. The Marquis of Queensbury term was adapted from prize-fighting because she felt that it typified the physical and mental contest waged between worker and manager "according to the rules of the game." "Transitory" management referred to all forms in the interim stage between the traditional and the installation of scientific management. "Scientific," with synonyms of "measured functional," "ultimate," or the "Taylor plan of management," described the goal toward which all firms should be striving.

Dr. Gilbreth compared and contrasted these three styles of management according to how they affected individuality, functionalization, measurement, analysis and synthesis, standardization, records and programs, teaching, incentives, and welfare. On individuality, she noted that psychologists up to that time had been largely concerned with the "psychology of the crowd." Comparatively little work had been done on the psychology of the individual. Under traditional management, individuality was stifled by the power of the central figure; under scientific management, it became a fundamental principle in selection, incentives, and in overall consideration of worker "welfare," *i.e.*, "general well-being,

[37] L. M. Gilbreth, *The Psychology of Management: The Function of the Mind in Determining, Teaching and Installing Methods of Least Waste*, New York: Sturgis and Walton Co., 1914; reissued in 1921 by the Macmillan Co., p. 1.

mental, physical, moral and financial."[38] The object of scientific management was to develop each man to his fullest potential by strengthening his personal traits, special abilities, and skills. The focus was upon how management could develop the individual for their mutual benefit, not upon his use and exploitation as under the Marquis of Queensbury type.

Functionalization promoted worker welfare by improving skills through specialization, enabling greater pride in output and higher wages; measurement insured that the individual received the product of his labors; standardization improved morale and prevented the worker from becoming a machine; and teaching overcame fear and instilled pride and confidence in the worker. Traditional management relied solely on rewards and punishment while scientific management attempted to enlist worker cooperation. The rewards under scientific management differed because they were predetermined, insuring against fear of rate cutting, were prompt rather than delayed under profit sharing, and "personal" in the sense that the worker was rewarded for his efforts and not by his class of work. Under scientific management, the worker gained "mental poise and security" rather than the anxiety created by traditional management. Concerning welfare, scientific management promoted regular work, encouraged good personal habits, and fostered the physical, mental, moral, and financial development of the worker.

Dr. Gilbreth was pioneering in the psychology of management; she did not have the benefit of a half century of empirical evidence and statistical sophistication that has been the evolution of the field of psychology. The state of the art in psychology was embryonic also: Wilhelm Wundt was fathering experimental psychology; Hugo Munsterberg was opening the vistas of industrial psychology; Ebbinghaus was experimenting with the memorization of nonsense syllables; and William James was developing his theories of emotions and habit formation. Dr. Gilbreth's work was more management than psychology; nevertheless, it illustrated concern for the worker and attempted to show how scientific management would foster and not stifle the individual workman. It is not easy to be on the foremost fringes of a new idea. But someone must be there

[38] *Ibid.*, p. 30.

or all frontiers vanish. The Gilbreths were in the vanguard and the field of management is indebted to them.

EFFICIENCY THROUGH ORGANIZATION: HARRINGTON EMERSON

Harrington Emerson (1853–1931) was a Presbyterian minister's son who believed in the Protestant virtues of thrift and the economical use of resources. Educated at the Royal Bavarian Polytechnik in Munich, he was symbolic of the new breed of "efficiency engineers" who were bringing new methods of time and cost savings to the burgeoning American industry. Emerson began as a troubleshooter for the General Manager of the Burlington Railroad and went on from there to become a consultant to the Santa Fe Railroad, which was on the verge of a serious work stoppage. In three years (1904–1907), Emerson was able to restore harmonious labor relations, reduce costs 25 per cent, and yield the company $1.5 million in annual savings.[39] At this point in his career, Emerson perceived the need for applications of his efficiency concepts in areas other than the railroads. His work was largely independent of the Taylor movement although he had been corresponding with Taylor from 1903 onward. *The Engineering Magazine* was one of the earliest forums for the new management movement and in 1908 and 1909 it published a series of articles by Emerson which were later issued as a single volume to become the basis of his system.[40]

Waste and inefficiency were the evils that Emerson saw pervading the entire American industrial system. His experience had shown that railroad repair shops averaged 50 per cent efficiency and that preventable labor and material wastes were costing the railroad industry $300,000,000 annually (hence his well-publicized testimony of a million dollars a day savings). Inefficiency was not confined to the railroads but could be found in manufacturing, agriculture, and education. National productivity was not a function of the abundance or of the lack of natural resources among

[39] Biographical data and the early work of Harrington Emerson is from "High Priest of Efficiency," *Milestones of Management*, Vol. 1, editors of *Business Week*, 1964, pp. 8–9.

[40] Harrington Emerson, *Efficiency as a Basis for Operations and Wages*, New York: Engineering Magazine, 1911 (copyright 1909 by John R. Dunlap).

different countries but the cause of prosperity was "ambition, the desire for success and wealth."[41] America had the wealth of resources and the stimulus of individual ambition for gain, yet amid all of this which had led to the rise of the United States as a world industrial power, she was losing her advantage due to inefficiency and wasted resource efforts. To Emerson, one of the greatest problems was the lack of *organization*. Only through proper organization could machines, materials, and human efforts be directed to improve efficiency and reduce waste.

Line and Staff Organization

Taylor's functional foreman ideas did not appeal to Emerson. He agreed with Taylor that the specialized knowledge of staff personnel was necessary but differed in how to bring this about. Influenced by his European education, Emerson admired the organizational efforts of General Von Moltke who had developed the general staff concept and made the Prussian army the tremendously efficient machine it was in the mid-nineteenth century.[42] The theory of the general staff concept was that each subject vital to military efforts was studied to perfection by a separate staff specialist and that the combined wisdom of these specialists emanated from a supreme general staff to advise the commander.

Standing alone and unaided, the line organization had serious deficiencies. Emerson sought to apply these staff principles to industrial practice to bring about "complete parallelism between line and staff, so that every member of the line can at any time have the benefit of staff knowledge and staff assistance."[43] Each firm was to have a "chief of staff" and four major subgroupings of staff head under him: one for "men" to "plan, direct, and advise" on everything pertaining to the well-being of employees; a second to advise on "structures, machines, tools, and other equipment"; a third for "materials" to include their purchase, custody, issue, and handling; and the fourth for "methods and conditions" to include standards, records, and accounting. Staff advice was available to all organizational levels and focused on planning: "It is the business of staff,

---

[41] *Ibid.*, p. 37. *Cf.* McClelland's thesis in Chapter 2.

[42] *Ibid.*, pp. 64–66. Karl von Clausewitz noted the use of the general staff concept in the Prussian Army as early as 1793. Karl von Clausewitz, *On War*, New York: Random House, 1943, p. 489; originally published in 1832.

[43] Emerson, *Efficiency as a Basis for Operations and Wages*, p. 69.

not to accomplish work, but to set up standards and ideals, so that the line may work more efficiently."[44] The distinction between Emerson and Taylor is thus apparent: instead of making one person responsible for and with authority over each particular shop function, Emerson leaves supervision and authority to the line which operates on the basis of planning and *advice* by the staff. This shift maintained the advantages of specialized knowledge without the disadvantages of splitting the chain of command.

Principles of Efficiency

Emerson made other contributions in the areas of cost accounting, the use of Hollerith punch card tabulating machines in accounting records, and in setting standards for judging worker and shop efficiency. He devised an incentive system which paid the worker a 20 per cent bonus for 100 per cent efficiency (the standard time); above the 100 per cent efficiency level the worker received in addition his wages for the time he saved plus the 20-per cent bonus. For example, at 100-per cent efficiency, the bonus was 20 cents per $1.00 of wages; at 120-per cent efficiency, 40 cents per $1.00 of wages; and 140-per cent, 60 cents.[45]

Emerson's efficiency work was somewhat overshadowed by the Taylor system and in part this was due to the railroad rate hearings. Emerson was one of the witnesses and his studies of railroad efficiency were used by Louis Brandeis to show that the railroads did not need a rate increase if they applied the methods of the newly named "scientific management." Subsequent to the hearings, Emerson published his *Twelve Principles of Efficiency*, which became another landmark in the history of management thought. A chapter was devoted to each of the twelve principles and, broadly conceived, the first five concerned relations with men and the remainder concerned methods, institutions, and systems. The "principles" were not isolated ones but interdependent and coordinated to form a structure for building a management system. In the Preface, Emerson stated his basic premise:

"It is not labor, not capital, not land, that has created modern wealth or is creating it today. It is *ideas* that create wealth, and what is wanted is

[44] *Ibid.*, p. 112.
[45] *Ibid.*, pp. 193–196. A table for computing bonus at all levels is found on p. 195. At 120 per cent, for example, 40 cents = 20 cents for bonus and 20 cents for working 20 per cent more efficiently.

more ideas—more uncovering of natural reservoirs, and less labor and capital and land per unit of production."[46]

Ideas were the dominant force and these must be focused on eliminating waste and creating a more efficient industrial system. Principles were the instruments to reach this goal and the basis of all principles was the line-staff form of organization because Emerson felt that "the industrial hook-worm disease is defective organization."[47]   The first principle was "clearly defined ideals." This principle made explicit the need for agreement among all organizational participants as to ideals and to pull in a "straight line." He did not use the term "objectives" as modern authors do, but "ideals" meant essentially the same thing. He hoped to reduce intra-organizational conflict, vagueness, uncertainty, and the aimlessness which arose when people did not understand and/or share a common purpose. Second, "common sense"; this principle exhorted managers to take a larger view of problems and their relationships and to seek special knowledge and advice wherever it could be found. Third, "competent counsel" was related to the second principle in that it pertained to building a competent staff force. "Discipline" became the fourth and provided for obedience and adherence to organizational rules. It was a foundation for the other eleven principles and made the organization a system rather than anarchy. The fifth and final principle pertaining to men was the "fair deal." The fair deal depended upon the ability of the manager to establish a system of justice and fairness in all dealings with the worker. It was not a patronizing or altruistic relationship but one of mutual advantage.

The seven principles pertaining to methods were more mechanistic and largely self-explanatory: "reliable, immediate, accurate, and permanent records" (information and accounting systems); "despatching" [sic] (planning and routing of work); "standards and schedules" (methods and times for tasks); "standardized conditions"; "standardized operations"; "written standard practice instructions"; and "efficiency reward" (the incentive plan). Each principle was liberally sprinkled with examples of Emerson's consulting experience and formed a thorough, though often redundant, statement of his system.

[46] Harrington Emerson. *The Twelve Principles of Efficiency*, New York: Engineering Magazine, 1913, p. x.
[47] *Ibid.*, p. 29.

Harrington Emerson achieved renown in his own time and his consulting firm endures today. He testified before the House Committee on Taylorism and other efficiency systems, served as one of the experts on the Hoover Committee, which published *Elimination of Waste in Industry*, helped found the Efficiency Society (1912), and through his associates tried to bring more ethical practices to the field of management consulting by forming the Association of Consulting Management Engineers (1933). Harrington Emerson was a pioneer in spreading the gospel of efficiency.

THE GOSPEL IN NON-INDUSTRIAL ORGANIZATIONS: MORRIS COOKE

While Taylor, Barth, the Gilbreths, Gantt, and Emerson were searching for efficiency in industrial enterprises, Morris Llewellyn Cooke (1872–1960) was extending the gospel of efficiency to educational and municipal organizations. After receiving a B.S. in Mechanical Engineering from Lehigh University (1895), Cooke went to work in industry and was soon applying a "questioning method" to the wastes of industry long before he met or heard of F. W. Taylor.[48] As Taylor began to publish and be known more widely, Cooke became an avid reader and defender of what Taylor was espousing. He eventually met Taylor and evidently impressed him, since Taylor asked Cooke to become a member of a committee studying the administrative effectiveness of the A.S.M.E. Taylor personally financed the study and paid Cooke's salary; during the year-and-a-half study their friendship grew and Cooke became one of the "insiders" in the scientific management movement. Distrustful of the so-called new breed of "efficiency engineers," Taylor designated only four men as his disciples, Barth, Gantt, H. K. Hathaway, and Cooke. Once, on one of his assignments, Cooke saw a sign over the workers' entrance to a factory reading "Hands Entrance"; he asked the owner "where do the heads and hearts enter?"—the sign was promptly removed.[49] Perhaps he was being flippant, but he made his point—scientific management called for more than "hands."

[48] An excellent biography of Cooke is by Kenneth E. Trombley, *The Life and Times of a Happy Liberal: Morris Llewellyn Cooke*, New York: Harper and Row, 1954.

[49] *Ibid.*, p. 10.

In 1909, the president of the Carnegie Foundation for the Advancement of Teaching wrote Taylor asking for help in "an economic study" of administration in educational organizations. Taylor sent Cooke and the resulting study was a bombshell in the academic world.[50] Although only physics departments were studied since it was believed that they were representative of the existing level of teaching and research, Cooke included nothing in his final report that he did not feel applied to other departments as well. The report was quite lengthy and detailed and Cooke attempted something that few had been, or are today, eager to do, *i.e.* measure the cost of input efforts and the resulting output in teaching and research.

His findings were quite upsetting: inbreeding (hiring your own graduates) was widespread; management practices in education were even worse than the acknowledged poor state of industrial practice; committee management was a curse; departments enjoyed excessive autonomy which worked against sound university coordination; professional pay should be based on merit and not longevity; and life tenure for professors should be scrapped and unfit teachers retired. Cooke recommended a "student hour" (one hour in class or laboratory per single student) as a standard to gauge the efficiency of professional effort. Professors should spend more time in teaching and research, leaving administration to specialists and not to committees. Assistants should be used more widely, allowing the higher-priced talent to take more complex jobs. Salary increases should be based on merit or efficiency and the costs of teaching and research should be more closely controlled by the central administration.

Initial reactions to the report were predictable: the president of the Massachusetts Institute of Technology said it read "as if the author received his training in a soap factory."[51] Nevertheless, some changes did come about and, though there are still inefficiencies and abuses, educational administration has made some progress, except perhaps, in the realm of committees.

The educational study had marked Cooke as an iconoclast, and there is no evidence that he was dismayed by the criticism he received. Following in Taylor's path, he knew the inevitability of

[50] M. L. Cooke, *Academic and Industrial Efficiency,* New York: Carnegie Foundation for the Advancement of Teaching, Bulletin No. 5, 1910.

[51] Trombley, p. 11.

resistance. In 1911, a newly elected reform mayor of Philadelphia asked Taylor to help out with municipal administration. Once more, Taylor sent Cooke into the breach. Cooke had been itching for reform ever since he had been bullied by a machine politician while Cooke was a poll watcher for the reform party. In the new administration, Cooke became the director of Public Works and brought scientific management to the governance of Philadelphia. In four years he saved the city over $1 million in garbage collection costs, achieved a $1¼ million reduction in utility rates, fired 1,000 workers who were inefficient, established pension and benefit funds, opened channels of communication for workers and managers, and moved municipal administration from smoke-filled rooms into the sunshine. His book *Our Cities Awake* put forth his case for better-managed municipalities through application of the principles of scientific management.[52] He successfully established a "functional management" organization patterned after Taylor's ideas, revamped budgeting procedures, hired numerous "experts" to replace political favorites, espoused management of the city by a professional "city manager," and sought to replace committees by individuals who had responsibility and authority. He called for "cooperation" by offering an early idea of participation in management decision making:

Here then is a work [job] in which we can all have a hand, a work which will always be ineffectually done if it is confined to well-educated and highly trained men at the top . . . administrative leadership will in the future more and more consist in getting the largest possible number "into the play" in having the great body of employees increasingly critical in their judgments about both their own work and the work which is going on around them.[53]

Cooke saw that it was not the system, but the *confidence* of the people in the system that made scientific management effective.

After his work in Philadelphia and the pleas for municipal reform, Cooke opened his own consulting firm in 1916. Like the other pioneers, he contributed his knowledge to the War Department during World War I. Always concerned with gaining the cooperation of labor, he became increasingly interested in the growing national labor movement. He became a close friend of and adviser to Samuel Gompers, president of the American Federation of Labor. Cooke saw his task as that of bringing the labor and

[52] M. L. Cooke, *Our Cities Awake*, New York: Doubleday and Co., 1918.
[53] *Ibid.*, p. 98.

management factions together in a time when they were becoming more antagonistic. His advice was that labor was just as responsible for production as management; increased production improved the lot of both and it would form an effective barrier against both unemployment and low wages.[54] This thesis was repeated in Mr. Cooke's last book, co-authored with Philip Murray.[55] During the administration of Franklin D. Roosevelt, Cooke held numerous positions, chief among them administrator of the Rural Electrification Administration and of the New York State Power Authority. He also served as a trouble-shooter for President Harry S. Truman; and when Cooke was asked by his biographer to list his lifetime accomplishments, he replied: "Rural electrification, inexpensive electricity in our homes, progress in labor-management relations, conservation of our land and water and scientific management in industry."[56] To scientific management Morris Cooke had brought new ideas to develop the harmonious cooperation between labor and management. He wanted more participation by workers, but most of all he sought to enlist the aid of the leaders of organized labor. If scientific management was to make any headway in the twentieth century, it required a man like Cooke to open the new vistas in non-industrial organizations and to gain the support of the American labor movement.

SUMMARY

The adolescence of a movement is analogous to life's teen-age years in growth, rebellion, and the search for the mellowing of adulthood. From Taylor's notion of science in management at Midvale and Bethlehem to the maturity of the movement in the 1920's, scientific management had its adolescence of diversity in the individuals examined in this chapter. Carl Barth was the true believer who became a faithful executioner of Taylor's orthodoxy. Henry Gantt began under Taylor's guidance, contributed significantly, and then strayed from the flock in his later years. The Gilbreths added refinement to Taylor's time study, enlarged

---

[54] Trombley, pp. 90–91.

[55] M. L. Cooke and Philip Murray, *Organized Labor and Production,* New York: Harper and Row, 1940. Murray was President of the Congress of Industrial Organizations (CIO) and the United Steel Workers of America.

[56] Trombley, p. 249.

the study of fatigue, and emphasized the psychology of scientific management.   Harrington Emerson polished Taylor's notions of efficiency, rejected his functional-foremen and wage-incentive schemes, and brought national recognition to the movement at the Eastern rate hearings.   Morris Cooke, nurtured by Taylor, brought the system to academic and municipal undertakings and sought a *rapprochement* between scientific management and organized labor.   The gospel of efficiency had its doctrine, but cracks were beginning to appear in the edifice as changing times brought new emphases.

8

Scientific Management in Europe and America

While Taylor and his associates furnished the impetus for scientific management, there were a number of individuals who were bringing the movement to its maturity along a number of dimensions. First, there was the immediate acceptance and applicability of scientific management in Europe, especially as an aid to management in World War I. Second, there was emerging recognition of the need to formalize the study of management in college curricula as well as in educating the industrial leader. Finally, there were numerous installations of scientific management in industry and a general spreading of its influence on other disciplines. This chapter will examine scientific management along these dimensions as well as explore a number of other individuals who were adding to, amending, and otherwise bringing the notion of science in management to its maturity.

SCIENTIFIC MANAGEMENT GOES ABROAD

Whereas the Industrial Revolution began in Europe and spread to America, the "scientific management revolution" began in America and spread abroad. As early as 1907, Taylor's time study methods were being introduced in France and World War I brought Europe's immediate attention to the possibilities of using scientific management to improve productivity.

Taylorism and Fayolism

The Frenchman Henri Fayol published his *Administration Industrielle et Générale* in 1916. Fayol's work, though recognized in Europe, remained in the intellectual shadow of Taylorism during the early part of the twentieth century. This was due to two primary forces: (1) the immediate applicability of Tayloristic efficiency devices to the French war effort; (2) the translation and popularization of Taylor's work by Henri Le Chatelier and Charles de Freminville. Georges Clemenceau, France's Minister of War, ordered all plants engaged in the war effort to study and apply Taylor's methods of systematic management. Despite America's intense interest in management, Henri Fayol was unknown until other times and other cultural conditions could bring his ideas to the fore. To Le Chatelier fell the task of propagating Taylorism in French-speaking Europe. He translated *The Principles of Scientific Management*, became a close friend of Taylor, and a leading exponent of his views in Europe. Le Chatelier added little to management thought himself; his contributions consisted in the elucidation of Taylor's philosophy, principles, and methods, and this did much to demonstrate the validity of scientific management in Europe.[1] Charles de Freminville was of lesser renown than Le Chatelier but likewise contributed to pioneering the management movement in France. As president of the Comité de l'Organisation Française, which served as the focal point for all activities devoted to the advancement of management in France, he helped fuse (for France) the two pioneering lives of Fayol and Taylor.[2]

The International Scientific Management Movement

The seeds having been sown, scientific management was soon to find other proponents who sought to bring its ideas and techniques under an ever-widening circle of influence. Edward Albert Filene (1860–1937) had pioneered in applying scientific methods to retail distribution in his family's Boston store. He had employed Frank Gilbreth as a consultant on employee training and evaluation and had attempted through other devices to bring science as well

---

[1] Lyndall Urwick and E.F.L. Brech, *The Making of Scientific Management; Thirteen Pioneers*, Vol. 1, London: Sir Isaac Pitman and Sons, 1951, pp. 93–103.
[2] *Ibid.*, pp. 105–110.

as human concern to retailing. In 1927, Filene was instrumental in forming the International Management Institute, located at Geneva, Switzerland, as an organization dedicated to spreading information about management abroad. The Institute's first Director was Lt. Col. Lyndall Urwick, who will be discussed in more detail later, and the office began functioning as a clearing house for international management. Unfortunately, the effort was short-lived. With the rise of Adolf Hitler to power, financial backers withdrew the organization's source of support and the Institute closed in 1933.[3]

The international management movement received mixed acceptance and underwent various transformations in various countries. In England, Taylorism was not well received. Taylor had engendered some bitterness with British manufacturers over patent rights to high speed steel and organized labor posed opposition so formidable that it made scientific management almost a negligible force.[4] In other countries, the international scientific management movement passed through various stages: first, the "propagandizing" and translations of men such as Le Chatelier; second, adaptation by various countries to meet their own needs; and finally, adjustment through various committees, conferences, and international organizations.[5] Different countries had varying political and economic structures which made it difficult to apply Taylorism in its pure form. Consequently, managers often grasped the mechanics of time study, incentive schemes, and so on, without applying the philosophy. Europe, having a long history of organized labor of an often radical nature, also encountered more resistance from unions than America. Further, an "anti-American" sentiment led to less-than-favorable reception before and during the War. The 1920's were marked, however, by a widespread recognition of the need for efficiency, and Taylorism was adapted to fit varying national goals. For example, the Germans stressed coordination between educational institutions and industry; the English emphasized industrial psychology and fatigue research;

---

[3] For further information on Filene, see Urwick, Golden Book, pp. 85–88; and Tom Mahoney, The Great Merchants, New York: Harper and Row, 1949, pp. 76–99.

[4] Urwick and Brech, The Making of Scientific Management, p. 111.

[5] Paul Devinat, Scientific Management in Europe, Geneva: International Labor Office, 1927.

the Swedes were primarily interested in standardization and sim-
plification; and the Russians charted their five-year plans on Gantt
charts and studied American mass production techniques.

European interest in Gantt's charts was stimulated by the work
of Wallace Clark, who popularized them and provided a basis for
the European "productivity movement." Before Gantt, however,
Poland's Karol Adamiecki had developed a "harmonogram" which
was a graphical device for simultaneously charting several complicated operations and thus enabling their harmonization.[6]
According to Mee, the harmonogram was similar to the idea of a
PERT network. The harmonogram, developed in 1896, received
some acceptance and use in Poland and Russia but Adamiecki's work
was never translated into English. In brief, scientific management
caught the fancy of Europe and translations flowed in that direction, but not vice versa. Taylor overshadowed Fayol, and Gantt
was accepted before Adamiecki; the industrial climate in Europe
was ready for the ideas of scientific management but it took other
times to bring recognition to Europe's own sons.

FORMALIZING THE STUDY OF MANAGEMENT

Academic and editorial interest signaled a maturity of the scientific management movement in the texts, management handbooks, journals, professional associations, and in the college
curricula beginning in the early 1900's. Despite Taylor's belief
that one had to "live" management and learn through shop experience, the study of industrial management was becoming more
formalized.

Education for Industrial Management

Harlow S. Person brought academic recognition to the Taylor
movement long before it became popular. In 1905, before the
Harvard entry into the management field, Dartmouth College
began the teaching of management *per se* under Person's guidance
at the Amos Tuck School of Administration and Finance. Later,
as dean, Dr. Person played host to the first scientific management

6 John Mee, "History of Management," *Advanced Management—Office Executive*,
Vol. 1, No. 10 (October, 1962), pp. 28–29.

conference in the United States.[7] Dr. Person had a broadening effect on the Taylor movement as president of the Taylor Society (successor to the Society to Promote the Science of Management). Dr. Person extended the group's membership and its range of interests and took a broad view of industrial education. He tried to dissipate the prevailing notion that scientific management was merely the use of a stopwatch and methods analysis; in his view, educators should emphasize the philosophy of scientific management and focus on the creative study of leadership in industry.

Dr. Person also gave early recognition to the need to bring the social scientist into the study of management. His thesis was that the manager and the worker were so closely entwined in everyday activities that they failed to see larger relationships; however, the social scientist would be able to take a larger, more objective view of industrial evolution in order to chart a future course of action for research and practice.[8] Person also made a distinction between "administration" and "management," lending a philosophical subtlety to the propagation of scientific management He viewed administration as the moral, social, and political aspects of running an enterprise, while management dealt with the technical aspects. Hence management could be more "scientific" while science in administration would be more difficult to achieve.[9] Through his own writings and those he edited, Dr. Person became a significant figure in refining scientific management thought.[10]

Louis D. Brandeis, who eventually was to serve as an associate justice on the Supreme Court, had brought the spotlight to bear on scientific management through the railroad rate hearings. In later work Brandeis continued to stress scientific management as a solution to American industrial problems. He was "anti-bigness" and felt that industry could be more efficient, more competitive,

[7] *Scientific Management,* Addresses and discussions of the conference on Scientific Management held October 12–14, 1911. Hanover, N.H.: Amos Tuck School of Administration and Finance, Dartmouth College, 1912.

[8] H. S. Person, "The Manager, the Workman, and the Social Scientist," *Bulletin of the Taylor Society,* Vol. 3, (February, 1917), reprinted in Edward E. Hunt (ed.), *Scientific Management Since Taylor,* New York: McGraw-Hill Book Co., 1924, pp. 226–237.

[9] H. S. Person, "Scientific Management," *Bulletin of the Taylor Society,* Vol. 4 (October, 1919), pp. 8–14.

[10] See for example H. S. Person (editor), *Scientific Management in American Industry,* New York: Harper and Row, 1928.

and more professional through scientific management.[11]   An early collection of readings by Clarence Bertrand Thompson of the Harvard School did much to explain scientific management by presenting original materials from the pioneers, articles by practitioners, and criticisms of the movement.[12]   It was a well balanced work and performed a great service to industrialists and academicians in the early scientific management era.

Also among those contributing to early management education was Leon Pratt Alford (1877–1942).   He was trained as an electrical engineer, worked in industry, became Editor-in-Chief of the influential journals *American Machinist, Industrial Engineering, Management Engineering,* and *Manufacturing Industries,* and pioneered the concept of "management handbooks" as an editor and vice president for the Ronald Press Company.[13]   His role in management education has not been generally acknowledged by management historians; nevertheless, his influence in the journals, on various professional committees, and in his books, was substantial. Among Alford's early writings was an attempt to provide a correct interpretation of "science" in management.   Writing with Alexander Hamilton Church, he deplored the term scientific management in that it was interpreted to mean that there was "a science rather than an art of management."[14]

The weakness of the Taylor approach, in Alford and Church's view, was that it superseded the art of leadership by substituting an "elaborate mechanism" or system.   This did not mean that the mechanism was useless but rather that it overlooked the dynamic possibilities of effective leadership.   Alford thought that Taylor's

[11] An excellent biography is Alpheus Thomas Mason, *Brandeis: A Free Man's Life,* New York: The Viking Press, 1956.   See Chapters 20 and 21 for Brandeis and the hearings.   Brandeis himself wrote *Scientific Management and the Railroads,* New York: Engineering Magazine, 1911; *Business: A Profession,* Boston: Small, Baynard and Co., 1914; and *The Curse of Bigness,* New York: Viking Press, 1934.

[12] C. B. Thompson (editor), *The Theory and Practice of Scientific Management,* Cambridge, Mass.: Harvard University Press, 1914.   The death of C. Bertrand Thompson (1882–1969), is noted in the *Academy of Management Journal,* Vol. 12, No. 1 (March, 1969), p. 66.

[13] An excellent biography, including a complete bibliography of Alford's work, may be found in William J. Jaffe, *L. P. Alford and the Evolution of Modern Industrial Management,* New York: New York University Press, 1957.

[14] A. H. Church and L. P. Alford, "The Principles of Management," *American Machinist,* Vol. 36, No. 22, (May 30, 1912), pp. 857–861.   Reprinted in Harwood F. Merrill (ed.) *Classics in Management,* New York: American Management Association, 1960, pp. 197–214.

so-called "principles" were too mechanical, and to remedy this he (and Church) proposed three broad principles: (1) the systematic use of experience; (2) the economic control of effort; and (3) the promotion of personal effectiveness. The first emphasized both personal experiences of executives plus scientific studies; the second was based on subprinciples of division of labor, coordination, "conservation" (least effort expended to a given end), and remuneration; and the third stressed personal rewards, developing contented workers, and promoting the worker's physical and mental health. From these three broad regulative principles, a truly scientific basis for the art of management could be discovered.

Alford's call for art plus science in management is a reflection of his admiration of Henry Laurence Gantt, about whom he prepared an excellent biography. In the style of Gantt, Alford pleaded for industrial engineers to become involved in leading the economy toward "service" to the community and toward better relations between employers and employees. Alford continued to stress this theme as a member of the prestigious American Engineering Council and contributed to the better known works of this group such as the reports on *The Elimination of Waste in Industry*, *The Twelve Hour Shift*, and *Safety and Production*. Parallel to his efforts on the Council, Alford turned to disseminating management knowledge through the device of "management handbooks." The specialists that Alford brought together to contribute to the handbook read like a 1924 *Who's Who in Management Engineering*: Wallace Clark, C. W. Lytle, J. Roe, George Hageman, and Dexter S. Kimball, to name a few. The pioneering concept of the handbook was to organize information on all facets of administering and operating business and industrial enterprises.[15]   It was through the handbook and his other publications that L. P. Alford sought to develop both the art and science of management.[16]

Dexter S. Kimball (1865–1952) was another influential figure in education for industrial management. As professor of machine design and construction at Cornell's Sibley College of Engineering, he became enthralled by Taylor's ideas and became one of Amer-

---

[15] L. P. Alford (ed.) *Management's Handbook*, New York: Ronald Press Co., 1924; and later, *Cost and Production Handbook*, New York: Ronald Press Co., 1934.

[16] See also: L. P. Alford, *Laws of Management Applied to Manufacturing*, New York: Ronald Press Co., 1928, and *Principles of Industrial Management*, New York: Ronald Press Co., 1940.

ica's first management professors. His course on "Works Administration" began in 1904; in it he taught the application of scientific management to plant location, equipment policies, plant organization, coordination, control of production, and labor compensation.[17] Kimball expanded the concept of scientific management in production and called for the scientific study of the distribution side of enterprise.[18]

Another who followed this "works administration" approach was John Richards. Richards, whose works were never published, gave a series of lectures in 1895 and 1896 on "works administration" before engineering students at Leland Stanford Junior University (Palo Alto, California).[19]

Early management education was largely of this works administration–industrial engineering genre. The number of institutions offering such courses on a regular basis increased from none in 1900 to ten in 1922 and to thirty-five in 1931.[20] The typical course outline for the period included such subjects as: designing the proper organizational structure, policies for plant and equipment, motion and time study, wage incentives and payment schemes, procurement, materials handling, materials control, and "industrial relations." Men like Norris Brisco at Columbia, Hugo Diemer at Penn State, A. G. Anderson at Illinois, Richard Lansburgh at the Wharton School, and Erwin Haskell Schell at the Massachusetts Institute of Technology were formalizing the study of management.[21] While their approaches were largely shop oriented à la Taylor and their view of leadership largely that of a "trait" approach, they

[17] His lectures were published in text form in *Principles of Industrial Organization*, New York: McGraw-Hill Book Co., Inc., 1913.

[18] D. S. Kimball, "Another Side of Efficiency Engineering," in C. B. Thompson, pp. 734–740.

[19] Richard J. Whiting, "John Richards—California Pioneer of Management Thought," *California Management Review*, Vol. 6, No. 2 (Winter, 1963), pp. 35–38.

[20] C. W. Lytle, "Collegiate Courses for Management: A Comparative Study of the Business & Engineering Colleges" (1932), cited by Jaffe, p. 233 and p. 294.

[21] The following represents a sample of such early management texts: A. G. Anderson, *Industrial Engineering and Factory Management*, New York: Ronald Press Co., 1928; Norris A. Brisco, *Economics of Efficiency*, New York: Macmillan Co., 1914; Hugo Diemer, *Factory Organization and Administration*, New York: McGraw-Hill Book Co., 1910; John C. Duncan, *The Principles of Industrial Management*, New York: Appleton-Century-Crofts, 1911; H. P. Dutton, *Factory Management*, New York: Macmillan Co., 1924; E. B. Godwin, *Developing Executive Ability*, New York: Ronald Press Co., 1915; E. D. Jones, *The Administration of Industrial Enterprises*, New York: Longmans, Green and Co., 1916; R. H. Lansburgh, *Industrial Management*, New York: John Wiley and Sons, 1923; and E. H. Schell, *The Technique of Executive Control*, New York: McGraw-Hill Book Co., 1924.

served to bring the study of industrial management to its apogee in the 1920's.

The Impact of Scientific Management on Other Disciplines

Beyond the industrial engineering flavor of management thought, education for general management responsibilities began to take on new dimensions. Stimulated by scientific management, other disciplines began to reflect the search of efficiency through science. William H. Leffingwell applied the principles of scientific management to office management.[22] The University of Chicago's Dr. Leonard D. White picked up where Morris Cooke had left off and made numerous contributions to public administration.[23] White was the first to teach public administration in the classroom and also pioneered in personnel management for governmental offices. In marketing, Arch W. Shaw, Ralph Starr Butler, Louis D. H. Weld, Paul T. Cherington, and Paul D. Converse were pioneering the scientific study of that field.[24]

In accounting, John H. Williams in 1922 conceived the idea of a "flexible budget" as an instrument for administrative control throughout the organization.[25] James O. McKinsey (1889–1937) also sought to expand upon traditional notions of accounting and pioneered in the development of budgets as planning and controlling aids. F. W. Taylor had deplored the traditional post-mortem uses of accounting and McKinsey furthered this notion by viewing accounting information as an aid to management rather than as an end in itself. For McKinsey, the budget was not a set of figures but a way of placing responsibility and measuring performance.[26] As

[22] William Henry Leffingwell, *Scientific Office Management*, Chicago: A. W. Shaw Company, 1917.

[23] Leonard D. White, *Introduction to the Study of Public Administration*, New York: Macmillan Co., 1926; and L. D. White, *The City Manager*, Chicago: University of Chicago Press, 1927.

[24] For the extent of the influence of scientific management on these pioneers, see Joseph C. Seibert, "Marketing's Role in Scientific Management," in Robert L. Clewett (ed.), *Marketing's Role in Scientific Management*, Chicago: American Marketing Association, 1957 pp. 1–3; Robert Bartels, *The Development of Marketing Thought*, Homewood, Ill.: Richard D. Irwin, 1962; and Paul D. Converse, *The Beginnings of Marketing Thought in the United States*, Austin: Bureau of Business Research, University of Texas, 1959.

[25] John Howell Williams, *The Flexible Budget*, New York: McGraw-Hill Book Co., 1934.

[26] James O. McKinsey, *Budgeting*, New York: Ronald Press Co., 1922; *Organization*, New York: Ronald Press Co., 1922; *Budgetary Control*, New York: Ronald Press Co., 1922; and *Managerial Accounting*, Chicago: University of Chicago Press, 1924.

a one-time Professor at the University of Chicago and later as a Senior Partner of McKinsey and Co., McKinsey was also influential in the early days of the American Management Association. The A.M.A. was founded in 1923 as sort of an adult extension university for practicing managers. Its objective was to broaden the study of management to encompass not only production and personnel but to include sales, financial, and other facets of managerial responsibilities.[27] In brief, education for management responsibilities was beginning to shift from that of production shop management toward a broader view encompassing allied areas.

Taylorism in Industrial Practice

Many industrialists played a large role in putting Taylor's theories to the test in their own factories. Henry S. Dennison, president of the Dennison Manufacturing Company, pioneered in employee selection, created an early "Personnel Office," and made his plant a testing ground for scientific management. Henry P. Kendall, Manager of the Plimpton Press of Norwood, Massachusetts, was an early promoter of scientific management in the printing industry. He thought that plants could become efficient by being "systematized" but that a greater long-run effect could be achieved only if the philosophy of scientific management was fully accepted by all parties.[28] James Mapes Dodge pioneered the link-belt conveyor which became the basis for belt assembly line operations and the Link-Belt Company (Philadelphia) was one of the major installations of the Taylor system.[29] Wilfred Lewis, president of the Tabor Manufacturing Company (Philadelphia), a machine-tool producer, was an authority on gearing and a friend of metric reform. Taylor's system, installed at Tabor, increased output 250 per cent.[30] Horace King Hathaway was General Manager of the Tabor Company and assisted Taylor in the installation. Hathaway advocated careful planning before installation, including an

[27] For more detailed information on the A.M.A. and its founders, see Urwick, *Golden Book*, pp. 238–251 (Alvin Earl Dodd); pp. 245–247 (Sam A. Lewisohn); and pp. 267–270 (James O. McKinsey).

[28] H. P. Kendall, "Unsystematized, Systematized, and Scientific Management," in C. Bertrand Thompson, *op. cit.*, pp. 103–131.

[29] See George P. Torrence, *James Mapes Dodge*, New York: Newcomen Society of North America, 1950; and James M. Dodge, "A History of the Introduction of a System of Shop Management," in Thompson, pp. 226–231.

[30] Wilfred Lewis, "An Object Lesson in Efficiency," Thompson, pp. 232–241; see also H. K. Hathaway "Wilfred Lewis," *Bulletin of the Taylor Society*, Vol. 15 (February, 1930), pp. 45–46.

extensive program of educating the workers and supervisors as to the principles and purposes of the Taylor system.[31]   George Babcock, with the assistance of Carl Barth, pioneered scientific management in the automobile industry at the Franklin Motor Car Company from 1908–1912.   He also initiated an employee counseling program there long before Mayo and Roethlisberger did so at Western Electric.[32]

Organization and Management

During this era, the study of organization was largely production-shop-oriented and focused on designing a formal structure of authority-activity relationships.   The early factory system, based upon the widespread division of labor, demanded the coordination of efforts, and the grouping of activities into departments satisfied that need.   Military, governmental, and church hierarchical models permeated early industrial organizational thought.   Daniel McCallum prepared America's first organizational chart and Joseph Slater Lewis pioneered in the same task for British industry.[33]   Emerson continued in the military tradition but Taylor had sought modification through his functional foremen.   Taylor's functional foreman concept did not become widely accepted but there was widespread recognition among others that new organizational forms were necessary.

In 1909 Russell Robb gave a series of lectures on organization at the newly formed Harvard Business School in which he attempted a compromise between the old military style and the new conditions of industry.[34]   His thesis was that the objectives of business differed from that of the military and therefore the organizational emphasis had to differ.   Much could be learned from the military framework of fixing responsibility and authority,

[31] H. K. Hathaway, "Prerequisites to the Introduction of Scientific Management," Thompson, pp. 270–278.

[32] George D. Babcock, *The Taylor System in Franklin Management*, New York: Engineering Magazine Company, 1917.

[33] Joseph Slater Lewis, *The Commercial Organization of Factories*, London: Spon Books, 1896.

[34] Russell Robb, *Lectures on Organization*, privately printed, 1910, Chapter 1 is reprinted in Harwood E. Merrill, pp. 161–175.   Mr. Robb was an engineer with Stone & Webster, Inc. of Boston, managers of public service corporations.   Further insights into his life and writings may be found in Edmund R. Gray and Hyler J. Bracey, "Russell Robb: Management Pioneer," *S.A.M. Advanced Management Journal*, Vol. 35, No. 2 (April, 1970), pp. 71–76.

of clearly defining duties and channels of communication, and of providing for order and discipline. However, the military stressed control and discipline, that being essential to its objectives, to an extent not necessary in industry. The industrial organization, built upon an extensive division of labor, needed to provide for coordination of effort to greater extent than the military. Success in industry was not based upon obedience but economy of effort; therefore the industrial organization had to be different. More stress had to be placed on worker and manager selection and training, processes had to be arranged for economy, and the manager must be aware that a "great factor in organization is 'system,' the mechanism of the whole."[35] An industrial organization was more than a machine based on order and discipline and must be infused with *esprit de corps* by leadership. Structure, discipline, and definitions of authority and responsibility were not enough; the industrial organization had to take into account "system . . . records and statistics . . . *esprit de corps*, cooperation, and team play."[36]

Webster Robinson, professor at the University of California, sought universal "fundamentals" of industrial organizations which were:

1. "Policies"—ranging from general to specific and guiding all effort.
2. "Function"—the specialization of labor.
3. "The Right Man: The Right Place"—proper selection and assignment of duties.
4. "Direction"—purpose and objectives defined for all.
5. "Supervision"—which followed through to insure compliance with "direction."
6. "Control."
7. "Delegation and coordination of authority and responsibility."
8. "Incentives."[37]

While Robb had emphasized the organic whole of the organization, Robinson was more concerned with the operative aspects of organization or what might be more closely akin to "principles" of organization.

In industrial practice, certain giant enterprises were developing organizational ideas that were to endure and to influence corporate structures for some time. At the DuPont Company the death of

[35] Robb, *Lectures*, p. 173.
[36] *Ibid.*, p. 175.
[37] Webster Robinson, *Fundamentals of Business Organization*, New York: McGraw-Hill Book Co., 1925.

General Henry DuPont created the need for "systematic management" to replace what Ernest Dale has called the "Caesar" style (one man rule) of the General. Hamilton McFarland Barksdale became president of DuPont and applied scientific management there as early as 1912. Barksdale stressed the human factor and was using psychological tests for personnel selection in 1910. He also pioneered in separating the line and staff functions, in developing uniform objectives and policies for the company, in the concept of decentralization of authority, and in the development of managerial talent.[38] The organizational legacy of DuPont carried over to the emerging General Motors Corporation. William C. Durant conceived the idea of creating General Motors out of an amalgam of motor car and parts producers. The union was unwieldy and General Motors was plucked from the brink of financial disaster by an infusion of DuPont money in 1920. In 1923, Alfred P. Sloan, Jr., became General Motor's President and, influenced by the DuPont system, created the concept of decentralized administration and operations with centralized control and review. By decentralizing operations and centrally coordinating control, the separate parts of General Motors could work toward a common end. Establishment of this multidivisional structure enabled organizational units to grow larger without the encumbrances of organizing by function.[39]

The concept of decentralization into product divisions required yet another pioneering idea, that of profit center accountability. DuPont's treasurer, Donaldson Brown, created the idea of controlling through accounting responsibility by linking the various organizational subunits to a planned rate of return on controllable expenses.[40] Each division or unit, given a certain amount of resource investment, could then have its performance measured and controlled by judging the rate of return on investment. The result was a correlation between efforts expended and results

[38] Ernest Dale, *The Great Organizers*, New York: McGraw-Hill Book Co., 1960. See also: Ernest Dale and Charles Meloy, "Hamilton McFarland Barksdale and the DuPont Contributions to Scientific Management," *Business History Review*, Vol. 36 (Summer, 1962) pp. 127–152.

[39] The General Motor's story is a classic and is examined, to name only a few, by: Alfred D. Chandler, Jr., (ed.) *Giant Enterprise*, New York: Harcourt, Brace Jovanovich, 1964; Peter Drucker, *The Concept of the Corporation*, New York: John Day Co., 1946; and Alfred P. Sloan, Jr., *My Years with General Motors*, New York: Doubleday & Co., 1963.

[40] Ernest Dale, *The Great Organizers*, p. 260.

obtained which enabled central management to judge and compare the effectiveness of each product division.   Donaldson Brown left DuPont to join General Motors and instituted basically the same system for Sloan.   Together, they created an organizational style widely emulated as other organizations grew too large to follow the previous centralized authority, responsibility by function, structure.

Breakthroughs were appearing in concepts of organizing during this period.   While some still focused on organizing the production function, others were taking a larger view.   Russell Robb sought an "organic whole" in the organization and Webster Robinson searched for universals in organizations.   At DuPont and General Motors, decentralization was emerging as a solution to greater size and complexity in organizations.

Management: Synthesis and Functions

In 1914, two years before the appearance of Henri Fayol's description of the elements or functions of management, Alexander Hamilton Church (1866–1936) put forth a functional approach to the study of management.[41]   Church began his career in England, became a consultant in cost accounting systems, and moved to America at the turn of the century.   Tutored by J. Slater Lewis, one of England's management pioneers, Church sought a broader approach to the study of management than he saw existing in Taylor's approach.[42]   To Church, every industrial undertaking consisted of two elements: (1) the "determinative" element, which fixed the manufacturing and distribution policies of the firm; and (2) the "administrative" element which took the policy as determined and gave it practical expression through buying, manufacturing, and selling.   In making these two elements operational, the manager used two fundamental "instruments": (1) *analysis*, consisting of cost accounting, time and motion study, routing, machine layout, and planning; and (2) *synthesis*, combining men, functions, machines, and all activities effectively to achieve some useful result.   In Church's view, Taylor's ideas were analytical and formed a restricted view of the task of management.   Manage-

---

[41] A. H. Church, *The Science and Practice of Management*, New York: Engineering Magazine, 1914.

[42] Joseph A. Litterer, "Alexander Hamilton Church and the Development of Modern Management," *Business History Review*, Vol. 35 (Summer 1961). p. 214.

ment should be concerned with total efficiency, not just with the efficiency of the production unit, of stores, or of any other single unit in isolation. This regard for the whole led Church to derive five "organic functions" of management:

1. Design, which *originates.*
2. Equipment, which provides physical *conditions.*
3. Control, which specifies duties, and which *orders.*
4. Comparison, which measures, records, and *compares.*
5. Operation, which *makes.*[43]

"Organic" was a physiological analogy meaning that these functions were essential, independent, and yet closely coordinated. Performance of the whole could be adversely affected if any of the parts were malfunctioning, just as in the human body. The manager needed knowledge of these functions just as the doctor needed knowledge of anatomy and physiology. Concerning the functions themselves, design was essentially planning; control was basically coordination, initiating orders, and supervising to insure compliance; and comparison was setting standards and measuring performance. The organic functions of Church do not have the logical appeal of Fayol's nor do they appear as universal in design due to Church's predilection toward manufacturing concerns. In a later book, Church stated that "it is not, of course, possible to teach executive ability."[44] The executive aspirant needed certain physical and moral traits and when he learned from his predecessors and had the experience, he would become effective. Again, Church lacked the foresight of Fayol but his notion of examining the organization as a whole and his "organic functions" earn him his place in management history.

An Early Philosopher

Every man is a philosopher whether he knows it or not. Philosophy reflects the values one holds and while some hold values consciously, others do not. Taylor was a philosopher, even though he had no pretensions as such. So was Gantt and many others who wrote and spoke of developing new values and creeds for an industrial age. Oliver Sheldon (1894–1951) was the first to lay claim to

---

[43] Church, pp. 37–38.
[44] A. H. Church, *The Making of an Executive,* New York: Appleton-Century-Crofts, 1923, p. 2.

developing explicitly a "philosophy of management."[45]   Sheldon began and ended his business career with Rowntree & Company, Ltd., an English chocolate manufacturing company headed by B. S. Rowntree.   Sheldon had undoubtedly read H. L. Gantt and his notion that business had a larger responsibility of "service" to society.   Sheldon stated his own rationale for a philosophy:

. . . we should devise a philosophy of management, a code of principles, scientifically determined and generally accepted, to act as a guide, by reason of its foundation upon ultimate things, for the daily practice of the profession.[46]

Adoption of isolated principles was not adequate to Sheldon's thesis; he sought a body of managers who would develop common motives, common ends, a common creed, and a common fund of knowledge.   The basic premise of his philosophy, like that of Gantt, was that of "service" to the community:

Industry exists to provide the commodities and services which are necessary for the good life of the community, in whatever volume they are required. These commodities and services must be furnished at the lowest prices compatible with an adequate standard of quality, and distributed in such a way as directly or indirectly to promote the highest ends of the community.[47]

This combination of the efficiency values of scientific management with the ethics of service to the community was the responsibility of each manager.   Each manager must adopt three principles: (1) "that the policies, conditions, and methods of industry shall conduce to communal well-being"; (2) that "management shall endeavor to interpret the highest moral sanction of the community as a whole" in applying social justice to industrial practice; and (3) that "management . . . take the initiative . . . in raising the general ethical standard and conception of social justice."[48]

    In applying these principles, management must maintain industry upon an *economic* basis and consider both human *and* technical efficiency.   This duality of efficiency was based upon: (1) scientific methods of work analysis; and (2) development of human potentialities to the greatest extent possible.   In Sheldon's philosophy, the economic basis of service, the dual emphasis on human and technical efficiency, and the responsibility of management

[45] Oliver Sheldon, *The Philosophy of Management*, London: Sir Isaac Pitman & Sons Ltd., 1923.
[46] *Ibid.*, p. 283.
[47] *Ibid.*, p. 284.
[48] *Loc. cit.*

to provide social justice would all lead to a "science of industrial management" of benefit to all parties. Management, through the application of science in work and cognizant of its responsibility for justice, served by being both technically and humanly efficient.

SUMMARY

Scientific management was a significant force in industry, in academia, and in other countries. In bringing the movement to its maturity, a number of individuals played relatively minor, though important, roles. Harlow Person began teaching management as a separate subject, Louis Brandeis called for a widening of the use of scientific management in professionalizing business, and individuals such as C. B. Thompson, Dexter Kimball, and L. P. Alford were bringing education for industrial management into the classroom as well as into industry. In Europe, the reaction was mixed; scientific management achieved international acclaim and recognition but took on varied forms in practice. Taylorism overshadowed the work of Fayol, for awhile, and became the *zeitgeist* of this era. The movement had its adherents as well as its dissenters. It was along all of these dimensions that scientific management reached its apogee of influence in college curricula, in industry, and in the international management movement.

9

The Origins of Industrial
Psychology and
Sociology

Scientific management was sired and nurtured in an era which stressed science as a way of life and living. It is not surprising, therefore, that the credo of scientific investigation would spread to many areas and shift them from traditional, intuitive, pseudo-scientific bases to more empirical, rational ones. Progress needs a spark and this chapter will examine how scientific management provided the ethic for industrial psychology and led to the emergence of personnel management as a discipline. Eras in management thought typically blend into one another and find their roots in earlier theory. Hence we will also find concurrent developments in sociology which anticipated and formed the intellectual basis for a subsequent era in evolving management thought.

PSYCHOLOGY AND THE INDIVIDUAL

Before the advent of scientific management, psychology was largely introspective, *i.e.*, based on the premise that man could learn what he needed to know about others by studying himself. Pseudosciences such as astrology, physiognomy, phrenology, and graphology were abundant as managers sought to select personnel on the basis of the movement and position of the stars, on their physical characteristics, on the basis of bumps on the skull, and on handwriting analysis.[1] Even in such reputable consulting firms as that of Harrington Emerson, Katherine H. M. Blackford, a physician, emphasized the study of physiognomy and graphology as aids to selection. She advocated the study of facial and hair coloring, the shape of noses, facial expressions, and head proportions such as "convex and concave faces," and other "psychophysical" variables in selecting employees. She found nine such psychophysical variables and also concluded that handwriting analysis, like the person's voice, was an expression of a person's character and should be taken into account.[2]

Elsewhere, psychology was escaping its introspective, pseudoscience beginnings. When Wilhelm Wundt opened his Leipzig laboratory in 1879, the scientific method first appeared in psychology. Wundt did not entirely abandon introspection but began to examine behavior through controlled experiments. As the father of experimental psychology, he opened the way for applied and eventually industrial psychology. Wundt was searching for "psychological man," just as Taylor sought economic man, through studying the individual for universal mainsprings of human conduct. Observation of human behavior, combined with the emergence of the psychoanalytical theories of Freud, soon led to a widespread search for instincts to explain behavior and thought. Man was not rational as Adam Smith had postulated but controlled by instincts and, by understanding these instincts, the secrets of man's hitherto unexplored mind could be opened for examination. Thorstein Veblen laid great stress on the instinct for workmanship; William James thought there were twenty-eight separate instincts; and Ordway Tead discovered ten.[3]

The disparities and disagreements among the lists of instincts soon proved that this approach was futile, and instinct theory was dismissed as an over-simplified view of man. However, the human variabilities which were noted in the attempts to develop instinct

---

[1] Cyril Curtis Ling, *The Management of Personnel Relations: History and Origins,* Homewood, Ill.: Richard D. Irwin, 1965, pp. 232–233.

[2] Katherine H. M. Blackford, *The Job, The Man, The Boss,* New York: Doubleday and Co., 1915, Chapter 7, p. 176 and p. 184.

[3] Ordway Tead, *Instincts in Industry: A Study of Working Class Psychology,* Boston: Houghton Mifflin Co., 1918. Tead's list consisted of the parental, sex, workmanship, possession, self-assertion, submissiveness, herd, pugnacity, play, and curiosity instincts.

theory led to the recognition of individual differences.   The study *of* man had to study *the* man and it was here that the psychologists found their alliance with scientific management.

The Birth of Industrial Psychology

Scientific management gave industrial psychology its ethic, its scope, and its direction for research.   The earliest objective of industrial psychology was

the maximum *efficiency* of the individual in industry and his optimum *adjustment* . . . in the belief that, in the final analysis, the maximum efficiency of that individual in the industrial situation can only be achieved by insuring his most satisfactory adjustment in that situation.[4]

While the engineer studied mechanical efficiency, the industrial psychologist studied human efficiency with the same goal in mind of improved overall greater productivity.   Acceptance by industry of the heretofore ivory-tower psychologist was facilitated by the psychologist's interest in efficiency.

Hugo Munsterberg (1863–1916) was the father of industrial psychology.   Born in Danzig and educated in Wundt's Leipzig laboratory, he was soon enticed to America by William James, the great Harvard psychologist.[5]   In 1892, Munsterberg established his psychological laboratory at Harvard, which was to become the foundation stone in the industrial psychology movement.   His interests were far-ranging, including the application of psychological principles to crime detection, to education, to morality, and to philosophy.   In 1912 he published *Psychologie und Wirtschaftleben*, which was translated as *Psychology and Industrial Efficiency* in 1913.[6]   In the spring of that year, he visited with President Wilson, Secretary of Commerce Redfield, and Secretary of Labor W. B. Wilson in Washington to win them to the idea of creating a government bureau dedicated to scientific research in the application of psychology to the problems of industry. National interest in scientific management was high and Munster-

---

[4] Morris S. Viteles, *Industrial Psychology*, New York: W. W. Norton and Co., 1932, p. 4.

[5] A sympathetic but interesting account of Herr Doktor Munsterberg may be found in Margaret Munsterberg, *Hugo Munsterberg: His Life and Work*, New York: Appleton-Century-Crofts, 1922.

[6] Hugo Munsterberg, *Psychology and Industrial Efficiency*, Boston: Houghton Mifflin Co., 1913.

berg sought to put science in the study of human behavior at the same level of national concern. According to Munsterberg:

> While today the greatest care is devoted to the problems of material and equipment, all questions of the mind . . . like fatigue, monotony, interest, learning . . . joy in work . . . reward . . . and many similar mental states are dealt with by laymen without any scientific understanding.[7]

Even though the government bureau never materialized, Munsterberg's research efforts sought to answer certain perplexing industrial questions:

> We ask how we can find the men whose mental qualities make them best fitted for the work which they have to do; secondly, under what psychological conditions we can secure the greatest and most satisfactory output from every man; and finally how we can produce most completely the influences on human minds which are desired in the interests of business. In other words, we ask how to find the best possible work, and how to secure the best possible effects.[8]

Munsterberg's *Psychology and Industrial Efficiency* was directly related to Taylor's proposals and contained three broad parts: (1) "The Best Possible Man"; (2) "The Best Possible Work"; and (3) "The Best Possible Effect." Part one was a study of the demands jobs made on men and the necessity of identifying those men whose mental qualities made them best fitted for the work they had to do. Part two sought to determine "psychological conditions" under which the greatest and most satisfactory output could be obtained from every man. Part three examined the necessity of producing the influences on human needs which were desirable for the interests of the business. For each of these objectives, Munsterberg outlined definite proposals for the use of tests in worker selection, for the application of research on learning in training industrial personnel, and for the study of psychological techniques which increased the worker's motives and reduced fatigue. In character with experimental psychology, Munsterberg illustrated his proposals with his own evidence gathered from the study of trolley motormen, telephone operators, and ship's officers.

Taylor and others, such as Harlow Person, had envisioned contributions from psychologists for research into the human factor. Munsterberg fitted into this scheme and the ethic of scientific management was readily apparent in (1) the focus on the individual,

[7] Margaret Munsterberg, p. 250.
[8] Hugo Munsterberg, pp. 23–24.

(2) the emphasis on efficiency, and (3) the social benefits to be derived from application of the scientific method. As Taylor had called for a mental revolution and the recognition of the mutuality of interests between employees and employers, Munsterberg noted:

> We must not forget that the increase of industrial efficiency by future psychological adaptation and by improvement of the psychophysical conditions is not only in the interest of the employers, but still more of the employees; their working time can be reduced, their wages increased, their level of life raised.[9]

Lillian Gilbreth's pioneering work in the *Psychology of Management* lacked the empirical evidence presented by Munsterberg but nonetheless fitted the same theme. Concern for the human factor was increasing and it was within the ethics and objectives of scientific management that it began. After Munsterberg, other industrial psychology texts appeared and followed a fairly definite pattern: first, developing a "psychological point of view of industry" by pointing out the need to study human behavior; second, establishing the roots and justification of the industrial psychology movement in scientific management; and finally, examining such recurring subjects as fatigue, vocational guidance, improving efficiency through testing and placement, and overcoming "industrial unrest" through understanding the human factor.[10]

Personnel: The Emergence of a Discipline

The focus on individual differences and the concern for efficiency created widespread interest in the human problems of industry. In the early days of the factory, the personnel or "employment" function was the responsibility of the line manager, typically the foreman. The growth of organizations and increased concern for the worker eventually led to the development of staff specialists who aided the line manager in finding, testing, training, and performing other personnel functions such as administering the wage program. B. F. Goodrich developed the first "employ-

[9] Hugo Munsterberg, pp. 308–309.
[10] Typical works would include: Frank Watts, *An Introduction to the Psychological Problems of Industry*, London: Allen and Unwin, 1921; Charles S. Myers, *Mind and Work: The Psychological Factors in Industry and Commerce*, New York: G. P. Putnam's Sons, 1921; and Charles S. Myers, *Industrial Psychology*, New York: People's Institute, 1925. Charles Samuel Myers, inspired by Munsterberg, pioneered industrial psychology in England.

ment" department in America (1900); National Cash Register established a "labor department" in 1902; and Plimpton Press, one of Taylor's first installations, had a personnel department in 1910.[11] Munsterberg's concern for finding the "best possible man" was the beginning of "scientific" personnel management and in turn touched off a vocational guidance and personnel testing and placement movement.

Walter Dill Scott (1869–1955) received his Ph.D. under Wundt at Leipzig in 1900.[12] In America, Scott turned his efforts to psychological research into advertising, to the selection and placement of salesmen,[13] and eventually to helping devise a system for classifying and testing officer candidates for the Army. In his early work Scott focused on the psychology of persuasion and on proper personnel selection to enhance industrial efficiency.[14] From this work, Scott turned to a broader view of personnel and pioneered in formalizing the emerging "personnel management" function.[15]

The early developmental period of vocational guidance efforts had few well-developed tools and techniques for personnel administration. World War I led to greater refinement, and the postwar period found great strides in the management of personnel. Henry Ford, faced with a tight labor market and a worker turnover rate of 10 per cent, formed an early personnel department in 1914 called the "Sociological Department."[16] The $5.00 wage, announced the same year, was "neither charity nor wages, but profit sharing and efficiency engineering."[17] Ford feared that the easy money of $5.00 per day would lead the workers astray, so he employed one hundred investigator—"advisers"—who visited the workers' homes to insure that their homes were neat and clean, that they did not

[11] Henry Eilburt, "The Development of Personnel Management in the United States," *Business History Review*, Vol. 33, No. 3, (Autumn, 1959), pp. 345–364.

[12] Edmund C. Lynch, "Walter Dill Scott: Pioneer Industrial Psychologist," *Business History Review*, Vol. 42, No. 2. (Summer, 1968), p. 150.

[13] Scott's contributions to advertising and marketing thought were many; see: Robert Bartels, *The Development of Marketing Thought*, Homewood, Ill.: Richard D. Irwin, 1962, pp. 46–48.

[14] W. D. Scott, *Influencing Men in Business*, New York: Ronald Press Co., 1911; and W. D. Scott, *Increasing Human Efficiency*, New York: Macmillan Co., 1911.

[15] W. D. Scott and R. C. Clothier, *Personnel Management: Principles, Practices, and Point of View*, Chicago: A. W. Shaw Co., 1923. (Revised in 1931, 1941, 1949, and 1954).

[16] Loren Baritz, *The Servants of Power*, p. 33.

[17] Henry Ford, quoted by Baritz, *loc. cit.*

drink too much, that their sex life was without tarnish, and that they used their leisure time profitably. The sociological department was a far cry from modern concepts of personnel management, but its formation symbolized the notion that concern for the human element was the very best investment a business firm could make. Investment in the human factor and the study of the psychological side of work was sound business practice and was reminiscent of Robert Owen's plea almost a century earlier for managers to pay as much attention to humans as to their machines.

The war experiences with the refinement of psychological tests, plus a tight labor market, and growing labor unrest in the post-war period as evidenced by the Wobblies (I.W.W.) and the Bolsheviks in Russia, spurred many firms to emulate the personnel departments of Ford and other companies. The early personnel and employment management texts followed the theme that concern for people would lead to greater prosperity for all. Farseeing industrialists such as James Hartness of Jones and Lamson Machine Company pointed out that management approaches were too mechanistic and relied too heavily on the efficiency engineers. Greater increases in efficiency must come through psychology in the work place as well as from engineering and economics.[18]   In England, Benjamin Seebohm Rowntree (1871–1954) brought to his York Cocoa Works an interest in human welfare which stopped slightly short of paternalism. Rowntree employed a sociologist in a "psychological department" who supervised company education, health, canteens, housing, and recreation.[19]   Mary Follett, (who will be discussed later) chose Rowntree's firm as a prime example of how a business should develop a social philosophy. Rowntree also influenced the lives and ideas of two other significant contributors to management thought, Oliver Sheldon and Lyndall Urwick.

Interest in the human side of enterprise and in the potentialities of personnel administration would lead to significant changes in assumptions about man in organizations. For instance, Ordway Tead partially recovered from his "instinct" explanation of work

---

[18] James Hartness, *The Human Factor in Works Management*, New York: McGraw-Hill Book Co., 1912.
[19] Urwick and Brech, pp. 58–70. See also B. S. Rowntree, *The Human Factor in Business*, London: Longmans, Green, and Co., 1921.

behavior to co-author an early personnel text with Hency C. Metcalf.[20] They concluded that instincts and inborn tendencies still had a great deal to do with human conduct but that advances in personnel research were opening new vistas enabling more scientific selection, placement, and training. Executives should adopt a "personnel point of view," which assumed that there was a cause and effect relationship in behavior which could be studied for purposes of guiding human conduct.[21] Proper work habits could be formed, emotions controlled, and creative leadership could lead to reduced conflict and improved morale.

The typical personnel management text of this era examined such subjects as job analysis, writing job descriptions and specifications, psychological tests, interviewing and selecting employees, merit rating, promotion policies, analyzing labor turnover, training, and dealing with problems such as tardiness and absences. The training of foremen was also included but relatively little attention was paid to developing higher management. "Industrial democracy" and employee representation were often mentioned but in the 1920's the stress was largely on company unions, partially due to some residue of Taylorism and partially to the fact that the twenties were a paternalistic, "union-busting" decade.

The 1920's witnessed a decline in psychological testing and an upswing in company paternalism and welfare schemes designed to woo worker loyalty. Man became the firm's most important asset, not out of sentimentality nor moral uplift, but based on the view that concern for employee welfare would increase worker efficiency. Personnel departments proliferated and worker welfare schemes were designed with the hope that workers would reciprocate by expressing their appreciation through higher productivity. Psychological testing had proved inadequate to the task of selection since research had failed to show any correlation between tests and job success.[22] An early employment manager noted that tests were unscientific, administered by amateurs, used as a substitute

[20] Ordway Tead and Henry C. Metcalf, *Personnel Administration: Its Principles and Practice,* New York: McGraw-Hill Book Co., 1920.

[21] Ordway Tead, *Human Nature and Management: The Applications of Psychology to Executive Leadership,* New York: McGraw-Hill Book Co., 1929, p. 9.

[22] For example, Henry C. Link suggested that more effort should be devoted to testing *tests* rather than men. H. C. Link, *Employment Psychology,* New York: Macmillan Co., 1921.

for judgment, and were little better than fortune telling for predicting human success.[23] Quacks abounded, throwing reputable psychologists into disrepute, as firms sought quick and simple solutions to human problems. After 1925 the testing fad declined and managers had less faith in measuring traits that would predict greater efficiency. Eventually this breach would be filled by the ethic of human relations as the road to greater productivity.

FOUNDATIONS OF SOCIAL MAN: THEORY AND RESEARCH

Scientific management did not neglect the human factor, as it is frequently alleged, but focused on the individual. There were reasons for this, as we shall see later, but changing cultural conditions and new theories were emerging in the scientific management era to lay the foundations for a new emphasis in evolving management thought.

Sociology and Industry

The social side of man and the human relations movement, while gaining their greatest thrust from the Hawthorne research, were finding their roots in earlier sociological theory. Max Weber, Émile Durkheim, and Vilfredo Pareto formed an intellectual triad of sociological theorists of the nineteenth century. Max Weber, who will be discussed in more detail later, established sociology as a field of inquiry and was concerned with the relationship between economics and society. Émile Durkheim's first book, his doctoral dissertation on *The Division of Labor*, was published in 1893.[24] He divided societies into two primary types, *mechanical*, or those dominated by a collective consciousness; and *organic*, or those characterized by specialization and division of labor and societal interdependence. Mechanical societies were bound together by friendliness, neighborliness, and kinship; however, such solidarity did not exist in organic societies and led to anomie or a state of confusion, insecurity, and "normlessness." According to Durkheim, restoration of social solidarity in organic societies must

[23] Mary Barnett Gilson, *What's Past is Prologue*, New York: Harper & Row, 1940, p. 64.

[24] É. Durkheim, *De la Division du travail Social*, Paris: F. Alcan, 1893; translated by George Simpson, New York: Free Press, 1947.

come through the law and a new "collective consciousness" which created values and norms and imposed them on the individual. In organic societies men must cooperate, "love" one another, and be willing to sacrifice self to the group in order to promote solidarity. In Durkheim there arises the antithesis of Adam Smith's self-interest as the basis for exchange. Instead, Durkheim would substitute the group as the source of values and norms and as the new collective consciousness. It was in Durkheim's anomie that Elton Mayo found a new prescription for industrial solidarity.

Vilfredo Pareto (1848–1923) was the father of the notion of "social systems."[25] By social system Pareto meant the state which society takes both at a specified moment and in the successive transformations which it undergoes within a period of time. Pareto was a "macro" sociologist and concerned with larger societal systems but his ideas were later adopted by Elton Mayo and the human relationists in their own analytical framework. Pareto's theories were introduced to Mayo and the Hawthorne researchers by Lawrence J. Henderson, a physiologist in the research group.[26]

William G. Scott further traced the comparison between Pareto and the Mayo group and found that Pareto's ideas of the social system, of logical and non-logical behavior, of equilibrium, of the functions of language, and of the circulation of the elite were all adopted by the Hawthorne researchers.[27] For example, Pareto's social system viewed society as a cluster of interdependent but variable units. The human relationists were concerned with the interdependence of the social and physical aspects of the work environment and viewed the system as something which must be considered as a whole because each part bore some interdependent relationship to every other part.

Aside from the pioneering work of Pareto and Durkheim, a major school of sociological theory called "social behaviorism" was forming during the scientific management era. This school introduced the idea of the "social person" as the object of study and established social psychology as a fundamental branch of sociol-

[25] Vilfredo Pareto, *The Mind and Society,* translated by Andrew Bongiorno and Arthur Livingston, New York: Harcourt Brace Jovanovich 1935.

[26] John B. Knox, "Sociological Theory and Industrial Sociology," *Social Forces,* March, 1955, cited by W. G. Scott, *Organization Theory,* p. 38. Henderson's study of Pareto may be found in L. J. Henderson, *Pareto's General Sociology,* Cambridge, Mass.: Harvard University Press, 1935.

[27] W. G. Scott, Figure 1–3, pp. 40–41.

ogy.[28]   Charles Horton Cooley contributed the "looking glass self" or the idea that the social self arises reflectively in terms of one's reactions to the opinions of others.   Through group experiences the person forms his first notions of both self and social unity. George Herbert Mead fathered social psychology by suggesting that one learns his own self through a process of taking the role of others in interaction situations.   Society entered every person through the process of interaction and the self is constantly being reshaped through these encounters.

In psychology, the notion of *Gestalt* was coming into prominence due to the work of the Austrian Christian von Ehrenfels (1890) and the German Max Wertheimer (1912).   Prior to the Gestalt idea, Martindale characterized psychological theories as "mechanistic" in that they tended to emphasize fundamental units of study, e.g. an element, a particle, or an individual.   Gestalt psychology, on the other hand, represented an "organismic" approach which emphasized not the parts or units but the patterns, wholes, configurations, etc., which made the whole appear to be more than the sum of its parts.[29]   From these beginnings, Gestalt theory would pervade the ideas of social systems, group dynamics, and other behavioral research right up to the modern-day notion of general systems theory.

Some Early Empirical Investigations

The group and social facets of man were gaining recognition in sociological theory and in the Gestalt idea of configurations and systems.   Empirical investigations into the human facet of industrial life were sparse but becoming more frequent.   Whiting has uncovered the work of Paul Goehre, a German theological student, who took a job in a factory to investigate working conditions in 1891.   Goehre observed that the workers took more pride in producing a complete unit of work rather than an unidentifiable fragment, that higher productivity occurred when supervisors instilled a feeling of group interdependence and teamwork, and that there were informal group pressures for adherence to its norms. Lower morale and lower efficiency were the result when men were

[28] Don Martindale, *The Nature and Types of Sociological Theory*, Boston: Houghton Mifflin Co., 1960, pp. 285–435.
[29] *Ibid.*, pp. 451–453.

isolated and felt a lack of "community of labour [sic]". According to Whiting, Goehre has formed a "missing link" between Robert Owen and the more modern human relationists.[30]

In the post-Taylor era, two other individuals were developing some unique ideas on motivation. Henri DeMan anticipated by more than three decades Frederick Herzberg's methods of probing worker motivation. DeMan asked both wage earners and salaried workers in various parts of Germany to make a statement "concerning their own feelings about their daily work."[31] DeMan concluded that there was a natural instinct in man to find "joy in work." In this drive, positive motives were instincts for "activity," "self-assertion," to be "constructive," and a longing for "mastery" (power). The negative factors which inhibited this natural impulse for joy in work were found: (1) in the job itself in factors such as detailed work, monotony, reduction of worker initiative, fatigue, and poor working conditions; and (2) in "social hindrances" such as the dependent position of the worker, unjust wage systems, speed-ups, insecurity of livelihood, and lack of social solidarity. DeMan's sample (seventy-eight subjects) was limited but his findings bear a remarkable similarity to Herzberg's later "motivation-hygiene" theory in many respects. DeMan felt that work itself was a motivator and that management's job was to remove the "hindrances" which prevented the worker from finding joy in work.

Whiting Williams quit his white collar job as personnel director of the Hydraulic Pressed Steel Company to become a blue collar "industrial hobo" to study working conditions first-hand. Williams worked in coal mines, ship building, iron mines, oil refineries, and a multitude of other industries to gauge the temper of the times. By living and working with his research sample, Williams was able to form some very definite impressions about labor-management relations: (1) that workers restricted output ("stringing out the job") because they perceived scarce job opportunities and employers tended to hire and lay off indiscriminately; (2) that unions arose out of worker concern for security and the unions

---

[30] Richard J. Whiting, "Historical Search in Human Relations," *Academy of Management Journal*, Vol. 7, No. 1 (March, 1964), pp. 45–53. Goehre's work was translated in English as *Three Months in a Workshop*, London: Swan Sonnenschein & Company, 1895.

[31] Henri DeMan, *Joy In Work*, translation by Eden Paul, New York: Holt, Rinehart and Winston, 1929, p. 9.

would not have made much progress if employers had evidenced concern for this worker need; (3) that long factory hours (12-hour shifts in steel) made both workers and foremen grouchy and tired, causing interpersonal conflict; and (4) that the workers listened to radical agitators because employers failed to speak "of the plans and purposes, the aims and ideals—the character of the company."[32]

In later writings, Williams argued that pay was relative in the worker's view; *i.e.* it was not the absolute amount of pay but the amount in relation to what others were receiving that counted. Hence incentive plans were less than effective as motivators. The "mainspring" of men was the " . . . wish to enjoy the feeling of our [the worker's] worth as persons among other persons."[33] "Togetherness" in thinking, feeling, and working in groups was important to the worker. It was from his peers that the worker drew his social sustenance, security, and his concept of self-worth. A worker chose to "get along" with his co-workers because he could always find another job but could not always move from the community. From the employer, and especially the foreman, he expected recognition and treatment conducive to preserving self-worth. It was not the paternalistic clubs, cafeterias, and recreation activities that won worker loyalty, but successful relations with the foreman as a representative of management. Williams recommended an Eleventh Commandment, "Thou Shalt Not Take Thy Neighbor For Granted" and urged management to change from appeals to fear to appeals to "hope and surety of reward."[34] Latent in Williams' study of the worker was Cooley's "looking glass self" and the group as the primary social unit. Williams' experiences had taught him that the worker was not the rational economic man as assumed by many. The worker acted on the basis of emotion, sought to maintain social status, and considered the nature of his job more important than any pecuniary considerations.

The view and analysis of man as a social being did not begin at Western Electric. From Durkheim's identification of *anomie*, through Pareto's analysis of the social system, through the social

[32] Whiting Williams, *What's on the Worker's Mind*, New York: Charles Scribner's Sons, 1920, pp. 283–290.

[33] Whiting Williams, *Mainsprings of Men*, New York: Charles Scribner's Sons, 1925, p. 147.

[34] Williams, *What's on the Worker's Mind*, pp. 312–313.

behaviorists such as Mead and Cooley, through the Gestaltists, and to the empirical evidence of Whiting Williams and others, economic man was on the wane and social man began to wax.

SUMMARY

Industrial psychology was a spin-off of scientific management and academic and industrial interest was stimulated in vocational guidance, personnel testing for selection, and individual motivation. A secondary theme of the period was a growing interest in worker behavior, and social scientists began to add new dimensions to understanding man in industry. Times were changing and the social facet of man, including his interactions, his needs for security, and his drives for social solidarity, began to appear. In theory and practice, Durkheim, Pareto, Whiting Williams, and others were laying the intellectual foundations for a new era in evolving management thought.

10

The Emergence of
Administrative Theory

History rarely measures the full contribution of a man during his own lifetime. Epitaphs are often prematurely written and other times bring added appreciation to men such as the two presented in this chapter. Both of our subjects lived during the latter nineteenth and the early twentieth centuries; both wrote during the scientific management era in America; both were Europeans; and both made lasting contributions to the evolution of management thought. One was a practicing manager and one an academician; one was trained in the physical sciences, the other in the social sciences; and neither was accorded the full measure of his contribution until some decades after his death. Henri Fayol, the French manager-engineer, fathered the first theory of administration through his study of the management process. Max Weber, the German economist-sociologist, sired a theory of organizations through his conception of bureaucracy as the ideal of technical efficiency. Both sought to generalize theory and practice; yet it was the task of others to bring full appreciation to the impact of their thinking on modern management.

HENRI FAYOL: THE MAN AND HIS CAREER

Henri Fayol (1841–1925) was born of a family of the French *bourgeoisie* and in 1860 graduated from the National School of

Mines at St. Etienne.[1] Trained as a mining engineer, Fayol joined the Commentary-Fourchambault Company in 1860 and spent his entire career with that coal-mining and iron foundry combine before retiring in 1918. In 1888, the company was in dire financial straits and headed for bankruptcy when Henri Fayol was named the Managing Director. As the coal pits of Commentary neared exhaustion, the pits and iron works at Décazeville were procured in 1892 and the new combine became known as "Comambault." Faced with the overall problems of the new combine, Fayol was able to bring the company from near bankruptcy to an unassailable financial position by the time of his retirement at the age of seventy-seven.

During his lifetime, Fayol made significant technical contributions to geology and metallurgy as well as to the field of management. He was awarded the Delasse Prize in 1893 for his technical accomplishments, the Gold Medal of the Society for the Encouragement of Industry, and was a member of the Legion of Honour. From his own experiences, Fayol began to formulate his ideas of administrative theory as early as 1900 when he read a paper on administration before the International Mining and Metallurgical Congress. In this particular paper, he indicated the importance of the administrative function but did not present the "elements" of management for which he later became famous. In 1908, he prepared a paper for the Jubilee of the Society of Mineral Industry in which he put forth his fourteen "general principles" of administration. His first mention of the "elements" of administration came in 1916 with the publication of his *Administration industrielle et générale*.[2] The first English translation was by Coubrough and appeared in 1930 under the auspices of the International Management Institute at Geneva.[3] One of Fayol's other papers, "The Administrative Theory of the State," was translated in

---

[1] The original source of personal data on Fayol is the *Dictionnaire de l'organization et de Science du Travail*, published by the Comité National de l'organization française, and translated by J. A. Coubrough in Henri Fayol, *Industrial and General Administration*, Geneva: International Management Institute, 1930, pp. 4–5. Further insights in a more readily accessible form may be found in Lyndall Urwick and E. F. L. Brech, *The Making of Scientific Management* (Vol. I), pp. 39–47, and L. Urwick's "Foreword" to Henri Fayol, *General and Industrial Management*, (translation by Constance Storrs) London: Sir Isaac Pitman and Sons, 1949, pp. v to xxix.

[2] Published as a monograph by The Societé de l'Industrie Minérale in 1916 and in book form by Dunod Frères (Paris) in 1925.

[3] The title was translated by Coubrough as *Industrial and General Administration*.

1923 and published in America in 1937 as a part of a collection entitled *Papers on the Science of Administration*.[4] However, America was not thoroughly exposed to Fayol's theory until 1949 when Pitman's of London published a translation by Constance Storrs.[5]

Ignorance of Fayol's work was not limited to the United States; even in France his work was largely overshadowed by that of Taylor, due to the efforts of Henry Le Chatelier and Charles de Freminville. Le Chatelier had translated and popularized Taylor in France and the contributions of scientific management to the French war effort were substantial. From Fayol's retirement (1918) to his death in 1925, he founded and presided over the meetings of the Center of Administrative Studies, a group formed to promote the advancement of *"Fayolisme."* Shortly before his death, this group merged with the Le Chatelier-de Freminville or *"Taylorisme"* group to form the Comité National de l'Organisation Française.

This merger was significant in that it brought the two main French schools of management together. Early interpretations of Fayol had placed his work in competition or contrast with Taylor's. Fayol insisted that this was not so and that the two were complementary in the sense that both sought to improve management through different avenues of analysis. In comparing the lives of these two men, one can see the reasons for their different perspectives.

These two fountainheads of management thought were quite dissimilar in many respects; and, though both were born of relatively well-to-do parents and both were educated as engineers, their similarities soon vanish. Fayol was born and educated to the managerial elite in a French culture which stressed position based on tradition. Social classes were more distinct and the French manager achieved success through genetics and long and faithful service. Taylor started at the bottom and worked his way up in the open culture of America and the functioning Protestant ethic. Fayol faced no hostile organized labor, never encountered the resistance of installing his system into a plant, and never appeared before any investigating committees. Taylor started as a worker and worked his way up while Fayol started as a junior executive and

---

[4] Edited by Luther Gulick and Lyndall Urwick; pp. 99–114.
[5] The title was translated by Storrs as *General and Industrial Management*.

from the beginning identified with the management group. Taylor began by implementing his methods in the shop and then generalized from them while Fayol built his system of general management from the executive viewpoint and then applied them to lower organizational elements. Taylor died relatively young amidst much turmoil and controversy. Fayol lived a long life, did not publish his major work until he was seventy-five, and avoided the boiling waters of controversy. Taylor's star shone brightly while Fayol's was eclipsed, awaiting other times and other men who could write his proper epitaph.

Management or Administration?

Fayol intended to write a four-part treatise on administration which would have included: Part I, the necessity for and possibility of teaching management: Part II, the principles and elements of management; Part III, his personal observations and experiences; and Part IV, the lessons of the war. Parts III and IV never appeared but the beginnings were enough to establish Fayol's stress on the importance of management in all undertakings, "large or small, industrial, commercial, political, religious, or any other."[6] This "universality" of management marked a major contribution since it proposed to overcome parochial views and set the study of management apart as a study in itself.[7] Fayol began by identifying six groups of activities found in all industrial undertakings: (1) "technical," such as production and manufacture; (2) "commercial," or buying, selling and exchange; (3) "financial," or the search for and optimum use of capital; (4) "security," or the protection of property and persons; (5) "accounting," or stocktaking, balance sheets, costs, and statistics; and (6) "managerial," or "planning, organization, command, co-ordination, and control."[8] Of the six activities, Fayol devoted his attention only to managerial activities since the others were commonly understood.

[6]Henri Fayol (the Storrs' translation), p. xxi. Except where specifically noted, the Storrs' translation will be used since it is more readily available.

[7] Cf. Taylor's introduction to Principles: "Third . . . to show that the fundamental principles of scientific management are applicable to all kinds of human activities, from our simplest individual acts to the work of our great corporations . . ." (p. 7). Fayol certainly knew of Taylor's work via Le Chatelier who translated it in the Revue de Metallurgie (1911). Thus Taylor perceived a universality of the methods and philosophy of scientific management but not the universality of the managerial functions as Fayol developed them.

[8] Fayol (Storrs), pp. 3–6.

At this point, it is necessary to develop an analysis of the variations which appear between Fayol's original French, Coubrough's 1930 translation, and Storrs' 1949 rendition.   Lyndall Urwick criticized the Storrs' translation for substituting the word "management" for "administration" but acceded to this change since it was "accurate and convenient" in modern terminology.[9] However, a comparison of these three editions will indicate how the course of management thought might have been changed by the translation of only *one* word.

In the original French, Fayol developed his *"fonction administrative"*:

J'ai donc adopté la définition suivante:
Administrer, c'est prévoir, organiser, commander, coordonner et contrôler;
Prévoir, c'est-à-dire scruter l'avenir et dresser le programme d'action;
Organiser, c'est-à-dire constituer le double organisme, matériel et social, de l'entreprise;
Commander, c'est-à-dire faire fonctionner le personnel;
Coordonner, c'est-à-dire felier, unir, harmoniser tous les actes et tous les efforts;
Controler, c'est-à-dire veiller à ce que tout se passe conformément aux règles établies et aux ordres donnés.[10]

Coubrough rendered this as:

I have, therefore, adopted the following definition: To *administrate* is to plan, organize, command, coordinate and control.
To plan means to study the future and arrange the plan of operations.
To organize means to build up the material and human organization of the business, organizing both men and materials.
To command means to make the staff do their work.
To co-ordinate means to unite and correlate all activities.
To control means to see that everything is done in accordance with the rules which have been laid down and the instructions which have been given.[11]

In the Storrs' version:

Therefore I have adopted the following definition: To *manage* is to forecast and plan, to organize, to command, to co-ordinate and to control.   To foresee and provide means examining the future and drawing up the plan of action. To organize means building up the dual structure, material and human, of the undertaking.   To command means maintaining activity among the personnel.   To co-ordinate means binding together, unifying and harmonizing all activity and effort.   To control means seeing that everything occurs in conformity with established rule and expressed command.[12]

---

9 "Foreword," *ibid.*, pp. xii–xiii.
10 Fayol, p. 11.
11 Fayol (Coubrough) p. 9, Italics added.
12 Fayol (Storrs), pp. 5–6. Italics added.

The major distinction between the translations of Fayol's *"administrer"* is in Coubrough's "to administrate" and Storrs' "to manage." How did Fayol distinguish between management and administration? In the original French:

La fonction *administrative* se distingue nettement des cinq autres fonctions essentielles.

Il importe de ne pas la confondre avec le gouvernement.

Gouverner, c'est conduire l'entreprise vers son but en cherchant à tirer le meilleur parti possible de toutes les ressources dont elle dispose; c'est assurer la marche des six fonctions essentielles.

L'administration n'est que l'une des six fonctions dont le gouvernement doit assurer la marche. Mais elle tient dans le rôle des grands chefs une si grande place qu'il peut parfois sembler que ce rôle est exclusivement administratif.[13]

According to Coubrough:

It is important not to confuse *administration* with *management.* *To manage* an undertaking is to conduct it towards its objective by trying to make the best possible use of all the resources at its disposal; it is, in fact, to ensure the smooth working of the six essential functions. Administration is only one of these functions, but the managers of big concerns spend much of their time on it that their jobs sometimes seem to consist solely of administration.[14]

And, the Storrs' translation:

The *managerial* function is quite distinct from the other five essential functions. It should not be confused with *government.* *To govern* is to conduct the undertaking towards its objective by seeking to derive optimum advantage from all available resources and to assure the smooth working of the six essential functions. Management is merely one of the six functions whose smooth working government has to ensure, but it has such a large place in the part played by higher managers that sometimes this part seems exclusively managerial.[15]

Thus Fayol made a definite distinction between *administrer* and *gouverner* which Coubrough interprets as "to administer" and "to manage" and which Storrs renders as "to manage" and "to govern." To a Frenchman, *gouverner* is a general function of steering or guiding a totality toward a goal; for example, the captain of a ship, the head of a state, or the chief of an enterprise. Depending on the context of the writer, *gouverner* may become steering a ship, governing a state, or *managing* an enterprise. On the other hand, *administrer* also means to manage but is less comprehensive

[13] Fayol, pp. 11–12. Italics added.
[14] Fayol (Coubrough), p. 9. Italics added.
[15] Fayol (Storrs), p. 6. Italics added.

and applies to executing smaller matters. Briefly stated, Coubrough's translation is the better of the two and Storrs' rendering of *gouverner* as "to govern" was not appropriate in the business context of Fayol's writing.[16]

The point in this comparative analysis is to clear up some semantic problems. For many, management is "getting things done through people" and this view has persisted because of the Storrs' translation:

> The managerial function finds its only outlet through the members of the organization (body corporate). Whilst the other functions bring into play material and machines the managerial function operates only on the personnel.[17]

Coubrough's version reads:

> The administrative function is only concerned with the human part of an undertaking; while the other functions control material and machines, the administrative function only affects the personnel.[18]

If one accepts Fayol's original intent to distinguish between *administrer* and *gouverner*, then the Storrs' translation which confined the definition of management to working with and through people was an erroneous one (Figure 10-1). Fayol's intent was to establish management as an overall function of conducting an undertaking "towards its objective by trying to make the best possible use of all the resources at its disposal . . . to ensure the smooth working of the six essential functions. Administration is only one of these functions . . ."[19] Alas, this was not the case; and the Storrs' translation became the standard translation of Fayol.[20]

Managerial Skills and Abilities

Fayol did not develop a discussion of this general "management" function separate from his "administrative elements." In presenting the abilities needed by a manager, he did stress the idea that each manager would need "special knowledge" which

---

[16] The author is indebted to Dr. Joseph Allaire, Chairman, Department of Modern Languages, Florida State University, for his assistance in comparing, translating and making the above distinctions.

[17] Fayol (Storrs), p. 19.

[18] Fayol (Coubrough) p. 19.

[19] Fayol (Coubrough) p. 9.

[20] This author prefers the Coubrough translation but will confine himself in the following pages to using the Storrs' terminology in order to preserve historical continuity and to keep the material within the commonly accepted frame of reference of the reader.

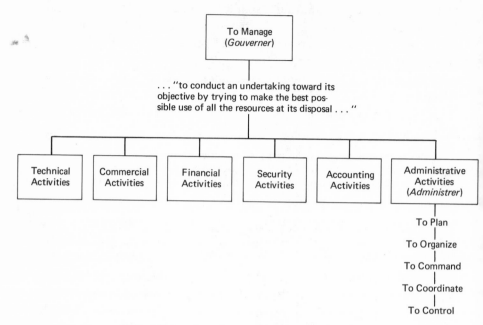

Fig. 10-1. Fayol's "management" function.

was peculiar to any function, such as technical, financial, and so on. In general, every manager needed these qualities and abilities:

1. Physical qualities: health, vigour, address.
2. Mental qualities: ability to understand and learn, judgement, mental vigour and adaptability.
3. Moral qualities: energy, firmness, willingness to accept responsibility, initiative, loyalty, tact, dignity.
4. General education: general acquaintance with matters not belonging exclusively to the function performed.
5. Special knowledge: that peculiar to the function, be it technical, commercial, financial, managerial, etc. . . .
6. Experience: knowledge arising from the work proper. It is the recollection of lessons which one has oneself derived from things.[21]

Fayol then graphed the relative importance of requisite abilities for personnel, depending on their location in the management hierarchy. At the worker level, technical ability was most important; but as one moved up the scalar chain, the relative importance of managerial ability increased while the need for technical ability decreased. The higher the level of authority, the more dominant

[21] Fayol (Storrs), p. 7.

became the need for managerial ability. Ability in commercial, financial, security, and accounting matters also diminished in importance farther up the scalar chain. In terms of differences in the size of the enterprise, the manager of a small firm must have relatively more technical ability, while in larger concerns, the upper levels needed managerial rather than technical ability.

The distinction between the relative importance of abilities was crucial to Fayol's development of the notion of *teaching* management. Regarding the proliferation of large firms and other organizations, he noted that future leadership must receive managerial training rather than clinging to the past precepts of education for technical, commercial, etc. abilities. Schools did not teach management and it was assumed by industrial leaders that practice and experience were the only pathways to a managerial position. The reason for the absence of management teaching was the "absence of theory." Each manager followed his own methods, principles, and personal theories, but no one had ever tried to fit the acceptable precepts and experiences into a general framework of administrative theory. Management knowledge came through osmosis and generalized concepts were lacking. Fayol had built his case for theory: (1) the fact that management was a separate ability applicable to all types of undertakings; (2) that this ability was sorely needed as one moved up the management hierarchy; and (3) the premise that managerial abilities could be taught.

The Principles of Management

The notion of "principles" of management is often misunderstood and subject to controversy. Fayol's conception of a principle was not as rigidly based as one might conceive of a rule or law in the physical sciences. He used the term "principles" very reluctantly:

For preference I shall adopt the term principles whilst dissociating it from any suggestion of rigidity, for there is nothing rigid or absolute in management affairs, it is all a question of proportion. Seldom do we have to apply the same principle twice in identical conditions; allowance must be made for different and changing circumstances . . .

Therefore principles are flexible and capable of adaptation to every need; it is a matter of knowing how to make use of them, which is a difficult art requiring intelligence, experience, decision and proportion. Compounded of tact and experience, proportion is one of the foremost attributes of the manager. There is no limit to the number of principles of management, every rule or managerial procedure which strengthens the body corporate or facilitates its functioning has a place among the principles so long, at least, as experience confirms its worthiness. A change in the state of affairs can be responsible for change of rules which had been engendered by that state.[22]

Fayol's principles were derived from those that he used "most frequently" in his own experience. They were not immutable but served as "lighthouses" to show the way to theory. Fayol's famous fourteen principles were:

1. Division of work.
2. Authority.
3. Discipline.
4. Unity of command.
5. Unity of direction.
6. Subordination of individual interests to the general interest.
7. Remuneration.
8. Centralization.
9. Scalar chain (line of authority).
10. Order.
11. Equity.
12. Stability of tenure of personnel.
13. Initiative.
14. *Esprit de corps.*[23]

Divsion of work was the classic idea of specialization of labor and the advantages which accrued in reducing waste, increasing output, and easing the task of job training. Like Taylor, Fayol thought that division of labor was not limited to technical work but could apply also to a "specialization of functions and separation of powers,"[24] *i.e.*, to managerial effort also.

Authority was defined as "the right to give orders and the power to exact obedience."[25] Fayol distinguished between the *formal* authority held by the manager by the virtue of his office or rank and *personal* authority which was "compounded of intelligence, experience, moral worth, ability to lead, past services, etc."[26] A good manager would *complement* his official authority with personal authority. Further, authority and responsibility were corollaries in the sense that wherever authority was exercised, responsibility arose. Fayol stated the classic case for authority

22 *Ibid.*, p. 19.
23 *Ibid.*, pp. 19–20. Note: Coubrough translated number five as "unity of management" and number nine as "the hierarchy."
24 *Ibid.*, p. 20.
25 *Ibid.*, p. 21.
26 *Ibid.*, p. 21.

being commensurate with responsibility and this principle has appeared throughout management literature to become as inseparable as Mary and her little lamb.

Discipline was in essence based on obedience and respect between the firm and its employees. It was essential to success and based on respect rather than fear. Poor discipline was inevitably the result of poor leadership and good discipline came from good leaders, clear agreements between management and labor regarding rules, and the judicious use of sanctions (penalties).

Unity of command, Fayol's fourth principle, brought him into opposition to Taylor's functional foremen. The principle that "For any action whatsoever an employee should receive orders from one superior only" was fundamental to Fayol's concept of an organization. Just as no man can serve two masters, dual command was a threat to authority, discipline, and stability.

Unity of direction meant "one head and one plan for a group of activities having the same objective."[27] Unity of direction came from a sound organization structure and was essential to "unity of action, coordination of strength, and focusing of effort."[28]

The subordination of individual interests to the general interest principle was a plea to abolish "ignorance, ambition, selfishness, laziness, weakness and all human passions" which caused conflict when the individual or a group tried to prevail over the organization. The *remuneration of personnel* principle was Fayol's version of economic man. After discussing day wages, piece rates, bonuses, and profit sharing, he concluded that the mode of payment was dependent upon many factors and that the objective was to "make the personnel more valuable . . . and also to inspire keenness."[29] His analysis certainly fell short of suggesting a clear concept of a remunerative principle or of any clear notion of motivation. The principle of *centralization* was more lucid and showed some brilliant insights into organization:

Centralization is not a system of management good or bad of itself, capable of being adopted or discarded at the whim of managers or of circumstances; it is always present to a greater or less extent. The question of centralization or decentralization, is a simple question of proportion, it is a matter of finding

27 *Ibid.,* p. 25. Coubrough rendered this as "unity of management" which was "one manager and one plan for all operations which have the same object in view." (p. 23).
28 *Ibid.,* p. 25.
29 *Ibid.,* p. 32.

the optimum degree for the particular concern.   In small firms, where the manager's orders go directly to subordinates there is absolute centralization; in large concerns, where a long scalar chain is interposed between manager and lower grades, orders and counter-information too, have to go through a series of intermediaries.   Each employee, intentionally or unintentionally, puts something of himself into the transmission and execution of orders and of information received too.   He does not operate merely as a cog in a machine. What appropriate share of initiative may be left to intermediaries depends on the personal character of the manager, on his moral worth, on the reliability of his subordinates, and also on the condition of the business.   The degree of centralization must vary according to different cases.   The objective to pursue is the optimum utilization of all faculties of the personnel.[30]

The continuum of possibilities for centralization and decentralization, the possible communication distortions in the scalar chain, and the variables affecting the degree of decentralization were pillars for evolving theory.   Fayol's notion of the centralization-decentralization continuum was explicit: "everything which goes to increase the importance of the subordinate's role is decentralization, everything which goes to reduce it is centralization."[31]

The *scalar chain* was "the chain of superiors ranging from the ultimate authority to the lowest ranks."[32]   It showed the routing of the line of authority and the channels for the transmission of communications.   To counter possible communication delays caused by the unity of command principle, Fayol developed his "gang plank" which allowed communications to cross lines of authority but only when it was agreed to by all parties and superiors were kept informed at all times.[33]   Thus Foreman F, desiring to communicate with Foreman P, could do so directly without reporting upward (F through E to A) and having that message in turn transmitted downward to P.   The gang plank (see Fig. 10-2) permitted swift, sure lateral communications without overloading circuits and preserved the unity of command principle.

Order, the tenth principle, insured a place for everything and everything in its place.   It applied to materials, shop cleanliness, and to personnel.   For people, it was each to his task and that task set neatly into a structure of activities.   *Equity* resulted from kindliness and justice and provided a principle for employee relations.   The twelfth principle, *stability of tenure of personnel*, sought

[30] *Ibid.*, p. 37.
[31] *Ibid.*, p. 34.
[32] *Ibid.*, p. 34.
[33] *Ibid.*, p. 34.   Coubrough translated Fayol's *passarelle* as a "bridge" (p. 28).

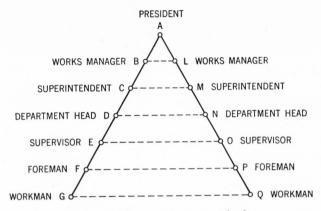

Fig. 10–2. Fayol's gang plank.

to provide for orderly personnel planning and provisions to replace the human resource. *Initiative* as a principle exhorted individuals to display zeal and energy in all efforts. Finally, *esprit de corps* stressed building harmony and unity within the firm. "Dividing enemy forces to weaken them is clever, but dividing one's own team is a grave sin against the business."[34]

Fayol's fourteen principles represented building blocks for his discussion of the elements of management. They were intended as guides to theory and practice and were not exhaustive in scope nor to be interpreted as rigid in application. The early factory system reflected many of these principles in practice but it was Fayol's contribution to codify them into a conceptual schema. So much of our present management literature has been built upon Fayol's ideas and terminology that we cannot see the uniqueness of his insights. For his time and in the context of the paucity of management literature, his ideas were fresh, illuminating, and milestones on the path of the evolving discipline of management.

The Elements of Management: Planning

Henri Fayol did not use the term "process" to describe the manager's functions but chose instead "elements of management." The first element and one he stressed a great deal was *prévoyance* or *planning*. To Fayol, "managing means looking ahead" and fore-

[34] *Ibid.*, p. 40.

sight was an essential element of management.[35] Any plan of action rested upon: (1) the firm's resources, *i.e.*, the buildings, tools, materials, personnel, sales outlets, public relations, etc.; (2) the nature of present work in process; and (3) future trends in all activities of the firm whose occurrence could not be predetermined. In developing the plan of action, Fayol put forth an early concept of participation:

> The study of resources, future possibilities, and means to be used for attaining the objective call for contributions from all departmental heads within the framework of their mandate, each one brings to this study the contribution of his experience together with recognition of the responsibility which will fall upon him in executing the plan.[36]

Such participation insured that no resource was neglected and it promoted managerial interest in the plan. More attention would be given to planning by lower echelon managers since they had to execute what they themselves had planned. A good plan of action had the characteristics of *unity* (one overall plan followed by specific plans for each activity); *continuity* (both short range and long range); *flexibility* (to bend to unexpected events); and *precision* (eliminating as much guesswork as possible). Based on these characteristics, Fayol advised a series of separate plans which would all together comprise one entire plan for the firm. Daily, weekly, monthly, annual, five-year, and ten-year forecasts (or plans) were prepared and redrafted as time passed or as conditions changed.

Fayol's stress on long-range planning was a unique contribution to management thought and his ideas are as important today as they were for his own time. He also displayed some unique insights into national planning for the French nation. The French government planned and budgeted on an annual basis with little or no regard for long-term development; the result was hand-to-mouth operations and a lack of exercise of fiscal responsibility by the chiefs of state. Fayol attributed the blame to "instability of tenure" for the prime minister and evidently this failing has been a continuing one for the French government. This first element of management, a combined function of planning and forecasting, was to be universal in applicability and a fundamental building block for all organizations.

---

[35] *Ibid.*, p. 43.
[36] *Ibid.*, p. 48.

Organizing

Organizing, the second element, included provisions for the structuring of activities and relationships as well as the procurement, evaluation, and training of personnel. As this element evolved, later writers split Fayol's organizing element into two elements, organizing and staffing (or human resource administration). For Fayol, to organize a business meant "to provide it with everything useful to its functioning: raw materials, tools, capital, personnel" and it was the duty of management to "see that the human and material organization is consistent with the objective, resources, and requirements of the concern."[37] The organization structure must be so arranged that it provided unity of direction toward the objective of the firm. The proper structure defined duties clearly, encouraged initiative and responsibility, harmonized activities and coordinated efforts, and insured control without an "excess of regulation, red tape, and paper control."[38]

In organization theory, the organizational "pyramid" is a product of functional growth. Functional growth is horizontal in that more people are added to functions as the organizational workload expands; scalar growth is vertical and caused by the need to add layers of supervision to direct and coordinate lower echelons. Each addition of workers in functional growth brings in fresh foremen and in turn these added supervisors require the addition of higher levels of management, resulting in continued scalar growth. Fayol built his functional and scalar growth processes on the basis of fifteen workers to a foreman and a ratio of four superiors to every other superior. For example, fifteen workers required one manager, sixty workers required four superiors, and in turn these four required one common manager. The organization grew in simple geometrical progression whose first term was fifteen (workers) and a common ratio of four; by following this progression, Fayol envisioned a method of keeping the number of levels in an organization to a minimum. An organization of 251,658,240 people for example, would require only thirteen levels of management. Fayol advocated a relatively narrow span of management throughout the organization. Whatever his level of authority, one manager was to have direct command over a small number of subordinates, "less

[37] *Ibid.*, p. 53.
[38] *Ibid.*, p. 54.

than six, normally" according to Fayol, and only the first line supervisor would have more. At the foreman's level, Fayol judged him to be capable of handling twenty or thirty men, provided "the work is simple."[39]

On the subject of staff, Fayol visualized a group of men who had the "strength, knowledge, and time" to assist a manager by acting as a "sort of extension of the manager's personality."[40] The staff was to take orders only from the general manager and Fayol compared it to the military concept of the general staff. The functions of the staff were to aid in carrying out the manager's personal duties such as correspondence, interviews, conferences, etc., to aid in liaison and control, to gather information and assist in formulating future plans and to "search for improvements." The latter function of the staff was unique to Fayol; he postulated that operating management had neither the time nor the energy to devote to long-term research because they were too absorbed in current and weighty problems of running the business. The staff, freed of daily cares, could search for better work methods, perceive changes in business conditions, and concern itself with long range matters.

Fayol's staff concept brought him into direct opposition to Taylor's functional foremen. Fayol agreed with Taylor's goal, i.e., the necessity for specialized assistance, but disagreed with the means. Functional foremen negated the unity-of-command principle and to Fayol this was treading on dangerous ground. Order must be maintained and this was possible only if one man was clearly responsible to one other person: "So . . . let us treasure the old type of organization in which unity of command is honored. It can, after all, be easily reconciled . . . with the assistance [i.e., staff] given to superintendents and foremen."[41]

Organization charts were a *sine qua non* of every enterprise. The preparation of a formal organization chart enabled one to visualize the organization as a whole, specified lines of authority, provided channels of communication, prevented the overlapping or encroachment of departments, avoided dual command situations, and clearly assigned duties and responsibilities. The chart itself was a managerial instrument for analyzing relationships be-

[39] *Ibid.*, p. 98.
[40] *Ibid.*, p. 63.
[41] *Ibid.*, p. 70.

tween departments, for specifying individuals and their tasks, and for making modifications in the organization. Fayol did not completely develop his ideas or methods of departmentalizing operations since this was to be reserved for Part III of his work, which was never finished. Turning from the organizational framework, Fayol developed the rudiments of a personnel or staffing function which consisted of selection, evaluation, and training. Selection was examined only briefly and was viewed as a function of finding the qualities and knowledge in people to fill all levels of the organization. The consequences of poor selection was "commensurate with the rank of the employee"; Fayol advised that the length of time spent on selection should be increased as the level of position being filled rose. Evaluation of both managers and workers was based on similar essential characteristics but varied according to the level within the organization:

1. "Health and physical fitness" were essential to all personnel.
2. "Intelligence and mental vigour" became more important further up the hierarchical chain. Mental vigour, as Fayol used the term, was the ability to "deal simultaneously with many varied manifold subjects" and was essential for higher managers.
3. "Moral qualities," such as initiative, acceptance of responsibility, loyalty, and discipline were important at all levels.
4. "General education," i.e., knowledge apart from job knowledge, was necessary if one wished to rise in the organization.
5. "Management knowledge" or that concerned with the elements of planning, organizing, command, coordination, and control became increasingly important as one moved up the organizational ladder.
6. "Knowledge of other functions" was necessary as one's responsibility expanded to include other spheres of activity[42]

Fayol confined himself to describing qualities and did not examine problems of evaluating performance, nor did he recommend methods and procedures for its conduct. Like Taylor's, his view of the personnel function was limited; this is not in criticism, however, since personnel practices of the day were very rudimen-

[42] *Ibid.,* pp. 76–77.

tary in all cases. Training was dealt with at length primarily because Fayol had an axe to grind. He advocated a diminution of technical training and an increased teaching of managerial knowledge. Contemporary education was based on the premise that the value of engineers and industrial leaders bore "a direct relationship to the number of years devoted to the subject of mathematics."[43] Fayol deplored the emphasis on mathematics: "Long personal experience has taught me that the use of *higher* mathematics counts for nothing in managing businesses . . ."[44] Basic mathematics helped train the mind but further study should be devoted to management rather than more mathematics. Fayol sought balance and advised young engineers to study people, "their behavior, character, abilities, work, and even their personal interests."[45] For Fayol, *everyone* should study management for it was necessary in the home as well as in industrial and nonindustrial undertakings.

Command

Command, Fayol's third element, had as its object "to get the optimum return from all employees of his unit in the interest of the whole concern."[46] Command was an art which rested upon certain personal qualities and knowledge of general principles of management. The manager who exercised command should:

1. Have a thorough knowledge of his personnel.
2. Eliminate the incompetent.
3. Be well versed in the agreements binding the business and its employees.
4. Set a good example.
5. Conduct periodic audits of the organization and use summarized charts to further this.
6. Bring together his chief assistants by means of conferences, at which unity of direction and focusing of effort are provided for.
7. Not become engrossed in detail.
8. Aim at making unity, energy, initiative and loyalty prevail among the personnel.[47]

Most of these aspects of command are self-explanatory and, together with the fourteen principles, form a fairly coherent picture of Fayol's concept of leadership. He deemed conferences a very use-

---

[43] *Ibid.*, p. 83–84.
[44] *Ibid.*, p. 84. Later he referred to "higher" mathematics as special studies such as calculus.
[45] *Ibid.*, p. 91.
[46] *Ibid.*, p. 97.
[47] *Ibid.*, p. 97–98.

ful device for insuring unity of direction and stressed that the chief must be constantly aware of all business activities. The *caveat* to avoid being engrossed in detail was not antithetical to keeping informed. The manager should be aware of everything but he did not neglect large problems while lavishing his attention on small ones. Through use of his staff, by proper definition of the organization, and through the use of oral and written reports, the manager could maintain direction and control of the main business issues. To achieve initiative, the manager should allow subordinates "the maximum share of activity consistent with their position and capability, even at the cost of some mistakes . . ."[48] This was mostly delegation and not full blown participation in management since a sound organization could be used to circumscribe activities to prevent too much initiative at the wrong times and in the wrong places. However, Fayol did recognize the importance of such delegated participation as a useful device for developing young managers.[49]

Coordination and Control

Coordination, viewed by Fayol as a separate element of management, meant "to harmonize all the activities of a concern so as to facilitate its working, and its success."[50] Later writers have stressed the role of coordination in all elements rather than treating it as a separate one. To Fayol, coordination was a balancing act of keeping expenses equivalent to revenues, of maintaining equipment to meet production goals, and of insuring that sales and production were consonant. Organization and planning facilitated coordination by specifying duties, establishing schedules, and focusing responsibilities on the objective. Command instilled initiative and the conferences between the manager and his subordinates provided a clearing house for airing problems, progress, and plans. The conference was a quick, simple way of keeping informed and of insuring organizational cohesion. Liaison officers, typically staff personnel, should be used to enhance coordination in the interim between conferences and in the care of establishments located far from the main office. The liaison position supplemented coordination but did not replace the direct responsibility of the chief.

[48] *Ibid.*, p. 103.
[49] *Ibid.*, p. 103.
[50] *Ibid.*, p. 103.

Control consisted of "verifying whether everything occurs in conformity with the plan adopted, the instructions issued, and the principles established."[51]   The objective of control was to identify errors in order to correct them and to prevent recurrence. Control was to be applied to people, objects, and activities. Effective control was based on prompt action followed by sanctions if necessary.   Control was impartial and Fayol advised separation of the inspector from those being inspected to insure independence of the control element.

A Final Note

Henri Fayol had the orientation of the top manager.   He was not as philosophical as Taylor, nor did he stress mechanics to the same extent.   Of the five elements he developed for his theory of administration, planning and organizing received the majority of his attention.   The stress on these two was not necessarily an imbalance but illustrated the primacy that Fayol gave to these elements with respect to the performance of the others.   Planning and organizing set the stage by making forecasts, developing a plan of action, establishing an organization, and selecting personnel.   In Fayol's terms: "The organization, having been formed, must be set going, and this is the mission of command."[52]   Command actuated the plans and the organization; coordination kept the parts of the organization in harmony; control checked up on plans and instructions with respect to actual performance; and the cycle was renewed as new plans were made in light of past operations.

It is easy to underestimate the work of Fayol.   His ideas and terminology are so commonplace to present management literature that they are taken for granted.   Yet his notion of an administrative theory applicable to all types of organized undertaking was an important milestone in this history of management.   Though Taylor did suggest the applicability of a science of management to a multitude of activities, Fayol receives the credit for "universality" because he was much more explicit and far reaching.   Taylor had more confidence in "principles" than Fayol, who saw them as flexible guides for action and not as immutable laws.

[51] *Ibid.*, p. 107.
[52] *Ibid.*, p. 97.

The "universality" of management principles was also tempered by Fayol. The manager who operated solely on the principles and who was armed only with knowledge of the elements would not be effective. In essence, the manager needed to know more than how to plan, organize, command, coordinate, and control. He had to have some knowledge of the business activities (technical, commercial, etc.) which he was managing, even if he were the chief executive. The elements did not operate in a vacuum but were applied to *something* which for Fayol were the essential activities and resources of the firm.

BUREAUCRACY: MAX WEBER

The life and work of Max Weber (1864–1920) runs chronologically parallel to that of Henri Fayol and Frederick Taylor. Born to a life of affluence in Germany in a family of considerable social and political connections, Weber was an intellectual of the first degree with far-ranging interests in sociology, religion, economics, and political science.[53] As a professor, editor, consultant to government, and author, he established himself as one of the leading scholars of his period. *The Protestant Ethic and the Spirit of Capitalism* was one of his major works but his interests also led him to consider the relationships between economic organizations and society. Weber was a theorist who introduced a significant number of new interpretations and emphases which were unique to the economic-historical discussions of the time. His contributions greatly facilitated understanding of the relationships and the continuity between nineteenth century family-firm capitalism, which he called "patrimonial," and the emerging era of the large scale organization of industry and big governmental units in Europe of Weber's day.

Bureaucracy as the Ideal

Weber perceived the need to establish a rational basis for the administration of large-scale undertakings and the result of his work was the conception of *bureaucracy* as an ideal organizational

[53] Biographical information on Max Weber is based on Hans Gerth and C. Wright Mills, *From Max Weber,* New York: Oxford University Press, 1946; and Reinhard Bendix, *Max Weber: An Intellectual Portrait,* Garden City, N.Y. Doubleday & Co., 1960.

arrangement. "Ideal," to Weber, did not mean desirable, but the "pure form" of organization.[54] Combinations or alloys of various organizational arrangements would appear in practice but Weber wanted to characterize an ideal type for the purpose of theoretical analysis. The bureaucratic ideal would serve as a normative model to ease the transition from small-scale entrepreneurial ("patrimonial") administration to large-scale professional administration. Weber's conceptualization of bureaucracy merits substantial consideration for naming him the "father of organization theory."

Though other writings of Weber were translated earlier (i.e. Frank Knight's translation of Weber's *Economic History* in 1927 and Talcott Parsons' rendition of *The Protestant Ethic* in 1930), his work on bureaucracy was not rendered into English until 1947. However, Chester Barnard, who will be discussed later, was influenced by Talcott Parsons and read Weber in the German.[55] Weber's writings thus formed a partial foundation for Barnard's own analysis of the formal organization. Weber was the intellectual progenitor of the formal analysis of organizational structures. He was concerned with designing a blueprint structure of authority—activity relationships which would facilitate the attainment of the objective of an organization.

Kinds of Authority

Weber postulated three *pure* types of legitimate (*i.e.*, socially acceptable) authority: (1) rational-legal authority which rested on "legality" or the "right of those elevated to authority . . . to issue commands"; (2) a "traditional" type which rested on a belief "in the sanctity of immemorial traditions and the legitimacy of the status of those exercising authority under them"; and (3) "charismatic" authority which was based "on devotion to the specific and exceptional sanctity, heroism, or exemplary character of an individual person . . ."[56] In the case of rational-legal authority, the obedience of subordinates was owed to the legally estab-

---

[54] S. M. Miller (ed.), *Max Weber*, New York: Thomas Y. Crowell Co., 1963, p. 10.

[55] The author is indebted to Professor William B. Wolf for his indication of the influence of Parsons on Barnard. Letter to author, December 16, 1970.

[56] A. M. Henderson and Talcott Parsons (editors and translators), *Max Weber: The Theory of Social and Economic Organization*, New York: Free Press, 1947, p. 328. In reality, Weber would recognize that authority may be legitimated on a combination of these so-called "pure" types.

lished hierarchy such as a business, a state office, military unit, or any other organization. It was obedience to the authority of an established *position* or rank. In traditional authority, obedience was due to the *person* who occupied the traditionally sanctioned position of authority. In charismatic authority (*i.e.*, charisma from the early Christian concept of "the gift of grace"), the leader was obeyed by virtue of the follower's personal trust and belief in his powers or revelations.

Some form of authority is the cornerstone of any organization. Without authority of some type, no organization can be guided toward an objective; authority brings order to chaos. Of the three pure types of authority, Weber said that rational-legal must provide the basis for a bureaucracy, since it: (1) provided a basis for *continuity* of administration; (2) was "rational", *i.e.*, the member occupying the administrative office was chosen on the basis of *competence* to perform his duties; (3) the leader was provided a legal means for exercising authority; and (4) all authority was clearly defined and carefully delimited to the functions necessary to accomplish the organization's task.[57] In contrast, tradition as legitimate authority would be less efficient since the leaders were not chosen on the basis of competence and since the administrative unit would act to preserve traditions of the past. Likewise, charisma as authority was too emotional and irrational in the sense that it avoided rules and routine and depended upon mystique and divine revelations.

The Administrative System

Weber's concept of the best administrative system is strikingly analogous to that of Taylor. For both men, management or administration meant the exercise of control on the basis of knowledge. Both sought technical competence in leaders who would lead by virtue of fact and not whim, by ability and not favoritism. The essential elements of Weber's ideal bureaucracy were:

1. A division of labor in which authority and responsibility were clearly defined for each member and were legitimatized as official duties.

2. The offices or positions would be organized in a hierarchy

---

[57] *Ibid.*, p. 330–331.

of authority resulting in a chain of command or the scalar principle.

3. All organizational members were to be selected on the basis of technical qualifications through formal examinations or by virtue of training or education.

4. Officials were appointed, not elected. (With the exception in some cases of the chief of the whole unit. For example, an elected public official.)

5. Administrative officials worked for fixed salaries and were "career" officials.

6. The administrative official was not an owner of the unit being administered.

7. The administrator would be subject to strict rules, discipline, and controls regarding his conduct of his official duties. These rules and controls would be impersonal and uniformly applied in all cases.[58]

For Weber, bureaucracy embodied the ideal administrative system and was not rule-encumbered inefficiency as the term has come to connote in modern parlance:

> Experience tends universally to show that the purely bureaucratic type of administrative organization—that is, the monocratic variety of bureaucracy— is, from a purely technical point of view, capable of attaining the highest degree of efficiency and is in this sense formally the most rational known means of carrying out imperative control over human beings. It is superior to any other form in precision, in stability, in the stringency of its discipline, and in its reliability. It thus makes possible a particularly high degree of calculability of results for the heads of the organization and for those acting in relation to it. It is finally superior both in intensive efficiency and in the scope of its operations and is formally capable of application to all kinds of administrative tasks.[59]

Weber perceived a spreading of the growth of large scale organizations in the church, state, the military, in political parties, in economic enterprises, and in all types of organizations. The growth of these large undertakings required a rationalization in administration. In Weber's view, capitalism had played a major role in the development of bureaucracy. Capitalism created an urgent need for stable, strict, intensive, and calculable administration. It was this need which gave bureaucracy a crucial role in society as the central element in any kind of large-scale organization.

[58] Adapted from *ibid.*, pp. 329–333.
[59] *Ibid.*, p. 337.

From a historical perspective, Weber's writings reflected what he saw as a breakup of tradition-based society. The process of industrialization in Germany had been rapid but largely constrained by the strong political regime of the Junkers. Germany stood at the crossroads between the old family-based business system and the rapid rise of large-scale enterprise. Weber's response to the breakup of tradition was to rationalize organizations to provide efficiency for a new capitalistic state. In essence, Weber was the Adam Smith of Germany.[60] Whereas Adam Smith had struck a blow to destroy the mercantile policies of England which were retarding the development of capitalism, Weber's attack on tradition and the use of political control in the economy, which was to be replaced by administration by knowledge and technical competence, was a similar thrust to advance capitalism. Bureaucracy was conceived as a blueprint for efficiency which would emphasize rules rather than men, and competence rather than favoritism.

Bureaucracy and Organization Theory

As the sire of organization theory, Weber paved the way for others to examine the ideal of bureaucracy versus its practice. Gradually, there has emerged a concern with the "informal organization" or the nonblueprinted operations of an organization. Etzioni has credited Weber with influencing the modern "structuralists" who have sought to integrate the classical, formalized approach to organizations with the human-relations-oriented, informal organizational analysts.[61] Based on Weber's search for legitimacy of authority to reduce the alienation caused by the use of formal authority, the structuralists have sought to solve the organizational dilemmas of rationality versus nonrationality, management versus the worker, and the formal versus the informal organization.

Weber's conception of the ideal has considerable merit and has inspired further examination of the sought versus the unsought consequences of organizational activities. The sociologists Robert Merton, Philip Selznick, and Alvin Gouldner have questioned the ideal and established models to show the dysfunc-

---

[60] S. M. Miller, p. 6.

[61] Amitai Etzioni, *Modern Organizations*, Englewood Cliffs, N.J.: Prentice-Hall, 1964, p. 41 and pp. 51–55.

tional consequences of bureaucracy.[62] The analysis of dysfunctions, or the "unanticipated" responses on the part of organizational members, did not deny the proposition that bureaucracies were more efficient but served to show what occurred when humans with all their idiosyncracies were added to the ideal blueprint.

Weber's work on bureaucracy remained largely unrecognized in America until the 1940's and 1950's. Like Fayol, he had to wait until cultural conditions created the need to think in terms of administrative theory. As organizations grew in size and complexity, men began to search for a theory of organizations. In their search they discovered Max Weber and his bureaucratic ideal.

SUMMARY

The emergence of administrative theory took place in two forms; one, Fayol's contribution of a universal process of managerial activities; and two, Weber's search for a blueprint of idealized structural arrangements for the purpose of insuring technical efficiency. From different backgrounds and perspectives, both Fayol and Weber attempted to present administrative schemes for coping with large-scale organizations. Henri Fayol stressed education for management rather than technical training, the importance of planning and organizing, the on-going phases of command, coordination, and control, and perceived from his experiences a universality of managerial functions. He distinguished between "management" as an integrating force and "administration" which worked solely through people. Max Weber took an administrative viewpoint in his bureaucratic ideal. He sought to avoid leadership and organization by tradition and charisma, to establish a rational-legal basis for authority, and to present orderly arrangements for the selection of personnel and the execution of activities. Both Weber and Fayol had history's misfortune of having to wait until others could give them their proper credit in the evolution of management thought.

[62] The Merton, Selznick, and Gouldner models may be found in James G. March and Herbert A. Simon, *Organizations,* New York: John Wiley & Sons, 1958, pp. 36–47.

11

Scientific Management and Organized Labor

There was never any doubt about Taylor's stand on organized labor. His insistence on science rather than bargaining in determining wages and working conditions and his preference for dealing with the individual worker rather than the union intermediary was to bring a surfeit of criticism. Our purpose here is to examine the critics, the opposing philosophies of organized labor and scientific management, and the changing tides in labor-management relations during this era.

THE STANCE OF ORGANIZED LABOR

Preceding the publicity given scientific management by the railroad hearings, organized labor had paid scant attention to Taylor and his followers. The existing philosophy of the American Federation of Labor, as represented by Samuel Gompers, was to bargain for more wages and to achieve gains for labor through "power" and not productivity.[1] As public interest was aroused by the possibilities of increasing national productivity through scientific management, labor leaders were stirred from their former positions. The strike at the Watertown Arsenal and the subsequent House investigation were results of organized labor's in-

---

[1] Jean Trepp McKelvey, *AFL Attitudes Toward Production: 1900–1932,* Ithaca, N.Y.: Cornell Studies in Industrial and Labor Relations, Vol II, 1952, pp. 6–11.

creased interest in and hardened attitudes toward the new vogue of efficiency engineering. Conceptually, the evolution of relations between organized labor and scientific management may be classified into rather discrete time periods: (1) a period of vitriolic hostility from 1911 to 1915; (2) an informal truce during the war production years 1916–1918; and (3) a new era of revisionism in management and cooperation on the part of labor lasting up to the Great Depression.

The Hoxie Report

The early position of organized labor *vis-à-vis* scientific management found its critical articulation in an investigation by the U.S. Commission on Industrial Relations. The chief investigator was Robert Franklin Hoxie, professor of political economy at the University of Chicago, and his assistants were Robert G. Valentine, an investigator and consultant in labor problems who was to represent management's viewpoint, and John P. Frey, editor of the *International Molder's Journal*, representing labor.[2] The purpose of the study was to investigate all systems of shop management including Taylor's, Gantt's, and Emerson's and the final report was the most comprehensive statement of the relations between scientific management and labor for that era.[3] The investigators examined thirty-five shops employing scientific management during the period January to April 1915. In addition, they consulted one hundred and fifty industrial leaders, labor officials, and authorities on scientific management, including Taylor, Gantt, and Emerson.

An early inkling of controversy occurred when Hoxie insisted on making no distinction between the theory and the practice of scientific management. To Hoxie, scientific management was what was practiced, regardless of the ideas and theories it advocated; to Taylor, scientific management "ceased to exist" if its principles and philosophy were violated in practice. Hoxie's

---

[2] Though calling himself a consultant to management on labor relations, Valentine had only brief experience in industry and that in banking. He taught English at the Massachusetts Institute of Technology and was at one time Assistant Commissioner of Indian Affairs. L. Urwick and E. F. L. Brech, *The Golden Book of Management*, London: Newman Neame Ltd., 1956, p. 163.

[3] Robert F. Hoxie, *Scientific Management and Labor*, New York: Appleton-Century-Crofts, 1915.

distinction did not impress Taylor and this undoubtedly led to his unfavorable reception of the report and the inclusion of a separate statement on his position in the appendix.[4]

The core of the Hoxie report was the analysis of the practice of scientific management in 1915. Contrary to the view that acceptance of the movement was widespread, Hoxie found a marked degree of diversity among the various shops studied. In the shops which were supposed to represent scientific management in practice, *not one* had a complete and faithful installation of either the Taylor, Gantt, or Emerson systems. Further, the systems which did appear did not conform precisely to the ideas and principles of the scientific management advocates since each management had modified the system to fit the idiosyncrasies of its own firm as it perceived them. This diversity led to an analysis of various features of the theory and how they became modified in practice. First, Hoxie found that practice violated the precepts of careful study and analysis prior to installation of any efficiency system. The lack of individuals trained in time study methods, coupled with employer pressure for quick payouts, resulted in hasty and incomplete job study. Standardization of tools, methods, and work conditions were lacking in most shops studied. The fault fell equally on management and on the efficiency engineer. Management's prevailing attitude was to opt for quick returns with small regard for the long-range outcome and with little concern for or knowledge of the impact of the system on the workers. On the other side, the efficiency experts who offered their services worked for the short run and did not have "the ability or the willingness to install scientific management in accordance with the Taylor formula and ideals."[5] Hoxie did not specifically fault Taylor or his close followers, but indicated that there were others who were picking and choosing from his system and discarding and violating the spirit and principles of what Taylor advocated.

Second, the concept of functional foremen found few adherents in practice. Some firms made the attempt but soon re-

---

[4] *Ibid.*, Appendix II, pp. 140–149. Mr. Gantt, in Appendix III (pp. 150–151), and Mr. Emerson, in Appendix IV (pp. 152–168), also filed their positions regarding Taylor's claims. The three do not present a unified theory of the movement but do agree on the fundamental aims of scientific management.

[5] *Ibid.*, p. 29.

turned to the military, line type of organization. Hoxie found that in practice the Taylor ideal of substituting obedience to knowledge and fact for obedience to personal authority had not come about. The old-time foremen continued to retain and use arbitrary authority to the detriment of fair dealing with the worker as Taylor had envisioned. In a third area of inquiry, Hoxie found that little or no progress was being made with respect to the scientific selection of workmen. "Labor heads," an early designation for the employment or personnel manager, were poorly trained and of "doubtful experience and capacity."[6] The work of the labor heads was further complicated by the ubiquitous presence of line-staff conflict. Line foremen and superintendents clung tenaciously to their traditional prerogatives and worked overtly and covertly to nullify the advice and assistance of the personnel managers. With due respect to scientific management, Hoxie noted that these problems also existed in other establishments and was not confined to those firms being studied. Personnel selection, and indeed the entire personnel function, was in a rather embryonic state in all shops, not just those attempting the scientific management system. Although initial selection was no better in scientific management shops, the overall general class of workmen did appear to be higher through some ill-defined process of weeding out. Hoxie did not examine the reasons; but one is led to conclude that the incentive schemes, standards of work, or some form of the first-class-man concept was evolving in scientifically managed shops.

Instruction and training of workmen was another area where practice fell far short of theory. There were few attempts to execute the Taylor precept of "setting each man to the highest task for which his physical and intellectual capacity fits him." Learning proceeded by trial and error, specially trained instructors were scarce, and instruction more often than not focused on attaining the standard rather than on learning the job. Despite these faults, Hoxie concluded that training practices in scientific management shops were generally better than what could be found elsewhere in industry.

A fifth area, and one of greater criticism, was in the use of time study and task setting. It was here that Hoxie found the

6 *Ibid.*, p. 32.

greatest diversity in practice and the most deviations from scientific inquiry. Standards and incentive rates were often established after only a cursory inquiry and led to a variety of inaccuracies and injustices. In theory, time study is supposed to yield a quantitative measure of performance by deriving standard times taken to perform a task. In practice, qualitative factors caused by the time study engineer's judgment and experience tended to make the results less and less scientific. To the elementary times recorded from observation, allowances must be added to cover fatigue, unnecessary delays, "human necessities" (personal time), and possible errors in the work of the observer. Rather than substituting "exact knowledge for prejudiced opinion in the setting of the task" as Taylor had advocated, Hoxie found some seventeen variables which could be affected by the judgment and subjectivity of the person doing the study. In general, the time study personnel were poorly trained, inexperienced, and often set rates based upon management's desires and not upon true scientific inquiry and observation.

Once more, the criticisms were not lodged against the concept of time study and Taylorism *per se*, but against the use of stop watches by untrained, inexperienced observers. Hoxie found the typical time study engineers to be technicians with little knowledge of the subject of fatigue who displayed little understanding of the psychology and temperament of workers. They were "prevailingly of the narrow-minded mechanical type, poorly paid, and occupying the lowest positions in the managerial organization."[7] Some employers recognized the limitations of time study and were attempting to improve; to others, time study became "religion" and was leading to over-strain, exhaustion, and underpayment of the workman. On this question of time study, Hoxie was the most pessimistic. He saw no future for time study, even under the most enlightened management.[8]

Incentive schemes also came under close scrutiny. Hoxie

[7] *Ibid.*, pp. 5–6.
[8] Professor Hoxie's doubts about time study are reinforced by modern prolabor writers. For example, see William Gomberg, *A Trade Union Analysis of Time Study*, New York: Prentice-Hall, 1948. Mr. Gomberg was Director of the Management Engineering Department of the International Ladies' Garment Workers Union. His position is that physiological, mechanical, psychological and sociological variables make time study "unscientific" and therefore the results of time study should be used for further bargaining and not as *the* standard.

found no pure adoptions of either the Taylor, the Gantt, or the Emerson plans. The Taylor differential piece rate plan was infrequently encountered and most plans were modifications of the Gantt and Emerson plans. Taylor had maintained that once rates were established they must never be cut "without an absolute change in the direction governing the work and the time demanded for doing it." In practice however, employers often interpreted very liberally the phrase "absolute change"; slight changes were made in tools, jigs, or materials in order to justify re-study of the job and rate cuts. Hoxie did not give evidence of the prevalence of this practice but noted that some managers were unscrupulous and eager to take advantage of the worker.[9] It must be added however, that this may occur under any system and was not the fault of scientific management. While Taylor maintained that scientific management would protect the worker against overspeeding and exhaustion, Hoxie found no evidence in practice that it in fact did so. Of course, this would be expected since the Taylor precepts which would protect the worker, *i.e.*, standardization of tools, methods, and conditions, substitution of knowledge for guess-work, careful studies of fatigue, proper instruction, admonitions against rate-cutting, rest periods, etc., were all being evaded in practice. Without these safeguards, the spirit of scientific management was putty in the hands of the unscrupulous.

Philosophies in Conflict

On a broader plane, Hoxie tried to reconcile the opposing views of unions and Taylor regarding industrial democracy. Taylor maintained that scientific management was the essence of industrial democracy. Taylor's argument hinged upon harmony and the mutuality of interest between labor and management. Individuals were stimulated and rewarded on the basis of effort, discipline fell under scientifically derived laws and not under autocratic, driving management, and protests were to be handled by reliance upon scientific inquiry and mutual resolution. On the other hand, organized labor declared that scientific management was essentially autocratic by forcing the employee to conform to the employer's concept of fairness and by limiting the

[9] Hoxie, p. 86.

democratic safeguards of the workers. Scientific management, according to the union view, monopolized knowledge and power in the hands of management by denying the worker a voice in setting work standards and in determining wage rates and conditions of employment. It introduced a "spirit of mutual suspicion" among workers and destroyed the "solidarity and cooperative spirit of the group" by emphasizing the individual worker. It destroyed unions, the protection that unions gave workers, and in turn obviated the collective bargaining process.

The result, in Hoxie's view, was an inevitable, fundamental conflict between organized labor and scientific management. Hoxie maintained that Taylor's philosophy was a "Utopian ideal" which would not be practical until management knew more of worker psychology, was able to stabilize and regularize employment to a greater extent, and would recognize the need to build "group solidarity" (i.e., through organized labor). Channels must be opened for grievances, presumably through union representation, and management must accept worker (and union) participation in decision making. In Hoxie's words, "with rare exceptions, then, democracy under Scientific Management cannot and does not exist apart from unionism and collective bargaining."[10] The rare exceptions were the "very few" managers who were truly democratic in spirit and practice; but for most managers, Hoxie characterized them as benevolent despots or solid autocrats. Hoxie concluded that scientific management was not promoting industrial democracy: "In practice, Scientific Management must, therefore, be declared autocratic; in tendency, a reversion to industrial autocracy, which forces the worker to depend on the employer's conception of fairness, and limits the democratic safeguards of the workers."[11]

In fairness to Taylor, Hoxie attempted to pinpoint the causes of the shortcomings of scientific management in practice. In part these were caused by the infancy and immaturity of the movement since all new social and industrial ideas fall short of the ideal in their younger days. On this point Hoxie was optimistic that many of these shortcomings would disappear in time. More specifically, Hoxie blamed management for seeking shortcuts to efficiency, he faulted Taylor for trying to generalize his machine shop experience to all types and sizes of industries, and indicted efficiency experts who were guilty of selling patent medicine panaceas to employers in dire financial straits and eager to improve performance. "So the Scientific Management shingles have gone up all over the country, the fakirs have gone into the shops, and in the name of Scientific Management have reaped temporary gains to the detriment of . . . the employer and the worker."[12]

Criticisms of the Hoxie Report

Those who criticize are also open to criticism. What can be said of the research methodology of the Hoxie team? Professor Hoxie and his associates made numerous attempts to be fair to Taylor by noting that practice fell far short of theory. However, the predilections of Hoxie, Frey, and Valentine toward labor yielded a research bias which is inescapable. There is also evidence that the methodology of the research group was less than meticulous. Mary Barnett Gilson, who was Employment Manager at Clothcraft Company of Cleveland, one of the shops included in the study, wrote that Hoxie was "brilliant" but "prejudiced."[13] When Hoxie and Frey visited Clothcraft, they held a short interview with the president, Mr. Richard Feiss, and some of his managers, took some notes, but never visited the factory area itself. They promised to return to see the working conditions but never did. Miss Gilson also wrote that Mr. Frey was especially antagonistic during the interview because Clothcraft had no union. If this encounter at Clothcraft was characteristic of the researchers' conduct at the other thirty-four shops in the study, one must conclude that the Hoxie group was less than thorough. The investigation lasted only four months (January to April 1915) and could have been conducted only in a superficial manner. It is unfortunate that those who had the best opportunity to do a thorough empirical investigation of scientific management in its early days approached this chance with closed minds and hasty feet.

Hoxie took the position that industrial democracy could come only through the process of collective bargaining. He saw no

---

[12] *Ibid.*, p. 117.
[13] Mary B. Gilson, *What's Past is Prologue*, New York: Harper & Row, 1940, p. 93.

other avenue, included no possibility for an educated, enlightened management, and seemed dedicated to the proposition that labor and management interests were inalterably opposed for all times and in all places. He brought no true bill against union leadership nor its membership for soldiering or resistance. On this count, his examination was less than equitable.

In later work, Professor Hoxie began to equivocate on whether the philosophies of scientific management and trade unionism were reconcilable or inalterably opposed. He maintained: "We surely cannot afford to give up the vast possibilities of increased productiveness which Scientific Management holds out"; further, "Scientific Management holds out possibilities of substantial benefits to labor."[14] The paradox he was unable to resolve was based on an essential philosophical incompatibility between labor and scientific management. In organized labor's case, it "can function successfully only through the maintenance of a fixed industrial situation and conditions." On the other hand, "Scientific Management can function successfully only on the basis of constant and indefinite change of industrial conditions."[15] In the final analysis, the proper application of scientific management "would spell the doom of effective unionism as it exists today."[16]

Was Taylor a Utopian idealist? Was the fault with Taylor or with those who grasped at the straws of expediency and forgot the philosophy? From the Hoxie study, one is led to conclude that American management failed in the pressures of the moment to thoroughly understand and apply the Taylor system. Many are called to be mechanics, but there are few who can execute a grand design. Both labor and management were guilty of checkmating Taylor's call for a mental revolution. To Hoxie's credit one must indicate that he stimulated an interest in bringing practice closer to the high ideals of scientific management.

CHANGING TIMES IN LABOR—MANAGEMENT RELATIONS

The ideas of scientific management inspired both faithful adherents and determined antagonists. From within and with-

[14] Robert F. Hoxie, *Trade Unionism in the United States,* New York: Appleton-Century-Crofts, 1924. p. 324. Published posthumously since Professor Hoxie took his own life in June, 1916.
[15] *Ibid.,* p. 341.
[16] *Ibid.,* p. 348.

out the movement, new ideas to meet new demands were coming to the fore. The Hoxie report provided a seedbed for others who were beginning to explore new vistas for scientific management, pointing out the positive features, and yet also beginning to nurture the seeds of dissent to be reflected later in a revisionist movement.

Defenders and Revisionists

H. H. Farquhar was pro-Taylor, yet had some interesting insights into the unexplored opportunities of the scientific management movement.[17] For Farquhar, the positive aspects of scientific management were both technical and human: on the technical side, it resulted in greater productivity at no greater worker exertion, led to more efficient utilization of equipment and materials, improved regularity of production, and enhanced the power and stimulus of scientific knowledge gained through investigation. On the human side, scientific management improved industry by better worker selection and training, higher wages, reduction of worker turnover, greater worker security, and by allowing a wider scope for individual initiative.

After putting forth the positive contributions, Farquhar examined "neglected opportunities." He indicated that these were not so much criticisms as guides for future work in management. First, he questioned whether or not "we have given sufficient weight to the question of personality in management . . ." and had forgotten that management was an art which required human direction and control. Second, he asked whether or not enough stress had been given to the fact that scientific management required better leadership than any other management system. Instead of developing leaders, management had focused on "carefully outlined procedures" and substituted them for the lack of leadership abilities. Finally, he wondered whether or not scientific management, by focusing on the individual as an individual, had "obscured the possibility of making that individual and his fellows more productive and more contented through

---

[17] H. H. Farquhar, "Positive Contributions of Scientific Management," in E. E. Hunt (ed.), *Scientific Management Since Taylor*, New York: McGraw-Hill Book Co., 1924, pp. 37–59. Originally published in the *Bulletin of the Taylor Society*, Vol. 9, No. 1, (February 1924). Professor Farquhar at the time was Assistant Professor of Industrial Management at the Harvard Graduate School of Business Administration.

recognizing the psychological benefits to be gained through group dealings"? Farquhar felt that it was unfortunate that Taylor stressed soldiering and the profit motive of the individual workman "almost to the exclusion of other instincts and motives in life and which at heart, he [Taylor] knew every workman is interested."[18] Taylor was an engineer, not a psychologist, and, though he knew from his own experience the values of being a "regular fellow" in the group, he did not write extensively on the problems of man in groups. Farquhar, though a defender of scientific management, was one of the first to question the omission of the social and group facet of man in industrial research.[19]

H. B. Drury (of the Ohio State University) was primarily a defender of scientific management and only secondarily a revisionist. He noted that total productivity improved 100 per cent at Midvale, 50–75 per cent at Bethlehem and on the Santa Fe, 250 per cent at the Tabor Manufacturing Company, 200 per cent at Link-Belt, and that substantial savings accrued at the Watertown Arsenal, in the cotton industry (Gantt), and in the construction industry (Gilbreths).[20] Under the guidance of scientific management pioneers, substantial improvements were achieved without labor strife or widespread worker displacement.

In answering the critics, Drury pointed out that organized labor was fighting scientific management because unions would have difficulties in recruiting membership if science replaced bargaining over terms and conditions of employment. Point by point, Drury examined and answered the allegations of the Hoxie report. First, scientific management did not have as its goal the placement of all industrial jobs on piecework. Taylor, in testimony before the Industrial Relations Commission, had said that only 17 per cent of the nation's industrial workers held jobs appropriate for the use of piece rate incentives.[21] Therefore, the

---

[18] *Ibid.*, pp. 48–49.

[19] Professor F. J. Roethlisberger indicates that the Hawthorne research team was not influenced in its research by Professor Farquhar's writing. Letter to author, January 28, 1969.

[20] Horace B. Drury, *Scientific Management: A History and Criticism*, New York: Columbia University Press, 1915, pp. 163–168. Drury noted that there were sixty installations of the Taylor system and two hundred of the Emerson system by 1912 (pp. 144–146).

[21] *Ibid.*, p. 166. It is interesting to note that a modern researcher says 27% of the 11½ million U. S. workers in manufacturing were paid on some incentive basis in 1959. L. Earl Lewis, "Extent of Incentive Pay in Manufacturing," *Monthly Labor Review*, Vol. 83, No. 5, May 1960. Lewis found variations among industries but the percentages of workers on incentives were fairly constant over time.

unions had little to fear that piece rates and incentive schemes based on time study would be applied to all jobs. Second, job monotony and routinization of work had actually made the worker more productive and better paid. If men were to be judged automatons in a factory, then the blame must be placed on the process of industrialization and not on scientific management. Third, there was no evidence that scientific management *per se* led to overwork and exploitation of employees. Greater output came from better methods and not greater worker exertion. Neither the Congressional investigating committee nor the Hoxie group found evidence of overwork or injury to worker health in factories where Taylors' procedures were strictly followed.[22] Fourth, there was no evidence that scientific management led to greater industrial strife. Drury noted that most opposition came from labor leaders and not from the workers. At Watertown Arsenal for example, the workers were told to resist by the labor leaders. At the Frankford Arsenal, "several hundred" workers petitioned to continue the installation of the Taylor system even though instructed to the contrary by their leadership.

Finally, Drury felt that scientific management was more aware of the human element in management than any previous management method:

[Scientific Management] is based upon the principle that cheerful workmen are more profitable than sullen ones, that to fit the work to the man is better than to try to fit the man to the work, that the individual is a more satisfactory unit of study and administration than the mass.[23]

In conclusion, Drury was much less critical than Hoxie and therefore must be classified primarily as a defender of scientific management. As a revisionist, he did not accept the movement as a final answer to industrial problems. He saw scientific management as a stage in industrial evolution, not entirely original and not yet complete. Progress and study would yield more "science" in management to replace the autocracy of driving and whimsical practices. His prognosis was that scientific management would not dominate American industry but that it would

---

[22] Drury, p. 190. Based upon his own studies and upon his own experiences as a worker, Stanley Mathewson concluded that a vast majority of managers of the times were not autocrats. Further, he maintained that the charge that scientific management exploited the worker was the "myth" of "popular magazine writers." S. B. Mathewson, *Restriction of Output Among Unorganized Workers*, New York: Viking Press, 1931, p. 151.

[23] Drury, p. 202.

become transformed and differentiated as industry turned more and more toward scientific investigation. His forecast was particularly perceptive; management did turn toward more investigation, especially in the social facet of the workplace, and subsequently in applying more rigorous quantitative tools.

The Hoxie report, coming on the heels of the Congressional investigation, represented a turning point in the evolution of management thought. The war years had brought an uneasy truce but after the war a new breed was rising in counterpoint to the Taylor movement to bring a series of changes in management philosophy, especially with regard to labor relations. In varying degrees, a number of people were instrumental in reformulating the "official" viewpoint of scientific management toward labor. Robert G. Valentine, a member of the Hoxie team, was one early revisionist who attempted a *rapprochement* between unions and scientific management as represented by the Taylor Society. Viewed with suspicion by the Taylorites but praised by union leadership, he argued that the labor-management relationship was properly one of "consent." Consent was based on worker participation, and especially union participation, in reaching all decisions affecting labor.[24] Ordway Tead, a former partner in Valentine's consulting firm, urged the formation of company unions in order to get worker participation.[25] The American Federation of Labor was opposed to this viewpoint although company unions did achieve some large measure of acceptability during the 1920's. Although Tead and Valentine pushed for worker and union participation in management, the major intellectual break over Taylor's union position was by Morris L. Cooke. Cooke became friendly with labor leaders, especially the patriarch Gompers, and was the most influential in opening up a new era for labor-management relations. Cooke proposed to "humanize" management by advocating collective bargaining over rates, standards, and all matters affecting worker welfare. This break by one of Taylor's disciples was hailed by labor leaders but condemned by such stalwarts as Harrington Emerson.[26]

[24] R. G. Valentine, "The Progressive Relation Between Efficiency and Consent," *Bulletin of the Society to Promote the Science of Management*, Vol. 2, No. 1, January 1916, pp. 28–29.

[25] Ordway Tead, *Instincts in Industry: A Study of Working Class Psychology*, Boston: Houghton Mifflin Co., 1918, pp. 56–58 and pp. 218–220.

[26] Milton J. Nadworny, *Scientific Management and the Unions: 1900–1932*, Cambridge, Mass., Harvard University Press, 1955, pp. 116–117.

Additional strength to labor's position came with the publication of *Waste in Industry*. Originally proposed by then Secretary of Commerce Herbert Hoover and appearing a decade after the appearance of Taylor's *Principles*, this report undertook an appraisal of the progress of industrial management in reducing the national waste that Taylor had decried in his original work. In its essence, the report left a very gloomy view of American management by stating that ". . . over 50 per cent of the responsibility for these wastes can be placed at the door of management and less than 25 per cent at the door of labor, while the amount chargeable to outside contacts is least of all."[27] The chief causes of low productivity were faulty material control, faulty production control, lack of cost control, lack of research, ineffective workmanship, and faulty sales policies. The report was more of an indictment of American management's failure to use known methods and procedures and not a criticism of scientific management itself. In view of Professor Hoxie's findings about the uneven acceptance of scientific management methods and almost a complete rejection of the requisite mental revolution, the *Waste in Industry* report is not surprising in its conclusions.

Labor leaders welcomed the conclusions that the responsibility for waste lay primarily with management and not with labor. Further, the report suggested that others (labor, owners, the buying public, and trade associations) could contribute to waste elimination by "cooperating" with management. This became a signal to Samuel Gompers to push for union participation in helping management eliminate waste.[28] The practical implications of this marked change in union attitudes toward waste elimination and improvement of industrial practices were to lead to an era of labor-management cooperation, a phenomenon so far largely confined to the 1920's. The wheel was to come full circle in the relations between organized labor and management.

The Union-Management Cooperation Era

It would be easy, almost too easy, to attribute the change in labor leadership attitudes to the influence of men such as Morris

[27] *Waste in Industry,* Federated American Engineering Societies, New York: McGraw-Hill Book Co., 1921, p. 9.
[28] Jean T. McKelvey, p. 70.

Cooke. The *rapprochement* of labor and scientific management also was based in the economic conditions of the Twenties. While younger men in the Taylor society did change the pure alloy of Taylor's attitudes concerning unions, the unions themselves were facing unusual environmental pressures. A short, steep depression in the early 1920's weakened unions; further, companies were becoming increasingly paternalistic, management was waging intense drives for the open shop, and government and the courts were becoming increasingly hostile to unionism. Americans saw radicals and Bolsheviks in every picket line and reacted against any concerted effort to change the *status quo*. Accordingly, union membership suffered, declining from around five million in 1920 to three and one half million in 1921.[29]   In this relatively hostile environment, labor leadership adopted the protective coloration characterized by a decade of union-management cooperation.

Numerous examples and industries can be cited to illustrate the shifting sands of labor-management relations. The clothing unions, under the capable leadership of Sidney Hillman, were among the first segments of organized labor to agree to cooperation and to implementation of scientific management techniques. The Rochester Plan, composed of nineteen manufacturers representing the Clothiers' Exchange of Rochester and the Amalgamated Clothing Workers of America, was an attempt to guarantee certain rights to both labor and management under a collective agreement. Management had the right of an open shop and the right to install efficiency techniques; in turn, labor's rights were to bargain collectively, to elect bargaining representatives, and to participate through "price committees" in the fixing of piece rates.[30]   This early attempt was successful and modern clothing unions are the most favorable advocates of piece rates set through collective bargaining.

The railroads also developed extensive plans for cooperation, first on the Baltimore and Ohio and then later the Chesapeake and Ohio, the Chicago and North Western, the Canadian National Railway, and others. In each instance the union implicitly accepted the principles of scientific management and partici-

---

[29] Nadworny, p. 122.
[30] Meyer Jacobstein, "Can Industrial Democracy Be Efficient? The Rochester Plan," *Bulletin of the Taylor Society*, Vol. 5. No. 4 (August 1920), reprinted in E. E. Hunt, pp. 212–221.

pated through joint union-management shop committees in improving work routing and scheduling, hiring practices, and job analysis.[31]   As in the garment industry, scientific management had gained greater acceptance than previously possible under resistant leadership.   When William Green succeeded Gompers as AFL President in 1925, he increased the emphasis on cooperation.   The AFL hired its own management consultant and in a 1930 statement of "Labor's Principles of Scientific Management," urged complete acceptance of scientific management.   Using "management research" departments within the union, labor leadership emphasized that the worker actually *needed* the management engineer.[32]   This "new unionism" completed a cycle in organized labor-scientific management relations.   Except for worker participation through unions and recognition of the union's right to bargain, Frederick Taylor's *Principles* were now accepted as valid by the labor world.

The AFL abandoned the idea of union-management cooperation in 1932.   The new political regime promised better days for labor and union efforts turned from cooperating with management to influencing legislation in order to insure its survival and strength.   The crash in 1929 and the deepening deterioration of economic conditions doomed most cooperative schemes to failure. Thus ended an era in scientific management.   The era began with the adamant Taylor who wanted to substitute scientific knowledge for bargaining, and the movement was re-directed by the revisionists who wanted worker and union participation. Spurred by adverse economic conditions, the labor movement itself began its move toward almost complete acceptance of Taylorism.   The 1920's are remembered for Babe Ruth, bathtub gin, short skirts, the Charleston, and Al Capone: it was during this decade that unions found a haven in scientific management.

SUMMARY

The publicity which brought scientific management into the national spotlight also aroused the ire of organized labor.   Orga-

---

[31] Otto S. Beyer, "Experiences with Cooperation between Labor and Management in the Railway Industry," *Wertheim Lectures on Industrial Relations* (1928), Cambridge, Mass., 1929.
[32] Nadworny, p. 138–139.

nized labor and the proponents of scientific management found themselves bound up in a fundamental conflict of philosophies. On the one hand, labor felt that scientific management meant autocracy in the workplace and placed the worker at a disadvantage *vis-à-vis* management. Taylor recognized the abuses in practice which violated the spirit of the mental revolution. However, he felt that the worker, and everyone else, would benefit the most from scientifically determined pay and standards, from individualized treatment of the worker, and from a spirit which tried to create more rather than fighting over the division of the surplus. In the end, both positions were being reshaped. Labor, influenced by the economic and political environment, came to accept a modified version of Taylorism. The scientific management movement, influenced by the revisionists, also changed in response to new demands for industrial cooperation.

12

Scientific Management in Retrospect

The death of Taylor was the demise of a man and not that of an idea. Bedeviled and discouraged in his latter days, Taylor must have felt that he had failed in his life's work. From its orthodox conception, scientific management was evolving inexorably as new men and ideas came forth in an ever changing cultural environment. Interacting to form a giant web of currents and eddies of change, very substantial economic, social and political forces shaped the emergence, course, and progress of the scientific management movement. In examining the cultural environment of scientific management, economic, social, and political forces are separated for expository purposes, although in reality they were interacting and mutually reinforcing. Within this framework, the whys and wherefores of Frederick W. Taylor and his intellectual heirs will form a more coherent picture.

THE ECONOMIC ENVIRONMENT: FROM THE FARM TO THE FACTORY

In 1800, 90 per cent of America drew its sustenance from agriculture; by 1900, the proportion was 33 per cent, and by 1929, 20 per cent. The transformation from an agrarian to an industrial nation placed America at the world's helm in output of products and services, in wages, and in the standard of living of its citizens. The typical citizen who awakened on the morning of January 1, 1900, saw little change between the old and the new centuries. Yet the change was there and America had in reality moved into a new era. The accumulation of resources, though moving at varying speeds in various industries, was culminating in a new phase. New industries, in their embryonic stage in the latter part of the nineteenth century, were growing to influence and eventually dominate the course of American life. Spindletop (near Beaumont, Texas) ushered in a new era for petroleum; chemical discoveries were proliferating and the DuPont firm opened up synthetic fibers with an "artificial silk" later called rayon; at Kittyhawk in 1903, the airplane industry was launched; and in steel, meat packing, electricity, rubber, tobacco, agricultural implements, and retailing, corporate giants began to take shape. These large-scale industrial forms presaged profound changes for Mr. and Mrs. Citizen-Consumer.

The automobile was one technological advancement which brought about substantial economic and social change during this period. Exhibited at the Paris Exposition in 1896 by the German Nicholas Otto, the gas-buggy was soon to become more than an amusement. Basic industries such as petroleum, steel, rubber, and glass were given added impetus by the automobile. Spin-off industries in tourist inns and restaurants, garages, and highway construction were created. The automobile gave man a new mobility, a new freedom of movement which led to a decentralization of the cities into suburban living and posed a new threat to older, established forms of transportation. The new economics of the automobile industry was based on a minute division of labor and on the interchangeability of parts. Henry Ford and his associates took these old ideas and transformed them into a logic of mass production on an assembly line basis which could be called the Second Industrial Revolution. Mass production yielded cost savings which in turn were passed on to the consumer via lower prices. In 1910, the "Model T" cost the consumer $950; by 1924 the purchase price was $290 and Ford was selling over one and one quarter million cars. Using lowered product price to expand the market and the greater market to achieve greater production savings, Ford divided work into small elements and personified Adam Smith's idea that the market was the only force limiting the division of labor. Ford's startling announcement of a $5 day wage in 1914 (when the average wage in the auto industry was $2.40 a day) operated on two premises: (1) that the best workers could be attracted and retained; and (2) that the worker needed the wherewithal to buy industry's output. In large part an economic man concept, it brought success to Ford and lent credence to Taylor. Although Ford lost his domination of the automobile industry as consumer preferences changed, his introduction of the logic of mass production had a lasting impact on American thought.

Administratively, the new economics of mass production demanded an even sharper focus on the development of management. Large accumulations of resources were requisite to meet the demands of mass markets and mass distribution. As the industrial giants grew, the men who had built the empires were passing from the helm and being replaced by a new breed of salaried manager. The personalized, informal structures of the family business yielded to the logic of size in industrial administration. No longer could the owner-entrepreneur depend upon his own supervision or on "departmentation by kinship."[1] Technology demanded specialized knowledge and staff personnel were added to handle engineering, production, purchasing, legal affairs, and other functional activities. Motives changed from the risk of loss or possibility of gain in one's equity as an entrepreneur to those germane to a salaried manager. This separation of ownership and management required the development of an enlarged fund of managerial talent trained or wise in the administration of industrial affairs.

Support for this growing need for professional managers was also found in economic theory. Alfred Marshall (1842–1924), of the "neoclassical school" of economic thought, indicated the differential advantage that management could provide:

> A manufacturer of exceptional ability and energy will apply better methods, and perhaps better machinery than his rivals: he will organize better the manufacturing and the marketing sides of his business; and he will bring them into better relation to one another. By these means he will extend his business; and therefore he will be able to take greater advantage from the specialization both of labour and of plant. Thus he will obtain increasing return and also increasing profit . . .[2]

---

[1] "Departmentation by kinship" refers to the early practice of setting up one department or division within the firm for every son or relative of the entrepreneur.

[2] Alfred Marshall, *Principles of Economics* (eighth edition), New York: MacMillan Co., 1949, p. 614. First published in 1890.

Marshall wrote of the "earnings of management" in his theory of distribution, of marginal analysis, and thereby laid the basis for managerial economics. The theoretical basis of economics would provide for a more systematic way of analyzing the problems of industry.

The Rationalization of Resource Utilization

Chandler has noted that Phase I (the resource accumulation phase) was complete in American industry by the beginning of World War I. Industrial growth in the latter nineteenth century had created the giant enterprise, and in the first two decades of the twentieth century it was the task of the salaried manager to design and implement the appropriate administrative structures. The large corporation demanded a formal structure of relationships between the firm's activities and personnel and required also a formalization of administrative procedures. Culmination of the resource accumulation phase meant that the typical corporation of the early twentieth century was faced with basically two problems: (1) the need to reduce unit costs by improving productive techniques and processes; and (2) the need to facilitate planning, coordination, and appraisal of performance.[3]

This set the stage for Phase II, the rationalization of resource utilization. The work of Taylor and other scientific management writers was focused on meeting the industrial needs of the economic environment with respect to rationalizing resource utilization. The rational, scientific approach to problem solving was the foundation of scientific management. Time and motion study set standards, intended to reduce fatigue, and sought to eliminate wasted motions; it was a logical approach to work design rather than whimsical or rule-of-thumb methods. The "first-class man" and the scientific selection of personnel were attempts to provide a better match between people's abilities and job requirements. The Taylor piece-rate incentive sought to boost production and lower per unit labor costs even while paying higher wages. The functional foremen were to bring specialized, expert advice and leadership; the separation of planning and doing was a concept designed to improve the planning of work; and the exception

[3] A. D. Chandler, *Strategy and Structure*, pp. 386–390. Chandler noted these problems but made only a passing reference to Taylor and the scientific management movement (p. 24).

principle sought to focus managerial attention on critical performance problems. Even Taylor's philosophy of a "mental revolution" was an attempt to reduce friction and to rationally bring together the interests of labor and management into a mutually rewarding whole.

Those who followed in Taylor's wake also followed this rationalization-of-resource-utilization theme. The Gilbreth's sought motion economy and waste reduction and their "systems" books were detailed how-to-do-it procedures manuals. Gantt's work provided visual aids for scheduling, routing, dispatching, and control of work. Carl Barth, Morris Cooke, and the others who followed the gospel of efficiency theme all focused on basically this same problem of productive efficiency. Harrington Emerson, among others, wrote of efficiency through organization, a matter of some consequence to industrialists of that period. Stated succinctly, the economic milieu of the era created and accounted for the appeal of Taylor and scientific management.

Economically, scientific management was a product of its environment in the sense that it grew out of the pressing needs of industry for efficiency. Resources were accumulated, phase I completed, and rationalization of resource utilization (phase II) became important. Many have criticized the scientific management era as characteristic of a "machine civilization" or a mechanistic view of man in industry. According to Daniel Bell, for example, the enterprise was rigidly structured to obey three "logics": (1) the "logic of size" based on large-scale production in a central work place: (2) the "logic of measured time" or the scientific determination of work standards: and (3) the "logic of hierarchy" resulting in a passage of control of work and the work pace from the worker to the management.[4] In Bell's opinion, Taylorism resulted in a "social physics" which reduced the social facet of man to solely physical laws and determinants. Human movement was detached from the human and made abstract through motion study. Science in enterprise made the worker passive, dependent, and removed all thought from his job. Bell represents one school of modern criticism whose thesis is that scientific management built a one-dimensional machine model of man and organizations.

[4] Daniel Bell, *Work and Its Discontents: The Cult of Efficiency in America,* Boston: Beacon Press, 1956. pp. 3–10.

Whatever the merits of such criticism, it simply does not portray the whole story. Placed in the cultural imperatives of his era, Taylor was meeting a legitimate need of industry. The "logics" which Bell uses in criticism were the logics that created scientific management. Taylor was not a social scientist and never claimed to be; his forte was efficiency, which was the watchword of the day. As cultural conditions changed, views on Taylorism were revised accordingly and management thought assumed new forms. The social scientist of today may find fault with Taylor but the historian must see the man from the perspective of his times.

Increasing Industrial Efficiency

The post-Taylor period witnessed great gains in industrial efficiency. Although the 1921 *Waste in Industry* report castigated American management, the period 1919–1929 was one of increasing productivity. One historian attributes the increase to (1) the methods of mass production, (2) Taylorism, and (3) better and cheaper sources of power.[5] In manufacturing, the number of man hours input per unit fell from an index number of 74 in 1919 to 42 in 1929 (1899=100) for a gain in efficiency of 43%. While output per person was rising rapidly, unemployment remained low, wages were rising, and the purchasing power of the dollar was relatively stable.[6] The prosperous 1920's held forth the promise of economic abundance for all. A great outpouring of products from the industrial machine and gains in real income gave the consumer more than ever before. The 1920's canonized the salesman and Madison Avenue. The ambitious young man avoided prosaic occupations, took sample case in hand, and sold Everyman the wares of abundance. "The business of America is business," said the taciturn Calvin Coolidge to capsulize the era. Retailing giants such as Woolworth's, the A and P, and Sears, Roebuck invaded every hamlet so that Mr. Everyman could dress, eat, and partake of America's goods in a manner never before possible in history.

[5] George Soule, *Prosperity Decade: From War to Depression*, New York: Holt, Rinehart and Winston, 1947, pp. 127–128. Professor Soule did not rank nor assign any weights to the influence of these three factors.

[6] Solomon Fabricant, *Labor Savings in American Industry: 1899–1939*, New York: National Bureau for Economic Research, pp. 43–46 and p. 50.

Economically, America came of age in this period. Large-scale administrative structures were required to cope with the economics of mass production and mass distribution. Rationalization of resource usage was required and scientific management became the conventional wisdom to fill that void. It was an age of concern for economic efficiency. With a tremendously productive industrial system, rising real wages, low-level unemployment, and mass marketing and distribution, America had never known such abundance. Many were buying stocks and land in sunny climes such as Florida and California to prepare for early retirement with their affluence. In October of 1929, there were only a few who thought that anything could go wrong; and after all, these were the pessimists who had not grasped the American dream.

THE SOCIAL ENVIRONMENT: FROM HORATIO ALGER TO BABBITT

Between the Civil War and World War I, Horatio Alger Jr. wrote more than one hundred books for boys with such piquant titles as *Bound to Rise, Luck and Pluck, Sink or Swim,* and *Tom, the Bootblack.* At least twenty million copies were sold and "Horatio Alger" became a synonym for a success story.[7] The typical plot was the tale of a young but poor hero, beset by the unscrupulous on all sides, who worked his way to wealth by the virtues of diligence, honesty, perseverance, and thrift. Quite often he was befriended by a benevolent benefactor who recognized his latent talent for capital accumulation and aided him in his climb to the pinnacle of the financial world. The hero of Alger's books was a personification of McClelland's "high achiever" and of Riesman's "inner-directed" man who had his own gyroscope to keep him on the path to success.[8] He exhibited the virtues of self-control, hard-work, and frugality of the Protes-

---

[7] The life of Horatio Alger Jr. (1832–1899) formed an interesting paradox to the type of novels he wrote. He wrote success stories of rags to riches yet he himself was neither born poor nor did he die rich. About fifteen of the twenty million copies of his books were sold after his death. Frederick Lewis Allen, "Horatio Alger, Jr.," The *Saturday Review of Literature,* Vol. 18, No. 21 (September 17, 1938), pp. 3–17.

[8] McClelland, in *The Achieving Society,* found that *n* achievement increased regularly from 1800 to 1890, peaked, and declined thereafter. See also David Riesman, *The Lonely Crowd,* Garden City, N.Y.: Doubleday and Co. 1950, pp. 28–32.

tant ethic and of Ben Franklin's Poor Richard.[9]   The hero learned in the school of hard knocks and no formal schooling could prepare him for success in business.   Charles M. Schwab, a protégé of Andrew Carnegie, stated the case:

If the college man thinks that his education gives him a higher social status, he is riding for a fall.   Some college men . . . have pride in their mental attainments that is almost arrogance.   Employers find it difficult to control, guide, and train such men.   Their spirit of superiority bars the path of progress.[10]

Elbert Hubbard sketched the traits of the man who was desired by industry in his "A Message to Garcia."   In this story, Rowan was asked to carry a message from the President of the United States to the insurgent Cuban General Garcia during the Spanish-American War.[11]   Without questioning and whining, Rowan took the initiative and, operating on a minimum of guidance, got the message through.   This display of the virtues of a self-starting, self-directed, highly motivated man exemplified the business ideal. The ideal was that of individual effort and initiative with a minimum of guidance from without.

Early scientific management theory was consonant with the social values of reward for individual effort and the classical virtues of rational man directed by his own self-interest.   Utilitarian economics, then in vogue, held that each individual rationally calculated what was to his own advantage based on the seeking of pleasure and the avoidance of pain.   Each worker, like every other human being, was motivated by his own self-interest.   In the classical period of economics, this self-interest was largely the monetary reward that came from work, giving rise to the idea of "economic man." Before Taylor, management by incentives had failed largely because management had not cleared the obstacles for gain from the worker's path and had indulged in rate cutting when earnings became too high.   Taylor's conception of a management which facilitated worker effort by study and proper job design was sup-

---

[9] An interesting anthology of success stories based on these virtues is Moses Rischin, *The American Gospel of Success,* New York: Quadrangle Books, 1965. Rischin discusses such individuals as Cotton Mather, Benjamin Franklin, Clarence B. Randall, and Billy Graham.

[10] Charles M. Schwab, "The College Man in Business," in Altha G. Saunders (ed.) *The Literature of Business,* revised edition, New York: Harper & Row, 1923, p. 5.

[11] Elbert Hubbard, "A Message to Garcia," *ibid.,* pp. 190–194.

posed to open the door and free the worker's basic drive for economic rewards. Rate-cutting was not in management's self-interest because it only served to force the worker to return to his former habits of soldiering. The mental revolution between labor and management was the recognition of mutual self-interest. From management's vantage, a rational system of work, proper incentives, no cutting of rates, and leadership by knowledge and not by "drive" would lead to lower costs and higher profits. From the worker's viewpoint, he would recognize that standards had been properly established by scientific study and that by following instructions and procedures, he would be able to rationally calculate that he could best serve his own self-interest by following Taylor's system.

The ideals of scientific management were compatible with the prevailing views of man, his needs, and his aspirations. As Hugh Aitken has so capably pointed out, scientific management was a manifestation of the rationalist's philosophies of the eighteenth century and earlier. All phenomena, including human activity, were subject to rational laws, and scientific management was an attempt to apply these laws to man at work.[12] The notion of a rational, economically motivated man and the spirit of scientific inquiry leading to the reduction of all activity to physical laws were both commonly held concepts deeply rooted in the culture.

The "Collision Effect"

Cultural change, that third eternal inevitability like death and taxes, is always difficult to pinpoint historically. But times were changing and the milieu of scientific management slowly assumed new dimensions that affected the course of management thought. Two disparate yet strangely congenial forces were forming to mark a new era in American cultural thought: (1) the closing of the frontier and (2) the rise of progressivism. America of the early twentieth century was in the turmoil of urbanization and industrialization. The noted historian, Frederick Jackson Turner, identified four forces which were tending to reshape American economic, social, and political ideals: (1) the exhaustion of the supply of free land and the closing of the West; (2) the concentration of wealth and power in the hands of a few fundamental indus-

---

[12] Hugh G. J. Aitken, *Taylorism at Watertown Arsenal*, Cambridge, Mass.: Harvard University Press, 1960, pp. 15–16.

tries; (3) the political expansion by America into territories beyond her own borders; and (4) the rise of Populism.[13]   The West in America typified the ideals of individualism, economic equality, freedom to rise on one's own initiative, and democracy. Whenever social conditions became too oppressive or capital pressed upon labor or political restraints became too great, the West provided an avenue of escape.   When the "safety valve" of the West closed, new institutional arrangements were necessary to attain the American ideal of democracy which had long been provided for by the West.

William G. Scott has built on Turner's thesis and has called the culmination of these cultural forces the "period of collision" (Figure 12-1). The "collision effect" was characterized by conflict and resulted from forces which had drawn people into an inescapable proximity and dependency upon one another. Left unmitigated, the collision effect would have led eventually to social and psychologi-

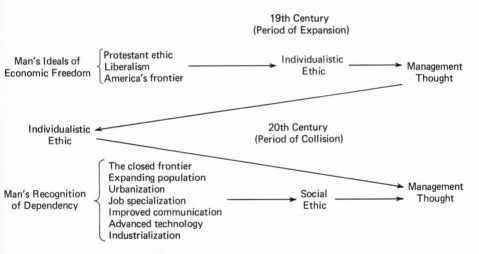

Fig. 12–1. Management thought in a changing culture. (Adapted from William G. Scott, *Organization Theory: A Behavioral Analysis for Management.* Homewood, Ill.: Richard D. Irwin, Inc., 1967, p. 53. Copyright © 1967 Richard D. Irwin, Inc.; by permission. This diagram appeared originally in William G. Scott, *The Social Ethic in Management Literature.* Bulletin No. 4, Bureau of Business and Economic Research, Georgia State College, Atlanta, Georgia, 1959, p. 10.)

[13] Frederick Jackson Turner, *The Frontier in American History,* New York: Holt, Rinehart and Winston, 1921, pp. 244–247.

cal degeneration. However, Scott's thesis was that the decline of the "individualistic ethic" of the period of expansion was slowly being replaced by a "social ethic" which substituted human collaboration for human competition "with a prayer that a social philosophy would lead to industrial harmony."[14] Basic to this search were Taylor's notions of "harmony, not discord," "cooperation, not individualism," and the "mental revolution" on the part of both labor and management.

There were elements of both the individualistic and the social ethics in Taylor's philosophy. In Scott's analysis, the social ethic began with the group as a source of value while the individualistic ethic started with the person as the primary value. Taylor's "cooperation, not individualism" would suggest that he accepted the social ethic. However, man is neither purely individualistic since he normally desires social intercourse, nor is he purely group-oriented because of his own ego needs. Taylor's philosophy bridged the gap between the two ethics by stressing the mutuality of interests and collaboration at work (the social ethic) coupled with individually based economic incentives and the selection and development of each person to the highest extent possible (the individualistic ethic). Taylor was clearly in touch with the problems of the industrialized society of the period. Though not known nor regarded as a social philosopher, he clearly perceived the industrial dilemma and proposed one means of alleviating the detrimental effects of the disharmonies of urbanization and industrialization.

Taylorism and the Progressives

The Populist-Progressive movement was a parallel development which attempted to provide a broader base for democracy in order to mitigate the perils of the collision effect. It is a strange quirk of history that Taylor would never have been considered by modern critics "progressive," yet his work and philosophy eventually became imbedded in Progressive thought. Progressivism had its roots in the Populist movement of the seventies and eighties. Whereas Populism was overwhelmingly rural and provincial, Progressivism was urban, middle-class, and nationwide.[15] Both were

---

[14] W. G. Scott, *The Social Ethic*, p. 9.

[15] Richard Hofstadter, *The Age of Reform*, New York: Vintage Books, 1955, p. 131. Hofstadter traced the reform movement in America from Populism, through Progressivism, to the "New Deal."

reform movements and Progressivism picked up where the Populism of William Jennings Bryan left off. For both movements, the central problem was to "restore" equality of opportunity by removing the interventions of government which benefitted large-scale capital and by replacing those interventions with ones which favored men of little or no capital.[16] Populism waned because it was based on support from a declining segment of the population, the rural areas. Progressivism, both a social and a political force, succeeded because it was concerned with labor, small businessmen, and the urban population. The Progressives sought to enfranchise women, elect United States Senators by direct popular vote, aid lower-income groups, establish a minimum wage, enact workmen's compensation laws, encourage trade unions, and enact a federal income tax.

There was probably little in the Progressive platform which would have appealed to F. W. Taylor but reform movements have a facility for making a union of odd couples. Scientific management caught the Progressive's eye at the Eastern rate hearings. Brandeis, a leading Progressive, helped coin the catchy title which made efficiency synonymous with morality and social order. The public could be "saved" from a rate increase if efficiency was introduced and labor and management denied unwarranted gains. Everyone could benefit from lower costs and higher wages if industrial leaders would accept Taylor's precepts. It was here that the Progressives' romance with scientific management began.[17] The reformers did not wish to root out capitalism but sought orderly change in the structure of industry vis-à-vis the public. Some reformers, like the Socialist Eugene Debs, wanted to replace the whole system. More moderate men, like Louis Brandeis, Herbert Croly, and Walter Lippman, thought that efficiency through science and leadership by professional experts would bring social order and harmony. Each envisioned a professionalization of business leadership which would remove the manager from the "cesspool of commercialism" and turn him into an "industrial statesman."[18] The appeal of scientific management to these men was that it offered

[16] Eric F. Goldman, *Rendezvous with Destiny*, New York: Vintage Books, 1952, p. 59. This is another excellent history of the Progressive reform movement.
[17] Samuel Haber, *Efficiency and Uplift: Scientific Management in the Progressive Era 1890–1920*, Chicago: University of Chicago Press, 1964, pp. 54–56.
[18] Walter Lippman, *Drift and Mastery*, New York: Mitchell Kennerly, Publisher, 1914, pp. 10–11. See also Louis Brandeis, *Business—A Profession*, Boston: Small, Baynard & Co., 1914.

leadership by expertise and knowledge and would hence rise above class prejudice and rule by drive and whim. The high wages and low costs promised by efficiency systems would check the greed of the employer and the laziness of the employee. Finally, scientific management showed that the interests of the employer and the employee were identical and the wastes of class conflict therefore unnecessary.[19]

The major snag between the Progressives and scientific management resided in Taylor's view of unions. To Progressives, unions were instruments of social and economic reform and men like Robert G. Valentine envisioned trade unions eventually being replaced by enlightened consumer unions in their evolution toward true industrial democracy.[20] The transition period was to be marked by a *rapprochement* between scientific management and organized labor based on "efficiency and consent." The revisionist movement was therefore a means whereby the Progressives could reconcile Taylorism with their own goals. Once the union view was resolved, the Progressives felt that scientific management had much to offer as a social force. The Progressives sought "industrial betterment" or "industrial welfare" which was an uneven mixture of philanthrophy, humanitarianism, and business acumen.[21] Industrialists such as John H. Patterson of National Cash Register set the pattern for the industrial welfare movement.[22] Such schemes for welfare and paternalism had the objectives of preventing labor problems and improving performance by providing hospital clinics, lunchrooms, bath houses, profit sharing, recreational facilities, and a host of other devices to woo worker loyalty. To this group, human happiness was a business asset and it was the wise, profit-minded employer who nurtured worker loyalty to the firm through various employee welfare schemes. The efficiency engineers, especially Taylor, complemented the work of the betterment or welfare proponents by linking efficiency and morality.[23] For Taylor, hard work led to morality and well-being; for the industrial betterment advocates, morality and well-being yielded hard work.

[19] Haber, pp. 58–58 and 89–90.

[20] R. G. Valentine, "Scientific Management and Organized Labor," *Bulletin of the Society to Promote the Science of Management*, Vol. 1, No. 1 (January, 1915) pp. 3–9.

[21] Haber, p. 18.

[22] Samuel Crowther, *John H. Patterson: Pioneer in Individual Welfare*, Garden City, N.Y.: Doubleday and Co., 1923.

[23] Haber, p. 20.

This reciprocal work-welfare equation was the core of the romance between the Progressives and scientific management.   Societal uplift through efficiency was in vogue.

In retrospect, social forces were generating and sanctioning an efficiency craze during the Taylor era.   A proliferation of popular and technical literature appeared on efficiency in the home, in education, in conservation of natural resources, in the church, and in industry.   The noted psychologist H. H. Goddard thought that the efficiency of group endeavors was not a function so much of intelligence but of the proper assignment of men to a grade of work which met their mental capacity.[24]   This psychological notion of the "first-class man" reflected the grip of Taylor's ideas on the academic community.   American educational institutions, seeking reform and a broader base for their efforts, seized upon Taylorism and discovered the efficiency expert.[25]   Conservationists, spurred by President T. R. Roosevelt and William Howard Taft, also found comfort in the gospel of efficiency.[26]   Feminists saw a saving grace in efficiency which would release the woman from the drudgery of housework and free her to assume her equal role in society.   The Reverend Billy Sunday recommended functional foremanship for the church so that each department could obtain expert advice and lasting results.[27]

This cultural fetish for efficiency was soon to wane.   By the 1920's, a marked shift had occurred from the individualistic ideal of Horatio Alger.   The gospel of production efficiency was dying as factories poured forth an abundance.   Prosperity reigned and a new gospel of consumption emerged with a heavy stress on sales and selling all Americans on the importance of being "middle class." Individuals such as Whiting Williams, Elton Mayo, and Mary Parker Follett were beginning to play down the emphasis on the individual and stress the importance of the group in industry.   The burgeoning discipline of personnel management emphasized industrial welfare, better selection, improving morale, and worker happiness as both a social and business asset.   Fictional critics of society

[24] Henry Herbert Goddard, *Human Efficiency and Levels of Intelligence,* Princeton, N.J.: Princeton University Press, 1920.

[25] An excellent study of Taylor's impact on education is Raymond E. Callahan, *Education and the Cult of Efficiency,* Chicago: University of Chicago Press, 1962.

[26] Samuel P. Hays, *Conservation and the Gospel of Efficiency,* Cambridge, Mass.: Harvard University Press, 1959.

[27] Haber, p. 63.

were deploring America's preoccupation with business and the vulgar, crass fellow Babbitt symbolized conforming mediocrity. There was security in conformity and man was becoming more conscious of his social relations and less aspiring in maximizing his individual return. The frontier was closed and new social values were replacing the Western ideal of rugged individualism. The seeds were sown for social man.

THE POLITICAL ENVIRONMENT: FROM ONE ROOSEVELT TO ANOTHER

The task of government and political institutions throughout time has always revolved around balancing two basic themes: (1) the need to establish equity and order to protect one man from another, and (2) the need to limit governmental power to protect man from the state. Political theorists like Machiavelli and Hobbes would see a central role for the state over man; Rousseau and Locke would seek a system of balances through which man could check the excesses of governmental power. Constitutional or representative government, the philosophy of Locke and Rousseau made manifest in America, makes consent of the governed the proper source of all legislative authority. Pluralism is characteristic of a constitutional society and it "seeks to diffuse power into many organizations and groupings and thus to prevent the development of imbalance of power and to assure the freedom of the individual from the tyranny of the one, the few, or the many."[28] The ballot box is the medium for making pluralism a reality. America of the late nineteenth century was seeking to perfect democracy and dissatisfied groups and individuals were responding to the collision effect with an outpouring of legislation to change the relations between man and state and between business and government. Founded on the premises of limited government, private property, freedom of economic opportunity, stress on individual initiative, and a government which should keep its hands off business, America was finding imbalances and imperfections between the ideals and practice of economic democracy. Instead of *laissez-faire* capitalism perpetuating itself as Adam Smith envisioned, business men were taking collective action to ration and monopolize the market, organized labor took on economic and political objectives, and special interest

[28] Richard Eells and Clarence Walton, *Conceptual Foundations of Business,* Homewood, Ill.: Richard D. Irwin, 1961, p. 363.

groups fought to expand their opportunity at the expense of other groups. Feeling powerless as individuals, collective action became more prevalent.[29]

The change in public attitude, that is, as espoused by the Progressives, was that government should look out for all interests of the people, not just a privileged few. Farm groups, especially the Grange movement, sought to protect themselves against the unholy alliance of the government bureaucrats who gave railroad franchises and the business men who bribed to get franchises and cheated to keep them. Workers organized through the Knights of Labor and later the American Federation of Labor in order to offset what they perceived to be an imbalance in bargaining power. Other groups sought subsidies, tariffs, and special legislation to enhance their own advantage. In 1900, there was no Department of Commerce, no Department of Labor, no Federal Reserve System, and no Federal Trade Commission. The United States Senate was composed of members elected by the various state legislatures and was a citadel of privilege. Women did not have the right to vote and immigrants were crowding into the cities. "Boss" rule prevailed in many cities and the muckrakers were only beginning their scathing attacks on governmental corruption and business malpractices. Upton Sinclair had not yet penned *The Jungle*, which aimed for the nation's heart, but hit its stomach and led to enactment of the Pure Food and Drug Act.

Business and the Progressives

The "Big Change" came in 1901 after the assassination of President McKinley and the succession of Theodore Roosevelt.[30] At first, the new President gave business men and the financial interests no cause for alarm. His well phrased first message to Congress did well to balance Teddy's own Progressive inclinations with a pro-business stance. Mr. Dooley, Peter Finley Dunne's fictional Irishman, aptly summarized President Roosevelt's position:

"Th' trusts," says he, "are heejus monsthers built up be th' inlightened intherprise in th' men that have done so much to advance progress in our beloved counthry" he says. "On wan hand I wud stamp thim undher fut; on th' other hand not so fast."[31]

[29] Samuel P. Hays, *The Response to Industrialism*, p. 190.
[30] Frederick Lewis Allen, *The Big Change*, New York: Harper & Row, 1952.
[31] Cited by Allen, *ibid.*, p. 85.

The honeymoon was brief. In 1902, President Roosevelt brought suit to dissolve the Northern Securities Company by invoking the Sherman Act. This direct blow at Northern Securities, a holding company set up by J. P. Morgan and Edward H. Harriman to control three major railroads,[32] opened a new era in government-business relations. Known as a prime proponent of conservation of natural resources as well as a "trust-buster," the first Roosevelt placed government in a new role as a regulator of business activity. Anti-trust suits were filed against the Beef Trust (1905), the Standard Oil Company of New Jersey (1906), and the American Tobacco Company (1907); and new legislation regulated the railroads (Elkin's Act in 1903 and Hepburn Act in 1906), and the telephone, telegraph and wireless industries (Mann-Elkins Act in 1910). Other state and federal legislative enactments sought to limit hours of work and regulate female and child labor. The Clayton Act and the Federal Trade Commission Act (1914) strengthened the Sherman Act and made more explicit other discriminatory business practices. The Federal Reserve Act (1913) created a more elastic currency and weakened the hold of big New York City banks over cash and reserves.

In retrospect, the political environment of the early scientific management era sought to bring a new balance between the power of business vis-à-vis the public. Though Taylor did not concern himself with the political environment to any large extent, his own battles with entrenched, resistant business leadership, for example Bethlehem Steel, indicate that he sought to replace management by privilege with management by science based on expertise. The mental revolution was to de-emphasize the division of the surplus and stress production for lower prices and higher wages. The romance of Taylor and the Progressives had political as well as social ramifications. Post-war America witnessed the decline of the Progressivism of Roosevelt and Woodrow Wilson and welcomed the "return to normalcy" of Warren Harding. America withdrew from the world arena of politics and turned inward to enjoy a decade of prosperity. Calvin Coolidge stated the tenor of the decade with his oft-quoted "The business of America is business." Congress and the Supreme Court relaxed controls over business, the influence of organized labor declined, sales were predominant over produc-

[32] The Northern Pacific, the Great Northern, and the Chicago, Burlington, and Quincy.

tion, company unions and industrial welfare schemes abounded, and revised Taylorism led to union-management cooperation.

Politically, the 1920's were a non-activist period. There was a brief restoration of the philosophy of *laissez-faire* and its belief in the self-regulating nature of an economy. Judge Gary held his famous dinners to get agreement on the price of steel, and banks and lending institutions gave free rein to finance whatever speculative impulse, be it land or stocks, the public might have. Blissfully ignoring the Florida land bust in 1926 and a downturn in economic activity in 1927, Mr. and Mrs. America enjoyed their bath-tub gin, rumble seats, jazz, and short skirts. The great collapse of 1929 signaled the end of an era. After that, America turned in desperation to the New Deal of Franklin Delano Roosevelt in the hope that government could do something, anything, to pull America from its cultural morass.

SUMMARY OF PART II

Figure 12-2 depicts the emergence, growth, and evolution of the scientific management era in a visual summary form. Scientific management was not an invention, it was a synthesis, a stage in evolving management thought. Charles Babbage could lay a valid claim for the paternity of a rational, systematic approach to management, but it was Frederick W. Taylor who gave systematic management a voice.

Taylor was the man of the hour, the *deus ex machina* who became the focal point for an idea. Scientific management was more than methods and time study; it was a much deeper philosophy of administering human and physical resources in a technologically advanced world where man had gained greater control over his environment than ever before. The Industrial Revolution had provided the impetus; Taylor provided the synthesis. As man gained greater power over his physical world, he sought to direct and guide the products of that greater prosperity to more rational ends. Taylor had an idea, a great idea, on how that might be done —by a mental revolution for all parties, founded on science and not whim, and leading to harmony and cooperation. Perhaps he was idealistic, even Utopian, but it would be wrong to criticize him for holding forth the promise of coupling industrial harmony, individual betterment, and greater productivity.

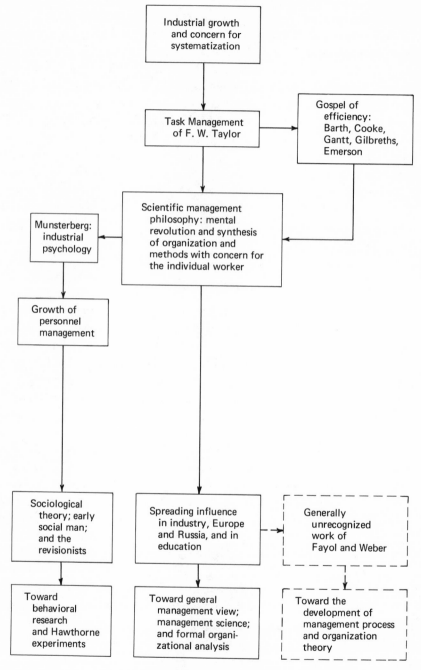

Fig. 12–2. Synopsis of the scientific management

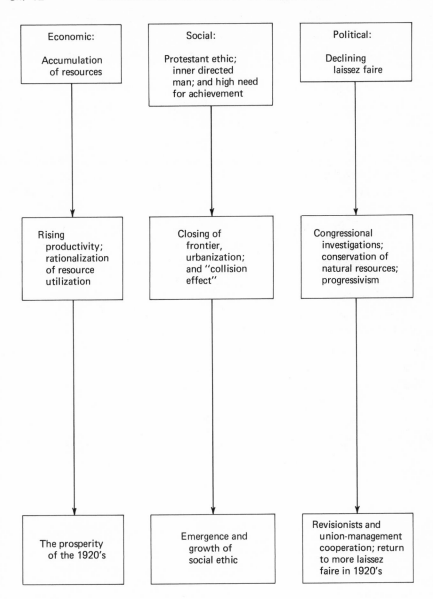

Economic:

Accumulation
of resources

Social:

Protestant ethic;
inner directed
man; and high need
for achievement

Political:

Declining
laissez faire

Rising
productivity;
rationalization
of resource
utilization

Closing of
frontier,
urbanization;
and "collision
effect"

Congressional
investigations;
conservation of
natural resources;
progressivism

The prosperity
of the 1920's

Emergence and
growth of
social ethic

Revisionists and
union-management
cooperation; return
to more laissez
faire in 1920's

era and its cultural environment.

Those who followed Taylor represented divergences from his orthodoxy. Some were major figures, leaving larger footprints in the sands of time, while others left merely tracings. But each in his own way provided for industrial education, for academic awareness of management, and for improved productivity and service to society by industry. Two of Taylor's contemporaries, Fayol and Weber, were to achieve acclaim only in more modern times; but all of those examined during this era reflected the imprint of Taylor's search for administrative rationality in a world of large enterprise.

The historical question of whether the man makes the times or *vice versa* cannot be begged. Certainly it is a mutually reciprocating force, an action-reaction throughout the history of man. Taylor and his followers were the products of an era which economically sought a rationalization of resource utilization, which socially sanctioned individual reward and effort, and which politically encouraged uplift through efficiency. In return, the men affected the times by giving voice to a movement toward material prosperity, toward industrial harmony to retard the collision effect, and toward making America into the world's economic and political leader. Scientific management was the child of its culture and in turn made its culture an adult of industrial, social, and political vigor.

III

THE SOCIAL MAN ERA

Eras in management thought never begin and end neatly in any particular year. Instead there is a blending of movements and the themes are played in a shifting of major and minor keys. The notion of a "social man era" reflects more of the philosophy which was emerging than any settled criterion for managerial action. Social man was born late in the scientific management era but did not achieve any large degree of recognition until the 1930's. In Part III, we will examine first the Hawthorne research and the emerging Mayoist philosophy which ushered in the human relations movement. Next, the work of Mary Parker Follett and Chester Barnard will be examined to illustrate some unique notions of authority and organizational integration. Then evolving management thought will be viewed in separate, parallel branches: one, the growth of widespread interest and research into industrial behavior; and two, the writings of a number of scholars who were slowly developing a top-management viewpoint of organizations. We will conclude Part III by examining the critics of the human relationists and by discussing the economic, social, and political environment of social man.

13

Serendipity at Western Electric

At times, many managers and professional students of the subject have held that there was a clear-cut cause and effect relationship between the quality of the physical work environment and the well-being and productivity of the worker. Surrounded by the proper ventilation, temperature, lighting and other physical working conditions, the worker would have the optimum environment for working on scientifically measured tasks while motivated by some wage incentive scheme. Other impediments to efficiency, such as fatigue and monotony, were believed in large measure to be due to improper job design, poor materials flow, working under stressful conditions, or other factors which posed environmental obstacles to workers' efforts. Fatigue, believed to be caused by the buildup of lactic acid toxins in the blood, could be reduced by removing wasted motions and by the introduction of scientifically determined rest periods. Some researchers even suggested that acid sodium phosphate pills taken daily were the panacea to all the ills of industrial fatigue. Illumination of the workplace was also believed important since it affected the quality, quantity, and safety of work. In 1924, the National Research Council of the National Academy of Sciences decided to determine the precise relationship between illumination and individual efficiency by initiating research at the Hawthorne Plant of Western Electric, the equipment-producing and supply arm of the American Telephone and Telegraph Company.

275

The Hawthorne Works employed 25,000 people at the time and the factory was located near Cicero on Chicago's dreary industrial west side.

In customary experimental style, the research began with the designation of two groups of female workers, each performing the same tasks and located in two rooms equally illuminated.[1]   One group, the "control," was to have no changes made in its illumination or work environment.   The other, consisting of six operatives, was the treatment group in which, by varying levels of illumination, the effects of lighting on efficiency could be scientifically determined.   The task in each group consisted of assembling telephone relays, a highly repetitive job.   Carefully designed, the research took into account room temperature and humidity as well as the level of illumination.   The researchers observed the groups and kept accurate records of production.   As the research proceeded, the results became more and more enigmatic.   Regardless of the level of illumination (even when in one instance it was reduced to almost the level of moonlight[2]), production in both the control and the experimental groups rose.   Puzzled, the researchers abandoned illumination as the significant variable and began manipulating methods of wage payments, rest periods, length of work day and work week as other possible causes of increased productivity.   During one period, moving from a group incentive plan to an individual piece rate plan resulted in a large increase in output.   The introduction of five-minute rest pauses at 10:00 A.M. and 2:00 P.M. also led to increases in productivity.   Shortening the work day, reducing the work week, and providing refreshments at the rest pauses all yielded increases in output.

Exasperated by their results, the researchers decided to abolish all "privileges" and to return to the conditions under which there were no rest pauses, no refreshments, and no shortened day or week, i.e., the original conditions of work with the sole exception that the individual piece-rate was retained.   Expecting the girls' spirits to be crushed, the researchers were amazed to find that "the daily and weekly output rose to a point higher than at any other

[1] Descriptions of this early research may be found in Elton Mayo, *The Human Problems of an Industrial Civilization*, New York: MacMillan Co., 1933, pp. 55–69; and in Fritz J. Roethlisberger and William J. Dickson, *Management and the Worker*, Cambridge, Mass.: Harvard University Press, 1939, pp. 15–86.

[2] At one point, the level of illumination was 0.06 of a foot candle. F. J. Roethlisberger and W. J. Dickson, p. 17.

time . . ."[3] Reinstatement of rest pauses and refreshments led to yet another boost in output to an all-time high. In brief, during the whole period of experimentation, individual output had risen from an average of 2,400 relays per week to 3,000 per week per worker.

These initial experiments of the National Research Council lasted from 1924 to 1927 and the results were so inconclusive that nearly everyone was prepared to abandon the whole project as useless. Output had increased but no one knew why. The illumination hypothesis was rejected; fatigue did not appear to be a factor, nor did there appear to be any consistent relationship between incentive schemes, hours of sleep, humidity or any of the other variables and worker output. George Pennock, Western Electric's superintendent of inspection, surmised that the key point was the interest shown in the workers by the experimenters.[4] But this was not considered totally conclusive and the management of Western Electric, at the urging of Pennock, decided to explore further the complexities of human reactions to the workplace. At that point, no one could have anticipated the scope and significance of what was to follow.

THE IVY LEAGUE COMES TO HAWTHORNE

During the winter of 1927–1928, Elton Mayo addressed a group of personnel men at the Harvard Club in New York City. In attendance was George Pennock, who told Mayo of the test room experiments and invited Mayo to come into the study as a consultant.[5] George Elton Mayo (1880–1949) was an Australian who had received his M.A. degree in Logic and Philosophy from the University of Adelaide in 1899. Mayo had taught logic and

---

[3] *Ibid.*, p. 65. Among those who were puzzled was the renowned scientist, Dr. Vannevar Bush. Bush, then Professor of Electrical Power Transmission at the Massachusetts Institute of Technology, took part in the original experiments and recalled that none of the researchers could explain the variations in output. Loren Baritz, citing correspondence with Dr. Bush, in *The Servants of Power*, p. 80.

[4] George Pennock, "Industrial Research at Hawthorne," *The Personnel Journal*, Vol. 8 (1930), p. 296. This was the first known appearance of the Hawthorne research in the management literature.

[5] Of the several accounts of how it all began, there is disagreement about who invited Mayo to Hawthorne. Loren Baritz in *The Servants of Power* cites correspondence from Mayo's personal files to the effect that it was T. K. Stevenson, Western Electric's Comptroller of Manufacturing (p. 90). In "The Fruitful Errors of Elton Mayo . . . ," *Fortune*, Vol. 34, No. 5 (November, 1946), Pennock is said to have extended the invitation.

philosophy at the Queensland University and later studied medicine in Edinburgh, Scotland.[6] While in Scotland, he became a research associate in the study of psychopathology; this experience was to serve as a basis for his later development as an industrial researcher. Under a grant from the Laura Spelman Rockefeller fund, Mayo emigrated to America and joined the faculty of the Wharton School of Finance and Commerce of the University of Pennsylvania. In his earliest industrial research, Mayo followed the conventional wisdom of the times and sought a relationship between working conditions and human performance in a textile mill near Philadelphia. By introducing rest pauses, Mayo was able to reduce turnover from 250 per cent to 5 per cent and improve efficiency. The work pauses, in Mayo's terms, reduced the "pessimistic reveries" of the workers, hence improving morale and productivity. Joining the Harvard faculty in 1926 as associate professor of industrial research, Mayo was about to embark on an intellectual journey that would reshape the course of management thought.

The Harvard Research Group

Intrigued by the initial results of the National Research Council experiments, which were then still incomplete, Mayo perceptively noted that "a remarkable change of mental attitude in the group" was the key factor in explaining the Hawthorne mystery.[7] In his opinion, the test room girls became a social unit, enjoyed the increased attention of the experimenters, and developed a sense of participation in the project.

The most significant change that the Western Electric Company introduced into its "test room" bore only a casual relation to the experimental changes. What the Company actually did for the group was to reconstruct entirely its whole industrial situation.[8]

With this recognition of the social milieu of industrial life, Mayo had opened the door to research into social man. Social man was the creation of group efforts in which Mayo became the focal point for collaborative research between company officials and the Harvard research group. Along with Mayo, Fritz Jules Roethlisberger (1898–   ) became a cornerstone in these efforts and a leading

---

[6] Personal data on Mayo are from Lyndall Urwick, *The Golden Book of Management,* pp. 220–224.

[7] Elton Mayo, pp. 71–72.

[8] *Ibid.*, p. 73.

exponent of the nascent philosophy of Human Relations. Roethlisberger received his A.B. degree from Columbia University in 1921 and his B.S. from the Massachusetts Institute of Technology in 1922. From 1922 to 1924 he was engaged in industrial practice as a chemical engineer and then he returned to Harvard to take his M.A. in 1925. He stayed on at Harvard to join the Industrial Research Department and soon became involved in the Hawthorne research. Roethlisberger served Harvard and human relations theory and practice for forty years before his retirement in 1967.[9]

In addition to the primary intellectual inspiration of Mayo and Roethlisberger, others also made significant contributions to the research group. For the company, G. A. Pennock, William J. Dickson (Chief of the Employee Relations Research Department), and Harold A. Wright (Chief of Personnel Research and Training) were the prime movers. From Academia, the roll call was to become a *Who's Who* in management research: W. Lloyd Warner, the anthropologist who was instrumental in designing the experiments designed to reveal the impact of the group upon the individual; T. North Whitehead, who did detailed statistical studies of the relay assembly room;[10] and L. J. Henderson, the physiologist who introduced the Harvard group to the work of Vilfredo Pareto.[11] Others were to follow but here was the beginning of a fateful voyage in management history.

Rejecting Traditional Hypotheses

The mythical Three Princes of Serendip did not find what they sought on their voyage but found things far more important than the original object of their search. Likewise, the Harvard group picked up the loose threads of the National Research Council experiments and found far more valuable insights into industrial man

[9] Biographical data on Professor Roethlisberger are from *Who's Who in America*, Chicago: A. N. Marquis Co., Vol. 35 (1968–69), pp. 1854–1855. Professor Roethlisberger is presently Wallace Brett Donham Professor of Human Relations, Emeritus. He received the Taylor Key in 1956 for his outstanding contributions to the field of management.

[10] T. N. Whitehead's work may be found in *Leadership in a Free Society*, Cambridge, Mass.: Harvard University Press, 1936; and *The Industrial Worker* (2 volumes), Cambridge, Mass.: Harvard University Press, 1938.

[11] Lawrence J. Henderson, *Pareto's General Sociology: A Physiologist's Interpretation*, Cambridge, Mass.: Harvard University Press, 1935. Henderson's work on Pareto provided a bond of interest between him and Chester I. Barnard and also influenced the work of another social systems analyst, George C. Homans.

than the original intent of the illumination studies. Mayo and his associates entered the Western Electric experiments in period ten of a thirteen-period project and immediately began to try to make sense of the previously incoherent results. The absence of a positive relationship between environmental changes, such as rest pauses, etc., and worker output led the Harvard group to examine the traditional hypotheses of management in an effort to find a new scope and role for management and the worker. Five hypotheses of management were proposed to explain the failings of the original illumination research: (1) that improved material conditions and methods of work were present in the test room, leading to greater output; (2) that rest pauses and shorter days had provided relief from fatigue; (3) that rest pauses had provided relief from the monotony of work; (4) that the individual wage payment incentive had stimulated increased output; and (5) that the changes in supervisory techniques, *i.e.*, improved interpersonal relations, had improved attitudes and output.[12]   One by one, each hypothesis was tested. The first explanation was rejected since some working conditions, *e.g.*, the level of illumination, had been purposely deteriorated and yet production had increased. Second, rest pauses and length of work day did not explain the results since output still increased after all of these "privileges" were taken away. The third hypothesis, relief from monotony, was less conclusive since monotony was deemed a state of mind and could not be assessed on the basis of output data alone. The researchers knew that worker attitudes had improved, probably due to their being singled out as a special group receiving increased attention, but were loath to attribute the large rise in output to this factor alone.

The hypothesis of incentive payments struck at the core of traditional management theories of motivation and merited a deeper examination. Two new groups were formed, a second relay test assembly group and the mica splitting test room. Five experienced relay assemblers were selected to form a new group for study. Prior to the experiment, they were on a group incentive plan and for the first nine weeks of the experiment they were placed on an individual incentive plan. Initially total output went up, leveled off (for all but one worker whose output decreased), and then remained constant at the new higher level (112.6 per cent over the

---

[12] Roethlisberger and Dickson, pp. 86–89.

base period of 100 per cent). After returning to the original group incentive plan for a period of seven weeks, the second relay assembly group's performance dropped to 96.2 per cent of the initial base of 100 per cent before the experiment. The mica splitters had always been on an individual incentive system and the only change in the experiment was to place a selected group in a special observation room while retaining the same incentive plan. Rest pauses and the length of the work-day were varied, as they had been in the earlier experiments, and changes in output noted. The mica splitting experiment lasted fourteen months and average hourly output rose 15 per cent.

In explaining the results of these two groups, the researchers rejected wage incentives as a cause of increased output. Although total output increased 12.6 per cent in the second relay assembly group, the researchers concluded that this was due to a desire on the part of the new group to equal the record of increase of the first relay assembly test group in the original experiments. Since the mica splitters had retained the same incentive scheme throughout the experiment, and since average hourly output had increased, the increase had to be due, in the researchers' opinion, to factors other than the payment scheme.[13] The conclusions they reached, which can be viewed as tenuous, were that it was not wages but improved morale, supervision, and interpersonal relations that led to greater output in both groups. This conclusion formed the fifth hypothesis and the bulk of Roethlisberger and Dickson's book was devoted to examining the influence of improved interpersonal relations on industrial behavior.

The Interviewing Program

The "new man" of industry was to be socially motivated and controlled. Improvements in efficiency and morale were postulated to be due to improved social or human conditions rather than material or environmental conditions. This did not mean that all previous thought was completely erroneous but that management must be concerned with both the technical *and* the social facets of work. In a sense the Harvard group had rediscovered Robert Owen who had admonished the mill owners to pay as much attention to their people as to their machines. While their methodology may

[13] Roethlisberger and Dickson, p. 158–60.

be suspect, their findings opened a new direction for management thought.

In the early experiments, the researchers removed the workers from the factory floor, placed them in special test rooms, and assumed many of the supervisory functions. This shift in control from the former line supervisor to the experimenters created a new social situation for the worker. As Mayo noted, the experimenters created a "freer and more pleasant working environment" under an experimenter-turned-supervisor "who is not regarded as the 'boss'."[14] The change in the quality of supervision was not a difference in its closeness but in the special attention given the workers with regard to their sentiments and motives. This special attention of experimenter for the subject conjures up the charge of the "Hawthorne effect" or the notion that the observers biased the experiment by their personal involvement. The experimenter (observer), who became the *de facto* supervisor, altered the previous managerial practices. Workers were advised and consulted about changes, their views were listened to sympathetically, and their physical and mental health became matters of great concern to the experimenters. As the research progressed, it became less of a controlled experiment and more inclined toward creating "a social situation" in which workers felt free to air their problems and one in which they established new interpersonal bonds with their co-workers and superiors.

It would be fallacious to reject the Western Electric research findings on the basis that the observer biased the experiment. On the contrary, the significance of the Hawthorne work was that it opened new vistas in which the supervisor was called upon, and could be trained, to play a different role, one far removed from personal, idiosyncratic traits and one which enabled him to take a personal interest in the subordinate and to play the role as the experimenter played it. What was this new role and how did it evolve? A turning point in the experiments was the initiation and conduct of the interviewing program which was initially a plan for improving supervision. Since the test room studies had demonstrated a close relationship between employee morale and supervision, the Harvard group set out to re-educate the supervisors by

[14] Elton Mayo, p. 78.

teaching them to play the role as the observer-supervisor had played it.

The basic premise of the interviewing program was that the new supervisory role was one of openness, of concern, and of willingness to listen. The observers had noted that the girls were "apprehensive of authority" but once the experimenter became more concerned with their needs, they lost their shyness and fear and talked more freely to company officials and to the observers. The girls developed a greater zest for work and formed new personal bonds of friendship both on the job and in after-hours activities. Their improved morale seemed to be closely associated with the style of supervision and with greater productivity. This link between supervision, morale, and productivity became the foundation stone of the Human Relations movement.

The interviewing program was quite lengthy and will be summarized for its unique features, rather than catalogued. The initial concept of the interviews was to have workers respond to directed questions about management's programs and policies, how well they were treated by their boss, working conditions, etc.; however, this patterned interview led to more serendipity at Hawthorne. The interviewers found to their surprise that the workers wanted to talk about things other than those included in the patterned format. What the workers thought was important was *not* those things deemed significant by the company or the investigators! Realizing this, the procedure was changed to a non-directive technique in which the interviewer allowed the worker to express his mind whether or not it was thought important to the interviewer. The interviewer's job was to keep the worker talking and the average length of interview went from thirty minutes to one and one-half hours. After this change, workers expressed the opinion in follow-up interviews that working conditions had improved (although they had not changed) and that wages were better (even though the wage scale was the same). In short, the opportunity to "let off steam" made the workers *feel* better about their situation even though it had not changed.

The "complaints" gathered in the interviews were thoroughly investigated and found generally to be irrelevant to the facts.[15] This

---

[15] Roethlisberger and Dickson, p. 255 *passim.*

separation of fact and sentiment led the researchers to conclude that there were two levels of complaints, the *manifest* or material content versus the *latent* or psychological form of the complaint. For example, one interviewee was preoccupied with the noise, temperature, and fumes in his department. Further examination revealed that his latent concern was the fact that his brother had recently died of pneumonia and the worker feared that his own health might be impaired. In another case, complaints about a low piece rate were traced not to verification of this fact but to a worker's concern for medical bills arising from his wife's illness. In essence, "Certain complaints were no longer treated as facts in themselves but as *symptoms* or indicators of personal or social situations which needed to be explored."[16] From the researchers' viewpoint, worker preoccupation with personal concerns inhibited his performance, a conclusion which Mayo had called "pessimistic reveries" in his early research. The outcome of the interviewing program was supervisory training in the need to listen and understand the personal problems of workers. The supervisors were trained to be interviewers, to listen rather than to talk, and "to exclude from their personal contacts with employees any moral admonition, advice, or emotion."[17] Supervisory use of this non-directive interviewing technique enabled the supervisor to handle more intelligently worker's personal problems, to locate those factors affecting worker performance, and to remove events or factors in the worker's social or physical environment which were affecting his performance. The new supervisor was to be more people oriented, more concerned, less aloof, and skilled in handling social and personal situations. The product of this human relations style of leadership was to be better morale, fewer "pessimistic reveries," and improved output.

Group Behavior: The Bank Wiring Room

The final phase of the research program at Western Electric ran essentially chronologically parallel to the interviewing program and concerned the study of informal group behavior in the bank wiring room. The discovery of the informal organization and its machinations should not be solely attributed to the Harvard group. Frederick W. Taylor was keenly aware of systematic soldiering and

16 *Ibid.*, p. 269.   Italics added.
17 *Ibid.*, p. 323.

group pressures; Whiting Williams had recounted his own experiences of informal relationships and attitudes toward work; and
Stanley Mathewson had made an extensive study of pressures leading to restriction of output.[18] Despite these early recognitions of
group pressures, the Harvard group was apparently surprised that
"attention had been called to the fact that social groups in shop
departments were capable of exercising very strong control over
the work behavior of individual members."[19] Restriction of output
was a new discovery to the researchers since they "had hitherto
been unaware of its implications for management practice and employee satisfactions."[20] Knowledge builds on knowledge; and the
failure of the researchers to glean from prior writings on informal
group behavior is a fault, although it should not detract from the
significance of their own research.

The group chosen for study was isolated in an observation room
and was composed of male operatives who assembled switches for
central office switchboard equipment. The "bank wiring" task
involved three groups of workmen whose work was highly interrelated: (1) the wiremen who wired the terminals; (2) the soldermen who solidified the connections; and (3) the inspectors who
judged the quality of their work. In total, nine wiremen, three
soldermen, and two inspectors were the objects of study. Wage
payments were based on a group incentive plan which rewarded
each worker on the basis of the total output of the group and would
necessarily stress the need for collaborative effort. One of the first
things noted by the researchers was that the workers had a clear-cut
notion of what comprised a "fair day's work" and that this was *lower*
than management's standard of output. If output exceeded that
informal standard, the workers expected a cut in the wage rate or
an increase in the "bogey" (*i.e.* management's standard) upon which
the incentive was based. The worker therefore faced two dangers:
one, high output which led to rate cuts or increased bogeys; or two,
low output which resulted in arousing the ire of the supervisor.
Group sentiment prevailed upon each worker not to exceed the
informal output agreement and hence become a "rate buster" nor
should he injure his fellow workers by parasitically falling below the

[18] Stanley B. Mathewson, *Restriction of Output Among Unorganized Workers*,
New York: Viking Press, 1931.
[19] Roethlisberger and Dickson, p. 379.
[20] *Ibid.*, p. 380.

standard and becoming a "rate chiseler." To enforce the group norm, the members engaged in some interesting intra-group disciplinary devices such as sarcasm, ridicule, and "binging." "Binging" involved a rather firm blow upon the upper arm of the object of disfavor and was used to enforce all violations of group norms. Avoiding bruises became a motivator and workers engaged in numerous subterranean devices to maintain informal group membership. For example, on high output days, a worker would hide the surplus and report only what conformed to the norm; later he would slow down, and take the previous surplus units from his cache and turn them in. Three facts neatly summarize the Harvard researchers' discoveries: (1) that restriction of output was deliberate and set by the group regardless of management's notion of expected output; (2) that workers smoothed out production reports to avoid the appearance of working too fast or too slowly; and (3) that the group developed its own devices to bring recalcitrant members into line.

A second facet of the bank wiring room research was the assessment of interpersonal relations for the purpose of studying social structure or group "configuration." In this phase the Harvard group could lay claim to far more originality than was possible in its study of restriction of output. Analysis of social relations in the bank wiring room revealed two cliques or informal groups within the formal structure. The formal structure consisted of three work groups of three wiremen each, one solderman serving each group, and with the inspection duties split between the two inspectors. The circles (Figure 13-1) indicated the presence of the two cliques A and B and the members of those sets. Wireman W_2 was shown with dotted lines to indicate that he was not a member of Clique A. Clique A was called the "front group" and worked toward the front of the observation room and Clique B was the "back group" because of their physical location. In analyzing these cliques, the researchers attempted to isolate the factors determining clique membership. Physical location (front and back) was one factor but did not govern; neither was occupation a determining factor since Clique A contained wiremen, solderers, and an inspector. Members of the same clique engaged in intra-group activities such as "games" (betting, binging, etc.), by trading jobs, and by helping one another even though company policy forbade all of these activities. Each

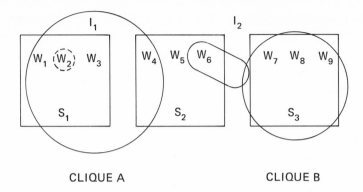

CLIQUE A   CLIQUE B

Key:
W = Wireman, S = Solderman, I = Inspector

Fig. 13–1. Internal organization of the bank wiring room. (Adapted from Roethlisberger and Dickson, *op. cit.*, p. 509. Copyright 1939 by the President and Fellows of Harvard College; by permission.)

clique excluded members from the other clique in these particular activities, and Clique A considered itself "superior" to Clique B.

Wiremen W_2 and W_5, solderer S_2, and inspector I_2 were "isolates" who did not participate in clique activities and were excluded for various reasons: S_2 had a speech impediment and did not contribute to social interaction; W_2 was self-reliant and a non-conformist; W_5 was ostracized from the group because he "squealed" to the foreman about group activities which violated company policy. The inspector "isolate" (I_2) was excluded because he took his inspection duties very seriously whereas I_1 often pointed out errors without formally charging them against the worker and acted more like one of the boys than did I_2. In the final analysis, certain sentiments seemed to govern clique membership:

(1) You should not turn out too much work. If you do, you are a 'rate-buster'.

(2) You should not turn out too little work. If you do, you are a 'chiseler'.

(3) You should not tell a supervisor anything that will react to the detriment of an associate. If you do, you are a "squealer".

(4) You should not attempt to maintain social distance or act officious. If you are an inspector, for example, you should not act like one.[21]

[21] *Ibid.*, p. 522.

What was to explain the variations in output between the relay assembly test room and the bank wiring room? In the former case the girls had increased their productivity but in the latter, restriction was the rule. Both groups were observed but the role of the observer was different. In the relay assembly experiment, the observer took the girls into his confidence, asked for suggestions, and encouraged participation in decisions affecting their welfare. In the bank wiring room however, the observers merely watched impassively while the workers perpetuated the same informal schemes practiced in the past. The eventual explanation of the differences in output would add ammunition to the Harvard group's arsenal of arguments for new managerial skills. In explaining the cliques, new vistas for social systems would be opened.

The researchers found that the cliques performed two functions for the workers: (1) it protected them from internal indiscretions of members, such as rate busting or chiseling; and (2) it protected them from the outside interference of management officials who would attempt to raise standards, cut rates, or stop their "games." The group was an instrument for controlling the activities and sentiments of the workers. Analogous to the findings of the interview program that in studying group behavior one had to separate fact from sentiment, the Harvard group began an exploration of the "facts" as the workers perceived them versus actual company practices as the researchers saw them. In regard to restriction of output, the researchers concluded that the fear of depression and layoff was not the sole reason for soldiering since workers restricted output in both good *and* bad times. Restriction was not a depression phenomenon and actually worked to the worker's detriment since restriction increased unit cost and might therefore actually induce management to make changes in rates, standards, or technology to offset the higher costs. Since the management of Western Electric had a long record of fair dealing with the workers, the researchers deemed the turning inward of the groups for protection to be "non-logical" and a worker misconception of reality.

Failing to find that mismanagement or general economic conditions caused the informal groups to form, the Harvard researchers sought an explanation by viewing the bank wiring room as part of a larger social organization. Relations with extra-departmental personnel, such as "efficiency men" and other "technologists," were viewed as disturbing since their actions could impinge on worker welfare. The technologist tended to follow a "logic of efficiency" which the workers perceived as an interference and a constraint on their activities. Further, supervisors (as a class) represented authority and the power to discipline to insure that the worker conformed to management rules. Apprehensive of such authority, the worker resisted supervisory attempts to force work behavior into an efficiency mold. Again, the researchers concluded that this was nonlogical behavior on the worker's part but stressed that management must recognize this and take into account "sentiments" along with the logic of efficiency. This position resulted in the admonition to management to view every organization as a "social system." The logic of efficiency in the technical system failed because it omitted the sentiments and nonlogical components of the social system.

The Organization as a Social System

The development of the social-system viewpoint must be classified as a major contribution of the Hawthorne research. The technical aspect of needs for efficiency and economic return should be viewed as being interrelated with concern for the human aspect of every organization. The employee has physical needs to be satisfied; but, more importantly, he has social needs. These needs arise from early social conditioning and persist through organizational life in relations with fellow workers and others in organizations. Events and objects in the physical work environment "cannot be treated as things in themselves. Instead they have to be interpreted as carriers of social value."[22] For example, a physical desk has no social significance; but if people who have desks are the ones who supervise others, then the desk becomes a status symbol and a carrier of social value. Other items, such as type of clothing worn, age, sex, seniority, and so on can also take on social significance. The researchers concluded that since man was not motivated by facts and logic, sentiments about things of social value became very powerful considerations in dealing with personnel.

The existence of the formal organization with its rules, orders, and payment plans, coupled simultaneously with an informal organization with its bases of sentiments and human interactions, posed problems for management. The informal organization should not be viewed as "bad" but as a necessary, interdependent aspect of the

[22] *Ibid.*, p. 557.

formal organization. Viewing the organization as a social system enabled management to attack the conflict between the "logic of efficiency" demanded by the formal organization and the "logic of sentiments" of the informal organization.[23]   The manager should strive for an equilibrium between the technical organization and the human one by securing the economic goals while "maintaining the equilibrium of the social organization so that individuals through contributing services to this common purpose obtain personal satisfactions that make them willing to cooperate."[24]

In short, the outcome of the Hawthorne research was a call for a new mix of managerial skills.   These skills were ones which were crucial to handling human situations: first, diagnostic skills in understanding human behavior and second, interpersonal skills in counseling, motivating, leading, and communicating with workers. Technical skills alone were not enough to cope with the man discovered at the Hawthorne Works.

A NEW VIEW OF INDUSTRIAL MAN

The new view of industrial man à la Mayo and Roethlisberger was in reality a new social philosophy for an industrial civilization. Mayo's education reveals the basis for this new emerging interpretation of man in industry.   For a short time, Mayo had studied medicine and, though he never received a medical degree, he developed an interest in "psychopathology," the scientific study of mental disorders.   Two individuals were in the vanguard of analyzing psychopathological thought, Pierre Janet of the French school, and Sigmund Freud, the originator of psychoanalysis.   Mayo claimed more affinity to Janet, including writing a scholarly work on his theories.[25]   Janet was of the opinion that the primary mental disorder was "obsession" or preoccupation with certain ideas to such an extent that the individual could not cope with them even though he knew such ideas to be irrational or untrue.   The Freudians called this "compulsion" and Mayo thought the work of Janet and that

[23] *Ibid.*, pp. 556–564.   "Logic of sentiments" was a contradiction since Roethlisberger and Dickson concluded that sentiments were nonlogical.

[24] *Ibid.*, p. 569.   The authors acknowledged their indebtedness to Chester Barnard (who will be discussed later) for this distinction.

[25] Elton Mayo, *Some Notes on the Psychology of Pierre Janet,* Cambridge, Mass.: Harvard University Press, 1948.

of Freud were complementary.[26] The essence of Mayo's obsession-compulsion interpretation was that individuals were incapacitated by their obsessions to such a degree that they were inflexible in their responses to life, including their personal, social, and industrial behavior. Obsessions, by reducing one's ability to adapt, had dysfunctional consequences for the worker and the supervisor. Although Mayo never once concluded that any large number of the workers at Hawthorne were severe cases, he did think that the interviewing program had demonstrated that minimal levels of obsession (or preoccupation) existed in the sense that "conditions of work tended in some way to prevent rather than facilitate a satisfactory personal adaptation."[27]

In Mayo's view, workers had been unable to find satisfactory outlets for expressing personal problems and dissatisfactions in their work life. This blockage had led to "pessimistic reveries" and preoccupations with personal problems at a latent level which emerged on the manifest level as apprehension of authority, restriction of output, and a variety of other forms of behavior which reduced morale and output. To Mayo, industrial life caused a sense of personal futility which led to social maladjustment and eventually to obsessive, irrational behavior:

> Human collaboration in work, in primitive and developed societies, has always depended for its perpetuation upon the evolution of a non-logical social code which regulates the relations between persons and their attitudes to one another. Insistence upon a merely economic logic of production . . . interferes with the development of such a code and consequently gives rise in the group to a sense of human defeat. This human defeat results in the formation of a social code at a lower level and in opposition to the economic logic. One of its symptoms is "restriction".[28]

It was from this psychopathological analysis of industrial life that Mayo and Roethlisberger formed the philosophical rationale for the human relations movement.[29] The goal was effective human collaboration; the means was the restoration of a social code to facilitate adjustment to industrial life.

[26] Elton Mayo, *Human Problems*, pp. 107–110.

[27] *Ibid.*, p. 114.

[28] *Ibid.*, pp. 120–121.

[29] Professor Roethlisberger also adopted this obsession-compulsion approach of Janet and Mayo. See F. J. Roethlisberger, "The Nature of Obsessive Thinking", *Man-In-Organization: Essays of F. J. Roethlisberger*, Cambridge, Mass.: Belknap Press of Harvard University Press, 1968, pp. 1–19. This paper was originally written in June, 1928 but was not published until 1968.

Anomie and Social Disorganization

To develop his thesis for human collaboration, Mayo borrowed Émile Durkheim's anomie as the basic premise for a new view of industrial man. In traditional societies man knew his place and his future and there was social solidarity. The domestic system, built around the family and kinship, gave man an identity in work as well as in his social life. The factory system and the process of industrialization destroyed this solidarity through widespread division of labor, increased social and physical mobility and the growth of large-scale organizations in which the manner of dealing with interpersonal relations shifted from a personal, friendship base to one of an impersonal nature. The result was a normless, rootless mode of life in which individual identities were lost along with the social bonds that provided continuity and purpose to man's existence. This anomie led to social disorganization in personal lives and in communities and effected a general overall sense of personal futility of defeat and disillusionment.[30] Social invention to cope with industrial changes had not kept pace with technical inventions. It was this "social lag" that caused the widespread sense of futility and the resultant social disorganization. Rapid economic growth, such as that American had experienced both before and after the turn of the century, had disturbed "communal integrity."

Mayo argued that the advance of a technically oriented society placed undue emphasis upon engineering and yielded a technological interpretation of the meaning of work in the sense that achievement criteria were based on the economic logic of efficiency. Social needs of individuals were pushed into the background, thereby reducing the individual's "capacity for collaboration in work."[31] Managerial emphasis on the logic of efficiency stifled the individual's desire for group approval, for social satisfactions, and for social purpose gained through communal life. Drawing from Pareto's notion of an "elite," Mayo postulated that the administrative elite was technically oriented and that "in the important domain of human understanding and control, we are ignorant of the facts and their nature."[32] The "new administrator" must be one who effectively restored opportun-

---

[30] Mayo, *Human Problems,* pp. 128–131.
[31] *Ibid.,* p. 166.
[32] *Ibid.,* p. 177.

ities for human collaboration in work and in life by recognizing man's need for social solidarity. This would be accomplished by training in the human and social aspects of industrial organization, by developing "listening" and counseling skills, and by recognizing and understanding the nonlogical side of the social code. The human problem, as Mayo perceived it, was that administrators thought that the answers to industrial problems resided in technical efficiency, when in fact, the problem was a social and human one.

The Rabble Hypothesis

Elton Mayo was concerned with the human, social, and political problems of an industrial civilization, and a preponderance of his productive writing era was marked by substantial conflict in a world characterized by depression, war, and social upheaval. In the foreword to *The Social Problems of an Industrial Civilization,* he wrote:

> . . . the atomic bomb arrives at this moment to call our attention both to our achievement and our failure. We have learned how to destroy scores of thousands of human beings in a moment of time: we do not know how systematically to set about the task of inducing various groups and nations to collaborate in the tasks of civilization.
> It is not the atomic bomb that will destroy civilization. But civilized society can destroy itself . . . if it fails to understand intelligently and to control the aids and deterrents to cooperation.[33]

In his *Social Problems,* and later in *The Political Problems of an Industrial Civilization,*[34] Mayo was concerned with the failure of social and political institutions to provide means for effective human collaboration in the huge aggregations of men and materials which characterized a mass-producing society. Overemphasis on technical progress and material life to the neglect of human and social life would be the downfall of civilization. Mayo traced the roots of this problem to faulty economic and political theory and laid the blame at the feet of David Ricardo and his "rabble hypothesis." In Mayo's view, the offender was *laissez-faire* economics and Ricardo's interpretation of society, which held that:

[33] Boston: Division of Research, Graduate School of Business Administration, Harvard University, 1945, p. xvi.

[34] Boston: Division of Research, Graduate School of Business Administration, Harvard University, 1947.

1. Natural society consists of a horde of unorganized individuals.

2. Every individual acts in a manner calculated to secure his self-preservation and self-interest.

3. Every individual thinks logically, to the best of his ability, in the service of this aim.[35]

Since man was brutal, and unthinking except in the service of his own interest, the necessary corollary to cope with this "rabble" man was the absolute state. This centralization of power was characteristic of Hobbes and Machiavelli; for Mayo, the era of Hitler and Mussolini was a continuation of this rabble hypothesis. Mayo attempted to refute the rabble hypothesis by: (1) postulating that it was collaboration with others, not competition among a disorganized horde, that was important; (2) stating that every individual acted to protect his *group* status and not his self-interest; and (3) repeating the Hawthorne findings that thinking was guided more by sentiment than by logic. The Hawthorne research was used by Mayo to support all of these positions in the sense that the research found group collaboration and group sentiments to override the logic of efficiency.

In all fairness to David Ricardo it must be noted that his "rabble hypothesis" was much less explicit than Mayo's interpretation. Ricardo, like Malthus, was one who earned for economics the title of "the dismal science" and he wrote in a gloomy world in which perhaps society did appear to be a horde to one from the educated class. Likewise, it was inappropriate to classify Ricardo's views of society with the *laissez-faire* of Adam Smith. Where Ricardo saw chaos, Smith saw order; in place of tragedy, Smith saw progress.[36] In linking the rabble hypothesis to *laissez-faire,* Mayo served his own purpose and not that of valid criticism. In linking it to Ricardo, he gave the gloomy prophet less than he deserved.

Aside from improper attributions, Mayo's idea was that the world must rethink its concepts of authority by abandoning the notion of unitary authority from a central head, be it the state, the church, or the industrial leader. Drawing heavily from Chester Barnard, Mayo concluded that authority should be based on social skills in securing *cooperation* rather than technical skill or expertise. By building from small groups to larger ones, and by basing leader-

[35] Elton Mayo, *Social Problems,* p. 40.

[36] Robert L. Heilbroner, *The Worldly Philosophers,* New York: Simon and Schuster, 1961, especially pp. 75–84.

ship on securing cooperation, social solidarity could be restored and democracy preserved. It was through the group that the horde could be avoided.

Developing the New Leadership

Elton Mayo had set the stage for social man by seeking a new leadership buttressed by social and human skills which would overcome anomie, the rabble hypothesis, and social disorganization. In its very essence, Mayoism espoused the same goal as Taylorism, that of collaboration and cooperation in industry. The means to this goal differed but the end which both anticipated was the recognition of a mutually beneficial relationship between the worker and management. It is not a question of who was right, Taylor or Mayo, but more significantly, whose ideas most logically followed the cultural premises of the times.

In Chapter 12, Taylor's views were seen to be logically consistent with his economic, social, and political environment. Begging the question on Mayo at this point and reserving that analysis for Chapter 18, let us examine the implementation of this philosophy of social man. The "new" leader was to be one who acted as an investigator of social sentiments for the furtherance of collaborative efforts to achieve organizational goals. Since man spent so much time in a group, and since many of his satisfactions were the product of cooperative effort, management must focus its efforts on the maintenance of group integrity and solidarity. The group became the universal solvent and now it was management's task to find the universal container.

A marked shift for the leader of social man was in the basic assumption about why people work. Money or economic motivation was deemed of secondary importance in stimulating higher productivity. Instead:

> Whether or not a person is going to give his services whole-heartedly to a group depends, in good part, on the way he feels about his job, his fellow workers, and supervisors . . .[37]

Money formed only a small part of satisfaction and the worker reported that he wanted

[37] F. J. Roethlisberger, *Management and Morale,* Cambridge, Mass.: Harvard University Press, 1942, p. 15.

. . . social recognition . . . tangible evidence of our social importance . . . the feeling of security that comes not so much from the amount of money we have in the bank as from being an accepted member of the group.[38]

The Hawthorne evidence seemed to support this view that workers did not respond rationally to calculate the pleasure to be derived from meeting the bogey and earning the bonus reward but instead conformed to group pressures to restrict output. If workers did not respond to an economic calculus, the manager found his job more complex. He had first to insure the economic function of the business by meeting production goals and keeping costs down. Second, he had to fulfill a *social* function to satisfy individual and group needs. For the human relationists, satisfaction of the social function led to fulfillment of the economic function. The manager satisfied needs and the worker reciprocated by increasing output. In a catchphrase—"satisfied workers are productive workers."

The foreman as the primary point of contact between the worker and management played a particularly crucial, and often conflicting role.[39] The problem for industrial leadership revolved around the premise that it was a rare supervisor who possessed both technical-economic skills and human relations skills. The ability to meet the logic of efficiency was different from the ability to meet the non-logic of worker sentiments. Supervisors tended to confuse fact with sentiment and, as the Harvard research group had found in the interviewing program, assumed that what the worker told them was the way things really were. Communications and listening skills hence became an important part of the supervisor's tool kit.[40] The answer to preparing leaders for the new human relations role was training at all levels to teach skills in human understanding of logical and nonlogical behavior, understanding of the sentiments of the worker through listening and communications skills, and developing the ability to maintain an equilibrium between the economic needs of the formal organization and the social needs of the informal organization. Equilibrium became the keynote of organizational effectiveness. Through the social structure, the worker

---

[38] *Ibid.*, pp. 24–25.

[39] See Roethlisberger's often reprinted "The Foreman: Master and Victim of Double Talk," in *Man-in-Organization*, pp. 35–58.

[40] The literature of the human relationists on communications is quite exhaustive. To sample the main ideas, see: F. J. Roethlisberger, "Barriers to Communication between Men," in *Man-in-Organization*, pp. 154–159; and F. J. Roethlisberger, "The Administrator's Skill: Communication," in *ibid.*, pp. 160–175.

obtained the recognition, security, and satisfactions which made him willing to cooperate and contribute his services toward the attainment of the organization's objectives. Disequilibrium occurred when technical change was introduced too fast and/or when management was out of touch with worker sentiments. This was the new leadership, one which could distinguish fact from sentiment and one which balanced economic logic and the nonlogic of sentiment.

Organized Labor and the Mayoists

Conspicuous by its absence in the writing of Mayo and others of the early human relations movement is the subject of organized labor. During the course of the 20,000 interviews at Hawthorne, no employee mentioned the subject of unions. The Hawthorne Works had successfully resisted organizing efforts and only in 1937 did a company union form.[41] It is true that most of the 1920's and part of the 1930's were periods of low union influence in industry. However, it is strange that the human relationists with their emphasis on group solidarity omitted unions from their view of industrial society. Loren Baritz, among others, has suggested that the Mayoists were anti-union and pro-management. "Cooperation" meant worker cooperation on management's terms. While this conclusion may not be perfectly accurate, the Mayoists were less than explicit on the role of unions. Apparently, the Mayoists thought that management could obviate the necessity for union representation by substituting human-relations-oriented supervisors who would fill the worker's needs for security, recognition, and the expression of grievances.

Organized labor, apparently unaware of the Mayoists' views, did not lash out initially at the Mayoists as they had at Taylor. Scientific management was a threat to union leadership, explicitly striking at the core of unionism; Mayoism was more subtle, posed no explicit threat, and passed over the head of union leaders rather than hitting them in the gut as Taylor had. After initial apathy, the publication *Ammunition* of the United Auto Workers in 1949 lashed out petulantly at Mayoism:

The prophet is Elton Mayo, a Harvard University professor who has been prying into the psychiatric bowels of factory workers since around about 1925 and who is the Old Man of the movement. The Bible is his book, the Human

[41] Loren Baritz, p. 113.

Problems of an Industrial Civilization. The Holy Place is the Hawthorne Plant of the Western Electric Company (the wholly owned subsidiary of one of the nation's largest monopolies, the AT and T). At Hawthorne, Ma Bell, when she wasn't organizing company unions, allowed Professor Mayo to carry on experiments with a group of women workers for some nine years . . .

For these nine years about every kind of experiment a very bright Harvard professor could think of was tried on the women. Everything you do to white mice was done to them, except their spines and skulls were not split so the fluid could be analyzed . . .

What did make them produce and produce and produce with ever-increasing speed was the expression of interest in their personal problems by the supervisor; interviews by psychiatrically trained social workers and (later on) the way they were paired off with friendly or unfriendly co-workers.

Now obviously this is the greatest discovery since J. P. Morgan learned that you can increase profits by organizing a monopoly, suppressing competition, raising prices and reducing production.[42]

Labeling the Hawthorne researchers as "cow sociologists" (contented workers give more "milk"), this union view contained much of the same illogical venom that characterized the hearings on the Taylor system.

A Final Note

Further criticisms by organized labor and Academia will be examined in Chapter 17. At this point, it is necessary only to draw some parallels between Taylor and Mayo as representatives of two major approaches to solving industrial problems. To this author, it is amazing to note the high degree of similarity of goals between the two men. Both perceived industrial conflict between the worker and management and put much of the onus on management; both sought a harmony or mutuality of interests between labor and management, Taylor through a mental revolution and Mayo through human collaboration. In this sense their goals are strikingly similar though their means to these ends differed. Both sought higher productivity and agreed that the worker must have the attention and aid of management in order to achieve that goal. Whereas Taylor would place on management the responsibility to reduce obstacles to higher performance through study, planning, and organizing, Mayo would increase the social skills of the supervisor. With this striking similarity in goals, the means to these ends bear the brunt of the dissimilarities. Taylor focused on the individual worker, Mayo on

[42] From "Deep Therapy on the Assembly Line," quoted by Loren Baritz, pp. 114–115.

the worker as a group member; Taylor was not concerned so much with interpersonal relations, the Mayoists were; Taylor thought that the physical work environment was a major impediment to higher productivity, the Mayoists thought it was the social environment; and Taylor thought that, given the opportunity, man would seek to opitimize his economic return, while the Mayoists downgraded the lure of money and stressed group membership. The training, backgrounds, and cultural perspectives of these two men do much to explain their dissimilarities. Taylor the engineer operated in an environment which demanded efficiency. Mayo was trained in logic and philosophy and was intrigued by psychopathology. Mayo lived in an era of different cultural imperatives. But more must be said of that matter later.

SUMMARY

Embarking upon a voyage to explain the mysterious discrepancy between traditional assumptions about work behavior and observed behavior, the Hawthorne researchers disclosed new facets of industrial man. Output was not related to physical conditions of work but to how people were treated and how they felt about their work, their supervisors, and their co-workers. Economic motives became suspect and social motives paramount. The Mayoists concluded that man was more responsive to his peer group than to management controls, that man obtained his basic sense of identity through relationships with others, and that it was through social relations that man could restore meaning to industrial life. The new leader for the new industrial man needed social, not technical skills. He should maintain an equilibrium between the logic of efficiency and the nonlogic of worker sentiments. By separating fact from sentiment and by developing listening and human skills, the human-relations-oriented supervisor could overcome the dysfunctions of anomie and restore group solidarity, and thereby achieve a dualization of satisfying both human social needs and organizational economic needs.

14

The Search for
Organizational
Integration

The Western Electric Research provided the impetus for the study of social man and social systems. Outside the Harvard circle, two individuals made significant contributions to the development of new ideas regarding the nature of authority, the necessity for coordination of effort, the resolution of conflict, and the design of organizations which would provide maximum opportunities for cooperative effort. One was a political philosopher turned business sage who never met a payroll in her life; the other, a utility executive whose hobby was classical piano and the work of Johann Sebastian Bach. Together, they were integrators who provided insightful links between the scientific management and the social man eras.

MARY PARKER FOLLETT: THE POLITICAL PHILOSOPHER

Born in Boston in 1868 and educated at the Thayer Academy and the Annexe at Harvard (later renamed Radcliffe College), Mary Parker Follett brought a wide variety of interests and knowledge to bear upon management thought before her death in 1933.[1]

---

[1] Biographical information on Miss Follett may be found in Henry C. Metcalf and Lyndall Urwick (ed.), *Dynamic Administration: The Collected Papers of Mary*

Trained in philosophy and political science, Mary Follett became interested in vocational guidance, adult education, and in the emerging discipline of social psychology. Chronologically, Follett belonged to the scientific management era; philosophically and intellectually, she was a member of the social man era. She had a foot in each world and served as a link between the two eras by generalizing from Taylor's concepts and by anticipating many of the conclusions of the Hawthorne researchers.[2]

In order to understand Mary Follett, one must examine her philosophical predilections. She was an ardent admirer of Johann Fichte (1762–1814),[3] the German philosopher who espoused a nationalism in which the freedom of the individual had to be subordinated to the group. Fichte did not think that man had free will but that he was bound up in an interpersonal network to which all men were committed. Thus man's ego belonged to a wider world of egos, making the ego a social one, until all together swelled up into one "Great Ego" which was part of a common life among all men.[4] Fichte's philosophy was made manifest in Follett's *The New State*, in which she challenged the prevailing political assumptions of her era.[5] Follett's thesis was that "we find the true man only through group organization. The potentialities of the individual remain potentialities until they are released by group life. Man discovers his true nature, gains his true freedom only through the group."[6]

The "group principle" was to be the "new psychology" and was designed to renounce the old ideas that man thought, felt, and

Parker Follett, New York: Harper and Row, 1940, pp. 9–29; and in L. Urwick, *The Golden Book of Management*, London: Newman Neame, 1956, pp. 132–137.

[2] Robert J. Daiute, *Scientific Management and Human Relations*, New York: Holt Rinehart and Winston, 1964, p. 30. Other useful sources on her philosophy are: Joel M. Rosenfeld and Matthew J. Smith, "Mary Parker Follett: The Transition to Modern Management Thought," *Advanced Management Journal*, Vol. 31, No. 4 (October, 1966), pp. 33–37; and Eliot M. Fox, "Mary Parker Follett: The Enduring Contribution," *Public Administration Review*, Vol. 28 (November–December, 1968), pp. 520–529.

[3] Urwick, *Golden Book*, p. 133.

[4] Henry D. Aiken, *The Age of Ideology*, New York: New American Library, 1956, pp. 54–60. Fichte was a disciple of Immanuel Kant and in his early years followed Kantian notions of rationalism and the absolutely inalienable rights of the individual. In his later years, Fichte broke with Kant, turned to nationalism and statism, and became part of the "romantic" revolt against reason.

[5] Mary Parker Follett, *The New State: Group Organization the Solution of Popular Government*, London: Longmans, Green and Co., 1918.

[6] *Ibid.*, p. 6.

acted independently. Group man lived in association, not as a separate ego, and individuals were created by reciprocal social intercourse. This view demonstrated her acceptance of Gestalt psychology and reflected Charles Horton Cooley's idea of the enlargement of the social self through association and the social "looking glass." Using phrases such as "togetherness," "group thinking," and "the collective will," Miss Follett sought a new society which would be based upon a group principle and not upon individualism. The underlying rationale was not to destroy the individual but was based upon her premise that only through the group could the individual find his "true self." Following the group principle, she concluded that a person's "true self is the group-self" and that "man can have no rights apart from society or independent of society or against society."[7] In negating the notion that the purpose of government is to protect individual rights, she proposed a new concept of democracy:

Democracy then is a great spiritual force evolving itself from men, utilizing each, completing his incompleteness by weaving together all in the many-membered community life which is the true theophany.[8]

For Follett, democracy was the development of a social consciousness, not individualism, and she felt that "the theory of government based on individual rights no longer has a place in modern political theory."[9] The new and true democracy was to build from small neighborhood groups, to community groups, to state groups, to a national group, and eventually to an international group "will." Without really coming to grips in this book with the problems of groups in conflict, she had faith that men could create a new "social consciousness" and live together peaceably in the "World State."[10] She demonstrated little confidence in ballot-box democracy, believing that this idea reflected crowd psychology and "right" being defined by the sheer weight of numbers.

In *Creative Experience*, Follett followed the same theme: that through conference, discussion, and cooperation, people could evoke each other's latent ideas and make manifest their unity in the pursuit of common goals. Relying heavily upon Gestalt psychology, which held that every psychological situation has a specific character apart from the "absolute" nature of the component parts, *i.e.*, the "whole"

---

[7] *Ibid.*, p. 137.
[8] *Ibid.*, p. 161, "Theophany" is "the visible manifestation of God or a god."
[9] *Ibid.*, p. 172.
[10] *Ibid.*, pp. 359–360. *cf.* Fichte's "Great Ego."

is a configuration greater than the sum of the parts, she felt that through group experiences the individual could reach a greater release of his own creative powers.[11]   The goal of group effort was an *integrative unity* which transcended the parts.   In essence, she began to answer the questions of group conflict which she failed to examine in *The New State*.   She hypothesized that any conflict of interests could be resolved in any one of four ways: "(1) voluntary submission of one side; (2) struggle and the victory of one side over the other; (3) compromise; or (4) integration."   Both one and two were clearly unacceptable because they involved the use of force or power to *dominate*.   Compromise was likewise futile because it postponed the issue and because the "truth does not lie 'between' the two sides."[12]   *Integration* involved finding a solution which satisfied both sides without compromise and domination. In a later lecture she gave her best examples of this concept of integration:

Let us take some very simple illustration.   In the Harvard Library one day, in one of the smaller rooms, someone wanted the window open, I wanted it shut. We opened the window in the next room, where no one was sitting.   This was not a compromise because there was no curtailing of desire; we both got what we really wanted.   For I did not want a closed room, I simply did not want the north wind to blow directly on me; likewise the other occupant did not want that particular window open, he merely wanted more air in the room . . . Let us take another illustration. A Dairymen's Co-operative League almost went to pieces last year on the question of precedence in unloading cans at a creamery platform.   The men who came down the hill (the creamery was on a down grade) thought they should have precedence; the men who came up the hill thought they should unload first.   The thinking of both sides in the controversy was thus confined within the walls of these two possibilities, and this prevented their even trying to find a way of settling the dispute which would avoid these alternatives.   The solution was obviously to change the position of the platform so that both up-hillers and down-hillers could unload at the same time.   But this solution was not found until they had asked the advice of a more or less professional integrator.   When, however, it was pointed out to them, they were quite ready to accept it.   Integration involves invention, and the clever thing is to recognize this, and not to let one's thinking stay within the boundaries of two alternatives which are mutually exclusive.[13]

The search for integrative unity, for commonality of will, and for human cooperation earned Mary Follett an international reputation as a political philosopher. *Creative Experience* was widely read by

[11] Mary Parker Follett, *Creative Experience*, London: Longmans, Green and Company, 1924, Chapter 5.

[12] *Ibid.*, p. 156.

[13] H. C. Metcalf and L. Urwick, pp. 32–33.   Copyright 1940, Harper and Row; by permission.

businessmen of the day and Miss Follett was drawn even more closely to the problems of industrial administration. In 1924–1925, she was asked to give a series of lectures in New York to a group of business executives under the auspices of the Bureau of Personnel Administration. It was from these lectures and subsequent work that she made the transition from a political to a business philosopher.

The Business Philosopher

If one views administration as a universal phenomenon, the processes which underlie political administration would necessarily apply to business as well. The same problems of achieving unity of effort, of defining authority and responsibility, of achieving coordination and control, and of developing effective leadership exist. It was toward the goal of drawing this parallel that Mary Parker Follett turned her attention. First, from *Creative Experience* she developed further the ideas of "constructive conflict" and the integrative unity of business. Since domination and compromise led to further strife and futility, integration was paramount in all business activities. In dealing with labor, she deplored the notion of collective bargaining because it rested on the relative balance of power and inevitably ended in compromise. Bargaining meant that there were two sides to fight over and both parties tended to lose sight of that which they had in common. In taking sides, *e.g.*, pro-labor or pro-management, positions solidified and the parties failed to see the business as a "functional whole" for which they had joint responsibilities. This collective responsibility began at the departmental level where workers were to be given group responsibilities:

> When you have made your employees feel that they are in some sense partners in the business, they do not improve the quality of their work, save waste in time and material, because of the Golden Rule, but because their interests are the same as yours [the manager's][14]

In Miss Follett's view, this was not a reciprocal back-scratching arrangement, but a true feeling on the part of both labor and management that they served a common purpose. She suggested that in the past an artificial line was drawn between those who managed and those who were managed. In reality, there was no line and

[14] *Ibid.*, p. 82.

all members of the organization who accepted responsibility for work at any level were contributing to the whole. Beyond the view of the firm as a unity, all should recognize the relation of the firm to its environment of creditors, stock-holders, customers, competitors, suppliers, and the community. This larger view of the firm and its environment would enable an integrative unity of society and the economy. Integration then became an associative principle applicable to all levels of life.

Integration as a principle of conduct would be less than fully effective unless people re-thought their concepts of authority and power. It was in this second area that Follett sought to develop "power with" instead of "power over" and "co-action" to replace consent and coercion. When there was an "order giver" and an "order taker", integration was difficult to achieve. The role of "boss" and "subordinate" created barriers to recognizing the commonality of interests. To overcome this, Follett proposed to "depersonalize" orders and to shift obedience to the "law of the situation":

> One *person* should not give orders to another *person*, but both should agree to take their orders from the situation. If orders are simply part of the situation, the question of someone giving and someone receiving does not come up.[15]

The rationale for the law of the situation was based on scientific management in the sense that Taylor's functional management sought obedience to facts determined by study and not based on the will of one person. In a paper for the Taylor Society, Follett put it this way:

> If, then, authority is derived from function, it has little to do with hierarchy of position as such. . . . We find authority with the head of a department, with an expert . . . the dispatch clerk has more authority in dispatching work than the President . . . authority should go with knowledge and experience . . .[16]

By shifting authority to knowledge, personal confrontations could be avoided as each person felt the dictates of the situation and thereby acted with less friction in achieving an integrative unity. Miss Follett admired this facet of scientific management, which divorced the person from the situation because it was good psychology in dealing with subordinates. For her, the essence of good human relations was creating the feeling of working *with* someone

[15] *Ibid.*, p. 59.
[16] "The Illusion of Final Authority," *Bulletin of the Taylor Society*, Vol. 2, No. 5 (December, 1926), p. 243.

rather than working *under* someone. In practice this became "power-with" versus "power-over" in her terms. Management should not exercise power over the worker, nor should the worker through unions exercise power over management. Jointly exercised power was "co-active," not coercive. The analogy she used was that "you have rights *over* a slave, you have rights *with* a servant."[17] Displaying a number of insights into the psychology of power, she rejected both the authoritarian's striving for power and Gandhi's "non-cooperation" as being insidious uses of power. Gandhi's concept of power through humility and non-violence was still the desire for "power-over." It was conflict, a search for bending the will of the British to his own movement. Integration and constructive conflict could not be found in any effort to dominate.

In all forms of life, from interpersonal relations to the handling of international disputes, "power-over" had to be reduced and obedience had to be shifted to the law of the situation. The basis for such integration was what she called "circular response." By this she meant a process based on the opportunity for each party to influence the other and through open interaction, over a period of time, "power-with" could be obtained. For labor and management it would come through open disclosure of costs, prices, and market situations. In international affairs, diplomacy became disclosure, not withholding, and facts, not triumphs. Demands for power were demands to share in control, especially for the labor movement; yet the demands focused on getting power without accepting responsibility. Employee representation plans were designed to share power by wresting it from management. Management, in retaliation, strove to retain all power and this led to inevitable industrial conflict. For Mary Follett, this struggle for power overlooked the mutual interests of both parties. She thought that "final authority" was an illusion based on a false premise of power; authority accrued in the situation, not the person or his position. Likewise, "final responsibility" was an illusion. Responsibility was inherent in the job or function performed and was "cumulative" in the sense that it was the sum of all individual and group responsibilities in a system of cross-relationships. At the individual level, a person was responsible *for* work, not *to* someone. At the departmental level, the responsibility for work was jointly

[17] Metcalf and Urwick, p. 101. Italics added.

shared by all those who contributed with the manager merely *interweaving* the various individual and group responsibilities. The chief of the organization also had cumulative responsibility for interweaving interdepartmental work.

In this second area of analysis, Miss Follett had put forth some iconoclastic notions of authority and responsibility. Traditional notions of the military or other organizations that authority was "power-over" and that responsibility accrued at the source of final authority were rejected. Authority resided in the situation, not the person or position. Logically then, responsibility was inherent in the function performed and accumulated in interweaving functions. This was heady material for thought from this modest spinster to the corporate manager.

Two facets of her philosophy have been explored: (1) the reduction of conflict through an integration of interests; and (2) the necessary corollary of obeying the law of the situation. A third facet of her philosophy concerned building the underlying psychological processes necessary to achieving goals through co-ordinating and controlling effort. Follett's view of control reflected her Gestalt psychology of dealing with wholes and the total situation to achieve unity. Control was impossible to achieve unless there was unity and cooperation among all elements, material and people, in a given situation. Any situation was out of control when interests were not reconciled. The basis for control resided in self-regulating, self-directing individuals and groups who recognized common interests and controlled their tasks to meet the objective. The manager did not control single elements, but complex interrelationships, not persons, but situations, and the outcome was a productive configuration of a total situation. How was this configuration achieved? Mary Follett called for a new philosophy of control which (1) was "fact-control rather than man-control," and (2) "correlated control" rather than "super-imposed control."[18] Each situation generated its own control because it was the facts of the situation and the interweaving of the many groups in the situation that determined appropriate behavior. Most situations were too complex for central control from the top to function effectively; therefore controls were to be gathered or "correlated" at many

[18] Mary Parker Follett, "The Process of Control," in L. Gulick and L. Urwick (ed.) *Papers on the Science of Administration,* New York: Institute of Public Administration, Columbia University, 1937, p. 161.

points in the organizational structure. This interweaving and correlation was to be based upon coordination which Follett saw as:

1. Co-ordination as the reciprocal relating of all the factors in a situation.
2. Co-ordination by direct contact of all the responsible people concerned.
3. Co-ordination in the early stages.
4. Co-ordination as a continuing process.[19]

These were considered the "four fundamental principles of organization" and involved the conclusion that the organization *was*
control since the purpose of organizing and coordination was to insure controlled performance. Coordination achieved unity and
unity was control. For an illustration, Miss Follett took the age-old
conflict between the purchasing agent who desired to reduce the
cost of purchased materials and the production manager who maintained that he needed better material with which to work. If they
followed the principle of early and continuous coordination, each
could see the reciprocal problems and would turn their search toward finding or developing a material which met both of their
requirements. Neither sacrificed his goals and unity was achieved
for their particular departments, for the firm, and for the consumer
or the community. This synthesis of interests was self-regulation
through coordination to achieve integration. The final facet of Miss
Follett's business philosophy concerned the type of leadership it
would take to make her system work. Leadership would no longer
be based on power but on the reciprocal influence of leader on
follower and follower on leader in the context of the situation. The
primary leadership task was defining the *purpose* of the organization; the leader should

. . . make his co-workers see that it is not *his* purpose which is to be achieved,
but a common purpose, born of the desires and the activities of the group.
The best leader does not ask people to serve him, but the common end. The
best leader has not followers, but men and women working with him.[20]

Company purposes were to be integrated with individual and group
purposes and this called for the highest caliber of executive leadership. The leader did not depend upon commands and obedience
but upon skills in coordinating, defining purposes, and in evoking
responses to the law of the situation. Recognizing that mere exhortation would not achieve this new definition of leadership, Miss
Follett called for executive development aimed at: (1) developing

---

[19] *Ibid.*, p. 161. Also in Metcalf and Urwick, p. 297.
[20] Metcalf and Urwick, p. 262.

more science in making both physical and human decisions; and
(2) developing a motive of service to the community. The combination of science and service would lead to a "profession" of management which enlisted knowledge for the service of others. To
those who aspired to be managers, she advised:

Men must prepare themselves as seriously for this profession as for any other.
They must realize that they, as all professional men, are assuming grave
responsibilities, that they are to take a creative part in one of the large
functions of society, a part which, I believe, only trained and disciplined men
can in the future hope to take with success.[21]

The notion of service was not to be substituted for the motive of
profit but integrated into a larger professional motive:

We work for profit, for service, for our own development, for the love of creating
something. At any one moment, indeed, most of us are not working directly
or immediately for any of these things, but to put through the job in hand in
the best possible manner. . . . To come back to the professions: can we not
learn a lesson from them on this very point? The professions have not given
up the money motive. I do not care how often you see it stated that they
have . . . Professional men are eager enough for large incomes; but they have
other motives as well, and they are often willing to sacrifice a good slice of
income for the sake of these other things. We all want the richness of life
in the terms of our deepest desire. We can purify and elevate our desires, we
can add to them, but there is no individual or social progress in curtailment of
desires.[22]

A Final Note

Are the elements of Mary Parker Follett's business philosophy
the idyllic notions of a political philosopher? The naturalistic
simplicity of men living and working together without the use of
coercion and without the need to sacrifice oneself through compromise is certainly worthy of merit for man, the reasoning being.
Integration, moving to a broader plane for a solution, would call
for much more creativity and imagination than one commonly
witnesses in daily industrial, academic, political, and social life.
Nevertheless, the goal is a worthy one and should be considered to
be akin to Taylor's "mental revolution" and Mayo's call for human
collaboration. Depersonalization of authority and obedience to the
law of the situation would certainly sound the death knell for
tyranny and autocracy. However, perceiving and defining the law
of the situation would be most difficult in a world of one-up-

[21] *Ibid.*, p. 131. Coypright 1940, Harper and Row; by permission.
[22] *Ibid.*, p. 145. Copyright 1940, Harper and Row; by permission.

manship. Organizational control based on a perceived unity of purposes would make the world of the manager much more palatable. However, reward systems in practice often run counter to measuring one's contribution to total effort. A knowledgeable business leadership, dedicated to improving practices through science and service, is a recurrent plea throughout the evolution of management thought. Perhaps the ideals of Mary Follett can be attained, perhaps not. If not, it would be because too few heeded the pleas of this feminine philosopher.

THE ERUDITE EXECUTIVE: CHESTER I. BARNARD

Chester Irving Barnard was a sociologist of organizations without portfolio. Born in Malden, Massachusetts, in 1886, he personified the Horatio Alger ideal of the farm boy who made good.[23] On a scholarship to Harvard, he supplemented his income by tuning pianos and running a small dance band. He studied economics at Harvard, completed the requirements in three years (1906–1909), but failed to receive a degree because he lacked a laboratory science. Since he had already passed the course with distinction, he was "too busy" and thought it pointless to take the laboratory section. Even without a bachelor's degree, he did well enough to earn seven honorary doctorates for his life-long labor in understanding the nature and purpose of organizations. Barnard joined the Statistical Department of the American Telephone and Telegraph system in 1909 and in 1927 became the President of New Jersey Bell. His unbounded enthusiasm for organizational work carried him into voluntary work in many other organizations: for example, he helped David Lilienthal establish the policies of the Atomic Energy Commission, he served the New Jersey Emergency Relief Administration, the New Jersey Reformatory, the United Service Organization (president for three years), the Rockefeller Foundation (president for four years), and was president of the Bach Society of New Jersey. Barnard was a self-made scholar who applied the theories

[23] Biographical information is based on William B. Wolf, *How to Understand Management: An Introduction to Chester I. Barnard*, Los Angeles: Lucas Brothers Publishers, 1968; Professor Wolf was President of the Academy of Management in 1971. For other information on Barnard, see *Who's Who in America*, Vol. 20 (1938–39), Chicago: A. N. Marquis Co., p. 247; and "Composer of Management Classics," *Milestones of Management*, Vol. II, by the Editors of *Business Week*, pp. 16–17.

of Vilfredo Pareto (whom he read in the original French edition), Kurt Lewin, Max Weber (whom he read in the original German edition), and the philosophy of Alfred North Whitehead in the first in-depth analysis of organizations as cooperative systems. By the time of his death in 1961, this Harvard "drop-out" had earned a place in history as a management scholar.

The Nature of Cooperative Systems

Barnard's best known work, *The Functions of the Executive*,[24] was an expansion of eight lectures given at the Lowell Institute in Boston in November and December of 1937. His explicit purpose for the lectures was to develop a theory of organizations and to stimulate others to examine the nature of cooperative systems administered by executives. To Barnard, the search for universals in organizations had been obstructed by too much emphasis on the nature of the state and the church and their concomitant stress on the origin and nature of authority. He complained that most research focused on social unrest and reform and included "practically no reference to formal organization as the concrete social process by which social action is largely accomplished."[25] Social failures throughout history were due to the failure to provide for human cooperation in formal organizations. Barnard said that the "formal organization is that kind of cooperation among men that is conscious, deliberate, and purposeful."[26]

By examining the formal organization, it was possible to provide for cooperation and accomplish basically three goals: (1) to insure the survival of an organization by "the maintenance of an *equilibrium* of complex character in a continuously fluctuating environment of physical, biological, and social materials, elements, and forces" within an organization; (2) to examine the external forces to which such adjustments must be made; and (3) to analyze the functions of executives at all levels in managing and controlling formal organizations.[27] Barnard's notion of including both internal equilibrium and external adjustment was an original view and brought criticism from those who adhered to the traditional view

[24] Chester I. Barnard, *The Functions of the Executive*, Cambridge, Mass.: Harvard University Press, 1938.
[25] *Ibid.*, p. 3.
[26] *Ibid.*, p. 4.
[27] *Ibid.*, p. 6. Italics added.

of intra-organizational analysis. Barnard rejected this traditional view of an organization having boundaries and comprising a definite number of members; he included in his concept of organizations investors, suppliers, customers and others whose actions contributed to the firm even though they might not be considered "members" of the firm itself.[28]

Barnard's construction of a cooperative system began with the individual as a discrete, separate being; however, he noted that humans do not function except in conjunction with other humans in an interacting social relationship. As individuals, people can *choose* whether or not they will enter into a specific cooperative system. They made this choice based on their purposes, desires, impulses of the moment, or by considering whatever alternatives were available. These were "motives," and the organization, through the executive function, modified individual actions and motives through influence and control. However, this modification might not always attain the goals sought by the organization nor by the person. The disparity between personal motives and organizational motives led Barnard to his "effective"-"efficient" dichotomy. A formal system of cooperation required an objective or purpose; and, if cooperation was successful, the goal was attained and the system was *effective*. The matter of efficiency was different; cooperative efficiency was the result of individual efficiencies since cooperation was entered into only to satisfy "individual motives." *Efficiency* was the degree to which individual motives were satisfied and only the individual could determine whether or not this condition was being met.[29]

Cooperation within formal organizations afforded possibilities for expanding the powers of the group beyond those which the individual alone could accomplish, *e.g.* moving a stone, producing an automobile, building a bridge, etc. People cooperated in order to do what they could not do alone; and, when the purpose was attained, their efforts were effective. However, individuals also had personal motives, and the degree to which they continued to contribute to formal efforts was a function of the satisfactions or dissatisfactions they personally derived. If their motives were not

---

[28] Barnard's rebuttal to his critics appeared in the *Harvard Business Review*, Spring, 1940, and is reprinted in C. I. Barnard, *Organization and Management*, Cambridge, Mass.: Harvard University Press, 1948, pp. 111–113.

[29] *The Functions of the Executive*, p. 44.

satisfied, they withheld efforts or withdrew from the system, and from their point of view the system was inefficient. In the final analysis, "the only measure of the efficiency of a cooperative system is its capacity to survive"; by this Barnard meant its ability to continue to offer enough inducements to satisfy individual motives in the pursuit of group purposes.[30] Viewed in modern terms, the formal organization must renew its energy or acquire negative entropy by offering net satisfactions to contributing members. If it was inefficient, it could not be effective and therefore would not survive. For Barnard this was a universal principle of organization theory and one which was recognized by the Hawthorne researchers and by most organizational theorists thereafter. This attempt to bridge the requirements of the formal organization with the needs of the socio-human system was a landmark in management thought which persists to this day.

Formal Organizations: Theory and Structure

Barnard defined an organization as "a system of consciously coordinated personal activities or forces" and used this to encompass all types of organizations, military, fraternal, religious, academic, business, or whatever.[31] Variations existed between organizations in terms of the physical or social environment, the number and kinds of persons involved, or in the bases upon which persons contributed to the organization. These variations, however, did not negate the universality of his definition of a *formal* organization as "a system of consciously coordinated activities or forces of two or more persons."[32] The organization consisted of human beings whose activities were coordinated and therefore became a system. The system was to be treated "as a whole because each part is related to every other part included in it in a significant way."[33] Levels of systems existed, ranging from departments or subsystems in the firm to a conglomeration of many systems forming "society" as a whole. Regardless of the level of the system being analyzed, all contained three universal elements: (1) willingness to cooperate; (2) common purpose; and (3) communication.

An organization cannot, by definition, exist without persons.

[30] *Ibid.*, pp. 55–57.
[31] *Ibid.*, p. 72.
[32] *Ibid.*, p. 73.
[33] *Ibid.*, p. 77.

In Barnard's terms, willingness to cooperate was indispensable and "means self-abnegation, the surrender of control of personal conduct, the depersonalization of personal actions."[34]   People must be willing to contribute to a system's objectives; but the intensity and timing of this willingness fluctuated, since it was based on the satisfactions or dissatisfactions experienced or anticipated by organizational members.   The organization must provide adequate inducements, both physical and social, to offset the sacrifices individuals made by foregoing alternative systems and participating in the existing one. For the individual his willingness was the joint effect of "personal desires and reluctances" to participate; for the organization, it was the joint effect of "objective inducements offered and burdens imposed."[35]   The net result was subjective and largely individual; hence the need for organizations to be efficient in Barnard's terminology.   Securing willingness involved the "economy of incentives" and this consisted of two parts: (1) offering objective incentives; and (2) changing subjective attitudes through persuasion.   Objective incentives were material ones (money), nonmaterial (prestige, power, *etc.*), and "associational" (social compatibility, participation in decision making, etc.).   Barnard evaded the question of which these devices was more effective (or more efficient), by stressing the subjectivity of individual motives.   Persuasion, or changing attitudes, was a subjective incentive method which sought by precept, example, and suggestion to condition the motives of individuals.   It was not coercion but inculcation of ideas designed to nurture cooperation.   Appeals to loyalty, *esprit de corps*, belief in organizational purpose, and other abstractions would fit into this category.

Purpose, the second universal element, was a corollary to willingness to cooperate.   Willingness could not be induced unless organizational members knew what efforts would be required of them and what satisfactions might accrue as a result of cooperating.   The executive must inculcate members with the common purpose or objective of the organization.   It was not necessarily what the purpose meant personally to the member, but what he perceived as its meaning to the organization as a whole.   Organizational motives and personal motives differed and the individual contributed not because his personal motives were the same as the organization's, but be-

[34] *Ibid.*, p. 84.
[35] *Ibid.*, pp. 85–86.

cause he felt that his personal satisfactions would come from accomplishing the purpose of the organization.

The process by which these first two universal elements became dynamic was through *communication*. All activity was based upon communication, and Barnard developed some "principles": (1) that *"channels of communication should be definitely known"*; (2) that *"objective authority requires a definite formal channel of communication to every member of an organization"*, i.e., everyone must report to or be subordinate to someone; and (3) that *"the line of communication must be as direct or short as possible"* in order to speed communications and reduce distortions caused by transmission through many channels.[36] Barnard developed other principles but these will suffice to capture the essence of the stress he placed on communications, which he well might be expected to do, considering his industrial background.

Identification of these three universal elements in the formal organization led Barnard to seek universals in the "informal organization." He defined the informal organization as "the aggregate of the personal contacts and interactions and the associated groupings of people" which were not a part of nor governed by the formal organization.[37] Without structure, and often without conscious recognition of joint purpose, informal groupings arose out of job-related contacts and in turn established certain attitudes, customs, and norms. Informal organizations often created conditions leading to formal organizations and vice versa. Barnard found three functions served by the informal organization: (1) communication; (2) maintenance of cohesiveness in the formal organization by regulating willingness to serve; and (3) maintenance of feelings of personal integrity and self respect. These functions appeared to be universal and made the informal organization an indispensable part of the formal organization. Informal activities served to make the organization more efficient and also facilitated effectiveness.

The Acceptance Theory of Authority

One of Barnard's most unusual ideas was his theory of authority. He defined authority as "the character of a communication [order] in a formal organization by virtue of which it is accepted by a con-

[36] *Ibid.*, pp. 175–177.
[37] *Ibid.*, p. 115.

tributor to or 'member' of the organization as governing the action he contributes." According to this definition, authority had two aspects: (1) the personal, subjective *acceptance* of a communication as being authoritative; and (2) the objective, formal "character in the communication by virtue of which it is accepted."[38] In Barnard's theory, the source of authority did not reside in "persons of authority" or those who gave the orders but in the acceptance or non-acceptance of the authority by the subordinate. If the subordinate disobeyed an order, he rejected the authority.

This notion was antithetical to all previous concepts of authority which had been based upon some hierarchy of rank or upon the power of organizational position. Whereas Follett would depersonalize authority and obey the law of the situation, Barnard retained the personal aspect but gave it a bottom-up interpretation. For Barnard, the individual must assent to authority and would do so if four conditions were met: (1) he could and did understand the communicated order; (2) he believed that the order was consistent with the purpose of the organization at the time of his decision; (3) he believed that the order was compatible with his personal interest as a whole; and (4) he was mentally and physically able to comply with the order.

To explain how an organization could function on such a unique concept of authority, Barnard developed a "zone of indifference" for each individual within which orders were accepted without questioning authority. The zone of indifference might be narrow or wide depending upon the degree to which the inducements outweighed the burdens and sacrifices for the individual. If a subordinate thought the order ran counter to his personal moral code, for instance, he had to weigh the advantages of staying employed against his own personal value system. Not all cases would be this clear-cut and Barnard admitted to many borderline possibilities; however, the individual must still balance the inducements versus the sacrifices to make the decision. In joining organizations, the Army for example, certain "rules of the game" are pre-established and in those matters the zone of indifference would undoubtedly widen.

The objective aspect of authority was more closely akin to traditional ideas. It rested on the presumption that orders and

[38] *Ibid.*, p. 163.

communications were authoritative and had a "potentiality of assent" when they came from superior positions. In one case, the order might be accepted because authority was imputed to the superior regardless of his personal abilities; this was formal authority or the authority of position. In another, the order might be accepted because the subordinate had respect for and confidence in the individual because of his personal ability and not because of his rank or position; Barnard called this the "authority of leadership."

When the authority of leadership was combined with the authority of position, the zone of indifference became exceedingly broad. Nevertheless, Barnard stressed that "the determination of authority remains with the individual."[39] In retrospect, much more can be imputed to Barnard's acceptance theory than actually exists. In a free society, individuals always have the choice to go along with the costs and benefits of directives with regard to compliance or not to do this. As long as labor is not conscripted, the acceptance theory is valid. What appears to be so striking in Barnard's theory is in reality another way of stating that all organizations depend upon leadership which can develop the capacity and willingness of members to cooperate.

The Functions of the Executive

In Barnard's analysis, executives operated as interconnecting centers in a communications system and sought to secure the coordination essential to cooperative effort. Communications was a central value in all of Barnard's writings and undoubtedly his views were influenced by his own industrial experience in the Bell System. To Barnard, executive work

is not *of* the organization, but the specialized work of *maintaining* the organization in operation . . . The executive functions serve to maintain a system of cooperative effort. They are impersonal. The functions are not, as so frequently stated, to manage a group of persons.[40]

The executive function to Barnard was analogous to the brain and nervous system in relation to the rest of the body:

It exists to maintain the bodily system by directing those actions which are necessary more effectively to adjust to the environment, but it can hardly

[39] *Ibid.*, pp. 173–174.
[40] *Ibid.*, pp. 215–216.

be said to manage the body, a large part of whose functions are independent of it and upon which it in turn depends.[41]

Barnard postulated three executive functions: (1) to provide a system of communication; (2) to promote the securing of essential personal efforts; and (3) to formulate and define purpose. In providing for communication, the executive must define organizational duties, clarify lines of authority and responsibility, and consider both formal and informal means of communication. Informal communications provided for organizational maintenance by allowing issues to be raised and discussed without forcing decisions and without overloading executive positions. The second executive function was to bring people into a cooperative relationship and to elicit their contributions to the organization. This was largely the task of recruiting and selecting those personnel who could best contribute and who would work together compatibly. It also included what Barnard called maintenance "methods": (1) the maintenance of morale; (2) the maintenance of a scheme of inducements; and (3) the maintenance of "schemes of deterrents" such as supervision, control, inspection, education, and training which would insure the viability of the cooperative system.

The third executive function, formulation of purpose and objectives, has already been examined in some depth. Slightly enlarging this function, Barnard included the functions of decision making and delegation. Delegation was a decision involving both the ends sought and the means to those ends. The results were decisions about the placement of various responsibilities and authority within the cooperative system so that individuals would know how they contributed to the ends sought. Decision making had two facets: (1) analysis, or the search for the "strategic factors" which would create the set or system of conditions necessary to accomplish the organization's purposes; and (2) synthesis, or the recognition of the interrelationships between elements or parts which together made up the whole system. As a capstone to the executive functions, Barnard postulated an "executive process" which was "the sensing of the organization as a whole and the total situation relevant to it."[42] This was the "art" of managing and was the *integration* of the whole with respect to internal equilibrium and adjustment to external conditions. Working from the micro level to the macro,

[41] *Ibid.*, p. 217.
[42] *Ibid.*, p. 235.

Barnard viewed all aspects of society as one large cooperative system. Every organization must secure personal and other services from its environment and "can survive only as it secures by exchange, transformation, and creation, a surplus of utilities in its own economy."[43]   The industrial organization for example, must produce both physical utilities and social utilities in order to survive:

Thus in every organization there is a quadruple economy: (1) physical energies and materials contributed by members and derived by its work upon the environment and given to its members; (2) the individual economy; (3) the social utilities related to the social environment; and (4) a complex and comprehensive economy of the organization under which both material services and social services are contributed by members and material things are secured from the environment, and material is given to the environment and social satisfactions to the members.   The only measure of this economy is the survival of the organization.   If it grows it is clearly efficient, if it is contracting, it is doubtfully efficient, and it may in the end prove to have been during the period of contraction inefficient.[44]

The moving creative force in this organization was moral leadership.   Leaders must hold some moral code, demonstrate a high capacity for responsibility, and be able to create a moral faculty in others.   Seeking a philosophical plane, Barnard concluded:

Executive responsibility, then, is that capacity of leaders by which, reflecting attitudes, ideals, hopes, derived largely from without themselves, they are compelled to bind the wills of men to the accomplishment of purposes beyond their immediate ends, beyond their times.   Even when these purposes are lowly and the time is short, the transitory efforts of men become a part of that organization of living forces that transcends man unaided by man; but when these purposes are high and the wills of many men of many generations are bound together they live boundlessly.

For the morality that underlies enduring cooperation is multidimensional. It comes from and may expand to all the world, it is rooted deeply in the past, it faces toward the endless future.   As it expands, it must become more complex, its conflicts must be more numerous and deeper, its call for abilities must be higher, its failures of ideal attainment must be perhaps more tragic; but the quality of leadership, the persistence of its influence, the durability of its related organizations, the power of the co-ordination it incites, all express the height of moral aspirations, the breadth of moral foundations.

So among those who cooperate the things that are seen are moved by the things unseen.   Out of the void comes the spirit that shapes the ends of men.[45]

---

[43] *Ibid.*, p. 245.
[44] *Ibid.*, pp. 251–252.   Copyright 1938 by the President and Fellows of Harvard College; by permission.
[45] *Ibid.*, pp. 283–284.   Copyright 1938 by the President and Fellows of Harvard College; by permission.

Chester Barnard was an erudite executive who drew upon his own experiences and upon sociological theory in order to build a theory of cooperative systems. His effective-efficient dichotomy was an attempt to synthesize the ever present conflict between organizational objectives and needs for economy of effort with the human's personal objectives and needs for satisfaction. His theory of authority, his call for moral leadership, and his identification of universal elements in both the formal and the informal organization were all significant contributions to evolving management thought.

SUMMARY

Mary Parker Follet and Chester Barnard were bridges between eras. Follett ushered in a group view of man and Gestalt psychology while living and working in the scientific management era. Barnard put forth an analysis of the formal organization yet introduced the role of the informal organization in achieving an equilibrium. Both operated more on a philosophical plane and sought to create a spirit of cooperation and collaboration. Both were concerned with the individual, not *per se*, but as he achieved his being through cooperative group efforts. Both sought to reshape previous concepts of authority, both emphasized cooperation and unity, and both concluded that it was professional, moral leadership which would enhance the effectiveness of organizations and the well-being of man.

15

People and Organizations

This and the succeeding chapter will examine two branches of developing management thought from about 1930 to the early 1950's. This chapter will focus on the growth and refinement of the human relations movement as it passed through micro and macro phases. The micro phase will reflect a significant amount of empirical research which led to substantial modifications in previously held views about man in organizations. The macro phase will be characterized by a number of individuals who were building theoretical constructs of social systems analysis which were precursory steps for the later development of organization theory. The title of this chapter, "People and Organizations," indicates the human orientation of this branch of thought, with the structural aspects of organizations assuming a secondary subject of inquiry. Chapter 16, on the other hand, will examine a parallel branch of thought in which organizations and organizational structures assume a primary importance while the human element received relatively less emphasis.

PEOPLE AT WORK: THE MICRO VIEW

Although social scientists had started to probe human behavior in industry in the first three decades of the twentieth century, it was not until the 1930's and 1940's that the greatest outpourings of behavioral research would appear. Whereas the engineer appeared to dominate the scientific management movement, the human relations movement was interdisciplinary, drawing from the contributions of sociologists, psychologists, and anthropologists. A basic premise in their research into the social facet of man was a Gestaltist notion that all organizational behavior involved some human "multiplier effect." Each individual, himself highly variable and complex due to his unique genetic composition and his family, social, and work experiences, became even more variable and complex when placed in interaction with other unique individuals. This multiplier effect meant that new means had to be devised to analyze, explain, predict, and control human behavior.

Developing Constructs for Group Analysis

Two individuals, Jacob L. Moreno and Kurt Lewin, paved the way in developing means for analyzing group behavior and their notions were frequently used in research during this era. Moreno provided a new analytical tool, *sociometry*. Moreno stated its purpose as follows:

> A process of classification, which is calculated to bring individuals together who are capable of harmonious interpersonal relationships and so create a social group which can function at the maximum efficiency and with a minimum of disruptive tendencies and processes.[1]

Moreno felt that the psychological activities of groups were not due to chance and that groups could be studied through the application of quantitative methods which probed the evolution and patterning of attitudes and interactions. For purposes of analysis, Moreno classified the basic attitudes which people showed toward one another as attraction, repulsion, and indifference.[2] In Moreno's sociometry, the members of the group to be studied were asked to indicate those with whom they would, and would not, like to associate. The resulting chart was called a *sociogram* which mapped the pairings and rankings of the individual's preferences for other individuals. These mutual preferences were to be considered dynamic, not static, and changing as members of the group changed and as problems facing the group changed. For example, in the New York Training School for Girls, where his

---

[1] J. L. Moreno, *Who Shall Survive?: A New Approach to Human Interrelations,* Washington, D.C.: Nervous and Mental Disease Publishing Co., 1934, p. 11.

[2] Cf. Karen Horney's "moving toward people," "moving against people," and "moving away from people." K. Horney, *Our Inner Conflicts,* New York: W. W. Norton and Co., 1945.

basic sociometric research was conducted, Moreno found that different pairings appeared depending upon whether the expressed choice was for a roommate or a workmate. This task-versus-friendship preference formed a foundation for important distinctions in industrial research. In industry, sociometric research has sought to combine work groups such that they would be superior in quality and quantity of work as well as conducive to higher morale for the participants.[3]

Psychodrama and sociodrama were also the contributions of J. L. Moreno and together these ideas formed a basis for "role playing" techniques and for the analysis of interpersonal relations. Psychodrama, being both a method of diagnosis and of treatment of psychopathology, consisted of placing a person or patient "on stage" to act out his deepest psychic problems with the aid of other "actors" and a therapist.[4] The focal person (a patient or trainee) was mentally taken out of his immediate environment by means of a specially contrived situation and forced to play a role in which it was almost impossible to keep his private ego and personal needs and sentiments from emerging. Scarcely aware that he was expressing his own true self, something he might be loath to do if asked to do so explicitly, he displayed overtly in the role situation whatever his psychopathology might be. Since other actors were also in the situation, he exposed his manner of dealing with others in the role play. Once exposed, therapy could begin on whatever deviations in behavior were disclosed. Further, psychodrama was a *cathartic* experience, enabling the actor to release and relieve his innermost doubts, anxieties, and other disorders.

Sociodrama, an outgrowth of psychodrama, focused on the group as the method of analysis whereas psychodrama focused on individual therapy. Sociodrama was based on the assumption that the contrived group was already organized by a set of previously held social and cultural roles. Catharsis and therapy were oriented toward understanding social and cultural roles such as supervisor-worker, negro-white, American-Oriental, *etc. Role reversal*, or taking the role of the opposite social or cultural group, for example, a white supervisor playing the role of a black worker, could be

[3] For example, see Raymond H. Van Zelst, "Sociometrically Selected Work Teams Increase Production," *Personnel*, Vol. 5 (1952) pp. 175–185. See also: J. L. Moreno (ed.) *The Sociometry Reader*, New York: Free Press, 1960.

[4] J. L. Moreno, *Psychodrama and Sociodrama*, Boston: Beacon Press, 1946, pp. 177–178.

used to broaden role flexibility and create an understanding of opposite or alien members. In brief, it was group psychotherapy designed to reduce resentments, frustrations, and misunderstandings. Moreno's work would serve to supplement the counseling and interpersonal relations aspects of the human relations movement by providing methods for studying and changing a person's or group's behavior *vis-à-vis* other persons or groups. Psychology and psychoanalysis, both essentially concerned with the isolated individual, were inadequate for analyzing group behavior, which was the subject matter most frequently encountered in studying industrial behavior.

Another important construct for analyzing group behavior was that of "group dynamics." Credit for originating this concept is generally given to Kurt Lewin (1890–1947), a Jewish psychologist who fled Hitler's Germany in the early 1930's. Lewin studied at the University of Berlin under Max Wertheimer, one of the founders of the Gestalt movement. Lewin's own notions were subsumed under the heading of "field theory," which held that group behavior was an intricate set of symbolic interactions and forces which not only affected group structure but also modified individual behavior. A group was never at a "steady state" of equilibrium but was in a continuous process of mutual adaptation which Lewin called "quasi-stationary equilibrium." An analogy might be that of a river flowing within its banks; it appears relatively stationary but there is nevertheless gradual movement and change. In developing his field theory, Lewin borrowed the term "topology" from geometry and applied it to the study of groups. Topology is a branch of geometry which deals with problems of continuity rather than size or shape; topological space is a set of objects or points with a definite relation to one another. Lewin saw behavior as a function of the person and his environment or "field" and sought to find some corollaries in psychological topology.[5] Using terms such as "life space," "space of free movement," and "field forces," *i.e.* tensions emanating from group pressures on the individual, Lewin and his associates embarked on a series of investigations into resistance to change and the effects of leadership on groups. For example, Lewin, Lippitt, and White examined the effects of "democratic," "authoritarian," and *laissez-faire*" leadership on boy's groups and demonstrated that

---

[5] For more on Lewin's uses of topology, see: R. W. Leeper, *Lewin's Topological and Vector Psychology*, Eugene: University of Oregon Press, 1943.

authoritarian leadership impaired initiative and bred hostility and aggressiveness while other styles were more effective in creating better morale and attitudes.[6] In research on changing family food habits during World War II, Lewin found that changes were more easily induced through group discussion than through individual methods. This was a new idea about the introduction of change, the idea that change would be facilitated when people thought *they* had discovered the need for change themselves rather than through being told to change.[7]

The emergence of group dynamics and the work of Kurt Lewin formed a significant milestone in evolving management thought. In 1945, Lewin founded the Research Center for Group Dynamics at the Massachusetts Institute of Technology; after his death, the Center was moved to the University of Michigan in 1948. Besides fathering group dynamics, Lewin opened up and added to the study of subordinate participation in decision making and the use of the group to achieve changes in behavior. One of Lewin's disciples, Dr. Leland P. Bradford, established at Bethel, Maine (1947) the first "sensitivity training" or human relations laboratory, called the National Training Laboratory. The essence of this sensitivity training was to achieve changes in behavior through "gut level" interactions which led to increased interpersonal awareness.

Briefly, Moreno and Lewin brought a new focus to the group rather than the individual. Their work, reflecting Gestalt psychology, led to further studies of social change, social control, collective behavior, and in general the effects of the group on the individual. Research moved from the static state of the individual in isolation to the dynamic state of the individual in interaction with others.

The Growth of Human Relations Research and Training

The 1930's had witnessed the emergence of a more favorable political climate for organized labor in which explicit recognition

[6] K. Lewin, R. Lippitt, and R. K. White, "Patterns of Aggressive Behavior in Experimentally Created 'Social Climates,'" *Journal of Social Psychology,* Vol. 10 (1939) pp. 271–299. For some application of group dynamics to industrial leadership situations, see: K. Lewin, *Resolving Social Conflicts,* New York: Harper and Row, 1948, pp. 125–141.

[7] For a summary of the applications of group dynamics work, see Dorwin Cartwright, "Achieving Change in People: Some Applications of Group Dynamics Theory," *Human Relations,* Vol. 4 (1951) pp. 381–392.

of the role of the worker in industry was required. The passage of the National Labor Relations Act in 1935 (the Wagner Act) and the formation of the C.I.O. brought a new emphasis to collective bargaining. Morris Cooke found a better environment for his *rapprochement* between labor and management which would insure industrial peace and productivity through collective bargaining.[8] The theme became that of "industrial democracy," which was to mean in essence the application of human relations in the industrial setting in conjunction with organized labor.[9] Accordingly, a number of centers began to appear which would pave the way for the new "industrial human relations." In 1943, an interdisciplinary group at the University of Chicago formed the Committee on Human Relations in Industry. Drawing its members from business (Burleigh Gardner), sociology (William Foote Whyte), and anthropology (W. Lloyd Warner), this committee was to characterize the new style of interdisciplinary behavioral research.

Industrial relations centers also came into vogue. The first was the New York State School of Industrial and Labor Relations at Cornell (1945); others were to follow, such as the Yale Labor-Management Center and the Institute of Labor and Industrial Relations at the University of Illinois. In 1946, Rensis Likert, himself a psychologist and statistician, founded the Institute for Social Research at the University of Michigan.[10] In 1947, a group of academicians, labor leaders, and others interested in advancing the state of knowledge in personnel and industrial relations, formed the Industrial Relations Research Association. It was in these centers and associations that a growing body of research literature on industrial behavior began.

Human relations training came into vogue during this period and was oriented toward overcoming communications barriers and enhancing interpersonal skills. The pathway to opening hidden talents in leaders resided in group-oriented techniques such as role playing, non-directive counseling, group discussion methods,

[8] Morris L. Cooke and Philip Murray, *Organized Labor and Production,* New York: Harper and Row, 1940.

[9] Clinton S. Golden and Harold J. Ruttenberg, *The Dynamics of Industrial Democracy,* New York: Harper and Row, 1942.

[10] After the death of Kurt Lewin, The Institute for Social Research formed two divisions, the Survey Research Center and the Research Center for Group Dynamics.

and eventually the evolution of sensitivity training. Carl Rogers, a clinical psychologist at the University of Chicago, refined the non-directive counseling techniques of the Harvard group.[11] Michigan's Professor Norman Maier was one of the foremost advocates of "group-in-action" training techniques. For Maier, "group decision" was:

> A way of controlling through leadership rather than force.
> A way of group discipline through social pressure . . .
> Permitting the group to jell on the idea it thinks will best solve a problem . . .
> Pooled thinking.
> Cooperative problem solving.
> A way of giving each person a chance to participate in things that concern him in his work situation.
> A method that requires skill and a respect for other people.[12]

In role playing and cases, technically oriented supervisors were asked to take on new role dimensions, to consult the group, and to discuss various decision alternatives in order to develop human relations skills. Case problems for training in human relations skills were growing in use in industrial and business school education. Many of these cases were adaptable to role-playing situations or otherwise lent themselves to sharpening the students' perceptiveness into human behavior or in developing interpersonal ability. Harvard, as might be expected because of the influence of Mayo and Roethlisberger, pioneered with its "Administrative Practices" course under the leadership of Edmund P. Learned.[13] Training to secure teamwork and to develop sensitive leaders led to a plethora of texts as managerial and employee education reached a new high in management history. The war had placed great emphasis on the need for trained managers; teamwork and group leadership notions were in vogue and academic institutions sought to fill an industrial void which called for both productive and satisfied workers.[14] Founded upon the Mayoist's call for socially skilled supervisors, enhanced by the ideas and techniques of Moreno and

---

[11] Carl P. Rogers, *Counseling and Psychotherapy,* Boston: Houghton Mifflin Co., 1942.

[12] Norman R. F. Maier, *Principles of Human Relations,* New York: John Wiley and Sons, 1952.

[13] The enduring casebook growing out of this course was John D. Glover and Ralph M. Hower, *The Administrator,* Homewood, Ill.: Richard D. Irwin, 1949, and revised in 1952, 1957, and 1963.

[14] See, for example: Earl G. Planty, William S. McCord, and Carlos Efferson, *Training Employees and Managers for Production and Teamwork,* New York: Ronald Press Co., 1948.

Lewin, and carried out in research centers and associations, human relations training reached its apogee in the 1940's and early 1950's.

CHANGING ASSUMPTIONS ABOUT MAN AT WORK

The Hawthorne experiments instigated a new thesis in evolving management thought. The Mayoists tilted with prior views about the nature of man's motivation, the role of the supervisor in eliciting human collaboration, and the importance of sentiments and informal activities at work. Investigations in the post-Hawthorne era furthered these challenges to previous ideas about the role of the manager. As an overview, these changing assumptions about man at work may be categorized as follows: (1) new ideas about motivation; (2) changing notions about the benefits to be derived from the division of labor; and (3) obtaining greater employee commitment to organizational goals through participation in decision making.

Men and Motivation

Abraham H. Maslow opened up the possibility of a multi-dimensional approach to motivation by proposing a theoretical hierarchy of man's needs. In 1943, Maslow identified at least five sets of these needs: "physiological," "safety," "love," "esteem," and "self-actualization" needs.[15] These basic needs were related to one another and were arranged in a hierarchy of "prepotency" (*i.e.* urgency of the drive). The most basic drives were physiological and, when these needs were satisfied, prepotency diminished and the next higher need emerged to dominate behavior. Once a need was gratified, it no longer motivated behavior. In Maslow's theory, a person moved up the "ladder" of needs as each level was satisfied and he could move in a reverse direction if a lower-order need was threatened or removed. Since man was a perpetually wanting animal, all needs were really never fully gratified. The top rung of the hierarchy was self-actualization or "what a man *can* be, he *must* be."[16] This was self-fulfillment or man's attainment of what he had the potential of becoming.

---

[15] A. H. Maslow, "A Theory of Human Motivation," *Psychological Review*, Vol. 50 (1943), pp. 370–396. Maslow later expanded and refined these early notions in *Motivation and Personality*, New York: Harper & Row, 1954.

[16] "A Theory of Human Motivation," p. 380.

The essence of Maslow's contribution was in the evolutionary, dynamic qualities of the nature of man's needs. In a subsistence level economy, physiological needs would appear to predominate. As the economy moved beyond that stage, other needs would become more important. The human relationists made the assumption that the American economy had in fact moved to a higher level of need priority. Fritz Roethlisberger stated the case for this position:

> People at work are not so different from people in other aspects of life. They are not entirely creatures of logic. They have feelings. They like to feel important and to have their work recognized as important. Although they are interested in the size of their pay envelopes, this is not a matter of their first concern. Sometimes they are more interested in having their pay reflect accurately the relative social importance to them of the different jobs they do. Sometimes even still more important to them than maintenance of socially accepted wage differentials is the way their superiors treat them . . . In short, employees, like most people, want to be treated as belonging to and being an integral part of some group.[17]

Accordingly, the new focus of motivational efforts was to be on the social aspects of the workplace and on the group. Adhering to the Mayo thesis that industry must promote collaboration and social solidarity, individual incentive plans began to receive less prominence while group plans achieved more.

One such plan was the Scanlon plan, named after Joseph N. Scanlon, a steelworker, later union official, and eventually a professor at the Massachusetts Institute of Technology.[18] Scanlon's bailiwick was the La Pointe Steel Company, a marginal producer which was on the brink of bankruptcy in 1938. Scanlon, in consultation with steelworker officials, worked out a union-management productivity plan which provided that the workers would get a bonus for tangible savings in labor costs. The plan succeeded in saving La Pointe from bankruptcy and spread to other firms. The heart of the Scanlon plan was in a suggestion plan and production committees that sought methods and means to reduce labor costs. There were no individual awards for suggestions, and the first principle of the whole plan was group oriented. Cooperation and collabora-

---

[17] F. J. Roethlisberger, from a speech entitled "The Human Equation in Employee Productivity," presented to the Personnel Group of the National Retail Dry Goods Association, 1950. Cited by Malcolm P. McNair, "Thinking Ahead: What Price Human Relations?", *Harvard Business Review*, Vol. 35, No. 2 (March–April, 1957), p. 17.

[18] Frederick G. Lesieur (ed.), *The Scanlon Plan: A Frontier in Labor-Management Cooperation*, published jointly by M.I.T. and John Wiley & Sons, 1958.

tion were stressed over competition and everyone benefitted from the suggestions of any one individual. Rewards were plant- or company-wide, encouraging union-management cooperation to reduce costs and share benefits. The traditional suggestion system rewarded the individual, but under Scanlon's notion, the group was rewarded.

The Scanlon plan had great appeal to labor because it could save jobs in failing firms such as La Pointe and because it explicitly required union participation in the production committees which sought to solve pressing problems. According to Scanlon, such participation was not to create a "feeling" of belonging or a "sense" of participation, but management's explicit recognition of a definite role for the worker and union representatives in suggesting improvements. It was not profit sharing because it did not establish any fixed percentage of profits, nor was it based on profits which were made available to employees. The Scanlon plan was and is unique in these many respects: (1) a group reward for suggestions; (2) joint committees for discussion and proposing labor-saving techniques; and (3) the worker's sharing in reduced costs, not increased profits *per se*.

While the Scanlon plan typified the industrial human relations approach to motivation, economic man did not pass entirely from the industrial scene. James F. Lincoln pleaded for and gave experience-based confirmation of appeals to the individual in his *Incentive Management*.[19] Lincoln thought that people were giving up freedom for security, that they were relying on someone else (the government) to assume the responsibility for this security, and that pride in work, self-reliance and other time-tested virtues were declining. The proper answer to this decline, in Lincoln's view, was to return to the "intelligent selfishness" of individual ambition. Man was not primarily motivated by money, nor by security, but by recognition for his skill. Lincoln's plan sought to develop each man to his highest ability and then to reward him with a "bonus" for his contribution to the success of the company. Over a period of sixteen years (1935–1950), including the Depression, the "average total bonus for each factory worker in that time has exceeded $40,000."[20] This bonus was over and above the

---

[19] James F. Lincoln, *Incentive Management: A New Approach to Human Relationships in Industry and Business,* Cleveland, Ohio: Lincoln Electric Co., 1951.
   [20] *Ibid.,* p. 111.

worker's other wages which were comparable to wage levels in the Cleveland area. At Lincoln Electric there was no history of work stoppages, labor turnover was almost non-existent, individual productivity was five times as great as that for all manufacturing, dividends per share were constantly rising, product prices were steadily declining, and worker bonuses continued high.[21] The individual incentive plan at Lincoln Electric is still in effect today and is as successful as ever.[22] Individual incentives à la Lincoln Electric were a minority case, however, and motivational research and advice during this era emphasized factors other than economic ones and stressed the group as the focal point for managerial stimulation.

Job Enlargement

A second facet of changing assumptions about man at work was a growing revolt against the division of labor. Walker and Guest found that the assembly line worker rebelled against the anonymity of his work even though he declared himself satisfied with his rate of pay and his job security.[23] Having met these more basic needs, the workers sought to avoid the mechanical pacing of the conveyor belt, the repetitiveness of work, and the deskilling of their jobs. Feeling that they were mere cogs in the machine, discouraged about their inability to influence the quality of their work, and unable to fully engage in social interaction due to mechanical pacing of the line, workers were dissatisfied with industrial life. As a result of these pioneering efforts, job enlargement and job rotation assumed a new focus in studies of industrial behavior. Job enlargement served to relieve monotony, to enhance skill levels, and to increase the workers' feeling of commitment to the total product. In essence, this enrichment of job *content* was deemed a better motivating device than wages or security.[24] The

[21] *Ibid.*, Appendix, pp. 251–289.

[22] In 1968, for example, a total of $15,130,000 was distributed to 1,889 employees (an average of slightly over $8,000 per worker) in addition to regular pay, normal fringe benefits, and overtime. Correspondence with the Company, May 16, 1969. In 1969, $16,544,000 was distributed to 1,973 employees (slightly over $8,000 per worker). Correspondence with the Company, December 5, 1969.

[23] Charles R. Walker and Robert H. Guest, "The Man on the Assembly Line," *Harvard Business Review*, Vol. 30, No. 3, (May–June, 1952), pp. 71–83.

[24] *Ibid.*, p. 77. Cf. Whiting Williams, *Mainsprings of Men*, pp. 58–60, who noted in 1925 that the "nature" of the job was more important than wages. Henri DeMan also noted the worker's search for "joy in work" through the nature of the task itself.

economic benefits of the division of labor as espoused by Adam Smith and Charles Babbage began to become suspect as the human relationists sought means to overcome industrial anomie through job enlargement.

Participation in Management

A third area of changing assumptions may be broadly viewed as a "power-equalization" thesis. This was an exhortation to play down the importance of the organizational hierarchy and to give a greater voice to subordinates through participation. Operating on the premise that worker participation would yield a greater commitment to organizational goals and would also further individual and group satisfactions, researchers sought to design work arrangements which would permit the involvement of subordinates in decision making. James C. Worthy, drawing upon his experiences in the Sears, Roebuck organization, argued for "flatter," less complex organizational structures, which maximized administrative decentralization and thereby led to improved subordinate attitudes, encouraged individual responsibility and initiative, and provided outlets for individual self-expression and creativity.[25]

William B. Given, Jr. and Charles P. McCormick were two industrialists who sought to apply the human relations philosophy to their organizations.[26] Using the catch-phrase "bottom up management," Given sought to develop and apply a philosophy of participation which essayed "to release the thinking and encourage the initiative of all those down from the bottom up . . ."[27] The notion involved widespread delegation of responsibility and authority, considerable managerial freedom in decision making, a free interchange of ideas at all levels, and the corollary acceptance of the fact that managers grow by having the freedom to fail. Recognizing that a "push from the top" was occasionally needed, Given tried to confine "top down" management to setting policy, clarifying goals, and providing training programs for subordinates who needed them.

[25] James C. Worthy, "Organizational Structure and Employee Morale," *American Sociological Review*, Vol. 15 (April, 1950), pp. 169–179. A similar thesis by Worthy appeared in "Factors Influencing Employee Morale," *Harvard Business Review*, Vol. 28, No. 1 (January–February, 1950).

[26] Given was president of the American Brakeshoe Company and McCormick, president of McCormick and Company, producers and distributors of spices.

[27] W. B. Given, Jr., *Bottom Up Management,* New York: Harper and Row, 1949, pp. 3–4.

McCormick's plan of participation became a model for developing junior executive boards in three score or more companies by 1938.[28] The McCormick Multiple Management Plan used participation as a training and motivational method in the early Depression years with the selection of seventeen promising younger men from various departments to form a junior board of directors. The board was given free access to financial and other company records, encouraged to elect its own officers and told that "every recommendation they made for the advancement of the business would have the serious consideration of the company."[29]   The junior board met with the senior board once a month and at that time submitted its suggestions which were generally accepted and acted upon to a greater extent than McCormick himself had expected. In fact, McCormick attributed company success during the lean depression years to the efforts of the junior board.   One example involved the redesign of the traditional bottle for extracts which McCormick expected his older executives to wish to retain.   The junior board conducted a market investigation, took housewives' ideas into account, and came up with a new design which had immediate acceptance by the senior board and in the marketplace.

The junior board evidenced other successes such as seeking out other capable young men and "sponsoring" them as protégés for further development.   This early identification of management talent led to better appraisal methods, and the junior board members graduated to the senior board at an average rate of one man per year.   Success with the junior board led to the creation of two others, the sales and factory boards, which operated essentially as the junior board for the sales and production departments.   In brief, the entire system of boards involved a number of advantages: (1) it opened communication channels for the "Young Turks"; (2) it involved them in decision making; (3) it provided a means for identifying and developing executives; (4) it relieved senior board members of a great deal of detailed planning and research; and, last but not least, provided for interlocking arrangements between various departments to coordinate and follow-through on company activities.   The McCormick plan as participation in action has real-

[28] Charles P. McCormick, *Multiple Management*, New York: Harper and Row, 1938, p. viii.   McCormick's sequel, *The Power of People*, New York: Harper and Row, 1949, indicated further success and international acceptance in nearly four hundred companies.   The plan is still in use and is successful; see "Miniboards Give Spice Maker Zest," *Business Week*, May 10, 1969, pp. 174–176.

[29] *Multiple Management*, p. 5.

ized the ideals of Follett's integration and Barnard's effectiveness and efficiency.

Participation in decision making received greater and greater acclaim over this period of analysis. Participation was viewed as democracy in action, opening communication channels, diffusing authority, and motivating people to give a greater commitment of themselves to organizational goals.[30] Participative management was a challenge to hierarchical, unilateral authority and sought to bring group forces into play.

Another aspect of the psychology of participation came with early efforts to apply Lewinian concepts in overcoming resistance to change. The Harwood Manufacturing Company inspired some early research on using participation to overcome resistance to change.[31] Hypothesizing that resistance to changes in work standards and methods were the result of a combination of individual reactions to frustration and group-induced pressures, Coch and French manipulated three schemes for introducing change: no participation, participation through representatives chosen by the workers, and total participation. Total participation in change resulted in faster attainment of the new production rate, lower turnover, and reduced worker aggression. Interpreting these results, the researchers concluded that management must effectively communicate the need for change and must stimulate group participation in planning change. By involving the worker in change, resistance was lowered, new social structures could emerge, and the costs of change in terms of turnover and relearning skills could be minimized.

Coch and French's research in achieving organizational change was based on the theoretical work of Kurt Lewin. They used the notion of quasi-stationary equilibrium in their analysis, and with other researchers turned to group dynamics theory in order to solve human relations problems. The *group* became the focal point for achieving change, and discussion of change and group reinforcement of attitudes was deemed much more effective than appealing to individual instincts. In brief, post-Hawthorne work was challenging prior assumptions by postulating: (1) that man

---

[30] See Gordon W. Allport, "The Psychology of Participation," *The Psychology Review*, Vol. 53, No. 3 (May, 1945), pp. 119–127.

[31] Lester Coch and John R. P. French, Jr., "Overcoming Resistance to Change," *Human Relations*, Vol. 1 (1948), pp. 512–532.

was primarily motivated by social and group needs; (2) that over-division of labor furthered anomie and could be allayed by job enlargement; and (3) that a greater commitment to organizational goals could be obtained and satisfactions enhanced by participation in decision making.

New Dimensions of Leadership

Early management thought held that the success or failure of the enterprise was due to the traits or characteristics of the manager-entrepreneur-leader. One either had the knack or he failed. Taylor identified the necessary qualities of foremen and, finding these qualities poorly distributed in the population, developed his functional foreman concept. Fayol wrote of the need for managerial knowledge, for technical skills, and for the proper moral, mental, and physical qualities of managers. He was much more optimistic than his predecessors that managerial skills could be taught. The Mayoists felt that the past had placed too much stress on the technical skills of the manager and that training should focus on the development of inter-personal skills. Chester Barnard wrote of leadership from a viewpoint of inducing others to follow and accept authority. Kurt Lewin and his associates appear to have been the first to view leadership as ranging along a continuum of possible "styles" from "*laissez-faire*" to "*democratic*" to "*authoritarian*." T. W. Adorno and his associates made a significant impact on leadership literature in 1950 with *The Authoritarian Personality*.[32] This behemoth volume, influenced by the anti-Semitism of Fascism, tried to relate personality structure with leadership, followership, morals, prejudices and politics. The F scale ("Fascist Scale"), developed as a part of the book, became an instrument for analyzing leadership styles as well as follower's preferences for leaders.

Empirical research, however, was beginning to challenge these personal "trait" and unidimensional views of leadership. As early as 1945, the Institute for Social Research at the University of Michigan under the direction of Rensis Likert began a series of empirical studies in a variety of organizations in order to determine what kinds of organizational structures and what principles and methods

---

[32] T. W. Adorno, Else Frenkel-Brunswick, D. J. Levinson, and R. M. Sanford, *The Authoritarian Personality*, New York: Harper and Row, 1950.

of leadership resulted in the highest productivity, the least absenteeism, the lowest turnover, and the greatest job satisfaction. Over a period of years, this research led to the identification of two different leadership "orientations": (1) an *employee orientation* in which the supervisor stressed interpersonal relationships on the job; and (2) a *production orientation* in which the supervisor focused on getting out production and was more concerned with the technical aspects of the job.[33] The Michigan studies found that an "employee orientation," coupled with relatively "general" rather than "close" supervision, led to superior productivity, greater group cohesiveness, higher morale, less worker anxiety, and lower worker turnover.[34] The supervisor obtained higher productivity by building a team spirit, by showing concern for the worker, and by shifting from a close, production-oriented style to a looser, employee-centered, supportive style.

Chronologically parallel to the Michigan studies, the Ohio State University Bureau of Business Research began a series of investigations which would lead to the development of a "situational" approach to leadership. Professors Ralph M. Stogdill and Carroll L. Shartle formed the core of the research efforts but were aided by numerous others in analyzing leaders and their interaction with the group. Relying heavily on sociometric techniques, the researchers explored members' perceptions of the organization, status, measures of group performance, characteristics of groups, and effective leader behavior in various group situations.[35] The Ohio State findings put forth a two-dimensional view of leadership: (1) an "initiating structure" dimension in which the leader acted

[33] The bulk of this research and the findings may be found in Rensis Likert, *New Patterns of Management,* New York: McGraw-Hill Book Co., 1961.

[34] In addition to Likert's work, see: Nancy Morse, *Satisfactions in the White-Collar Job,* Ann Arbor, Mich.: Institute for Social Research, 1953; Robert Kahn and Daniel Katz, "Leadership Practices in Relation to Productivity and Morale," reprinted in Dorwin Cartwright and Alvin Zander, *Group Dynamics: Research & Theory,* Evanston, Ill.: Row, Peterson & Company, 1960, pp. 554–571; and S. F. Seashore, *Group Cohesiveness in the Industrial Work Group,* Ann Arbor: Survey Research Center, University of Michigan, 1954.

[35] The extent of this research is quite large; for only a sample, see: Ralph M. Stogdill and Carroll L. Shartle, *Methods in the Study of Administrative Leadership,* Columbus: Ohio State University, Bureau of Business Research Monograph No. 80, 1955; R. M. Stogdill *Leadership and Structures of Personal Interaction,* Monograph No. 84, 1956; J. K. Hemphill, *Situational Factors in Leadership,* Ohio State University, Bureau of Educational Research Monograph No. 32, 1950; Ellis L. Scott, *Leadership and Perception of Organization,* Monograph No. 82, 1956; and Donald T. Campbell, *Leadership and Its Effects Upon the Group,* Monograph No. 83, 1956.

to further the work objectives of the group; and (2) a "considera-tion" dimension in which the emphasis was on the needs of the followers and upon interpersonal relationships.

The analogies between the Ohio State and the Michigan studies of leadership are substantial: (1) both held a new view which was antithetical to a trait or a single-continuum approach; and (2) both identified two dimensions of leader behavior. One dimension was a production-oriented, initiating structure (task-oriented) axis; and another was an employee-oriented, consideration (interpersonal-relations-oriented) axis. The two dimensions did not appear to be mutually exclusive; that is, a leader could combine a high initi-ating structure with high consideration. The advances in under-standing leadership were in viewing every leadership situation as one of interaction between the leader and the group. Instead of a single style which led to the best results, there were more dimen-sions in every situation. Eventually this two-dimensional model of leader behavior would lead to a "grid" of possibilities, but more of that later.

In brief, the micro facet of people and organizations may be characterized as the generation and extension of significant research into industrial behavior. The emphasis was on man in the group, on social motivation, on redesigning organizational tasks to yield greater worker satisfaction, on participation in decision making, and on developing new dimensions of leadership.

PEOPLE AT WORK: THE MACRO VIEW

On the macro side, research was building into some essential notions of human behavior from a larger viewpoint. There were a number of attempts to conceptualize and theorize about what was being discovered about man at work and the results were pre-cursory steps to the later development of organization theory.

The Search for Fusion

One of the earliest and most perceptive studies of the inter-action of the social system with the technical-work system was a study of restaurants by William Foote Whyte.[36] A key concept in

---

[36] W. F. Whyte, *Human Relations in the Restaurant Industry*, New York: McGraw-Hill Book Co., 1948.

his analysis was that of *status*, or the relative prestige of a job in a person's eyes or in the regard of others.   The restaurant was characterized by many levels of job status, ranging from low-status bus-boys and dishwashers to relatively high-status cooks.   Whyte found that the flow of work of taking customer orders, of food preparation, and of serving the food posed a number of human relations problems.   Cooks, typically male, held a higher set of culturally derived status distinctions; on the other hand, waitresses, considered lower status, were typically in the position of *initiating* work for the cooks by placing customers' orders to be filled.   Since those who initiated work for others were traditionally held to be in a higher status (*e.g.,* supervisors initiate work for subordinates), it was inevitable that conflicts would occur when a lower status person initiated work for a higher status one. The conflict was mediated by placing orders on "spindles" and the use of higher counters such that the initiation of work was depersonalized.   In this way the cook could remove and prepare the order under the pretext that it had not come from a lower-status person but from the spindle.[37]

Whyte developed other nuances of status on the job, such as differentiations among cooks who prepared different types of dishes, but his main argument focused on the use of social science knowledge to improve performance as well as human relations by (1) understanding the nature and functioning of the social system, and (2) developing teamwork through incentives which fostered collaboration rather than conflict.   In brief, Whyte's work was a contribution to the analysis of the interaction of the work system with the social system in an effort to reduce interpersonal frictions which arose when these two systems met.

Another significant step in developing a macro view was an empirical investigation of a New England telephone company by E. Wight Bakke of Yale University.[38]   Bakke sought to determine how the company and the union were bound together in an intricate social system.   He found five major elements or "bonds of organization": (1) the functional specifications or the organization's

---

[37] *Ibid.,* p. 69–76. See also Elias H. Porter, "The Parable of the Spindle," *Harvard Business Review,* Vol. 40, No. 3 (May–June, 1962), pp. 58–66. The "Spindle" was an ideal application of M. P. Follett's ideas; it depersonalized authority and required all to obey the "law of the situation."

[38] E. Wight Bakke, *Bonds of Organization: An Appraisal of Corporate Human Relations,* New York: Harper & Row, 1950.

definitions of jobs and departmental relations; (2) the status-system bond, which placed people in a vertical hierarchy of authority and deference with respect to direction; (3) a communication system, which accomplished the transmission of essential information; (4) the reward and penalty system, which provided incentives and controls in order to achieve organizational objectives; and (5) the organization charter bond, which included all those elements that contributed to giving the organization a "character" or a quality of entity. Through analysis of these bonds, Bakke sought to provide an understanding of the interaction between the formal system of relationships and the informal one. Bakke concluded that all five bonds could be analyzed to demonstrate that the formal and informal systems interacted to influence human behavior and that any initiation of change would affect both sides of the equation.

In later work, Bakke sought to classify the process by which the two systems, formal and informal, could be brought into conjunction. The elements of this "fusion process" were: (1) the "socializing process" by which the organization determined the person's "position" in the organization and the "function" he performed; and (2) the "personalizing process" which was the individual's determination of the "standing" he wanted to obtain in the organization and the "conduct" he expected of himself. Fusion occurred when formal position and informal standing interacted to define the members' status and when formal function and informal conduct interacted to determine the member's role.[39]

Bakke was not giving answers to specific human relations problems but proposing a conceptual diagnostic tool for organizational analysis. In perspective, it was a building block for the later analysis of socio-technical systems. The Tavistock Institute (London) was also responsible for a number of studies concerning the factory both as a social system and as a part of the broader social community. One extensive case study of the Glacier Metal Company was based on Lewin's field theory and sought to examine industrial changes as they moved through work groups into the larger community.[40]

---

[39] E. W. Bakke, *The Fusion Process*, New Haven, Conn.: Labor and Management Center, Yale University, 1953; and E. W. Bakke, *Organization and the Individual*, New Haven, Conn.: Labor and Management Center, Yale University, 1952, pp. 14–18.

[40] Elliott Jacques, *The Changing Culture of a Factory*, London: Tavistock Publications, 1951.

Such longitudinal research into the on-going firm was rare, and the results indicated the general theme of studying organizations as interacting socio-technical systems. While the Tavistock studies largely reaffirmed the theories of Barnard, they did provide empirical data for studying and coping with social adaptation to technological and organizational changes.

Technological change disrupts the social system, a factor that should be considered in any initiation of change by management. A classic instance was the introduction of new technology in the British coal industry following World War II.[41] The new technology required a break-up of small work groups which had high cohesiveness and the substitution of specialized, larger groups working in shifts. The logic of efficiency, *i.e.*, the economic benefits of the new long wall method, resulted in severe emotional disturbances for the workers, low productivity, and an increasing sense of anomie. The object lesson in this case was that the imperatives of efficiency disrupted the social organization to such an extent that all of the hoped-for advantages of the new system could not come about. Technological changes cannot be effective unless there are corresponding provisions to redesign the system of social relationships.

New Tools for Macro Analysis

Herbert A. Simon (of Carnegie-Mellon) opened a new dimension in organizational analysis with his *Administrative Behavior*, which became an introduction to a later pioneering contribution in organization theory.[42] Simon was primarily concerned with decision making from the standpoint of the logic and psychology of human choice. He postulated that insights into the structure and function of an organization could best be gained by analyzing the manner in which the decisions and behavior of employees were influenced within and by the organization. All administrative activity was group activity; an organization took from the individual some of his decision-making autonomy and substituted for it an organizational decision-making process. To Simon, this was necessary since it was impossible for any single isolated individual to

---

[41] E. L. Trist and K. W. Bamforth, "Some Social and Technical Consequences of the Longwall Method of Coal-Getting," *Human Relations*, Vol. 4 (1951), pp. 6–38.

[42] Herbert A. Simon, *Administrative Behavior*, New York: MacMillan Co., 1945. Revised in 1947 and 1957.

reach any high degree of objective rationality. Decision making then became the result of the participation of many groups in the organization, rather than decisions residing in the scalar chain, and the effect was a "composite" decision.[43] This latter notion appears to be closely related to Mary Parker Follett's interweaving of individual and group decisions into a "cumulative" responsibility. Throughout his work, Simon reflected primarily the influence of Chester Barnard, especially on authority, inducements, and communications, and the ideas of Miss Follett to a lesser degree. Simon's contribution came through his central theme that to study organization one must study the complex network of decisional processes, which were all directed toward influencing human behavior. By studying the distribution and allocation of decision making functions, one could comprehend the influences on human behavior, the human choices with respect to organizational inducements, and the establishment of an effective and meaningful equilibrium between the freedoms afforded the individual to make the decision on the job and the necessity for the organization to impose restrictions on the individual's freedom. Professor Simon's *Administrative Behavior* was an insightful link between Chester Barnard and later refinements in organization theory.

L. J. Henderson's work on Pareto formed the foundation for another step forward in the analysis of social systems by Harvard's George C. Homans. Homans attended Henderson's seminar on Pareto and co-authored a scholarly work on Pareto which formed the basis for the development of his own view of socio-technical systems in *The Human Group*.[44] Homans divided the total social system of a group into an "internal system" and an "external system" (Figure 15-1). The external system was composed of forces or environmental factors, such as policies, job definitions, work flow, etc., outside the group. The internal system consisted of elements within the social life of the group which could influence the external system. Conversely, the external system impinged on the internal system resulting in an interaction between the formal and informal organizations. Further, Homans categorized various

[43] *Ibid.*, p. 221. Professor Simon says that the term was suggested to him by Chester Barnard. In retrospect, the notion sounds more like Follett than Barnard.

[44] The results of Henderson's seminar may be found in George C. Homans and Charles P. Curtis, Jr., *An Introduction to Pareto: His Sociology*, New York: Alfred A. Knopf, 1934; the more modern work in George C. Homans, *The Human Group*, New York: Harcourt, Brace Jovanovich, 1950.

SOCIAL SYSTEM

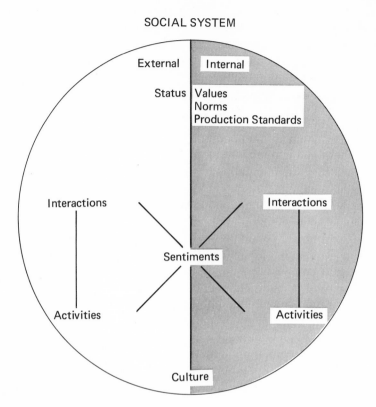

Fig. 15–1. Homan's conceptual framework. (Adapted from Joseph A. Litterer [ed.], *Organizations: Structure and Behavior*, New York: John Wiley and Sons, 1963, p. 144. Copyright © 1963, John Wiley and Sons, Inc.; by permission.)

dimensions of group behavior which interacted and could be found in both the internal and the external system: (1) *activities*, or what was formally required of members or behavior which informally emerged; (2) *interactions*, or any transaction between any two or more group members which could be either organizationally prescribed or informally originated; and (3) *sentiments*, an intangible, elusive concept which had to be inferred from observing behavior.[45]

Using the Hawthorne Bank Wiring Room experiment for one example, Homans demonstrated how these three dimensions

[45] Homans, *The Human Group*, pp. 34–40.

interacted in the two systems. Formal activities were the expectations and the work system devised by management for the Wiring Room; informal activities were restriction of output, "horseplay," games, and other non-sanctioned activities. Formal interactions were specified by job assignments and work flow among wiremen, soldermen, and inspectors; informal interactions and communications led to the formation of cliques A and B. Sentiments of management were essentially that the workers would act in their self-interest to earn wages; on the other hand, informal sentiments in the internal system tended more toward friendship and group acceptance. Homans proceeded to pair dimensions, such as the influence of interactions on sentiments, etc., to show the reciprocal influence of the external and the internal systems. While the Homans' model was exceedingly broad and some of its dimensions elusive, it provided a building block for further developments in organization theory.

Talcott Parsons, the well-known Harvard economist-sociologist, also played his role in this emerging field of social systems analysis. Parsons received his doctorate from Heidelberg, wrote his dissertation on Max Weber, and introduced Chester Barnard to Weber's bureaucracy. In an early work, Parsons drew together the ideas of Weber, Pareto, Alfred Marshall, and Durkheim and developed a "voluntaristic theory of social action."[46] His ideas influenced Barnard's search for a theory of "cooperative systems" and Parsons has provided further work in social systems analysis.[47] In brief, a number of individuals were paving the way for organization theory and a view of the organization as a socio-technical system.

SUMMARY

While Mayo and Roethlisberger had opened the door to human relations research in industry, it was the task of others to bring these notions to fruition. The "people and organizations" facet of evolving management thought was presented in two phases: (1) the micro level of inquiry into sociometry, group dynamics, participation in decision making, leadership, and the motivational appeals to group man; and (2) the macro search for analytical tools and

---

[46] Talcott Parsons, *The Structure of Social Action*, New York: McGraw-Hill Book Company, 1937.
[47] Talcott Parsons, *The Social System*, New York: Free Press, 1951.

conceptual models to explain the interactions of the formal and informal aspects of organizations.

The human relationists and their behavioral descendants were to bring about a substantial number of amendments to previously held concepts of management. Among them were: (1) an increasing emphasis on the social, group-belonging needs of man; (2) the desire to enlarge and enrich jobs to dispel the discouraging side-effects of over-specialization of labor; (3) a marked decline in the emphasis on the hierarchy of authority and a call for "bottom up," participative management; (4) an increasing recognition of the informal side of the organization and the role of worker sentiments and informal activities; and finally, the development of means to study the interaction of the formal and the informal organizations.

The group was the process, social man the product. Management was exhorted to turn its attention to the social side of man, to get people involved, and to thereby couple worker satisfaction and higher productivity. Social man may have been born at Hawthorne, but his nurturance and elementary education were at Yale, Harvard, Michigan, M.I.T., Illinois, and Ohio State.

16

Organizations and People

Chronologically parallel to the developments at Western Electric, the writings of Chester Barnard, and the empirical work in human relations, another stream of management thought focused on the structure and design of organizations. People were not entirely omitted from the equation but were placed in a relatively subordinate role to other problems of managerial concern. This chapter, covering the period from the advent of the Great Depression to 1951, will show an evolution through two phases: (1) interest in and concern for organizational structure, authority, coordination, span of control, and other issues relevant to organizational design; and (2) an increasing concern for a top administrative viewpoint which preceded renewed interest in the work of Henri Fayol.

ORGANIZATIONS: STRUCTURE AND DESIGN

The impact of the economic holocaust of 1929 on management thought has never been fully examined. While Chapter 18 will attempt such an examination, the focus here will be on one set of theorems, the use of organizational design, to alleviate human want and misery. The Mayoist school put forth another set, that of group solidarity and human collaboration. The authors examined below felt that the efficient design and operation of organizations was another possible alternative for industry.

The Affable Irishman: James D. Mooney

During the cold, dark days of the Depression, the exhortation *Onward Industry!* reflected the premise that through organizational efficiency, the lot of mankind could be improved. *Onward Industry!*, the joint efforts of a General Motors executive, James D. Mooney, and a Fordham history professor, Alan C. Reiley, was an attempt "to expose the *principles of organization,* as they reveal themselves in various forms of human group movement, and to help industry to protect its own growth through a greater knowledge and use of these principles."[1] While joint authorship existed, it later became evident that the organizational aspect of the book was due to Mooney while Reiley assumed a lesser role and contributed primarily to the historical analysis of organizations. James Mooney was president of the General Motors Export Corporation and traveled over the world as a goodwill ambassador and negotiator for the General Motors Corporation. Described as "affable" and an "experienced diplomat," Mooney completed high school through correspondence, received a degree in mining engineering from Case Institute (1908), joined General Motors in 1920, and rose through the organization to head its Export Corporation.[2] Mooney was selected by President Roosevelt as his personal, secret emissary to Hitler when there were attempts to stop the war in 1939 and 1940 before America became involved. Failing in this, Mooney was given a special G.M. assignment to convert the company to defense production. He left G.M. in 1942 to head the U.S. Navy Bureau of Aeronautics and after the war became president and chairman of the board of Willys Overland Motors. Just before Mooney's death in 1957, it was finally revealed that since 1937 Mooney had been serving in another role of reporting to the Office of Naval Intelligence on activities in Europe. Perhaps James D. Mooney was the only contributor to management thought who was a spy!

In *Onward Industry!,* Mooney and Reiley set out to develop

[1] James D. Mooney and Alan C. Reiley, *Onward Industry!: The Principles of Organization and their Significance to Modern Industry,* New York: Harper and Row, 1931, p. xiii. This book was revised by Mooney and Reiley in 1939 and retitled *The Principles of Organization.* Mooney revised the book again in 1947. References below will distinguish between *Onward Industry!* and the revised edition where appropriate.

[2] Personal insights into Mooney are from "Drawing the Rules from History," *Milestones of Management,* Vol. I, by the Editors of *Business Week,* pp. 10–11.

principles of organizational efficiency which would meet industrial objectives of "profit through service" which they viewed as an obligation to contribute to "the alleviation of human want and misery."[3] Productive efficiency, though necessary, was not enough to insure the goal of industrial service. The entire organization, both production and distribution, must be efficient in terms of providing for organized group effort toward organizational aims and purposes. For Mooney and Reiley the efficient organization was based on formalism, which "means the efficient coordination of all relationships."[4] There is no evidence that either Mooney or Reiley had ever heard of Max Weber, the German who sought bureaucracy as the ideal, but the purposes and methods of these two sets of organizational theorists are more similar than dissimilar. Mooney and Reiley defined what they meant by organization: "Organization is the form of every human association for the attainment of a common purpose."[5] To clarify the role of management in organizations, they made this distinction:

Management is the vital spark which actuates, directs, and controls the plans and procedure of organization. With management enters the personal factor, without which no body could be a living being with any direction toward a given purpose. The relation of management to organization is analogous to the relation of the psychic complex to the physical body. Our bodies are simply the means and the instrument through which the psychic force moves toward the attainment of its aims and desires.[6]

Using the body-mind analogy for organization and management, Mooney and Reiley formulated their principles of organization and put them in a framework of "principle," "process," and "effect." The first principle was that of coordination, which meant "the orderly arrangement of group effort, to provide unity of action in the pursuit of a common purpose."[7] Coordination was a broad principle which contained all the principles of organization. Coordination found its own principle or foundation in *authority* or "the supreme coordinating power." This did not mean autocracy but the source of responsibility for direction. Authority was a "right" which inhered legitimately in the organization as opposed to

[3] Mooney and Reiley, *Onward Industry!*, p. xiii.
[4] *Ibid.*, p. xv.
[5] *Ibid.*, p. 10.
[6] *Ibid.*, p. 13.
[7] J. D. Mooney, *The Principles of Organization*, (revised edition) New York: Harper and Row, 1947, p. 5. The substance of Mooney's revision and the original *Onward Industry!* differ only slightly; the former being more concise and definitive.

power, which was an individual possession. In government, for example, authority represented *de jure* governments, while power represented *de facto* governments. Since coordination implied an aim or objective, every member of the organization must understand this common purpose, and Mooney and Reiley called this *doctrine* or the "definition of the objective."[8] This was similar to the religious concept of creed, but for industry it meant the attainment of "surplus through service" which was the objective of business. The greater the members' understanding of the organization's doctrine, the greater the degree of teamwork and the accomplishment of objectives.

The second principle was the *scalar* one, which meant that there was a hierarchy of degrees of authority and corresponding responsibility in every organization. Every organization, even of two people, had a scalar chain of superior to subordinate and thereby one found the scalar principle in operation. The scalar principle had its own principle in *leadership*, which "represents authority." Leadership was not always the "supreme authority" but was "the form that authority assumes when it enters into process."[9] The essence of this was that leaders were designated through the process of *delegation* which conferred authority on a subordinate by a superior. Delegation always meant the conferring of authority, whether it be authority over people or authority for task performance. Conversely, authority always carried with it responsibility for accomplishing what was authorized. The "effect" of this scalar principle was *functional definition*, which defined and assigned a task for each subordinate along the scalar chain.

The third principle, the *functional principle*, was not the same idea as functional definition but was the "distinction between different kinds of duties."[10] Every organization had functional differentiation in the sense that people performed different kinds of duties such as production, sales, lathe operations, security, *etc.* To cite Mooney:

In every organized undertaking there must be some function that determines its objective, another that moves to its attainment, and a third that makes interpretative decisions in accordance with those rules of procedure that have been predetermined. These functions, which may be called the *determinative*, the *applicative*, and the *interpretative*, are related as principle, process, and

8 *Ibid.*, p. 10.
9 *Ibid.*, p. 15.
10 *Ibid.*, p. 25.

effect. In secular government they are known as the *legislative*, the *executive*, and the *judicial* functions.[11]

Every duty, function, or individual job involved either determination of what was to be done, the doing of that thing, or deciding on questions which arose in that performance.

Mooney also made a delineation of staff service as contrasted with authority or command. The task of staff service was to advise or counsel and it had three phases:

> The *informative* phase refers to those things which authority should know in framing its decisions: the *advisory*, to the actual counsel based on such information; the *supervisory*, to both preceding phases as applied to all the details of execution. It is through this last phase that the informative and advisory phases become operative throughout an entire organization.[12]

According to Mooney, there should never be any confusion about line and staff because line represented "the authority of *man*; . . . Staff, the authority of *ideas*."[13] Line commanded, staff advised, and Mooney envisioned no potential conflict in line-staff relations as long as this was kept in mind.

Mechanically, Mooney and Reiley's principles resembled Weber's bureaucratic hierarchy, his rational-legal notion of authority, and his requirement for specifically defined duties and responsibilities. Mooney and Reiley made no reference to Weber and, since Weber's work had not been translated into English at this time, it must be assumed that they independently developed their format for efficiency through the proper organizational structure.

Following their section on the principles of organization, Mooney and Reiley examined the history of organizations to demonstrate these principles in operation. Most probably the work of the historian Reiley, they examined Greece, Rome, and other ancient civilizations and rulers to show the scalar process and other principles. Though largely a description of governments and the military, the Catholic Church came in for some close scrutiny by the two Irish Catholics. The first principle, coordination, found its authority in God, by whom it was delegated to the Pope as the supreme coordinating authority. The scalar principle operated from the pope, through the cardinals (who were often both line and staff), to the bishops and priests in the delegation of authority.

---

[11] *Ibid.*, p. 26. Copyright 1947, Harper and Row; by permission.
[12] *Ibid.*, p. 33. Copyright 1947, Harper and Row; by permission. Italics added.
[13] *Ibid.*, p. 34.

Functional definition, though less clear, was based on a division between the secular and the regular clergy, who may or may not perform certain acts of consecration. In the development of staff, the Church operated on a *compulsory staff service* concept. Under this rule, a superior must consult the elder monks even on minor matters. On matters of major importance, he must consult everyone for advice. This concept did not abridge his line authority but compelled him to consult everyone before rendering a decision. The superior could not refuse to listen. In industry, the compulsory staff principle would not protect the manager from errors in judgment but it would serve to allay errors of knowledge.

Briefly, Mooney and Reiley were concerned with the mechanisms of organization structure and design. The human element was not missing entirely but was relegated to a secondary role. For organization theory, Mooney and Reiley became a building block for a formalistic view of organizations.

Texts, Teachers, and Trends

A number of individuals continued the industrial engineering type of texts for management education and reflected more of a shop management view of organizations. Some were unique in their approach but for the most part they continued to stress production layout, scheduling, materials handling, organizing the shop, production control and other largely technique-oriented subjects. One unique approach was that of Henry Dennison (1877–1952) who had been a pioneer in the installation of the Taylor system in his own firm. The title of Dennison's book, *Organization Engineering*, is misleading for it advocated a design of organizational structure which was diametrically opposed to Mooney and Reiley's approach.[14] Dennison began with the idea that organization engineering was "making a success of group life" and built the organization structure up from groups of men who, under capable leadership, resolved their frictions and unified their motives in a single direction. Instead of designing the structure and tasks first, Dennison would find "like-minded" people, group

---

[14] Henry S. Dennison, *Organization Engineering*, New York: McGraw Hill Book Co., 1931. The Dennison Manufacturing Company was one of the first installations of Taylor's system. For an excellent history, see E. P. Hayes and Charlotte Heath, *History of the Dennison Manufacturing Company*, Cambridge, Mass.: Harvard University Press, 1930.

them, and develop the total organization structure last. In this sense, Dennison actually anticipated by a decade or more the behavioralists who were advocating sociometrically selected work teams or other mutual-choice devices to group workers by compatibility.

Dennison proposed seven factors necessary for effective teamwork: (1) a knowledge of common purpose; (2) a desire for a common purpose; (3) a desire on the part of the employees to help each other; (4) some degree of functional definition; (5) a knowledge of what a person's teammates were doing; (6) a knowledge of what teammates were supposed to do; and (7) a knowledge of how to help them.[15] Leadership was more than command or directing and included "helping," which reflected the influence of Gantt and Taylor on Dennison.

Dennison's view of motivation was also unique:

Four general groups of tendencies which may actuate a member of any organization are: (1) regard for his own and his family's welfare and standing; (2) liking for the work itself; (3) regard for one or more members of the organization and for their good opinion, and pleasure in working with them; and (4) respect and regard for the main purposes of the organization . . . Only when impelled by the four combined can all of man's power be brought into steady and permanent play.[16]

Dennison would modify jobs so that more satisfaction would be obtained from them. He did not develop any notion of job enlargement but was on the fringe of later behavioral theory, which sought to make work satisfying. He recognized informal groups and their influence on restriction of output and proposed non-financial incentives which, when properly mixed with economic incentives, built loyalty. Principles of organization were not to be "sacred in and of themselves" and the final organization structure should be flexible to strengthen group performance, not to ossify it. Authority and responsibility should be clearly defined and a sound organization structure furthered organizational efficiency if it were flexible enough to meet changing group and organizational needs, i.e., if it promoted "success of group life." Dennison also recognized limits to and variations in the number of men to whom the executive could give his attention. The span of control, in his view, "seldom runs beyond six to twelve people."[17]

[15] Dennison, pp. 38–40.
[16] Ibid., pp. 63–64.
[17] Ibid., pp. 137–138.

Similar to Dennison's uniqueness in organizational design was Henry P. Dutton who defined organization as "the art of applying resources effectively to the accomplishment of a purpose."[18] For Dutton, all of management was largely subsumed under the subject of organization; included were topics that would later resemble the management process. Dutton called this a "cycle of activity," which included: (1) *information,* the gathering of facts through the scientific method and through creative thinking; (2) *decision,* selection of a course of action from among alternatives; (3) *dispatch,* initiating the action dictated by the decision; (4) *performance*; and (5) *progress records, reports and follow-up,* that is, checking on performance for corrective action and supplying information for a new spiral of action. Such a cycle omitted many elements of what came to be known as the management process, but Dutton did stress the need for creative thinking and the circular nature of the manager's task.

Other contributions during the 1930's were more production-oriented. C. Canby Balderston and his associates defined management as "the art and science of organizing, preparing and directing human effort applied to control the forces and to utilize the materials of nature for the benefit of man."[19] They said that all managers, regardless of the type of enterprise, were concerned with four basic elements: men, money, machines, and material. They proceeded to analyze product design, physical facilities and equipment, power, heat, light, ventilation, inventory control, production control, and other shop-oriented subjects. Organization was treated within a formal framework in the Mooney and Reiley style; and personnel management, an emerging subject of consideration during the era, was one of the few subjects which appeared outside the shop management boundaries. One clue to the changing notions about management appeared in the 1949 revision of this work in which the authors defined management as "the stimulating, organizing, and directing of human effort to utilize effectively materials and facilities to attain an objective."[20] L. P. Alford,

[18] Henry P. Dutton, *Principles of Organization,* New York: McGraw-Hill Book Co., 1931, p. 1.

[19] C. Canby Balderston, Victor S. Karabasz, and Robert P. Brecht, *Management of an Enterprise,* New York: Prentice-Hall, 1935, p. 5. Professors Balderston and Brecht of the Wharton School, University of Pennsylvania, later became influential in forming the Academy of Management and Professor Brecht served as President of the Academy 1941–1947.

[20] Same authors plus Robert J. Riddle, 1949, p. 6.

mentioned earlier, continued the tradition of industrial engineering-oriented management.[21] Ralph M. Barnes, a student of Dexter Kimball at Cornell, began what has continued to be an industrial engineering approach to setting standards, simplifying work methods, and devising wage schemes.[22] Professor William Mitchell of the University of Chicago fell into the production management category, dealing with production, plant investment, and control of operations.[23]

On the academic front, many were sensing a need for a synthesis in management education. Professors E. H. Anderson of the University of Alabama and G. T. Schwenning of the University of North Carolina perceived the fragmentary nature of management literature and made a contribution by attempting to "appraise and synthesize" the work of others.[24] Though few new ideas were introduced, their synthesis and extensive bibliography provides a valuable research insight into this era. Anderson and Schwenning did note however, the appearance of Coubrough's 1930 translation of Henri Fayol's work, although they did not give it more than a passing glance. In 1936, Charles L. Jamison of the University of Michigan and William N. Mitchell of Chicago invited a group of management teachers to the University of Chicago's Quadrangle Club for the purpose of discussing the formation of a society to advance the philosophy of management.[25] Enough interest was evoked for Wharton's Balderston to invite the group to Philadelphia for another conference in 1937. R. C. Davis of Ohio State wrote the Constitution in 1940–1941, officers were elected, and the Academy of Management began formal operations in 1941. The objectives of the academy were stated as follows:

> The Academy is founded to foster the search for truth and the general advancement of learning through free discussion and research in the field of management. The interest of the Academy lies in the theory and practice of management, both administrative and operative. It is concerned also

[21] L. P. Alford, *Principles of Industrial Management for Engineers*, New York: Ronald Press Co., 1940.

[22] Ralph M. Barnes, *Motion and Time Study*, New York: John Wiley and Sons, 1937. Revised in 1940, 1949, 1958, 1963, and 1968.

[23] William N. Mitchell, *Organization and Management of Production*, New York: McGraw-Hill Book Co., 1939.

[24] E. H. Anderson and G. T. Schwenning, *The Science of Production Organization*, New York: John Wiley and Sons, 1938.

[25] Preston P. LeBreton, "A Brief History of the Academy of Management," in the Appendix of Paul M. Dauten, Jr. (ed.) *Current Issues and Emerging Concepts in Management*, Boston: Houghton Mifflin Co., 1962, pp. 329–332.

with the theory and practice of operative management as it relates to the work of planning, organizing, and controlling the execution of business projects. It is also concerned with activities having to do with the forming, directing, and coordinating of departments and groups which are characteristic of administrative management. It is not concerned primarily with specialized procedures for the control and execution of particular kinds of projects that are significant chiefly in narrow segments of a business field.

The general objectives of the Academy shall be therefore to foster: (a) A philosophy of management that will make possible an accomplishment of the economic and social objectives of an industrial society with increasing economy and effectiveness. The public's interest must be paramount in any such philosophy, but adequate consideration must be given to the legitimate interests of Capital and Labor. (b) Greater understanding by Executive leadership of the requirements for a sound application of the scientific method to the solution of managerial problems, based on such a philosophy. (c) Wider acquaintance and closer co-operation among such persons as are interested in the development of a philosophy and science of management.[26]

Academy membership was restricted to professors, although a few businessmen could be selected. The outbreak of World War II and consequent travel restrictions held Academy activities dormant until 1947 when annual meetings were resumed. Jamison, as founder, presided from 1936–1940; Brecht was President from 1941–1947, and Davis became President in 1948. The academy reflected the increased awareness for the necessity of teaching management and for bringing together diverse ideas into a search for management theory.

Another trend appeared which indicated an increasing awareness of the relationship of industry to society as a whole. In 1928, Arthur G. Anderson of the University of Illinois had published *Industrial Engineering and Factory Management*.[27] This first edition was essentially of the works administration-industrial engineering approach which was typical of that era. In 1942, Merten J. Mandeville (University of Illinois), and John M. Anderson (of Minneapolis-Honeywell, Inc.), became co-authors with A. G. Anderson and introduced a larger view of the management function, which stressed the need for management to relate effectively to its public. In the authors' view, management must assume its social responsibility and promote both economic and social progress through productive and distributive efficiency as well as through

---

[26] *Ibid.*, p. 330.

[27] A. G. Anderson, *Industrial Engineering and Factory Management*, New York: Ronald Press Co., 1928.

emphasis on "the human side" of the company.[28] Discussing relations with customers, stockholders, the public at large, and
employee relations, the authors took more of an environmental view
of management than was apparent in any other management text
since Gantt. Although a large portion of the remainder of the book
was devoted to traditional production subjects, it did reflect an
increasing concern for a larger view of the management function.

Building Blocks for Administrative Theory

In 1937, Luther Gulick and Lyndall Urwick assembled a series
of papers which reflected the divergences in management thought
during the era under consideration.[29] This landmark in management literature contained essays by James D. Mooney, Henri Fayol,
Henry Dennison, L. J. Henderson, T. N. Whitehead, Elton Mayo,
Mary Parker Follett, John Lee, V. A. Graicunas, and the editors
themselves. It included the first American rendition of Henri
Fayol's work, including Urwick's comparison of Fayol with
Mooney,[30] and an early account of the Hawthorne research.[31]
Despite the inclusion of Follett and the Harvard experimenters, the
whole of the collection was formalistic in terms of organization
theory.

Luther Gulick was Director of the Institute of Public Administration at Columbia University and served as a member of President
Roosevelt's Committee on Administrative Management which
attempted, without much success, to reform and reorganize the
federal bureaucracy.[32] Amplifying Fayol's version of the process
which appeared in the same collection, Gulick developed his
famous POSDCORB, which was his view of the functions of the
executive. The initials represented the following activities:

[28] Anderson, Mandeville, and Anderson, *Industrial Management,* (revised edition),
New York: Ronald Press Co., 1942, p. 3. Professor Mandeville became President of
the Academy of Management in 1959.

[29] Luther Gulick and Lyndall Urwick (eds.), *Papers on the Science of Administration,* New York: Institute of Public Administration, Columbia University, 1937.

[30] Henri Fayol, "The Administrative Theory of the State," (translation by Sarah
Greer), *ibid.,* pp. 99–114 and pp. 115–130.

[31] L. J. Henderson, T. N. Whitehead, and Elton Mayo, "The Effects of Social
Environment," *ibid.,* pp. 143–158.

[32] *Report of the President's Committee on Administrative Management,* Washington, D.C.: U. S. Government Printing Office, 1935. This report called for a
restructuring of governmental agencies and offices to eliminate overlapping duties and
to provide for more effective measures of executive responsibility.

*P*lanning, that is working out in broad outline the things that need to be done and the methods for doing them to accomplish the purpose set for the enterprise;

*O*rganizing, that is the establishment of the formal structure of authority through which work subdivisions are arranged, defined, and coordinated for the defined objective;

*S*taffing, that is the whole personnel function of bringing in and training the staff and maintaining favorable conditions of work;

*D*irecting, that is the continuous task of making decisions and embodying them in specific and general orders and instructions and serving as the leader of the enterprise;

*C*o-ordination, that is the all important duty of interrelating the various parts of the work;

*R*eporting, that is keeping those to whom the executive is responsible informed as to what is going on, which thus includes keeping himself and his subordinates informed through records, research, and inspection;

*B*udgeting, with all that goes with budgeting in the form of fiscal planning, accounting, and control.[33]

Gulick visualized his process as universal but his description of the functions was primarily applied to governmental administration. Gulick's contribution was not found in his version of the process, even though this is most easily recalled, but in his theory of departmentation which appears to be unique in the management literature for that time. Gulick began with the premise that the major purpose of organization was coordination. He then formulated a "principle of homogeneity" which required the grouping of similar activities under one head; otherwise friction and inefficiency would result. In grouping activities by this principle, Gulick noted four primary methods: (1) *purpose*, or function performed such as "furnishing water, controlling crime or conducting education"; (2) the *process* being used, such as "engineering, medicine . . . stenography, statistics, accounting"; (3) *persons* or *things* dealt with or served, such as "immigrants, veterans, Indians . . ."; and (4) the *place* where the service is being rendered.[34] In Gulick's scheme, these would be major groupings or primary levels of departmentation and any one could be chosen depending upon which best served the organization's objectives. For example, if the primary level chosen was by place (i.e. geographical), the secondary level might be grouped by purpose, process, clientele, or even again by place. The same would be true for the third level and so on. Any decision about how to group activities must follow

[33] Luther Gulick, "Notes on the Theory of Organization," Gulick and Urwick, p. 13. Italics added.

[34] *Ibid.*, p. 15 and pp. 21–31.

the principle of homogeneity, insure coordination, and maintain flexibility as the organization grew or as its objectives changed. While Mooney and Reiley stressed "functionalism" or the distinction between kinds of duties, Gulick demonstrated how these duties and activities could be grouped into homogeneous departments in order to assure coordination. It was on this point that Luther Gulick made his primary contribution to management and organization theory.

Lieutenant Colonel Lyndall Fownes Urwick (1891–   ), co-editor with Gulick of the *Papers on the Science of Administration,* has earned his place in management history. Educated at Oxford, he served in a distinguished manner in Her Majesty's Army and government in World Wars I and II, was Organizing Secretary of Rowntree and Company (1920–1928), was elected and served as Director of the International Management Institute in Geneva (1928–1933), and was Chairman of Urwick, Orr and Partners, Ltd., management consultants in London until his retirement.[35] Influenced to a great degree by B. S. Rowntree and Oliver Sheldon of the Cocoa Works, Col. Urwick has written on a wide range of subjects such as his collaboration with E. F. L. Brech on biographical sketches of pioneers in scientific management, with Henry Metcalf on Mary Follett's papers, with Gulick, and on his own on various aspects of organizations. Although his writings have spanned many decades, his work in the late 1920's and 1930's was heavily oriented along formalism in organization theory.[36] He identified eight principles applicable to all organizations: (1) the "principle of the objective," or that all organizations should be an expression of a purpose; (2) the "principle of correspondence," that authority and responsibility must be co-equal; (3) the "principle of responsibility," that responsibility of higher authorities for work of subordinates is absolute; (4) the scalar principle; (5) the "principle of the span of control," concluding that no superior can supervise directly the work of more than five or six subordinates whose work interlocks; (6) the "principle of specialization,"

---

[35] No author, *L. Urwick: A Bibliography,* London: Urwick, Orr and Partners, 1957.

[36] See L. Urwick "Principles of Direction and Control," John Lee (ed.) *A Dictionary of Industrial Administration,* London: Sir Isaac Pitman and Sons, 1928; L. Urwick, *Management of Tomorrow,* London: Nisbet and Co., 1933, in which he developed a "Pure theory of organization"; and L. Urwick, *Scientific Principles of Organization,* New York: American Management Association, 1938.

or limiting one's work to a single function; (7) a coordination principle; and (8) the "principle of definition," or a clear prescription of every duty.[37]

Urwick's discovery of Henri Fayol's elements led him to compare Fayol with Mooney and Reiley in a search for broader "principles of administration." He applied Mooney and Reiley's "principle, process, and effect" to Fayol's fourteen principles and concluded that these independent developments in organization theory were remarkably correlated and that they suggested a possible avenue of integration for administrative theory.[38] In later work, Urwick expanded his search for a synthesis by deriving twenty-nine major principles and a host of subprinciples by integrating his own ideas with those of Fayol, Mooney and Reiley, Taylor, Follett, and V. A. Graicunas.[39] He was optimistic that a general theory of administration could be attained and his own work has represented a substantial step in that direction.

The Span of Control

While Gulick and Urwick were publicizing and synthesizing the work of Fayol and Mooney and Reiley, V. A. Graicunas was furnishing mathematical proof to support the concept of a narrow span of control.[40] Graicunas, a French management consultant, was largely influenced by the British General Sir Ian Hamilton who expressed the military view of the span of control:

> . . . As to whether the groups [of subordinates] are three, four, five, or six, it is useful to bear in mind a by-law; the smaller the responsibility of the group member, the larger may be the number of the group—and *vice versa* . . . the nearer we approach the supreme head of the whole organization, the more we work towards groups of six.[41]

Graicunas observed that industrial managers were hampered by trying to supervise too many subordinates; this was due, in part, to their desire "to enhance their prestige and influence" by adding

---

[37] L. Urwick, *Scientific Principles of Organization*, New York: American Management Association, 1938.

[38] See L. Urwick, "The Function of Administration with Special Reference to the Work of Henri Fayol," in Gulick and Urwick (ed.), pp. 115–130.

[39] L. Urwick, *The Elements of Administration*, New York: Harper and Row, 1944.

[40] V. A. Graicunas, "Relationship in Organization," in Gulick and Urwick, pp. 181–187.

[41] Sir Ian Hamilton, *The Soul and Body of an Army*, London: Arnold Publishing House, 1921, p. 229.

sections and departments to their responsibilities.[42] Such ego
bolstering could be deadly from the standpoint of delays, lack of
coordination, and confusion from trying to control too many
subordinates. Graicunas indicated two factors to support his argument for a narrow or limited span of control: (1) the psychological principle of "span of attention" which stated that the human
brain could only cope with so many variables at any one time; and
(2) his own development of "cross relationships" and "direct group
relationships" in addition to "direct single relationships." On this
second point, Graicunas described these relationships in this way:

> In almost every case the superior measures the burden of his responsibility
> by the number of direct single relationships between himself and those he
> supervises. But in addition there are direct group relationships and cross re-
> lationships. Thus, if Tom supervises two persons, Dick and Harry, he can
> speak to them as a pair. . . . Further what Dick thinks of Harry and what Harry
> thinks of Dick constitute two cross relationships which Tom must keep in mind
> in arranging any work over which they must collaborate in his absence . . . Thus,
> even in this extremely simple unit of organization, Tom must hold four to six
> relationships within his span of attention:
>
> Direct Single Relationships
>   Tom to Dick and Tom to Harry 2
> Direct Group Relationships
>   Tom to Dick with Harry and Tom to Harry with Dick 2
> Cross Relations
>   Harry with Dick and Dick with Harry 2
>   Total Relationships .... 6[43]

With the addition of these different sets of relationships,
Graicunas postulated that when the number of direct single relationships increased arithmetically with the addition of one subordinate the corresponding increase in the number of direct group
and cross relationships caused the total number of relationships to
increase in exponential proportion. Where n represented the number of persons supervised, Graicunas derived a formula to show
this growth:

$$\text{Total relationships} = n(\frac{2^n}{2} + n - 1)$$

or, if there were three subordinates in direct single relationship,
then:

$$\text{Total} = 3(\frac{2^3}{2} + 3 - 1), \text{ or } 3 \times 6 = 18$$

[42] Graicunas, p. 183.
[43] *Ibid.*, p. 184.

Further, to show the growth as subordinates were added:

$$n = 1 \quad 2 \quad 3 \quad 4 \quad 5 \quad 6 \quad 7 \quad 8 \quad 9 \quad 10 \quad 11 \quad 12$$
$$\text{total} = 1 \quad 6 \quad 18 \quad 44 \quad 100 \quad 222 \quad 490 \quad 1080 \quad 2376 \quad 5210 \quad 11374 \quad 24708$$

The significance of this geometric growth was that increasing n from 4 to 5 increased working capacity 20 per cent whereas the increase in the "possible" number of relationships increased 127 per cent or from 44 to 100. Hence Graicunas argued that the span of control should be limited to a "maximum of five and most probably, only four."[44] Exceptions to this decision rule were permissible in the case of routine work at lower organizational elements where workers worked relatively independently of others, where they had little or no contact with others, and where supervisory responsibilities were less complex and therefore allowed a wider span of control. However, at upper levels, where responsibility was greater and often overlapped, the span should be less. Graicunas noted also that "it is not possible to assign comparable weights to these different varieties of relationship," suggesting that he was aware that not all interaction possibilities were operative at all times. If some interactions were not required, for example, if Dick need not interact with Harry, or if the job was routine and interaction not crucial, then the number of relationships would be less and the span might be wider. Graicunas was using mathematics to prove a point. His formula represented "maximum possible" relationships, not what might actually be operative at one given point in time. His advice, highly influenced by military and governmental needs for control and coordination, reflected his formalistic concern for organizational efficiency and should not be generalized to other situations where other variables, such as subordinate motivation or development, might be of greater import.

TOWARD A TOP MANAGEMENT VIEWPOINT

A second facet of this era involved developments which were shifting management thought from a shop-management, production orientation to a larger view of the administrative function. The design of organization structures and the search for organizational

---

[44] *Ibid.*, p. 185.

principles were still subjects for discussion; however, organizations *per se* were beginning to take a back seat to the study of administration. Ralph C. Davis is an excellent example of this transition period in evolving management thought.

Ralph C. Davis: Pater Familiae et Magister

Ralph Currier Davis (1894–   ) received his mechanical engineering degree in 1916 from Cornell where he studied under the pioneering Dexter Kimball.[45] After becoming a registered industrial engineer he went to work on the industrial engineering staff of the Winchester Repeating Arms Company where, as he puts it, "I quickly discovered that I knew practically nothing about management."[46] His experiences were soon enriched by observing Carl Barth, Dwight Merrick, and members of the staff of A. Hamilton Church's consulting firm, who were all on assignment at Winchester. In 1923, Davis was invited to the Ohio State University to establish a Department of Management in the College of Commerce and Administration. His first book was in the traditional shop level, "operative management" orientation. Davis stated that the fundamental functions and principles of factory management were universal in their application and that a sound organization was essential:

> In developing the organization, consideration should be given to (1) the fundamental functions to be performed and their relation to one another, (2) the proper division of responsibility, (3) the definite location of responsibility, (4) the proper functioning of the system, (5) the flexibility of the organization, (6) provision for future growth, (7) personal characteristics and abilities, (8) the creation of an ideal, and (9) the quality of the leadership.[47]

Davis also questioned the wisdom of Taylor's functional foremen:

> The employee in a functionalized organization must look to a number of executives for instructions. This may impair discipline by permitting him to play off one executive against another. Furthermore, it is difficult to draw sharp lines between many of the functions of management, and accordingly there is danger of conflict of authority between the various functions . . . Finally,

---

[45] Biographical information is based on personal correspondence, Ralph C. Davis to author, May 18, 1969; and on John F. Mee, *"Pater Familiae et Magister"* (Father of Family and Teacher), *Academy of Management Journal*, Vol. 8, No. 1 (March, 1965), pp. 14–23.

[46] R. C. Davis to author, May 18, 1969.

[47] R. C. Davis, *The Principles of Factory Organization and Management,* New York: Harper and Row, 1928, p. 41.

the Taylor division of functions is adapted chiefly to shop conditions. It cannot be applied readily to the other units of the organization, as, for example, the purchasing department.[48]

On personnel, Davis reflected the industrial psychology orientation of the period by stressing job analysis and scientific selection of workers: "Psychological methods have a scientific basis and seem to offer the only real hope for the development of scientific methods for the selection of applicants."[49]

In 1927, Davis was asked by General Motors to set up a Department of Management in the General Motors Institute at Flint, Michigan. It was at General Motors from 1927–1930 that he was exposed to the philosophies and principles of Donaldson Brown and Alfred P. Sloan, Jr., and from that time on he began to formulate his "administrative" approach to management as opposed to his previous "operative" or shop-level approach. Davis' approach was further reshaped by his acquisition (in 1930 or 1931) of Coubrough's translation of Henri Fayol's *Industrial and General Administration*.[50] In 1934, this melding of ideas led Davis to develop his own "organic functions" of management as planning, organizing, and controlling.[51] R. C. Davis' life and work illustrate the ecology of evolving management thought over a span of more than four decades. His 1928 work was largely a shop level, "operative"-oriented approach to management; in 1934, he developed his own organic functions of planning, organizing, and controlling; and in 1940, he developed the management process further but still devoted a large portion of this book to production shop subjects.[52] His notions of management theory and practice were clearly in transition when he published *The Fundamentals of Top Management* in 1951.[53] In this effort, he moved almost entirely to an "administrative management" viewpoint.

[48] *Ibid.*, pp. 47–48 and p. 50.

[49] *Ibid.*, p. 338.

[50] R. C. Davis to author, September 11, 1971.

[51] R. C. Davis, *The Principles of Business Organization and Operation*, Columbus, Ohio: H. L. Hedrick, 1935, pp. 12–13. John Mee has suggested that Davis' idea of "organic functions" reflected the influence of Alexander Hamilton Church. Church developed some "organic functions" of management in 1914 and Davis had encountered Church's ideas at the Winchester Repeating Arms Company. John Mee to Author, August 26, 1969.

[52] Ralph C. Davis, *Industrial Organization and Management*, New York: Harper and Row, 1940. This book was a substantial revision of his 1928 text and its third edition appeared in 1957.

[53] Ralph C. Davis, *The Fundamentals of Top Management*, New York: Harper and Row, 1951.

In *Fundamentals,* Davis defined management as "the function of executive leadership" and stressed the need for "professional" managers who had a sound philosophy of management with respect to leadership and the relations between business and the community. Since the business organization was largely an economic institution, its objectives were "any values that the business organization is required or expected to acquire, create, preserve, or distribute."[54] Organizational objectives were constrained by community ideals or commonly held standards of business conduct. Executive leadership was a motivating force that stimulated and directed the members of the organization toward the satisfactory achievement of its objectives.

In developing the management process, Davis viewed his organic functions as universally applicable to all types of enterprises. Planning was the "specification of the factors, forces, effects and relationships that enter into and are required for the solution of a business problem" and provided "a basis for economical and effective action in the achievement of business objectives."[55] Planning was mental work of a creative nature which facilitated understanding and accomplishment of the organization's mission. Organizing included "any process that results in the antecedent provision of the necessary basic conditions for successful business accomplishment" and involved "bringing functions, physical factors, and personnel into proper relationships with one another . . ."[56] Organization rested on authority which was "the right to plan, organize, and control the organization's activities . . ."[57] This represented the traditional formal view of authority as the right to command and decide, which Davis found to be legitimatized ultimately in organized society. For example, society upholds the right of private property; individuals exercise this right through stock ownership in a company and delegate the management of their property to the board of directors who in turn delegate authority down through the scalar chain. With respect to the functional grouping of activities and his examination of other aspects of organizing, Davis reflected the formalism of Mooney and Reiley and other writers of this genre. He did not examine

[54] *Ibid.,* p. 10.
[55] *Ibid.,* p. 43.
[56] *Ibid.,* p. 238.
[57] *Ibid.,* p. 281.

the informal organization, made no mention of the Western Electric research, and in general made few references to the behavioral research being carried out during that era.

Control was defined "as the function of constraining and regulating activities that enter into the accomplishment of an objective."[58] Davis identified eight control functions: routine planning, scheduling, preparation, dispatching, direction, supervision, comparison, and corrective action. In this scheme, he did make a useful distinction by indicating the importance of *timing* in phases of control. For instance, routine planning, which provided information for the execution of plans, was a phase of control. On the other hand, creative planning involved advance planning of a general nature and was part of the organization's total planning function. The phases of control were: (1) *preliminary* control, which included routine planning, scheduling, preparation and dispatching; and (2) *concurrent* control, or direction, supervision, comparison, and corrective action. Preliminary control tried to design in advance constraints and regulations which would assure proper execution of the plan; on the other hand, concurrent control operated while performance was in progress. Corrective action completed the control cycle and began the preliminary phase again by identifying deviations and by replanning or taking other actions to prevent recurrence of deviations. While many of his predecessors had written of control, Davis presented a much more insightful and comprehensive view of this function.

In comparing Davis and Fayol, we note that each had his own uniqueness. Both stressed the universality of management, both recognized the necessity and importance of teaching management, and both held to a formalized view of management. Fayol's process added command and coordination to planning, organizing, and controlling. Davis did not include command but included it under a more descriptive label of "executive leadership" which permeated all other functions. Likewise, Davis treated coordination as operating throughout his organic functions and not separate as regarded by Fayol. On the other hand, Fayol developed staffing as a subfunction of organizing while Davis paid relatively less attention to the personnel function.

[58] *Ibid.*, p. 663.

Analyzing Top Management

World War II mobilized vast productive capabilities and the post-war period found American enterprise trying to cope with the problems of managing operations on a larger scale than ever before. Top management faced greater responsibilities in determining common ends toward which efforts must be directed, in maintaining the coordination of functions, in relating growing and emerging activities brought about by new products, processes, and markets, and in harmonizing, measuring, and controlling the results of these efforts. It was toward these new responsibilities of top management that administrative analysts turned their attention. One pioneering work examined the top management of thirty-one "blue chip" companies for the purpose of compiling the state of the management art with respect to long-range planning and objectives, organization, staffing, and controlling.[59] The authors found that only about half of their sample prepared detailed plans for periods up to a year in advance and that very few companies developed fully integrated systems of plans for the firm as a whole. Very few companies developed long-range objectives and the authors stated that "one of the greatest needs observed during the course of this study is for more adequate planning and clarification of future objectives, both near-term and long-range."[60] The authors traced this failing to inadequate organizational arrangements in which jurisdictions, responsibilities, and relationships were ill-defined, staff departments poorly conceived and coordinated, and in which committees, that bane of all organizational work, were poorly designed and used for the wrong tasks. In staffing, "many companies" left provisions for key management personnel development and succession "largely to providence."[61] Control practices brought little solace; only one-half of the companies studied used budgetary control as a means of planning and subsequently for measuring "over-all results of efforts."

It is difficult to evaluate the authors' findings since they failed

[59] Paul E. Holden, Lounsbury S. Fish, and Hubert L. Smith, *Top Management Organization and Control*, Stanford, Calif.: Stanford University Press, 1941.

[60] *Ibid.*, p. 4. Another book during this era which focused on the nature of and need for planning was Edward H. Hempel, *Top Management Planning*, New York: Harper and Row, 1945.

[61] Holden, Fish, and Smith, pp. 6–8.

to fully develop their own explanation of the discrepancy between apparently poor management practices on the one hand and success in the "blue chip" category on the other. The thirty-one companies sampled were studied for seven months and six months were taken for analysis. Perhaps such a short period of study explains the variance in that no long-range changes could be noted; or perhaps early war prosperity enabled successful performance regardless of managerial ability. Whatever the explanation, the Holden, Fish, and Smith report demonstrated increasing concern for a top management viewpoint with respect to objectives, planning, organization, staffing, and controlling.[62]

Executive leadership as a subject of analysis was appearing with increasing regularity during the 1940's. Professor Sune Carlson conducted an empirical study of executive communications and concluded that they occupied a major portion of the manager's time.[63] Stanford University's Robert A. Gordon presented a broader study of 155 larger corporations in which he focused on the direction and coordination of America's big business. Noting the separation of ownership and management of the large corporation and that many American industries were dominated by one or by a few large firms, Gordon stressed the need for "professionalization" of management. The era of the entrepreneurial motive of profit from managing one's own investment had passed and the new era was one dominated by salaried managers hired by the board of directors. The result was a lessening of the profit motive in corporations leading to inflexibility and bureaucracy in decision making.[64] Gordon saw dangers in this increased insulation of the decision-makers from ownership, especially with respect to the establishment of a self-perpetuating oligarchy of an executive group which placed its own interests above the interests of stockholders and others whose welfare was involved. Gordon's answer to this corporate leadership dilemma was dynamic, professional executives who were responsive to the needs of the groups the organization served.

[62] In a more recent follow-up study of fifteen leading corporations, many improvements in managerial practices were noted, especially with respect to long-range planning, executive development, and management information systems. See Paul E. Holden, Carlton A. Pederson, and Gayton E. Germane, Top Management, New York: McGraw-Hill Book Co., 1968.

[63] Sune Carlson, Executive Behavior, Stockholm, Sweden: Strombergs, 1951.

[64] Robert A. Gordon, Business Leadership in the Large Corporation, Washington, D.C.: The Brookings Institution, 1945.

Professors Peterson and Plowman, Jackson Martindell, and Alvin Brown also sought the top management viewpoint characteristic of this era. Peterson and Plowman focused on organization, policy, executive leadership, and the board of directors.[65] Jackson Martindell formulated what was to become a continuing series of publications on appraising managerial competence in organizations.[66] Through his "management audit" approach, Martindell established criteria for the purposes of evaluating management practices. His criteria included: (1) the economic function of a company; (2) its organization structure; (3) the health of its earnings growth; (4) its practices with regard to fairness to stockholders; (5) its research and development practices; (6) its fiscal policies; (7) the value contributed by the board of directors; (8) the company's productive efficiency; (9) its sales organization; and (10) an evaluation of the executive abilities of the company. The method of evaluation consisted of allocating points for performance ratings in each of the ten areas, summing these points for an overall evaluation, and then comparing the excellence of any particular company with the score obtained from companies in similar industries. While Martindell's techniques have been refined over the years, his approach was significant in that it sought to establish means for evaluating and comparing overall company practices from a top management viewpoint.

Alvin Brown, an executive of the Johns-Mansville Corporation, was more organizationally oriented but also tried to weave in some administrative functions. Brown defined organization as a "means to more effective concerted endeavor" and thought that principles of organization were universally applicable to all types of human effort.[67] Brown identified ninety-six principles of organization, classifying them under headings such as purpose of organization, scope of organization, responsibility, delegation, authority, self-coordination, phases of administration, and so on. For instance, principle nine was that "responsibility cannot be shared with

[65] Elmore Peterson and E. Grosvenor Plowman, *Business Organization and Management,* Chicago: Richard D. Irwin, 1941 (revised in 1948, 1952, 1956, and 1962, with Joseph M. Trickett added as a co-author).

[66] Jackson Martindell, *The Scientific Appraisal of Management,* New York: Harper and Row, 1950.

[67] Alvin Brown, *Organization of Industry,* New York: Prentice-Hall, 1947, p.v. This book was an enlargement of his *Organization: A Formulation of Principle,* New York: Hibbert Printing Co., 1945. Alvin Brown was President of the Academy of Management in 1957.

another"; principle twenty-five read "authority includes all means necessary and proper for the performance of responsibility": and the list continued to principle ninety-six that "whereas organizational principle [i.e. theory] is a science, the practice of organization is an art." Brown was more concerned with organizational structure, viewing it as a means to more effective administration. Organization was the handmaiden of administration which consisted of the phases of *planning, doing,* and *seeing*.[68] This administrative process was cyclical and overlapping in that planning was a mental process of anticipating and specifying activities, "doing" was the physical execution, and "seeing" was confirmation that planning and doing were consonant in contributing to organizational purposes. The organization structure was the body in which the planning, doing, and seeing phases came to life. Brown's ideas reflected the formalistic approach to organizations typical of others examined in this chapter. His search for a science of organizational principles, his classification of these principles, and his differentiation between organization and administration were a prelude to a search for management principles in succeeding eras.

SUMMARY

Whereas the Mayoists sought greater productivity and satisfaction based on building social solidarity and collaboration, the individuals examined in this chapter were more concerned with the proper structuring of activities and relationships in order to reach essentially the same ends. These "formalists" postulated that people worked better when they knew what was expected of them and that they would be more satisfied and productive under those conditions. Hence these "formalists" stressed organizational structure and design as a means to both employee satisfaction and organizational productivity. Their efforts were characterized by a search for *principles of organization* and eventually by the quest for broader *principles of administration.* Mooney and Reiley extricated rules of organization from history to increase organizational efficiency and thereby alleviate "human want and misery"; Henry Dennison built his structure from compatible work groups aimed toward flexible overall structures which would make work

[68] *Ibid.,* pp. 205–207.

more satisfying; and Gulick, Urwick, Graicunas and others also tended toward formalizing relationships to reduce confusion and foster certainty and predictability. While this stress on organization structure and on management of production operations persisted for much of the period, Ralph C. Davis personified the shift in management thinking from the operative to the administrative viewpoint with his organic functions of management. Gulick and Urwick brought Henri Fayol to the fore and Urwick in turn attempted to synthesize administrative theory. Gordon and others were displaying an increasing awareness of the large-scale administrative problems in the 1940's. The stage was being set for a new focus on the functions of the manager.

17

Social Man and the Critics

The Hawthorne research did not inspire any investigating commission, congressional inquiry, nor any direct recriminations and strikes by organized labor. Mayo did not have his Hoxie, Senator Wilson or Redfield, nor any confrontations such as the Watertown Arsenal. Nevertheless, every thesis generates its own antithesis (as Hegel saw it) and the Mayoists have had their share of criticism.

HAWTHORNE REVISITED

William H. Knowles reviewed the literature in 1958 and classified the criticisms of the human relations adherents under these categories: (1) their lack of scientific validity; (2) their overemphasis on the group; (3) their view of the nature of conflict; (4) their focus on group decision making; (5) their view of democracy; (6) their mysticism; (7) their evangelism; and (8) their methods of training for human relations skills.[1] Henry Landsberger performed for human relations the function that Horace B. Drury did for scientific management. Landsberger furnished an extensive list of critical reviews of *Management and the Worker* up to 1958 and put forth a defense of that work. Landsberger identified four separate areas of criticism: (1) the

[1] William H. Knowles, "Human Relations in Industry: Research and Concepts," *California Management Review*, Vol. 1, No. 1 (Fall, 1958); reprinted in S. G. Huneryager and I. L. Heckman (ed.); *Human Relations in Management* (2nd ed.), Cincinnati, Ohio: South-Western Publishing Co., 1967, pp. 31–58.

Mayoists' view of society as one characterized by anomie, social disorganization, and conflict; (2) their acceptance of management's views of the worker and management's "willingness to manipulate workers for management's ends"; (3) their failure to recognize other alternatives for accommodating industrial conflict, such as collective bargaining; and (4) their specific failure to take unions into account as a method of building social solidarity.[2] Since these reviews, more fuel has been added to the fire. The following analysis will build upon the work of Knowles and Landsberger by adding more recent criticisms and will combine the critical evaluations of social man into three broader conceptual categories: (1) the premises from which the Mayoists worked; (2) their methodology; and (3) their conclusions regarding the care and feeding of social man.

The Premises of Industrial Civilization

Mayo and Roethlisberger both began with a view of industrial society characterized by anomie. Man, bound up in his obsessive-compulsive "pessimistic reveries," needed identification with his fellow man and constructive outlets for his latent fears and frustrations. Industrial civilization, though making giant strides in technological progress, had created a cultural lag by diminishing the importance of collaborative social skills. The Mayoists' response was to build from small group structures to a view of man in a larger social system. A number of critics have questioned these assumptions about the nature of industrial society and the Mayoists' view of social systems. Daniel Bell felt that the Harvard group lacked adequate basic hypotheses about the nature of the industrial system: "There is no view of the larger institutional framework of our economic systems within which these relationships arise and have their meaning."[3] Among the specific omissions, Bell cited changes in class structure with respect to an increase in white collar and technical workers, a shift in technology which de-graded the skilled worker and tended to replace the unskilled worker, and a leveling of jobs in which workers became largely semi-skilled machine tenders. In short, the Mayoists viewed the firm as a closed social system and overlooked the impact of technological and economic

[2] Henry A. Landsberger, *Hawthorne Revisited*, Ithaca, N.Y.: Cornell Studies in Industrial and Labor Relations, Volume IX, Cornell University, 1958, pp. 29–30.

[3] Daniel Bell, "Exploring Factory Life," *Commentary*, January, 1947, p. 86.

changes which had a direct bearing upon the status of workers in the total industrial system.

Bell also charged that the Mayoists considered themselves "social engineers" who managed not men but a social system in an effort to "adjust" the worker so that the human equation fitted the industrial equation. Since pride in work and the satisfactions of craftmanship had been destroyed by the process of industrialization, the Mayoists felt that man must find his satisfactions in human association. Bell said that to think that contented workers were productive workers was to equate human behavior with "cow sociology," i.e., that contented cows give more milk.[4] Counseling at Hawthorne, for which Bell used the colorful phrase "ambulatory confessors," was to be the new method of controlling humans.[5] When employees exposed their innermost doubts and fears, they were more susceptible to managerial manipulation. The socially skilled supervisor could move from the use of authority to coerce humans to psychological persuasion for worker "manipulation as a means of exercising dominion."[6] Another facet of Bell's criticism was that the human relations' style of supervision was to replace thinking about improving work itself. Social man, relieved of "pessimistic reveries" by the catharsis of counseling, would feel better and forget all of his other problems. Bell recalled a folktale to make this point:

A peasant complains to his priest that his little hut is horribly overcrowded. The priest advises him to move his cow into the house, the next week to take in his sheep, and the next week his horse. The peasant now complains even more bitterly about his lot. Then the priest advises him to let out the cow, the next week the sheep, and the next week the horse. At the end the peasant gratefully thanks the priest for lightening his burdensome life.[7]

In short, Bell challenged what he perceived to be a basic premise of Mayoism—that the worker still was to be regarded as a means to an end of industrial productivity. The new means were social skills but the end was still manipulation of the worker. Instead of

[4] Daniel Bell. *Work and Its Discontents: The Cult of Efficiency in America,* Boston: Beacon Press 1956, p. 25.

[5] *Ibid.,* p. 26. Professor Ghiselli also warned that employee counseling could be an "invasion of privacy." Individuals may reveal their innermost secrets to a psychiatrist, but not to their boss. Edwin E. Ghiselli, "Human Relations Revisited," *Public Personnel Review,* Vol. 21, No. 3 (July, 1960), pp. 193–198.

[6] Bell, p. 28.

[7] *Ibid.* p. 26.

restoring man's pride in workmanship and allaying anomie, human relations substituted a catharsis for the worker rather than striking at the root of the problem, the nature of work itself. On this latter point, Bell's criticism has much merit.

Another attack on premises came from those who maintained that the Mayoists presented a naive view of societal conflict. According to these critics, the Mayoists assumed that a commonality of interests could be found between labor and management when in fact society was much more complex in terms of conflict between classes and interest groups. Some tensions and conflict were inevitable in every human situation and some may even be necessary. The goal should not be to eliminate conflict and tension but to provide healthy outlets for resolution.[8] The Mayoists' notion of a conflict-free state of equilibrium was a worthy goal but too idealistic for modern critics. The Mayoists, like the Taylorists, found faddists and perversions of their original intentions. The human relations cult which followed the original conception of man as a social being often concluded that the goal of their efforts was to keep everyone happy in a conflict-free state of equilibrium with resultant worker-management marital bliss. When bliss was attained, higher productivity was the corollary. As William Fox put it:

Among the guilty are the "human relationists" with an inadequate concept of human relations, who mistakenly preach participation, permissiveness, and democracy for all, and those employers who confuse popularity with managerial effectiveness and misinterpret the Golden Rule in dealing with their subordinates . . . Many mistakenly regard it [human relations] as an "end" toward which the organization shall endeavor rather than as what it should be—a "means" for achieving the organization's primary service objectives.[9]

According to Fox, the regard for human relations as an end rather than a means misled the manager to think that a conflict-free state and worker contentment would automatically lead to company success when in fact the company might fail. Human relations could not be substituted for well-defined goals, policies, high

[8] Landsberger, pp. 30–35. See also Bernard Sarachek, "Elton Mayo's Social Psychology and Human Relations," *Academy of Management Journal*, Vol. 11, No. 2 (June, 1968), pp. 189–197.

[9] William M. Fox, "When Human Relations May Succeed and the Company Fail," *California Management Review*, Vol. 8, No. 3 (Spring, 1966), reprinted in Max S. Wortman and Fred Luthans (eds.), *Emerging Concepts in Management*, New York: Macmillan Co., 1969, p. 184.

standards of performance, and other administrative functions which were necessary to organizational goal attainment.

In brief, the challenges to the basic premises of the Mayoist's were: (1) that they displayed a lack of awareness of larger social and technological systems; (2) that they accepted a premise that the worker could be manipulated to fit into the industrial equation; (3) that they assumed that cooperation and collaboration were natural and desirable and thus overlooked more complex issues in societal conflict; and (4) that they confused means and ends in assuming that the goal of contentment and happiness would lead to harmonious equilibrium and organizational success.

The Research Methodology

The modern management researcher is much more sophisticated in statistics and research methodology than the group of men who entered the Western Electric plant in 1927. The bulk of human relations thought was based on relatively few studies, and these studies were full of intellectual pitfalls in the view of a more sophisticated audience.[10] References have already been made to the small samples upon which sweeping conclusions were reached and to the classic "Hawthorne effect" of biasing one's own results by observing and participating in the experiment. Industrial research is full of cracks and crevices and the researcher is pinioned between the need for the controlled experiments of a laboratory versus the empirical reality of on-going activity. Seen in this light, one can forgive the human relations researchers some of their peccadilloes but not all of them.

The Mayoists' conclusions regarding man's motivation is a particularly pressing issue. William Foote Whyte concluded that Elton Mayo destroyed the orthodox theory of the economic motivation of workers.[11] Alex Carey of the University of New South Wales has used data from Roethlisberger, Dickson, and T.N. Whitehead

---

[10] Knowles, op. cit., pp. 45–46, said that the bulk of the literature on human relations had based its conclusions on primarily four sources: the original Hawthorne study, the Harwood Manufacturing Company, the Glacier Metal Company (English), and the University of Michigan Survey Research Center's comparative studies of the Prudential Life Insurance Company, the Detroit Edison Company, the Baltimore and Ohio Railroad, and the International Harvester Company. Knowles commented that the human relationists "got a lot of mileage" out of these studies; ibid., p. 46.

[11] W. F. Whyte, "Human Relations Theory—A Progress Report," Harvard Business Review, Vol. 34, No. 5. (September–October, 1956), pp. 125–132.

to challenge whether or not this was true.[12]   For purposes of review without repeating too much of the discussion in Chapter 13, the original experiments took a small group of female relay assemblers and subjected them to various changes in working conditions, including a new incentive scheme and a "new" supervisor (observer).   Output increased but the Harvard researchers wanted to isolate the cause in order to test their five hypotheses regarding the puzzling results.   They formed a second relay assembly group which was to be placed on a new incentive plan and a group of mica splitters who would have new supervision but who would retain their old individual incentive plan.   In the second relay group, output rose 12.6 per cent but the experiment was abandoned at the end of nine weeks because other girls who were not in the experiment wanted to go on the same individual incentive scheme as the experimental group.   After abandoning the incentive plan, output dropped 16 per cent.   However, the researchers rejected economic incentives as the explanation of these variations in output by saying: ". . . it is difficult to conclude whether the increase in output was an immediate response to the change in wage incentive or was merely representative of the top level of a more or less upward swing [in output]."[13]

The mica splitters were already on individual incentives.   This scheme was retained but all the changes introduced in the original experiments such as new supervision, separate rooms, shortening of hours, and rest pauses were made in the mica group.   Thus the only variable held constant in the mica splitters experiment was the individual incentive scheme.   Average hourly output rose 15.6 per cent over a period of fourteen months among the mica splitters.[14]   Since the incentive scheme had not been changed, the researchers concluded that it was supervision and not wages that caused the increase.   On this point, Carey demurred by noting that the researchers changed their methods of reporting increases in output.   In both relay assembly group experiments, both "average hourly output" and "increase in total output" had been used to describe results.   However, in the mica splitting experi-

---

[12] Alex Carey, "The Hawthorne Studies: A Radical Criticism," *American Sociological Review*, Vol. 32, No. 3 (June, 1967), pp. 403–416. A similar criticism is by A. J. M. Sykes, "Economic Interest and the Hawthorne Researchers," *Human Relations*, Vol. 18 (1965).

[13] Roethlisberger and Dickson, p. 133.

[14] *Ibid.*, p. 148, Table XV.

ment, *only* "average hourly output" was used. If "total output" had been used in measuring mica splitting results, the outcome would have been zero or less because output per hour went up 15.6 per cent while the weekly hours worked decreased by 17 per cent from 55½ to 46½.[15] In effect, Carey's point was that total output was constant (or less) and that the new supervision and other changes had no effect since the old individual scheme was retained. By changing their measurement base, the researchers had shown an increase in output due to the "new supervision" when in fact there had been no increase in total output.

To capsulize Carey's comparison of the three experiments: (1) in the original relay assembly experiments a piecework incentive was introduced and total hours decreased 4.7 per cent from beginning to end and total output was up 30 per cent; (2) in the second relay group total output rose 12.6 per cent under the individual incentive but fell 16 per cent when the incentive scheme was abandoned; and (3) among the mica splitters, incentives were held constant, hours were reduced, and there was no increase and perhaps even a decrease in total output. Hence Carey concluded that it was completely erroneous for the Harvard group to decide that wages were not a variable and that it was spurious research methodology to change the way of computing and reporting increases in output.[16]

Carey also chastized the researchers for their claims of "friendly supervision." First, the group selected "cooperative" girls who were willing to participate in the experiments. Second, two girls from the original group began causing some problems and "were removed for a lack of cooperation, which would have otherwise necessitated greatly increased disciplinary measures."[17] After reviewing production records, Carey concluded that output did not increase until the two girls were dismissed and two "more cooperative" ones were added to the original group.[18] Was this "friendly supervision" or the old-time use of negative sanctions to increase output?

[15] Carey, p. 408. *Cf.* Roethlisberger and Dickson pp. 136–139.
[16] Carey, p. 410.
[17] T. N. Whitehead, *The Industrial Worker*, (Vol. I), p. 118. In *The Human Problems of an Industrial Civilization*, Mayo said they "dropped out" (p. 56); *cf.* Carey p. 411.
[18] Carey, p. 415.

Carey, having available a number of years of hindsight and a more sophisticated understanding of research methodology, has aimed a number of damaging charges at the conduct of the Hawthorne experiments. He considered the whole study to be "worthless," not only because of the manipulation of data, the rejection of economic incentives as a possible explanation, and the use of dismissals to get added productivity, but also because of a number of other points: (1) that the samples in all cases were extremely small and that no further attempts were made to increase sample size: (2) that no attempts were made to correlate output records of girls not in the experiment with those who were; and (3) that statistically reliable results were not obtainable from a sample of five, thus making generalization very tenuous. Carey maintained that the Hawthorne experiments were really consistent with the old view of economic incentives and the use of a firm hand in discipline in order to get higher output.

Peter Drucker, though not using the statistical, research methodological approach of Carey, also criticized the human relationists for their lack of "any awareness of the economic dimension."[19] In concluding that man was motivated by social and psychological satisfactions, the Harvard group lost sight of the whole man. They neglected the nature of work itself, focused instead on interpersonal relations, and thereby failed to find that man derived satisfactions from more than his fellowman.

In defense of the Hawthorne experimenters, Shepard has indicated that Carey overstated his case, in some instances supported the researchers' findings which he had criticized, and was wrong in rejecting the results of the Western Electric studies. Shepard maintained that Roethlisberger and Dickson's intent was to place monetary incentives in their proper perspective, i.e. as "carriers of social value."[20] Perhaps so, but many followers of the human relationists did not see this subtlety and this led to a rejection of economic motivators. Many of Carey's other criticisms remain unchallenged and, though critics often overstate their case, he served to bring new questions to some old findings.

[19] Peter Drucker, *The Practice of Management*, New York: Harper and Row, 1954, p. 279.
[20] Jon M. Shepard, "On Alex Carey's Radical Criticism of the Hawthorne Studies," *Academy of Management Journal*, Vol. 14, No. 1 (March, 1971), pp. 23–32.

Conclusions Regarding Social Man

Does everyone desire to participate in decision making, in group "games," and want to feel the comfort of security through belonging? Robert N. McMurry has maintained that "democratic management runs counter to human nature."[21] Some people prefer regimentation and are unwilling or unable to make positive contributions. Further, McMurry regarded group decision making as an illusion in which the autocracy of the group may be substituted for the autocracy of an individual. Group decisions stimulate the individual's dependency on the group and lead to conformity through denials of his own perceptions of reality because of a desire to conform to group pressures. In the interests of group harmony, disagreement may be stifled, thus reducing organizational innovation and progress. William H. Whyte has also decried the exaltation of the group to the detriment of the individual. For Whyte, the ethic of social man had its roots in three forms: (1) "scientism"; (2) "togetherness"; and (3) "belongingness." Whyte's criticisms were aimed at these three points: first, that advocates of the social ethic sought a science of man such as that available in the physical sciences; second, that the Mayoists sought to rebuild modern society along the same social bonds that were apparent in primitive societies; and finally, that the group was superior to the individual and all problems could be solved through collective efforts.[22] Consensus would replace creativity.

For Malcolm P. McNair, to speak of developing supervisory "human relations skills" often meant a "cold-blooded connotation of proficiency, technical expertness, calculated effect."[23] This danger of treating people with the same developed skills as one would develop for handling a machine reflected the idea of a cult of "people efficiency." McNair's indictment of the human relations approach was built around four themes: (1) that it ". . . encourages people to feel sorry for themselves, makes it easier to slough off responsibility, to find excuses for failure, to act like children"; (2) that it sapped individual responsibility by playing down the vir-

---

[21] Robert N. McMurry, "The Case for Benevolent Autocracy," *Harvard Business Review*, Vol. 36, No. 1, (January–February, 1958), p. 85.

[22] William H. Whyte, Jr., *The Organization Man*, Garden City, N.Y.: Doubleday & Co., 1956, p. 26, p. 40, *passim*.

[23] Malcolm P. McNair, "Thinking Ahead: What Price Human Relations?", *Harvard Business Review*, Vol. 35, No. 2 (March–April, 1957), pp. 15–23.

tues of self-discipline, will power, and self-control; (3) that it emphasized keeping everyone happy which resulted in conformity to group wishes and desires; and (4) that it developed a "one-sided" concept of the executive job. The executive needed more than "listening" and human relations skills to be effective in accomplishing organizational goals. In teaching human relations as a separate skill, McNair saw the dangers of compartmentalizing knowledge when in fact it should become an integral part of all managerial development, whether in marketing, management, or whatever. In essence, McNair concluded: "It is not that the human relations concept is wrong; it is simply that we have blown it up too big and have placed too much emphasis on teaching human relations as such at the collegiate and early graduate level . . . Let's treat people like people, but let's not make a big production of it."[24]

Many critics called for a better mix of managerial skills but one which would avoid the "evangelism" and the "mysticism" which so often characterized human relations training. Evangelism represented a thesis that only human relations could "save Western Civilization from impending doom".[25] The doom theme was an old one, having its roots in the revulsion of the Romantic philosophers at the perceived ravages of the Industrial Revolution. For social philosophers such as Durkheim, Mayo, and Toynbee, advancing technology and the specialization of labor destroyed social cohesiveness and yielded a loss of pride in work for mankind. Increased interpersonal competition and concern for material things destroyed primary groups, caused status anxiety, and created obsessive-compulsive reactions. The answer to "impending doom" was an evangelical zeal by the human relationists to play down material acquisitiveness, to rebuild primary groups, and to teach man to love his fellow man once more. The world could be saved by belongingness and man could once more find himself by losing himself in some larger entity. This mystical overtone, reflecting the Gestalt psychology of the totality, attributed wisdom to groups which could not be found in individuals. It was not the logic of efficiency but the ill-logic of sentiments which would save man from the brink. The moral uplift of scientific management had been efficiency; for the human relationists, it was belongingness and solidarity.

[24] *Ibid.*, p. 23.
[25] Knowles, p. 52.

The Mayoists were also placed under fire for a "promanagement antilabor bias." According to the critics, it was not man but management that the Mayoists sought to save. For example, Mary Barnett Gilson noted that:

> In all the more than six hundred pages describing the Western Electric experiments, costing hundreds of thousands of dollars and supported by some of the wealthiest groups of this country, no reference is made to organized labor except a short statement, unindexed, that it was so seldom mentioned by any workers that it was not considered sufficiently important to discuss. . .[26]

While it is true that the Mayoists made no reference to the role of organized labor, it would be unfair to conclude that this constituted an anti-labor bias. It was labor, the worker, who was the center of their concern when they called for the application of human relations skills.

The Critics: A Final Note

The multitude of criticisms against the Mayoist–human relations axis have been conceptualized into attacks on their premises, their methodology, and their conclusions regarding the nature and nurture of social man. In defense of the movement, Landsberger indicated that the Mayoists were much less dogmatic than the critics maintained and that they realized any conclusions "would bear the stamp of human imperfection."[27] According to Landsberger, the critics' attacks should have been directed toward those individuals and groups who seized upon the infant theories of human relations and attempted to fashion out of them "cookbook" techniques for management's handling of people. If this defense sounds familiar, it should; the Hoxie report noted that managers in practice grasped the techniques but not the philosophy of scientific management. Likewise, human relations as *the* means to avoid impending social, political, and industrial doom led to evangelic, missionary exhortations about "getting along with people." The results were frequently insincere, often abortive, and derisive terms like calling the human relationists "the happiness boys" were the result.

In response to the promanagement–antilabor bias, Landsberger

---

[26] M. B. Gilson, "Review of Management and the Worker," *American Journal of Sociology*, July, 1940, p. 101. See also Harold L. Sheppard, "The Treatment of Unionism in 'Managerial Sociology'," *American Sociological Review*, April, 1949, pp. 310–313.

[27] Landsberger, p. 49.

noted that the lag between the conduct of the interviews (1927–1932), and their publication (1939), explained the omission of unions. While *Management and the Worker* and the writings of Mayo omitted unions, Landsberger concluded that this did not automatically make them promanagement and antiunion. With respect to the omission of monetary incentives, Landsberger defended the researchers, as Shepard has, by stating that they did not omit them but instead held that wages were carriers of social value which should be viewed as only one aspect of a larger social phenomenon. In sum, Landsberger would conclude that the Hawthorne researchers were "not guilty," though they made their share of blunders, of most of the challenges of the critics. More serious challenges have been leveled since Landsberger's defense, especially the Carey analysis, and these pilgrimages to Hawthorne have served to bring a better perspective to the past.

SUMMARY

The critics have questioned a number of facets of the philosophy as well as the practice of the human relations–social man thesis. These were discussed in terms of attacks upon the premises, the methodology, and the conclusions regarding industrial man. The premises of Mayo and his associates were largely a product of the times, as we shall see in the next chapter. The methodology has only more recently been challenged and certainly leaves some doubt in terms of our modern insistence upon more rigorous research methods. However, the state of statistical knowledge at the time of the original experiments was rudimentary at best and we must recognize this state of the arts before issuing a wholesale indictment. In spite of all the limitations and shortsightedness, the Hawthorne experiments did signal a new direction in management thought. The experiments stimulated research, discussion, and a re-examination of managerial premises. In its time, the human relations movement witnessed all of the malpractices and misinterpretations to which any new idea usually falls prey. Today, the apogee of the movement has passed as the very research it stimulated is bringing fresh insights into human behavior.

18

Social Man in Retrospect

The ideas of men in the context of their times form an interesting topic for historical discussion. Within its cultural context, scientific management as the gospel of efficiency found its basis in the economic necessities of large scale corporate organizations, in the social sanction of individual achievement and the moral uplift of efficiency, and in political concern for national productivity and the conservation of resources. What can be said of the era from the advent of the Hawthorne experiments to the early 1950's? It has been postulated that management thought forms a more coherent picture when viewed in its changing cultural milieu of economic, social and political forces. Management is both a process in and a product of its environment. The social man era was an age of individual hopes dashed on the reefs of economic misfortune, of social collisions and maladies, and of political shifts heralding a transformation in traditional relationships. Though treated independently below, these cultural facets interacted to form the cultural milieu of social man.

THE ECONOMIC ENVIRONMENT: FROM DEPRESSION TO PROSPERITY

The "great crash" of 1929 found the winter of its discontent in earlier days. The 1920's were prosperous and characterized by price stability, a doubling of industrial productivity, and a 55 per cent rise in the real income of individuals.[1] Industrial efficiency

[1] David N. Alloway, *Economic History of the United States*, New York: Monarch Press, 1966, p. 29.

and mass production technology were holding costs down and increasing the purchasing power of the dollar. On the human front, economic and political chauvinism led to restrictions on immigration, largely at the behest of organized labor. Quotas were established for various nationalities and sources of cheap labor began to evaporate. As an economic corollary to the emerging political withdrawal and isolationism, America turned to protection tariffs with the Fordney-McCumber Tariff of 1922. For a short time, this protection afforded American industry and agriculture a respite from the rigors of competition. In the long run, American productive capacity began to outrun its ability to consume and, with foreign markets relatively closed, pressures began to build which would lead to corporate mergers and to excessive speculation. Installment buying and easy credit, though intended to stimulate consumption to take up the productive slack, instead increased personal indebtedness to a dangerously high level.

The 1920's also saw a wave of business consolidations. Antitrust legislation and Presidential activists had slowed the growth of trusts, pools, and holding companies but the post-war period saw a tripling in the rate of mining and manufacturing mergers. By 1925, the sixteen principal holding companies in the electrical energy field held 53 per cent of the nation's electrical productive capacity. Individuals like Samuel Insull were pyramiding company on company, borrowing and re-borrowing on the resultant leverage.[2] Corporations with over $80 million in assets controlled 80 per cent of the assets of stocks of corporations regularly traded on the New York Stock Exchange. In 1927, the two hundred largest non-financial corporations controlled over 45 per cent of the assets of all non-financial corporations.[3] According to Burns, the growth of giant enterprise led to a decline in the number of sellers, to a concentration of economic power in the hands of the few, and to a decline in competition.[4] This scramble for size to gain efficiencies of scale led to more consolidations, and big business was becoming Big Business. The public wanted a piece of this dynamic growth,

[2] An interesting account of the use of holding companies and their rise and downfall is Forrest McDonald, *Insull*, Chicago: University of Chicago Press, 1962.

[3] Gardiner C. Means, "The Growth in the Relative Importance of the Large Corporation in American Economic Life," *American Economic Review*, Vol. XXI (1931), pp. 10–42.

[4] Arthur Robert Burns, *The Decline of Competition*, New York: McGraw-Hill Book Co., 1936.

money was cheap, margin requirements were low, and it was this orgy of speculation that led to Black Friday, October 24, 1929. On that day, the stock market fell forty points and wiped out thirty billion dollars worth of inflated stock values.

For more than a decade following, all of American life was to be substantially changed by that crash which preceded the Great Depression. In 1929, forty-eight million persons were employed and the unemployment rate was 3.2%. By 1933, 30% of the nation's workers were without jobs.[5] Businesses were failing, unemployment rampant, incomes dropping, homes lost, family savings wiped out, and worst of all, national morale was at an all time low. Gone was the optimism of prosperity and promise; the old guideposts apparently had failed as "rags to riches" became the midnight pumpkin. Perhaps it was not the economic depression but the psychological one which left the lasting imprint on our forefathers.[6] Recovery from the economic morass was painfully slow, but from the social and psychological viewpoint, it was even slower. Feeling inept in adjusting to economic deprivation, people turned to the government for relief.

Attempts at Economic Recovery

The new political regime of Franklin Roosevelt promised freedom from fear, from want, and the other fears that bound America. President Hoover had tried the Reconstruction Finance Corporation in 1932 as a scheme to pump government funds into private business enterprise. President Roosevelt went much further with the "New Economics" of John Maynard Keynes. Keynesian economics was a challenge to the Protestant ethic dogma of thrift; Keynes held that savings which were withheld from consumption could lead to dislocation and underutilization of economic resources. Therefore the Federal Government should intervene and "prime" the pump to stimulate consumption and to provide for economic recovery. This new capitalism was also designed to destroy the financial control of Wall Street, to link government assistance with industrial capitalism, to aid agriculture and small business in the Progressive tradition, and to increase benefits to the workers who formed the chief electorate.

[5] Lloyd G. Reynolds, *Labor Economics and Labor Relations*, 4th ed., Englewood Cliffs, N.J.: Prentice-Hall, 1964, p. 339.

[6] See Caroline Bird, *The Invisible Scar*, New York: David McKay Co., 1966.

While Keynesians would hold that economic stimulation through government spending contributed to recovery, the Friedmanites have maintained that proper monetary action by the Federal Reserve could have prevented contraction of the money supply and allayed the Depression.[7] Robert Heilbroner concluded that World War II was the factor that really pulled America from its economic doldrums, not government pump-priming.[8] Economists may fuss and fume about proper remedial actions but in reality "what might have been" is a matter for other historians. The fact for management was that the government did become increasingly involved in economic life; though capitalism was preserved, with ownership and management remaining in the hands of private individuals, control and policy guidelines became more and more lodged in the hands of the dominant political party. The new concept of the corporation tied it more closely than ever before to the public interest with concomitant calls for "economic statesmanship" on the part of business leaders and for public regulation of corporate concentrations of power.

The Grass Roots and Bottom Up Movement

Economically it was to be the age of the "little man," the farmer, the worker, the small businessman, the unemployed, the hungry, and all others who were the waifs of economic misfortune. Somehow it was Wall Street and Big Business who were considered the primary contributors to the ills of the economy. Economic policy was to be from the "grass-roots" up in aiding the little man to counterbalance the concentration of power in Big Business. People were concerned that there was an economic elite and sought to democratize industry, to reduce power differentials, and to restore the influence of those at the base of the pyramid. Berle and Means noted the separation of ownership and management and pointed out that control was passing from the hands of owners to the hands of a select body of top corporate managers whose decisions affected the entire economy.[9] Kenneth Boulding warned of the moral dilemma caused by the conflict between the industrial

---

[7] Milton Friedman and Anna J. Schwartz, *The Great Contraction: 1929–1933,* Princeton, N.J.: Princeton University Press, 1965.

[8] Robert Heilbroner, *The Making of Economic Society,* p. 167.

[9] Adolf A. Berle, Jr. and Gardiner C. Means, *The Modern Corporation and Private Property,* New York: MacMillan Company, 1947.

aristocracy of a hierarchy of authority with the democratic ideal of equality.[10]   James Burnham foresaw that managers would become an elite ruling class in a "managerial society".[11]

For management scholars, the little man movement found its expression in "bottom up management," "multiple management," and participative leadership.   The Mayoists saw the root of economic problems in social problems.   For them, man's anomie was made manifest in his pessimistic reveries, in obsessive-compulsive behavior, in the turning inward of groups to protect themselves from management, and in the expressed needs of the workers to find social satisfactions on the job.   Once social solidarity was restored, primary groups rebuilt, communications channels opened, and social and psychological needs fulfilled, man could turn his efforts to being more productive.   Follett would certainly support this thesis in her call for depersonalizing authority, for integration, and for enlightened leadership.   Barnard indicated that an organization had to be efficient in terms of satisfying individual and group needs in order to be effective in meeting organizational goals.   Cooperation was a reciprocal process for both management and the worker.   From the "people and organizations" point of view, industrial problems were to be solved by democratizing the workplace and thereby improving human relationships within the organization.

Organization as the Answer

Whereas managerial concern for administrative structures to rationalize resource utilization dominated the first three decades of the twentieth century, industrial attention in the 1930's was primarily on survival.   For Mooney and Reiley, Brown, Gulick, Urwick, and others of the organizational bent, the solution resided in the proper, orderly arrangement of formal relationships.   People, preferring order and certainty, would function better within a well-structured system and management could better insure economic survival through the practice of sound organizational principles. In their cultural context, those who focused on people and those who focused on the organization were attempting to cope with the

[10] Kenneth E. Boulding, *The Organizational Revolution: A Study of the Ethics of Economic Organization*, New York: Harper and Row, 1953.

[11] James Burnham, *The Managerial Revolution*, New York: John Day Co., 1941.

massive social and industrial dislocations presented by the Depression.

The Depression delayed the development of any growth which would have moved industry into Phase III of Chandler's framework. Reduced sales and the general contraction in activity postponed any enlargement or elaboration of structures. However, the presence of excess productive capacity did stimulate interest in product diversification.[12] The advent of the war required industrial conversion to military production, and the post-war reconversion finally shifted the bulk of American industry into Phase III. Mobilization for the war effort had created both technological and managerial advancements. Vast productive resources had been gathered, training within industry had created a deeper pool of managerial talent, consumer products had been rationed, worker earnings were high, and the post-war era found America with a pent-up demand for products and services. With demand outrunning productive ability, America did not experience the anticipated post-war business slumps. The war had created new products, new technologies, new markets and a more highly skilled, broader-based labor force. Management thought was in transition in this era and the shift was from a production orientation to a top management viewpoint, which called for a changed executive role in balancing and coping with larger-scale enterprises and markets. Managers were seeking a broader, more flexible conceptual framework, a process of action upon which they could build for a more dynamic interplay of inputs and outputs. The work of R. C. Davis was cited previously to show this transition in thought; Henri Fayol was awaiting rediscovery, and others were writing with more emphasis on top management.

The post-war period promised a new era of prosperity, expansion, and diversification. The regained prosperity and the further growth of industry was to create a new focus in evolving management thought.

THE SOCIAL ENVIRONMENT: FROM BABBITT TO THE ORGANIZATION MAN

The economic temper of the times most certainly shaped the social values which came to dominate the period under analysis.

---

[12] Alfred Chandler, Jr., *Strategy and Structure*, p. 44.

Attitudes and aspirations are the founts of man's strength, and the crushing economic burden for many was a violation of the previously held precepts of abundance and success for Everyman. The 1920's had brought Madison Avenue to Peoria and Dubuque, and American productive ability and salesmanship presaged more than a car in every garage and a chicken in every pot. What happened to man's relations to man and the assumptions which guided his behavior in the troubled 1930's? Broadly viewed, two fairly distinct paths were reshaping social values: (1) a decline of the tenets of the Protestant ethic and the rise of a "social ethic"; and (2) a decline in the level of esteem given the businessman.

Shifting Social Values

The Lynds, in their famous study of the "typical" American city of the late 1920's, found a split in values between the "working class" man and the white collar man. For the worker, economic motives appeared to be primary:

> This dominance of the dollar appears in the apparently growing tendency among younger working class men to swap a problematic future for immediate "big money".[13]

While the workers measured social status by financial status and tended to hold to the traditional virtues of individualism, including a declining interest in belonging to organized labor, the businessmen represented a different outlook. The Lynds noted a decline in individualism among businessmen and a rapidly increasing conformity and "need to belong." In their follow-up study, made during the Depression, the Lynds found that "the insecurity during the depression has brought with it greater insistence upon conformity and a sharpening of latent issues."[14] Workers were turning to unions for collective action and businessmen combined to maintain the "open shop"; these "latent issues" sharpened class distinctions and engendered social bitterness. The economic catastrophe had brought about a shift in social values for the worker as well as the manager.

After the crash, of what value were the time-tested Protestant ethic virtues of thrift and hard work? Apparently nearly everyone

---

[13] Robert S. Lynd and Helen M. Lynd, *Middletown: A Study in Contemporary American Culture,* New York: Harcourt Brace Jovanovich, 1929, p. 81.

[14] Robert S. Lynd and Helen M. Lynd, *Middletown in Transition: A Study in Cultural Conflicts,* New York: Harcourt Brace Jovanovich, 1937, p. 427.

had been affected in some way, the loss of a job here, a savings account there, or a friend who had lost his shirt in the market. The new consciousness was that the disaster had struck the virtuous as well as the prodigals, the tycoon as well as the tyro, and the energetic as well as the feckless. People found their own fortunes intertwined with that of others in a pattern not subject to reason or justice. As time went on,

. . . there was a continuing disposition among Americans young and old to look with a cynical eye upon the old Horatio Alger formula for success; to be dubious about taking chances for ambition's sake; to look with a favorable eye upon a safe if unadventurous job, social insurance plans, pension plans . . . They had learned from bitter experience to crave security.[15]

This craving for security, this turning inward of man to his fellow man who shared the same tribulations, marked that generation as well as their children, and even perhaps another generation or more. Perhaps man has a natural reaction to form groups when faced with threatening circumstances—when these circumstances assume a major cultural impact, such as a depression, then man becomes more and more a group being. The presence of others must offer some psychological sense of relief under threatening or frustrating conditions. Erich Fromm has also noted this desire of man to escape the loneliness of standing alone. In Fascist Germany, to escape this loneliness, man turned to an authoritarian regime which made his decisions for him and which gave him a sense of identity, however evil it might have been. According to Fromm, this "need to belong" also pervaded American industrial life and an individual more frequently than not would be willing to give up self to conform to the group. While the Reformation and the Industrial Revolution drove man from the security of medieval life, enabling him to find freedom in the spiritual, political, and economic spheres of his life, industrialization created new threats to these new-found freedoms.[16] Man felt alone in the individualism of capitalism and the Protestant ethic and needed something larger than himself, God, the Nation, the Company, the Union, or Something with which to identify and lose self.

The conditions of the troubled 1930's must have compounded this desire for group affiliation as a source of strength. McClelland

[15] Frederick Lewis Allen, *The Big Change,* New York: Harper and Row, 1952, p. 132.

[16] Erich Fromm, *Escape from Freedom,* New York: Holt, Rinehart and Winston, 1941, pp. 7–10.

found in his studies that the need for achievement had increased in America from 1800 to 1890 but had decreased regularly since that date. The trade-off between the need for affiliation and the need for achievement took a dramatic shift from 1925 to 1950. In 1925, the need for affiliation was primarily a familial concern; by 1950, affiliation had become an *alternative* concern for economic achievement.[17]   By 1950 Americans were showing more concern for affiliative relationships and less concern for achievement.[18]

David Riesman and his associates have furnished additional evidence for this era by noting the shift from the "inner-directed" to the "other-directed" man. The inner-directed man represented the era of *laissez-faire* capitalism, the Protestant ethic, and emphasized self-direction and control. The "other-directed" man was characterized by high social mobility, emphasis on consumption rather than production, and on getting along and being accepted by others as the magic key to accomplishment.[19]   Riesman would call the Taylor period "job minded" and the other-directed man of the Mayoist era, "people-minded."[20]   For Riesman, the shift from the "invisible hand to glad hand" actually began about 1900. Up until that time *laissez-faire* and the Utilitarian philosophy of individualism had been the dominant force. After 1900, the closing of the frontier and restrictions on immigration began to bring less confidence in self-interest and a rise in confidence in "groupism."[21] The inner-directed man persisted for a period after 1900 but individuals began to feel more lonely in the crowd. One had to live where he was and was unable to move to a new frontier and to use the West as a safety valve. Most of the pressing problems of production began to disappear, and the problems of consumption became more apparent. Inner-directed individuals had to cope with a niggardly material environment; the new problems which arose following relative conquest of a hostile material environment were problems with people. The entrepreneur could deal face-to-face with most of his employees—he knew them, their problems, their likes and dislikes. Growth made industry less personal,

[17] David C. McClelland, *The Achieving Society*, p. 167.

[18] *Ibid.*, p. 166; and McClelland's "Business Drive and National Achievement," *Harvard Business Review*, Vol. 40, No. 4 (July–August, 1962), p. 110.

[19] David Riesman, Nathan Glazer, and Reuel Denney, *The Lonely Crowd*, New Haven, Conn.: Yale University Press, 1950, pp. 19–40.

[20] *Ibid.*, p. 151.

[21] *Ibid.*, pp. 151–152; and David Riesman, *Individualism Reconsidered*, New York: Free Press, 1954, p. 31.

replacing the personal style of the entrepreneur with the bureau-cratic style of the administrator. The personal touch of leadership was gone only to be replaced with the directives from the tech-nically trained specialists that an advanced industrial nation required. Social competence, the manipulation of people, began to assume a new importance, and technical skills were played down.

Individual loneliness in the organizational crowd led to the rise of "groupism" and social man. Progressive education began fitting the child to the group in the socialization process, and the parental socialization function was replaced by peer socialization. Small groups became the panacea for individual adjustment to the loneliness of industrialization. Getting along and being accepted was the magic key to accomplishment. A person was judged by what others thought of him, not what he thought of himself. The psychological gyroscope of inner-directed man began to waver and now needed the helping North Star of others.

The "Confusion of Souls"

Industrialization had not made man less religious but man found he could more easily segment his life into religious and non-religious duties. When God smiled on the division of labor, thrift, and success, man found a comfort in combining secular drives with spiritual grace. For one authority, the Depression caused a "con-fusion of souls" and a crisis for the Protestant ethic.[22] Self-help had failed and the notion of self-made man was rejected as the guarantee of economic order. Charity became a public rather than a private concern, and the power for the individual of the Prot-estant gospel of success fell into disfavor. Out of this confusion of souls and the debris of *laissez-faire*, the moral order needed to take on new dimensions. On the one hand there was the "mind cure" approach offered by Norman Vincent Peale in *The Power of Posi-tive Thinking*; on the other hand, the "getting along" cure of Dale Carnegie. Peale advised seeking the "inner power" of Christianity to cope with stress and crises. This turning inward helped man escape his loneliness and malaise by drawing upon the greater power of God. Carnegie established the personal-magnetism ethic

---

[22] Donald Meyer, *The Positive Thinkers: A Study of the American Quest for Health, Wealth and Personal Power from Mary Baker Eddy to Norman Vincent Peale*, Garden City, N.Y.: Doubleday & Co., 1965, pp. 233–237.

in 1936 with his *How to Win Friends and Influence People.*[23] This book, replete with "how-tos" of human relations, advised that the path to success resided in: (1) making others feel important through a sincere appreciation of their efforts; (2) making a good first impression; (3) winning people to your way of thinking by letting others do the talking, being sympathetic and "never tell a man he is wrong"; and (4) changing people by praising of good traits and giving the offender the opportunity to save face. Although *Management and the Worker* had not been published at that time, the Carnegie formula bore a striking resemblance to the rules the Harvard researchers laid down for the counselors in the interviewing program. For Carnegie the way to success was through winning the cooperation of others.

These "positive thinkers" stressed two ways out of the "confusion of souls": (1) drawing on the inward power of faith; and (2) drawing personal strength by winning the cooperation of others through personal magnetism. The social ethic of the times played down achievement by individual striving because the Protestant ethic had run its course. This new ethic was "others"-oriented with moral uplift coming not from efficiency but from getting along with others. For the most part, social man was sired, born, and nurtured in these trying times. Man sought belonging in the group, solace in association, and fulfillment in affiliation.

The Social Ethic

A second facet of this attempt to understand social man and his times must come through an analysis of the changing societal views toward the businessman and the manager. The businessman as represented in fiction may or may not be a barometer of his social esteem. Robert Kavesh has warned that the fictional businessman is generally portrayed in an unrealistic manner.[24] This is because of the writer's need to dramatize in contrasts and to gain sympathy for characters. While it would be impossible to hold the businessman to blame for the Depression era's hard times, it was evident

---

[23] Dale Carnegie, *How to Win Friends and Influence People,* New York: Simon and Schuster, 1936. Dale Carnegie was founder and president of the Dale Carnegie Institute of Effective Speaking and Human Relations.

[24] Robert A. Kavesh, *Businessmen in Fiction,* Hanover, N.H.: Amos Tuck School of Business Administration, 1955, p. 11. An exception that he noted, however, was Cameron Hawley's *Executive Suite.*

that he became through fictional writings the *symbol* of society's ills. The 1920's had canonized the businessman as hero and symbol of prosperity and the good life; when times turned turbulent, was it not fair to heap the blame on the "bankster" who robbed people of their homes and savings? While such charges were not entirely just, the businessman as portrayed in fiction undoubtedly became a convenient focal point for public wrath.

William G. Scott has noted that the novels of the 1930's and 1940's were of disillusionment with individualism. Individualism became futile and the novelists shifted the keynote to pleas for "humanitarianism and collectivism in the form of proletarian fiction".[25] The "hero" vanished to be replaced by a "they" who did things without reason and were beyond the control of mere mortals. "They" represented power, machines, and forces, not individual managers whom one could hold responsible. The corporation was a monster of oppression in which people and their lives were ground down piece by piece. Representative of this type of fiction were John Steinbeck's *Grapes of Wrath* and Nathaniel West's *A Cool Million*. For Steinbeck, it was not individuals but "they" who gave the migrants a hard time. For West, his hero of the Alger type found himself caught between the contending forces of "international bankers" and "world revolutionists" who slowly but surely destroyed his spirit of individualism and quest for free enterprise.

As the 1940's and 1950's unfolded, the manager completed the shift from the hero image by becoming more and more of an "organization man." In conformity there was security and the manager became a hero not because of "great or daring deeds, but because he tolerates grinding mediocrity and conformity".[26] In Marquand's *The Point of No Return*, Pawel's *From the Dark Tower*, and Sloan Wilson's *The Man in the Gray Flannel Suit*, the emphasis was on conformity and the futility of rebelling against the organization as a system. In Scott's thesis, these novelists portrayed the shift from the individualistic ethic to the "social ethic" in management literature. The reference point in the "social ethic" was the group and the collective nature of man in which

---

[25] William G. Scott, *The Social Ethic in Management Literature*, Atlanta: Bureau of Business and Economic Research, Georgia State College of Business Administration, 1959, p. 47.
[26] *Ibid.*, p. 50.

man found a need for collaboration and social solidarity. Not only did this occur in fiction, but also in the technical literature of Follett, the Mayoists, and others who were playing down the individual and reinforcing the group or collective nature of man.

The social ethic in fiction underscored conformity, depersonalization of the individual into a "they," and portrayed the corporation as a monster machine. In technical literature, the ideas of teamwork, participation, group decision making, small rather than large groups, committee management, the "interweaving of responsibilities," and democratic leadership were abundant. Scott's striking parallel between the fictional and technical writers of the social man era is food for thought. Taken together with the low esteem of the businessman as symbol of the corporate monster, it was understandable that the Mayoists and others sought to remodel organizations from the bottom up in order to meet man's needs. While the Mayoists and others would reform the organization through the group, the organizational engineers would reform the group through the organization. In their view, *Onward Industry!* was a rallying cry for coordinating and focusing group efforts, not to subdue the individual, but to release his potential. "Principles" were not only organizational rules, but also guides for human conduct toward a purpose. Mooney, Gulick, and others knew of man's need to belong and sought to provide that through organizational definition. To these writers, it was through structure and not catharsis that man could release his potential.

In another sense, some critics have held the business man and industrialization responsible for the ills of modern civilization. Intellectuals have maintained an uneasy truce with industrial life by idealizing agriculture and denigrating business. Jeffersonian and Jacksonian democracy were examples of the praise of an agricultural, small-unit, family-owned, ideal base of society. To be big was to be bad, and to live in the "city" was a sign of the decline of man. Why have the intellectuals idealized agriculture and sullied business? Kavesh perceptively noted that "the growth of cities is the history of business: the big business-man is the symbol of the city, and the city became the symbol of degradation."[27] This idea of non-city living still prevails; the first sign of success to the modern is the ability to escape the city by moving to the suburbs.

[27] Kavesh, p. 6.

Here he can escape the hurly-burly of the city and "farm" his 100 × 200 lot in some semblance of an agrarian existence.

Baritz has suggested that Mayo was one of those who was committed to an "Agrarian Golden Age":

> [Mayo] . . . believed that there was a mystical but direct relationship between farming and truth. . . . An industrial society, by definition, could not be virtuous, for as men lost sight of the soil they lost sight of nature; and in so doing, they lost sight of the meaning of life and fell victim to the glossy gadgetry of modern industrialism. For Mayo, then the problem of the modern factory was clear; how to make possible the re-creation of Agrarian Virtue, Agrarian Loyalty, and the Agrarian Sense of Community in the twentieth century's world of skyscrapers and subways, of smoke and steam?[28]

For Mayo, the answer was to rebuild social solidarity and collaboration through the small group. Once the communal integrity of agrarian life was re-established, man could cope with the evils of the city, the de-skilling of work, and the anomic de-personalization of factory routine. Perhaps the Australian Mayo was caught up in the American-Jeffersonian-Jacksonian democratic tradition. He was certainly influenced by Durkheim, who saw evils in industrial life much as Robert Owen had seen them in the early nineteenth century. While Durkheim admonished men to love one another unselfishly and Owen tried to build communal centers, Mayo accepted the parameters of industrialization and tried to rebuild man's interpersonal relations within that framework. The gloom of the Depression, World War II, and the threat of the atomic bomb would certainly cause Mayo to harken back to an Agrarian Golden Age in which man could find solace in small groups.

THE POLITICAL ENVIRONMENT: FROM FDR TO EISENHOWER

While the economic cycle had gone from the bust to boom and the social environment reflected increasing needs for affiliation, the political cycle saw an increasing role for government in individual and business affairs. No other period in American history has seen a political administration begin in such dire times, endure for such a long period, and cope with as many adversities as the tenure of Franklin Delano Roosevelt. Roosevelt, scion of a patrician family, cousin of former President Theodore Roosevelt, and paralyzed from the waist down by polio, brought a charisma to the

---

[28] Loren Baritz, *The Servants of Power*, p. 111.

American people in the depths of their despair. In his acceptance speech for the Democratic nomination, he had said "I pledge you, I pledge myself, to a New Deal for the American people." This became the slogan of the policies of the Roosevelt administration, which promised to reshuffle the old cards of society.

The New Deal

FDR saw as his first task that of restoring confidence to a stricken nation. A landmark of the lengths to which he went were the "first hundred days" (March 9, to June 16, 1933) in which a special session of Congress passed a multitude of bills enabling emergency legislation and giving Roosevelt tremendous political and economic powers. Roosevelt's keynote phrase, "The only thing we have to fear is fear itself," hoped to instill in the American people feelings of confidence and hope. In those first hundred days, legislation created such agencies as the Agricultural Adjustment Administration (A.A.A.), Civilian Conservation Corps (C.C.C.), Securities Exchange Commission (S.E.C.), Tennessee Valley Authority (T.V.A.), the Home Owners Loan Corporation (H.O.L.C.), the Federal Relief Act, the Railway Reorganization Act, the Federal Deposit Insurance Corporation (FDIC), and the National Industrial Recovery Act (NIRA).[29] The day of alphabet soup government had been created.

While some viewed the New Deal as "creeping socialism" and prophesied the end of capitalism, others saw the reforms as a necessary adjustment of capitalism while the motor was running in order to save free enterprise. Private enterprise endured, but in the process a lot of socialism did creep in. The restacking of the social, political, and economic order was to bring an activist role for government. Hands-off as a policy was defunct and the role of government increased in an effort to shift the balance of power as people perceived it from the financiers of Wall Street to the farmers, organized labor, and the "little man." One of FDR's "brain-trusters," Rexford Tugwell, wrote that the idyllic days of business doing what it willed was gone and that the new leadership of industry must recognize unions, democratize industry by encouraging participation, and keep in mind the "greatest good for the

[29] John Gunther, *Roosevelt in Retrospect*, New York: Harper & Row, 1950, pp. 278–280, and 283–287.

greatest number."[30] Tugwell felt that industry had failed to provide security for the working class and that government must fill this vacuum. The response to this craving for security was made manifest in a number of pioneering legislative acts: the Social Security Act of 1935 sought to provide for old-age assistance; the Fair Labor Standards Act of 1938 established a guaranteed minimum hourly wage for certain workers; and the Railroad Unemployment Insurance Act of 1938 was the first national unemployment protection. These and other acts marked the shift from Adam Smith's "invisible hand" to Riesman's "glad hand," from private to public charity, and from the Protestant ethic to the social ethic.

Augmenting the Position of Labor

The Roosevelt era was a bottom up view of society. The role of federal power achieved a new dimension in governmental-business relations that even the Progressives had not envisioned. The New Deal introduced a positive conception of public responsibility that emphasized federal responsibility for relief of want and employment, for individual security, for parity for farmers, for recognition of organized labor and for maintenance of industrial peace, and enlarged responsibilities for operation of the nation's credit system. It was a new age, a calling for a new balance of power which promised to restore society by: "new commitments, new interpretations of the American role."[31]

Of all the changes in the redress of power, none had more immediate significance for management thought than the new role for labor. The pro-management legal environment that prevailed in the 1920's and the reliance on union-management cooperation was abruptly altered in the 1930's. During this period, the New Deal addressed itself to remedying a perceived imbalance in labor-management relations and passed revolutionary legislation that greatly strengthened the position of organized labor. The first significant piece of labor legislation passed by the Congress was the Federal Anti-Injunction Act of 1932, more commonly referred to as the Norris-LaGuardia Act. This act, for all practical purposes, completely divested federal courts of injunctive powers in cases

[30] Rexford Guy Tugwell, *The Industrial Discipline*, New York: Columbia University Press, 1933, p. 158.

[31] Dexter Perkins, *The New Age of Franklin Roosevelt: 1932–1945*, Chicago: University of Chicago Press, 1957, p. 3.

growing out of a labor dispute. In 1933, Congress passed the National Industrial Recovery Act, the first in a series of New Deal enactments designed to lift the nation out of the depression of the 1930's. Section 7a of the NIRA, in similar but stronger language than that already existing in the Norris-LaGuardia Act, specifically guaranteed that "employees shall have the right to organize and bargain collectively through representatives of their own choosing . . . free from the interference, restraint, or coercion of employers. . . ." It further provided that "no employee and no one seeking employment shall be required as a condition of employment to join any company union or to refrain from joining, organizing or assisting a labor organization of his own choosing. . . ."

When the NIRA was declared unconstitutional by the Supreme Court in 1935 (*Schecter* vs. *U.S.*), Congress quickly replaced it with a law that was even more pleasing to organized labor. The National Labor Relations Act, more commonly known as the Wagner Act, was far more definitive in what it expected of collective bargaining than was the NIRA. The Wagner Act guaranteed employees "the right to self-organization, to form, join, or assist labor organizations, to bargain collectively through representatives of their own choosing, and to engage in concerted activities for the purpose of collective bargaining." In addition, it placed specific restrictions on what management could do by specifying five "unfair" management practices. To implement these provisions, the Act established a National Labor Relations Board which was granted the authority not only to issue cease-and-desist orders against employers violating the restrictions, but also to determine appropriate bargaining units and to conduct representation elections.

The passage of the Wagner Act marked a critical turning point in labor-management relations and created a new style of industrial unionism to supplant craft unionism. John L. Lewis, president of the United Mine Workers, led the fight for industrial unionism within the American Federation of Labor. Rebuffed, Lewis formed the Committee for Industrial Organization (known after 1938 as the Congress of Industrial Organizations) whose purpose came to be that of bringing workers into unions regardless of occupation or skill level. The newly founded CIO enjoyed almost instant success and was able to claim almost 4 million members as early as 1937. By 1941, virtually all the giant corporations in the mass-production industries had recognized the CIO-affiliated unions as bargaining agents for their employees. With the legal climate created by the New Deal legislation, union membership spurted from less than three million members in 1933 to more than eight million by 1939.

In retrospect, labor gained substantial power during the 1930's through legislation. The New Deal labor policy was part of a power-equalization drive designed to restore the voice of the "little man" in the industrial hierarchy. This new role for the worker fitted into the calls for teamwork, cooperation, and democratization of the workplace through worker participation. During the war, all shoulders were turned to the wheels of industry and differences temporarily laid aside. Employment regulation, such as through the War Labor Board, prevailed and in general enhanced the power of labor. After the war, numerous strikes led to the public opinion that labor had too much power and resulted in the passage of the Labor-Management Relations Act (Taft-Hartley Act) in 1947. While this act did bring about some redress in the balance of power, no longer was the employer able to pursue unilateral actions with respect to labor policies. In general, the whole environment of management had changed, not just with respect to labor, but also in all relations with government.

The political environment brought a new focus for management thought. The manager had a new set of variables with which to contend, new relationships to be managed, and a revised set of assumptions with respect to the balance of power. After World War II, the search for general administrative theory would emerge as a solution to the complexities of managing in the modern era.

SUMMARY OF PART III

Figure 18-1 depicts the cultural forces and the developments in the social man era. Scientific management was the dominant theme in the 1920's but there were the seeds of dissent of the revisionists and the beginnings made by sociologists and social psychologists who were bringing into play the ideas of behavioralism in management before the advent of the Hawthorne experiments. Mary Follett, though chronologically belonging to the scientific management era, served as an intellectual bridge to the emerging group approach to management's problems. The Hawthorne experiments and the subsequent writings of Mayo, Roethlisberger, Dick-

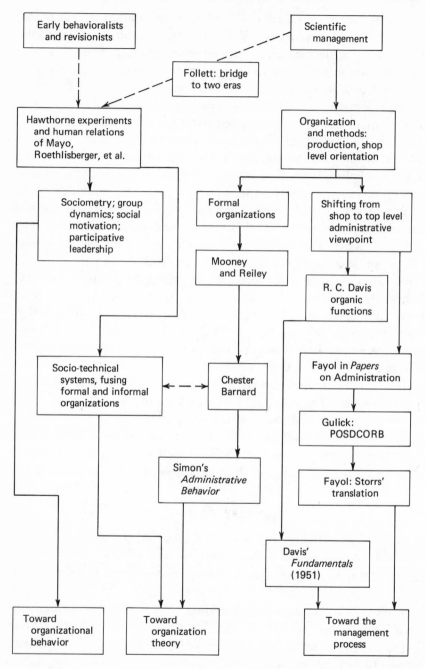

Fig. 18–1. Synopsis of the social man era

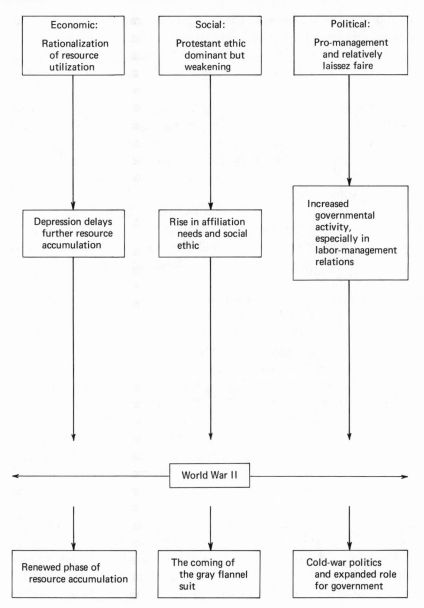

and its cultural environment.

son, and Whitehead brought the human relations movement to the forefront and led to the social man theme. The heirs of Taylor and scientific management found new dimensions in organizations and in the job of the manager in coping with the new *zeitgeist* of this era.

The Hawthorne experiments, beginning before but enduring through the early days of the Depression, brought about a shift in emphasis: (1) an increased concern for people rather than production; (2) exhortations to play down the rigidity of administrative structures in order to increase the fulfillment of man's needs; (3) less emphasis on wages and efficiency and more concern for man's interpersonal relations as motivators; and (4) more concern for the ill-logic of sentiments rather than the logic of efficiency. The human relations movement and the research which followed reflected several basic themes which were products of the cultural environment: (1) calls for social, human skills rather than technical skills; (2) emphasis on rebuilding man's sense of belonging through groups and social solidarity in order to overcome the "confusion of souls"; and (3) concern for equalizing power through unions, through participative leadership, and by fusing the formal organization with the social system of the factory.

The post-Hawthorne research assumed two separate yet congenial approaches: The "micro" researchers were establishing constructs for studying man-in-groups, were postulating a hierarchy of man's needs, and were viewing leadership as a group-interactive-situational phenomena. Along the "macro" branch, W. F. Whyte, George Homans, and E. W. Bakke were seeking to understand and to bring about an integration of the formal system with the informal system of sentiments, activities, and interactions. Each of these paths would lead to the "new humanism" and to the organization theory of the modern era.

Chronologically parallel to these developments in the human relations movement, the descendants of scientific management offered different types of solutions to the vexing problems of the Depression. Largely shop-management-oriented at the beginning, as in the case of R. C. Davis, this branch of management thought also began to assume new dimensions. On the one hand, organizational constructs were offered as one way out of the cultural impasse. Mooney and Reiley urged *Onward Industry!* and Chester Barnard presented a sociological study of the formal organization and attempted to synthesize these "formalists" with the human relationists with his "efficiency-effectiveness" dichotomy. Alongside the organizational approach to management's problems, the elements of a top level management viewpoint began to appear in the work of R. C. Davis, the translation of Fayol's process in the "Papers on Administration," and the efforts of Lyndall Urwick to synthesize principles of administration. A methods and analysis segment of scientific management was to receive increased recognition during World War II and would later emerge as operations research and management science in the modern era. Taken all together, the heirs of scientific management were establishing the foundations for the modern era of organization theory, the management process, and the search for quantification and systems in management.

In the cultural environment, management thought was shaped by the stressful times. Further economic growth was retarded by the Depression and the post-war boom was to create a need for a top-level administrative viewpoint. The Protestant ethic and the need for achievement, though not disappearing, declined in significance as man sought to find his identity and *raison d'être* through affiliation and getting along with others. People, not production, were the main concern of the administrator. Politically, an increased role for government and the growth, power, and legal protection afforded organized labor introduced new variables to be considered in managerial decision making. The world of management was much more complex than ever before with more advanced technology and communications, international markets, a broader-based, better-educated work force, and an increased awareness of the relationships between business and society. It was out of this age of confusion, trauma, and diversity that the modern era in management thought was about to begin.

IV

THE MODERN ERA

Nestled between the knowns of yesterday and the unknowns of tomorrow, the present is the twilight of history. It is difficult to put more recent developments in perspective; some years from now we will be able to look upon this era with the aid of historical analysis, see the course of progress after it has evolved, and be better able to place our contemporaries in a clearer perspective. It is not possible to examine the full extent of modern management writings for they are too diverse and too extensive for an in-depth analysis. Instead, we must be content to sketch the broad outlines of evolving management thought and try to perceive major trends, shifts, and influences in the modern era.

If one had to pick a general theme to depict the modern era, it would be one of a search for a Holy Grail, a quest to see which single or combination of "schools" of management thought have that authentic piece of the True Cross of management knowledge. In examining this modern diversity, we will analyze first the search for a unified body of knowledge through the "principles and process" approach to management. Next, the focus will be upon the evolution of a modern view of organizational humanism which will illustrate the search for harmony between the formal requirements of the organization and the informal dimensions of people in organizations. A search for order in management theory will be depicted as attempts to quantify variables in management decision making and efforts to bring order from chaos through general systems theory. These three objectives, unity, harmony, and order, characterize the quest of management scholars for a better understanding of the complex organizations and their societal interactions in the context of their environment. Finally, we will conclude by probing the lessons of history for evolving management thought. It is in this modern era that management thought experiences its adolescence of diversity and seeks the professional posture of maturity.

19

Principles and Process: The Search for Unity

Management scholars have sought to reduce the theory and practice of management to an orderly body of knowledge for some time. The "principles and process" approach represents one view of how a general theory of management might be developed. The management "process," that is, *what* the manager does in performing his job, provides a framework for theory. "Principles" allegedly describe *how* the manager should manage and represent building blocks for the body of knowledge. In Chapter 16 we saw an increasing concern for general management theory and postulated that this was necessitated by the further growth of organizations after World War II, by the proliferation of staff specialists, by the increased importance of new business functions beyond the realm of production and engineering, and by a greater awareness of relating management tasks to their more complex environment. If any one factor had to be chosen to explain the concern for a general theory, it had to be the increased number of variables to be taken into account in decision making. It was in this environment that management scholars turned from a shop-level management orientation to general management theory.

The first generation of the process approach to management thought consisted of the work of its intellectual progenitor, Henri Fayol; Ralph C. Davis and Luther Gulick were influenced by Fayol's elements and must be classified as "first generation" since their writings influenced more modern versions of the management process.   It was in the writings of these men that the functions of the manager were established as a recurring, interdependent cycle of activity which led to the accomplishment of organizational goals.   Though the elements included in the process differed among these authors, all saw management as a universal skill, applicable to all types of organizations and at all levels within the management hierarchy.   From these beginnings, new contributors whose names are more familiar to modern students began to reshape the existing body of management knowledge.   Less emphasis was placed on production management and more began to be placed on general management theory.

With this brief link to the past, the modern era of the process approach will be developed as: (1) the proliferation of "principles and process" approaches in a second generation of writers; (2) the appearance of some serious challenges to the nature and content of management education; (3) the increasing awareness of the environment and the responsibilities of managers; (4) the influx of ideas from the behavioral and quantitative sciences leading to a theory "jungle"; and (5) the development of systems theory in management as one hope for unity.   It was in this ebb and flow of ideas that the process approach to management theory was to be reshaped.

THE SECOND GENERATION

Variations In the Management Process

The first effort of a second generation of authors was that of William H. Newman of Columbia University.   In 1950, Newman had copyrighted materials as *Principles of Administration* which was later published as *Administrative Action: The Technique of Organization and Management.*[1]   Newman defined administration as "the guidance, leadership, and control of the efforts of a group of individuals toward some common goal" and developed a logical

---

[1] W. H. Newman, *Administrative Action: The Technique of Organization and Management,* Englewood Cliffs: N.J., Prentice-Hall, 1951.   Newman was president of the Academy of Management in 1951.

process of administration as a separate intellectual activity.[2] The elements in Newman's process were planning, organizing, assembling resources, directing, and controlling. For Newman, planning was determining what is to be done in advance of doing it. It "provides the basis for organization, assembling resources, direction, and control."[3] Planning involved recognizing the need for action, investigation and analysis, proposing action, and a decision. The outcome of the planning process was the development of three broad groups of plans: (1) goals or objectives, which defined purposes of organizational effort and made integrated planning easier; (2) "single-use plans" which established a course of action to "fit a specific situation and are 'used up' when the goal is reached"; and (3) "standing plans," which endured over time and were changed only as the occasion warranted. Newman's other elements of the process were:

[Organizing as] . . . grouping the activities necessary to carry out the plans into administrative units, and defining the relationships among the executives and workers in such units.

[Assembling resources as] . . . obtaining for the use of the enterprise the executive personnel, capital, facilities and other things needed to execute the plans.

[Directing as] . . . that vital step between preparation and actual operation; it is the issuing of instructions and otherwise indicating to subordinates what should be done.

[Controlling as] . . . seeing that operating results conform as nearly as possible to the plans.[4]

While Newman's version of the process was closely akin to Fayol's, it did have some unique features: (1) the distinction between the types of plans; (2) the "assembling resources" element; and (3) the treatment of coordination under directing rather than as a separate activity. Beyond this early contribution to the process approach, Professor Newman has made significant contributions to business policy and to the importance of objectives in "shaping the character" of an organization. He felt that the basic objectives of the firm should define its place or niche in the industry, define the firm's social philosophy as a business "citizen," and

[2] *Ibid.*, p. 1.
[3] *Ibid.*, p. 28.
[4] *Ibid.*, pp. 4–5. In his second edition (1963) Professor Newman substituted "Supervising" as a function instead of "Directing" and added motivation under supervising so that it included directing, motivating, and coordinating.

serve to establish the general managerial philosophy of the company.[5]

George Terry of Northwestern University was the first to call his book *Principles of Management.* Terry defined management as

the activity which plans, organizes, and controls the operations of the basic elements of men, materials, machines, methods, money, and markets, providing direction and co-ordination, and giving leadership to human efforts, so as to achieve the sought objectives of the enterprise.[6]

Terry's version of the process was:

[Planning as] . . . the determination of a proposed method of action. It is a methodic technique of looking ahead in order to anticipate possible hinderances and eliminate them before they take place.

[Organizing as] . . . the determination and arrangement of functions deemed necessary for attainment of the objective and an indication of the authority and responsibility assigned to individuals charged with the execution of the respective functions.

[Directing as] . . . the guidance of all efforts toward the stated objective. It points out the course to be followed. It identifies the channels through which each action is to take place.

[Co-ordinating as] . . . the orderly synchronization of efforts to provide the correct timing and sequence of execution resulting in harmonious and unified action to a common end.

[Controlling as] . . . the process of restraining, checking, and motivating efforts within desired channels so that the results achieved are within the designated limits established by the objective.[7]

Leading human efforts was a less definitive function but involved the utilization and development of an organization's personnel and required the proper application of influence so that every member of the organization desired to work toward organizational goals. Leading human efforts, treated apart from directing, involved more consideration of developing executives and developing proper attitudes in order to achieve results. In later editions, Terry combined the directing and leading human efforts functions into an "actuating" function which sought to instill a desire on the part of subordinates to internalize the organization's objectives. Later editions also stopped treating coordinating as a separate func-

---

[5] William H. Newman, "Basic Objectives Which Shape the Character of a Company," *Journal of Business of the University of Chicago,* Vol. 26, No. 4, (October, 1953), pp. 211–223; and the enduring policy book of W. H. Newman and James P. Logan, *Business Policies and Central Management,* (now in its sixth edition), Cincinnati, Ohio: South-Western Publishing Co., 1971.

[6] George R. Terry, *Principles of Management,* Homewood, Ill.: Richard D. Irwin, 1953. Terry was president of the Academy of Management in 1961.

[7] *Ibid.,* pp. 5–8, p. 81, pp. 147–8, and p. 267.

tion and recognized it as an integral part of all functions. Starting with six functions, Terry later reduced them to four; planning, organizing, actuating, and controlling. With respect to "principles," Terry defined a principle as "a fundamental statement providing a guide to action."[8] The principles, like Fayol's, were lighthouses to knowledge and not laws in the scientific sense. Among the principles that Terry offered were these:

[Principle of service:] The fundamental objective of every enterprise is service; it is eminently practical, stable, and sound.

[Principle of objective:] A clear and complete statement of the objective is essential, and it should be made known to all members of an enterprise affected by it so that management activities can be directed in a unified, orderly, gainful, and effective manner.

[Principle of Leadership:] Skillfully applied leadership contributes tremendously to smooth and successful group efforts.[9]

There were also principles and subprinciples for planning, policies, decision making, organizing, and other managerial tasks. In this first of many "principles and process" texts, Terry had established the theme for a search for a unified body of knowledge.

In 1954, the Department of the Air Force prepared and distributed for training and operational purposes Air Force Manual 25-1, *The Management Process*.[10] This manual established five functions of management: planning, organizing, coordinating, directing and controlling. Objectives, or "missions" in the military sense, were stressed a great deal as the foundation stone of all managerial activity. This governmental interest in the process was significant for two reasons: (1) it signaled a further interest in the study of management as a separate activity; and (2) it was recognition of the universality of management beyond the previous emphasis on the study of management in the business concern.

Management by Objectives

Outside the notion of a Fayolian process approach to management, Peter Drucker made an enduring contribution to understanding the role of the manager in a business society. In contrast to the "functions" of the manager which were prevalent in the process texts, Drucker developed three broader managerial func-

[8] *Ibid.*, p. 9.

[9] *Ibid.*, p. 54, p. 56, and p. 229.

[10] *The Management Process*, Air Force Manual 25–1, Washington, D.C.: United States Government Printing Office, 1954.

tions: (1) managing a business; (2) managing managers; and (3) managing workers and work. According to Drucker, in every decision the manager must put economic considerations first and management could justify its existence only through the economic results it produced:

> . . . management has failed if it fails to produce economic results. It has failed if it does not supply goods and services desired by the consumer at a price the consumer is willing to pay. It has failed if it does not improve or at least maintain the wealth producing capacity of the economic resources entrusted to it.[11]

Drucker recognized that there may be non-economic consequences of managerial decisions, such as happiness and improved community welfare, but he felt that these were by-products of the emphasis on economic performance. In striving for economic results, the first function of "managing a business" was of an entrepreneurial character, innovative in the Schumpetrian sense of creating markets and products rather than being passive and adaptive. The second function of "managing managers" introduced the notion of "management by objectives." Without explicit recognition of the fact, Drucker followed Mary Follett's idea of depersonalizing authority and obeying the law of the situation:

> A manager's job should be based on a task to be performed in order to attain the company's objectives . . . the manager should be directed and controlled by the objectives of performance rather than by his boss.[12]

Management by objectives was to replace management by drive, and control was to be self-control rather than control from above. Knowing the objectives of his unit and those of the enterprise, the manager could direct his own activities:

> The only principle that can do this is management by objectives and self control . . . it substitutes for control from outside the stricter, more exacting and more effective control from the inside. It motivates the manager to action not because somebody tells him to do something . . . but because the objective needs of his task demand it.[13]

In the third managerial function of managing the worker, Drucker advised treating the human as the most vital resource of the firm,

---

[11] Peter F. Drucker, *The Practice of Management*, New York: Harper and Row, 1954, p. 8.
[12] *Ibid.*, p. 137.
[13] *Ibid.*, p. 136.

engineering the work to fit the worker, giving the worker more control over his job, and restoring challenge and "wholeness" to the job.

". . . Getting Things Done Through Others"

While Drucker focused primarily on the practical aspects of management, others were continuing to further the use of the process to find management theory. Harold Koontz and Cyril O'Donnell of the University of California at Los Angeles defined management as "the function of getting things done through others."[14] This definition reflected the Storrs' rendition of Fayol's *administrer* as management and the Koontz and O'Donnell definition became one of the more widely held views of the task of management.[15] Koontz and O'Donnell furthered the Fayolian notion of the universality of management and sought in their book to provide a conceptual framework for the orderly presentation of the principles of management.

According to Koontz and O'Donnell, the manager was known by the work he performed, and that was planning, organizing, staffing, directing, and controlling. These authors pointed out that some authorities maintained that these functions were exercised in the sequence given, but in practice the manager actually used all five simultaneously. Therefore, Koontz and O'Donnell discussed the functions in a different sequence—namely organizing, staffing, directing, planning, and controlling:

[Organizing was] . . . the establishment, with necessary authority and with provision for coordination, of relationships between persons assigned the performance of specialized tasks for the achievement of enterprise objectives.
[Staffing] . . . encompasses the recruiting, selection, training, promotion and retirement of managers.
[Directing] . . . embraces those activities which are related to guiding and supervising subordinates.
[Planning was the] . . . function which involves the selection, from among alternatives, of enterprise objectives, policies, procedures, and programs.

[14] Harold Koontz and Cyril O'Donnell. *Principles of Management: An Analysis of Managerial Functions.* New York: McGraw-Hill Book Co., 1955, p. v. and p. 3. Koontz was president of the Academy of Management in 1963.
[15] In 1963 Koontz and O'Donnell defined management "as the accomplishment of desired objectives by establishing an environment favorable to performance by people operating in organized groups." (p. 1); and in 1968 as "the design or creation and maintenance of an internal environment in an enterprise where individuals, working together in groups, can perform efficiently and effectively toward the attainment of group goals." (p. 1).

[Controlling involved] . . . the measurement and correction of the performance of subordinates in order to make sure that enterprise objectives and the plans devised to attain them are accomplished.[16]

Koontz and O'Donnell stressed that each of these functions contributed to organizational coordination. However, coordination was not a separate function itself but was the result of effective utilization of the five basic managerial functions. In this first book, Koontz and O'Donnell offered a number of principles: in organizing, for example, "the principle of parity of authority and responsibility" and "the principle of unity of command"; in planning, "the principle of strategic factors"; and so on. The Koontz and O'Donnell principles and process approach has been an enduring, integral part of the search for a systematic body of management knowledge.

With the Koontz and O'Donnell offering and a revision by George Terry in 1956, the process appeared to be settling down to a four-function analysis of planning, organizing, directing, and controlling. Characteristic of this development was that of Dalton McFarland (of the Michigan State University) who interpreted management as a process by which resources were combined in achieving organizational goals. Management was performed by an executive who was "a person in an organization who possesses rank, status, and authority which permit him to plan, organize, control, and direct the work of others."[17] McFarland's effort reflected a greater concern for consideration of strategic and tactical factors in decision making, setting objectives, and in concern for the human resource as a utilizer of all other resources.

A Final Note

The period 1958–1960 marked a significant turning point for the evolution of the process school of management. Before examining the multitude of forces which would bring a number of changes to management theory, let us try to summarize and visualize the first and second generations of the search for theory

---

[16] *Ibid.*, pp. 83, 301, 36, 34 and 545. This order was changed in subsequent editions (1959, 1964, and 1968) to planning, organizing, staffing, directing, and controlling.

[17] Dalton E. McFarland, *Management Principles and Practices*, New York: Macmillan Company, 1958, p. 42 (revised editions in 1964 and 1970). Professor McFarland was president of the Academy of Management of 1965.

through the process.   In retrospect, the process approach was an attempt to identify management as a distinct intellectual activity which was universal in nature.   The search was for a generally agreed upon body of knowledge which could be distilled into principles and hence would lead to a general philosophy or theory of management.   The need for theory was evident: wider markets, advanced technology, widespread use of specialists, and larger, more intricate organizational forms demanded a more precise manner of handling human and physical resource problems.   The underlying technical, human, and managerial problems of the early factory system still were present but the fund of managerial talent needed to be expanded to handle ever increasing masses of resources in ever increasing numbers of business, governmental, and other types of organizations.   The search for unity through the process was the suggested answer to these problems.

As the process approach evolved, it began in classic simplicity with Fayol and Davis, became more diverse in the functions presented by Gulick, Newman, and Terry, and then began to settle down with more widespread agreement among AFM 25-1, Koontz and O'Donnell, and McFarland (Figure 19-1).

Of the managerial functions presented, planning, organizing, and controlling achieved the greatest agreement as to their applicability.

Managerial Functions	Fayol (1916)	Davis (1934)	Gulick (1937)	Newman (1951)	Terry (1953)	AFM 25-1 (1954)	Koontz and O'Donnell (1955)	Terry (1956)	McFarland (1958)
Planning	√	√	√	√	√	√	√	√	√
Organizing	√	√	√	√	√	√	√	√	√
Coordination	√		√	√	√	√			
Controlling	√	√		√	√	√	√	√	√
Command	√								
Directing			√	√	√	√	√		√
Leading Human Efforts					√				
Actuating								√	
Staffing	√*		√				√		
Assembling Resources				√					
Reporting			√						
Budgeting			√						

*Staffing was subsumed under the organizing function by Fayol.

Fig. 19–1.   The first and second generations.

A fourth function of the specified role of the manager in putting the bits and pieces together, starting the system, and keeping it together was a source of much disagreement in terminology. For some it was directing, for others supervising, leading, actuating, or whatever. Staffing, which Fayol had subsumed under organizing, was achieving some recognition as a separate function either explicitly for the human resource or more generally under the heading of "assembling resources." Coordination began and endured as a separate managerial function until 1954; afterwards, it became an integral part of the entire process. While scholars were settling down by 1958 to some degree of unanimity about the job of the manager, new developments in education, in other disciplines, and in the environment of management were beginning to impinge upon the process school and would lead to some changing notions about the manager's job.

RESHAPING THE PROCESS APPROACH

The forces that were to reshape the first and second generations of the process came from a variety of sources. As an overview we will examine: (1) some challenges to both business and management education; (2) an increasing awareness of environmental forces on the role of the manager; and (3) the profusion of inputs from quantitative methods and the behavioral sciences which would lead to the management theory "jungle." Following the discussion of these ideas, we will see that the third generation of the process approach began to take on some new dimensions.

Challenges to Management Education

In 1959, two reports on business education appeared which would have a significant impact on the development of management thought. Unlike the study of education by Morris Cooke for the Carnegie Fund in 1910, these reports were taken more seriously by educators. The Ford Foundation commissioned and financed a study by Robert A. Gordon of the University of California (Berkeley) and James E. Howell of Stanford University.[18] Likewise, the Carnegie Corporation sponsored a study by Frank

---

[18] R. A. Gordon and J. E. Howell, *Higher Education for Business*, New York: Columbia University Press, 1959.

C. Pierson of Swarthmore College.[19]   Although the authors of the two reports exchanged information, they reached their conclusions independently and both reports were sharp indictments of the state of business education in the United States.   Both reports noted that schools of business administration were in a state of turmoil in trying to define just what should be taught and how it should be done.   By adhering to outworn precepts of education, the business schools were not preparing competent, imaginative, flexible managers for an ever changing environment.   Schools overemphasized "vocationalism," *i.e.*, training for specific jobs, rather than preparing broadly educated individuals for maximum future growth in a business career.

While most schools claimed to be engaged in "professional education," the Gordon and Howell report questioned whether or not business was or could be a "profession."   They suggested four criteria for defining a profession:

First, the practice of a profession must rest on a systematic body of knowledge of substantial intellectual content and on the development of personal skill in the application of this knowledge to specific cases.   Second, there must exist standards of professional conduct, which take precedence over the goal of personal gain. . . .   A profession has its own association of members, among whose functions are the enforcement of standards, the advancement and dissemination of knowledge, and, in some degree, the control of entry into the profession.   Finally, there is some prescribed way of entering the profession through the enforcement of minimum standards of training and competence.[20]

Applying these criteria, the authors found that business was developing a body of knowledge and moving toward meeting the first criterion.   However, it had no clearly defined standards of conduct beyond those embodied in the law; it had no governing body or association; and there were no prescribed entry avenues for a business career.   Failing on criteria two, three, and four, and partially satisfying the first criterion, business was not a profession. The authors concluded that business was beginning to resemble a profession and they were hopeful that further progress in defining standards and systematizing knowledge would move business toward the "professional" end of career spectrums.

The path to developing a profession resided in changing the

[19] F. C. Pierson, *The Education of American Businessmen: A Study of University-College Programs in Business Administration*, New York: McGraw-Hill Book Co., 1959.
[20] Gordon and Howell, pp. 69–70.

content of the business school curriculum. More stress should be placed on a general education, especially in the humanities and the liberal arts; on an expansion of requirements in mathematics; and on extended study in the behavioral and social sciences. For management education, Gordon and Howell noted that there were at least four different aspects of the field of organization and administration: (1) managerial problem solving through the scientific method and quantitative analysis; (2) organization theory; (3) management principles; and (4) human relations.[21] Each played a part in the study of management and the authors recommended some integration of these ideas into a sequence of courses which would better prepare future leaders rather than leaving them with a fragmented picture of the tasks of management. Beyond the management area, the authors made numerous recommendations in other functional areas of business, in graduate education, and in teaching methodology. In total, both the Gordon and Howell and the Pierson reports were calling for a new shape in education for management and for business. Both reports led to scholarly introspection, debate, and a gradual reshaping of the area of study encompassed under the title of "management."

Increasing Environmental Awareness

The Ford and Carnegie reports instigated a host of changes in management curricula and thought. It must not be presumed that managerial awareness of its environment began in 1959 but it does appear that these reports provided a new stimulus for some old ideas. While an extensive analysis is not possible at this point, certain areas will be examined to show the changing views of the manager *vis-à-vis* his environment. The more significant changes came in quests for a profession of management, for a philosophy of management, for ethics, and for social responsibility in business. In practice, these four areas were interacting as scholars and practitioners sought a way out of diversity and a more solid foundation for systematizing managerial knowledge and behavior and for relating the business organization to its larger environmental context.

The notion of a profession or of being a "professional" has always connoted status beyond the ordinary. Business has been considered a base occupation by many cultures, by the Greeks and

21 *Ibid.*, pp. 179–182.

Romans especially, and those associated with business would prefer to be recognized as a more integral part of society and regarded as an essential part of carrying out societal goals. If business or management could be regarded as a profession, then the manager would feel that his role in society would be held in higher esteem. The 1960's witnessed an ever increasing body of literature on the pros and cons of management and business as a profession. Partially inspired by the Carnegie and Ford reports, partially a reaction to some highly questionable pricing practices in the electrical industry, and in part due to a deep concern for relating business to society, scholars sought to meet the missing criteria which would raise business to the level of a profession. Joseph Towle suggested that the Master of Business Administration degree be recognized as constituting the minimum prerequisite for entering the profession of management;[22] later, Professor Towle edited a volume of readings with the intent of integrating ethics into the "emerging profession of management."[23] The term "professional" began to crop up more frequently in articles and books as scholars proposed to treat management as a profession.[24] The aura was one of optimism and the theme presented was that through advancing knowledge, in professional associations for setting standards, and through ethical codes, management could truly become a profession.

A philosophy of management would be attractive to a management profession. Philosophy should serve to order knowledge, to provide values and premises, and to provide an epistemology or an answer to the question "how do we know?" R. C. Davis stated:

> The problem of greatest importance in the field of management is and probably will continue to be the further development of the philosophy of management. A philosophy is a system of thought. It is based on some orderly, logical statement of objectives, principles, policies and general methods of approach to the solution of some set of problems.[25]

[22] Joseph W. Towle, "The Challenge that Management is a Profession," in Paul Dauten (ed.) *Current Issues and Emerging Concepts of Management*, Boston: Houghton Mifflin Co., 1962, pp. 323–327. Towle was President of the Academy of Management in 1960.

[23] Joseph W. Towle (ed.), *Ethics and Standards in American Business*, Boston: Houghton Mifflin Co., 1964, especially Parts Four and Five.

[24] For example, see Louis A. Allen, *The Management Profession*, New York: McGraw-Hill Book Co., 1964; and Theodore Haimann, *Professional Management*, Boston: Houghton Mifflin Co., 1962.

[25] Ralph C. Davis, "Research in Management During the '50's," in Arthur E. Warner (ed.), *Research Needs in Business During the '50's*, Bloomington, Ind.: Business Report #13, 1950, p. 32.

For Davis, the premises of an American philosophy of management would be built upon private capitalism, the epistemology would be the spirit of scientific management, and orderly knowledge could be provided by sound business objectives and policies.[26] John Mee has stated that a management philosophy of the future "should provide managers and administrators with concepts, a scale of values, and a means to settle them without hindering the flow of economic and social progress."[27] Other scholars have taken various views of management philosophy, from pragmatic to metaphysical, and, though no clear-cut philosophy has emerged, the search continues for a deeper rationale and an orderly framework for management thought.[28]

Ethics, or agreements about codes of personal and interpersonal conduct, has been a subject of philosophers since time immemorial. Business transactions, so deeply imbedded in trust and confidence in one's fellow man, have been an integral part of this search for guides to conduct beyond the question of legal boundaries. The anti-trust prosecution of a number of electrical manufacturing companies in 1960 for price-fixing, coupled with the need for ethics in professionalism, touched off a number of inquiries into business ethics; the ferment has not abated to this day. The areas of inquiry were many: market collusion, conflict of interests, the morality of power, "reasonable" profits, advertising, and interpersonal relations, to name only a few. Father Baumhart revealed that more than 50 per cent of the businessmen he interviewed believed that other businessmen would violate a code of ethics, if one existed, if they thought that they would go undetected.[29] While everyone would agree on the need for a code of ethics, the literature fails to reveal any clear-cut unanimity of opinion about what exactly would be the standards and the content of such a code. Would the code

[26] Ralph Currier Davis, "Frederick W. Taylor and the American Philosophy of Management," *Advanced Management*, vol. 24, No. 4 (December, 1959), pp. 4–7. Also see: Stewart Thompson, *Management Creeds and Philosophies*, New York: American Management Association, 1958.

[27] John F. Mee, *Management Thought in a Dynamic Society*, New York: New York University Press, 1963, p. 84. Mee was president of the Academy of Management in 1952.

[28] An excellent review of the literature and some questions which must be posed for management philosophy are discussed in William D. Litzinger and Thomas E. Shaefer, "Perspective: Management Philosophy Enigma," *Academy of Management Journal*, Vol. 9, No. 4 (December, 1966), pp. 337–343.

[29] Raymond C. Baumhart, "How Ethical are Businessmen?" *Harvard Business Review*, Vol. 39, No. 4 (July–August, 1961), p. 19.

be applicable to an industry, a nation, a world? Would it be founded upon some Judeo-Christian or other religious base, or upon the "situation," or whatever? While the debate continues, this quest for ethics has revealed the challenges to management's desire to be a profession and to relate effectively to its environment.[30]

Social responsibility, or a broader concept of "business and society," has represented a fourth area in this increasing awareness of the manager's environment. The idea of a business or corporate "conscience" or of some awareness of the impact of decisions upon a broader environment is an old one. Robert Owen, Henry Gantt, Oliver Sheldon, and even "robber barons" like John D. Rockefeller and Andrew Carnegie held notions of social responsibility, service to the community, or a stewardship of wealth. To a large extent, post-World War II concern for social responsibility grew out of the criticisms of business during the Depression and from those who felt that too much power was concentrated in the hands of too few businessmen. Many have held that social responsibility should be commensurate with social power:

. . . if power and responsibility are to be relatively equal, then the avoidance of social responsibility leads to a gradual erosion of social power. To the extent that businessmen do not accept social responsibility opportunities as they arise, other groups will step in to assume these responsibilities.[31]

For the advocates, business has a stake in societal development and must give as well as partake of the largesse. They argue that profits may be foregone to some extent but that the long-run benefits will outweigh the costs, *i.e.* "social responsibility is good business." The alternatives to accepting responsibility could be more government intervention or further criticisms of business. In part, acceptance of social responsibility takes some of the wind out of the sails of the critics.

The question of what to include in social responsibility is a broad one and extends into hiring the hard core unemployed, to corporate giving to education, research, and other philanthropies,

---

[30] Suggested readings for a deeper inquiry would include: Thomas A. Petit, *The Moral Crisis in Management*, New York: McGraw-Hill Book Co., 1967; Raymond Baumhart, *Ethics in Business*, New York: Holt, Rinehart and Winston, 1968; Alvar and Carol J. Elbing, *The Value Issue of Business*, New York: McGraw-Hill, Book Co., 1967; and Robert T. Golembiewski, *Men, Management, and Morality: Toward a New Organizational Ethic*, New York: McGraw-Hill Book Co., 1965.

[31] Keith Davis, "Can Business Afford to Ignore Social Responsibility?" *Management Review*, Vol. 49 (July, 1960), p. 59.

to the firm as a citizen of the community, to air and water pollution abatement, and a host of other questions.[32] Not everyone agrees with the idea of social responsibility; such individuals hold that the business organization is an economic institution. To take on non-economic, social goals would violate the interests of the stock-holders, result in business imposing its views on others, and would be fundamentally subversive in a free enterprise economy.[33] The controversy will continue and our discussion here must be confined to a historical summary. The intent has been to show that these four factors, professionalism, philosophy, ethics, and social responsibility, were interacting to reshape the course of management thought. Together with the challenge to management education, a greater awareness of the environment of the manager and his responsibilities would have a large impact on management thought in the 1960's.

The Generation Gap

The new wine that was testing the strength of the principles and process container came not only from the educational and societal critics but also from an increasing accumulation of empirical research and new advances in other areas. From the social and behavioral scientists, new notions were arising about individual and group behavior and the human relationists were evolving toward different interpretations of man at work. March and Simon wrote *Organizations* (1958); modern organization theory was emerging. The former production management–engineering approaches were availing themselves of more elaborate mathemati-

[32] The literature of social responsibility and business and society is quite vast. For openers, see Richard Eells, *The Meaning of Modern Business,* New York: Columbia University Press, 1960; Richard Eells and Clarence Walton, *Conceptual Foundations of Business,* Homewood, Ill.: Richard D. Irwin, 1961 and 1969; Joseph W. McGuire, *Business and Society,* New York: McGraw-Hill Book Co., 1964; William T. Greenwood (ed.), *Issues in Business and Society,* Boston: Houghton Mifflin Co., 1964; Paul T. Heyne, *Private Keepers of the Public Interest,* New York: McGraw-Hill Book Co., 1968; and Keith Davis and Robert L. Blomstrom, *Business and Its Environment,* New York: McGraw-Hill Book Co., 1966.

[33] For examples of the critics, see: Milton Friedman, *Capitalism and Freedom,* Chicago: University of Chicago Press, 1962; Theodore Leavitt, "The Dangers of Social Responsibility," *Harvard Business Review,* Vol. 36, No. 5 (September–October, 1958), pp. 41–50; and Charles F. Phillips, Jr., "What is Wrong with Profit Maximization?" *Business Horizons* (Winter, 1963), in W. E. Schlender, W. G. Scott, and A. C. Filley (ed.), *Management in Perspective,* Boston: Houghton Mifflin Co., 1965, pp. 121–131.

cal models and tools and attempting to quantify the management equation. General systems theory, still inchoate, was establishing some rudimentary notions about the nature of the universe and its parts. While each of these modern developments will be dealt with in greater depth in Chapters 20 and 21, it is easy to visualize the forces that were reshaping the process approach (Figure 19-2).

While the Gordon and Howell report had noted the diversity of approaches to the study of management, it was Harold Koontz who delineated the differences and applied the catchy label of the "management theory jungle."[34] It was in this jungle that the gap between the second and the subsequent generations became painfully obvious. Koontz noted there were six main groups or "schools" of management thought:

1. The *management process* school "perceives management as a process of getting things done through and with people operating in organized groups." Often called the traditional or universalist

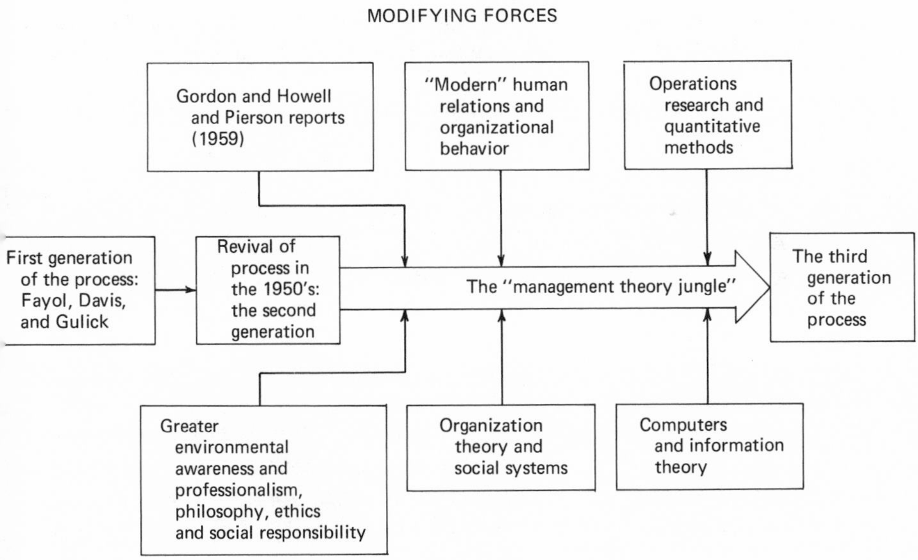

MODIFYING FORCES

Fig. 19–2. The generation gap.

[34] Harold Koontz, "The Management Theory Jungle," *Journal of the Academy of Management*, Vol. 4, No. 3 (December, 1961), pp. 174–188. See also: Harold Koontz, "Making Sense of Management Theory," *Harvard Business Review,* July–August 1962, pp. 24–30.

approach, this school was fathered by Henri Fayol and sought to identify and analyze the functions of the manager in order to bridge management theory and practice.

2. The *empirical* school identified management as the "study of experience" and used case analyses or Ernest Dale's "comparative approach" (in *The Great Organizers*) as vehicles for teaching and to draw generalizations about management. The basic premise of this school was that by examining the successes and failures of managers, understanding of effective management techniques would be furthered.

3. The *human behavior* school, variously called the human relations, leadership, or behavioral sciences approach, sought to study management as interpersonal relations since management was getting things done through people. This school used psychology and social psychology to concentrate on the "people" part of management.

4. The *social system* school saw management as a system of cultural interrelationships in which various groups interacted and co-operated. The sire of this approach was Chester Barnard and its adherents drew heavily upon sociological theory.

5. The *decision theory* school concentrated on analyzing and understanding who made decisions, how they were made, and the entire process of a selection of a course of action from among various alternatives. Economic theory, and especially the theory of consumer choice, represented the intellectual foundations of this approach to management.

6. The *mathematical* school viewed management as a "system of mathematical models and processes." This approach included the contributions of operations researchers, operations analysts, or management scientists who thought that management or decision making could be "expressed in terms of mathematical symbols and relationships."[35]

Koontz conceded that each of these schools had something to offer to management theory but suggested that the student of management should *not confuse content with tools*. For instance, the field of human behavior should not be judged the equivalent of the field of management, nor should a focus on decision making or mathematics be considered as encompassing the entire area of analysis. Preferably, each of these areas would provide insights and methods to aid the manager in performing his tasks and hence

[35] The preceding analysis was adapted from *ibid.*, pp. 177–182.

were tools and not schools. The causes of confusion and the "jungle warfare" between the various approaches were many: (1) "the semantics jungle" of varying uses and meanings of such terms as organization, leadership, management, decision-making, etc.; (2) problems in defining management as a body of knowledge since the term was used under such varying circumstances and in a variety of situations; (3) the "*a priori* assumption" or the tendency for some to cast aside the observations and analyses of the past since they were *a priori* in nature; (4) the misunderstanding of principles through trying to disprove a whole framework of principles when one was violated in practice; and (5) the "inability or unwillingness of management theorists to understand each other" caused by professional "walls" of jargon between disciplines and personal and professional desires to protect their own idea. or cult.[36] Koontz was hopeful that the jungle could be disentangled if these problems could be resolved.

The Quest for a Denouement

A direct result of the jungle article was a symposium of distinguished teachers and practitioners of management at the University of California, Los Angeles campus, in 1962. Koontz was the conference chairman and financial support came from the McKinsey Foundation and the Western Management Sciences Institute. The objective of the seminar was to convene a group of "eminent scholars with diverse research and analytical approaches to management, as well as perceptive and experienced practitioners of the managerial art from business, education and government."[37] Ernest Dale launched the conference by questioning the universality of management principles. Dale, deemed one of the "empirical school" by Koontz, put forth two arguments to refute the universal thesis: first he stated that the three best managed organizations (according to Jackson Martindell) were the Standard Oil Company of New Jersey, the Roman Catholic Church, and the Communist Party. Applying the doctrine of universality then meant that an executive "merry-go-round" of these three chief executives was possible. Since this was obviously not true, the

---

[36] The above is based on *ibid.*, pp. 182–186.
[37] Harold Koontz (ed.), *Toward a Unified Theory of Management*, New York: McGraw-Hill Book Co., 1964, p. xi.

"universality and transferability of management" was therefore negated.[38] Finally, Dale held that the notion of a universal manager was contradicted by actual experience. Businessmen faced great frustration when assuming government posts and military men going into industry were chosen for their value in securing government contracts and not for any managerial ability they might have.[39]

Dale's attack on the universalists was only the opening salvo. Roethlisberger was less critical, recognized the shortcoming of behavioral research, but felt that a general theory was possible if researchers turned some attention to explaining what previously had been found through experimentation.[40] Harvard University's Robert Schlaifer, representing the decision theorists, stated that he was "convinced that decision theory is not and never will be a *part* of a theory of management."[41] Herbert Simon disagreed with the Koontz jungle from the onset. Simon maintained that there was no jungle, no semantic confusion, and was "exhilarated by the progress we have made . . . toward creating a viable science of management and an art based on that science".[42] According to Simon, management theory was far from being a jungle and was becoming a beneficiary of and a contributor toward systems theory. The study of complex systems required a variety of inputs, from empiricists, decision theorists, behavioralists, *et al.* and the future of management held forth the promise of a synthesis in management science.

From these diverse views, further discussion yielded few new insights. In reporting his observations of the discussions, Tannenbaum noted that semantics were a major problem and that people preferred to "play it safe" by using their own jargon and speaking only from familiar ground. Simon defended the use of jargon as marking the growth of a discipline which needed a new vocabulary to express new ideas. R. C. Davis challenged Dale's description of

[38] *Ibid.,* pp. 26–27.

[39] *Loc. cit.* For a more comprehensive analysis of Dale's criticisms of the universalists, see E. Dale, *The Great Organizers,* New York: McGraw-Hill Book Co., 1960, pp. 5–11. A summary and analysis of more recent research may be found in John B. Miner, *Management Theory,* New York: Macmillan Co., 1971, Chapters 6, 7, and 8.

[40] *Toward a Unified Theory,* pp. 41–67.

[41] *Ibid.,* p. 68.

[42] *Ibid.,* p. 79.

a "classicist"; others engaged in extensive attempts to define terms; and Wilfred Brown capsulized much of the conference sentiment when he said: "Frankly, gentlemen, I have not been able to follow much of what's been said in the discussions."[43]

As Koontz concluded, "Semantic confusion was evident throughout the discussions."[44] As a denouement, Koontz proposed an "eclectic approach" which would maintain management as a discipline of its own but one which would enable management to support itself by drawing upon relevant findings of many other disciplines. Koontz was still hopeful that the functions of planning, organizing, staffing, directing, and controlling would form the core of the management discipline and, when buttressed by eclecticism, that the process approach would lead to a general theory. The U.C.L.A. symposium was indicative of the incoherent state of management theory. Perhaps the seminar topic should have been sub-titled "Is Anybody Listening?" Academicians could understand only those from their own specialty, practitioners could not understand academicians, and vice versa.

Koontz's perceptive analysis of the existing state of management theory in 1961 and the U.C.L.A. symposium encouraged a renewed interest in principles, universality, semantics, and other pressing problems in the search for a unified theory of management. In response to the jungle, some authors proposed new schemes although others were content to support the traditional, process approach while decrying the criticisms of the behavioralists. Waino W. Suojanen suggested that functional management theory (the process school) was appropriate to only certain types of organizations and that management must be viewed in biological terms as evolving toward more use of quantitative and behavioral sciences because of changing technology, the changing needs of people, and new types of research and development oriented organizations.[45] From his retirement home in Australia, Lyndall Urwick joined the fray and questioned Suojanen's implication that the

[43] *Ibid.*, p. 231. Mr. Brown was president of the Glacier Metal Co., Ltd., where a number of organizational systems studies were made.
[44] *Ibid.*, p. 238.
[45] Waino W. Suojanen, "Management Theory: Functional and Evolutionary," *Journal of the Academy of Management*, Vol. 6, No. 1 (March, 1963), pp. 7–17. For a similar thesis, see: Donald Austin Woolf, "The Management Theory Jungle Revisited," *Advanced Management Journal*, Vol. 30, No. 4 (October, 1965), pp. 6–15.

theories of the behavioral scientists were evolutionary and hence destined to supersede the functional theories of management.[46]

Some individuals were optimistic that a general theory could be developed. Frederick thought that, by drawing upon the best of all schools of thought, a coherent body of management thought could be developed along the same lines as Lord Keynes' *General Theory of Employment, Interest and Money*.[47] One author developed a taxonomic matrix patterned after the Periodic Table which would aid in classifying management concepts in order to aid the development of a general theory.[48] Gordon suggested a multiple approach to the problem, including an "ecological" approach, which would fuse various schools into a larger process of administration.[49]

The pessimists were in a minority, or at least less vocal. In addition to Suojanen's notion that the evolution of the behavioral sciences would supersede the functional approach, George S. Odiorne posited that management situations were too complex for precise principles and propositions that would yield a sound theory.[50] Others indicated that researchers and authors interjected too many of their own value judgments and worked from diametrically opposed premises and that these facts of academic reality seriously hampered any hope for unification.[51]

To a great extent, the controversy only proved what Koontz

[46] Lyndall F. Urwick, "The Tactics of Jungle Warfare," *Journal of the Academy of Management*, Vol. 6, No. 4 (December, 1963), pp. 316–329. Col. Urwick also attacked the behavioral scientists for contributing to much confusion in semantics and for rejection of past pioneering concepts. See Lyndall F. Urwick, "Have We Lost Our Way in the Jungle of Management Theory?" *Personnel*, Vol. 42, No. 3 (May–June, 1965), pp. 8–18.

[47] William C. Frederick, "The Next Step in Management Science: A General Theory," *Journal of the Academy of Management*, Vol. 6, No. 3 (September, 1963), pp. 212–219.

[48] Authur C. Laufer, "A Taxonomy of Management Theory: A Preliminary Framework," *Academy of Management Journal*, Vol. 11, No. 4 (December, 1968), pp. 435–442.

[49] Paul J. Gordon, "Transcend the Current Debate on Administrative Theory," *Journal of the Academy of Management*, Vol. 6, No. 4 (December, 1963), pp. 290–303. Gordon was President of the Academy of Management in 1969. A later, similar scheme to reconcile and integrate human and organizational values may be found in Edwin B. Flippo, "Interactive Schemes in Management Theory," *Academy of Management Journal*, Vol. 11, No. 1 (March, 1968), pp. 91–98.

[50] George S. Odiorne, "The Management Theory Jungle and the Existential Manager," *Academy of Management Journal*, Vol. 9, No. 2 (June, 1966), pp. 109–116.

[51] See Orlando Behling, "Unification of Management Theory: A Pessimistic View," *Business Perspectives*, Vol. 3, No. 4 (Summer, 1967), pp. 4–9.

had set out to do, that is, to show that there was a theory thicket. Often the proposed methods of disentanglement only led to more rain and the further growth of foliage. The jungle has not yet been penetrated, the machetes are becoming somewhat duller, and the hope for unity is still the Holy Grail.

THE THIRD GENERATION

Principles and process writers in the 1960's were the offspring of this era of diversity. If one were to choose a theme for their efforts, it would be that of integration, the search to bring various differing views into the process fold. Two facets of the third generation were apparent: (1) the eclectic "readings book" approach; and (2) the integrated process approach.

The Eclectics

One barometer of the confusion over defining just exactly what was the proper study of management was reflected in the number of "readings" books in the late 1950's, carrying over into the 1960's. The notion of a collection of articles by various authorities under the editorship of one or more men was not a new idea, for example, C. Bertrand Thompson and Harlow S. Person edited some excellent materials on scientific management. Thereafter, collections became less in vogue until a number of them started to reappear about 1958. The suggested explanation for this phenomenon is that these were attempts to provide vehicles for teaching management in the face of diversity in management knowledge.

The readings were generally eclectic, allowing the instructor or student to pick and choose if he preferred or to allow overall exposure to a number of ideas. Fremont Shull offered a collection encompassing defining the nature of management, approaches to management, and the functions of the manager; Richards and Nielander adopted a slightly different framework but dealt with developments in human relations, decision theory, and operations research as well as some of the managerial functions; Koontz and O'Donnell provided readings on management theory and managerial functions; and William Greenwood offered an interdisciplinary collection in response to the outcome of the U.C.L.A.

symposium.[52] Books of readings have continued throughout the 1960's and have provided one way of offering a diversity of views which would make management education more eclectic.

The Integrators

Principles-of-management texts also followed this theme of integrating diversity. Jucius and Schlender stated the objective of their book was "to present an eclectic picture of the manager."[53] Within the process framework, they sought to build more philosophy, behavioral, and decision theory ideas into the traditional approach. In collaboration with Summer, W. H. Newman put forth another effort at the process approach. Managing was ". . . getting things done by working with people and other resources . . ."[54] This required the manager to coordinate the activities of others and, therefore, management was a *social* process. Albers sought an "interdisciplinary" approach which would integrate such diverse areas as group dynamics, operations research, economic theory, electronic data processing, etc.[55] Haynes and Massie also took the interdisciplinary path and aimed "to relate traditional treatments of management and modern quantitative and behavioral research".[56] Haimann took the traditional functions of management and essayed to bring the contributions of the behavioral sciences into a conceptual framework of professionalism.[57]

The University of Florida's William Fox conceptualized one of the more unique offerings with "an integrated functional approach".

[52] Fremont A. Shull, Jr. (ed.) *Selected Readings in Management,* Homewood, Ill.: Richard D. Irwin, 1958. Revised with Andre L. Delbecq in 1962. Max D. Richards and William A. Nielander (ed.), *Readings in Management,* Cincinnati, Ohio: South-Western Publishing Co., 1958, revised in 1963 and 1969. Richards was president of the Academy of Management in 1967. Harold Koontz and Cyril O'Donnell (eds.), *Readings in Management,* New York: McGraw-Hill Book Co., 1959; revised in 1968. William T. Greenwood, *Management and Organizational Behavior Theories: An Interdisciplinary Approach,* Cincinnati, Ohio: South-Western Publishing Co., 1965.

[53] Michael J. Jucius and William E. Schlender. *Elements of Managerial Action,* Homewood, Ill.: Richard D. Irwin, 1960, p. vii. Jucius was president of the Academy of Management in 1950.

[54] William H. Newman and Charles E. Summer, Jr., *The Process of Management,* Englewood Cliffs, N.J.: Prentice-Hall, 1961, p. 9.

[55] Henry H. Albers, *Organized Executive Action,* New York: John Wiley and Sons, 1961; revisions were retitled *Principles of Management* and appeared in 1965 and 1969.

[56] W. Warren Haynes and Joseph L. Massie, *Management: Analysis, Concepts and Cases,* Englewood Cliffs, N.J.: Prentice-Hall, 1961, p. v (revised edition in 1969).

[57] Theo Haimann, *Professional Management,* Boston: Houghton Mifflin Co., 1962.

Fox wished to emphasize the *interaction* of the traditional management functions and stated that "managers must plan for planning activity, organize for it, and control it, and they must perform these same functions for control."[58]   Further, Fox brought in recent developments in quantitative and behavioral research to supplement the traditional functions.   Justin G. Longenecker sought "a blending of the newer concepts in organizational behavior with classical theory".[59]   Ernest Dale spent relatively little time on organizational behavior and devoted more space to management pioneers and new developments in computers and operations research.[60]   Franklin Moore remained more in the traditional stream but also emphasized to a great extent the organizing function and the effects that organization theory was having on modern business.[61]   Flippo attempted an integration of traditional and behavioral approaches to management by conceptualizing his analysis along the lines of "formal planning," "the human element" in planning; "formal organization," "informal organization," and so on using the formal-informal dichotomy.[62]   Richards and Greenlaw set out to integrate traditional concepts with quantitative and behavioral concepts and also reflected the growing importance of systems and information theory by viewing an "organization as an information-decision system."[63]   Reflecting more of a behavioral approach, Hicks essayed "to integrate the findings of behavioral science with classical theories of management . . . [and to] explain how managers can profitably use quantitative techniques of analysis in organizational problems."[64]   Filley and House have sought more empirical evidence and attempted to "make operational some of the relevant findings from research in the literature of sociology,

[58] William M. Fox, *The Management Process: An Integrated Functional Approach*, Homewood, Ill.: Richard D. Irwin, 1963, p. vii.

[59] Justin G. Longenecker, *Principles of Management and Organizational Behavior*, Columbus, Ohio: Charles E. Merrill Publishing Co., 1964, p. vii.

[60] Ernest Dale, *Management: Theory and Practice*, New York: McGraw-Hill Book Co., 1965, revised in 1969.   Dale was president of the Academy of Management in 1968.

[61] Franklin G. Moore, *Management: Organization and Practice*, New York: Harper & Row, 1964.   Moore was president of the Academy of Management in 1956.

[62] Edwin B. Flippo, *Management: A Behavioral Approach*, Boston: Allyn and Bacon, 1966 (revised in 1970).

[63] Max D. Richards and Paul S. Greenlaw, *Management Decision Making*, Homewood, Ill.: Richard D. Irwin, 1966, p. vii.

[64] Herbert G. Hicks, *The Management of Organizations*, New York: McGraw-Hill Book Co., 1967, p. vii.

psychology, political science, and economics, as well as that of business management itself."[65]

It is impossible to explore in full the work of each of the preceding authors, but the intent has been to characterize the management process approach in a period of transition during the 1960's. From the basic work of Fayol, subsequent generations have sought to bring greater depth, a broader scope, and a better conceptual framework to management theory. Those who were characterized as the third generation sought this framework in the process but it was to be supplemented by an interdisciplinary flavor.

THE FOURTH GENERATION

It would be presumptuous to conclude that the fourth generation has supplanted the third. The fourth generation label is merely an expository device, a conceptual handle to reflect what many have come to view as the most recent entry in the management theory sweepstakes.

The Systems Approach

General systems theory, actually beginning in 1937 with the ideas of Ludwig von Bertalanffy, was finally achieving recognition in general management theory in the 1960's. The origin and development of general systems theory will be examined at length in Chapter 21; it is sufficient to note here that the systems framework represented a newer quest for a general theory of management. In 1963, two separate publications marked the appearance of the systems approach to the manager's job. Seymour Tilles suggested that an organization was not merely a social system, nor an information-decision system, but an open-ended system of many interrelated parts.[66] Using the systems approach, the manager could define system objectives, establish criteria for evaluating systems performance, and better relate the firm to a variety of environmental systems. In essence, Tilles was using the systems framework to bring diverse subsystems into an integrated whole and also recog-

---

[65] Alan C. Filley and Robert J. House, *Managerial Process and Organizational Behavior,* Glenview, Ill.: Scott, Foresman and Co., 1969, preface.

[66] Seymour Tilles, "The Manager's Job: A Systems Approach," *Harvard Business Review,* Vol. 41, No. 1 (January–February, 1963), pp. 73–81.

nizing the influences of the external environment on managerial decision making.

Johnson, Kast, and Rosenzweig built upon the pioneering work of Bertalanffy and sought to integrate general systems theory and the process approach to management.[67]   These authors postulated that "managing by system" was a philosophical notion as well as a practical reality and that this blending of systems theory and management theory would lead to more effective management. Beyond these efforts, other authors sought to recast the principles and process approach into the general systems theory framework. Voich and Wren presented a view of the manager "as the motivating and linking mechanism in a *resource system* in which he plans, organizes, controls, and administers the resources available to him."[68]   For these authors, the organization was an interacting complex of physical, human, and information resources which could be viewed conceptually and managed as an input-output system.   Professor Sisk's approach was to combine "the familiar and traditional analysis of the management process . . . with the newer systems concept of management."[69]   Professors Haimann and Scott sought "to integrate the older, more traditional functional approach to management with newer contributions from systems theory and the behavioral sciences."[70]   This spilling over of systems theory into the traditional process approach has reflected an increasing concern for the increasingly complex environment of management and for an incorporation of behavioral, quantitative, information-theory, and systems-theory concepts into the traditional framework.

Comparative Management

Another facet of the search for theory has been the attempt to analyze and integrate administrative concepts from cross-cultural, cross-institutional, and cross-disciplinary points of view.   This movement, variously called "comparative management" or "com-

[67] Richard A. Johnson, Fremont E. Kast, and James E. Rosenzweig, *The Theory and Management of Systems,* New York: McGraw-Hill Book Co., 1963 (revised in 1967).

[68] Dan Voich, Jr., and Daniel A. Wren, *Principles of Management: Resources and Systems,* New York: Ronald Press Co., 1968, p. v.

[69] Henry L. Sisk, *Principles of Management: A Systems Approach to the Management Process,* Cincinnati, Ohio: South-Western Publishing Co., 1969, p. iii.

[70] Theo Haimann and William G. Scott, *Management in the Modern Organization,* Boston: Houghton Mifflin Co., 1970, p. vii.

parative administration," has been a reaction to the growth of multinational business organizations and to the need for management knowledge in such diverse fields as nursing, education, government, industry, librarianship, and other managerial settings. Various conferences have been held in attempts to bring together scholars from many disciplines and professions in order to find out what administrative concepts may be held in common.

The main thrust of interest in comparative management came with publications and conferences in 1965. Richard Farmer and Barry Richman were among the first to develop a "model" which would identify the critical elements in the management process as they applied to individual firms in varying cultures.[71] Negandhi and Estafen suggested three key variables of management "philosophy," "process," and "effectiveness" as they applied to cross-cultural settings.[72] The Silver Anniversary annual meeting of the Academy of Management in 1965 was devoted to the theme of "comparative administration" and Preston LeBreton, as president of the Academy in 1966, started a task force to further explore how comparative management theory could be expanded and refined. Since that time, LeBreton has continued to lead this search to so generalize management theory that future leaders would be trained to understand the "political, economic, cultural, and personal factors which influence the creation, behavior, and success of organizations."[73] While the 1962 U.C.L.A. symposium seemed more concerned with intra-management theory unity, the comparative management approach has sought a broader base across cultures, across professions, and across disciplines.[74] Viewed as an emerging phenomenon, this approach has been heavily influenced by general systems theory in management. Despite the relative newness of comparative management, it evidently has developed its

[71] R. N. Farmer and B. M. Richmann, *Comparative Management and Economic Progress,* Homewood, Ill.: Richard D. Irwin, 1965.

[72] Anant R. Negandhi and Bernard D. Estafen, "A Research Model to Determine the Applicability of American Management Know-How in Differing Cultures and/or Environments," *Academy of Management Journal,* Vol. 8, No. 4 (December, 1965) pp. 309–318.

[73] Preston P. LeBreton (ed.) *Comparative Administrative Theory,* Seattle: University of Washington Press, 1968, p. 377.

[74] See also: Ross A. Webber, *Culture and Management: Text and Readings in Comparative Management,* Homewood, Ill.: Richard D. Irwin, 1969; and J. Boddewyn, *Comparative Management and Marketing,* Glenview, Ill.: Scott Foresman and Co., 1969.

own theory thicket;[75] only future research will answer the question of whether or not Fayol's universality of management applies to a broader context.

A Final Comment

The preceding analysis has focused on the evolution of the process approach to management theory without examining in depth the rich body of literature in the modern era. Of course the task of writing history is never done, for each day brings new ideas, new evidence, and new ways of examining the tasks of the manager. It is difficult for the modern, so steeped in his own daily activities and so influenced by the current press of today's ideas, to sit back and put them in perspective. The zoom lens of history often leaves the near present slightly out of focus.

Despite these admitted limitations, the last twenty years of developments in the principles-process school still show a steady evolution. The changes have not been so much in the basic nature of the traditional functions of the manager as in the refinement of these ideas through experience, experiment, and discussion. Planning has evolved from a production planning–scheduling idea to a broader, organizational-systems-wide phenomenon. The notion of management by objectives has received increasing attention since Drucker's early work and more stress has been placed upon managerial performance appraisal by "results."[76]

Interest in long-range planning and planning theory has gained headway and the notion of planning for a system of orderly flows of resources rather than for traditional business functions has represented a new conceptual format for the planning process.[77] One new budgeting technique, Planning-Programming-Budgeting Systems (PPBS), has emerged from the systems concept to provide a means for allocating and focusing resource efforts on pro-

---

[75] See Hans Schollhamer, "The Comparative Management Theory Jungle," *Academy of Management Journal,* Vol. 12, No. 1 (March, 1969), pp. 81–97.

[76] George S. Odiorne, *Management by Objectives: A System of Managerial Leadership,* New York: Pitman Publishing Co., 1965.

[77] See Preston P. LeBreton and Dale Henning, *Planning Theory,* Englewood Cliffs, N.J.: Prentice-Hall, 1961; George A. Steiner, *Managerial Long-Range Planning,* New York: McGraw-Hill Book Co., 1963; D. W. Ewing, *Long-Range Planning for Management,* New York: Harper and Row, 1964; and E. Kirby Warren, *Long-Range Planning,* Englewood Cliffs, N.J.: Prentice-Hall, 1966.

gram objectives.[78] In brief, the planning function has evolved to a more refined state of knowledge in which more variables are taken into account, more information can be digested, and a broader planning format is possible.

The organizing function has moved from analysis of formal structures to reflect more of the informal organization, the idea of a socio-technical system, and the matrix and project methods of organizing for research and development activities. The staffing function has reflected increasing concern for executive development and succession and has begun to treat the problem as one of "human resource administration" rather than personnel management. Directing, leading, actuating—whatever the designation—has collected the findings of the behavioralists and placed more emphasis on participatory leadership, on motivation, and on communication. Controlling has become more concerned with the human problems caused by control systems, has brought in cybernetic or feedback concepts from information theory, and has moved to appraisal by results within the systems concept. From the early work of Henri Fayol and throughout the various generations, the process approach has become more eclectic, more interdisciplinary, but unity in theory has not yet been attained.

SUMMARY

Post-World War II management found renewed interest in general administrative theory. The development of expanded markets, the technological advances which followed wartime research, and the continued growth of organizations required managers to operate on a sounder theoretical base. Management was to become more than providing for production operations, more than merely business management, and more than the straightforward performance of a limited number of activities. It was in this environment that scholars and practitioners sought to provide management principles and an intellectual framework for managing through the process approach. The early 1950's found a wide variation in terminology, especially with respect to directing or

[78] For further information, see: David I. Cleland and William R. King, *Systems Analysis and Project Management,* New York: McGraw-Hill Book Co., 1968, Chapter 6; and David Novick (ed.) *Program Budgeting* (second edition) New York: Holt, Rinehart and Winston, 1969.

leading, and the second generation began to refine the Fayolian functions to fit modern organizations. Simplicity did not reign, however, as other areas spilled over into the process by contributing mathematical models, findings from the behavioral sciences, and the cybernetics of the computer age. The "jungle" was widely debated and the 1960's were characterized as an age of attempted integration of various new ideas into the traditional functions. The quest for unity has continued through the systems approach and comparative management. This unity has not come; perhaps it never will. Only the future and the hindsight it affords will bring this search into a better perspective. But the search continues, as it should, and if any lessons are to be learned from history, it is that we must learn to break down the walls of academic jealousy, to develop a better appreciation of our intellectual heritage, and to realize that we occupy only one point in time. Synthesis will come as we learn better to relate the technical and human problems of organizations.

20

Organizational Humanism: The Search for Harmony

Apace with the search for unity in management theory, modern behavioralists were gathering the harvest of the Western Electric and other researchers and sowing a new crop of ideas for managerial cultivation. The roots of concern for man in organizations may be traced historically to the "humanists" of the Renaissance who called for the overthrow of monolithic church authority, the participation and enlightenment of the citizenry, the breakup of rigid social structures, and the rediscovery of *man* as a unit of study. Throughout the preceding pages, we have seen varying views and assumptions about man *vis-à-vis* the organization. Robert Owen admonished the factory owners to pay as much attention to their "vital machines," their workers, as to their physical machines. Taylor, so often maligned by the modern behavioralists, was concerned with individual development and provided the roots for the empirical investigation of man's behavior when he wrote: "There is another type of scientific investigation which should receive special attention, namely, the accurate study of the motives which influence men."[1] The industrial psychology of Hugo

[1] F. W. Taylor, *Principles*, p. 119.

Munsterberg was the response to this call for better understanding of men at work. Others, such as Whiting Williams and Henri DeMan probed the human factor in industry. The roots of behavioralism were established before the Hawthorne studies; but that research, coming in such perilous days of industrial development, brought a new focus on man in organizations. This was social man and the Mayoists' call for the development of the manager's social skills.

The post-Hawthorne developments were presented as developing along two lines: (1) the micro analysis of human behavior in motivation, group dynamics, and leadership; and (2) the macro search for the fusion of the social and technical systems. This chapter will pick up where Chapter 15 left off and examine these micro and macro approaches as they evolved into modern views of man *vis-à-vis* the organization. Modern management makes more sense when viewed in the light of its foundations, and it will be seen that the modern behavioralists were engaged in a search for a harmony of man and organizations which began many years earlier. This search for harmony may be defined as the quest for a just adaptation of human needs and aspirations to the requirements and goals of the organization. Harmony means agreement between the parts of a design or composition which gives a pleasing unity of effect whether it be in music, art, or organizational life. This chapter will probe the modern quest to resolve the conflict between the logic of efficiency and the logic of sentiments, the search to meet human needs while fulfilling the objectives of organizations.

MAN AND ORGANIZATIONS

The human relations movement was interdisciplinary in nature, bringing in the contributions of sociology, psychology, social psychology, anthropology, and political science as the primary disciplines to help to develop a body of knowledge about the behavior of individuals at work. The human relationists gathered many to their bosom to stoke the fires of industrial harmony. As the movement evolved, however, we will see: (1) a decline in the interpretation of man's needs as being primarily social; and (2) the emergence of a new focus on man as a self-actualizing being.

Human Relations in Transition

In its early stages, the human relations movement bore the stamp of industrial sociology. Mayo and his associates were interested in rebuilding primary groups, in the factory as a social system, in status and role concepts, in the group as the source of human satisfaction, and in developing the social skills of the leader. The outcome of the Hawthorne studies was the establishment of various industrial relations centers, survey research centers, and other similarly titled organizations for carrying out behavioral research in industry. It was in these institutions that research was spawned which would eventually lead to the decline of social man.

The industrial sociologists attempted to overcome some of the criticisms levied against the Mayoists, and the early 1950's were to see the rise of "industrial human relations." Just as Robert Valentine and Morris Cooke tried to bring about a *rapprochement* between scientific management and organized labor, the post-Mayo revisionists quickly put unions into the human relations picture. Organized labor had made significant membership gains in the 1930's and 1940's and the 1950's brought the merger of the A.F.L. and the C.I.O. The industrial sociologists devoted more and more space to organized labor and examined industry as an *institution* of groups of social classes, workers, foremen, managers, *et al.*, who operated in a larger societal complex.[2]

A basic assumption which appeared to prevail in this approach to industrial human relations was that there was natural conflict between labor and management with respect to dividing the surplus created by an advanced technological society.[3] To the industrial human relationists, the answer to industrial conflict resided not in human relations training *per se* but in overcoming the conflicting interests and ideologies of management and the worker, usually

[2] Examples of this may be found in George Friedman, *Industrial Society*, New York: Free Press, 1955; Wilbert E. Moore, *Industrial Relations and the Social Order*, New York: Macmillan Co., 1951; Eugene V. Schneider, *Industrial Sociology*, New York: McGraw-Hill Book Co., 1957; Delbert C. Miller and William H. Form, *Industrial Sociology*, New York: Harper and Row, 1951; and W. Lloyd Warner and James O. Low, *The Social System of the Modern Factory*, New Haven, Conn.: Yale University Press, 1947.

[3] See Arthur Kornhouser, Robert Dubin, and Arthur M. Ross (eds.) *Industrial Conflict*, New York: McGraw-Hill Book Co., 1954; and various selections in Conrad M. Arensberg, et.al. (ed.), *Research in Industrial Human Relations*, New York: Harper and Row, 1957.

meaning the organized worker.   Industrial harmony would come through collective bargaining and from professional industrial relations specialists.[4]

In addition to bringing unions into the human relations fold, the human relations texts of the 1940's and early 1950's continued in the Mayoist tradition.   They typically postulated that the "feelings" of people were more important than the "logics" of organization charts, rules, and directives.[5]   Human relations was based on intangibles, not on hard scientific investigation, and there were no "final" answers, *i.e.*, nothing positive nor fixed in solutions to human problems.   In part, it was a rebellion against the absolutism of science and against the rigors of being responsible for one's actions. Malcolm McNair had criticized this lack of individual responsibility; an analogy might be that of the trend toward rehabilitating instead of punishing a criminal offender.   In general, the texts of the early 1950's emphasized feelings, sentiments, and collaboration.[6]   They were heuristic rather than specific or systematic, *i.e.* the texts encouraged others to investigate and discover for themselves rather than prescribing techniques.

The outpouring of behavioral research from various centers was to lead to the discoveries that: (1) the satisfied worker was not always the most productive worker; and (2) it was not necessarily the relationships between worker and manager nor the cohesiveness of the work group that led to higher productivity, but that it was the nature of work itself which was important.   The beginning of the end for orthodox human relations appeared in the criticisms being levied in the 1950's of the abuses and corruption of the "happiness boys."   For many, the term "human relations" represented "at best a rather pedestrian effort and at worst a cynical attempt to manipulate people."[7]   The behavioral sciences were seen as one way in which more powerful analytical and conceptual tools could be put to use in handling the problems of human

---

[4] See Ross Stagner, *The Psychology of Industrial Conflict*, New York: John Wiley and Sons, 1956; and William Foote Whyte's application of human relations to the bargaining problems of Inland Steel in *Pattern for Industrial Peace*, New York: Harper and Row, 1951.

[5] Schuyler D. Hoslett (ed.), *Human Factors in Management*, New York: Harper and Row, 1946, Preface.

[6] For example: Burleigh B. Gardner and David G. Moore, *Human Relations in Industry*, Homewood, Ill.: Richard D. Irwin, 1955.

[7] William G. Scott, *Human Relations in Management: A Behavioral Science Approach*, Homewood, Ill.: Richard D. Irwin, 1962, p. 4.

behavior. Through the use of behavioral sciences, one could study the role of the manager and view business as a social system to study the "whole man," not just social man, political man, or economic man.[8]

The decline of social man was found in these dimensions: (1) the industrial research which discovered that man was more complex than orthodox human relations had assumed; (2) the criticisms of human relations as being too "happiness" oriented; and (3) the growing sophistication of the behavioral science disciplines themselves. Post-World War II America witnessed human relations in transition, and social man declined in importance to be replaced by a more rigorous way of examining man in organizations.

The Changing Environment and the New Humanism

It is always difficult to pinpoint chronologically the decline of one set of ideas and the emergence of a new philosophy. However, there is evidence that the period from 1957–1960 can be specified as marking the emergence of a new philosophy concerning man in organizations. William G. Scott has called this emerging philosophy of the modern era "industrial humanism."

[Industrial humanism] has both a philosophy and an assortment of practices with which it proposes to change the conventional structure of work relationships and the content of work itself . . . with the goal of the restoration of the individual's opportunity for self-realization at work.[9]

In its essence, industrial humanism sought to offset the authoritarian tendencies of organizations, to provide for democracy and self-determination at work, to integrate individual and organizational goals, and to restore man's dignity at work. A more comprehensive and more descriptive term might be *organizational humanism*; and this phrase will be used to describe the new philosophy which was to replace the alleged softness and heuristic nature of the old human relations school.

What cultural phenomena are appropriate to mark this shift from social man to organizational humanism during the period 1957–1960? In the economic-technology sphere, two events serve as benchmarks: (1) the recession of 1957–58; and (2) the begin-

[8] Wilmar F. Bernthal, "Contributions of the Behavioral Science Approach," *Proceedings, Academy of Management Annual Meeting*, 1962, pp. 21–28.

[9] William G. Scott, *Organization Theory: A Behavioral Analysis for Management*, Homewood, Ill.: Richard D. Irwin, 1967, p. 43 and p. 258.

ning of the space age. Professor Megginson has noted that the human relations philosophy dominated until the recession of 1957–58. During the recession, the human relations philosophy failed to meet the economic criteria of productivity and profitability. Afterward, Megginson postulated that the new emphasis was on "human resources" rather than "human relations." The human resources philosophy "views the productivity of employees as being an economic resource of a firm or nation. The employee himself . . . is viewed according to the concept of human dignity."[10] This approach gave dual credence to economic efficiency while "recognizing and respecting the personal dignity of each human entity."[11]

The orbiting of Sputnik I thrust the world into the space age and America into a space race. In an effort to catch up, America began to fund large research and development programs. These programs generated the further development of computer-based information systems, the need for more quantitative bases for decisions, and the problems of managing engineers and scientists. The "professional" employee in research and development activities required new assumptions about motivation and leadership; the task of managing complex, interfacing projects demanded the rethinking of traditional line-and-staff organizational structures; and the requirements of a more highly technological, space-age economy required new modes of resource allocation and utilization.

Social values were in flux. Whereas the college students of the 1950's were accused of apathy, the new decade brought a new activism as institutions and their administrations began to be questioned more and more. Within business education itself, we have already discussed the soul-searching of the Gordon-Howell-Pierson reports. Curricula were being reshaped and there was a revival of interest in management as a profession, in ethics, in philosophy, and in the social responsibility of business. In the political realm, the Eisenhower years were closing and the new decade promised the vitality and vibrancy of the youthful President John F. Kennedy. There was the promise of civil rights, of help to the disadvantaged, and of the opportunity to serve through

---

[10] Leon C. Megginson, *Personnel: A Behavioral Approach to Administration*, Homewood, Ill.: Richard D. Irwin, 1967, p. 87; see also Raymond E. Miles, "Human Relations or Human Resources?", *Harvard Business Review*, Vol. 43, No. 4, (July–August, 1965), pp. 148–163.

[11] Megginson, *loc. cit.*

the Peace Corps. In short, the late 1950's were presaging the close of an era and the 1960's were promising to bring in more of a bottom up, power-equalizing humanism.

In management literature, the 1957–60 period saw a number of publications which reflected this shift in management thought. (These writings will be examined in depth below.) They followed a fairly consistent theme. In 1957, Keith Davis set the stage for what might be called "modern human relations"; in 1957 Chris Argyris put forth his "personality *versus* organization" hypothesis; in 1959 Frederick Herzberg published his "motivation-hygiene" theory; and in 1960 Douglas McGregor dichotomized "Theories X and Y." Others were to follow to modify our concepts of motivation, leadership, and organization, but the shift from social man to the new humanism of self-actualizing man was established during the 1957–1960 period.

Work and Self-Actualizing Man

One of the criticisms of the human relationists was their emphasis on social relations to the neglect of a focus on the nature of work and the satisfactions in work for man. When viewed as a cultural value, work has a spotted history. As Purcell has pointed out, the Greeks used the word *ponos*, meaning sorrow or burden for work; in medieval Europe, work was meaningful enough for men to derive their family names from their crafts and today we find names like Hunter, Weaver, Carpenter, Taylor, Miller, and so on. However, to derive names from jobs today, such as "Mike Machinist" or "Luella Keypuncher" would be folly.[12] The Protestant ethic saw work as an end in itself, not necessarily to be enjoyed but to serve as a sign of election and a means to achieving the grace of God. The critics of the Industrial Revolution and of the infant capitalism, such as Karl Marx, saw work as an imposition of the power of the exploiting capital class upon the working class. F. W. Taylor developed no explicit values for work but largely reflected the Protestant ethic that for each man there was a class of work at which he was best and, after assignment to that work, the worker would contribute the most to himself, to his employer, and

[12] Theodore V. Purcell, "Work Psychology and Business Values: A Triad Theory of Work Motivation," *Personnel Psychology*, Vol. 20, No. 3 (Autumn, 1967), pp. 235–236.

to the community. Mayo and his associates played down work as a duty, as a means to fulfillment, and as a central theme of industrial life in order to substitute interpersonal relations as a means of overcoming the anomie that industrial civilization had caused. Abraham Maslow established a hierarchy of needs for man in the early 1940's and extended this theory in his *Motivation and Personality.*[13] Maslow saw a dynamic interplay of needs in which the summit was the need for "self-actualization." It was in this drive for self-fulfillment, for man's being what he could be, that the modern behavioralists found blockages in previously held views of motivation, leadership, and organizations.

The modern era of organizational humanism has developed a new view of work, of man, and of how to achieve organizational harmony by designing organizations to allow man expression of what was assumed to be a natural urge to find satisfactions in work. In perspective, the themes developed by modern writers have mental health overtones as they seek to reduce organizational rigidity, as they strive to understand the personality needs of the healthy individual, and as they propose new managerial styles and philosophies to satisfy human needs while still fulfilling the formal goals of the organization.

Human Relations and Organizational Behavior

Nowhere was the evolution in human relations thought more evident than in the work of Arizona State's Professor Keith Davis, "Mr. Human Relations." In 1957 Davis defined human relations as "the integration of people into a work situation in a way that motivates them to work together productively, cooperatively, and with economic, psychological, and social satisfaction."[14] This view marked the beginning of a modern view of human relations which was more empirically rigorous in understanding organizational behavior and philosophically broader in understanding man's interaction in a more complex network of societal forces. Davis held that modern human relations really had two facets: one was con-

[13] A. H. Maslow, *Motivation and Personality*, New York: Harper & Row, 1954. An extension of this thinking may be found in A. H. Maslow, *Eupsychian Management*, Homewood, Ill.: Richard D. Irwin, 1965; by eupsychian, Maslow means "moving toward psychological health," (p. xi).

[14] Keith Davis, *Human Relations in Business*, New York: McGraw-Hill Book Co., 1957, p. 4.

cerned with understanding, describing, and identifying causes and effects of human behavior through empirical investigation; while the other facet was the application of this knowledge into operational situations. The first could be termed "organizational behavior" and the second facet was "human relations." Both facets were complementary in that one investigated and explained while the other was a way of thinking about people at work and applying behavioral insights into operating situations.[15]

In other work, Davis had developed techniques for the analysis of informal communications structures and has written extensively of the informal organization and of the social responsibility of business. The "modern" human relations of Keith Davis added economic and psychological facets to the social nature of man. He has brought unions into the equation, added broader consideration of societal forces, and based the new human relations era on a more rigorous empirical understanding.

Personality and Organization

Chris Argyris of Yale University had been a proponent of what had been variously called the "personality versus organization" hypothesis or the "immaturity-maturity" theory of human behavior. For Argyris there are some basic trends in the personality growth of healthy, mature individuals. From infancy to adulthood, there is a tendency for the "healthy" personality to develop along a continuum from immaturity to maturity by moving from being passive to being active; by moving from dependence to independence; by growing from a lack of awareness of self to awareness and control over self; and so on.[16] One could determine an individual's degree of self-actualization by plotting his position on the immaturity-maturity continuum. According to Argyris, the basic properties of the formal organization keep individuals immature and mediate against self-actualization. Criticizing Taylor and other organizational formalists, Argyris found four basic properties of the formal organization to be the seat of the prob-

---

[15] Davis' second edition was entitled *Human Relations at Work* (1962) and the third edition bore the title of *Human Relations at Work: The Dynamics of Organizational Behavior* (1967).

[16] Chris Argyris, *Personality and Organization: The Conflict between the System and the Individual,* New York: Harper and Row, 1957, p. 50.

lem: first, the specialization of labor limits individual initiative, chokes off self-expression, and requires an individual to use only a few of his abilities. "It inhibits self-actualization and provides expression for few, shallow, skin-surface abilities that do not provide the endless challenge desired by the healthy personality."[17] Second, the chain of command assumes that efficiency is a result of arranging the parts so that power and authority are lodged at the top and so that through a definite hierarchy of authority the top can control the bottom of the organization. The impact of this is to make the individuals dependent upon and passive toward the leader. The individual has little control over his working environment, develops a short time perspective, and is made dependent by the incentive and control systems. Third, the unity-of-direction principle means that the path toward the goal is directed and controlled by the leader. Problems develop when these work goals do not involve the employee, when he is not allowed to aspire to use more of his abilities, and when he is not allowed to define his own goals in terms of his inner needs. Finally, the span-of-control concept tends to decrease the amount of self-control and the time perspective of the individuals at the bottom of the ladder. By limiting the number of subordinates under one manager, closer control may be exercised and this presupposes immaturity of these individuals.

Using these four organizational "principles," Argyris built his case for the incongruency between the needs of the healthy personality and the requirements of the formal organization. Faced with the demands of the organization, the individual may engage certain defense mechanisms to adapt or to react: (1) he may leave the organization; (2) he may climb the organizational ladder to achieve more autonomy; (3) he may daydream, become aggressive, use projection, regress, or use other defense mechanisms; (4) he may become apathetic or noninvolved; and (5) he may create and formalize informal groups to sanction his own apathy, disinterest, restriction of output, aggression, and so on. Management, faced with the reactions of the worker, also reacts by using more autocratic, directive leadership, by tightening organizational controls, or by turning to "human relations." To Argyris, managers have

17 *Ibid.*, p. 59.

adopted pseudo-human relations in many cases in order to "sugar-coat" the work situation rather than trying to remove the causes of employee discontent.

From Argyris' prolific writings, one can see his proposals for designing organizations to reduce the incongruency and to achieve harmony between the personality and the organization. Job enlargement, an increase in the number of tasks performed by the employee along the flow of work or a lengthening of the time cycle required to complete one unit, is one way to give an individual a greater opportunity to use more of his abilities and to give him a greater sense of power and control over his work. Participative, employee-centered leadership decreases feelings of apathy, dependence, and submissiveness and helps the individual achieve self-actualization, while helping the organization meet its goals. In other areas, Argyris advises management to give employees a variety of experiences, to challenge them by giving them more responsibility, and to rely more on employee self-direction and self-control. Argyris requires a "reality-centered" leadership which has diagnostic skills, an awareness of self and others, and which keeps in mind at all times the worth of the individual and the worth of the organization. It is through awareness, understanding, and modification of organizational practices that the healthy individual can be nurtured in a healthy organization and that both can achieve their goals and needs. Harmony, then, for Argyris is not sweetness and light but the maturation of people in enlightened organizations.

Theories X and Y

Douglas McGregor (1906–1964) received his doctoral degree from Harvard University in 1935 and taught social psychology at Harvard from 1935 to 1937. He became an assistant professor of psychology at the Massachusetts Institute of Technology in 1937 and served that institution except for six years as president of Antioch College (1948–1954), until his death. As president of Antioch College, McGregor found that the precepts of the human relations model were inadequate for coping with the rigors and realities of organizational life.

I believed, for example, that a leader could operate successfully as a kind of adviser to his organization. I thought I could avoid being a "boss."

Unconsciously, I suspect, I hoped to duck the unpleasant necessity of making difficult decisions, of taking the responsibility for one course of action, among many uncertain alternatives, of making mistakes and taking the consequences. I thought that maybe I could operate so that everyone would like me—that "good human relations" would eliminate all discord and disagreement.

I couldn't have been more wrong. It took a couple of years, but I finally began to realize that a leader cannot avoid the exercise of authority any more than he can avoid responsibility for what happens to his organization.[18]

In *The Human Side of Enterprise*, McGregor made a significant shift in his ideas from the human relations philosophy to the new humanism. He challenged the "classical principles of organization" as being inappropriate, since they were largely based on the church and the military; as being unrelated to the modern influences of the political, social and economic milieu; and as being based on erroneous assumptions about human behavior.[19] McGregor felt that managerial assumptions about human nature and human behavior were all-important in determining the manager's style of operating. Based upon his assumptions about the nature of man, the manager could organize, lead, control, and motivate people in different ways. If the manager accepted one set of assumptions, he would tend to manage one way, or if he held a different set, he would manage another way. The first set of assumptions McGregor examined was Theory X, which was to represent the "traditional view of direction and control." Theory X assumptions were:

1. The average human being has an inherent dislike of work and will avoid it if he can . . .

2. Because of this human characteristic of dislike of work, most people must be coerced, controlled, directed, threatened with punishment to get them to put forth adequate effort toward the achievement of organizational objectives . . .

3. The average human being prefers to be directed, wishes to avoid responsibility, has relatively little ambition, wants security above all.[20]

McGregor thought that these X assumptions were the ones prevailing in modern industrial practice. He stated that he did not

[18] Douglas McGregor, "On Leadership," *Antioch Notes*, (May, 1954), pp. 2–3. Cited by Warren G. Bennis, "Revisionist Theory of Leadership," *Harvard Business Review*, Vol. 39, No. 1 (January–February, 1961), p. 34.

[19] Douglas McGregor, *The Human Side of Enterprise*, New York: McGraw-Hill Book Co., 1960, pp. 16–18.

[20] *Ibid.*, pp. 33–34. Theories X and Y were first published in *Adventures in Thought and Action*, Proceedings of the Fifth Anniversary Convocation of the School of Industrial Management, Massachusetts Institute of Technology, Cambridge, Mass., April 9, 1957; reprinted in Warren G. Bennis, Edgar H. Schein, and Caroline McGregor (editors), *Leadership and Motivation: Essays of Douglas McGregor*, Cambridge, Mass: M.I.T. Press, 1966, pp. 3–20.

intend to make a "straw man" for demolition with his Theory X but his polarization of X as encompassing all traditional management certainly led to such an interpretation by others. He did not name individuals nor delve into past management thought very deeply; if he had, he would have found that Theory X was not quite as prevalent as he assumed. While he did note a shift from "hard" X (presumably scientific management) to "soft" X (human relations), McGregor maintained that no fundamental shift in assumptions or managerial philosophies had occurred.

Theory Y was put forth as a "modest beginning for new theory with respect to the management of human resources." The assumptions of Theory Y were:

1. *The expenditure of physical and mental effort in work is as natural as play or rest.* The average human being does not inherently dislike work . . .

2. *External control and the threat of punishment are not the only means for bringing about effort toward organizational objectives. Man will exercise self-direction and self-control in the service of objectives to which he is committed.*

3. *Commitment to objectives is a function of the rewards associated with their achievement.* The most significant of such rewards, e.g., the satisfaction of ego and self-actualization needs, can be direct products of effort directed toward organizational objectives.

4. *The average human being learns, under proper conditions, not only to accept but to seek responsibility.* Avoidance of responsibility, lack of ambition, and emphasis on security are generally consequences of experience, not inherent human characteristics.

5. *The capacity to exercise a relatively high degree of imagination, ingenuity, and creativity in the solution of organizational problems is widely, not narrowly, distributed in the population.*

6. *Under the conditions of modern industrial life, the intellectual potentialities of the average human being are only partially utilized.*[21]

In a use of Mary Follett's terms, with a slight twist of Argyris, McGregor called Theory Y "the integration of individual and organizational goals" and held that it led to the "creation of conditions such that the members of the organization can achieve their own goals *best* by directing their efforts toward the success of the enterprise."[22] Under Theory Y, it was the essential task of management to unleash man's potential so that he could achieve his goals by directing his efforts toward those of the organization. It was "management by objectives" in the traditional sense but the

---

[21] *The Human Side of Enterprise,* pp. 47–48. Copyright 1960, the McGraw-Hill Book Company; by permission.
[22] *Ibid.,* p. 49.

motivation came from the *commitment* of people to the objectives of the organization. Managers who accepted the Y image of human nature would not structure, control, or closely supervise the work environment. Instead, they would attempt to aid the maturation of subordinates by giving them wider latitude in their work, encouraging creativity, using less external control, encouraging self-control, and motivating through the satisfactions which came from the challenge of work itself. The use of the authority of external control by management would be replaced by getting people *committed* to organizational goals because they perceived that this was the best way to achieve their own goals. A perfect integration was not possible, but McGregor hoped that an adoption of Y assumptions by managers would improve existing industrial practice.

McGregor has served as a bridge from the old view of human relations to the new organizational humanism. It was McGregor's fundamental belief that harmony could be achieved, not by being "hard" or "soft," but by changing assumptions about people in order to see that people could be trusted, that they could exercise self-motivation and control, and that they had the capacity to integrate their own personal goals with those of the formal organization. Edgar Schein, an associate of McGregor's, has held that he did not intend to set up Theory Y as a monolithic set of principles; instead, McGregor wanted Theory Y "to be a realistic view, in which one examined one's assumptions, tested them against reality, and then chose a managerial strategy that made sense in terms of one's diagnosis of reality."[23] Empirical verification of Theory Y is available but not in abundance. The Non-Linear Systems Company of Del Mar, California, a developer and producer of precision electronic instruments, has successfully applied Theory Y to its workers.[24]

To McGregor, how people were treated was largely a self-fulfilling prophecy; if the manager assumed that people were lazy and treated them as if they were, then they *would* be lazy. On the

---

[23] Edgar H. Schein, "Introduction," in Douglas McGregor, *The Professional Manager,* New York: McGraw-Hill Book Co., 1967, p. xi. Published posthumously, this work was edited for publication by Caroline McGregor and Warren G. Bennis. For a collection of McGregor's major works, see *Leadership and Motivation: Essays of Douglas McGregor,* edited by Warren G. Bennis and Edgar H. Schein with the collaboration of Caroline McGregor, Cambridge, Mass.: MIT Press, 1966.

[24] Arthur H. Kuriloff, "An Experiment in Management: Putting Theory Y to the Test," *Personnel,* Vol. 40, No. 6 (November-December, 1963), pp. 8–17.

other hand, if the manager assumed that people desired challenging work and exploited this premise by increasing individual
discretion, the worker would in fact respond by seeking more and
more responsibility.

The Motivation-Hygiene Theory

A high degree of consonance with Argyris and McGregor about
why people work has been put forth by Frederick Herzberg and his
associates. Based on extensive empirical investigation, Herzberg
set forth a "motivation-hygiene" theory of motivation which has
received both widespread support and many criticisms. The
research was designed to discover the importance of attitudes
toward work and the experiences, both good and bad, which workers
reported. Herzberg asked his research samples to respond to this
question: "Think of a time when you felt exceptionally good or
exceptionally bad about your job, either your present job or any
other job you have had . . . Tell me what happened."[25] Out of
the responses to this question and a series of follow-up questions,
Herzberg set out to discover the kinds of things which made people happy and satisfied on their jobs or unhappy and dissatisfied.
In analyzing his data, he concluded that people responded in such
a manner as to isolate two different kinds of needs which appeared
to be independent. When people reported unhappiness and job
dissatisfaction, they attributed this to their job environment or
the *job context*. When people reported happiness or satisfaction,
they attributed this good feeling to work itself or to the *job content*.

Herzberg called the factors which were identified in the job
context "hygiene" factors "for they act in a manner analogous to the
principles of medical hygiene. Hygiene operates to remove health
hazards from the environment of man. It is not curative: it is,
rather, a preventive."[26] The hygiene factors included "supervision,
interpersonal relations, physical working conditions, salaries, company policies, and administrative practices, benefits, and job security."[27] When these factors deteriorated below what the worker

[25] Frederick Herzberg, Bernard Mausner, and Barbara B. Snyderman, *The
Motivation to Work*, New York: John Wiley and Sons, 1959, Appendix I, p. 141. The
reader will recall from Chapter 9 that Henri DeMan asked a similar question in
1929 in his search for "joy in work."

[26] *The Motivation to Work*, p. 113.

[27] *Ibid.*, p. 113.

considered an acceptable level, job dissatisfaction was the result. However, when the job context was considered optimal by the worker, dissatisfaction was removed; but this did not lead to *positive* attitudes but to some sort of a neutral state of neither satisfaction nor dissatisfaction.

The factors that led to positive attitudes, satisfaction, and motivation were called the "motivators" or those things in the work itself which satisfied the individual's needs for self-actualization. The motivators were such factors as achievement, recognition for accomplishment, challenging work, increased job responsibility, and opportunities for growth and development. All of these factors were in the nature of the job itself and, if present, led to higher motivation for the worker. In this sense, Herzberg was saying that traditional assumptions of motivation about wage incentives, improving interpersonal relations, and establishing proper working conditions did not lead to higher motivation. They removed dissatisfaction, acted to prevent problems; but once these traditional "motivators" were optimal, they did not lead to positive motivation. According to Herzberg, management should recognize that hygiene was necessary but that once it had neutralized dissatisfaction, it did not lead to positive results. Only the "motivators" led people to superior performance.

In rebuttal to those who claimed success for wage incentive plans such as the Scanlon and the Lincoln Electric schemes, Herzberg said that money in these cases was actually a direct reward for recognition, achievement, and responsibility. It was not wage increases in an across-the-board manner (which would be a hygiene factor) but added earnings which were merited as a reward for growth, achievement, and responsibility. For Herzberg, "hygiene is not enough" and the motivation to work must come from job enrichment ("vertical loading" or job enlargement), from more challenging jobs and opportunities for growth, and from the supervisors who were aware of the need for recognition and achievement and gave employees chances for self-actualization.

Davis, Herzberg, McGregor, and Argyris form the pillars of this modern quest for organizational humanism. Harmony would not come from a mental revolution nor from social solidarity but from the use of the behavioral sciences to understand the nature and needs of man in organizations. Harmony was reciprocity, a psychological contract between man and his organization. It was a mutual agreement that said "I want to be productive, I want to prosper, I want to be recognized for what I achieve; give me that opportunity and the organization shall prosper also."

The Self-Actualizers and Their Critics

The self-actualizing-man thesis has not been without its critics. Robert Dubin has suggested that organizations are not as tyrannical as Argyris supposed and that to assume that work is the sole life interest of the worker, *i.e.*, he must derive his life satisfactions from his job, is erroneous.[28] George Strauss also has questioned the "personality vs. the organization" hypothesis by suggesting that the stated needs for self-actualization reflect the strong value judgments of professionals (*i.e.*, *Professors* Argyris, McGregor, and Herzberg) and do not necessarily apply to all segments of the population.[29] According to Strauss, the self-actualizers neglect economic motivation, assume that all people want to be independent and creative and, therefore, err by concluding that the job should be the primary mode of need satisfaction for everyone ("as it is for professors"). Strauss and Dubin would argue for flexible leadership styles and for giving opportunities for self-actualization where appropriate to the worker's abilities and aspirations. But where tasks were highly programmed and the organizational costs of self-actualization outweighed the gains, or when people did not desire to make work their central life interest, self-actualization would not be appropriate as a motivational device.

There has also been opposition to Herzberg's conclusions. The criticisms are basically twofold: one, that the research technique was faulty in that people are "more likely to attribute the causes of satisfaction to their own achievement and accomplishments on the job" while they, when asked by the interviewer, are "more likely to attribute their dissatisfaction, not to personal inadequacies or deficiencies, but to factors in the work environment."[30] A second set of criticisms have hinged upon the neatness and simplicity of

[28] Robert Dubin, "Person and Organization," in Robert Dubin (ed.), *Human Relations in Administration*, 3rd ed., Englewood Cliffs, N.J.: Prentice-Hall, 1968, pp. 90–93.

[29] George Strauss, "Some Notes on Power Equalization," in Harold J. Leavitt (ed.), *The Social Science of Organizations*, Englewood Cliffs, N.J.: Prentice-Hall, 1963, pp. 41–84.

[30] Victor Vroom, *Work and Motivation*, New York: John Wiley and Sons, 1964, pp. 127–129.

Herzberg's treatment of such a complex subject as motivation.[31] All of this has led Edgar H. Schein to conclude that a new era of management notions of motivation is in the offing since "man is a more complex individual than rational-economic, social, or self-actualizing man."[32] It is too early to see clearly the form of theory and research it would take to bring this multidimensional "complex man" into the limelight. It may be no more than recognition of the simple fact that we are all different and should be understood and treated as such.

LEADERSHIP: TASKS AND PEOPLE

The concern for human interrelationships and the necessity for managerial social skills endured for some time after the Western Electric research. Early behavioral research, such as that of the group dynamicists, tended to place leadership styles on a continuum of possibilities ranging from authoritarian to democratic and finally to *laissez-faire*. This clustering of leader-behavior modes reflected the idea that the authoritarian would use his formal authority, be production-oriented, and operate unilaterally in making decisions. The democratic or participative leader on the other hand would use his formal authority sparingly, be employee-centered, and involve his subordinates in the decision-making process.

Authority, an integral part of the leadership process, has undergone a steady evolution without any general sense of agreement. The "formalists" of organization theory, such as Max Weber, would legitimatize authority in the formal power to hold a position as granted by superior powers, be it the state or in the right to hold private property. Taylor thought that authority resided in knowledge, Follett advised obeying the "law of the situation," and

---

[31] See Theodore Purcell, "Work Psychology and Business Values," p. 239; and Orlando Behling, George Labovitz, and Richard Kosmo, "The Herzberg Controversy: A Critical Reappraisal," *Academy of Management Journal*, Vol. 11, No. 1 (March, 1968), pp. 99–108.

[32] Edgar H. Schein, *Organizational Psychology*, Englewood Cliffs, N.J.: Prentice-Hall, 1965, pp. 60–63. This more complex view of human behavior has spawned a "multidimensional approach" in more recent writings: see for example, Anthony G. Athos and Robert E. Coffey, *Behavior in Organizations: A Multidimensional View*, Englewood Cliffs, New Jersey: Prentice-Hall, 1968; and Billy J. Hodge and Herbert J. Johnson, *Management and Organizational Behavior: A Multidimensional Approach*, New York: John Wiley and Sons, 1970.

Barnard saw it in the acceptance by subordinates of the superior's orders.[33]   All of these latter views were in contrast to the authority of position and tended to play down the hierarchy. Participative leadership, espoused by human relationists and organizational humanists, also followed this theme. Harold Leavitt has called this approach "power equalization," that is, a movement to reduce the power and status differentials between the superior and the subordinate.[34]   The goal was to play down the organizational hierarchy of authority, to give the worker a greater voice in decisions, to encourage creativity, and to overcome apathy by getting people involved and committed to organizational goals.

The research which characterized this drive to equalize power has already been discussed in some detail. The Ohio State studies described two dimensions of leader behavior as "initiating structure" and "consideration". The University of Michigan studies, under the direction of the venerable Rensis Likert, isolated two dimensions called the "employee orientation" and the "production orientation." Likert found that "supervisors with the best records of performance focus their primary attention on the human aspects of their subordinate's problems and on endeavoring to build effective work groups with high performance goals."[35] Likert built his argument for a "new pattern" of leadership based on participative, "supportive" management.[36]

Participative management, as a manifestation of power equalization, gave employees a greater voice in setting goals, making decisions, and in obtaining more autonomy in their work. The manager

[33] An excellent review of differing notions of authority may be found in Robert J. Daiute, "Managerial Authority in Management Thought," *Advanced Management Journal*, Vol. 33, No. 4 (October, 1968), pp. 66–75.

[34] Harold J. Leavitt, "Applied Organizational Change: A Summary and Evaluation of the Power Equalization Approaches," Seminar in the Social Science of Organizations, Pittsburgh, June, 1962; cited by George Strauss, p. 41.

[35] Rensis Likert, *New Patterns of Management*, New York: McGraw-Hill Book Co., 1961, p. 7. There are a multitude of leadership books using basically this approach. One which emphasizes leadership as influence and the role of sensitivity training is Robert Tannenbaum, Irving R. Weschler, and Fred Massarik, *Leadership and Organization*, New York: McGraw-Hill Book Co., 1961; Eugene Emerson Jennings has written extensively on leadership, especially on executive stress, role ambiguities, and flexibility in leadership roles, see for example, E. E. Jennings, *The Executive, Autocrat, Bureaucrat, Democrat*, New York: Harper and Row, 1962, and *Executive Success: Stresses, Problems and Adjustment*, New York: Appleton-Century-Crofts, 1967; a psychoanalytic approach may be found in Abraham Zaleznik, *Human Dilemmas of Leadership*, New York: Harper and Row, 1966.

[36] A more recent work is Rensis Likert, *The Human Organization: Its Management and Value*, New York: McGraw-Hill Book Company, 1967.

became employee-centered, exercised a looser form of supervision, and tried to tap the creativity and commitment of his subordinates. By practicing participation, by involving the workers in matters that concerned them, management was to be repaid by higher productivity and the worker was supposed to exhibit higher morale, more cohesiveness, and to achieve greater satisfactions in his work.

Toward Adaptive Leadership

While Likert and others formed the primary support for participative management, empirical research often showed inconsistencies in the conclusion that this style was always best. Even Likert had found that high morale or high cohesiveness did not always lead to higher productivity nor did a production-centered supervisor always have a low producing section. As Likert stated it:

On the basis of a study I did in 1937, I believed that morale and productivity were positively related; that the higher the morale, the higher the production. Substantial research findings since then have shown that this relationship is much too simple.[37]

Often it was not a question of one or the other emphasis, *i.e.*, employee-centered or production-centered, but under what circumstances did one work better than the other? Could "initiating structure" and "consideration" be combined or balanced in some way? These questions which arose out of the Ohio State and the University of Michigan work opened new vistas for leadership research and formed the basis for the development of the "managerial grid" by Blake and Mouton (Figure 20-1).[38]

The "grid approach" was an attempt to avoid the extreme "either/or" styles of leadership, such as either scientific management or human relations, production-centered or people-centered, and even Theory X or Theory Y, by showing the possibilities for various blends of leadership styles. This grid of alternatives reflected two dimensions, "concern for people" on the vertical

[37] Rensis Likert, quoted in Warren G. Bennis, "Revisionist Theory of Leadership," *Harvard Business Review* (January–February, 1961), p. 31. The "revisionists," according to Bennis, attempted to reconcile classical management theory with modern behavioral sciences. He included such people as McGregor, Likert, Simon, and Zaleznik.

[38] Robert R. Blake and Jane S. Mouton, *The Managerial Grid*, Houston, Tex.: Gulf Publishing Co., 1964.

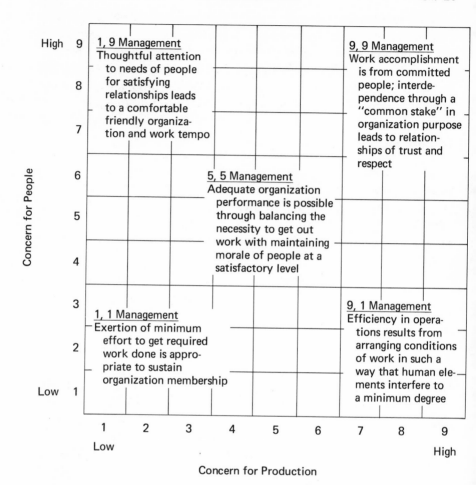

Fig. 20–1. The managerial grid. (Adapted from Blake and Mouton, *op. cit.*, Figure 1, p. 10. Copyright © 1964, Gulf Publishing Co., Houston, Texas. Used with permission.)

axis, and "concern for production" on the horizontal axis. Each axis was expressed in terms of a nine-point scale with the number 1 representing minimum concern and number 9 standing for maximum concern. Although a number of different managerial theories can be shown on the managerial grid, Blake and Mouton emphasize those at the four corners and in the middle. Each of these five theories defines a definite, but different, set of assumptions regarding how managers orient themselves for managing situations of production that involve people. Each theory is seen as a set of possible assumptions for using the organizational hierarchy to link people into production. Any set of assumptions is subject to change; and when a person changes his underlying managerial assumptions, his actual managerial practices shift accordingly. A given individual's style can be viewed as a dominant set of assumptions that guide his actions.

In the 9,1 style a high concern for production is coupled with a low concern for people, a basic assumption being that an organization cannot meet its needs for production and the personal needs of people at the same time. Heavy emphasis is placed on task and job requirements with the manager occupying a position of authority and being responsible for planning, directing, and controlling the actions of his subordinates so that production objectives of the enterprise are reached. The 9,1 motto is "Nice guys finish last."[39] The 1,9 style with minimum emphasis on production and maximum concern for people is also rooted in the assumption that production requirements are contrary to the needs of people but emphasis is on satisfying the needs of people. The 1,9 motto is "Nice guys don't fight."[40] The 1,1 managerial style also assumes an incompatibility between production requirements and the needs of people but the 1,1 manager experiences few dilemmas. In an attitude characteristic of those who have accepted defeat, he has learned to have little concern for either. The 5,5 approach also assumes a conflict between the organizational purpose of production and the needs of the people but the solution is a compromise between the two. The 5,5 approach recognizes the responsibility of the manager to plan, direct, and control; but the 5,5 manager does not command or direct so much as he leads, motivates, and communicates to get work done.

The 9,9 approach assumes that there is no necessary and inherent conflict between organizational purpose, production goals, and the needs of the people. Effective integration of people with production is possible by involving them and their ideas in determining the conditions and strategies of work. A basic aim is to promote the conditions that integrate creativity, high productivity, and high morale through concerted team action. Mutual understanding and agreement as to what the organization goals are and of the means by which they are to be attained are at the core of work

[39] *Ibid.*, p. 48.
[40] *Ibid.*, p. 80.

direction. People and production are interconnected in a real sense. The general theme is to create work conditions where people understand the problem, have stakes in the outcome, and where their ideas make a real contribution to the result obtained. Direction and control are achieved by working for understanding of and agreement by subordinates concerning organizational purposes and how to contribute to them. This approach assumes that, when individuals are aware of organizational purpose and of their real stakes in the outcome, there is no necessity for direction and control in an authority-obedience sense. Control and direction become self-control and self-direction. Blake and Mouton have shown how leadership styles could move along a continuum of possibilities based on managerial assumptions. In this respect, the grid largely reflects the urgings of other organizational humanists to build teamwork, self-direction and control, and to design work structures to get commitment from participants.

The Contingency Model

Another approach which has achieved widespread recognition is the "leadership contingency model" of Fred Fiedler.[41] Fiedler has moved away from many of the normative statements about the best or "ideal" leadership style to suggest that a number of leader behavior styles may be effective or ineffective depending on important elements of the situation. Fiedler has devoted over fifteen years to empirical testing of his model and many other researchers have contributed to its understanding and application.[42] To measure leadership style, Fiedler required a person (subject) to give a self-description and also a description of his least preferred co-worker and his most preferred co-worker. From this he derived "Assumed Similarity between opposites" (ASo) scores which indicated the differences or "distances" between the various descriptions. These ASo scores measured an attitude toward others which may best be described as emotional or psychological dis-

[41] Fred E. Fiedler, A Theory of Leadership Effectiveness, New York: McGraw-Hill Book Co., 1967.

[42] For example, see J. G. Hunt, "Breakthrough in Leadership Research," Personnel Administration, Vol. 30, No. 5 (September–October, 1967) pp. 38–44; and Walter Hill, "The Validation and Extension of Fiedler's Theory of Leadership Effectiveness," Academy of Management Journal, Vol. 12, No. 1 (March, 1969), pp. 33–47.

tance. A "high" ASo person tends to be concerned about his inter-personal relations, feels a need for the approval of his associates, and is less "distant" in describing himself and others. The "low" ASo person is relatively independent of others, is less concerned with feelings, and is willing to reject a person who cannot complete the assigned task. In essence, the high ASo is "consideration" oriented and the low ASo "task" oriented in terms of the Ohio State studies.

In various studies Fiedler further identified three major factors in the leadership situation: (1) "leader-member relations," or the degree to which a group trusted or liked or were willing to follow the leader; (2) the "task structure," or the degree to which the task was ill- or well-defined; and (3) "position power," or the formal authority as distinct from the personal power of the leader. Fiedler then developed various models to show how these variables inter-acted and concluded that "the appropriateness of the leadership style for maximizing group performance is contingent upon the favorableness of the group task situation."[43] The most favorable situation, for a leader, in which to influence his group is one in which he is well liked by the members (good leader-member relations), has a powerful position (high position power), and is directing a well-defined job (high task structure). The most unfa-vorable situation is one in which the leader is disliked, has little position power, and faces an unstructured task. As the model moves from a very favorable to a very unfavorable situation, Fiedler has concluded that (1) *task-oriented* (low ASo) leaders tend to per-form best in group situations which are either very favorable or very unfavorable to the leader, and (2) *relationships-oriented* (high ASo) leaders tend to perform best in situations which are inter-mediate in favorableness (Figure 20-2).

Hersey and Blanchard have extended Fiedler's model by adding an "effectiveness" dimension to the task and relationships dimen-sions.[44] This "tri-dimensional" model gives more emphasis to leader behavior as it is appropriate for various situations. Whether two- or three-dimensional, leadership models have evolved to encompass more variables and to lead to more flexible, adaptive views of effective leader behavior.

[43] Fiedler, *A Theory of Leadership Effectiveness*, p. 147.
[44] Paul Hersey and Kenneth H. Blanchard, *Management of Organizational Behavior*, Englewood Cliffs, N.J.: Prentice-Hall, 1969, pp. 76–80.

TASK-ORIENTED STYLE	RELATIONSHIP-ORIENTED CONSIDERATE STYLE	TASK-ORIENTED STYLE
Low Assumed Similarity or Least-preferred Co-worker Scores	High Assumed Similarity or Least-preferred Co-worker Scores	Low Assumed Similarity or Least-preferred Co-worker Scores
←———————	———————————	———————→
Unfavorable leadership situation	Situation intermediate in favorableness for leader	Favorable leadership situation

Fig. 20–2. Appropriate leadership styles for various situations. (Adapted from Fiedler, *op. cit.*, Figure 1—1. p. 14. Copyright © 1967, McGraw-Hill Book Company, Inc.; by permission.)

ORGANIZATIONS AND MAN

Post-World War II management was faced with burgeoning masses of physical and human resources which were growing into ever more and more complex patterns and relationships. Management was faced with mass markets growing into an international scale and with mass assemblages of people of varying personal needs, educational backgrounds, and degrees of specialized knowledge. It was an emerging age of technological advancement which would bring the world beyond the atomic age and into the space age. Through electronic communications and the mass media, managers were becoming more aware of different markets, of different cultures, and of the political and economic race between East and West. Faced with more complexities, managers sought better means of analyzing alternatives in order to yield more efficacious results. One avenue of this search was for a new theory of organizations. These organizational theorists assumed a more macro stance and saw a larger view in which the search for harmony was implemented by the redesign of organizations to fit man and his diverse needs. The theorists were concerned with the *processes* of organizations as goal-seeking entities and how these organizations might assume a more pleasing form in light of what the behavioral sciences were revealing about the nature of man.

This "organization and man" quest for harmony was different

from the organizational humanists only in the means to the end. In Part III we saw that the Mayoists and the organizational formalists, such as Mooney, Gulick, and others, took opposite stances regarding the problems of their times. The Mayoists sought to rebuild organizations through primary groups and thereby to yield satisfied, productive workers; the formalists sought to redesign organizations to achieve efficient, coordinated effort and thereby to release man's potential to produce. In a similar manner, the modern organizational theorists sought to redesign organizations while the humanists sought to reshape our assumptions about the nature and nurturance of man. In reality, they both held the goal of organizational harmony.

The Roots of Modern Organization Theory

Organizations are as old as man and the views of management scholars have reflected a steadily evolving notion of how organizations might work both more efficiently and more effectively in terms of Chester Barnard's dichotomy. Organization theory itself is a product of its cultural environment and finds its roots in evolving ideas about the economic and the human problems facing organizations. Early organizations such as the church, the military, and the state were faced with the problems of getting predictable results. They did not face the rigors of market competition, and organizational structures were designed to keep humans within the boundaries of administrative desire. Early entrepreneurs, faced with both the rigors of competition and the vagaries of their labor force, adopted the precepts of prior organizations in their early structures. Hence, such ideas as a limited span of control, unity of command, a clearly defined hierarchy of authority, division of labor, and other such formal, blueprinted notions made sense to these early organizational writers.

It was not out of malice toward men that they stressed the anatomy of the organizational structure but out of the economic imperatives of bringing the multiplicity of human and physical resources together in a profitable concordance. William G. Scott and Joseph Litterer have labeled early organization theory as the "classical" approach. In their view, it was concerned with the anatomy of organizations and the assumed rational behavior of man.[45] Among the classicists we would find Weber, Fayol, Mooney and Reiley, Gulick, Urwick, Barnard, and others who stressed organizational goals, the division of labor, the scalar chain, and the formal aspects of the structure. Barnard, though primarily a classicist, was breaking with some of these chains with his efficiency-effectiveness dichotomy.

A second stage in the development of organization theory came with the emergence of behavioralism and especially the Hawthorne studies. Scott has called this the "neo-classical" approach while Litterer used the phrase "the naturalistic school of organizations." This era sought to overcome the "deficiencies" of the classicists by recognizing the people as part of the organization. Through emphasis on the informal organization, on the illogic of sentiments, and on the interactions of individuals and groups, the neo-classicists brought to the fore the recognition that many events may occur in organizations which could not have been anticipated by the planning and organizing genius of the classicist.

The third stage in the evolution of organization theory found its genesis in the same 1957–1960 time period in which organizational humanism began. It was in this era that scholars began to play down the formal blueprints of Weber, Mooney, and other classicists and began to relax the notion of a rigid organizational structure. While the Mayoists wrote of people and omitted structure, the modern organizational theorists sought to preserve both people and structure. It was in this modern era that organization theory moved beyond bureaucracy.

Beyond Bureaucracy

Four books during the 1958–1960 period marked the decline of hierarchy and bureaucracy and the rise of flexibility as a goal of organization theory. First came the work of James March and Herbert Simon (1958); followed in short order by that of Marshall Dimock (1959), Mason Haire (1959), and John Pfiffner and Frank Sherwood (1960). These will be discussed below but their appearance coincident with the rise of organizational humanism illus-

---

[45] William G. Scott, "Organization Theory: An Overview and an Appraisal," *Journal of the Academy of Management*, Vol. 4, No. 1 (April, 1961), pp. 9–11; and Joseph A. Litterer (ed.), *Organizations: Structure and Behavior*, New York: John Wiley and Sons, 1963, pp. 3–4.

trates a marked shift in management thought from the classical and neo-classical eras.

March and Simon were the first to put forth a conceptual framework and a series of "propositions" about human behavior in order to present a "new" theory of organizations.[46] March and Simon were critical of the "classical" advocates of organization theory and presented F. W. Taylor and Luther Gulick as prime proponents of this approach. March and Simon concluded that the Taylor branch of classical theory was "physiological" in that Taylor was more concerned with task specialization and definition, motion and time study, fatigue, and the engineer's approach to organizations. Gulick and his group (such as Mooney and Reiley, Urwick and Fayol) were classified as "administrative management theorists" because they were concerned with broader notions of organization such as departmentalization, coordination, and other integrative schemes. March and Simon's indictment of these classicists was basically as follows: "First, in general there is a tendency to view the employee as an inert instrument performing the tasks assigned to him. Second, there is a tendency to view personnel as given rather than as a variable in the system."[47]

To March and Simon "traditional organization theory views the human organism as a simple machine."[48] In their view, the classicists failed on numerous counts by forming incomplete and inaccurate theories of motivation, by expressing little appreciation of intraorganizational conflict, and by omitting many significant elements of human behavior. The modifications which March and Simon sought to make in traditional organization theory were largely based on recent empirical discoveries in psychology and economics and upon the earlier theoretical derivations of Chester Barnard. Motivation was viewed as a "search process" among various "evoked alternatives" which would lead the organizational member to decide whether or not to participate in working toward the organization's goals. This decision to participate was based on the "inducements" offered by the organization which brought about "organizational equilibrium" in terms of earlier work by Barnard, and also by Simon in his Administrative Behavior. March

[46] James G. March and Herbert A. Simon (with the collaboration of Harold Guetzkow), Organizations, New York: John Wiley and Sons, 1958.
[47] Ibid., p. 29.
[48] Ibid., p. 34.

and Simon also examined different kinds of conflict in organizations, rational and non-rational problem solving, centralization and decentralization, and the problems of innovating within the confines of organizations which were typically programmed and routinized.

In essence, *Organizations* was a bold stroke against classical theory and a call for a new organizational design which recognized the limits of a decision maker's rationality, the need for understanding the human choosing process, and the need for a structure balanced with the needs and goals of organizational members. In depicting the classicist's views as a "machine-model" of organizations in which the human was merely a cog, March and Simon laid themselves open to questioning. It was naive on their part to capsulize Taylor's work as a machine model concerned only with the physiological organization of work. It is true that Taylor was an engineer and that he did not have much training in the behavioral sciences. It is also true that the behavioral sciences of Taylor's era were rather ill-conceived in comparison to modern standards and he, Gulick, and other early writers should not be indicted for the poor state of the behavioral arts. In rebuttal, Lyndall Urwick has cited Simon's own work:

> We have a rapidly expanding body of empirical knowledge about how decisions are actually made in organizations, including in recent years successful attempts to simulate some kinds of middle management decision making quite accurately with digital computers.[49]

To this Urwick has added: "In the light of his enthusiasm for the computer, who is Professor Simon to criticize other writers for adopting a 'machine-model of human behavior?' "[50]

However, the machine-model label has stuck to the classicists and March and Simon had opened new vistas in the search for modern organization theory. In the same vein others followed to show the way beyond bureaucracy. Marshall Dimock sought to overcome the stifling characteristics of bureaucracy through the vitality of leadership. In his view, bureaucracy inhibited the innovation which all modern societies required.[51] Mason Haire

[49] Herbert A. Simon, *The New Science of Management Decision,* New York: Harper and Row, 1960, p. 1.

[50] Lyndall F. Urwick, "Have We Lost Our Way in the Jungle of Management Theory?", *Personnel,* Vol. 42, No. 3, (May–June, 1965), p. 15–16.

[51] Marshall E. Dimock, *Administrative Vitality: The Conflict with Bureaucracy,* New York: Harper and Row, 1959.

established the field of modern organization theory as one which would include motivation, personality theory, communications and decision theory, and even biology and ecology.[52] Pfiffner and Sherwood sought a middle ground between the classical structural approach and the behavioral orientations through the concept of organizational "overlays."[53] These overlays (sociometric, functional, decision, power, and communications) were to be placed in the formal structure to reflect informal organizational events. In retrospect, these beginnings of modern organization theory were attempts to overcome the rigidity and formality of the classicists in order to substitute a more flexible, human view of organizations and man.

Toward Organizational Systems

Modern organization theory did not divorce itself entirely from the classicists and the neo-classicists, but the estrangement was enough to call for separate housekeeping. Organization theory became established as a separate area of study and sociologists and political scientists joined management scholars in the study of complex organizations.[54] The notion of a duality of human and work systems in organizations had been established earlier in the work of W. F. Whyte, E. W. Bakke, George Homans, and Eliot Jacques of the Tavistock Institute. The phrase "socio-technical systems" accurately describes this conceptual and analytical approach for the study of human work systems. Modern organization theory built upon these foundations as it sought through theorizing and empirical research to view the organization as a mutually interacting set of human, physical, and procedural variables in a complex system.

The "systems" view of organization has been a modification

---

[52] Mason Haire (ed.), *Modern Organization Theory*, New York: John Wiley & Sons, 1959.

[53] John M. Pfiffner and Frank P. Sherwood, *Administrative Organization*, Englewood Cliffs, N.J.: Prentice-Hall, 1960.

[54] For merely a sample, see: Philip Selznick, *TVA and the Grass Roots*, Berkeley: University of California Press, 1949; Robert K. Merton (ed.) *Reader in Bureaucracy*, New York: Free Press, 1952; Peter M. Blau, *Bureaucracy in Modern Society*, New York: Random House, 1956; Amitai Etzioni, *Modern Organizations*, Englewood Cliffs, N. J.: Prentice-Hall, 1964; Theodore Caplow, *Principles of Organization*, New York: Harcourt Brace Jovanovich, 1964; Robert Presthus, *The Organizational Society*, New York: Alfred A. Knopf, 1962; and Victor A. Thompson, *Modern Organization*, New York: Alfred A. Knopf, 1964.

of the traditional views of structure, authority, division of labor, handling change and conflict, and other common organizational problems. It has been a shift from the *form* or structure to the *process* and interaction of activities and people. Warren Bennis has led the way in proposals for change agents and the handling of organizational change.[55] Joseph Litterer has built his analysis of organizations from individual behavior to group behavior and thereby to formal and informal interactions in a socio-technical system.[56] William G. Scott took the systems view and stated that we are moving toward a "constitutional organization" in which there will be limits on the power of superiors to deal unilaterally and arbitrarily with their subordinates.[57] John Seiler has written of cybernetics, human and social "inputs," and the analysis of the organization as an interacting pattern of variables.[58] Carzo and Yanouzas have added quantitative analytical techniques to an open systems concept of organizations.[59] "Project management" has been a creation of the aerospace industry and has resulted in new "matrix" forms of organization. By cutting across functional lines, the matrix or project organization gives more flexibility in meeting predetermined goals.[60]

Flexibility rather than formality and process rather than form have been the keynotes of modern organization theory. The hierarchy of authority has fallen into greater disfavor, power is diffused, and managers are urged to use interpersonal influence rather than authority to get results. Social critics have had a field day with the ineptitudes of bureaucrats and bureaucracy. Parkinson's Law and the Peter Principle have become popular symbols of the disfavor of formality in organizational life.[61] There has not

[55] Warren G. Bennis, *Changing Organizations*, New York: McGraw-Hill, 1966.

[56] Joseph A. Litterer, *The Analysis of Organizations*, New York: John Wiley and Sons, 1965.

[57] William G. Scott, *Organization Theory: A Behavioral Analysis for Management*, Homewood, Ill.: Richard D. Irwin, 1968.

[58] John A. Seiler, *Systems Analysis in Organizational Behavior*, Homewood, Ill.: Richard D. Irwin, 1967.

[59] Rocco Carzo, Jr. and John N. Yanouzas, *Formal Organization: A Systems Approach*, Homewood, Ill.: Richard D. Irwin, 1967.

[60] For more complete discussions, see: John S. Baumgartner, *Project Management*, Homewood, Ill.: Richard D. Irwin, 1963; and David I. Cleland and William R. King, *Systems Analysis and Project Management*, New York: McGraw-Hill Book Co., 1968.

[61] C. Northcote Parkinson, *Parkinson's Law and Other Studies in Administration*, Boston: Houghton Mifflin Co., 1957; and Lawrence J. Peter and Raymond Hull, *The Peter Principle*, New York: William Morrow and Co., 1969. Here the authors

been a complete rejection of formality in organizations but a call for the recognition that some organizations need more flexibility than others.[62] Joan Woodward has found that organization structure is related to technologies of various types of manufacturing. Some structures are more appropriate than others depending upon whether the technology calls for job order, intermittent, or continuous manufacturing.[63] Like Woodward, Lawrence and Lorsch have postulated that no one form of organization is "best". They have developed a "contingency theory" which says that technological and market conditions have a large impact on company organization and that the type of organization chosen depends on the specific demands of the company environment.[64]

Modern research and writing has indicated a move toward flexibility, toward adaptation of the structure to fit technology, market, and other environmental factors. It has become in a sense an "organizational grid" of ideas about structure and people, moving along a continuum of possibilities in order to mix concern for structure and concern for the human element in some pleasing design. The shift in thought has gone from the bureaucratic ideal to the need for "adaptable" organizations; from the idealization of the scalar principle to the decline of the hierarchy in getting people involved in decisions; and from the needs for efficiency to the needs for coping with change and encouraging creativity. Modern organizations are much more complex in both internal structure and environmental constraints than those of Max Weber's day. It has been in response to these modern forces that organization theory has evolved to propose new strategies and structures.

A Final Note

The search for harmony between organizations and men has evolved through various approaches throughout history. The goals

---

have developed a modern lampooning of bureaucracy in the same vein as C. Northcote Parkinson. "Hierarchiology," or the study of hierarchies, has as its first principle that "in a hierarchy each employee tends to rise to his level of incompetence: every post tends to be occupied by an employee incompetent to execute its duties."

[62] See Gerald Bell, "Formality versus Flexibility in Complex Organizations," in Gerald Bell (ed.), *Organizations and Human Behavior*, Englewood Cliffs, N.J.: Prentice-Hall, 1967, pp. 97–106.

[63] Joan Woodward, *Industrial Organization: Theory and Practice*, London: Oxford University Press, 1965.

[64] Paul H. Lawrence and Jay W. Lorsch, *Organization and Environment: Managing Differentiation and Integration*, Homewood, Ill.: Richard D. Irwin, 1968.

of these approaches bear a remarkable similarity and the means to these ends bear the brunt of the differences. Man resisted regimentation even before the factory system and has sought rewards and satisfactions for his efforts. Organizations have had age-old problems of bringing together technology and people to serve an organizational end and the conflict between these sets of objectives has been readily apparent throughout these preceding pages. Scientific management sought a recognition of the mutuality of interests through a mental revolution in which the individual could be appropriately rewarded while contributing to the productivity of the enterprise. The human relationists' quest was for social solidarity through understanding of and concern for people who would reciprocate by being satisfied, productive workers. The organizational humanists advocated personal awareness, interpersonal competence, understanding of human nature and needs, and flexibility and balance in bringing harmonious relations between the man and the organization. Even though the major themes have offered differing avenues, each has sought in its own way to keep the "man" in management without neglecting the "manage" in management.

SUMMARY

Organizational humanism began during the 1957–1960 period. It emerged as a response to the alleged softness and to deficiencies in empirical research in the traditional human relations mode of thinking. It also emerged as a response to the shortcomings of the classical and neo-classical approaches to organization theory. As a philosophy, organization humanism has sought to bring a new focus on man and his varied needs, on work as a means of fulfillment, and on the process rather than the structuring of activities. As an operational technique, this humanism has challenged the assumptions we make about people and the motivational, leadership, and organizational styles most appropriate to the modern environment. Organizational humanism has sought a harmony in organizational life, a pleasing and productive arrangement of parts within the whole which would satisfy the requirements of man and the organization.

21

Quantification and Systems: The Search for Order

Numbers have always held a fascination for man; man has ascribed magical powers to some numbers, malignancy to others, and throughout history has used numbers to account for his flock of sheep as well as to reach for the stars. Having no intrinsic value in themselves, numbers have become symbols of man's quest for knowledge because they lend a preciseness and orderliness to man's environment. In observing nature, man also noted that there was a natural rhythm of the seasons, of the solar system, and of life and death in all things. His inquisitiveness led him to explore, to attempt to explain the inexplicable, and to search for a great force that bound the complexities observed in nature into some rational order of events. Man sought to bring order from chaos by searching for interrelationships between observed events and activities. Although man is curious and seeks variety in life, he also has a need for closure, a need to bring his observations into some unity of perception. He is basically an orderly, rational being who desires to control his environment in so far as that is possible.

For management, man's search for order has been expressed throughout history in attempts to rationalize and systematize the workplace and the organization's operations. The modern era of quantitative methods and systems theory has deep roots in prior management theory and this chapter will briefly trace those beginnings and modern developments in management's search for order.

THE QUEST FOR QUANTIFICATION

In the search for order and predictability, the scientific method has denoted a rational approach to problem solving through the statement of hypotheses, the accumulation of data, the identification of alternatives, and the testing, verification, and selection of a path of action based upon facts. In his break with the mystics who held that reality was unknowable, Aristotle established the foundations for the scientific method. After Greece and Rome fell, reason submerged to the Age of Faith during the Middle Ages only to re-emerge in the Renaissance and an Age of Reason. It was during this time that the foundations for modern mathematics and science were to be established. René Descartes (1596–1650) thought the world operated mechanistically and prescribed the use of mathematics to describe its movements. Isaac Newton (1642–1727) developed calculus and stated laws of motion and gravitation, furthering Descartes' conception of the world as a giant machine. There were others who saw an orderly universe and mathematics was to be the building block for bringing the parts together into one grand formula. The rediscovery of Aristotle during this time and the renewed interest in mathematics and in science led to the vast technological changes in man's environment known as the Industrial Revolution.

Charles Babbage, and to some extent Andrew Ure, applied a scientific approach to the solution of the problems of the burgeoning factory system. Industrialization demanded order and predictability and the engineers were a breed well equipped to cope with the scientific study and systematization of work. Scientific management and the work of Taylor, Barth, Gantt, the Gilbreths, Emerson, and others were the Age of Reason in twentieth century management thought. In the 1930's, scientific management declined in emphasis as society had problems beyond the production of goods with which to cope. World War II and the renewed growth of large-scale enterprise, however, created a new environment for management. It was in the modern era that new ideas were being formed to add to the tradition of Aristotle, Descartes, Babbage, and scientific management.

Operations Research

World War I had given widespread recognition and acceptance to the notion of science in management. Governments and industrial organizations seized on the precepts of scientific management in order to cope with the mass assemblages of resources required to carry on the war. Likewise, World War II brought about a union of managers, government officials, and scientists in an effort to bring order and rationality to the global logistics of war. The British formed the first "operations research teams" of various specialists in an effort to bring their knowledge to bear upon the problems of radar systems, anti-aircraft gunnery, anti-submarine warfare, the bombing of Germany, and civilian defense matters. One of the best known groups was under the direction of Professor P. M. S. Blackett, physicist, Nobel Prize winner, and co-developer of radar. Blackett's team, called "Blackett's circus," included "three physiologists, two mathematical physicists, one astrophysicist, one Army officer, one surveyor, one general physicist, and two mathematicians."[1] It was in groups such as this one that various specialists were brought together under one tent to solve the complex problems of the war and defense efforts.

In its conception, operations research was the application of scientific knowledge and methods to the study of complex problems with the stated purpose of deriving a quantitative basis for decisions which would accomplish the organization's objectives. While the British formed the first operations research groups, the Americans soon saw the potential of "operations analysis." Dr. James B. Conant, then Chairman of the National Defense Research Committee, and Dr. Vannevar Bush, then Chairman of the Committee on New Weapons and Equipment of the Joint Chiefs of Staff, saw the British groups in operation and were instrumental in forming similar staff groups for the United States Navy and the Eighth Bomber Command. The conclusion of the war did not bring the demise of operations research. The Army formed an Operations Research Office, the Navy established an Operations

---

[1] Florence N. Trefethen, "A History of Operations Research," in Joseph F. McCloskey and Florence N. Trefethen (ed.), *Operations Research for Management,* Baltimore: Johns Hopkins Press, 1954, p. 6.

Evaluation Group, and the newly formed Air Force established its Operations Analysis Division.[2]

Industrial organizations and private consulting firms also began to recognize that the methods of operations research were applicable to problems of a non-military nature. Arthur D. Little, Inc., a private consulting firm, was one of the first to seek industrial uses. Other firms, some old and some new, began to apply the operations research concept and professional societies and professional journals began to form the first wave of an operations research boom. The Operations Research Society of America was founded in 1952 and began publishing its journal *Operations Research*. In 1953, The Institute of Management Science (TIMS) stated its objectives as "to identify, extend, and unify scientific knowledge that contributes to the understanding of the practice of management" and began publishing the journal *Management Science*. It was merely a light staccato in the late forties and early fifties, but the environment of management was changing rapidly in its complexity after the war and managers and academicians were seeking a more orderly basis for decision making. The war had resulted in an unprecedented accumulation of resources, and firms were faced with advancements in scientific knowledge which led to new products and markets, new technologies, and new developments in transportation and communication.

Historically, it is interesting to note the closing gap between the resource accumulation and the rationalization of resource utilization phases. It took America over a hundred years of resource accumulation (phase I) before scientific management appeared as phase II. Dormant during the Depression, phase III, the renewal of resource accumulation, began in post-war America. In less than a decade, attempts were being made to re-rationalize resource utilization (phase IV) through the application of more science in managing.

The beginnings of operations research in industry came very naturally in the production management area. It was here that there were more structured kinds of problems and decisions for which decision rules could be rationally devised. There were problems of stocking the proper level of inventories, of scheduling production, of manufacturing in economical batches, of quality

---

[2] *Ibid.*, pp. 12–15. The reader will recall that Dr. Bush also participated in the original Hawthorne experiments under the aegis of the National Research Council.

control, of capital acquisition, and a host of other physical resource problems. For industrial practice:

> O.R. (Operations Research) in the most general sense can be characterized as the application of scientific methods, techniques, and tools to problems involving the operation of the system so as to provide those in control of the operations with optimum solutions to the problems.[3]

As such, operations research, or what some prefer to call management science, has direct lineal roots in scientific management. Indeed, the similarities are striking. Taylor, Gilbreth, and others spoke of the "one best way" as the objective of their scientific analysis. The modern management scientist has merely put the quest more euphemistically:

> The approach of optimality analysis is to take these alternatives into account and to ask which of these possible sets of decisions will come *closest* to meeting the businessman's objectives, *i.e.* which decisions will be best or *optimal*.[4]

The difference between the "one best way" and an "optimal" decision is a moot one. The old school and the new one have both sought through the scientific method to rationally evaluate alternatives in an effort to find the best possible decision. In Taylor's time, people had confidence that science could lead to societal perfectability; today, we are less confident in such a scheme and "optimal" sounds better to our ears than the "one best way."

Another striking similarity is that the moderns, like their predecessors, have sought to apply the scientific method in the analysis of human behavior. The Institute of Management Science has formed a functional interest group, the College on Management Psychology, and its purpose is "to investigate the processes of work and managing work by applying psychology, psychiatry, and the behavioral sciences in order to enhance our understanding of management." Hugo Munsterberg could not have stated the case more clearly. Modern behavioralists frequently view management science as a continuation of a mechanistic view of man and feel that the behavioral and quantitative approaches are mutually exclusive. However, we should remember that it was not the wheel which was man's great invention, but the axle. We need to search

---

[3] C. West Churchman, Russell L. Ackoff, and E. Leonard Arnoff, *Introduction to Operations Research*, New York: John Wiley and Sons, 1957, pp. 8–9.

[4] William J. Baumol, *Economic Theory and Operations Analysis*, Englewood Cliffs, N.J.: Prentice-Hall, 1961, p. 4.

for how these areas complement one another and how they might be brought together in some grand scheme.

Modern management science, inverted from scientific management, was not so much the search for a science *of* management as it was a striving for the use of science *in* management. It was here in quantitative methods, operations research, management science, or operations management that the tools of science were enlisted to help solve the age-old management problem of the optimum allocation of scarce resources toward a given goal.

Changing Times in Management Education

The Gordon and Howell report had been particularly critical of the state of business education with respect to mathematics. Sputnik launched the space age and new generations of computer technology were evolving to cope with the massive problem solving and information requirements of the 1960's. The business student, being prepared for leadership in a computerized space age, had had few if any requirements for mathematics in the typical business school curriculum. The 1960's saw a reversal of this state of affairs and schools began to require more and more statistics and mathematics of their students. The burgeoning appearance of quantitative methods in curricula brought a proliferation of new management specialities and eventually an enrichment in the semantic problems of the management theory jungle.

For many, the language of the operations researcher resembles the mumbo-jumbo of the witch doctor. There is the ritual of model building, the symbols to be manipulated during the ceremony, and the awe-inspiring incantation of magical phrases. To the uninitiated, the total ceremony inspires awe, fear, and reverence for the mathematical elite. Hence, there should be little wonder that the quantitative specialists had such an impact on traditional management theory. The 1950's saw a host of the new genre of production or operations management textbooks. Individuals like Russell Ackoff, C. West Churchman, Edward Bowman, Robert Fetter, Elwood Buffa, Jay Forrester, and others were bringing new ideas and techniques into management thought.[5]

[5] A suggestive but not comprehensive bibliography of the operations research approach to production management would include: Russell L. Ackoff, E. Leonard Arnoff, and C. West Churchman, *Introduction to Operations Research,* New York: John Wiley and Sons, 1957; Edward H. Bowman and Robert B. Fetter, *Analysis for*

The new language of management was heavily oriented toward statistics and mathematics. At its base was the scientific method of problem solving; the body was composed of specific techniques for quantifying variables and relationships; and its apex was the notion of a model which represented the variables and their relationships for the purposes of prediction and control. Techniques such as statistics, linear programming, waiting line or queueing theory, game theory, decision trees, the transportation method, Monte Carlo methods, and simulation devices were part and parcel of the new language.[6] Statistics and probability theory aided in sampling for quality control purposes and other uses; linear programming and its special techniques facilitated the choice of a desirable course of action given certain constraints; and queueing theory facilitated balancing the costs and the services of a machine or other service facility. Competitive strategies could be best understood by drawing upon game theory;[7] capital acquisitions could be simulated through computers and the use of probability theory; and quantitative models could be built and manipulated to test the impact of changes on one or more of the variables or the model as a whole.

Along with presenting the analytical techniques, serious attempts were being made to bring the operations research tools into a conceptual framework. The outcome of this was the "decision theorists," who sought to combine the economic concepts of utility and choice with the more modern quantitative tools. One early landmark attempt was by David Miller and Martin Starr, who stressed the executive's decision-making role in optimizing and sub-optimizing corporate goals and placed less emphasis on the

---

Production Management, Homewood, Ill.: Richard D. Irwin, 1957; Elwood S. Buffa, *Modern Production Management,* New York: John Wiley and Sons, 1961, 1965, and 1969; Jay W. Forrester, *Industrial Dynamics,* Cambridge, Mass.: M.I.T. Press, 1961; and Samuel B. Richmond, *Operations Research for Management Decisions,* New York: Ronald Press Co., 1968.

[6] In addition to references in the preceding footnote, the following would serve to explain more fully these techniques and their uses: Richard I. Levin and Rudolph P. Lamone, *Linear Programming for Management Decisions,* Homewood, Ill.: Richard D. Irwin, 1969; Daniel Teichroew, *An Introduction to Management Science: Deterministic Models,* New York: John Wiley & Sons, 1964; William T. Morris, *Management Science: A Bayesian Introduction,* Englewood Cliffs, N.J.: Prentice-Hall, 1968; and Harvey M. Wagner, *Principles of Management Science: With Applications to Executive Decisions,* Englewood Cliffs, N.J.: Prentice-Hall, 1970.

[7] The mathematically inclined might wish to read John von Neumann and Oskar Morgenstern, *Theory of Games and Economic Behavior,* Princeton, N.J.: Princeton University Press, 1944; a lighter approach to game theory is John McDonald, *Strategy in Poker, Business, and War,* New York: W. W. Norton and Co., 1950.

techniques.[8] Jay Forrester has been a pathfinder in attempts to design and simulate the entire operations and interactions of an enterprise.[9] In other developments, economic historians have sought to construct quantitative models of early and modern economies in order to better understand economic development.[10]

Statistical theory was substantially advanced in post-war America and probability theory became an important consideration in making managerial decisions. More esoteric ideas, such as those found in Bayesian statistics, added the subjective probability of events as a basis for the maximization of expected profit or utility in a decision. These more sophisticated decision making tools were to reshape notions of educating managers through changes in business school curricula and would also bring about a new variety of specialists with whom the manager had to communicate. Henri Fayol, who had found the use of "higher mathematics" of no value in his experience, probably would have had his ideas of management education severely shaken in the business school of the 1960's.

Henry Gantt would also be surprised to find what the new quantitative methods had done with his ideas. The reader will recall that Gantt, under pressure to handle complex industrial-military interactions in World War I, had devised a graphic method of scheduling and controlling activities. In 1956–57, the DuPont Company developed a computerized arrow diagram or network method for planning and controlling which became known as the Critical Path Method (CPM). This method used only one time estimate and included only activities (arrows).[11] In 1957–58, in managing the development of the Polaris missile, the United States Navy encountered much the same problems in project scheduling and evaluation as it had in Gantt's day with ship building. Together with the consulting help of Booz, Allen, and Hamilton, Inc., and the Lockheed Missile Systems Division (the prime contractor), the Navy devised the Program Evaluation and Review

[8] David W. Miller and Martin K. Starr, *Executive Decisions and Operations Research*, Englewood Cliffs, N.J.: Prentice-Hall, 1960. See also: David W. Miller and Martin K. Starr, *The Structure of Human Decisions*, Englewood Cliffs, N.J.: Prentice-Hall, 1967.

[9] Jay W. Forrester, *Industrial Dynamics*, Cambridge, Mass.: M.I.T. Press, 1961.

[10] For some exercises in "cliometrics," see *Purdue Faculty Papers in Economic History*: 1956–1966, Homewood Ill.: Richard D. Irwin, 1967.

[11] Russell D. Archibald and Richard L. Villoria, *Network-Based Management Systems (PERT/CPM)*, New York: John Wiley & Sons, 1967, pp. 12–15.

Technique (PERT). This technique used statistical probability theory to furnish three time estimates (pessimistic, most probable, and optimistic) and added "events" (circles) to the graphing of activities.

Taken together, these network techniques of PERT and CPM serve to plan a network of activities, their relationships, and their interaction along a path to a given completion date. They graph paths for the flow of activities, provide events as checkpoints, and focus managerial attention on a "critical path" or paths in an effort to keep the total project on course.[12] While these techniques are much more complex than this brief description implies, they are really little more than the Gantt chart concept enlarged and enriched by forty or more years of advancing management and statistical knowledge.

Quantification: A Final Note

While the preceding pages have barely scratched the surface of what is a substantial and growing body of literature, the links with the past and the trends should be fairly obvious. Modern operations research is a re-emergence of man's age-old quest for order, predictability, measurement, and control. In the development of management thought, the search for science in managing is an old one and reflects the search for certainty of performance in operations. The search for order through quantification is an attempt to quantify variables in industrial and organizational problems, to enhance the measurement and control of performance, and to construct abstract models to represent the real world in order to manipulate and test these models for the purpose of aiding decision making. Beginning as the province of the technical specialist, operations research has begun to provide a foundation block for general systems theory and has become an integral part of education for the manager of the future.

SYSTEMS

A second part of this search for order in the modern era came with the development of systems theory or systems approaches to the study of management. We will see that the systems concept

---

[12] For example, see Joseph Horowitz, *Critical Path Scheduling: Management Control Through CPM and PERT*, New York: Ronald Press Co., 1967.

is really an old one and that modern developments have been an amalgam of many disciplines in an effort to sharpen managerial skills, to develop an operative theory of management, and to provide a better conceptual framework for organizational design and operation.

Early Notions of Systems

A dictionary definition of a system is "an assemblage of objects united by some form of regular interaction or interdependence; an organic or organized whole."[13] Throughout history man has observed such an orderliness in nature. He saw an ecological balance in plant and animal life; he noted that the planets and stars operated predictably enough and he made gods of stars and used them to chart his own life forecast; he saw that small streams flowed into larger and still larger ones to flow to the sea; and he saw a rhythm in the coming and going of seasons so that he could plant and harvest his crops. Primitive man built his life activities around rituals which were a part of this natural order; such ceremonies gave him the security of order and predictability. For example, the Egyptians depended upon the orderliness of nature in the rise and fall of the Nile in order to transport the materials for the construction of the pyramids.

As man designed his organizations, he sought once more the orderliness in their operation that he observed in nature. Under the domestic system, entrepreneurs operated their various undertakings as a system built upon the receipt of orders for products, the "putting-out" of the work, and the return of the completed product. The early factory managers sought "systematic" management which would arrange the workplace, secure the proper flow of materials, and facilitate the performance of human effort in order to achieve some predictable result. Boulton and Watt designed a simplified inventory-production system by standardizing parts in such fashion that inventory level could be reduced to a minimum and customer reordering would be simplified. Taylor sought to systematize the selection of workers and the conditions of their jobs; Gilbreth wrote of "Field Systems" and "Concrete Systems"

[13] *Webster's New Collegiate Dictionary,* Springfield, Mass.: G. and C. Merriam Co., 1956, p. 863.

which were manuals for standardizing methods and procedures for work; and Gantt developed graphic aids to schedule, coordinate, and control the work of many agencies. Fayol separated management and administration and viewed management as the integration of all six functions of a business in directing it toward objectives. Mayo and his associates advised the manager to view his organization as a "social system" composed of many human parts; Lewin made "field theory" into a solid analytical tool; W. F. Whyte viewed the restaurant as a work-flow social system; and Bakke and Homans wrote of the need to study the interactions of both formal and informal components. Follett spoke of integrative unity and Barnard wrote of formal and informal communications and the need to maintain an equilibrium both within the organization and with elements outside the organization.

If we examine all of these early notions of systems, we can see that they have in common a number of characteristics: (1) there was always a goal or purpose for the organization, some reason for its existence whether it be tombs for the pharaohs, industrial products, governmental services, or social satisfactions; (2) there was some presumed inflow or input of materials, equipment, and human effort into the organization; (3) there was something being done in the organization to transform these inputs into some useful product or service to meet goals of the organization; and (4) there was some need to measure, to control, to acquire the necessary information about performance to see if plans were being carried out. Further, these early writers recognized the complex interactions which existed between the human and physical parts of the organization. There was a search to study the parts, to understand their interrelationships, and to so arrange the parts that they led to the desired outcome.

There is evidence that early management writers saw an interrelationship of parts and sought to bring these together into an organic whole or system. They sought to rationalize resource utilization, to understand human behavior, and to devise schemes whereby managers could bring the parts together. Some focused on organizational design, some on production processes, some on the factory as a social system, and others on the administrative activities performed by the manager in planning, organizing, and controlling work.

General Systems Theory

Although notions of systems existed, the major distinction between prior eras and the modern one was in the *way of thinking* or the *philosophy* of the systems approach. Here again we find deep roots in prior thought. It was in the early twentieth century that psychologists and sociologists began the "organismic" or Gestalt approach in theories of behavior. This was a break with the prior "mechanistic" or fundamental unit method of analysis. In 1926, a South African lawyer and general, Jan Christian Smuts, represented the coming *Zeitgeist* of following eras by noting a tendency toward "holism" (wholeness) in all form, matter, life, and personality. He spoke of "fields" before Kurt Lewin and put forth a synergistic view of the universe in noting that an organism consists of parts but is more than the sum of those parts.[14] Before Boulding, Smuts developed an idea of a "progressive grading" or levels of "holistic synthesis" (systems): (1) "mere physical mixtures," wherein the parts largely preserve their character; (2) chemical compounds, which form a new structure and the parts are not easily identifiable; (3) organisms, with central control of parts and organs; (4) "minds," with central control achieving a freedom and creativity; and (5) personality, the "most evolved" whole in the universe. Smuts' work represented a Gestalt view of the universe and must be considered as an attempt at what was to become the province of general systems theory.

Ludwig von Bertalanffy, a biologist, is credited with coining the phrase "general systems theory." Bertalanffy introduced the notion of "general systems theory" at a University of Chicago seminar in 1937 but did not publish his work until after the war.[15] He sought a unity of sciences which would go beyond merely relating physical phenomena at an atomistic level. He thought that it was possible to develop a systematic, theoretical framework for describing relationships in the real world and that different dis-

[14] Jan Christian Smuts, *Holism and Evolution,* New York: Macmillan Co., 1926, pp. 1–2 and p. 101.

[15] Ludwig von Bertalanffy, "General Systems Theory—A Critical Review," in Walter Buckley (ed.), *Modern Systems Research for the Behavioral Scientist,* Chicago: Aldine Publishing Co., 1968, p. 13. See also: Ludwig von Bertalanffy, *General Systems Theory: Foundations, Development, Applications,* New York: George Braziller, 1968; and Ludwig von Bertalanffy, *Organismic Psychology and Systems Theory,* Barre, Mass.: Clark University Press, 1968.

ciplines had similarities which could be developed into a "general systems model." Every science or discipline had a "model," *i.e.* a conceptual structure intended to reflect aspects of reality, but no *one* science had a monopoly on all knowledge since each science merely reflected a certain slice of reality. The goal, as Bertalanffy conceptualized it, was to search for parallelisms in disciplines and thereby be able to generalize a theoretical framework. Bertalanffy noted certain characteristics which were similar in all sciences: (1) the study of a whole, or organism; (2) that organisms tended to strive for a "steady state" or equilibrium; and (3) the "openness" of all systems in that the organism was affected by its environment and in turn affected its environment.[16]

Bertalanffy's efforts were the beginning piece in a jigsaw puzzle upon which others began to build. Norbert Wiener coined the word "cybernetics" from the Greek *kubernētēs* meaning steersman or helmsman.[17] The study of cybernetics showed that all systems could be designed to control themselves through a communications "loop" which "fed back" information allowing the organism to adjust to its environment. Of course, James Watt had developed the first cybernetic control device, the "fly-ball governor," as a method of automatically regulating the speed of a steam engine. However, Wiener was seeking to study language and messages in a human sense in order to understand man-machine interactions and their broader implications for society.[18] Along a parallel path, Shannon and Weaver were developing some concepts of information theory as it pertained to the encoding, transmitting, and decoding of messages, to channel capacity, and to the mathematical study of communications.[19]

The economist Kenneth Boulding built directly upon Bertalanffy's ideas and tried to integrate Wiener's cybernetics with the information theory of Shannon and Weaver. Boulding suggested that general systems theory was one way of developing a means for specialists to find a common denominator, a language

---

[16] Ludwig von Bertalanffy, "General Systems Theory: A New Approach to the Unity of Science," *Human Biology*, Vol. 23 (December, 1951), pp. 302–361. See also: Ludwig von Bertalanffy, *Problems of Life*, New York: John Wiley and Sons, 1952.

[17] Norbert Wiener, *Cybernetics*, Cambridge, Mass.: M.I.T. Press, 1948.

[18] Norbert Wiener, *The Human Use of Human Beings*, Boston: Houghton Mifflin Co., 1950.

[19] Claude E. Shannon and Warren Weaver, *The Mathematical Theory of Communication*, Urbana: University of Illinois Press, 1949.

through which they could communicate. Boulding developed nine levels of systems for analysis and these are listed here in order of increasing complexity: (1) frameworks (static); (2) clockworks (simple dynamic systems); (3) thermostat (cybernetics); (4) cell (open, self-maintaining); (5) plant (genetic-societal); (6) animal; (7) man; (8) social organizations; and (9) transcendental. For Boulding, general systems theory "aims to provide a framework or structure on which to hang the flesh and blood of particular disciplines and particular subject matters in an orderly and coherent corpus of knowledge."[20]

While Boulding left the ninth level ("transcendental") largely unexplored, C. West Churchman has developed some ideas in this realm of general systems theory and human values.[21] For Churchman, the "challenge to reason" comes in those areas which do not readily lend themselves to the scientific method and systems analysis.

The elements of general systems theory were flowing from a variety of sources and establishing a theoretical and philosophical framework for studying different levels of systems, for recognizing the openness of systems, for developing information feedback to maintain a relatively steady state, and for probing systems theory as a way of thinking Along with this framework, industrial technology was advancing to make the dreams of systems theory come at least fairly close to reality. One advancement in particular, the computer, made a significant contribution because of its ability to process masses of data, to simulate operations, to solve intricate problems, and to control production processes. Certain aspects of the development of the computer have already been discussed in the work of Charles Babbage, the Jacquard loom, and the punch card of Herman Hollerith. Hollerith had developed the punch card and sorter to aid the United States Census Bureau. He left the Bureau and formed the Tabulating Machine Company (1903) and from that company the International Business Machines Corporation emerged in 1912. It was not until 1944 that Harvard's Howard Aiken developed for IBM the first automatic sequence

[20] Kenneth E. Boulding, "General Systems Theory—The Skeleton of Science," *Management Science*, (April, 1956), pp. 197–208; reprinted in Peter R. Schoderbeck (ed.), *Management Systems*, New York: John Wiley and Sons, 1967, pp. 7–15.

[21] C. West Churchman, *Challenge to Reason*, New York: McGraw-Hill Book Company, 1968.

controlled computer, an electromechanical, but not an electronic, model.[22]

From its crude beginnings, the computer was soon to become an electronic marvel, a boon to managers, the bane of income tax evaders, and a constant companion of us all. It was the computer and all of its capabilities that arrived on the scene at the proper historical moment to aid the information theorists, the operations researchers, and the systems analysts in their work. Without the computer, systems theory would not have developed as rapidly as it did. With the computer, the complexities of mathematical models were simplified, simulation and game theory furthered, information systems enriched, and the automated control of factories made possible. The computer made possible a Third Industrial Revolution based on cybernetics. The First had replaced man labor with machine labor, the Second brought forth mass production through the assembly line, and the Third replaced man control of production processes with machine control.

Systems Theory and Management Theory

Beginning with Bertalanffy as a hope in 1937 and evolving through the work of Wiener, Boulding, and others, general systems theory was not to make its major impact on management thought until the 1960's. It is true that more and more pieces of the puzzle were being inserted from organization theory, management process theory, information theory, decision theory, the behavioral sciences, and operations research. However, these specialized areas of study were evolving toward more and more of a "systems approach" until "systems" was to become the catch-phrase of the modern era. Figure 21-1 presents a conceptual model of this impact that general systems theory had on modern management thought. The figure suggests much more neatness and simplicity than was apparent in the real world. In reality, each area of subject matter was reflecting portions of others in a reciprocal process of change and influence which tended to blend them together at certain points. The model does, however, serve as a convenient framework for the analysis which follows.

[22] Richard N. Schmidt and William E. Meyers, *Introduction to Computer Science and Data Processing*, New York: Holt, Rinehart and Winston, 1965, pp. 19–30.

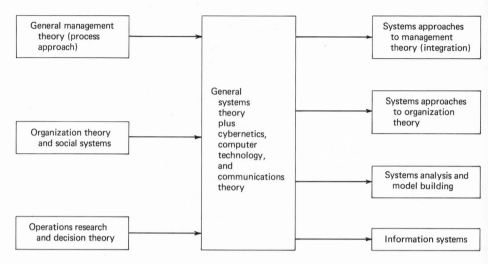

Fig. 21–1. Systems theory and management.

The year 1963 marked the first impact of general systems theory on the process approach to management. While portions of these influences were discussed in Chapter 19, the focus here will be on various attempts to use the systems approach as an integrative framework for studying the job of the manager. Seymour Tilles defined a system as a "set of interrelated parts" and noted that many people held limited views of management as a "social system," as a "data processing system," or as a system of "funds flows."[23] Tilles proposed a synthesis from a "systems point of view" which would divide the work of the manager into four basic tasks:

(1) Defining the company as a system.
(2) Establishing system objectives, which can be further broken down to:
   —Identifying wider systems.
   —Setting performance criteria.
(3) Creating formal subsystems.
(4) Systemic integration.[24]

In his analysis, Tilles discussed each of these parts of the manager's job .and concluded that the systems approach enabled the manager to have a conceptual framework for relating different specialties and parts of the company to one another. Further, the

[23] Seymour Tilles, "The Manager's Job: A Systems Approach," *Harvard Business Review*, Vol. 41, No. 1 (January–February, 1963), p. 74.
[24] *Loc. cit.*

systems approach provided an open-ended view of the manager's job which facilitated understanding of "how his company relates to its complex environment—to the other great systems of which it is a part."[25]   In many respects, Tilles' writings reflected as much of Chester Barnard as of Bertalanffy, but the groundwork was laid for further expansion of using the systems approach to the job of the manager.

Johnson, Kast, and Rosenzweig put forth a more comprehensive view of the systems approach as "a way of thinking about the job of managing . . . [which] provides a framework for visualizing internal and external environmental factors as an integrated whole."[26] Drawing more heavily on Bertalanffy and Boulding, the authors defined a system as "an array of components designed to achieve an objective according to plan."[27]   The business organization typified a system in that it was an open system which was influenced by and in turn influenced its environment, in that it strove to maintain a state of "dynamic equilibrium" of parts to whole, and because it was a dynamic interplay of both internal and external forces trying to satisfy goals of both the organization and of individual participants.

From their conceptual framework, the authors applied the systems approach to planning, organizing, controlling, and communications as integral parts of the manager's job.   They also suggested applications of the systems concept in weapon-systems management, rhochrematics or physical distribution management, automation, and data processing systems.   Implementation of systems management drew heavily from the techniques of management science, such as simulation, PERT, the Monte Carlo method, etc. Human systems were included in the authors' analysis; and, in retrospect, they presented a significant contribution to the evolution of management thought.   They sought to bring the physical, human, and informational aspects of the manager's job into one grand framework of a "way of thinking" by the manager about how to integrate all facets of the organization into an integrated whole.

Others also sought to apply the systems approach in order to integrate management process theory.   Voich and Wren concep-

[25] *Ibid.*, p. 81.

[26] Richard A. Johnson, Fremont E. Kast, and James E. Rosenzweig, *The Theory and Management of Systems*, New York: McGraw-Hill Book Co., 1963, p. 3 (revised edition, 1967).

[27] *Ibid.*, p. vii and p. 91.

tualized the organization as a complex input-output system in which the manager became a motivating and linking mechanism in applying the management process to a system of physical and human resources. In defining a system as "a purposeful, organized interrelationship of components in which the performance of the whole exceeds the individual outputs of all the parts", these authors presented a Gestalt and synergistic view of an organization.[28] For Voich and Wren, the systems approach (1) facilitated understanding of the organization as a whole rather than as a chaotic arrangement of parts; (2) permitted the analysis of resource flows toward objectives; (3) described the manager's job in terms of the allocation and utilization of resources; and (4) revealed an awareness of the environmental forces which affected managerial decision making. Sisk also presented a synergistic view by defining a system as being "composed of parts that are interrelated in a manner that forms a unified whole that is more than a mere summation of the parts."[29] From that point, Sisk used systems theory to show the interrelatedness of specific aspects of the job of the manager.

One branch of Figure 21-1, the influence of general systems theory on the management process, has been examined. This branch took the view that the job of the manager could be accommodated within the realm of the systems theory and that the systems view was a way of thinking about integrating management activities both internally and in relation to the organizational environment. As noted previously, systems theory formed one avenue of hope for unity in management theory.

A second stream of influence of general systems theory came through organization theory and systems approaches to organizational design. The Mayoists and other behavioralists conceived of organizations as social systems and the organizational theorists discussed in Chapter 20 were describing socio-technical systems. The Tavistock Institute furnished early views on the analysis of organizations as open systems in which there was a dynamic interplay between the work system and the human system.[30] The systems approach to organizations has been more recently char-

[28] Dan Voich, Jr. and Daniel A. Wren, *Principles of Management: Resources and Systems*, New York: Ronald Press Co., 1968, p. 21.

[29] Henry L. Sisk, *Principles of Management: A Systems Approach to the Management Process*, Cincinnati, Ohio: South Western Publishing Co., 1969, p. 12.

[30] See Chapters 15 and 20, and more recently: Eric J. Miller and Albert K. Rice, *Systems of Organization*, London: Tavistock Publications, 1967.

acterized by the application of management science concepts and systems models to earlier concepts of organization theory. For example, Carzo and Yanouzas have suggested such esoteric techniques as Markov chain analysis and waiting line theory as being applicable to the study of organizational design.[31] Seiler and his associates have proposed the analysis of human, social, technical, and organizational "inputs" as aids to designing complex organizational systems.[32] Kast and Rosenzweig have included a framework for "comparative organizational systems" which reflects the influence of both general systems theory and comparative management on organization theory.[33] In each of these more modern developments, one can see attempts to blend information technology, quantitative methods, socio-human factors, organizational technology, and management theory into the systems concept.

The concept of project management or the "matrix organization" has also become a part of organization theory. Emerging from the complexities of managing aerospace and other projects for the Department of Defense and the National Aeronautics and Space Administration, the project-management concept cuts across functional lines to concentrate responsibility for accomplishment upon a project manager. The project manager, who may be a government official or a manager from a contracting organization, has responsibility for various functions which contribute to a given objective. The project-management concept has also led to the development of planning-programming-budgeting systems (PPBS) which cut across functional lines to view activities as an integrated totality. Both organization theory and systems analysis areas have been affected by the development of the project-management concept.[34]

The operations research branch has felt the influence of systems theory and has responded with a host of "systems analysis"

---

[31] Rocco Carzo, Jr. and John N. Yanouzas, *Formal Organization: A Systems Approach*, Homewood, Ill.: Richard D. Irwin, 1967.

[32] John A. Seiler, *et al.*, *Systems Analysis in Organizational Behavior*, Homewood, Ill.: Richard D. Irwin, 1967.

[33] Fremont R. Kast and James E. Rosenzweig, *Organization and Management: A Systems Approach*, New York: McGraw-Hill Book Co., 1970.

[34] The literature of project management is substantial and two excellent basic beginning points for further study are: John Stanley Baumgartner, *Project Management*, Homewood, Ill.: Richard D. Irwin, 1963; and David I. Clelland and William R. King, *Systems Analysis and Project Management*, New York: McGraw-Hill Book Co., 1968.

techniques and models. One author defined systems analysis as "the selection of elements, relationships, and procedures to achieve a specific purpose."[35] As such, systems analysis has reflected a diversity of writings from many views such as organizational theory, management science, decision theory, and information systems. The systems-analysis approach may be characterized as providing problem-solving approaches, flow charting, simulation techniques, the use of computers, and the application of sophisticated operations research techniques.[36] To a large extent the systems analysts are making a specialty out of micro analysis of operations in contrast to more macro approaches in organization theory and in the systems approaches to the management process. Yet in another sense, the systems analysts have broadened the operations research branch, integrated into it a host of other analytical devices, and provided a link to the growth of information systems.

The final branch of this attempt to trace the influence of general systems theory on modern thought is in the development of management information systems. Information has always been crucial to management decision making, and the Egyptian scribe who recorded his master's inventory with a stylus on a clay tablet was a forerunner of the modern information specialist. The need for management information existed prior to the Industrial Revolution, was made more crucial as organizations grew, and became a subject of major importance in a twentieth century of electronic computers, automated production, and cybernetic controls. Information has become such a critical problem that some scholars have postulated a view of "the business organization as an information-decision system."[37] With an expanding view of the business environment and the doubling of our knowledge every five or so years, it is not surprising that information systems to

[35] Van Court Hare, Jr. *Systems Analysis: A Diagnostic Approach*, New York: Harcourt Brace Jovanovich, 1967, p. ix.

[36] To merely scratch the surface, one might sample: Claude McMillan and Richard F. Gonzalez, *Systems Analysis: A Computer Approach to Decision Models*, Homewood, Ill., Richard D. Irwin, 1965 and 1968; Stanford L. Optner, *Systems Analysis for Business Management*, (second edition) Englewood Cliffs, N.J.: Prentice-Hall, 1968; Richard J. Hopeman, *Systems Analysis and Operations Management*, Columbus, Ohio: Charles E. Merrill Publishing Co., 1969; and Stanley Young, *Management: A Systems Analysis*, Glenview, Ill.: Scott, Foresman and Co., 1966.

[37] Max Richards and Paul S. Greenlaw, *Management Decision Making*, Homewood, Ill.: Richard D. Irwin, 1966, p. vii.

cope with this expanding universe were necessary. Coupled with the computer and the development of cybernetics, a substantial body of literature has grown up around the theme of management information systems.[38] Wiener's concept of cybernetics has been expanded and refined in modern usage until the point has been reached where many activities are measured and controlled on a "real-time" basis, *i.e.* as the activity is actually occurring.[39]

The area of management information systems is but one of many whose development has been affected by general systems theory. Information has become a more vital resource than ever before to the successful management of the modern, more complex organization which operates in an environment of manifold economic, social, and political constraints. The generation, storage, and transmission of information is one of the most vexing problems of our present organizational society. Knowledge, proliferating rapidly each year, forms the base of all organizations, and the manager must constantly rely on information specialists in his decision making.

SUMMARY

This chapter has been characterized as a search for order through quantification and systems. The modern era has demanded that managers refine their decision-making methods, that they enlarge their conceptual schema, and that they seek better ways of allocating and utilizing their physical and human resources. Operations research was viewed as a modernized version of early scientific approaches to problem solving and of management's search to improve its ability to explain, predict, and control events. Systems theory was viewed as a quest for universal hooks from which would hang general theories to be gleaned from spe-

---

[38] Typical of these developments are: John F. Dearden and F. Warren McFarlan, *Management Information Systems*, Homewood, Ill.: Richard D. Irwin, 1966; Sherman C. Blumenthal, *Management Information Systems*, Englewood Cliffs, N.J.: Prentice-Hall, 1969; and Bartow Hodge and Robert N. Hodgson, *Management and the Computer in Information and Control Systems*, New York: McGraw-Hill Book Co., 1969.

[39] For example, see Robert V. Head, *Real-Time Business Systems*, New York: Holt, Rinehart and Winston, 1964; Stafford Beer, *Cybernetics and Management*, New York: John Wiley and Sons, 1959; and Stafford Beer, *Decision and Control*, New York: John Wiley and Sons, 1966.

cialized fields. In the areas of both quantification and systems, the search was for order, for measurement, for predictability, and for the antithesis of chaos.

Is it possible that general systems theory will become a second age of synthesis in evolving management thought? There is an indication that the "systems approach" is gaining relevance in management theory, in the study of organizations, in model building and simulation, and in the processing of information. Both quantitative and qualitative approaches to management's problems are drawing upon systems theory for part of their conceptual framework. Specialists still abound; yet there is the hope that from systems theory we can draw a grand parallel from the differentiated segments of the management theory jungle and thereby achieve unity, harmony, and order in our understanding of man-in-organizations.

22

The Past as Prologue

Lives of great men all remind us
We can make our lives sublime,
And, departing, leave behind us
Footprints on the sands of time;
—LONGFELLOW, *A Psalm of Life*

This has been a story about footprints, the men who left them, and the times in which these men lived. The past must not be buried but used as a foundation and guide for the footprints which will be made in the future. Within the practices of the past there are the lessons of history for tomorrow; there is a flow of events and ideas which link yesterday, today, and tomorrow in a continuous stream. We occupy but one point in this stream of time: we can see the distant past with a fairly high degree of clarity, but as we approach the present, our perspective becomes less clear. The future must be a projection, and a tenuous one at best. New ideas, subtle shifts in themes, and emerging environmental events all bring new directions to evolving management thought. The purpose of this concluding chapter is to present in summary form the past as a prologue to the future. Two broad areas will be examined: one, the evolving notions of the managerial functions; and two, the changing environment of management.

THE MANAGERIAL FUNCTIONS: PAST AND FUTURE

The managerial functions form a convenient framework for a summary discussion of the past and the future. While the preceding pages have focused on the chronological evolution of men, ideas, and movements, there is a stream of changing ideas about what the manager does which can be used to link the past to the future.

Planning

Planning in early organizations depended in large part upon the seasons and upon natural events. Construction projects, planting and harvesting, and the hunt were seasonal activities. State planning and control of economic enterprises was often rigidly practiced by the Egyptians, Romans, Greeks, and other early civilizations. There was no separation of powers between the economic and political spheres, and this command philosophy prevailed for centuries prior to the cultural rebirth. The overthrow of mercantilism and the emergence of the *laissez-faire* economic philosophy severed the state from its role in economic planning. The market, through the consumer, was deemed the best method of allocating scarce resources toward human ends.

With this break in tradition, planning assumed a new importance for the entrepreneur. He had to be creative and innovative in meeting market needs. Shorn of the monopolies and franchises granted under mercantilism, the entrepreneur had to assume greater risks and take more cognizance of the future. The factory required large-scale capital investments, work flows had to be arranged to meet the new industrial technology, and human resources had to be recruited and trained to meet the demands of the factory system. At best, planning was intuitive and based upon the technological dictates of a particular industry. The standardization and interchangeability of parts facilitated planning but in turn complicated the problem of coordinating the efforts of others in bringing the pieces together. The widespread division of labor, though facilitating training of an essentially unskilled work force, furthered the problems of coordinating efforts.

As textile, steel, railroad, and other industries expanded, the planning problems became more acute. In scientific management, Taylor and his co-workers placed great stress on the planning function because of its crucial import to the existing industrial environment. Standards, to be set through motion and time study, were essential for scheduling and for incentive schemes. Taylor's separation of planning and doing and his concept of functional foremen were ideas designed to bring expert knowledge to bear upon production scheduling, work flows, and production control. Harrington Emerson spoke of "ideals," an early notion of the importance of objectives in organizations. H. L. Gantt developed visual aids to planning and controlling and added time as a vital ingredient in the planning process. Henri Fayol identified planning and forecasting as the first step in a process of managerial actions and wrote of the need for "unity of direction" in plans and in leadership.

An industrial engineering production orientation to management planning persisted in the early work of R. C. Davis. In later work he wrote of routing, dispatching, and scheduling as planning subfunctions and stressed objectives along with his organic functions. James Mooney also wrote of the concept of "doctrine" or commonly shared purposes in organizations. As management thought moved into the forties and fifties, shifts began to appear in the concept of planning. The human relationists spoke of the need for "participation" in planning and other managerial activities. Participation, whether of the "bottom up" style or of "multiple management," was to bring greater psychological as well as economic benefits.

The management process approach, emerging from the pioneering work of Fayol, based the planning concept on a broader plane than just production. Planning became almost synonymous with decision making and was intended to incorporate all business activities instead of just production. Peter Drucker developed the notion of "management by objectives" which has become a key concept in the management literature. William Newman stressed the importance of objectives in shaping the company "character." In the late 1950's and early 1960's, scholars were showing a greater concern for integrating the formal aspects of planning with the informal, human problems connected with budgeting, planning, and controlling. Long-range planning, though an age-old problem, assumed new dimensions with the growth of automated factories, the advent of the computer age, and the proliferation of international markets. From the quantitative specialists, new ideas were emerging for more precise and economical ways of allocating scarce resources through more sophisticated statistical and mathematical procedures. Model building and simulation came into vogue in this computerized cybernetic age. The systems concept, building upon this vast history, has made planning the idea of planning for activity flows through PERT, rhochromatics, the matrix organization, and through planning-programming-budgeting systems (PPBS).

Thus the planning activity has evolved from a highly intuitive, command-oriented concept to one which is enriched by modern technology, by sophisticated aids, and by a broader understanding of man-machine interactions in a broader system. What, then, can be said of the future? Certainly there is no foreseeable diminution in the importance of the planning function to organized endeavors. The challenge will be to turn our accumulated knowledge of the planning function and the wealth and sophistication of our aids to planning to solve a variety of problems. We will be able to apply this knowledge and these tools to the more efficient utilization of physical resources and to the enhanced satisfaction of the human resource. We will be better able to train entrepreneurs and managers and to further the economic progress of underdeveloped nations. We will be in a better position to handle the complex interfaces between organizations and between the public and the private sectors of our economy.[1] Model building and simulation of complex systems will be a necessity in planning for the large-scale investments required in automated factories and in social investments. Economic and demographic forecasts will be enriched through better understanding of econometrics and of the behavioral sciences. A vast number of social problems, for example, urban development and ecological dilemmas, will lend themselves to systems analysis and design.[2] In the exploration of space and in probing the ocean depths, the systems approach to planning has been and will continue to be useful. The essence of the planning function itself will not change significantly in the future. But it will continue to evolve, as it has in the past, as man learns more and more about theories and methods of coping with the uncertainties of the future.

[1] An example of how this might be done in electrical "power pools" may be found in Daniel A. Wren, "Interface and Inter-organizational Coordination," *Academy of Management Journal,* Vol. 10, No. 1 (March, 1967), pp. 69–81.

[2] A pioneering work in the simulation and systems approach to urban problems is Jay W. Forrester, *Urban Dynamics,* Cambridge, Mass.: M.I.T. Press 1969.

Organizing

Throughout history man has found his own activities inextricably interwoven with organizations. Since man was not held in a very high esteem in many early cultures, he was usually deemed subservient to the dictates of the monarch, the military leader, or the central source of church dogma. Authority was legitimatized on the divine right of kings or upon biblical delegation to the successors of Peter. Organizational structures were designed to keep human behavior within predictable bounds through discipline, a central decision maker, central doctrine, and a rigid hierarchy of authority. The early entrepreneur could not depend upon doctrine, nor military discipline, nor divine right to legitimatize his authority; yet he adopted many of the precepts of organizational structures from the church, the state, and the military. The entrepreneur divided labor and created problems of coordination; so he established departments under the leadership of kinsmen or salaried managers and acted himself to both own and manage the organization. Finding his submanagers largely illiterate and often undependable, it is understandable that the entrepreneur tended to keep a tight rein on activities.

The railroads were really the first industry to pose organizational problems on a grand scale. Daniel McCallum and Henry Poor stuck basically to the centralized, rigid organizational structure. However, the human reaction in nineteenth-century America led to McCallum's resignation and to Poor's rethinking of the human versus the "system." As masses of resources continued to accumulate during America's dynamic industrial growth, the owner-manager began to give way to the salaried manager to a greater and greater extent. During the scientific management era, writers wrote extensively of structural and coordination problems and of the need to bring specialized advice and assistance to the work place. Taylor developed his scarcely used functional foreman concept; Emerson applied Prussian general staff ideas to industrial organizations; Fayol developed principles of organization; and Weber conceived bureaucracy as the epitome of technical efficiency. This era continued to stress the formal organization, although there was recognition of work restriction, morale, and other informal group phenomena.

The social man era really began to reshape substantially the thinking about organizations. On one hand, the Mayoists brought a new focus to informal groups, social needs, and interactions in a "social system." There were also the organizational formalists of the same era such as James Mooney, Luther Gulick, and Lyndall Urwick. For these formalists, the source of organizational authority resided in the right to hold private property and this right was then exercised through the scalar chain. Follett followed more in the Mayoist tradition in playing down formal structure, in obeying the law of the situation, depersonalizing authority, and in "interweaving" responsibility. Chester Barnard, even though primarily a formalist, tried to synthesize the formal and informal organizations through his effectiveness-efficiency dichotomy. Like Follett, he radically revised the concept of authority in basing it on the subordinate's acceptance of a directive. Participation in organizations became a keynote in Given's "bottom up" management and in McCormick's "multiple management." Whyte, Bakke and Homans wrote of human-work systems and laid the basis for socio-technical systems. Coexisting in the social man era, the formalists and the informalists both sought to improve the depressing environment: for one, it was through social skills and for the other, through sound principles of organization that the human problems of an industrial civilization could be overcome.

Compared with the past, the social man era witnessed the most radical departures from previously held concepts of organization and authority. The modern era has built upon both the classicists and the neo-classicists as it has evolved toward "organizational systems." This has been in large part due to the organizational humanists' view that man needs some structure in organized activity (which they say the neo-classicists neglected) but not so much that it would interfere with his self-actualization (which they saw in the "man-machine model" of the classicist). The result has been a decline in the worship of a hierarchy, the recognition of the human desire for power equalization in organizations, and the development of new organizational forms, such as the matrix or project organization, which emphasize flows of activities rather than structure. Decentralization, flexibility, and "contingency" organizational strategies have been the keynote of the modern era. The span of control has become the span of management, and managers have been exhorted to keep the span wide to flatten the organization. Job enlargement rather than specialization of labor is viewed as one way of restoring meaningfullness to man's work.

Given this heritage, what may we expect of future organizational structures and strategies? To illustrate the dangers of prediction, one might refer to Leavitt and Whisler's forecast in 1958 that the computer and new information technology would: (1) result in a recentralization of authority in the hands of top management; (2) move certain classes of middle management downward in status and compensation while other middle managers would move upward into the top management group; and (3) lead to an organization structure which would resemble a football balanced on the top of a church bell.[3] However, recent events have not supported this prediction. The project organization, cutting across functional lines and forming smaller task groups, has been one way of coping with size and information needs by focusing on specific projects. The conglomerate, a phenomenon of the 1960's, found under one corporate label a diversity of types of industries, and these have relied basically on decentralization and autonomy in performance. For instance, Textron, Litton, and Ling-Temco-Vought run two-billion-dollars-a-year operations with no more than 200 people on each of their central staffs.[4] Middle managers, supposed to wither on the vine, have proliferated and assumed new roles in digesting for top management the masses of information generated by information technology.

With this in mind, one approaches prognostication with more caution and less fervor. The growth of knowledge-oriented industries, for example, the research-and-development-oriented firms, would seem to indicate that the project organization is here to stay. Employing highly educated specialists who tend to use as their reference group their profession rather than the company, this type of firm will have to seek fluid structures and other inducements for organizational participation. C. P. Snow has indicated some of the problems which will occur in a clash between the "science"-oriented part of a culture and the literary, "non-science"-oriented portion.[5] The value orientations of the scientist are

[3] Harold J. Leavitt and Thomas L. Whisler, "Management in the 1980's," *Harvard Business Review*, Vol. 36, No. 6. (November–December, 1958), pp. 41–48.
[4] "The Seventies: Super but Seething," *Business Week*, December 6, 1969, p. 138.
[5] C. P. Snow, *Two Cultures and the Scientific Revolution*, Cambridge, England: University Press, 1959.

toward his profession while the non-scientist tends to be oriented toward the company. The clash is not only in values but in communications and understanding between the "two cultures." Managers will have to design organizations for prompt, flexible performance while overcoming or channeling conflicts between the scientist and the non-scientist.

Automation may not cause the organizational problems that were once anticipated. Daniel Bell, former labor editor for *Fortune,* has estimated that if automation were introduced into all of the factories that could use it, only 8 per cent of the labor force would be affected.[6] The growth of service-related industries, such as medical services, and of knowledge-related industries would certainly indicate a shift away from the industrial production firms of previous eras. For automated factories, the organizational problems will not be structural but one of making work meaningful.

As the public sector of the economy continues to grow *vis-à-vis* the private sector, as it appears that it will do, there will be an enlarged interest in comparative organizational theory. In federal, state, and local governments, in educational institutions, and in quasi-public organizations such as Comsat, there will be a search for sound organizational structures and strategies. This will provide fertile soil for comparative management and will lead to the further development of comparative organizational theory.

As international trade continues to expand, there will be a continuing interest in multinational organizational structures. The whole world will provide the framework for the organization and a particular country or area will be just a division of the total company. International operations will lead to another clash of cultures between the "home office" and the "foreign" subsidiary. The manager of the foreign branch may be indigenous to that country, but there will arise a need for a cultural interfacing with the "home office." Bilingual and bicultural managers or offices will be needed to explain the home office policies and operations to the market area being served, and vice versa.

Concern for maintaining relationships within a broader societal context, for example, in solving ecological problems, overcoming central city decay, and in providing jobs for hard-core unemployed, will also bring new dimensions to organization structures.

---

[6] Daniel Bell, *Work and Its Discontents,* Boston: Beacon Press, 1956, p. 49.

One avenue is that of liaison managers or offices who would act to interface the corporate organization with the Department of Health, Education, and Welfare, with a particular community, with other companies working on the same problem, or with the NAACP or other concerned groups. This interface manager or office would become an entry point for extra-organizational members and a contact point for purposes of planning and coordination.

Centralized authority and the hierarchy will continue to decline in the context of a better-educated, more mobile organizational member. Traditional line-and-staff distinctions will blur and fade in future organizations under the project management concept. Toffler has suggested that "ad-hocracy" will replace bureaucracy. His premise is that the organization of the future will have to be more fluid, more responsive, and that task forces, project groups, and transient teams will combine to solve problems and then disband only to be replaced by newly formed teams for newly emerging problems.[7] Whatever the form, the organizing function will continue to reflect the assumptions we make about people. As we continue to operate on the premises that people seek autonomy, desire challenges, are trustworthy, and are capable and desirous of assuming responsibility, the present trends of project organization, decentralization, and decline of hierarchy will continue.

Leadership

In order to gain a perspective, leadership may be viewed as an all-encompassing function of guiding the human resource toward organizational objectives. This function has been subsumed under many labels throughout the years: entrepreneurship, supervising, leading, directing, commanding, actuating, and so on. As such, leadership has been closely allied with notions about the skills or traits the leader-manager must have as well as how he goes about motivating people. In early organizations, leadership was the function of the eldest, the strongest, the most articulate, or often based upon some religious concept such as the divine right of kings. As such, leadership was often viewed as a function of custom and tradition or in many cases as one of the personal traits of the leader. Concepts of motivation were scarce at best: occupational and societal duties were expected to be ful-

---

[7] Alvin Toffler, *Future Shock*, New York: Random House, 1970, Chapter 7.

filled based upon tradition. Man was not expected to desire much beyond subsistence in this world. The command philosophy of leadership, as typified by Hobbes and Machiavelli, furthered the notion of centralized control to keep brute man in his place. The cultural rebirth was to shake man from these tradition- and command-based concepts and place a new emphasis on achievement in this world.

The early entrepreneurs acquired leadership positions through their power to command capital and their ability and zeal to transform this capital into productive enterprises. Within the factory system, the pressures for economies of scale soon forced entrepreneurs to hire salaried sub-managers and this was to lead to a number of problems in finding and developing talent and in motivating managerial performance. Adhering to the precepts of past organizations and to their own experiences, entrepreneurs thought that it was the personal idiosyncratic traits of the individual that led to leadership success or failure. The abilities and skills of the leader were not deemed transferable: managerial advice was based upon the industry or firm to be managed, and the early "texts" of James Montgomery and William Brown reflected this parochial view. Motivation in the early factory marked the first appearance of an "economic man" concept. Piece-work systems held forth the carrot, disciplinary fines provided the stick, and factory owners and religious officials combined to try to develop a factory "ethos" which would lead man to link his job performance to his measure of spiritual worth.

Charles Dupin was the first to suggest that managerial skills could be taught, suggestive of the idea that management was more than a function of personal traits. Economic-man concepts continued in vogue and Babbage and Ure exhorted the worker to accept the factory system as a means of improving his condition. Robert Owen urged a communal existence, had less confidence in the wage system, and fought to improve man's condition by improving his environment.

The scientific management era, following the growth of American industry and a continued rise in the employment of "professional," salaried, non-owning managers, viewed leadership as a function of knowledge. The best leader was the technical expert, and Taylor's functional foreman concept sought to provide specialized supervision for the worker. Gantt envisioned a leadership "elite" composed of industrial engineers. The factory ethos of that period was the "mental revolution," which was based on the premise that workers and managers would perceive that they had mutual interests in efficiency and productivity which would lead to high wages and low costs. In this age of Benthamite Utilitarianism, the economic-man concept was in tune with a cultural environment of individual reward based on individual effort. But within the scientific management movement there were also motivational concepts beyond those of economic gain. Gantt recognized the importance of morale and teamwork; Taylor admonished the leader to know his men and to build a personal rather than an impersonal system; and Lillian Gilbreth recognized the psychological factors bearing upon work.

Henri Fayol saw managerial skills as universal and teachable and identified the mix of skills needed as the manager moved up the scalar chain. Though his work was overshadowed by that of Taylor, Fayol's process and his notions of universality were to lead to the development of general administrative theory. By distinguishing between "management" as a total function of guiding the enterprise and "administration" as a cyclical sub-function of working through people, Fayol established a conceptual framework for the study of management.

The notion of social man found its roots in the early sociologists, such as Cooley and Mead, and in the work of Whiting Williams. There was a decline in the ethic of individual achievement motivation and a rise in the idea that man was primarily a social creature. This idea found its support in the work of the Mayoists and in the beginnings of human relations at the Hawthorne plant. This "new" view of man, though subjected to criticism, was that he was not motivated by money but by interpersonal relations and his need to belong. The cultural environment was perilous and the Mayoists sought to overcome industrial problems by building group solidarity and by developing social skills in managers. Thus the shift from the Taylor concept of a leader who led because he was technically the most competent was replaced by the notion that social skills were the most important to the manager.

The Mayoists spawned a number of ideas and research about leadership and motivation. Participatory, democratic leadership came into vogue, interpersonal skills were to be developed, and sensitive, socially skilled leaders were deemed the best. At Ohio State and Michigan, leadership took on a "situational" aura which played down the traits of the leader and emphasized the interaction of leader and led in the situation. Leadership was viewed as a continuum of possibilities with the democratic style as the most favorable.

The modern era brought another shift: motivation was to be found in challenge, responsibility, and in work itself in the idea of self-actualizing man. Argyris, McGregor, Herzberg and others sought to make work the source of satisfaction for the worker. Leadership ideas took a less drastic change: the situational approach led to the "grid" of Blake and Mouton and to the "contingency" model of Fiedler. The modern mix of skills required was that of adaptation, choosing the right style to fit the task structure and the abilities and attitudes of people. The ethos of the modern era was that of harmony, the bringing together of organizations and people in a Theory Y–self-actualizing notion of organizational productivity and human satisfaction.

There have been marked shifts in past notions of leadership and men. Our ideas have evolved as changing environmental conditions have reshaped our assumptions about people. What will the future bring? Certainly an advanced technological society will demand a variety of specialists who have higher educational and skill levels. Galbraith has called this growth of technical specialists the "technostructure".[8] In his view, the technostructure is the decision-making body and has replaced the owners and managers of the past as the decisive force in corporate management. Dealing with the better-educated specialist will mean that managers will need to rely more and more on making work meaningful since this type of worker will be more inclined to identify with his "profession" rather than the company. This will give rise to more problems of relating the scientist to the non-scientist as postulated in C. P. Snow's "two cultures."

Leadership development will become a more crucial issue both within America and in other parts of the world. The "black capitalist" has been proposed as one way of aiding the American Negro

[8] John Kenneth Galbraith, *The New Industrial State*, Boston: Houghton Mifflin Co., 1967, p. 71.

to have a piece of the action and a stake in economic advancement.[9] In Europe, American managerial ability is so superior to that of indigenous talent that it poses a threat to the economic goals of many nations.[10]   In underdeveloped nations, leadership and entrepreneurship are crucial to economic growth.   David McClelland maintains that the achievement motive can be taught and that the seeds of entrepreneurship can be implanted in underachieving groups and nations.[11]   In the future our leadership development programs will focus more and more on "underachievers" in an effort to furnish them with the attitudes and skills necessary for self-help advancement.

The mix of managerial skills will most probably not change drastically.   Managers will need some level of technical ability in order to communicate with and manage the work of specialists. Managerial skills in terms of the time-honored functions of planning, organizing, controlling, etc. will not change in their basic nature. One change which will most probably emerge will be a greater emphasis on *conceptual* skills for the manager of the future.   He will need to be able to see parts of his managerial situation, determine how these parts interact, and decide how to put all of these together in a total framework.   This will be more than a conceptualization of the firm as a system and will include the relation of the firm to a broader context.

Education for this skill mix will undoubtedly be difficult.   It will be at the polar extreme from the early idea of managing one type of industry.   It will most likely take the form of education through general systems theory or its intellectual spin-off, comparative management theory.   Emphasis will be placed on universal characteristics of organizations, on their interrelationships, and on visualization of management as a cross-cultural, cross-institutional phenomenon.   Education for management may shift from the business school setting, or the business school itself may evolve into a college of management arts and sciences.   While this may

[9] See, for example: Louis Allen, "Making Capitalism Work in the Ghettos," *Harvard Business Review*, Vol. 47, No. 3 (May–June, 1969), pp. 83–92; and Theodore Cross, *Black Capitalism: Strategy for Business in the Ghetto*, New York: Atheneum Publishers, 1969.

[10] An uneasy look at the situation in France is by J. J. Servan-Schreiber, *The American Challenge*, New York: Atheneum Publishers, 1968.

[11] David C. McClelland and David G. Winter, *Motivating Economic Achievement*, New York: Free Press, 1969.

sound chauvinistic coming from a teacher of management, we will come to see business and industry as a subset of a larger institutional framework. The public sector, (e.g., government, education, the military, and other nonprofit-oriented organizations), is continually growing in proportion to the private sector. This alone will demand a view of industrial organizations as a subset to the total concept of management.

Motivation will be a pressing problem of the future as it has always been. The advent of more leisure, the growth of automation, and the rise of service industries will move man further and further from physical work as it is presently conceived. Work, as we know it, will mean entirely different things to our children. There will not only be a physical removal of man's direct ties to a physical product but also an intellectual separation. More mental functions will be turned over to machines and man will be an observer rather than a participant. What will this mean to self-actualization? Certainly it will be difficult to obtain any pride or feeling of accomplishment while monitoring a machine. This will mean the decline of self-actualizing man on the job. Self-actualization of the future may be found in the family, in how we spend our leisure time, or in other creative pursuits off the job.

One author has suggested that the future manager will be evaluated "more in the light of value systems than for skills and proficiencies."[12] That is, managerial evaluation will be based upon contribution to social as well as to economic prosperity. Since we already have enough problems in measuring performance, the addition of these other intangible factors will certainly complicate the situation. Whatever the skills, however they are evaluated, and wherever they are applied, the leadership function will continue to be the crux of our age-old task of keeping the "man" as well as the "manage" in "management."

Human Resource Administration

The recruitment, selection, training, and administration of the human resource has a checkered history. Commonly called staffing or personnel management, this managerial function has grown into greater prominence over time. The early factory system posed

---

[12] John F. Mee, "Management Challenges of the 1970's," *Advanced Management Journal*, Vol. 34, No. 4 (October, 1969), p. 45.

all sorts of problems in inducing an agrarian worker to go into the factory, in teaching him the skills of an industrial civilization, in keeping his behavior within the parameters of sound, profitable practices, and in developing trustworthy salaried managers. The personnel function for many years was the responsibility of the line manager; it was not until around 1900 that "employment departments" and "labor chiefs" began to appear as a separate organizational function. Even the renowned scholar Henri Fayol treated staffing as a subfunction of organizing.

The industrial psychology of Munsterberg, arising out of the ethics of scientific management, was the first attempt to develop a scientific basis for personnel management; this was the first break with pseudoscientific selection and the search for "psychophysical" variables. Taylor sought a "first-class man" but it was Munsterberg who sought through testing and empirical study to place the man in the right job. Vocational guidance was an early theme of industrial psychology and personnel testing became the fad in the post World War I era. People were being recognized more and more as a valuable asset of the firm, and the personnel function, through such offices as Henry Ford's "sociology department," achieved more recognition. In large part, the theme of early personnel departments was worker "adjustment" to the industrial situation. During the 1920's, companies took on various welfare schemes, partly to combat incipient unionism, partly to instill worker loyalty to the company, and partly because it was felt that concern for the human asset was sound business procedure.

The growth of unionism in the 1930's led to expansion of the personnel function into industrial-relations-oriented activities. Industrial sociology, the product of the Mayoists, was amended as the "industrial human relations" of the 1940's. Industrial peace was viewed as a function of management's understanding and recognition of the role of unions in determining wages, hours, and conditions of employment.

For the management resource, early entrepreneurs looked for trustworthy, stable men who had the physical, social, or other personal attributes which would lead to success of the firm. This notion of managerial selection based on personal characteristics prevailed for an extended period. Under scientific management, Taylor had little confidence in any school (other than that of experience) for developing managers. Fayol made a major break with the personal trait–experience approach and thought that managerial skills could be taught in schools. However, there were few business schools and the general view still held that managers would best develop under the tutelage of an already proven manager. It was during the scientific management era that business schools began teaching management, and gradually these outputs would form a growing pool of talent for industry.

The human relations movement broadened education for management to include the development of social skills through the use of cases, incidents, and sensitivity training. The 1950's not only witnessed a renewed interest in general management theory but also the rapid growth of programs for industrial leaders commonly called "executive development" programs. Many industrialists returned to the classroom to renew their skills and reshape their attitudes to cope with the renewed growth of organizations.

The decline of the human relations philosophy in the late 1950's brought a new focus to the personnel function. The term "human resource administration" came more into vogue and scholars linked this philosophy to organizational humanism, to Rensis Likert's human asset accounting, and to the idea of productivity and efficiency through the satisfactions of work rather than through welfare-oriented, keep-people-happy schemes.

The future will bring into play many of the problems already commented upon with respect to future managerial skills and human motivation. A more affluent, leisure-oriented, better-educated work force will make selection and placement more difficult and retention more tenuous. Unions will continue to play both an economic and a political role in influencing managerial decisions. After experiencing a stagnation in membership growth, i.e., as a percentage of the total work force, unions have expanded their efforts into heretofore unexplored areas such as teachers, governmental employees, and other white collar workers. More organizations and managers of the future will find themselves engaged in the process of collective bargaining if these efforts succeed.

The bulk of future problems in human resource administration will lie in the area of social values. The 1960's saw pressing demands for employment quotas for minority groups, for equal employment opportunity legislation, for the abolition of employment tests in hiring because they allegedly discriminate against the culturally deprived, and for business to move into slum areas to set up factories and training programs. The National Alliance of Businessmen has moved vigorously to establish quotas for industries to hire the hard core unemployed. In practice, experiences under these programs have reflected many of the problems encountered by the early entrepreneurs in the factory system. The hard core unemployed have had little or no prior work experience, few usable skills, poor work habits (such as going on spending sprees after receiving a big check), and do not seem to be overly enthusiastic about the factory or office regimen. With a lowering of selection standards in order to bring the hard core into the factory, there will be more pressure for improved training, supervision, and motivation.

Employers will begin to "teach" a need for achievement; they will need to orient these workers into the "new" culture of the factory and will invest more time in being concerned with bringing these workers up to appropriate performance levels. Unions and management will have to reach agreements for "reverse seniority"; that is, providing security to long-term employees and laying them off during personnel cutbacks rather than the low seniority, newly hired, hard-core employees. Supervisors will need new attitudes and skills in handling the disadvantaged; larger investments will be made in training; work groups will need to be rebuilt; and management policies will have to be reshaped. The investment will be great, and hopefully the long-run return on our human capital will be commensurate with this investment. The future manager will find his human resource problems more closely aligned with both the social values and the political imperatives of the future.

Controlling

The managerial activity of controlling has existed since organized effort began. Controlling completes the managerial activity cycle by measuring and evaluating planned versus actual actions in order to take corrective action, if necessary. As such, controlling deeply reflects the premises of the controller. In pre-industrial societies, controlling was based on unilateral command and rigid discipline in view of the low esteem with which man was held. The factory brought into play more variables to be controlled, yet the entrepreneur could not rely upon the power of dogma, military regimen, nor upon state fiat to achieve control. Standardization of parts helped somewhat but the widespread division of labor and the unskilled work force which was unaccustomed to working to close tolerances impeded development of any sophisticated, reliable control systems. Accounting as a means of providing information for decision making was in a relatively gross state and cost accounting methods were undeveloped except for some early descriptive attempts by Charles Babbage.

Scientific management stressed controlling through empirical study to set accurate standards and made other advancements in measuring times and costs. As in the early factory, the emphasis was on the control of materials, schedules, and other facets of the production function. In this era, the first significant graphic aids to planning and controlling were developed by Gantt. The early factory owners and church officials had combined to urge a "factory ethos" upon the worker; under Taylor the "mental revolution" was to attempt to bring this same identity of managerial and worker goals. Though these attempts generally failed, they both sought an *internalization* of goals as both a motivating and as a control device. The premise that internal commitment to goals reduces the need for external control devices is thus an old one in management thought.

For the Mayoists, control was not an explicit function. Managers were to become aware of informal reactions to external control devices and how they affected the worker. The ill-logic of sentiments, once understood, would presumably lead the manager to modify any stringent use of external controls, to open communications channels, to develop his interpersonal skills, and to recognize the importance of group influences on the task of the manager. Mary Follett would depersonalize control to obey the law of the situation and Barnard would conclude that control was effective only to the extent that the group accepted managerial authority and standards. In general, the social man era was to lead to a softening of any rigorous notions of external control. Control was to become more of a democratic, internalized commitment to the inducements offered by management and the social skills the manager displayed.

R. C. Davis made a substantial contribution to the control function when he stressed the importance of timing. "Preliminary" control occurred through proper planning, preparation, and dispatching; "concurrent" control, on the other hand, operated while performance was in progress. Davis' notions of control added depth and practicality to the ideas of Fayol. The resurgence of interest in general management theory through the process approach broadened the concept of controlling beyond that of a production orientation. Controlling was viewed as completing a cyclical process of activities and as leading to replanning, resetting of objectives, and other kinds of corrective action.

The advent of the computer, the concept of cybernetics, and the growth of information systems combined to stress the role of feedback in managerial control. More sophisticated control devices were possible through computerized handling of masses of data such as PERT. Organizational humanism has been a modern attempt to reduce rigidity in organizational structures and to recognize the impact that controls have upon the human factor. The new "ethos" of the modern era has been self-actualizing man, again postulating that men should internalize the goals of the organization and see them as means to the satisfaction of their own needs and aspirations.

As long as our culture reflects the idea of man and his satisfactions as a primary organizational value, we will see an emphasis on self-direction, internalization, and self-control. Before industrialization, man was primarily a tool in the hands of central authorities. As these bonds were broken by the cultural rebirth, man's aspirations and well-being have been coming more and more into focus on organizational value. The future will continue to emphasize the impact of control systems on man, and there will be an ever continuing quest to balance the needs for order with a concern for humans.

Our youthful contemporaries seem less inclined to accept at face value the dictates of their elders. As these individuals begin to assume the responsibilities of a corporate life, there will be strains and tugs at previously cherished notions of evaluating and measuring performance. "Doing your own thing" may be the desire, but history shows a clash between this ideal and the realities of controlled performance toward group goals. On the other hand, history also shows that statism and centralized controls lead to a rebellion against increased conformity and to a diminution of innovation and individual achievement aspirations. Organizations, like political systems, will find a continuation of this clash of the individual versus the system. In its formative days, the Catholic Church centralized authority; yet today there are strains and stresses for autonomy. Russia has had some second thoughts about centralized planning and controlling. In America, the state has intervened to control more and more; in the future, we will see a continuing rebellion against this, the establishment, and the system.

The very control devices which have the potential for increased efficiency carry within them their own self-destruct mechanisms. As centralized control is made more possible, it is also made less palatable to the individual. As activities become more centralized for efficiency's sake, they also become less flexible in meeting local needs and in allowing for individual discretion. In short, the institutionalization of the control function has been enhanced by modern technological developments; yet a proliferation of rules, forms, and procedures and other accoutrements of institutionalization may lead to dysfunctional consequences for both the human and the organization.

There will be future pressures for efficiency in resource utilization and modern control concepts can contribute to this goal. Yet there will be the strain between the individual and the system and the dangers of losing sight of the goal of controlling and the means of controlling. Cybernation will make possible a greater emphasis on external control devices; yet human values decree internalization of goals and self-control. Boguslaw has viewed the systems concept as a device to extend the mastery of man over nature; indeed, this is an old theme which has persisted throughout the evolution of management thought. Yet the systems concept poses its greatest threat "precisely in its potential as a means for extending the control of man over man."[13] Will the systems designer of today and tomorrow form the new leadership elite which Henry Gantt envisioned in the "New Machine"? Or will the systems designer formulate pleasing arrangements of parts and whole which will preserve those human values which have been our quest for such a long time? It is in resolving this paradox that management will find the challenges of the future.

[13] Robert Boguslaw, *The New Utopians: A Study of Systems Design and Social Change*, Englewood Cliffs, N.J.: Prentice-Hall, 1965, p. 204.

THE CULTURAL ENVIRONMENT

Management thought is the synthesis of many disciplines and the product of many forces. Throughout our study we have seen how the impact of technology, the changing of cultural values, and the ebb and flow of men and institutional arrangements have affected management thought. What we think about the allocation and utilization of resources in goal-directed organized effort is heavily influenced by our culture. Yet we are not slaves, not passive, not pre-determined nor predestined to play our roles upon some great cultural stage. Our ideas in turn shape and change our environment in a historical action-reaction process of reciprocal interaction.

The Economic Environment

Management finds its roots in the economic problems of man. It is essentially an economic study in the broadest sense which is concerned with producing and distributing economic value in a directed manner. Management is not limited in its scope, however, to economic, *i.e.* business, institutions. Economic value must be created and sustained in all types of endeavors which seek to achieve some goal or goals with a certain amount of resource effort. Governments run on budgets financed by taxes which are not limitless. Churches operate on contributions which are not always forthcoming in abundance. Other organizations face this scarcity of resources and must engage in managerial activities to meet their manifold ends.

Management as an activity is also a resource. It carries the capability of producing value by guiding efforts more economically. There was a broad span of time before management became recognized as a legitimate factor in the process of creating value. Land and labor were first considered as the primary focus of economics; later captial was added as church strictures concerning usury loosened; but management has been viewed as a resource only recently. The nineteenth century brought some recognition of a managerial function, but it was not until the twentieth century that men began to isolate, identify, and study management as a separate function applicable to all types of organizations. It was here that we saw the problems of managing becoming so acute that they required a separate body of study.

Early societies had economic problems but sought their solutions either in past precepts or in a command philosophy of resource allocation. The market economy, as a part of the cultural rebirth, led to the generation of a new body of economic thought. A rapid advance in technology became the basis for a new economic order, the factory system. Here, coupled with steam power and changing cultural values, economics took on new dimensions. The factory system created both managerial and broader cultural problems. The managerial problems created the need to study management; the cultural problems created the first needs for managers to be responsible and aware of their environment.

Technology and science have evolved rapidly since the Industrial Revolution, and this advancement has continually placed greater pressures on management scholars and practitioners to cope with newer, more formidable problems. Advancements in power sources, communications, materials, transportation, and technology have removed the managerial activity from the domestic system to a world of international commerce. Chandler's cycle was used throughout this study to show how economic expansion led to changes in management thought. As resources are accumulated, managerial problems mount and forces arise which lead to a need to rationalize resource utilization. Administrative structures are formulated to meet industrial strategies and managers have had to cope with a dynamic economic environment in transportation, power, communications, and markets.

The early factory resulted in an accumulation of resources, and the first attempts at rationalization were made by Charles Babbage and Andrew Ure. The nineteenth century was depicted as the resource accumulation phase in American industry and scientific management was the response to this environmental pressure. Dormant during the Depression, the post-World War II world saw a renewal phase of resource accumulation. In a relatively rapid response, the reaction to this has been a search to re-rationalize resource utilization through operations research and more science in managing. But quantification could not provide the whole answer; there also arose the need for better relations with the human element *vis-à-vis* the system. Systems theory has been viewed as a modern attempt at synthesis, a more recent response to a rationalization of resource utilization.

This cycle of accumulation, rationalization, renewal, and renewed rationalization will hold true for the future as it has for the past. There will be, however, a diminished time lag between the phases of the cycle as our body of knowledge expands and our methods of communicating knowledge improves. While there may be a synthesis in systems, there will also be forces leading from a general systems framework back to specialized views. Mortal man can mentally conceptualize only so much. Each will pick a piece from the general systems model and study it in detail and in the process he may lose sight of the general systems attitude.

The future also holds a wealth of challenges in the advancement of science and in dynamic demographic factors. Science has advanced to a point where serious moral questions are being posed about heart transplants, artificial organs, and the possibilites of genetic manipulation through unraveling the RNA and DNA components of the genetic code.[14] A conservative estimate of United States population in the 1980's is 231 million people, with half of that population under the age of thirty. The gross national product will probably reach one trillion, four hundred billion dollars by 1980 and it will be composed largely of products which do not exist today.

> It is an extraordinary era in which we live. It is altogether new. The world has seen nothing like it before. I will not pretend, no one can pretend, to discern the end; but everybody knows that the age is remarkable for scientific research into the heavens, the earth; and perhaps more remarkable still is the application of this scientific research to the pursuits of life. The ancients saw nothing like it. The moderns have seen nothing like it until the present generation. The progress of the age has almost outstripped human belief.

The words of a modern? No, these were the words of Daniel Webster in November, 1847, upon the opening of a stretch of railroad track in Lebanon, New Hampshire. What we see and marvel at today will be accepted as commonplace by our children. This progress will not come without its costs. C. P. Snow has noted a resurgence of the "literary" intellectual, whom he calls the

[14] For a creative approach to the possibilities of scientific advancement, see Richard N. Farmer, *Management in the Future*, Belmont, Calif.: Wadsworth Publishing Co., 1967.

"natural Luddite," who scorns the material progress which science and technology have brought.[15] Toffler has suggested that we must avoid "Luddite paroxysms" yet keep technology responsible through such devices as a "technology ombudsman."[16] The challenge for the scientist and manager of the future will be to convince the intellectual Luddites, much as Babbage, Ure, and Dupin sought to do, that material advancement brings social betterment.

Organizational goals in the past have been largely economic ones. This did not preclude social goals, for example, early notions of social responsibility and service, but these were more frequently than not viewed as by-products of the economic goals. The future manager will find social values impinging more and more upon his economic decision making framework. This social overlay of values may work to the detriment of economic return, and managers will find some degree of schizophrenia and social vertigo in the decision making process. The task of future management thought is not an either/or proposition—either economic or social values—but one in the most enlightened sense of integration. In Taylor and Follett this notion of integration received varying interpretations. For Taylor, the "mental revolution" would bind all together in prosperity through efficiency; for Follett, it was the exercise of creativity in searching for a higher level solution to lead to mutual resolution without compromise or conflict. While these ideals have been held high before, it is the task of the future to make them operative. Indeed, it will be a formidable challenge, one worthy of our best minds, to bring forth a mix of cultural values which would lead to both economic and social progress.

The Social Environment

While management finds its roots in the economic necessities of efficient and effective resource utilization, it also finds its actions affected by social values. Humans are the primary input of the management model and the outputs are used to satisfy human aspirations. Both internally and externally, managers are affected by prevailing social values. Finding its justification in being essential to organized efforts, the activity of management becomes

---

[15] C. P. Snow, *The Two Cultures: And a Second Look,* Cambridge, England: University Press, 1964.

[16] Toffler, p. 381 and pp. 390–392.

inextricably interwoven with assumptions about people and about man's relation to other men.

Man has not been held as a primary value in many cultures. The tribe, the state, or other groups have often held that man must keep himself subservient to group or political needs. As evidence of this, slavery, the ownership of man by man, prevailed until relatively recently, historically speaking. Even the Greeks, who first flirted with democracy, thought that slavery was proper. It may or may not be historical coincidence, but the record shows that economic and social progress has been most rapid after enslavement ends. Early civilizations made little progress under slavery; and the feudal system, which was a more insidious enslavement device, kept society dormant. As man broke the bonds of feudalism, the monolithic authority of the church, and the dictates of the monarchy, he began to make economic and social progress.

An industrial society required a different set of assumptions about the nature of man: that he could have the freedom to choose his own government, that he could be self-directing, that he could pursue property and wealth as natural rights, and that he could devise means for the redress of grievances and injustices. It was in this context that individual liberty became a value, that the individual quest for wealth was morally sanctioned, and that creativity and innovation were encouraged. This individualism dominated the economic growth of the Industrial Revolution and fed the fires of industrialization. Even within America, it was the post-slavery era that led to the greatest growth in resource accumulation and great social mobility for those fleeing Europe.

Man's relations to man were bound up in traditional precepts for ages. Social customs and taboos were far more important than social progress, and it was the task of the tribe, the state, the church, or the feudal lord to preserve the social heritage. The cultural rebirth brought a re-definition of man *vis-à-vis* man. The social solidarity of the community based on the agrarian life was sorely shaken by urbanization and industrialization. New neighbors, new customs, new environs, and new jobs were the social crises for industrial man. The family, formerly a prime social and economic unit, was to begin disintegration as parents and children went on their different paths to work in the new factory. Socialization, formerly a task of the family, became the province of the factory, the educational system, and of peers in work groups.

Robert Owen made an early attempt to restore communal integrity in the face of the perceived ravages of industrialization. Yet industrialization proceeded, and man, guided by an inner gyroscope, furthered the specialization of labor, the factory system, and the expansion of markets. In rejecting the communal system of Owen, man accepted and furthered the notion of individualism. Man was not entirely plastic in the early factory; he resisted technological advancement, factory regimen, and managerial discipline. Yet he accepted an innovative motivational premise in the concept of economic motivation. The carrot, supported by the stick and the moralistic overtones of the factory ethos, was held forth as the way of individual betterment.

Profits, long deemed a cardinal sin, became morally sanctioned by the Protestant ethic. Commerce and trade, deemed ignoble by many prior civilizations, became a stepping stone for the ambitious young man to cross the turbulent waters of social class. The ingredients of this social mix thus condoned trade, profits, and individual achievement. Holes were being torn in the social fabric but that was the way of progress. Stagnancy worships the untorn cloth. But even as these tears were appearing, there were a few who were beginning to put forth new philosophies which would help man in his newly found relations. Babbage sought an early identification of the mutuality of interests through profit sharing; Ure and Dupin established classes to prepare young men for more rewarding professions; and Henry Poor sought through leadership to overcome the conflict between the individual and the system.

Scientific management was a philosophy for coping with the social problems as well as the industrial problems of the age. Rooted in utilitarian economics, in the rationalism of nineteenth-century philosophy, and in the Protestant virtues of individualism, scientific management was a call for an integration of all interests in society. The mental revolution called for men to take their eyes off of dividing the spoils and to work toward creating more and more. The primary benefits were economic, but the social benefits were many: lowered prices, higher wages, individuals doing the work at which they were best, and everyone, manager, worker, and society at large, benefiting from prosperity through efficiency.

Even during the apogee of scientific management thought, the credo of individualism, as personified in the Protestant and achievement ethics, was declining. The Depression and its aftermath was to bring a new focus in social values: affiliation needs became a trade-off for achievement needs; profits and efficiency declined as goals; self-help became government help; inner direction became other direction; and businessmen lost the esteem they had held previously. The Mayoists sought to rebuild social solidarity and to overcome a perceived cultural lag by exhortation to develop the social skills of the manager. Bottom-up management, in industry as well as in the Rooseveltian "little people" philosophy, became the goal. Getting along was valued before getting ahead. Man was a creature caught up in forces which he could not control and therefore someone else must help. The self-help doctrine was obsolete and the economic, social, and political climate was changing to offset the human dislocations of economic catastrophe.

In the modern era, social values appear to have shifted somewhat, but not much. Affiliation is still highly regarded but less so as self-actualization has moved to the forefront. Self-actualization is based on the social premise that man finds his dignity and fulfillment in the challenge, rewards, and satisfactions which come from work itself. The trend is still away from authoritarianism, except today it is the anti-establishment movement. Calls for power equalization have led to programs for the poor, the black, and all others deemed disadvantaged. Profits are not too highly regarded and businessmen are asked to assume social goals and to diminish economic profitability if necessary. Hiring the hard core unemployed, pollution control, and a host of other social issues have placed the manager in a potentially conflicting position of having to satisfy social demands while simultaneously keeping workers, customers, and creditors happy.

Peter Drucker has called these times "the age of discontinuity."[17] Drucker sees the discontinuities developing in new space age technologies, in the growth of the "knowledge industry," in the international development of economies, and in the political matrices of large organizations and ideological struggles. These discontinuities represent a break-up of previous bases and assumptions about economic arrangements for allocating resources, about

[17] Peter F. Drucker, *The Age of Discontinuity: Guidelines to Our Changing Society,* New York: Harper and Row, 1968.

social values, and about the nature and purpose of political institutions. It is in these stresses and strains on the cultural fabric that there will be continued pressures on leaders in all types of organizations.

The power equalization movement has not yet run its course, and the modern appearances of this phenomenon finds its roots in a disenchantment with urbanization and industrialization. The businessman has been closely identified with the city, and the city is deemed degrading by many. Our inner cities are decaying today, yet it is the business sector that has the resource capability to rebuild them. Youth is disenchanted with business, and yet it is in the business sector that the resources and the know-how are accumulated which can provide jobs, housing, reduce or eliminate pollution, and solve other pressing cultural problems. Profits are suspect, yet it is profitability which is the key to research and development, to investments, and to long-run prosperity and growth of the total economy. Productivity and efficiency are no longer the cultural goals that they once were, yet it is productivity that enables higher wages, lower costs, and market proliferation and expansion.

Founded by stoics, America is becoming an epicurean society. Thrift is no longer a virtue, and neither is wealth. The biblical precepts of rights and wrongs are being threatened by "situation" ethics. There is art without form, and music without harmony. It is in the future that the social fabric faces its most severe tests. It is in this uncertain future of shifting social values that management will have to summon forth its greatest energies of creativity and human understanding in the service of purposeful endeavors.

The Political Environment

The philosophical premises and the practical realities of the relation of man to state are also deeply imbedded in the assumptions made about human nature. Early political philosophy was based on the premise that man in a state of nature was basically an unreasoning brute who could be civilized only by some central authority. Organizational structures reflected this premise and legitimization of authority tended to be based upon some time hallowed or upon some mystical source of power. The divine right of kings, based upon Adam's God-given power to rule his children, was such a source of authority. Tribal taboos, enshrined in ceremonial rites and ancestral worship, formed another such source of authority. Machiavelli and Hobbes were the spokesmen of lodging supreme power in the prince or the state.

John Locke broke with this command philosophy and established the framework for constitutional government. Coupled with the Protestant ethic, the market ethic, and the philosophical age of enlightenment, the liberty ethic provided a new source of power and a new legitimization of authority. Political thought with respect to economic thought followed the premise of self-governing man, guided only by his own self interest in the pursuit of property, wealth, and happiness. This laissez-faire environment provided fertile soil for the Industrial Revolution, aided and abetted innovations in marketing and production, and gave a political sanction to the entrepreneur. But even as laissez-faire prevailed, there were early attempts through parliamentary investigations to check some of the abuses of power by individuals. Though generally unsuccessful, these efforts reflected a general scheme of societal checks and balances which constitutional government provided.

Early American political thought followed the laissez-faire precepts until the post-Civil War period. Increasing protests against an unholy alliance between government and business and against abuses by "robber barons" brought legislation to regulate business activities. First came legislation on the railroads, where the abuses were most severe, and then later in antitrust legislation. Labor legislation lagged somewhat behind the development of other regulatory agencies, but that too was soon to pass. Laws regulating hours, working conditions, and child and female labor were slow to gain credence by the courts as the proper province of governmental activity.

Recalling Pirenne's thesis at this point, the nineteenth century was still relatively laissez-faire but the twentieth century was to see an increasing role of government in business. The "new economics" placed government in a primary role through monetary and fiscal policy in efforts to stimulate economic recovery from the Depression. Labor legislation led to a spurt in union membership growth in the Rooseveltian "little man" philosophy. Post-World War II saw explicit recognition of the responsibility of the government to maintain high employment levels and sustained economic activity through the Employment Act of 1946. Some counterbalance to union power was achieved in the Taft-Hartley Act (1947) and in later labor legislation. The 1950's and 1960's found Keynesian economics in vogue, witnessed new legislation in regulating labeling, advertising, and packaging consumer products, and formed the beginnings of civil rights legislation. In the courts and in laws, the power equalization drive sought to aid the poor, to guarantee opportunities for education, and to provide for no discrimination in employment practices. Civil rights legislation, brought on in some cases by militancy, in some instances by civil disobedience, and in some degree by conscience, became the watchword of the late 1960's.

The political environment will continue to be exceedingly crucial in managerial decision making. Trade and tariff policy, foreign policy, defense spending, product regulation, wage-price guidelines, anti-trust legislation, employment practices, pollution control, urban problems, and governmental emphasis on other social projects will continue to shape the objectives of the business sector for some time to come. East-West tensions have turned the Cold War into a number of lukewarm wars. In juxtaposition to the early veneration of the "old man," this age is witnessing the killing of the old man as he is symbolized in the establishment. Political leaders and spokesmen are assassinated, the violent overthrow of government urged, and judicial and congressional ethics are of deep concern. It is in this age of militancy that power equalization threatens to become a new oligarchy of the power of the few over the many.

Perhaps the future will lend further credence to Pirenne's thesis. Perhaps there will be increasing governmental regulation and control to bring continuity from discontinuity, order from chaos. Perhaps this centralization and regulation will lead to a stifling equalization of all to the point where creativity and achievement lose their value.[18] To restore innovation and progress, there

---

[18] Durant makes a significant point for modern man: "Hence the dream of communism lurks in every modern society as a racial memory of a simpler and more equal life; and where inequality or insecurity rises beyond sufferance, men welcome a return to a condition which they idealize by recalling its equality and forgetting its poverty." Will Durant, *The Story of Civilization, Part I; Our Oriental Heritage,* New York: Simon & Schuster, 1935, pp. 18–19.

may have to come a withering away of state controls of economic activity. If so, the twenty-first century manager may find a new age of relatively *laissez-faire* political and economic philosophies.

SUMMARY

This has been a long journey which is only just beginning. Throughout this trip, management has been viewed as an activity essential to all organized efforts. Management finds its basis in the economic allocation and utilization of human and physical resources in order to attain organizational objectives. However, management is more than an economic activity—it is a conceptual function which must mold resources into a proper mix within the economic, social, and political facets of its environment. Management thought is the mirror reflection of managerial activity. Management thought brings form to function and philosophy to practice.

Fairly definite trends, forces, and philosophies have emerged in this conceptual analysis of evolving management thought. Management is both a product of and a process in its environment. Internally, management thought has passed through phases of differing emphases on the human and on the organizational and methods facets of the problems encountered in guiding goal-directed systems. Externally, management thought has been affected by evolving technology, by shifting assumptions about the nature of man, and by the dynamics of economic, social and political values.

Figure 22-1 is a somewhat sketchy summary of the broad swath that has been cut through this study of management. The modern era has seen a proliferation of approaches to management thought and an increasing awareness of the environment of management. Perhaps there will be an age of synthesis in systems theory, comparative management, or in some other conceptual scheme which has not yet been seen. Perhaps not, but it is this search that makes the study of management most worthy of intellectual and practical exercise. Management is one of the most dynamic of all disciplines; as technology, institutions, and people change, our ideas of management evolve in order to cope with man's oldest problem—the allocation and utilization of scarce resources to meet

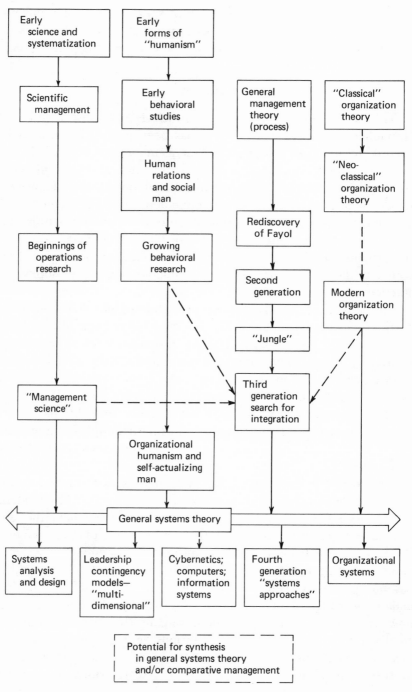

Fig. 22–1. Synopsis of the modern era

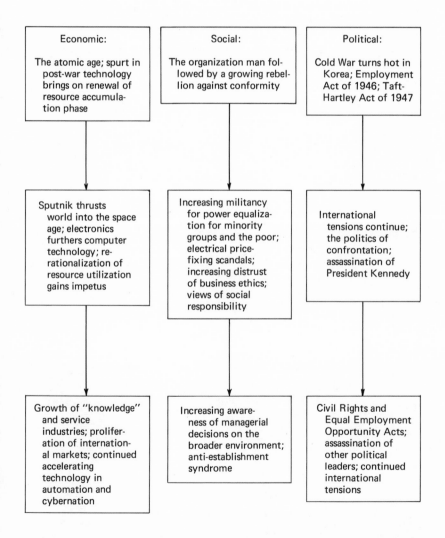

Economic:	Social:	Political:
The atomic age; spurt in post-war technology brings on renewal of resource accumulation phase	The organization man followed by a growing rebellion against conformity	Cold War turns hot in Korea; Employment Act of 1946; Taft-Hartley Act of 1947
Sputnik thrusts world into the space age; electronics furthers computer technology; re-rationalization of resource utilization gains impetus	Increasing militancy for power equalization for minority groups and the poor; electrical price-fixing scandals; increasing distrust of business ethics; views of social responsibility	International tensions continue; the politics of confrontation; assassination of President Kennedy
Growth of "knowledge" and service industries; proliferation of international markets; continued accelerating technology in automation and cybernation	Increasing awareness of managerial decisions on the broader environment; anti-establishment syndrome	Civil Rights and Equal Employment Opportunity Acts; assassination of other political leaders; continued international tensions

and the cultural environment.

the manifold desires of human society. Today is not like yesterday, nor will tomorrow be like today; yet today is a synergism of all our yesterdays, and tomorrow will be the same. There are many lessons in history for management scholars, and the most important one is the study of the past as prologue.

Selected Bibliography

PART I: EARLY MANAGEMENT THOUGHT

BABBAGE, CHARLES, *On the Economy of Machinery and Manufactures.* London: Charles Knight, 1832.

BEARD, MIRIAM, *A History of Business,* Vols. I and II. Ann Arbor: University of Michigan Press, 1962 and 1963.

BURNS, TOM and SAUL, S. B., *Social Theory and Economic Change.* London: Tavistock Publications, 1967.

CHANDLER, ALFRED D., JR., *Henry Varnum Poor: Business Editor, Analyst, and Reformer.* Cambridge, Mass.: Harvard University Press, 1956.

CHAPMAN, STANLEY D., *The Early Factory Masters.* New York: Augustus M. Kelley Publications, 1967.

CLARK, VICTOR, *History of Manufactures in the United States, 1607–1860.* New York: McGraw-Hill Book Co., 1916.

CLOUGH, SHEPARD B., *The Rise and Fall of Civilization: An Inquiry into the Relationship Between Economic Development and Civilization.* New York: McGraw-Hill Book Co., 1951.

COCHRAN, THOMAS C. and MILLER, WILLIAM, *The Age of Enterprise.* New York: Macmillan Co., 1944.

COOKE-TAYLOR, R. W., *Introduction to a History of the Factory System.* London: Richard Bentley and Sons, 1886.

COTTRELL, LEONARD, *The Anvil of Civilization.* New York: Mentor Book, New American Library, 1957.

DEANE, PHYLLIS, *The First Industrial Revolution,* London: Cambridge University Press, 1965.

DUPIN, CHARLES, *Discours sur le Sort des Ouvriers.* Paris: Bachelier, Librairie, 1831.

DURANT, WILL, *The Story of Civilization, Part I: Our Oriental Heritage.* New York: Simon and Schuster, 1935.

DURANT, WILL, *The Story of Civilization, Part II: The Life of Greece.* New York: Simon and Schuster, 1939.

DURANT, WILL, *The Story of Civilization, Part III: Caesar and Christ.* New York: Simon and Schuster, 1944.

DURANT, WILL, *The Story of Civilization, Part IV: The Age of Faith.* New York: Simon and Schuster, 1950.

EELS, RICHARD and WALTON, CLARENCE, *Conceptual Foundations of Business.* Homewood, Ill.: Richard D. Irwin, 1961.

GAGER, CURTIS H., "Management Throughout History," in *Top Management Handbook,* H. B. Maynard, (ed.) New York: McGraw-Hill Book Co., 1960.

GEORGE, CLAUDE S., JR., *The History of Management Thought.* Englewood Cliffs, N. J.: Prentice-Hall, 1968.

HAYEK, FRIEDRICH, *Capitalism and the Historians.* Chicago: University of Chicago Press, 1954.

HAYS, SAMUEL P., *The Response to Industrialism 1885–1914.* Chicago: University of Chicago Press, 1957.

HEILBRONER, ROBERT L., *The Making of Economic Society.* Englewood Cliffs, N. J.: Prentice-Hall, 1962.

HEILBRONER, ROBERT L., *The Worldly Philosophers: The Lives, Times, and Ideas of the Great Economic Thinkers.* New York: Simon and Schuster, 1953.

HOFSTADTER, RICHARD, *Social Darwinism in American Thought: 1860–1915.* Philadelphia: University of Pennsylvania Press, 1945.

HOSELITZ, B. F., *Sociological Aspects of Economic Growth,* New York: Free Press, 1960.

HUGHES, JONATHAN, *The Vital Few.* Boston: Houghton Mifflin Co., 1966.

LARSON, HENRIETTA, *Guide to Business History.* Cambridge, Mass.: Harvard University Press, 1948.

McCLELLAND, DAVID, *The Achieving Society.* New York: Van Nostrand Reinhold Co., 1961.

OLIVER, JOHN W., *History of American Technology.* New York: Ronald Press Co., 1956.

OWEN, ROBERT, *The Life of Robert Owen.* London: Effingham Wilson, 1857.

PARSONS, TALCOTT, and SMELSER, NEIL J., *Economy and Society: A Study in the Integration of Economic and Social Theory.* New York: Free Press, 1956.

PIKE, ROYSTON, *Hard Times: Human Documents of the Industrial Revolution.* New York: Praeger Publishers, 1966.

POLLARD, SIDNEY, *The Genesis of Modern Management: A Study of the Industrial Revolution in Great Britain.* Cambridge, Mass.: Harvard University Press, 1965.

ROLL, ERICH, *An Early Experiment in Industrial Organization.* London: Longmans, Green and Co., Ltd., 1930.

SCHUMPETER, JOSEPH A., *The Theory of Economic Development.* Cambridge, Mass.: The Harvard University Press, 1936.

SMELSER, NEIL J., *Social Change in the Industrial Revolution: an application of theory to the Lancashire Cotton Industry, 1770–1840,* Chicago: University of Chicago Press, 1959.

SMITH, ADAM, *An Inquiry into the Nature and Causes of the Wealth of Nations.* NEW YORK: Modern Library, 1937. Originally published in 1776.

SMITH, FREDERICK, *Workshop Management: A Manual for Masters and Men* (3rd. ed.) London: Wyman and Son, 1832.

SOMBART, WERNER, *Modern Capitalism.* London: T. Fisher Unwin, 1913.

TAWNEY, R. H., *Religion and the Rise of Capitalism.* London: John Murray, 1926.

TOYNBEE, ARNOLD, *The Industrial Revolution.* Boston: Beacon Press, 1956.

URE, ANDREW, *The Philosophy of Manufactures*. London: Charles Knight, 1835.

VEBLEN, THORSTEIN. *The Theory of the Leisure Class*. New York: Macmillan Co., 1899.

WEBER, MAX. *The Protestant Ethic and The Spirit of Capitalism*. New York: Charles Scribner's Sons, 1958.

PART II: THE SCIENTIFIC MANAGEMENT ERA

AITKEN, HUGH G. J., *Taylorism at Watertown Arsenal*, Cambridge, Mass.: Harvard University Press, 1960.

ALFORD, LEON R., *Henry Laurence Gantt, Leader in Industry*. New York: Harper and Row, 1934.

Alford, L. P., *Laws of Management Applied to Manufacturing*. New York: Ronald Press Co., 1928.

BARITZ, LOREN, *The Servants of Power*, New York: John Wiley and Sons, 1960.

BELL, DANIEL, *Work and Its Discontents: The Cult of Efficiency in America*. Boston: Beacon Press, 1956.

BENDIX, REINHARD, *Max Weber: An Intellectual Portrait*, Garden City, New York: Doubleday and Co., 1960.

BRANDEIS, LOUIS D., *Scientific Management and Railroads*. New York: Engineering Magazine Co., 1911.

CHURCH, ALEXANDER HAMILTON, *The Science and Practice of Management*. New York: Engineering Magazine Co., 1914.

CLARK, WALLACE, *The Gantt Chart*. New York: Ronald Press Co., 1922.

COOKE, M. L., *Our Cities Awake*. New York: Doubleday and Co., 1918.

COPLEY, FRANK B., *Frederick W. Taylor: Father of Scientific Management*, Vols. I and II. New York: Harper & Row, 1923.

DALE, ERNEST, *The Great Organizers*. New York: McGraw-Hill Book Co., 1960.

DeMAN, HENRI, *Joy In Work*. New York: Holt, Rinehart and Winston, 1929.

DRURY, HORACE B., *Scientific Management: A History and Criticism*. New York: Columbia University Press, 1915.

EMERSON, HARRINGTON, *The Twelve Principles of Efficiency*. New York: Engineering Magazine Co., 1913.

EMERSON, HARRINGTON, *Efficiency as a Basis for Operation and Wages*. New York: Engineering Magazine Co., 1911.

FAYOL, HENRI, *Administration Industrielle et Générale*, Paris: 1916 and 1925; English trans. by Coubrough (Geneva: 1930); and trans. by Storrs, London: Sir Isaac Pitman's and Sons, 1949.

FILIPETTI, GEORGE, *Industrial Management in Transition*. Homewood, Ill.: Richard D. Irwin, 1946.

GANTT, HENRY L., *Industrial Leadership*. New Haven Conn.: Yale University Press, 1916.

GANTT, HENRY L., *Organizing for Work*. New York: Harcourt Brace Jovanovich, 1919.

GANTT, H. L., *Work, Wages, and Profit*. New York: Engineering Magazine Co., 1910.

GILBRETH, FRANK B. and LILLIAN M., *Applied Motion Study*, New York: Sturgis and Walton Co., 1917.

GILBRETH, LILLIAN M., *The Psychology of Management*. New York: Sturgis and Walton Co., 1914.

GILSON, MARY B., *What's Past is Prologue*. New York: Harper and Row, 1940.

HABER, SAMUEL, *Efficiency and Uplift*. Chicago: University of Chicago Press, 1964.

Hearings before Special Committee of the House of Representatives to Investigate the Taylor and other Systems of Shop Management, under Authority of House Resolution 90 (1912).

HOXIE, R. F., *Scientific Management and Labor*. New York: Appleton Century-Crofts, 1915.

KAKAR, SUDHIR, *Frederick Taylor: A Study in Personality and Innovation*. Cambridge, Mass.: M.I.T. Press, 1970.

KIMBALL, D. S., *Principles of Industrial Organization*. New York: McGraw-Hill Book Co., 1913.

LING, CYRIL C., *The Management of Personnel Relations: History and Origins*. Homewood, Ill.: Richard D. Irwin, 1965.

MARTINDALE, DON, *The Nature and Types of Sociological Theory*. Boston: Houghton Mifflin Co., 1960.

MEE, J. F., *Management Thought in a Dynamic Society*. New York: New York University Press, 1963.

MEE, JOHN F., "A History of Twentieth Century Management Thought." PhD. dissertation, Department of Business Organization, Ohio State University, 1959.

METCALF, HENRY, *The Cost of Manufactures and the Administration of Workshops Public and Private*. New York: John Wiley and Sons, 1885.

MILLER, F. B. and COGHILL, M. A., *The Historical Sources of Personnel Work*. Bibliography Series No. 5. Ithaca, N. Y.: New York State School of Industrial and Labor Relations, Cornell University, September 1961.

MUNSTERBERG, HUGO, *Psychology and Industrial Efficiency*. Boston: Houghton Mifflin Co., 1913.

NADWORNY, MILTON J., *Scientific Management and the Unions: 1900–1932*, Cambridge, Mass.: Harvard University Press, 1955.

TAYLOR, FREDERICK W., *The Principles of Scientific Management*. New York: Harper & Row, 1911.

TAYLOR, FREDERICK W., *Shop Management*. New York: Harper & Row, 1903.

TILLETT, A., KEMPNER, T., and WILLS, G. (eds.), *Management Thinkers*. London: Penguin Books, 1970.

SHELDON, OLIVER, *The Philosophy of Management*. London: Sir Isaac Pitman and Sons, 1923.

STRAUSS, ANSELM (ed.), *The Social Psychology of George Herbert Mead*. Chicago: University of Chicago Press, Phoenix Books, 1956.

TEAD, ORDWAY, and METCALF, HENRY C., *Personnel Administration*. New York: McGraw-Hill Book Co., 1920.

THOMPSON, C. B. (ed.), *The Theory and Practice of Scientific Management*. Boston: Houghton Mifflin Co., 1917.

TROMBLEY, KENNETH E., *The Life and Times of a Happy Liberal: Morris Llewellyn Cooke*. New York: Harper and Row, 1954.

URWICK, LYNDALL (ed.), *The Golden Book of Management*, London: Newman Neame, 1956.

URWICK, LYNDALL and BRECH, E. F. L., *The Making of Scientific Management*, Vol. III. London: Management Publications Trust, 1951.

URWICK, LYNDALL and BRECH, E. F. L., *The Making of Scientific Management: Thirteen Pioneers*, Vol. I. London: Sir Isaac Pitman and Sons, 1948.

WEBER, MAX, *The Theory of Social and Economic Organization.* (Trans. by T. Parsons) New York: Free Press, 1947.

WILLIAMS, WHITING, *What's on the Worker's Mind.* New York: Charles Scribner's Sons, 1920.

WILLIAMS, WHITING. *Mainsprings of Men.* New York: Charles Scribner's Sons, 1925.

YOST, EDNA, *Frank and Lillian Gilbreth: Partners for Life.* New Brunswick, N. J.: Rutgers University Press, 1949.

PART III: THE SOCIAL MAN ERA

ALFORD, L. P., *Principles of Industrial Management for Engineers,* New York: Ronald Press Co., 1940.

ALLEN, FREDERICK L., *Only Yesterday.* New York: Harper and Row, 1931.

ANDERSON, A. G., *Industrial Engineering and Factory Management,* New York: Ronald Press Co., 1928.

ANDERSON, E. H., and SCHWENNING, G. T., *The Science of Production Organization,* New York: John Wiley and Sons, 1938.

BAKKE, E. W., *Bonds of Organization: An Appraisal of Corporate Human Relations.* New York: Harper and Row, 1950.

BARNARD, CHESTER I., *The Functions of the Executive.* Cambridge, Mass.: Harvard University Press, 1938.

BERLE, ADOLF A., JR., and MEANS, GARDINER C., *The Modern Corporation and Private Property.* New York: Macmillan Co., 1947.

BROWN, ALVIN, *Organization of Industry.* Englewood Cliffs, N. J.: Prentice-Hall, 1947.

BURNHAM, JAMES, *The Managerial Revolution.* New York: John Day Co., 1941.

CARNEGIE, DALE, *How to Win Friends and Influence People.* New York: Simon & Schuster, 1936.

CHANDLER, ALFRED, JR., *Strategy and Structure.* Cambridge Mass.: M.I.T. Press, 1966.

DAVIS, RALPH C., *The Fundamentals of Top Management.* New York: Harper and Row, 1951.

DAVIS, RALPH C., *The Principles of Factory Organization and Management.* New York: Harper and Row, 1928.

DAVIS, RALPH C., *The Principles of Business Organization and Operation.* Columbus, Ohio: H. L. Hedrick, 1935.

DENNISON, HENRY, *Organization Engineering* New York: McGraw-Hill Book Co., 1931.

EITINGTON, JULIUS: E., "Pioneers of Management: Personnel Management," *Advanced Management—Office Executive.* Vol. 2 (January, 1963).

FOLLETT, MARY PARKER, *Creative Experience.* London: Longmans, Green and Co., 1924.

FOLLETT, MARY PARKER, *The New State: Group Organization the Solution of Popular Government.* London: Longmans, Green and Co., 1918.

GARDNER, BURLEIGH B., and MOORE, DAVID G., *Human Relations in Industry.* Chicago: Richard D. Irwin, 1945.

GIVEN, W., *Bottom-up Management.* New York: Harper and Row, 1949.

HOLDEN, P. E., L. S. FISH, and H. L. SMITH, *Top Management Organization and Control.* Stanford, Calif.: Stanford University Press, 1941.

HOMANS, GEORGE C., *The Human Group.* New York: Harcourt Brace Jovanovich, 1950.

JACQUES, ELLIOTT, *The Changing Culture of a Factory.* London: Tavistock Publications, 1951.

KAVESH, ROBERT A., *Businessmen in Fiction.* Hanover, N. H.: Amos Tuck School, 1955.

LANDSBERGER, HENRY A., *Hawthorne Revisited.* Ithaca, N. Y.: New York State School of Industrial and Labor Relations, 1958.

LEWIN, K., *Resolving Social Conflicts,* New York: Harper and Row, 1948.

LINCOLN, JAMES F., *Incentive Management: A New Approach to Human Relationships in Industry and Business.* Cleveland, Ohio: Lincoln Electric Co., 1951.

LYND, ROBERT S. and LYND, HELEN M., *Middletown: A Study in Contemporary American Culture.* New York: Harcourt Brace Jovanovich, 1929.

MAIER, NORMAN R. F., *Principles of Human Relations.* New York: John Wiley and Sons, 1952.

MASLOW, A. H., "A Theory of Human Motivation," *Psychological Review,* Vol. 50 (1943).

MAYO, ELTON, *The Human Problems of an Industrial Civilization.* New York: Macmillan Co., 1933.

MAYO, ELTON, *The Social Problems of an Industrial Civilization.* Boston: Division of Research, Graduate School of Business Administration, Harvard University, 1945.

McCORMICK, CHARLES P., *Multiple Management.* New York: Harper and Row, 1938.

METCALF, HENRY C. and LYNDALL URWICK, *Dynamic Administration—The Collected Papers of Mary Follett.* New York: Harper and Row, 1942.

MOONEY, J. D., and A. C. REILEY, *Onward Industry.* New York: Harper and Row, 1931.

MOONEY, J. D. and A. C. REILEY, *The Principles of Organization.* New York: Harper and Row, 1939.

MORENO, J. L., *Who Shall Survive?: A New Approach to Human Interrelations.* Washington, D. C.: Nervous and Mental Disease Publishing Co., 1934.

PERKINS, DEXTER, *The New Age of Franklin Roosevelt: 1932–1945.* Chicago: University of Chicago Press, 1957.

RIESMAN, DAVID (and others), *The Lonely Crowd: A Study of the Changing American Character.* New Haven, Conn.: Yale University Press, 1950.

ROETHLISBERGER, F. J., *Man-in-Organization.* Cambridge, Mass.: Belknap Press of Harvard University Press, 1968.

ROETHLISBERGER, F. J., *Management and Morale.* Cambridge, Mass.: Harvard University Press, 1941.

ROETHLISBERGER, F. J., and DICKSON, W. J., *Management and the Worker.* Cambridge, Mass.: Harvard University Press, 1939.

SCOTT, WILLIAM G., *The Social Ethic in Management Literature.* Atlanta: Georgia State College of Business Administration, 1959.

SIMON, HERBERT A., *Administrative Behavior. A Study of Decision-Making Processes in Administrative Organization.* New York: Macmillan Co., 1947.

STOGDILL, R. M., *Methods in the Study of Administrative Leadership.* Columbus: Ohio State University, Bureau of Business Research, 1955.

URWICK, L., *The Elements of Administration*, New York: Harper and Row, 1944.

URWICK, L., *Scientific Principles of Organization*, New York: American Management Association, 1938.

WHITEHEAD, T. N., *The Industrial Worker*. 2 Vols. Cambridge, Mass.: Harvard University Press, 1938.

WHYTE, WILLIAM F., *Human Relations in the Restaurant Industry*. New York: McGraw-Hill Book Co., 1948.

WHYTE, WILLIAM H., JR. *The Organization Man*. Garden City, N. Y.: Doubleday & Co., 1956.

PART IV: THE MODERN ERA

ACKOFF, RUSSELL L., ARNOFF, LEONARD E., and CHURCHMAN, C. WEST, *Introduction to Operations Research*. New York: John Wiley and Sons, 1957.

ALBERS, HENRY H., *Organized Executive Action*. New York: John Wiley and Sons, 1961.

ALLEN, LOUIS A., *The Management Profession*. New York: McGraw-Hill Book Co., 1964.

ARGYRIS, CHRIS, *Personality and Organization*. New York: Harper and Row, 1957.

BEER, STAFFORD, *Cybernetics and Management*. New York: John Wiley and Sons, Inc., 1959.

BLAKE, ROBERT R., and MOUTON, JANE S., *The Managerial Grid*. Houston, Tex.: Gulf Publishing Co., 1964.

BOWMAN, EDWARD H., and FETTER, ROBERT B., *Analysis for Production Management*. Homewood, Ill.: Richard D. Irwin, 1957.

BROSS, IRWIN D., *Design for Decision*. New York: MacMillan Co., 1953.

BUFFA, ELWOOD S., *Modern Production Management*. New York: John Wiley and Sons, 1961, 1965, and 1969.

CLELAND, DAVID I., and KING, WILLIAM R., *Systems Analysis and Project Management*. New York: McGraw-Hill Book Co., 1968.

DALE, ERNEST, *Management: Theory and Practice*. New York: McGraw-Hill Book Co., 1965 and 1968.

DAUTEN, PAUL M., JR., *Current Issues and Emerging Concepts in Management*. New York: Harper and Row, 1964.

DAVIS, KEITH and BLOMSTROM, ROBERT L., *Business and Its Environment*. New York: McGraw-Hill Book Co., 1966.

DAVIS, KEITH, *Human Relations in Business*. New York: McGraw-Hill Book Co., 1957, 1962, and 1967.

DIEBOLD, JOHN and GEORGE TERBOUGH, *Automation—the Advent of the Automatic Factory*. New York: Van Nostrand Reinhold Co., 1952.

DRUCKER, PETER, *The Practice of Management*. New York: Harper and Row, 1954.

FARMER, RICHARD N., *Management in the Future*. Belmont, Calif.: Wadsworth Publishing Co., 1967.

FENN, DAN H., JR. (ed.), *Management In a Rapidly Changing Society*. New York: John Wiley and Sons, 1964.

FILLEY, ALAN C., and HOUSE, ROBERT J., *Managerial Process and Organizational Behavior*. Glenview, Ill.: Scott, Foresman and Co., 1969.

FLIPPO, EDWIN B., *Management: A Behavioral Approach*. Boston: Allyn and Bacon, 1966 and 1970.

FORRESTER, JAY W., *Industrial Dynamics*. Cambridge, Mass.: M.I.T. Press, 1961.

FOX, WILLIAM M., *The Management Process: An Integrated Functional Approach*. Homewood, Ill.: Richard D. Irwin, 1963.

GALBRAITH, JOHN KENNETH, *The New Industrial State*. Boston: Houghton Mifflin Co., 1967.

GOLDWIN, R. A. (ed.), *Toward the Liberally Educated Executive*. New York: Fund for Adult Education, 1957.

GOLEMBIEWSKI, ROBERT T., *The Small Group: An Analysis of Research Concepts and Operations*. Chicago: University of Chicago Press, 1962.

GORDON, R. A., and HOWELL, J. E., *Higher Education for Business*. New York: Columbia University Press, 1959.

HAIRE, MASON (ed.), *Modern Organization Theory*. New York: John Wiley & Sons, 1959.

HAYNES, W. WARREN, and MASSIE, JOSEPH L., *Management Analysis, Concepts and Cases*. Englewood Cliffs, N. J.: Prentice-Hall, 1961.

HERZBERG, F., MAUSNER, B., and SNYDERMAN, B. B., *The Motivation to Work*. New York: John Wiley & Sons, 1959.

HERZBERG, F., *Work and the Nature of Man*. Cleveland, Ohio: World Publishing Co., 1960.

HICKS, HERBERT G., *The Management of Organizations*. New York: McGraw-Hill Book Co., 1967.

HODGE, BILLY J., and JOHNSON, HERBERT J., *Management and Organizational Behavior: A Multidimensional Approach*. New York: John Wiley & Sons, 1970.

JOHNSON, RICHARD A., KAST, FREMONT E., and ROSENZWEIG, JAMES E., *The Theory and Management of Systems*. New York: McGraw-Hill Book Co., 1963.

JUCIUS, MICHAEL J., and SCHLENDER, WILLIAM E. *Elements of Managerial Action*. Homewood, Ill.: Richard D. Irwin, 1960.

KOONTZ, H. and O'DONNELL, C., *Principles of Management*. New York: McGraw-Hill Book Co., 1955, 1959, 1964, and 1968.

KOONTZ, H. (ed.). *Toward a Unified Theory of Management*. New York: McGraw-Hill Book Co., 1964.

LEBRETON, PRESTON P., *Comparative Administrative Theory*. Seattle: University of Washington Press, 1968.

LIKERT, RENSIS, *The Human Organization: Its Management and Value*. New York: McGraw-Hill Book Co., 1967.

LIKERT, RENSIS, *New Patterns of Management*. New York: McGraw-Hill Book Co., 1961.

LITTERER, JOSEPH A., *The Analysis of Organizations*. New York: John Wiley and Sons, 1965.

MARCH, JAMES G., and SIMON, HERBERT A., *Organizations*. New York: John Wiley and Sons, 1958.

MASLOW, A. H., *Motivation and Personality*. New York: Harper and Row, 1954.

MCCLELLAND, DAVID C. and WINTER, DAVID G. *Motivating Economic Achievement*. New York: Free Press, 1969.

MCFARLAND, DALTON E., *Management Principles and Practices*. New York: MacMillan Co., 1958, 1964, and 1970.

McGregor, Douglas, *The Human Side of Enterprise*. New York: McGraw-Hill Book Co., 1960.

McMillan, Claude, and Richard F. Gonzalez, *Systems Analysis—An Approach To Decision Models*. Homewood, Ill.: Richard D. Irwin, 1966.

Megginson, Leon C., *Personnel: A Behavioral Approach to Administration*. Homewood, Ill.: Richard D. Irwin, 1967.

Miller, David, and Starr, Martin K., *Executive Decisions and Operations Research*. Englewood Cliffs, N.J.: Prentice-Hall, 1966.

Miller, David, and Starr, Martin K. *The Structure of Human Decisions*. Englewood Cliffs, N. J.: Prentice-Hall, 1967.

Moore, Franklin G., *Management: Organization and Practice*. New York: Harper and Row, 1964.

Morris, William T., *Management Science in Action*. Homewood, Ill.: Richard D. Irwin, 1963.

Newman, William H., *Administrative Action: The Techniques of Organization and Management*. Englewood Cliffs, N. J.: Prentice-Hall, 1951 and 1960.

Newman, William H., and Summer, Charles E., Jr., *The Process of Management*. Englewood Cliffs, N. J.: Prentice-Hall, 1961.

Optner, Stanford L., *Systems Analysis for Business Management*. Englewood Cliffs, N. J.: Prentice-Hall, 1965.

Pfiffner, J. M. and Sherwood, F. P., *Administrative Organization*. Englewood Cliffs, N. J.: Prentice-Hall, 1960.

Presthus, Robert, *The Organizational Society*. New York: Alfred A. Knopf, 1962.

Prince, Thomas R., *Information Systems for Management Planning and Control*. Homewood, Ill.: Richard D. Irwin, 1966.

Richards, Max D., and Greenlaw, Paul S., *Management Decision Making*. Homewood, Ill.: Richard D. Irwin, 1966.

Roy, Robert H., *The Administrative Process*. Baltimore: Johns Hopkins Press, 1958.

Scott, William G., *Organization Theory: A Behavioral Analysis for Management*. Homewood, Ill.: Richard D. Irwin, 1967.

Selznick, Philip, *Leadership in Administration*. Evanston, Ill.: Row, Peterson & Co., 1957.

Shartle, Carroll, *Executive Performance and Leadership*. Englewood Cliffs, N. J.: Prentice-Hall, 1956.

Simon, Herbert A., *The New Science of Management Decision*. New York: Harper and Row, 1960.

Snow, C. P., *The Two Cultures: And A Second Look*. Cambridge, England: University Press, 1964.

Snow, C. P., *Two Cultures and the Scientific Revolution*. Cambridge, England: University Press, 1959.

Terry, George, *Principles of Management*. Homewood, Ill.: Richard D. Irwin, 1953, 1956, 1960, 1964, and 1968.

Voich, Dan Jr., and Wren, Daniel A., *Principles of Management: Resources and Systems*. New York: Ronald Press Co., 1968.

von Neumann, John and Morgenstern, Oskar. *Theory of Games and Economic Behavior*. Princeton, N. J.: Princeton University Press, 1944.

Wiener, Norbert, *Cybernetics*. Cambridge, Mass.: M.I.T. Press, 1948.

Wiener, Norbert, *The Human Use of Human Beings*. Boston: Houghton Mifflin Co., 1950.

WOODWARD, JOAN, *Industrial Organization: Theory and Practice*. London: Oxford University Press, 1965.

YOUNG, STANLEY, *Management: A Systems Analysis*. Glenview, Ill.: Scott, Foresman, and Co., 1966.

ZALEZNIK, ABRAHAM, *Human Dilemmas of Leadership*. New York: Harper and Row, 1966.

Author and Name Index

Subject Index